Race and Ethnic Relations in the United States

Readings for the 21st Century

Christopher G. Ellison
University of Texas, Austin

W. Allen Martin
University of Texas, Tyler

Foreword by Joe R. Feagin
University of Florida

Roxbury Publishing Company
Los Angeles, California

Library of Congress Cataloging-in-Publication Data

Race and ethnic relations in the United States: readings for the 21st century/
Christopher G. Ellison, W. Allen Martin [editors].
  p. cm.
  Includes bibliographical references.
  ISBN 0-935732-80-2
  1. United States—Ethnic relations.   2. United States—Race relations. I. Ellison,
Christopher G., 1960- . II. Martin, W. Allen, 1948- .
E184.A1R236   1999
305.8' '00973—dc21

96-49904
CIP

RACE AND ETHNIC RELATIONS IN THE UNITED STATES:
Readings for the 21st Century

Publisher and Editor: Claude Teweles
Copy Editors: Anton Diether, Renée Burkhammer, and Dawn VanDercreek
Production Editors: James Ballinger, C. Max-Ryan, and David Massengill
Production Assistants: Sacha A. Howells, Joyce Rappaport, and Colleen O'Brien
Typography: Synergistic Data Systems
Cover Design: Marnie Deacon Kenney

*The introduction to the section "Asian Americans" was written by Wendy Ng of San
Jose State University. The introduction to the section "Renegotiating Identities, Rethinking Categories" was written by Melissa Landers-Potts and Trellis Smith, with the
assistance of Velma McBride Murry, all of the University of Georgia. The introduction
to the section "Interracial and Interethnic Conflict" was written by Velma McBride
Murry and the Editors.*

Printed on acid-free paper in the United States of America. This paper meets the standards
for recycling of the Environmental Protection Agency.

ISBN: 0-935732-80-2

ROXBURY PUBLISHING COMPANY
P.O. Box 491044
Los Angeles, California 90049-9044
Tel: (213) 653-1068 • Fax: (213) 653-4140
Email: roxbury@crl.com

Contents

Asian Americans

Native Americans

Sources and Consequences of Residential Segregation

Affirmative Action

Diversity in Higher Education

Crime and Criminal Justice

Interracial and Interethnic Conflict

The Conflict Over Immigration

Renegotiating Identities, Rethinking Categories

Foreword

Joe R. Feagin
University of Florida

In the Declaration of Independence, the young Thomas Jefferson asserted that "We hold these truths to be self-evident, that all men are created equal, that they are endowed by their creator with certain unalienable rights, that among these are life, liberty, and the pursuit of happiness." Jefferson, though a slaveholder and admitted racist, helped to set in motion a long struggle for human rights that has continued to the present day. These revolutionary ideas have inspired movements for human rights by many groups, including those disenfranchised by the original U.S. Constitution. The most important human rights statement of our era, the Universal Declaration of Human Rights, was passed by the United Nations in 1948. Extending the language of Jefferson, this Declaration affirms that "all human beings are born free and equal in dignity and rights" and are entitled to basic rights "without distinction of any kind, such as race, color, sex, language, religion, political or other opinion, national or social origin, property, birth or other status" (United Nations 1948). This internationally accepted statement of principle proclaims that all human beings have equal rights, including the right not to be discriminated against. These are rights that human beings own independently of particular societal and governmental conditions. In the nation that launched this rights revolution, however, the task of providing full human rights for all—of eliminating all racial, ethnic, gender, and class discrimination—remains to be accomplished. The historical and contemporary contexts of this task, as well as its magnitude, are made clear in the readings in this book.

In this well-crafted anthology, two of the nation's talented sociologists, Christopher G. Ellison and W. Allen Martin, have gathered up-to-date assessments of the conditions faced by people of color, with particular emphasis on African Americans, Latino Americans, Asian Americans, and Native Americans. They have also focused part of this reader on critical issues churning at the core of U.S. society, including residential apartheid, affirmative action, multiculturalism, interracial conflict, immigration debates, and racial issues in criminal justice. Between today and the middle of the twenty-first century, most of the racial-ethnic "haves," particularly affluent white Americans, will need to adjust their perspectives and practices dramatically to fit the increasingly multiethnic, multiracial world in which we all will live. Currently, white Americans are a statistical minority in many cities, and by about the year 2060, they will become a minority in the nation. People of color will become the majority in U.S. economic, educational, and political institutions. The march of this population transition cannot be stopped. Those Americans, young and old, who cultivate a deeper understanding of this nation's racial-ethnic inequalities and conflicts—and develop their own perspectives and practices in a thoroughly egalitarian and pro-human-rights direction—will be the ones best able to contribute positively to and prosper in the society of the future.

Introduction

More than half a century ago, Swedish social scientist Gunnar Myrdal and his colleagues termed the issue of race relations "An American Dilemma." By this they referred to the fundamental contradiction between our nation's rhetorical commitment to equality, freedom, and due process under the law for all citizens and the reality of segregation, prejudice, and structural inequality that confronted racial and ethnic minorities every day. Undoubtedly, much has changed since Myrdal et al.'s description of American racial problems. In the wake of the civil rights movement of the 1950s and 1960s, *de jure* racial segregation ended and sweeping new laws were passed in an attempt to ban discrimination and guarantee equal access and fair treatment for people of all sectors of society. By many indicators, the quality of life for racial and ethnic minorities has improved substantially in recent decades. Yet despite these very real changes, the problems of discrimination, prejudice, and inequality remain deeply embedded within the fabric of our society.

As we rapidly approach the twenty-first century, several critical trends and developments have intensified public concern over race and ethnic relations in the United States. Recognizing the significance of renewed tensions, President Clinton initiated a "national dialogue" on race and ethnicity, including several "town hall meetings" in various parts of the country. Among the issues that concern many Americans, recent opinion polls show that Americans—and especially African Americans—harbor pessimistic views of the current racial/ethnic climate. The nation remains deeply divided over the best ways to combat racism and discrimination, and to reduce racial/ethnic inequality. For instance, a number of court decisions and political initiatives aim to curtail the use of affirmitive action in state government employment, contracts and procurement policies, and higher education. Many observers worry that these steps may threaten African American and Latino/a gains in education and professional arenas. The growing population of restrictive immigration reforms, manifested most clearly by the passage of Proposition 187 by California voters, strikes some observers as thinly-veiled anti-Latino/a and anti-Asian sentiment. And certainly the events surrounding the Rodney King incident and the trial of O.J. Simpson underscored the intensity of African American frustration with a white-dominated legal and judicial justice system that, in the eyes of many Americans, has treated persons of color unfairly.

As this reader goes to press, events continue to illustrate the continuing importance and volatility of race and ethnic relations in the U.S. For instance, throughout 1997-98, Americans have been shocked and outraged by vicious hate crimes against persons of color, including a spate of arsons targeting African American churches. In one East Texas town, a popular African American man was chained to a pickup truck and dragged to his death, allegedly by three local European American (white) men with criminal records. Highly-charged political activities continue to make news as well. By a hefty electoral majority, and with non-trivial Latino/a support, California voters have recently approved Proposition 229, which halts bilingual education in that state's public schools. Immigration issues also remain extremely important. Despite the objections of hi-tech industries, pending legislation in congress would sharply restrict the ability of businesses to hire immigrants with scarce and valuable expertise. And according to very recent news accounts, spurred by the findings of academic studies and the persistent appeals of human rights organizations, the Immigration and Naturalization Service (INS) is pledging to look for ways to reduce the high levels of mortality among undocumented migrants who attempt unauthorized crossings of the U.S.–Mexico border.

These developments, and others too numerous to mention, testify to the growing concern over race and ethnic relations in American society. Mirroring this public alarm, academics have in recent years produced a wealth of new scholarship on these issues. Although this anthology cannot be fully inclusive—the volume of new work is simply too great—we want to introduce students to some of the best recent thinking and research.

We have planned this anthology based on our own experience in teaching courses on race and ethnic relations and on conversations with colleagues around the country. Surveying the materials currently on the market, we became convinced that there was a need for an anthology that focuses squarely on race and ethnicity in the contemporary United States—the experiences of specific populations, as well as the public debates that are reshaping race and ethnic relations today. This reader will acquaint students with influential ideas and new research developed by the leading figures in the area of racial and ethnic relations. Indeed, a number of the pieces included here have already achieved the status of contemporary classics in the field. While many contributors are social scientists, we also include several pieces by top opinionmakers (e.g., Brimelow, Glasser, and Steele) who have helped to shape current debates over affirmative action, welfare reform, diversity in higher education, and other key issues.

This anthology is designed to stand alone or to complement the group-by-group coverage that remains the core of most major texts in the area of racial and ethnic relations, including the best-selling works in that genre. At the same time, this reader addresses the kinds of contemporary issues and political debates (e.g., immigration policy and diversity in higher education) mentioned above, which receive limited attention in most core texts. We hope that this combination of group-specific materials and issue-oriented articles will be useful to instructors using a wide variety of texts and course blueprints.

A good reader should focus on current topics and materials, especially in the rap-idly changing area of racial and ethnic relations. Because it is not feasible to cover every significant controversial topic in an anthology of this type, we have chosen to emphasize eight major areas of interest to social scientists, policymakers, and the general public. The selections in this reader represent very current approaches to the study of racial and ethnic relations. Further, a number of our selections focus on issues that are frequently overlooked in other collections, such as the problems of racism on college campuses (e.g., Feagin and Steele), the human rights consequences of immigration policy (Dunn), the impact of the "war on drugs" (Tonry), the constructed meaning of whiteness (Frankenburg), and numerous others.

Although this anthology is not designed to focus primarily on the intersection of various social parameters—as some readers on race, class, and gender do—it would be inappropriate to study racial and ethnic relations without acknowledging social class and gender variations in the experiences of various groups today. Consequently, the selections in this volume provide substantial coverage of the key stratification issues that confront various minority populations and call attention to the distinctive circumstances and experiences of women in diverse communities.

Students are best served by a reader that presents contemporary debates from varied theoretical and political perspectives. This is an even more salient concern in light of recent allegations that courses on racial and ethnic relations tend to promote political indoctrination rather than social science analysis. This book is intended to promote debate by presenting strongly opposed but powerfully argued positions on key issues (e.g., Glasser and Steele on affirmative action).

To be effective pedagogically, an anthology must be appealing and accessible to both students and instructors. For this reason, these selections have been carefully edited to minimize academic jargon and unnecessary methodoligical detail. Moreover, this reader focuses on topics that are directly relevant to the lives of students, such as higher education, affirmative action, and crime and criminal justice. Brief section introductions are designed to link the various selections and to provide background information about the issues under consideration.

This volume is organized in two major sections. The first section consists of articles on the contemporary experiences of African Americans, Latino/a Americans, Asian Americans, Native Americans, and European Americans, respectively. The ordering of groups within this section does not imply any judgment about their relative importance. While a number of the readings explore issues that are germane to specific minority populations (e.g., the "model minority" stereotype of Asian Americans), many selections also address more general themes, including: (1) the impact of social change and economic restructuring on life chances within various racial and ethnic populations; (2) the intersection of race and ethnicity, social class, and gender in shaping the experiences of various racial and ethnic groups; and (3) the politics of labelling and the negotiation and construction of identities in the contemporary United States.

The second major section is composed of articles that address significant public controversies. Contributions focus on the following specific issues: (1) continuity and change in the forms of prejudice and discrimination faced by peoples of color; (2) the promise and pitfalls of affirmative action policies; (3) the causes and consequences of residential segregation; (4) race and ethnic relations on college and university campuses; (5) disparities in criminal victimization, perpetration, and treatment in the criminal justice system; (6) the growing conflicts among racial and ethnic groups in urban contexts; (7) the controversies surrounding immigration reform; and (8) the negotiation and changing character of racial and ethnic identities.

The articles in these subsections are written from a variety of theoretical and political perspectives. Our goal is to expose students to a wide range of views and arguments on each of these topics. Although our choices will not satisfy every instructor, we have worked within the limited available space to offer diverse materials that should serve as a springboard for stimulating lectures, class discussions, and personal reflections.

An appreciation of America's unique racial and ethnic mosaic and an awareness of the complexity of contemporary intergroup relations are keys to competent citizenship as we prepare to enter the twenty-first century. We hope this reader will make a modest contribution toward achieving these goals.

Acknowledgements

A number of individuals deserve acknowledgement for their assistance with this anthology. Several thoughtful colleagues offered valuable advice regarding articles to be included and issues to be addressed. They include: Frank Bean, John Sibley Butler, Timothy Dunn, Gil Cardenas, Dale McLemore, Arthur Sakamoto, Darren Sherkat, Mark Warr, and Craig Watkins, and no doubt others as well. Special thanks are due to Wendy Ng, Velma McBride Murry, Melissa Landers-Potts, and Trellis Smith for their help in crafting introductions to three sections in this book. We would also like to thank the following reviewers—Gerry R. Cox (South Dakota School of the Mines); Kevin Delaney (Temple University); E. Joel Heikes (Southwest Texas State University); Michael Hood (Mercer University); Reid Luhman (Eastern Kentucky University); Jack E. Niemonen (University of South Dakota); and Gary Sandefur (University of Wisconsin)—for their helpful suggestions, many of which were incorporated into the volume. In addition, Phoebe Moore helped by providing a student's perspective on many of the selections that we considered for inclusion. We wish to thank Claude Teweles, publisher-editor of Roxbury Publishing Company, for his patience and encouragement during the longer-than-anticipated process of completing the book, and various members of his staff for their careful attention to a wide range of editorial and production issues. We also want to acknowledge the secretarial contributions of Jody Mullins and Charlotte Chambers at the University of Texas-Tyler. Finally, and most importantly, we are grateful to our families—Sharon Sandomirsky, and Debra, Zachary, and Michelle Martin—for their love and patience while we finished work on this anthology.

Part I

Racial and Ethnic Populations in the United States

African Americans

The civil rights movement of the 1950s and 1960s brought about tremendous changes in laws and social attitudes. More than 30 years later, however, statistics reveal dramatic gaps between European Americans (whites) and African Americans in various indicators of the quality of life, including earnings and wealth, health and personal well-being, and life expectancy, among many others (O'Hare, Pollard, Mann, and Kent 1991). Such inequalities, encountered across many areas of life experience, fuel a persistent frustration with the status quo.

Scholars have long debated whether these inequalities are mainly due to race or class—that is, whether they result from antiblack discrimination or reflect the long legacy of generally lower socioeconomic standing among African Americans. Hotly debated by W.E.B. DuBois, Oliver Cox, and others in the early twentieth century, this issue has been broached with new vigor by William Julius Wilson. In a landmark volume provocatively titled *The Declining Significance of Race: Blacks and Changing American Institutions* (1980), Wilson has argued that the contemporary African American population is increasingly diverse, and that two key segments of this population now have dramatically different experiences and future prospects. On the one hand, a growing African American middle class enjoys unprecedented opportunities to pursue the American dream. On the other hand, expanding numbers of urban poor—sometimes termed the ghetto "underclass"—face a desperate future, with bleak prospects for improvement in their employment opportunities and living conditions.

A number of factors have contributed to the remarkable contemporary growth of the African American middle class (Wilson 1980). Obviously, the advent of anti-discrimination regulations has been pivotal. Civil rights legislation passed in the 1960s outlawed many forms of discrimination, and subsequent affirmative action initiatives stimulated the hiring and promotion of African Americans by public sector bureaucracies and major private sector firms, beginning with those companies which contracted with the federal government. In addition, the dramatic expansion of the size and scope of the government in the 1960s and 1970s fostered growth in the African American middle class (Collins 1983).

Wilson and other scholars tend to identify middle-class African Americans on the basis of three criteria: (a) household incomes (or current earnings); (b) education levels (i.e., whether at least one adult in the household is a college graduate); and (c) occupational attainment (i.e., whether at least one adult is employed in a professional, managerial, technical, or administrative position). By 1990 approximately 13 percent of African American men and 19 percent of African American women held managerial and professional jobs, while 17 percent of African American men and 39 percent of African American women were employed in technical and administrative positions (O'Hare et al. 1991). While these figures lag behind those for whites—African American males are especially underrepresented in managerial and professional jobs—the ranks of the African American middle class have expanded dramatically since the heyday of the civil rights era (Farley and Allen 1987). Given the long history of labor market discrimination against African American males, the role of working women has been critical to this development (Geschwender and Carroll-Seguin 1990).

However, some observers prefer to use another set of criteria to identify the African American middle class: net worth, or the total value of assets (i.e., home equity, savings, investments such as retirement accounts, stocks and bonds, real estate, and inherited resources) once debts and liabilities have been subtracted (Oliver and Shapiro 1995). They argue that this offers a more accurate picture of financial power and security—for instance, the ability of households to borrow for investments, education, and business startups, and the capacity of households to absorb temporary emergencies and reversals of fortune. And racial differences in net worth are striking: for white households, the median net worth in 1988 was estimated to be $43,279; the corresponding figure for African American households was $4,169. Moreover, nearly half (46.9 percent) of white households had a net worth of $100,000 or more, as compared with only around 15 percent of African American households (O'Hare et al. 1991).

These figures reflect the insecurity and vulnerability of the first-generation African-American middle class, many members of which tend to carry more debt and enjoy less inherited wealth than their white counterparts (Landry 1987). Further, equity in a home is the single largest asset for most Americans, but the rate of home ownership for African Americans is only about two-thirds that of the total US population. Even among those who own their home, the amount of equity owned by African Americans is only approximately 60 percent of the national average (O'Hare et al. 1991), and persistent patterns of residential segregation (see Section 7, this volume) are believed to contribute significantly to this gap.

Moreover, some scholars have warned of the fragility of the African American middle class, arguing that it is especially vulnerable to macroeconomic downturns and political changes. According to Collins (1983, 1997), for instance, a significant portion of this middle class has been politically constructed by affirmative action guidelines and similar initiatives aimed at increasing opportunities for African Americans. Some public- and private-sector employees were hired specifically to fulfill hiring goals or quotas. Others have public-sector positions in which they deal mainly with African Americans or other minority group members (e.g., employees in welfare and social service bureaucracies). Still other jobs derive indirectly from the pursuit of equal-opportunity goals (e.g., civil rights law firms) or servicing affirmative action programs (e.g., minority-owned firms that benefit from contract set-aside provisions).

One frequent concern is that large-scale government budget cuts and policy shifts could eliminate significant numbers of public-sector jobs, including many that are now staffed by minority workers. Moreover, growing popular and political opposition to affirmative action and related initiatives could also sharply reduce the occupational and earnings gains of middle-class African Americans and black executives in the private sector (Collins 1989). Consistent with this view, one study finds that labor market discrimination against younger cohorts of African Americans may have increased since the mid-1970s, when Wilson conducted his initial analysis of middle-class growth, due perhaps to more conservative social and political climates (Cancio et al. 1996), although others dispute this claim (Farkas and Vicknair 1996). Further, Collins (1997) suggests that the politically constructed jobs of many African American executives may seem especially expendable in an era of corporate downsizing and restructuring.

Rosy evaluations of the African-American middle class often give short shrift to the phenomenon of systematic and institutional discrimination. A plethora of routine practices within schools, corporations, and other settings work against African Americans. Such practices are sometimes intended to discriminate, as with membership barriers against African Americans erected by some social clubs, which serve to keep minorities on the outside of informal business and professional networks. But other practices also have the effect of placing African Americans at a disadvantage, even though they are ostensibly "colorblind." Examples include "objective" employment requirements, such as extensive previous work experience or advanced educational credentials, which disproportionately few African Americans can present.

Although Wilson and others write of a "declining significance of race," the personal experiences of many upwardly mobile African Americans indicate that race continues to shape their life chances and perceptions (Willie 1989). The kinds of incidents reported by Feagin (this volume; Feagin and Sikes 1994), and recently investigated by various print and television journalists, show that even middle-class standing and resources do not insulate African Americans from overt and covert racist treatment in public settings. Cose (this volume) discusses subtle forms of racism and their effects on African Americans in the corporate world. At least one recent study shows that being a "token Black" in a white-dominated workplace can lead to specific forms of job-related stress, and to higher levels of depression and anxiety among upwardly mobile African Americans (Jackson, Thoits, and Taylor 1995).

As scholars and community leaders debate the current standing of the African-American middle class, public attention has been riveted on the dismal fortunes of the ghetto poor in many major cities, especially in the northeastern and midwestern U.S. Clearly the high level of poverty among African Americans has become a major national issue. For the past two decades African American poverty rates have stagnated, remaining around 30–35 percent. And we should bear in mind that our current methods of measuring poverty may be inadequate; some researchers estimate that "real" levels of African American poverty are much higher than official statistics indicate (Wilson 1991). Studies suggest that African Americans living below the official poverty line are actually poorer than their white counterparts. The dire straits of poor African Americans surface in statistics on household assets: in 1990, approximately 30 percent of African Americans had zero or negative net worth, as compared with only around 5 percent of whites (O'Hare et al. 1991; Oliver and Shapiro 1995).

While there has always been urban poverty among African Americans, recent decades have witnessed a growing concentration of this poverty and an intensification of other patterns that are increasingly seen as serious social problems (e.g., long-term unemployment, violent crime, drug abuse, housing deterioration, family disruption, out-of-wedlock births) within minority neighborhoods. Of the poor African Americans who resided in the central cities of metropolitan areas in 1990, nearly three-fourths lived in high poverty neighborhoods (O'Hare et al. 1991).

What has caused this downward spiral for entire neighborhoods of African Americans? According to many observers, the main problem is the exodus of stable, high-paying blue-collar jobs, especially in manufacturing industries (Wilson 1996). Numerous firms—indeed, entire manufacturing sectors (e.g., durable consumer goods, electronics)—left the central cities of the "snowbelt" during the 1970s and 1980s, headed for suburbs, "sunbelt" (i.e., southern and southwestern) areas, and even offshore (e.g., East Asia, the Caribbean), mainly in search of cheaper labor. Many of the firms that did remain in "snowbelt" cities used technology to reduce the need for low-skilled labor (Wilson 1996).

In virtually every "snowbelt" metropolitan area, the number of entry-level jobs requiring less than a high school degree declined during the 1970–85 period (Kasarda 1989). To be sure, the number of jobs requiring college education increased, but these positions were largely beyond the reach of inner-city minority residents. These high-end service positions (e.g., advertising, computer services) were taken by mostly white professionals who lived in gentrified urban areas or commuted in from suburbs. While some low-end service jobs (e.g., janitorial, food service) were also created during this period, some argue that there were not enough to keep pace with the need, while others note that these positions were also unattractive to many ghetto residents, due to their low wages and benefits. In short, these processes are believed to have resulted in a "spatial mismatch" of skills and jobs; the skill levels of nearby residents were apparently incompatible with the needs of employers.

According to Wilson, the loss of stable blue-collar jobs had devastating effects on African-American communities and neighborhoods in urban areas. In his view, one key factor has been the flight of the African American middle class from these blighted neighborhoods (Wilson 1987). The departure of individuals who have succeeded through education and conventional employment has meant the loss of role models for youths. In addition, the loss of stable working and middle classes has undermined institutions, such as social clubs, neighborhood groups, and other voluntary associations. In some areas, even the influence of churches—long the mainstays of African-American communities—has been reduced. Perhaps most importantly, these changes mean that young people tend to lack the social connections that can give them the "inside track" on job openings, because their neighborhood friends are often unemployed (Wacquant and Wilson, this volume). Some speculate that these neighborhood dynamics can contribute to feelings of powerlessness and hopelessness among residents, which may in turn become a self-fulfilling prophecy (Wilson 1991).

Given this analysis of the causes of urban blight, Wilson and others call for several policy initiatives aimed at easing these problems. They advocate stronger and more innovative partnerships between schools and private firms to overcome the "network gap" which separates young people from job skills, knowledge of openings, and good work habits (Wilson 1987). Many scholars and policymakers also support urban enterprise zones, which provide various types of incentives (e.g., tax abatements, waivers of some regulations, new infrastructure considerations) for firms that relocate to those neighborhoods and hire and train employees who live nearby. Some hope to improve mass transit facilities, so that inner-city workers can find and keep jobs more easily in suburban communities. Still others propose encouraging the migration of some urban residents to other regions of the U.S. with low unemployment rates and plentiful job opportunities (Kasarda 1989).

While Wilson's work on the ghetto poor has gained currency among many policymakers and the general public, some scholars reject his major arguments. For instance, Massey and Denton argue that high levels of residential segregation played a major role in the concentration of African-American poverty within certain neighborhoods; by limiting the housing choices available to poor minorities, the structure of segregation may have confined the devastating impact of job losses to a small number of vulnerable neighborhoods which lacked the resources to rebound (Massey and Denton 1993). Supporters of this analysis endorse a mix of regulations and incentives aimed at promoting the desegregation of residential neighborhoods.

Conservative analysts maintain that the flawed values and deviant lifestyles of many inner-city residents are the primary causes of urban misery today. Doubting the wisdom or effectiveness of government initiatives, many indict the welfare state for "encouraging" welfare dependency and "rewarding" out-of-wedlock births, and they support welfare cutbacks. Because they believe that the urban poor lack both a vigorous work ethic and a sober view of their civic obligations, conservatives often favor reforms that require recipients of government assistance to work in exchange for their checks (Mead 1989). However, skeptics have long branded such "workfare" programs as "slavefare."

Deciding whether "flawed" values underlie the growth of the underclass is an important and contentious task. Jencks (1991) has pointed out that by virtually any indicator, levels of urban poverty have not risen in recent years. Instead, the key features of current ghetto poverty are (a) its concentration in a relatively small number of hard-hit neighborhoods and (b) the correlation of this poverty with "deviant" lifestyle choices, especially those adopted by women, such as out-of-wedlock childbearing. This leads some to suspect that discussions about policies vis-á-vis the "urban underclass" have less to do with alleviating poverty than with stigmatizing ("bashing") certain patterns of family life now common among urban African Americans. However, some suggest that these practices (e.g., female-headed households) may have deep roots in African American history and culture. They may also reflect creative responses of women (Jarrett, this volume) to the relative dearth of marriageable African American males (e.g., due to high rates of male incarceration, homicide, etc.) in these areas (Raley 1996). To some scholars and policymakers, this suggests the need to make more resources available in these areas, rather than to cut back.

Many observers from across the political spectrum also call for more volunteerism—by churches, social clubs, and individuals—to mentor young people, and to promote positive values of faith and nuclear family life. In addition, scholars and politicians have endorsed various "empowerment" initiatives, such as promoting tenant ownership of dilapidated public housing complexes. Some observers suggest that one key to reducing ghetto poverty may be to encourage small business startups by inner city residents, drawing upon the rich (but often ignored) heritage of entrepreneurship among African Americans (Butler 1991).

Some researchers caution that racial discrimination plays an important role in producing and sustaining ghetto poverty, over and above the effects (if any) of structural economic shifts or subcultures of poverty. In one widely heralded study, Kirschenman and Neckerman (1991) interviewed mostly white employers in the Chicago area, and found that they consider race frequently—along with other markers such as neighborhood of residence and high school—when making employment decisions. In contrast to those who argue that appropriate jobs are absent from the inner city, these authors conclude that white employers simply avoid hiring most young African Americans, who are perceived through the most unflattering ghetto images as unqualified and unreliable troublemakers. This argument draws indirect support from recent sophisticated studies of the microlocation of jobs within inner-city areas, which tend to show that African Americans actually reside near ample numbers of entry-level jobs with minimal skill requirements—the kinds of jobs for which inner-city youths would be eligible—and that African Americans have shorter projected commuting distances than whites (Cohn and Fossett 1996). Such findings raise the possibility that dis-

crimination is responsible for high African-American unemployment.

Wilson and his colleagues have performed a vital service by drawing attention to the plight of the ghetto poor in northeastern and midwestern cities. At the same time, it is important to recognize that African-American poverty rates are alarmingly high in the nonmetropolitan South. Roughly one-quarter of African-American adults in the U.S. reside in the small towns and rural areas of the South, where dramatic social and economic inequality between the races persists too often, and where the benefits of rural development (e.g., relocated manufacturing industries) have largely bypassed minorities (Lichter 1989). Further, while it is true that sunbelt cities tend to have fewer high-poverty areas than their snowbelt counterparts, several of these cities (e.g., Los Angeles) have experienced substantial losses of stable, relatively high-skilled blue-collar jobs, and many (e.g., Los Angeles, Houston, Atlanta) also have significant pockets of concentrated misery (Bullard 1989).

Despite the substantial changes in laws and social attitudes since the heyday of the civil rights movement, whites and African Americans, on average, still confront vastly unequal opportunities and life chances. The articles in this section offer differing perspectives on the struggles, frustrations, and triumphs of African Americans, while summoning all Americans who believe in expanded opportunity and racial justice to redouble their efforts in pursuit of those ideals.

References

Bullard, R.D. (ed). 1989. *In Search of the New South: The Black Urban Experience in the 1970s and 1980s.* Tuscaloosa: University of Alabama Press.

Butler, J.S. 1991. *Entrepreneurship and Self-Help Among Black Americans: A Reconsideration of Race and Economics.* Albany: SUNY Press.

Cancio, A.S., T.D. Evans, and D.J. Maume, Jr. 1996. "Reconsidering the Declining Significance of Race: Racial Differences in Early Career Wages." *American Sociological Review* 61: 541–556.

Cohn, S., and M. Fossett. 1996. "What Spatial Mismatch? The Proximity of Blacks to Employment in Boston and Houston." *Social Forces* 75: 557–574.

Collins, S. 1983. "The Making of the Black Middle Class." *Social Problems* 30: 369–382.

——. 1989. "The Marginalization of Black Executives." *Social Problems* 36: 317–331.

——. 1997. *Black Corporate Executives: The Making and Unmaking of the Black Middle Class.* Philadelphia: Temple University Press.

Farkas, G., and K. Vicknair. 1996. "Appropriate Tests of Racial Wage Discrimination Require Controls for Cognitive Skill: Comment on Cancio, Evans, and Maume." *American Sociological Review* 61: 557–560.

Farley, R., and W. Allen. 1987. *The Color Line and the Quality of Life in America.* New York: Russell Sage Foundation.

Feagin, J.R., and M. Sikes. 1994. *Living with Racism.* Boston: Beacon Press.

Geschwender, J., and R. Carroll-Seguin. 1990. "Exploding the Myth of African American Progress." *Signs* 15: 285–299.

Jackson, P.B., P.A. Thoits, and H.F. Taylor. 1995. "Composition of the Workplace and Psychological Well-Being: The Effects of Tokenism on America's Black Elite." *Social Forces* 74: 543–558.

Jencks, C. 1991. "Is the American Underclass Growing?" Pp. 28–100 in *The Urban Underclass*, edited by C. Jencks and P. Petersen. Washington: Brookings Institution.

Kasarda, J. 1989. "Urban Industrial Transition and the Underclass." *Annals of the American Academy of Political and Social Science* 501: 26–47.

Kirschenman, J., and K. Neckerman. 1991. " 'We'd Love to Hire Them, But. . .' The Meaning of Race for Employers." Pp. 203–232 in *The Urban Underclass*, edited by C. Jencks and P. Petersen. Washington: Brookings Institution.

Landry, B. 1987. *The New Black Middle Class.* Berkeley: University of California Press.

Lichter, D.T. 1989. "Race, Employment Hardship, and Inequality in the American Nonmetropolitan South." *American Sociological Review* 54: 436–447.

Massey, D., and N. Denton. 1993. *American Apartheid: Segregation and the Making of the Urban Underclass.* Cambridge, MA: Harvard University Press.

Mead, L. 1989. "The Logic of Workfare: The Underclass and Work Policy." *Annals of the American Academy of Political and Social Science* 501: 156–169.

O'Hare, W.P., K.M. Pollard, T.L. Mann, and M.M. Kent. 1991. *African Americans in the 1990s.* Washington: Population Reference Bureau.

Oliver, M.L., and T.M. Shapiro. 1995. *Black Wealth/White Wealth: A New Perspective on Racial Inequality.* New York: Routledge.

Raley, R.K. 1996. "A Shortage of Marriageable Men? A Note on the Role of Cohabitation in Black-White Differences in Marriage Rates." *American Sociological Review* 61: 973–983.

Willie, C.V. (ed.) 1989. *Caste and Class Controversy on Race and Poverty: Round Two of the Willie/Wilson Debate*, 2nd. ed. Dix Hills, NJ: General Hall.

Wilson, W.J. 1980. *The Declining Significance of Race: Blacks and Changing American Institutions*, rev. ed. Chicago: University of Chicago Press.

——. 1987. *The Truly Disadvantaged: The Inner City, the Underclass, and Public Policy.* Chicago: University of Chicago Press.

——. 1991. "Studying Inner-City Social Dislocations: The Challenge of Public Agenda Research." *American Sociological Review* 56: 1–14.

——. 1996. *When Work Disappears: The New World of the Urban Poor.* New York: Alfred Knopf.

1

The Continuing Significance of Race:

Antiblack Discrimination in Public Places

Joe R. Feagin

Aspects of Discrimination

Discrimination can be defined in social-contextual terms as "actions or practices carried out by members of dominant racial or ethnic groups that have a differential and negative impact on members of subordinate racial and ethnic groups" (Feagin and Eckberg 1980, pp. 1–2). This differential treatment ranges from the blatant to the subtle (Feagin and Feagin 1986). Here I focus primarily on blatant discrimination by white Americans targeting middle-class blacks. Historically, discrimination against blacks has been one of the most serious forms of racial/ethnic discrimination in the United States and one of the most difficult to overcome, in part because of the institutionalized character of color coding. I focus on three important aspects of discrimination: (1) the variation in sites of discrimination; (2) the range of discriminatory actions; and (3) the range of responses by blacks to discrimination.

Sites of Discrimination

There is a spatial dimension to discrimination. The probability of experiencing racial hostility varies from the most private to the most public sites. If a black person is in a relatively protected site, such as with friends at home, the probability of experiencing hostility and discrimination is low. The probability increases as one moves from friendship settings to such outside sites as the workplace, where a black person typically has contacts with both acquaintances and strangers, providing an interactive context with greater potential for discrimination.

In most workplaces, middle-class status and its organizational resources provide some protection against certain categories of discrimination. This protection probably weakens as a black person moves from those work and school settings where he or she is well-known into public accommodations such as large stores and city restaurants where contacts are mainly with white strangers. On public streets blacks have the greatest public exposure to strangers and the least protection against overt discriminatory behavior, including violence. A key feature of these more public settings is that they often involve contacts with white strangers who react primarily on the basis of one ascribed characteristic. . . .

The Range of Discriminatory Actions

. . . In my data, discrimination against middle-class blacks still ranges across this continuum: (1) avoidance actions, such as a white couple crossing the street when a black male approaches; (2) rejection actions, such as poor service in public accommodations; (3) verbal attacks, such as shouting racial epithets in the street; (4) physical threats and harassment by white police officers; and (5) physical threats and attacks by other whites, such as attacks by white supremacists in the street. Changing relations between blacks and whites in recent decades have expanded the repertoire of discrimination to include more subtle forms and to encompass discrimination in arenas from which blacks were formerly excluded, such as formerly all-white public accommodations.

Black Responses to Discrimination

. . . Middle-class strategies for coping with discrimination range from careful assessment to withdrawal, resigned acceptance, verbal confrontation, or physical confrontation. Later action might include a court suit. Assessing the situation is a first step. Some white observers have suggested that many middle-class blacks are paranoid about white discrimination and rush too quickly to charges of racism (Wieseltier 1989, June 5). . . . But the daily reality may be just the opposite, as middle-class black Americans often evaluate a situation carefully before judging it discriminatory and taking additional action. This careful evaluation, based on past experiences (real or vicarious), not only prevents jumping to conclusions, but also reflects the hope that white behavior is not based on race, because an act not based on race is easier to endure. After evaluation one strategy is to leave the site of discrimination rather than to create a disturbance. Another is to ignore the discrimination and continue with the interaction, a "blocking" strategy. In many situations resigned acceptance is the only realistic response. More confrontational responses to white actions include verbal reprimands and sarcasm, physical counterattacks, and filing lawsuits. Several strategies may be tried in any given discriminatory situation. In crafting these strategies middle-class blacks, in comparison with less privileged blacks, may draw on middle-class resources to fight discrimination. . . .

Responses to Discrimination: Public Accommodations

Two Fundamental Strategies: Verbal Confrontation and Withdrawal

In the following account, a black news director at a major television station shows the interwoven character of discriminatory action and black response. The discrimination took the form of poor restaurant service, and the responses included both suggested withdrawal and verbal counterattack.

He [her boyfriend] was waiting to be seated. . . . He said, "You go to the bathroom and I'll get the table. . . ." He was standing there when I came back; he continued to stand there. The restaurant was almost empty. There were waiters, waitresses, and no one seated. And when I got back to him, he was ready to leave, and said, "Let's go." I said, "What happened to our table?" He wasn't seated. So I said, "No, we're not leaving, please." And he said, "No, I'm leaving." So we went outside, and we talked about it. And what I

said to him was, you have to be aware of the possibilities that this is not the first time that this has happened at this restaurant or at other restaurants, but this is the first time it has happened to a black news director here or someone who could make an issue of it, or someone who is prepared to make an issue of it.

So we went back inside after I talked him into it and, to make a long story short, I had the manager come. I made most of the people who were there (while conducting myself professionally the whole time) aware that I was incensed at being treated this way. . . . I said, "Why do you think we weren't seated?" And the manager said, "Well, I don't really know." And I said, "Guess." He said, "Well I don't know, because you're black?" I said, "Bingo. Now isn't it funny that you didn't guess that I didn't have any money (and I opened up my purse) and I said, "because I certainly have money. And isn't it odd that you didn't guess that it's because I couldn't pay for it because I've got two American Express cards and a Master Card right here. I think it's just funny that you would have assumed that it's because I'm black." . . . And then I took out my card and gave it to him and said, "If this happens again, or if I hear of this happening again, I will bring the full wrath of an entire news department down on this restaurant." And he just kind of looked at me. "Not [just] because I am personally offended. I am. But because you have no right to do what you did, and as a people we have lived a long time with having our rights abridged. . . ."

This example provides insight into the character of modern discrimination. The discrimination was not the "No Negroes" exclusion of the recent past, but rejection in the form of poor service by restaurant personnel. The black response indicates the change in black-white interaction since the 1950s and 1960s, for discrimination is handled with vigorous confrontation rather than deference. The aggressive black response and their white backtracking [suggest] that black-white interaction today is being renegotiated. It is possible that the white personnel defined the couple as "poor blacks" because of their jeans, although the jeans were fashionable and white patrons wear jeans. In comments not quoted here the news director rejects such an explanation. She forcefully articulates a theory of rights—a response that signals the critical impact of civil rights laws on the thinking of middle-class blacks. The news director articulates the American dream: she has worked hard, earned the money and credit cards, developed the appropriate middle-class behavior, and thus has under the law a *right* to be served. There is defensiveness in her actions too, for she feels a need to legitimate her status by showing her purse and credit cards. One important factor that enabled her to take such assertive action was her power to bring a TV news team to the restaurant. This power marks a change from a few decades ago when very few black Americans had the social or economic resources to fight back successfully.

This example underscores the complexity of the interaction in such situations, with two levels of negotiation evident. The negotiation between the respondent and her boyfriend on withdrawal vs. confrontation highlights the process of negotiating responses to discrimination and the difficulty in crafting such responses. Not only is there a process of dickering with whites within the discriminatory scene but also a negotiation between the blacks involved. . . .

Discrimination in public accommodations can occur in many different settings. A school board member in a northern city commented on her experiences in retail stores:

[I have faced] harassment in stores, being followed around, being questioned about what are you going to purchase here. . . . I was in an elite department store just this past Saturday and felt that I was being observed while I was window shopping. I in fact actually ended up purchasing something, but felt the entire time I was there—I was in blue jeans and sneakers, that's how I dress on a Saturday—I felt that I was being watched in the store as I was walking through the store, what business did I have there, what was I going to purchase, that kind of thing. . . . There are a few of those white people that won't put change in your hand, touch your skin—that doesn't need to go on. . . . I find my best weapon of defense is to educate them, whether it's in the store, in

a line at the bank, any situation, I teach them. And you take them by surprise because you tell them and show them what they should be doing, and what they should be saying and how they should be thinking. And they look at you because they don't know how to process you. They can't process it because you've just shown them how they should be living, and the fact that they are cheating themselves, really, because the racism is from fear. The racism is from lack of education.

This excessive surveillance of blacks' shopping was reported by several respondents in our study and in recent newspaper accounts (see Jaynes and Williams 1989, p. 140). Several white stereotypes seem to underlie the rejection discrimination in this instance—blacks are seen as shoplifters, as unclean, as disreputable poor. The excessive policing of black shoppers and the discourtesy of clerks illustrate the extra burden of being black in public places. No matter how affluent and influential, a black person cannot escape the stigma of being black, even while relaxing or shopping. There is the recurring strain of having to craft strategies for a broad range of discriminatory situations. Tailoring her confrontation to fit the particular discrimination, this respondent interrupted the normal flow of the interaction to call the whites to intersubjective account and make a one-way experience into a two-way experience. Forced into new situations, offending whites frequently do not know how "to process" such an aggressive response. Again we see how middle-class blacks can force a reconstruction of traditional responses by whites to blacks. The intensity of her discussion suggests that the attempt to "educate" whites comes with a heavy personal cost for it is stressful to "psych" oneself up for such incidents. . . .

Middle-class black parents often attempt to protect their children from racial hostility in public places, but they cannot always be successful. A manager at an electronics firm in the Southwest gave an account of his daughter's first encounter with a racial epithet. After describing racist graffiti on a neighborhood fence in the elite white suburb where he lives, he described an incident at a swimming pool:

I'm talking over two hundred kids in this pool; not one black. I don't think you can go anywhere in the world during the summertime and not find some black kids in the swimming pool. . . .Now what's the worst thing that can happen to a ten-year-old girl in a swimming pool with all white kids? What's the worst thing that could happen? It happened. This little white guy called her a "nigger." . . . And what initiated that, they had these little inner tubes, they had about fifteen of them, and the pool owns them. So you just use them if they are vacant. So there was a tube setting up on the bank, she got it, jumped in and started playing in it. . . . And this little white guy decided he wanted it. But, he's supposed to get it, right? And he meant to get it, and she wouldn't give it to him, so out came all these racial slurs. So my action was first with the little boy. "You know you're not supposed to do that. Apologize right now. Okay, good. Now, Mr. Lifeguard, I want him out of this pool, and you're going to have to do better. You're going to have to do better, but he has to leave out of this pool and let his parents know, okay?"

Taking his daughter back the next day, he observed from behind a fence to make certain the lifeguard protected her. For many decades black adults and children were excluded from public pools in the South and Southwest and many pools were closed during the early desegregation period. These accommodations have special significance for middle-class black Americans, and this may be one reason the father's reaction was so decisive. Perhaps the major reason for his swift action was because this was the first time that his daughter had been the victim of racial slurs. She was the victim of cutting racist epithets that for this black father, as doubtless for most black Americans, connote segregated institutions and violence against blacks. Children also face hostility in public accommodations and may never shake this kind of experience. At a rather early point, many black parents find it necessary to teach their children how to handle discriminatory incidents. . . .

Careful Situation Assessments

We have seen in the previous incidents some tendency for blacks to assess discriminatory incidents before they act. . . .

The complex process of evaluation and response is described by a college dean, who commented generally on hotel and restaurant discrimination encountered as he travels across the United States:

When you're in a restaurant and . . . you notice that blacks get seated near the kitchen. You notice that if it's a hotel, your room is near the elevator, or your room is always way down in a corner somewhere. You find that you are getting the undesirable rooms. And you come there early in the day and you don't see very many cars on the lot and they'll tell you that this is all we've got. Or you get the room that's got a bad television set. You know that you're being discriminated against. And of course you have to act accordingly. You have to tell them, "Okay, the room is fine, [but] this television set has got to go. Bring me another television set." So in my personal experience, I simply cannot sit and let them get away with it [discrimination] and not let them know that I know that that's what they are doing. . . .

When I face discrimination, first I take a long look at myself and try to determine whether or not I am seeing what I think I'm seeing in 1989, and if it's something that I have an option [about]. In other words, if I'm at a store making a purchase, I'll simply walk away from it. If it's at a restaurant where I'm not getting good service, I first of all let the people know that I'm not getting good service, then I [may] walk away from it. But the thing that I have to do is to let people know that I know that I'm being singled out for a separate treatment. And then I might react in any number of ways—depending on where I am and how badly I want whatever it is that I'm there for.

. . . The dean's interview highlights a major difficulty in being black—one must be constantly prepared to assess accurately and then decide on the appropriate response. This long-look approach may indicate that some middle-class blacks are so sensitive to white charges of hypersensitivity and paranoia that they err in the opposite direction and fail to see discrimination when it occurs. In addition, as one black graduate student at a leading white university in the Southeast put it: "I think that sometimes timely and appropriate responses to racially motivated acts and comments are lost due to the processing of the input." The "long look" can result in missed opportunities to respond to discrimination.

Using Middle-Class Resources for Protection

One advantage that middle-class blacks have over poorer blacks is the use of the resources of middle-class occupations. A professor at a major white university commented on the varying protection her middle-class status gives her at certain sites:

> If I'm in those areas that are fairly protected, within gatherings of my own group, other African Americans, or if I'm in the university where my status as a professor mediates against the way I might be perceived, mediates against the hostile perception, then it's fairly comfortable. . . . When I divide my life into encounters with the outside world, and of course that's ninety percent of my life, it's fairly consistently unpleasant at those sites where there's nothing that mediates between my race and what I have to do. For example, if I'm in a grocery store, if I'm in my car, which is a 1970 Chevrolet, a real old ugly car, all those things—being in a grocery store in casual clothes, or being in the car—sort of advertises something that doesn't have anything to do with my status as far as people I run into are concerned.
> Because I'm a large black woman, and I don't wear whatever class status I have, or whatever professional status [I have] in my appearance when I'm in the grocery store, I'm part of the mass of large black women shopping. For most whites, and even for some blacks, that translates into negative status. That means that they are free to treat me the way they treat most poor black people, because they can't tell by looking at me that I differ from that.

This professor notes the variation in discrimination in the sites through which she travels, from the most private to the most public. At home with friends she faces no problems, and at the university her professorial status gives her some protection from discrimination. The increase in unpleasant encounters as she moves into public accommodations sites such as grocery stores is attributed to the absence of mediating factors such as clear symbols of middle-class status—displaying the middle-class symbols may provide some protection against discrimination in public places.

An east coast news anchorperson reported a common middle-class experience of good service from retailers over the phone:

> And if I was seeking out a service, like renting a car, or buying something, I could get a wonderful, enthusiastic reaction to what I was doing. I would work that up to such a point that this person would probably shower me with roses once they got to see me. And then when I would show up, and they're surprised to see that I'm black, I sort of remind them in conversation how welcome my service was, to put the embarrassment on them, and I go through with my dealings. In fact, once my sister criticized me for putting [what] she calls my "white-on-white voice" on to get a rental car. But I needed a rental car and I knew that I could get it. I knew if I could get this guy to think that he was talking to some blonde, rather than, you know, so, but that's what he has to deal with. I don't have to deal with that, I want to get the car.

Being middle-class often means that you, as many blacks say, "sound white" over the phone. Over the phone middle-class blacks find they get fair treatment because the white person assumes the caller is white, while they receive poorer (or no) service in person. Race is the only added variable in such interpersonal contact situations. Moreover, some middle-class blacks intentionally use this phone-voice resource to secure their needs.

Responses to Discrimination: The Street

Reacting to White Strangers

As we move away from public accommodations settings to the usually less protected street sites, racial hostility can become more fleeting and severer, and thus black responses are often restricted. The most serious form of street discrimination is violence. Often the reasonable black response to street discrimination is withdrawal, resigned acceptance, or a quick verbal retort. The difficulty of responding to violence is seen in this report by a man working for a media surveying firm in a southern industrial city:

> I was parked in front of this guy's house. . . .This guy puts his hands on the window and says, "Get out of the car, nigger.". . . So, I got out, and I thought, "Oh, this is what's going to happen here." And I'm talking fast. And they're, "What are you doing here?" And I'm, "This is who I am. I work with these people. This is the man we want to put in the survey." And I pointed to the house. And the guy said, "Well you have an out-of-state license tag, right?" "Yea." And he said, "If something happened to you, your people at home wouldn't know for a long time, would they?" . . . I said, "Look, I deal with a company that deals with television. [If] something happens to me, it's going to be a national thing. . . . So, they grab me by the lapel of my coat, and put me in front of my car. They put the blade on my zipper. And now I'm thinking about this guy that's in the truck [behind me], because now I'm thinking that I'm going to have to run somewhere. Where am I going to run? Go to the police? [laughs] So, after a while they bash up my headlight. And I drove [away].

Stigmatized and physically attacked solely because of his color, this man faced verbal hostility and threats of death with courage. Cautiously drawing on his middle-class resources, he told the attackers his death would bring television crews to the town. This resource utilization is similar to that of the news director in the restaurant incident. Beyond this verbal threat his response had to be one of caution. For most whites threatened on the street, the police are a sought-after source of protection, but for black men this is often not the case.

At the other end of the street continuum is nonverbal harassment such as the "hate stare." . . . A middle-class student with dark skin reported that on her way to university classes she had stopped at a bakery in a white residential area where very few blacks live or shop. A white couple in front of the store stared intently and hatefully at her as she crossed the sidewalk and entered and left the bakery. She reported that she had experienced this hate stare many times. The incident angered her for some days thereafter, in part because she had been unable to respond more actively to it.

In between the hate stare and violence are many other hostile actions. Most happen so fast that withdrawal, resigned acceptance, or an immediate verbal retort are the reasonable responses. . . .

It seems likely that for middle-class blacks the street is the site of recurring encounters with various types of white malevolence. A vivid example of the cumulative character and impact of this discrimination was given by another black student at a white university, who recounted his experiences walking home at night from a campus job to his apartment in a predominantly white residential area:

> So, even if you wanted to, it's difficult just to live a life where you don't come into conflict with others. Because every day you walk the streets, it's not even like once a week, once a month. It's every day you walk the streets. Every day that you live as a black person you're reminded how you're perceived in society. You walk the streets at night; white people cross the streets. I've seen white couples and individuals dart in front of cars to not be on the same side of the street. Just the other day, I was walking down the street, and this white female with a child, I saw her pass a young white male about 20 yards ahead. When she saw me, she quickly dragged the child and herself across the busy street. What is so funny is that this area has had an unknown white rapist in the area for about four years. [When I pass] white men tighten their grip on their women. I've seen people turn around and seem like they're going to take blows from me. The police constantly make circles around me as I walk home, you know, for blocks. I'll walk, and they'll turn a block. And they'll come around me just to make sure, to find out

where I'm going. So, every day you realize [you're black]. Even though you're not doing anything wrong; you're just existing. You're just a person. But you're a black person perceived in an unblack world. [This quote includes a clarification sentence from a follow-up interview.]

. . . Unable to "see" his middle-class symbols of college dress and books, white couples (as well as individuals) have crossed the street in front of cars to avoid walking near this modest-build black student, in a predominantly white neighborhood. Couples moving into defensive postures are doubtless reacting to the stigma of "black maleness." The student perceives such avoidance as racist, however, not because he is paranoid, but because he has previously encountered numerous examples of whites taking such defensive measures. Many whites view typical "street" criminals as black or minority males and probably see young black males as potentially dangerous. . . . When I discussed this student's experiences with a prominent black journalist in a northeastern city, he reported that whites sometimes stop talking—and white women grab their purses—on downtown office-building elevators when he enters. These two men had somewhat different responses to such discrimination, one relatively passive and the other aggressive. In a follow-up interview the student reported that he rarely responded aggressively to the street encounters, apart from the occasional quick curse, because they happened too quickly. Echoing the black graduate student's comments about processing input and missed opportunities, he added: "I was basically analyzing and thinking too much about the incident." However, the journalist reacts more assertively; he described how he turns to whites in elevators and informs them, often with a smile, that they can continue talking or that he is not interested in their purses.

On occasion, black middle-class responses to street hostility from white strangers are even more aggressive. A woman who now runs her own successful business in a southwestern city described a car incident in front of a grocery store:

We had a new car . . . and we stopped at 7-11 [store]. We were going to go out that night, and we were taking my son to a babysitter. . . . And we pulled up, and my husband was inside at the time. And this person, this Anglo couple, drove up, and they hit our car. It was a brand new car. So my husband came out. And the first thing they told us was that we got our car on *welfare*. Here we are able-bodied. He was a corporate executive. I had a decent job, it was a professional job, but it wasn't paying anything. But they looked at the car we were driving, and they made the assumption that we got it from welfare. I completely snapped; I physically abused that lady. I did. And I was trying to keep my husband from arguing with her husband until the police could come. . . . And when the police came they interrogated them; they didn't arrest us, because there was an off-duty cop who had seen the whole incident and said she provoked it.

Here we see how some whites perceive blacks, including middle-class blacks, in interracial situations. The verbal attack by the whites was laced with the stereotype about blacks as welfare chiselers. This brought forth an angry response from the black couple, which probably came as a surprise to the whites. Note too the role of the off-duty police officer. The respondent does not say whether the officer was white or black, but this detail suggests that certain contexts of discrimination have changed—in the past a (white) police officer would have sided with the whites. . . . This respondent also underscores her and her husband's occupational achievements, highlighting her view that she has attained the American middle-class ideal. She is incensed that her obvious middle-class symbols did not protect her from verbal abuse. . . .

Responses to Discrimination by White Police Officers

Most middle-class blacks do not have such governmental authority as their personal protection. In fact, white police officers are a major problem. Encounters with the police can be life-threatening and thus limit the range of responses. A television commentator recounted two cases of police harassment when he was working for a survey firm in the mid-1980s. In one of the incidents, which took place in a southern metropolis, he was stopped by several white officers:

"What are you doing here?" I tell them what I'm doing here. . . . And so me spread on top of my car. [What had you done?] Because I was in the neighborhood. I left this note on these peoples' house: "Here's who I am. You weren't here, and I will come back in thirty minutes." [Why were they searching you?] They don't know. To me, they're searching, I remember at that particular moment when this all was going down, there was a lot of reports about police crime on civilians. . . . It took four cops to shake me down, two police cars, so they had me up there spread out. I had a friend of mine with me who was making the call with me, because we were going to have dinner together, and he was black, and they had me up, and they had him outside. . . . They said, "Well, let's check you out." . . .

It's like, if they can stop me, why wouldn't I go to jail, and I could sit in there for ten days before the judge sees me. I'm thinking all this crazy stuff. . . . Again, I'm talking to myself. And the guy takes his stick. And he doesn't whack me hard, but he does it with enough authority to let me know they mean business. "I told you stand still; now put your arms back out." And I've got this suit on, and the car's wet. And my friend's hysterical. He's outside the car. And they're checking him out. And he's like, "Man, just be cool, man." And he had tears in his eyes. And I'm like, oh, man, this is a nightmare. This is not supposed to happen to me. This is not my style! And so finally, this other cop comes up and says, "What have we got here Charlie?" "Oh, we've got a guy here. He's running through the neighborhood, and he doesn't want to do what we tell him. We might have to run him in." [You're "running through" the neighborhood?] Yeah, exactly, in a suit in the rain?! After they got through doing their thing and harassing me, I just said, "Man this has been a hell of a week.". . .

Scattered evidence suggests that by the time they are in their twenties, most black males, regardless of socioeconomic status, have been stopped by the police because "black-

ness" is considered a sign of possible criminality by police officers (Moss 1990; Roddy 1990, August 26). This treatment probably marks a dramatic contrast with the experiences of young white middle-class males. In the incident above the respondent and a friend experienced severe police maltreatment—detention for a lengthy period, threat of arrest, and the reality of physical violence. . . . The middle-class suits and obvious corporate credentials (for example, survey questionnaires and company car) did not protect the two black men. . . .

Conclusion

I have examined the sites of discrimination, the types of discriminatory acts, and the responses of the victims and have found the color stigma still to be very important in the public lives of affluent black Americans. The sites of racial discrimination range from relatively protected home sites, to less protected workplace and educational sites, to the even less protected public places. The 1964 Civil Rights Act guarantees that black Americans are "entitled to the full and equal enjoyment of the goods, services, facilities, privileges, advantages, and accommodations" in public accommodations. Yet the interviews indicate that deprivation of full enjoyment of public facilities is not a relic of the past; deprivation and discrimination in public accommodations persist. Middle-class black Americans remain vulnerable targets in public places. Prejudice-generated aggression in public places is, of course, not limited to black men and women—gay men and white women are also targets of street harassment (Benokraitis and Feagin 1986). Nonetheless, black women and men face an unusually broad range of discrimination on the street and in public accommodations. . . .

Particular instances of discrimination may seem minor to outside white observers when considered in isolation. But when blatant acts of avoidance, verbal harassment, and physical attack combine with subtle and covert slights, and these accumulate over months, years, and lifetimes, the impact on a black person is far more than the sum of the individual instances. . . .

The cumulative impact of racial discrimination accounts for the special way that blacks have of looking at and evaluating interracial incidents. One respondent, a clerical employee at an adoption agency, described the "second eye" she uses:

I think that it causes you to have to look at things from two different perspectives. You have to decide whether things that are done or slights that are made are made because you are black or they are made because the person is just rude, or unconcerned and uncaring. So it's kind of a situation where you're always kind of looking to see with a second eye or a second antenna just what's going on.

The language of "second eye" suggests that blacks look at white-black interaction through a lens colored by personal and group experience with cross-institutional and cross-generational discrimination. . . . What many whites see as black "paranoia" (e.g., Wieseltier 1989, June 5) is simply a realistic sensitivity to white-black interaction created and constantly reinforced by the. . . types of cumulative discrimination cited above.

Blacks must be constantly aware of the repertoire of possible responses to chronic and burdensome discrimination. . . . Another respondent was articulate on this point:

. . . if you can think of the mind as having one hundred ergs of energy, and the average man uses fifty percent of his energy dealing with the everyday problems of the world—just general kinds of things— then he has fifty percent more to do creative kinds of things that he wants to do. Now that's a white person. Now a black person also has one hundred ergs; he uses fifty percent the same way a white man does, dealing with what the white man has [to deal with], so he has fifty percent left. But he uses twenty-five percent fighting being black, [with] all the problems being black and what it means. Which means he really only has twenty-five percent to do what the white man has fifty percent to do, and he's expected to

do just as much as the white man with that twenty-five percent. . . . You just don't have as much energy left to do as much as you know you really could if you were free, [if] your mind were free.

The individual cost of coping with racial discrimination is great, and . . . you cannot accomplish as much as you could if you retained the energy wasted on discrimination. This is perhaps the most tragic cost of persisting discrimination in the United States. In spite of decades of civil rights legislation, black Americans have yet to attain the full promise of the American dream.

References

Benokraitis, Nijole, and Joe R. Feagin. 1986. *Modern Sexism: Blatant, Subtle and Covert Discrimination.* Englewood Cliffs: Prentice-Hall.

Feagin, Joe R., and Douglas Eckberg. 1980. "Prejudice and Discrimination." *Annual Review of Sociology* 6:1–20.

Feagin, Joe R., and Clairece Booher Feagin. 1986. *Discrimination American Style* (rev. ed). Melbourne, FL: Krieger Publishing Co.

Jaynes, Gerald D., and Robin Williams, Jr. (eds.). 1989. *A Common Destiny: Blacks and American Society.* Washington, DC: National Academy Press.

Moss, E. Yvonne. 1990. "African Americans and the Administration of Justice." Pp. 79–86 in *Assessment of the Status of African-Americans,* edited by Wornie L. Reed. Boston: University of Massachusetts, William Monroe Trotter Institute.

Roddy, Dennis B. 1990, August 26. "Perceptions Still Segregate Police, Black Community." *The Pittsburgh Press,* p. B1.

Wieseltier, Leon. 1989, June 5. "Scar Tissue." *New Republic,* pp. 19–20.

2

A Dozen Demons

Ellis Cose

...In the workplace, the continuing relevance of race takes on a special force, partly because so much of life, at least for middle-class Americans, is defined by work, and partly because even people who accept that they will not be treated fairly in the world often hold out hope that their work will be treated fairly—that even a society that keeps neighborhoods racially separate and often makes after-hours social relations awkward will properly reward hard labor and competence. What most African Americans discover, however, is that the racial demons that have plagued them all their lives do not recognize business hours—that the stress of coping extends to a nonwork world that is chronically unwilling (or simply unable) to acknowledge the status their professions ought to confer.

The coping effort, in some cases, is relatively minor. It means accepting the fact, for instance, that it is folly to compete for a taxi on a street corner with whites. It means realizing that prudence dictates dressing up whenever you are likely to encounter strangers (including clerks, cops, and doormen) who can make your life miserable by mistaking you for a tramp, a slut, or a crook. And it means tolerating the unctuous boor whose only topic of party conversation is blacks he happens to know. But the price of this continual coping is not insignificant. In addition to creating an unhealthy level of stress, it puts many in such a wary state of mind that insults are seen where none were intended, often complicating communications even with sensitive, well-meaning whites who unwittingly stumble into the racial minefield.

What is it exactly that blacks spend so much time coping with? For lack of a better phrase, let's call them the dozen demons. This is not to say that they affect blacks only; as will become clear, members of other racial minority groups are often plagued by them as well. Nor is it to say that there are only twelve, or that all black Americans encounter every one. Still, if you're looking for a safe bet, you could not find one more certain than this: that any random gathering of black American professionals, asked what irks or troubles them, will eventually end up describing, in one guise or another, the following items.

1. *Inability to fit in*. During the mid 1980s, I had lunch in the Harvard Club in Manhattan with a newsroom recruiter from the *New York Times*. The lunch was primarily social, but my companion was also seeking help in identifying black, Hispanic, and Asian-American journalists he could lure to the *Times*. Though he had encountered plenty of people with good professional credentials, he was concerned about an attribute that was torturously difficult to gauge: the ability to fit into the often bewildering culture of the *Times*. He was desperate to hire good minority candidates, he said, yet hiring someone who could produce decent copy was not enough. He wanted people with class, people who could be "*Times* people."

As we talked, it became clear that he was focusing on such things as speech, manners, dress, and educational pedigree. He had in mind, apparently, a certain button-down sort, an intellectual, nonthreatening, quiet-spoken type—something of a cross between, William F. Buckley and Bill Cosby. Someone who might be expected to have his own membership at the Harvard or Yale Club. Not surprisingly, he was not having much success. That most whites at the *Times* fit no such stereotype seemed not to have occurred to him. I suggested, rather gingerly, that perhaps he needed to expand his definition of a "*Times* person," that perhaps some of those he was eliminating for seemingly superficial reasons might have all the qualities the *Times* required.

Even as I made the argument, I knew that it was unpersuasive. Not because he disagreed—he did not offer much of a rebuttal—but because he and many similarly placed executives almost instinctively screened minority candidates according to criteria they did not apply to whites. The practice has nothing to do with malice. It stems more, I suspect, from an unexamined assumption that whites, purely because they are white, are likely to fit in, while blacks and other minority group members are not. Hence, he found it necessary to search for specific assurances that those he brought into the fold had qualities that would enable them, despite their color, to blend into the great white mass.

2. *Exclusion from the club.* Even the ability to fit in, however, does not necessarily guarantee acceptance. Many blacks who have made huge efforts to get the right education, master the right accent, and dress in the proper clothes still find that certain doors never seem to open, that there are private clubs—in both a real and a symbolic sense—they cannot join. . . .

In 1990, in testimony before the U.S. Senate Judiciary Committee, Darwin Davis, senior vice president of the Equitable Life Assurance Society, told of the frustrations he and some of his black friends had experienced in trying to join a country club. "I have openly approached fellow executives about memberships. Several times, they have said, 'My club has openings; it should be no problem. I'll get back to you.' Generally, one of two things happens. They are too embarrassed to talk to me or they come right out and tell me they were shocked when they made inquiries about bringing in a black. Some have even said they were told to get out of the club if they didn't like the situation as it is."

Davis, a white-haired, elegant, and genial raconteur who loves to play golf, told the Senate panel that his interest was not merely in the game but in the financial costs of exclusion. He was routinely reduced to entertaining golf-playing clients at a public course with poor facilities. "The best I can offer my client is a hamburger and a beer in a plastic cup. My competitor takes this client. . .where they have a great lunch and drinks, and use of the locker room and showers. Then, they get their shoes shined. I am out of the ball game with this client." Whenever he found out that a customer played golf, he became "anxious because I know I am on thin ice." It was "disheartening and demeaning," he added, "to know that it doesn't matter how

hard I work, how proficient an executive I become, or how successful I become. I will be denied this one benefit that success is supposed to confer on those who have achieved."

Two years after his testimony, Davis told me his obsession with private clubs sprang in part from concerns about his children. Several years before, he had visited a club as a guest and happened to chance upon a white executive he knew. As they were talking, he noticed the man wave at someone on the practice range. It turned out that he had brought his son down to take a lesson from the club pro. Davis was suddenly struck by a depressing thought. "Damn!" he said to himself. "This is being perpetuated all over again. . . . I have a son the same age as his. And when my son grows up he's going to go through the same crap I'm going through if I don't do something about this. His son is learning how to . . . socialize, get lessons, and do business at a country club." His own son, Davis concluded, would "never ever be able to have the same advantages or even an equal footing."

3. *Low expectations.* Shortly after I arrived to take over the editorial pages of the New York *Daily News,* I was visited by a black employee who had worked at the paper for some time. More was on his mind than a simple desire to make my acquaintance. He had also come to talk about how his career was blocked, how the deck was stacked against him—how, in fact, it was stacked against any black person who worked there. His frustration and anger I easily understood. But what struck me as well was that his expectations left him absolutely no room to grow. He believed so strongly that the white men at the *Daily News* were out to stymie black achievement that he had no option but failure, whatever the reality of the situation.

Even those who refuse to internalize the expectation of failure are often left with nagging doubts, with a feeling, as journalist Joe Boyce puts it, "that no matter what you do in life, there are very few venues in which you can really be sure that you've exhausted your potential. Your achievement is defined by your color and its limitations. And even if in reality you've met your fullest potential, there's an aggravating, lingering doubt . . . because you're never sure. And that makes you angry."

During the late 1970s, I met a Harvard student, Mark Whitaker, who was interning for a summer in *Newsweek's* Washington bureau. Whitaker made it clear that he intended to go far. He had it in mind to become editor of *Newsweek.* I didn't know whether to be amused by his arrogance, awed by his ambition, or amazed by his naivete. I asked Whitaker—the product of a mixed (black/white) union—whether he had considered that his race might hold him back. He answered that maybe it would, but that he was not going to permit his color to smother his aspirations. He would not hold himself back. If he was to be stopped, it would be by someone else.

More than a decade later, when Whitaker had become a *Newsweek* assistant managing editor, I reminded him of our earlier conversation. He laughed his precocious comments off, attributing them to the ignorance and arrogance of youth. We both knew better, of course—just as we knew that many young blacks, for a variety of reasons, never even reach the point of believing that success was within their grasp.

Conrad Harper, former head of the Association of the Bar of the City of New York and a partner in Simpson Thacher & Barlett, said that throughout the years he had seen plenty of young associates "bitterly scarred by not being taken first as lawyers . . . but always first as African Americans." He had also seen affirmative action turned into a stigma and used as a club to beat capable people down. If someone's competency is consistently doubted, "the person begins to question his own abilities." The result, he added, is not only a terrible waste of talent, but in some cases psychological damage.

4. *Shattered hopes*. After two years toiling at an eminent law firm, the young associate walked away in disgust and became a public defender. For more than a year after leaving, he was "so filled with rage, I couldn't even talk about it much." A soft-spoken Mexican American, he bristles with emotion as he recalls those years.

He believes that he and other minority group hires simply never got a shot at the big assignments, which invariably went to white males. This sense of disappointment, he makes plain, was felt by all the nonwhites in his class. He remembers one in particular, a black woman who graduated with honors from Yale. All her peers thought she was headed for the stars. Yet when she was rated periodically, she was never included in the first tier but at the top of the second.

If he had been alone in his frustration, he says, one could reject his complaint as no more than a case of sour grapes. "But the fact that all of us were having the same kinds of feelings" means something more systemic was at work. He acknowledges that many whites had similar feelings, that in the intensely competitive environment of a top law firm, no one is guaranteed an easy time. But the sense of abandonment, he contends, was exacerbated for nonwhites. By his count, every minority group member who entered the firm with him ended up leaving, having concluded that nonwhites—barring the spectacularly odd exception—were not destined to make it in that world.

5. *Faint praise*. For a year and a half during the early 1980s, I was a resident fellow at the National Research Council-National Academy of Sciences, an august Washington institution that evaluates scientific research. One afternoon, I mentioned to a white colleague who was also a close friend that it was a shame the NRC had so few blacks on staff. She replied, "Yes, it's too bad there aren't more blacks like you."

I was stunned enough by her comment to ask her what she meant. She answered, in effect, that there were so few really intelligent blacks around who could meet the standards of the NRC. I, of course, was a wonderful exception. Her words, I'm sure, were meant as a compliment, but they angered me, for I took her meaning to be that blacks (present company excluded) simply didn't have the intellect to hang out with the likes of her.

My colleague's attitude seemed to disallow the possibility of a better explanation for the scarcity of blacks than the supposedly low intellectual quality of the race. Perhaps there were so few blacks at the NRC—because they simply were not sought out, or because they were encouraged to believe, from childhood on, that they could never master the expertise that would land them in such a place. The ease with which she dismissed such possibilities in favor of a testimonial to my uniqueness disappointed and depressed me.

Blacks who have been singled out as exceptions often experience anger at the whites who commend them. One young woman, a Harvard-trained lawyer with a long list of "firsts" behind her name, had another reason for cringing whenever she was held up as a glistening departure from the norm for her race. "I don't like what it does to my relationships with other blacks," she said.

6. *Presumption of failure*. A year or so prior to my Harvard Club chat with the *Times* recruiter, I was visited at my office (then in Berkeley, California) by a *Times* assistant managing editor. I took him to lunch, and after a few drinks we fell into a discussion of people at the *Times*, among them a talented black editor whose career seemed to have stalled. Was he in line, I asked, for a high-level editorship that would soon be vacant? My companion agreed that the editor would probably do very well in the job, but then he pointed out that a black person had never held such a post at the *New York Times*. The *Times* would have to think hard, he indicated, before changing that, for they could not afford to have a black journalist fail in such a visible position. I didn't know whether the man even wanted the job (he later told me he might have preferred something else); I know that he didn't get it, that (at least in the eyes of one *Times* assistant managing editor in 1985) his prior work and credentials could not offset the questions raised by his color. Failure at the highest levels of the *Times* was a privilege apparently reserved for whites.

The *Times'* executive's reasoning reminded me of an encounter with a newspaper editor in Atlanta who had contacted me several years earlier. He had an editorial writer's position to fill and was interested in giving me a crack at it. I was intrigued enough to go to Atlanta and spend an evening with the man. We discovered we shared many interests and friends and hit it off famously. Still, I wondered: Why in the world was he recruiting me? Interesting though Atlanta might be, and as well as he and I got along, there had never been much chance that I would leap at the job. In no way did it represent a career advancement, and the editor's budget would barely permit him to pay the salary I was already making. As the evening wore on, I put the question to him bluntly. Why did he not offer the job to someone in his newsroom for whom it would be a real step up? His answer I found more than a little unsettling. One black person, he said, had already come on staff and not performed very well. He could not afford another black failure, so he had gone after someone overqualified in an attempt to buy himself insurance.

I'm sure he was not surprised that I turned the job down. . . . I don't doubt . . . that similar preconceptions still exist, that before many executives even ask whether a minority person can do a job, they ask whether they are prepared to take a flyer on a probable failure.

7. *Coping fatigue*. When Armetta Parker headed for Midland, Michigan, to take a job as a public relations professional at the Dow Chemical Company, she assumed that she was on her way to big-time corporate success. A bright, energetic black woman then in her early thirties, Parker had left a good position at a public utility in Detroit to get on the Fortune 100 fast track.

"Dow was everything I expected and more, and everything I expected and less," she says. The town of nearly forty thousand had only a few hundred black families, and virtually no single black people her own age. Though she expected a certain amount of social isolation, "I didn't expect to get the opportunity to take a really hard look at me, at what was important to me and what wasn't." She had to face the fact that success, in that kind of corporate environment, meant a great deal of work and no social life, and that it also required a great deal of faith in people who found it difficult to recognize competence in blacks. . . .

Nonetheless, Parker did extremely well, at least initially. Her first year at the company, she made it into "The Book"—the roster of those who had been identified as people on the fast track. But eventually she realized that "I was never going to be vice president of public affairs for Dow Chemical." She believed that her color, her gender, and her lack of a technical degree all were working against her. Moreover, "even if they gave it to me, I didn't want it. The price was too high." Part of that price would have been accepting the fact that her race was not seen as an asset but as something she had to overcome. And her positive traits were probably attributed to white genes, she surmised, even though she is no more "white" than most American blacks. Even her way of talking drew attention. Upon meeting her, one colleague remarked with evident pleasure and astonishment, "You don't speak ghettoese." She had an overwhelming sense that what he meant was "You're almost like us, but not enough like us to be acceptable." . . . She realized that "good corporate jobs can be corporate handcuffs. You have to decide how high of a price you're willing to pay."

8. *Pigeonholing*. Near the end of his brashly brilliant tenure as executive editor of the *Washington Post*, Ben Bradlee observed how much both Washington and the *Post* had changed. Once upon a time, he told me, one would not have thought of appointing a black city editor. Now one could not think of not seriously considering—and even favoring—a black person for the assignment.

Bradlee, I realized, was making several points. One was about himself and his fellow editors, about how they had matured to the extent that they valued all managerial talent—even in blacks. He was also acknowledging that blacks had become so central to Washington's political, economic, and social life that a black city editor had definite advantages, strictly as a function of race. His third point, I'm sure was wholly unintended but clearly implied: that it was still possible, even for the most enlightened management, to classify jobs by color. And logic dictates that if certain managerial tasks are best handled by blacks, others are best left to whites.

What this logic has meant in terms of the larger corporate world is that black executives have landed, out of all proportion to their numbers, in community relations and public affairs, or in slots where their only relevant expertise concerns blacks and other minorities. The selfsame racial assumptions that make minorities seem perfect for certain initially desirable jobs can ultimately be responsible for trapping them there as others move on.

9. *Identity troubles*. The man was on the verge of retiring from his position as personnel vice president for one of America's largest companies. He had acquired the requisite symbols of success: a huge office, a generous compensation package, a summer home away from home. But he had paid a price. He had decided along the way, he said matter-of-factly, that he could no longer afford to be black.

I was so surprised by the man's statement that I sat silent for several seconds before asking him to explain. Clearly he had done nothing to alter his dark brown complexion. What he had altered, he told me, was the way he allowed himself to be perceived. Early in his career, he had been moderately outspoken about what he saw as racism within and outside his former corporation. He had learned, however, that his modest attempts at advocacy got him typecast as an undesirable. So when he changed jobs, he decided to disassociate himself from any hint of a racial agenda. The strategy had clearly furthered his career, even though other blacks in the company labeled him an Uncle Tom. He was aware of his reputation, and pained by what the others thought, but he had seen no other way to thrive. He noted as well, with evident pride, that he had not abandoned his race, that he had quietly made it his business to cultivate a few young blacks in the corporation and bring their careers along; and could point to some who were doing very well and would have been doing considerably worse without his intervention. His achievements brought him enough pleasure to balance out the distress of not being "black."

Putting aside for the moment what it means to be "black," the fear of being forced to shed one's identity in order to prosper is not at all uncommon. Georgetown University law professor Anita Allen tells of a worried student who asked whether her diction would have to be as precise as Allen's if she was to be successful as a lawyer. She feared, it seemed, not merely having to change her accent, but being required to discard an important part of herself.

10. *Self-censorship and silence*. . . . [M]any blacks find their voices stilled when sensitive racial issues are raised. A big-city police officer once shared with me his frustration at waiting nineteen years to make detective. In those days before affirmative action, he had watched, one year after another, as less qualified whites were promoted over him. And each year he had swallowed his disappointment, twisted his face into a smile, and congratulated his white friends as he hid his rage—so determined was he to avoid being categorized as a race-obsessed troublemaker. And he had endured other affronts in silence, including a vicious beating by a group of white cops while carrying out a plainclothes assignment. As an undercover officer working within a militant black organization, he had been given a code word to whisper to a fellow officer if the need arose. When he was being brutalized, he had screamed out the word and discovered it to be worthless. His injuries had required surgery and more than thirty stitches. When he was asked by his superior to identify those who had beat him, he feigned ignorance; it seems a fellow officer had preceded his commander and bluntly passed along the message that it was safer to keep quiet.

Even though he made detective years ago, and even though, on the side, he managed to become a successful businessman and an exemplary member of the upwardly striving middle class, he says the anger still simmers within him. He worries that someday it will come pouring out, that some luckless white person will tick him off and he will explode, with tragic results. Knowing him, I don't believe he will ever reach that point. But I accept his fear that he could blow up as a measure of the intensity of his feelings, and of the terrible cost of having to hold them in.

11. *Mendacity*. Even more damaging than self-imposed silence are the lies that seem an integral part of America's approach to race. Many of the lies are simple self-deception, as when corporate executives claim their companies are utterly color-blind. Some stem from unwillingness to acknowledge racial bias, as when people who have no intention of voting for a candidate of another race tell pollsters that they will. And many are lies of business, social, or political convenience, as was the case with Massachusetts Senator Edward Brooke in the early 1970s.

At the time, Brooke was the highest-ranking black politician in America. His name was routinely trotted out as a vice presidential possibility, though everyone involved knew the exercise was a farce. According to received wisdom, America was not ready to accept a black on the ticket, but Brooke's name seemed to appear on virtually everyone's list. During one such period of vice-presidential hype, I interviewed Brooke for a newspaper profile. After asking the standard questions, I could no longer contain my curiosity. Wasn't he tired, I asked, of the charade of having his name bandied about when no one intended to select him? He nodded wearily and said yes, he was.

To me, his response spoke volumes, probably much more than he'd intended. But I took it as his agreement that lies of political convenience are not merely a nuisance for those interested in the truth but a source of profound disgust and cynicism for those on whose behalf the lies are supposedly told.

12. *Guilt by association*. In the mid 1980s, I was unceremoniously tossed out of Cafe Royale, a restaurant that catered to yuppies in San Francisco, on the orders of a maitre d' who apparently mistook me for someone who had caused trouble on a previous occasion. I sued the restaurant and eventually collected a few thousand dollars from its insurance company. But I will never forget the fury I experienced at being haughtily dismissed by an exalted waiter who would not suffer the inconvenience of having to distinguish one black person from another.

My first real understanding of how poisonous such an attitude could be came to me at the age of twelve or thirteen, when I went to Marshall Field's department store in downtown Chicago in search of a Mother's Day gift. While wandering from one section of the store to another, I gradually became aware that someone was shadowing me. That someone, I ascertained, was a plain-clothes security guard. Apparently I fit his profile of a shoplifter. For several minutes, I roamed through the store, trying to ignore him, but he was determined not to be ignored. Little by little, he made his surveillance more obvious, until we were practically walking in lock step. His tactics unsettled me so much that I could no longer concentrate on shopping. Finally, I whirled to face him.

He said nothing, merely glared as my outrage mounted. *How dare he treat me like a criminal*, I thought, *simply because I'm black.* I screamed something at him, I don't remember what. Whatever it was, it had no effect; he continued to stare at me with a look somewhere between amusement and disdain. I stalked out of the store, conceding him the victory, burning with anger and humiliation. . . .

[Many commentators argue] that America's cities have become so dangerous, largely as a result of young black thugs, that racial discrimination is justified—and is even a necessary tool of survival when directed at young black men.˙ . . .

This rationalization strikes me, to put it mildly, as dangerous. For it inevitably takes one beyond the street, and beyond those black males who are certifiably dangerous. It quickly takes one into society at large, where blacks in no way connected with street crime find themselves victims of street-crime stereotypes. Members of the law-abiding black middle class also have sons, as do those countless African Americans without substantial financial resources who have tried to pound into their children, from birth, that virtue has it rewards, that there is value in following a moral path and shunning the temptations of the street. . . .

Countless members of the black middle class are in fact volunteering every spare moment in an attempt to do whatever they can (working in homeless shelters, volunteering in literacy programs, serving as formal mentors) to better the lives of those in the so-called underclass. At the same time, however, many who belong to America's black privileged class are struggling with problems of their own that are largely unseen or dismissed.

3

The Cost of Racial and Class Exclusion in the Inner City

Loïc J. D. Wacquant
William Julius Wilson

After a long eclipse, the ghetto has made a stunning comeback into the collective consciousness of America. Not since the riots of the hot summers of 1966–68 have the black poor received so much attention in academic, activist, and policymaking quarters alike.[1] Persistent and rising poverty, especially among children, mounting social disruptions, the continuing degradation of public housing and public schools, concern over the eroding tax base of cities plagued by large ghettos and by the dilemmas of gentrification, the disillusions of liberals over welfare have all combined to put the black inner-city poor back in the spotlight. Owing in large part to the pervasive and ascendant influence of conservative ideology in the United States, however, recent discussions of the plight of ghetto blacks have typically been cast in individualistic and moralistic terms. The poor are presented 'as a mere aggregation of personal cases, each with its own logic and self-contained causes. Severed from the struggles and structural changes in the society, economy, and polity that in fact determine them, inner-city dislocations are then portrayed as a self-imposed, self-sustaining phenomenon.

This vision of poverty has found perhaps its most vivid expression in the lurid descriptions of ghetto residents that have flourished in the pages of popular magazines and on televised programs devoted to the emerging underclass.[2] Descriptions and explanations of the current predicament of inner-city blacks put the emphasis on individual attributes and the alleged grip of the so-called culture of poverty.

This article, in sharp contrast, draws attention to the specific features of the proximate social structure in which ghetto residents evolve and strive, against formidable odds, to survive and, whenever they can, escape its poverty and degradation. We provide this different perspective by profiling blacks who live in Chicago's inner city, contrasting the situation of those who dwell in low-poverty areas with residents of the city's ghetto neighborhoods. Beyond its sociographic focus, the central argument running through this article is that the interrelated set of phenomena captured by the term "underclass" is primarily social-structural and that the ghetto is experiencing a "crisis" not because a "welfare ethos" has mysteriously taken over its residents but because joblessness and economic exclusion, having reached dramatic proportions, have triggered a process of hyperghettoization.

Indeed, the urban black poor of today differ both from their counterparts of earlier years and from the white poor in that they are becoming increasingly concentrated in dilapidated territorial enclaves that epitomize acute social and economic marginalization. . . .

[The] growing social and spatial concentration of poverty creates a formidable and unprecedented set of obstacles for ghetto blacks. . . .

The purpose of this article is to begin to highlight this specifically sociological dimension of the changing reality of ghetto poverty by focusing on Chicago's inner city. . . .

Deindustrialization and Hyperghettoization

Social conditions in the ghettos of Northern metropolises have never been enviable, but today they are scaling new heights in deprivation, oppression, and hardship. The situation of Chicago's black inner city is emblematic of the social changes that have sown despair and exclusion in these communities. . . . [An] unprecedented tangle of social woes is now gripping the black communities of the city's South Side and West Side. In the past decade alone, these racial enclaves have experienced rapid increases in the number and percentage of poor families, extensive out-migration of working- and middle-class households, stagnation—if not real regression—of income, and record levels of unemployment. As of the last census, over two-thirds of all families living in these areas were headed by women; about half of the population had to rely on public aid, for most adults were out of a job and only a tiny fraction of them had completed college.[3]

The single largest force behind this increasing social and economic marginalization of large numbers of inner-city blacks has been a set of mutually reinforcing spatial and industrial changes in the country's urban political economy[4] that have converged to undermine the material foundations of the traditional ghetto. Among these structural shifts are the decentralization of industrial plants, which commenced at the time of World War I but accelerated sharply after 1950, and the flight of manufacturing jobs abroad, to the Sunbelt states, or to the suburbs and exurbs at a time when blacks were continuing to migrate en masse to Rustbelt central cities; the general deconcentration of metropolitan economies and the turn toward service industries and occupations, promoted by the growing separation of banks and industry; and the emergence of post-Taylorist, so-called flexible forms of organizations and generalized corporate attacks on unions—expressed by, among other things, wage cutbacks and the spread of two-tier wage systems and labor contracting—which has intensified job competition and triggered an explosion of low-pay, part-time work. This means that even mild forms of racial discrimination—mild by historical standards—have a bigger impact on those at the bottom of the American class order. In the labor-surplus environment of the 1970s, the weakness of unions and the retrenchment of civil rights enforcement aggravated the structuring of unskilled labor markets along racial lines,[5] marking large numbers of inner-city blacks with the stamp of economic redundancy. . . .

As the metropolitan economy moved away from smokestack industries and expanded outside of Chicago, emptying the Black Belt of most of its manufacturing jobs and employed residents, the gap between the ghetto and the rest of the city, not to mention its suburbs, widened dramatically. By 1980, median family income on the South and West sides had dropped to around one-third and one-half of the city average, respectively, compared with two-thirds and near parity 30 years earlier. Meanwhile, some of the city's white bourgeois neighborhoods and upper-class suburbs had reached over twice the citywide figure. . . .

A recent ethnographic account of changes in North Kenwood, one of the poorest black sections on the city's South Side, vividly encapsulates the accelerated physical and social decay of the ghetto and is worth quoting at some length:

> In the 1960's, 47th Street was still the social hub of the South Side black community. Sue's eyes light up when she describes how the street used to be filled with stores, theaters and nightclubs in which one could listen to jazz bands well into the evening. Sue remembers the street as "soulful." Today the street might be better characterized as soulless. Some stores, currency exchanges, bars and liquor stores continue to exist on 47th. Yet, as one walks down the street, one is struck more by the death of the street than by its life. Quite literally, the destruction of human life occurs frequently on 47th. In terms of physical structures, many stores are boarded up and abandoned. A few buildings have bars across the front and are closed to the public, but they are not empty. They are used, not so secretly, by people involved in illegal activities. Other stretches of the street are simply barren, empty lots. Whatever buildings once stood on the lots are long gone. Nothing gets built on 47th. . . . Over the years one apartment building after another has been condemned by the city and torn down. Today many blocks have the bombed-out look of Berlin after World War II. There are huge, barren areas of Kenwood, covered by weeds, bricks, and broken bottles. . . .[6]

Fundamental changes in the organization of America's advanced economy have thus unleashed irresistible centrifugal pressures that have broken down the previous structure of the ghetto and set off a process of hyperghettoization.[7] By this, we mean that the ghetto has lost much of its organizational strength—the "pulpit and the press," for instance, have virtually collapsed as collective agencies—as it has become increasingly marginal economically; its activities are no longer structured around an internal and relatively autonomous social space that duplicates the institutional structure of the larger society and provides basic minimal resources for social mobility, if only within a truncated black class structure. And the social ills that have long been associated with segregated poverty—violent crime, drugs, housing deterioration, family disruption, commercial blight, and educational failure—have reached qualitatively different proportions and have become articulated into a new configuration that endows each with a more deadly impact than before.

If the "organized," or institutional, ghetto of forty years ago . . . imposed an enormous cost on blacks collectively,[8] the "disorganized" ghetto, or hyperghetto, of today carries an even larger price. For, now, not only are ghetto residents, as before, dependent on the will and decisions of outside forces that rule the field of power—the mostly white dominant class, corporations, realtors, politicians, and welfare agencies—they have no control over and are forced to rely on services and institutions that are massively inferior to those of the wider society. Today's ghetto inhabitants comprise almost exclusively the most marginal and oppressed sections of the black community. Having lost the economic underpinnings and much of the fine texture of organizations and patterned activities that allowed previous generations of urban blacks to sustain family, community, and collectivity even in the face of continued economic hardship and unflinching racial subordination, the inner-city now presents a picture of radical class and racial exclusion. It is to a sociographic assessment of the latter that we now turn.

The Cost of Living in the Ghetto

Let us contrast the social structure of ghetto neighborhoods with that of low-pov-

erty black areas of the city of Chicago. . . . Given that the overall poverty rate among black families in the city is about one-third, these low-poverty areas can be considered as roughly representative of the average non-ghetto, non-middle-class, black neighborhood of Chicago. . . . Extreme-poverty neighborhoods comprise tracts with at least 40 percent of their residents in poverty. . . . These tracts make up the historic heart of Chicago's black ghetto: over 82 percent of the respondents in this category inhabit the West and South sides of the city, in areas most of which have been all black for half a century and more, and an additional 13 percent live in immediately adjacent tracts. Thus when we counterpose extreme-poverty areas with low-poverty areas, we are in effect comparing ghetto neighborhoods with other black areas, most of which are moderately poor, that are not part of Chicago's traditional Black Belt. Even though this comparison involves a truncated spectrum of types of neighborhoods,[9] the contrasts it reveals between low-poverty and ghetto tracts are quite pronounced. . . .

The Black Class Structure In and Out of the Ghetto

The first major difference between low- and extreme-poverty areas has to do with their class structure. . . . A sizable majority of blacks in low-poverty tracts are gainfully employed: two-thirds hold a job, including 11 percent with middle-class occupations and 55 percent with working-class jobs, while one-third do not work.[10] These proportions are exactly opposite in the ghetto, where fully 61 percent of adult residents do not work, one-third have working-class jobs and a mere 6 percent enjoy middle-class status. For those who reside in the urban core, then, being without a job is by far the most likely occurrence, while being employed is the exception. Controlling for gender does not affect this contrast, though it does reveal the greater economic vulnerability of women, who are twice as likely as men to be jobless. Men in both types of neighborhoods have a more favorable class mix resulting from their better rates of employment: 78 percent in low-poverty areas and 66 percent in the ghetto. If women are much less frequently employed—

42 percent in low-poverty areas and 69 percent in the ghetto do not work—they have comparable, that is, severely limited, overall access to middle-class status: in both types of neighborhood, only about 10 percent hold credentialed salaried positions or better. . . .

As we would expect, there is a close association between class and educational credentials. Virtually every member of the middle class has at least graduated from high school; nearly two-thirds of working-class blacks have also completed secondary education; but less than half—44 percent—of the jobless have a high school diploma or more. Looked at from another angle, 15 percent of our educated respondents—that is, high school graduates or better-have made it into the salaried middle class, half have become white-collar or blue-collar wage earners, and 36 percent are without a job. By comparison, those without a high school education are distributed as follows: 1.6 percent in the middle class, 37.9 percent in the working class, and a substantial majority of 60.5 percent in the jobless category. In other words, a high school degree is a *conditio sine qua non* for blacks for entering the world of work, let alone that of the middle class. Not finishing secondary education is synonymous with economic redundancy.

Ghetto residents are, on the whole, less educated than the inhabitants of other black neighborhoods. This results in part from their lower class composition but also from the much more modest academic background of the jobless: fewer than 4 in 10 jobless persons on the city's South Side and West Side have graduated from high school, compared to nearly 6 in 10 in low-poverty areas. It should be pointed out that education is one of the few areas in which women do not fare worse than men: females are as likely to hold a high school diploma as males in the ghetto—50 percent—and more likely to do so in low-poverty areas—69 percent versus 62 percent.

Moreover, ghetto residents have lower class origins, if one judges from the economic assets of their family of orientation.[11] Fewer than 4 ghetto dwellers in 10 come from a family that owned its home and 6 in 10 have parents who owned nothing, that is, no home,

business, or land. In low-poverty areas, 55 percent of the inhabitants are from a home-owning family while only 40 percent had no assets at all a generation ago. Women, both in and out of the ghetto, are least likely to come from a family with a home or any other asset—46 percent and 37 percent, respectively. This difference in class origins is also captured by differential rates of welfare receipt during childhood: the proportion of respondents whose parents were on public aid at some time when they were growing up is 30 percent in low-poverty tracts and 41 percent in the ghetto. Women in extreme-poverty areas are by far the most likely to come from a family with a welfare record.

Class, Gender, and Welfare Trajectories in Low- and Extreme-Poverty Areas

If they are more likely to have been raised in a household that drew public assistance in the past, ghetto dwellers are also much more likely to have been or to be currently on welfare themselves. Differences in class, gender, and neighborhood cumulate at each juncture of the welfare trajectory to produce much higher levels of welfare attachments among the ghetto population. . . .

In low-poverty areas, only one resident in four is currently on aid while almost half have never personally received assistance. In the ghetto, by contrast, over half the residents are current welfare recipients, and only one in five have never been on aid. . . .

None of the middle-class respondents who live in low-poverty tracts were on welfare at the time they were interviewed, and only one in five had ever been on aid in their lives. Among working-class residents, a mere 7 percent were on welfare and just over one-half had never had any welfare experience. This same relationship between class and welfare receipt is found among residents of extreme-poverty tracts, but with significantly higher rates of welfare receipt at all class levels: there, 12 percent of working-class residents are presently on aid and 39 percent received welfare before; even a few middle-class blacks—9 percent—are drawing public assistance and only one-third of them have never received any aid, instead of three-quarters in low-poverty tracts. But it is among the jobless that the difference between low- and extreme-poverty areas is the largest: fully 86 percent of those in ghetto tracts are currently on welfare and only 7 percent have never had recourse to public aid, compared with 62 percent and 20 percent, respectively, among those who live outside the ghetto.

Neighborhood differences in patterns of welfare receipt are robust across genders, with women exhibiting noticeably higher rates than men in both types of areas and at all class levels. The handful of black middle-class women who reside in the ghetto are much more likely to admit to having received aid in the past than their male counterparts: one-third versus one-tenth. Among working-class respondents, levels of current welfare receipt are similar for both sexes—5.0 percent and 8.5 percent, respectively while levels of past receipt again display the greater economic vulnerability of women: 1 in 2 received aid before as against 1 male in 5. This gender differential is somewhat attenuated in extreme-poverty areas by the general prevalence of welfare receipt, with two-thirds of all jobless males and nine in ten jobless women presently receiving public assistance.

The high incidence and persistence of joblessness and welfare in ghetto neighborhoods, reflecting the paucity of viable options for stable employment, take a heavy toll on those who are on aid by significantly depressing their expectations of finding a route to economic self-sufficiency. While a slim majority of welfare recipients living in low-poverty tracts expect to be self-supportive within a year and only a small minority anticipate receiving aid for longer than five years, in ghetto neighborhoods, by contrast, fewer than one in three public-aid recipients expect to be welfare-free within a year and fully one in five anticipate needing assistance for more than five years. This difference of expectations increases among the jobless of both genders. For instance, unemployed women in the ghetto are twice as likely as unemployed women in low-poverty areas to think that they will remain on aid for more than five years and half as likely to anticipate getting off the rolls within a year.

Thus if the likelihood of being on welfare increases sharply as one crosses the line between the employed and the jobless, it remains that, at each level of the class structure, welfare receipt is notably more frequent in extreme-poverty neighborhoods, especially among the unemployed, and among women. This pattern is confirmed by the data on the incidence of food assistance . . . and strongly suggests that those unable to secure jobs in low-poverty areas have access to social and economic supports to help them avoid the public-aid rolls that their ghetto counterparts lack. Chief among those are their financial and economic assets.

Differences in Economic and Financial Capital

A quick survey of the economic and financial assets of the residents of Chicago's poor black neighborhoods . . . reveals the appalling degree of economic hardship, insecurity, and deprivation that they must confront day in and day out.[12] The picture in low-poverty areas is grim; that in the ghetto is one of near-total destitution. . . .

Due to meager and irregular income, those financial and banking services that most members of the larger society take for granted are, to put it mildly, not of obvious access to the black poor. Barely one-third of the residents of low-poverty areas maintain a personal checking account; only one in nine manage to do so in the ghetto, where nearly three of every four persons report no financial asset whatsoever from a possible list of six and only 8 percent have at least three of those six assets. . . . Here, again, class and neighborhood lines are sharply drawn: in low-poverty areas, 10 percent of the jobless and 48 percent of working-class blacks have a personal checking account compared to 3 percent and 37 percent, respectively, in the ghetto; the proportion for members of the middle class is similar—63 percent—in both areas.

The American dream of owning one's home remains well out of reach for a large majority of our black respondents, especially those in the ghetto, where barely 1 person in 10 belongs to a home-owning household, compared to over 4 in 10 in low-poverty areas, a difference that is just as pronounced within each gender. The considerably more modest dream of owning an automobile is likewise one that has yet to materialize for ghetto residents, of which only one-third live in households with a car that runs. Again, this is due to a cumulation of sharp class and neighborhood differences: 79 percent of middle-class respondents and 62 percent of working-class blacks have an automobile in their household, contrasted with merely 28 percent of the jobless. But, in ghetto tracts, only 18 percent of the jobless have domestic access to a car—34 percent for men and 13 percent for women.

The social consequences of such a paucity of income and assets as suffered by ghetto blacks cannot be overemphasized. For just as the lack of financial resources or possession of a home represents a critical handicap when one can only find low-paying and casual employment or when one loses one's job, in that it literally forces one to go on the welfare rolls, not owning a car severely curtails one's chances of competing for available jobs that are not located nearby or that are not readily accessible by public transportation.

Social Capital and Poverty Concentration

Among the resources that individuals can draw upon to implement strategies of social mobility are those potentially provided by their lovers, kin, and friends and by the contacts they develop within the formal associations to which they belong—in sum, the resources they have access to by virtue of being socially integrated into solidary groups, networks, or organizations, what Bourdieu calls "social capital."[13] Our data indicate that not only do residents of extreme-poverty areas have fewer social ties but also that they tend to have ties of lesser social worth, as measured by the social position of their partners, parents, siblings, and best friends, for instance. In short, they possess lower volumes of social capital.

Living in the ghetto means being more socially isolated: nearly half of the residents of extreme-poverty tracts have no current partner—defined here as a person they are married to, live with, or are dating steadily—and one in five admit to having no one who would qualify as a best friend, compared to 32 percent and 12 percent, respectively, in low-poverty areas. It also means that intact marriages are less frequent. . . . Jobless men are much less likely than working males to have current partners in both types of neighborhoods: 62 percent in low-poverty neighborhoods and 44 percent in extreme-poverty areas. Black women have a slightly better chance of having a partner if they live in a low-poverty area, and this partner is also more likely to have completed high school and to work steadily; for ghetto residence further affects the labor-market standing of the latter. The partners of women living in extreme-poverty areas are less stably employed than those of female respondents from low-poverty neighborhoods: 62 percent in extreme-poverty areas work regularly as compared to 84 percent in low-poverty areas.

Friends often play a crucial role in life in that they provide emotional and material support, help construct one's identity, and often open up opportunities that one would not have without them—particularly in the area of jobs. We have seen that ghetto residents are more likely than other black Chicagoans to have no close friend. If they have a best friend, furthermore, he or she is less likely to work, less educated, and twice as likely to be on aid. Because friendships tend to develop primarily within genders and women have much higher rates of economic exclusion, female respondents are much more likely than men to have a best friend who does not work and who receives welfare assistance. Both of these characteristics, in turn, tend to be more prevalent among ghetto females.

Such differences in social capital are also evidenced by different rates and patterns of organizational participation. While being part of a formal organization, such as a block club or a community organization, a political party, a school-related association, or a sports, fraternal, or other social group, is a rare occurrence as a rule—with the notable exception of middle-class blacks, two-thirds of whom belong to at least one such group—it is more common for ghetto residents—64 percent, versus 50 percent in low-poverty tracts—especially females—64 percent, versus 46 percent in low-poverty areas—to belong to no organization. As for church membership, the small minority who profess to be, in Weber's felicitous expression, "religiously unmusical" is twice as large in the ghetto as outside: 12 percent versus 5 percent. For those with a religion, ghetto residence tends to depress church attendance slightly—29 percent of ghetto inhabitants attend service at least once a week compared to 37 percent of respondents from low-poverty tracts—even though women tend to attend more regularly than men in both types of areas. Finally, black women who inhabit the ghetto are also slightly less likely to know most of their neighbors than their counterparts from low-poverty areas. All in all, then, poverty concentration has the effect of devaluing the social capital of those who live in its midst.

Conclusion: The Social Structuring of Ghetto Poverty

. . . Our conclusion, then, is that social analysts must pay more attention to the extreme levels of economic deprivation and social marginalization as uncovered in this article before they further entertain and spread so-called theories about the potency of a ghetto culture of poverty that have yet to receive rigorous empirical elaboration. Those who have been pushing moral-cultural or individualistic-behavioral explanations of the social dislocations that have swept through the inner city in recent years have created a fictitious normative divide between urban blacks that, no matter its reality—which has yet to be ascertained[14]—cannot but pale when compared to the objective structural cleavage that separates ghetto residents from the larger society and to the collective material constraints that bear on them.[15] It is the cumulative structural entrapment and forcible socioeconomic marginalization resulting from the historically evolving interplay of class, racial, and gender domination, together with sea changes in the organization of American capitalism and failed urban and social policies, not a "welfare ethos," that explain the plight of today's ghetto blacks. . . .

Endnotes

1. For instance, Sheldon H. Danziger and Daniel H. Weinberg, eds., *Fighting Poverty: What Works and What Doesn't* (Cambridge, MA: Harvard University Press, 1986); William Kornblum, "Lumping the Poor: What *Is* the Underclass?" *Dissent*, Summer 1984, pp. 275–302; William Julius Wilson, *The Truly Disadvantaged: The Inner City, the Underclass and Public Policy* (Chicago: University of Chicago Press, 1987); Rose M. Brewer, "Black Women in Poverty: Some Comments on Female-Headed Families," *Signs: Journal of Women in Culture and Society*, 13(2):331–39 (Winter 1988); Fred R. Harris and Roger W. Wilkins, eds., *Quiet Riots: Race and Poverty in the United States* (New York: Pantheon, 1988). Martha A Gephart and Robert W. Pearson survey recent research in their "Contemporary Research on the Urban Underclass," *Items*, 42(1–2):1–10 (June 1988).

2. William Julius Wilson, "The American Underclass: Inner-City Ghettos and the Norms of Citizenship" (Godkin Lecture, John F. Kennedy School of Government, Harvard University, Apr. 1988), offers a critical dissection of these accounts.

3. A more detailed analysis of social changes on Chicago's South Side is in William Julius Wilson et al., "The Ghetto Underclass and the Changing Structure of Urban Poverty," in *Quiet Riots*, ed. Harris and Wilkins.

4. Space does not allow us to do more than allude to the transformations of the American economy as they bear on the ghetto. For provocative analyses of the systemic disorganization of advanced capitalist economies and polities and the impact, actual and potential, of postindustrial and flexible-specialization trends on cities and their labor markets, see Scott Lash and John Urry, *The End of Organized Capitalism*, (Madison: University of Wisconsin Press, 1988); Claus Offe, *Disorganized Capitalism: Contemporary Transformations of Work and Politics*, ed. John Keane (Cambridge: MIT Press, 1985); Fred Block, *Revising State Theory: Essays on Politics and Postindustrialism* (Philadelphia: Temple University Press, 1987); Donald A. Hicks, *Advanced Industrial Development* (Boston: Oelgeschlager, Gun and Hain, 1985); Barry Bluestone and Bennett Harrison, *The Great U-Turn* (New York: Basic Books, 1988); Michael J. Piore and Charles F. Sabel, *The Second Industrial Divide: Possibilities for Prosperity* (New York: Basic Books, 1984).

5. See, for instance, Norman Fainstein, "The Underclass/Mismatch Hypothesis as an Explanation for Black Economic Deprivation," *Politics and Society*, 15(4):403–52 (1986–87); Wendy Wintermute, "Recession and 'Recovery': Impact on Black and White Workers in Chicago" (Chicago: Chicago Urban League, 1983); Bruce Williams, *Black Workers in an Industrial Suburb: The Struggle against Discrimination*, (New Brunswick, NJ: Rutgers University Press, 1987).

6. Arne Duncan, "The Values, Aspirations, and Opportunities of the Urban Underclass" (B.A. honors thesis, Harvard University, 1987), pp. 18 ff.

7. See Gary Orfield, "Ghettoization and Its Alternatives," in *The New Urban Reality*, ed. P. Peterson (Washington, DC: Brookings Institute, 1985), for an account of processes of ghettoization; and Wacquant and Wilson, "Poverty, Joblessness and Social Transformation," for a preliminary discussion of some of the factors that underlie hyperghettoization.

8. Let us emphasize here that this contrast between the traditional ghetto and the hyperghetto of today implies no nostalgic celebration of the ghetto of yesteryear. If the latter was organizationally and socially integrated, it was not by choice but under the yoke of total black subjugation and with the threat of racial violence looming never too far in the background. See Arnold Hirsch, *Making the Second Ghetto: Race and Housing in Chicago, 1940–1960* (New York: Cambridge University Press, 1983), for an account of riots and violent white opposition to housing desegregation in Chicago in the two decades following World War II. The organized ghetto emerged out of necessity, as a limited, if creative, response to implacable white hostility; separatism was never a voluntary development, but without a protection against unyielding pressures from without, as shown in Allan H. Spear, *Black Chicago: The Making of a Negro Ghetto, 1890–1920* (Chicago: University of Chicago Press. 1968).

9. Poverty levels were arbitrarily limited by the sampling design: areas with less than 20 percent poor persons in 1980 were excluded at the outset, and tracts with extreme levels of poverty, being generally relatively underpopulated, ended up being underrepresented by the random sampling procedure chosen.

10. Class categories have been roughly defined on the basis of the respondent's current occupation as follows: the middle class comprises managers, administrators, executives, professional specialists, and technical staff; the working class includes both blue-collar workers and noncredentialed white-collar workers; in the jobless category fall all those who did not hold a job at the time of interview.

11. And from the education of their fathers: only 36 percent of ghetto residents have a father with at least a high school education, compared to 43 percent among those who live outside the ghetto. The different class backgrounds and trajectories of ghetto and non-ghetto blacks will be examined in a subsequent paper.

12. Again, we must reiterate that our comparison excludes *ex definitio* the black upper- and the middle-class neighborhoods that have mushroomed in Chicago since the opening of race relations in the 1960s. The development of this "new black middle class" is surveyed in Bart Landry, *The New Black Middle Class* (Berkeley: University of California Press, 1987).

13. Pierre Bourdieu, "The Forms of Capital," in *Handbook of Theory and Research for the Sociology of Education*, ed. J. G. Richardson (New York: Greenwood Press, 1986). The crucial role place by relatives, friends, and lovers in strategies of survival in poor black communities is documented extensively in Carol B. Stack, *All Our Kin: Strategies for Survival in a Black Community* (New York: Harper & Row, 1974). On the management of relationships and the influence of friends in the ghetto, see also Elliot Liebow, *Tally's Corner: A Study of Negro Streetcorner Men* (Boston: Little, Brown, 1967); Ulf Hannerz, *Soulside: Inquiries into Ghetto Culture and Community* (New York: Columbia University Press, 1969); Elijah Anderson, *A Place on the Corner* (Chicago: University of Chicago Press, 1978); Terry Williams and William Kornblum, *Growing Up Poor* (Lexington, MA: Lexington Books, 1985).

14. Initial examination of our Chicago data would appear to indicate that ghetto blacks on public aid hold basically the same views as regards welfare, work, and family as do other blacks, even those who belong to the middle class.

15. Let us emphasize in closing that we are not suggesting that differences between ghetto and non-ghetto poor can be explained by their residence. Because the processes that allocate in individuals and families to neighborhoods are highly socially selective ones, to separate

neighborhood effects—the specific impact of ghetto residence—from the social forces that operate jointly with, or independently of, them cannot be done by simple controls such as we have used here for descriptive purposes. On the arduous methodological and theoretical problems posed by such socially selective effects, see Stanley Lieberson, *Making It Count: The Improvement of Social Theory and* *Social Research* (Berkeley: University of California Press, 1985), pp. 14–43 and passim.

4

Living Poor:

Family Life Among Single Parent, African-American Women

Robin L. Jarrett

... Recent increases in the number of households headed by poor African-American women, the result of non-marital, adolescent childbearing, have encouraged researchers to once again debate the relationship between family structure, race, and poverty. Like past discussions, both structural and cultural arguments have been advanced to explain changing household and family formation patterns. Recent quantitative studies (see Baca Zinn 1990b; Marks 1991; Patterson 1981 for an overview), as well as past ethnographic research (see Jarrett in press for an overview), offer support for the structural argument, challenging the cultural position. These data indicate that economic forces are closely correlated with female headship and non-marital childbearing among poor African-American women. The structural perspective correctly documents the link between economic forces and family patterns. But it obscures many of the processes associated with living in poverty.

This paper expands on the structural explanation by describing the ways that African-American women live in poverty, dynamically adapting to larger economic forces. I use qualitative interview data to explore the following question: How do poor African-American women, in their daily lives, respond to conditions of economic marginality?...

Family Structure, Race, and Poverty: 'Female Householder, No Husband Present'

At the heart of the deterioration of the fabric of Negro society is the deterioration of the Negro family. It is the fundamental source of the weakness of the Negro community. . . . In essence, the Negro community has been forced into a matriarchal structure which, because it is so out of line with the rest of the American society, seriously retards the progress of the group as a whole. (Moynihan 1965, 29)

. . . Under the new rubric of the "underclass debate," researchers have returned to old questions of the relationship between family structure, race, and poverty (Katz 1989; Piven et al. 1987; Wilson and Aponte 1985). Little consensus exists on its key dimensions—such as size, origins, defining characteristics—or if in fact, such a group exists. Most researchers, however, use the term "underclass" to convey a group of minority poor who represent a persistent and more dangerous form of poverty (see Auletta 1982; Glasgow 1980; Lemann 1986; Mead 1986; Murray 1984; Ricketts and Sawhill 1988). . . .

Two conceptual frameworks, the cultural and the structural, provide competing arguments to explain changes in family patterns. The cultural explanation maintains that changing household and family formation patterns among low-income African Americans are the result of deviant values. Researchers cite various factors generating distinctive values, but cultural formulations that stress the role of liberal welfare reforms in exacerbating deviant values have been particularly influential (Mead 1986; Murray 1984). The basic argument is that ghetto-specific norms differ from their mainstream counterparts, positively endorsing single motherhood, out-of-wedlock childbearing, welfare dependency, male irresponsibility, criminal behavior, low mobility aspirations, and, more generally, family instability (Auletta 1982; Lemann 1986; Mead 1986; Murray 1984; see also Cook and Curtin 1987 for an overview).

The structural explanation argues that demographic shifts in household and family formation patterns reflect larger economic trends. Researchers cite macro-structural changes in the economy—including the decline in entry-level jobs, the relocation of jobs away from the inner-city, and the mismatch between job requirements and employee skills—and parallel declines in rates of male employment, marriage, and childbearing within marriage as evidence of external or situational pressures on family life. The fundamental thesis is that economic factors impede the construction and maintenance of mainstream family patterns: they encourage poor African-American women to forego marriage, bear children out-of-wedlock, head their own households, and rely on welfare income (Darity and Meyers 1984; Joe 1984; Staples 1985; Testa et al. 1989; Wilson 1987). . . .

The structural perspective challenges the culture of poverty argument and documents the association between economic factors and family patterns. Nevertheless, it is flawed in two critical ways. First, it assumes the superiority of the two-parent household (Cerullo and Erlien 1986). The structural perspective uses an idealized, if not mythic, model of the nuclear family to assess poor African-American families (Reed 1988). Consequently, it fails to acknowledge the diversity of family forms as well as their viability among the poor and nonpoor alike (Baca Zinn and Eitzen 1992; Thorne and Yalom 1982; Williams 1992b; see also Baca Zinn 1990a). Second, the structural perspective takes an economic deterministic position and ignores the role of human agency. It posits a direct and unmediated relationship between economic factors and family patterns. Moen's and Wethington's (1992:243) general critique of structural models is applicable: the inordinate concentration on external factors encourages the overgeneralized view that families are "at the mercy of forces beyond their control, their responses constrained to the point of total conformity to structural forces." Consequently, we know little about how poor women actually respond to conditions of economic marginality. . . .

Despite its conceptual limitations, the structural perspective has received consistent empirical support. This suggests that the continued rejuvenation of the cultural perspective reflects larger racial divisions within U.S. society, rather than actual findings from academic research (Gresham 1989; Wilkerson and Gresham 1989; Rainwater and Yancey 1967; Suttles 1976). These observations highlight the need to move beyond stagnant debates that center on improperly conceptualized cultural models (Gans 1969; Leacock 1971; Rainwater 1987; Swidler 1986) as well as on deterministic and overgeneralized structural models.

Sample and Methodology: 'Research Touched By Human Hands'

. . . The data reported in this paper derive from a series of focus group interviews (see Jarrett 1993 for a detailed methodological discussion). The interviews were broadly conceived as an exploratory examination of how *women* in poor families adapt to conditions of poverty. I concentrated on various aspects of family life, including family formation patterns, household living arrangements, childcare and socialization patterns, intergenerational relations, male-female relations, and welfare, work, and social opportunities.

Ten focus groups, comprised of a total of 82 low-income African-American women, were conducted between January and July 1988. Each focus group session lasted approximately two hours and was held with groups of no more than 8–10 women. The tape-recorded discussions were relatively unstructured but topically oriented, allowing for comparisons across groups. The ten focus group interviews conducted represent a larger than average number for such research projects and fell within the upper range for serious research (see Calder 1977; Hedges 1985).

The criteria for selection of the women was based on the profiles of women discussed in the current underclass debate. They included: 1) never-married mothers, 2) who received AFDC, and 3) lived in high poverty or economically transitional neighborhoods in the city of Chicago. Most of the women were in their early to middle twenties and began their childbearing careers as adolescents. A purposive sample was drawn from Chicago-area Head Start programs since such programs are located in low-income communities and serve women fitting the above profiles.

A team of research assistants transcribed and coded the interviews thematically by topical area. The initial codes were based on the broad topical areas guiding the research but were expanded to include unanticipated information that emerged in the discussion. Once this task was completed, key issues and themes were identified for each area.

The Empirical Data: 'In Their Own Words'

. . . In this section, I present empirical data that offer insights on the lives of real women and that address the limitations of the structural framework. As a point of departure, I examine the normative and behavioral dimensions of familial roles among the sample of never-married, African-American mothers. The concentration on the conflict between norms and behaviors provides a dynamic example of how women who hold conventional aspirations concerning family patterns respond in their daily lives. Around this broad topic, I explore four issues: 1) Marriage, the ideal; 2) Marriage, the reality; 3) Economic impediments to conventional marriage; and 4) Alternatives to conventional marriage.

Marriage, the Ideal: 'Everybody Wants To Be Married'

Women consistently professed adherence to mainstream patterns. For virtually all of the women interviewed, legal marriage was the cornerstone of conventional family life. Marriage represented a complex of behaviors, including independent household formation, economic independence, compatibility, and fidelity and commitment that were generally associated with the nuclear family. Representative excerpts from group members illustrate:

Independent Household Formation:

. . . He lives with his grandmother. I don't want to move into his grandmother's

home. I live at my mother's. I don't want him to move in there. When we get married, I want us to live in our own house, something we can call ours.

Economic Independence:

. . . He's always nagging me to get married. I ask him: "Are you going to be able to take me off aid and take care of all four of my children?" So when I say that he just laugh.

Compatibility:

I think a person should never get married unless it's for love. . . . [If] you want to spend the rest of your life with that person, you all [should] have a good understanding. If you marry somebody just because you pregnant, just because you have four or five kids by them, or because society or whoever pressured you into it, you goin' to become mean and resentful. And if that person turns out to not be what you thought or that marriage turns out to be something less than you hoped it would be, it's not goin' to be worth it. . . .

Fidelity and Commitment:

If I get married, I believe in being all the way faithful.

I want you to take care of me. I'm not looking to jump into bed and call this a marriage. I want you to love me, care for me, be there when I need you because I'm going to be there for you when you need me. . . .

Nita, a mother of two children, provided one of the most eloquent statements on the meaning of marriage. She said:

I would love to be married. . . . I believe I would make a lovely wife. . . . I would just love to have the experience of being there married with a man. I imagine me and my children, my son a basketball player . . . playing for the [Chicago] Bulls. My daughter . . . playing the piano, have a secretary job and going to college. . . . Me, I'm at home playing the wifely duties. This man, not a boy, coming home with his manly odors. . . . My husband comes home, takes off his work boots and have dinner. . . . I would like to have this before I leave this earth, a husband, my home, my car.

Likewise, Charmaine, who despite her own unmarried status, firmly asserted:

I think everybody wants to get married. Everybody wants to have somebody to work with them. . . . and go through life with . . . I would like to be married. I want to be married. I'm not gonna lie. I really do.

Women, despite their insistent statements concerning the importance of marriage as the cornerstone of mainstream family life, were well aware of the unconventionality of their actual behaviors. Women openly acknowledged that their single status, non-marital childbearing, and in some cases, female-headship, diverged from mainstream household and family formation patterns. Tisha said with a mixture of humor and puzzlement:

Is this what it's supposed to be like? So, I'm going backwards. Most people say, "Well, you go to school, you get married, and you have kids." Well, I had my kids. I'm trying to go to school and maybe, somewhere along the line, I'm going to catch up with everybody else. . . .

Women's observations in this study are consistent with past ethnographic research (Aschenbrenner 1975; Clark 1983; Holloman and Lewis 1978; Ladner 1971; Stack 1974; see also Anderson 1976). Even in Lee Rainwater's (1970) study of the . . . notorious Pruitt-Igoe housing project in St. Louis, impoverished residents routinely professed adherence to mainstream values concerning marriage and family. He observed:

The conventionality and ordinariness of Pruitt-Igoeans' conception of good family life is striking. Neither in our questionnaire nor in open-ended interviews or observational contexts did we find any consistent elaboration of an unconventional ideal. In the working class, a good family life is seen to have at its core a stable marriage between two people who love and respect each other and who rear their children in an adequate home, preferably one that has its own yard. If only things went right, according to most Pruitt-

Igoeans, their family life would not differ from that of most Americans. (Rainwater 1970:48)

Marriage, the Reality: 'That's a Little White Girl's Dream'

Women were pessimistic about actually contracting family roles as defined in the mainstream manner. Their aspirations for conventional family roles were tempered by doubt and, in some cases, outright pessimism.

Karen's comment reflected her sense of uncertainty:

I would like to get married one day . . . to somebody that's as ready as I am. . . . But it's so scary out here. You scared to have a commitment with somebody, knowing he's not on the level. . . . They ready to get their life together; they looking for a future.

Denise [said:]

I used to have this in my head, all my kids got the same daddy, get married, have a house. That's a little white girl's dream. That stuff don't happen in real life. You don't get married and live happily ever after. . . .

Women's experiences were augmented by the experiences of others. Through the processes of observation of and comparison to older women in the community, younger women gauged their chances of contracting ideal family forms. Comments from Regina and Tennye, respectively, illustrated this:

A good husband has a good job where I can stay home with the family, raise the kids like on TV. But then it's hard. You don't find too many, not like when our mothers was coming up.

I don't think I'll ever find a husband because of the way I feel. I want it like my mother had it. [My father] took care of us. She been married to him since she was sixteen. He took care of her, took her out of her mother's house. She had four kids, he took care of all the kids.

These comments suggest that even as younger women compare themselves with older women, conventional patterns remain their reference point. Women's views also signal their awareness of declining opportunities for attaining mainstream family patterns within impoverished African-American communities.

Women's first-hand experiences indicate a more general point. Economic forces are not experienced in impersonal ways; nor are they experienced by solitary individuals, as implied by the structural perspective. Economic constraints are, instead, mediated through social relationships and interaction processes. Individuals ponder their situations with others in similar circumstances. As a result of his own ethnographic work, Hannerz (1969) critiqued the mechanistic components of the structural argument:

> [It] is made to look as if every couple were left on its own to work out anew a solution to problems which have confronted many of both their predecessors and their contemporaries in the black community (Hannerz 1969:76).

His comment also suggests that the generational persistence and reaffirmation of particular strategies occur because the socioeconomic conditions that support them are still operant (cf. Franklin 1988). This point is aptly illuminated by Myesha and Pam, whose circumstances mirrored their mothers':

> My father wasn't around. But you know he tried. . . . He calls [me] now. Well, with my boyfriend, he [may] stay by my side. If he leaves, he just leave. . . . So, if my mama could do it, I know I can raise Daniel [my son].

> My mother had eight of us. I sympathize with what she go through because she doesn't get any help. But she raised us all by herself and we doing okay. It's a lot of women that don't need no man to help raise her kids because I know I can take care of mine by myself.

Economic Impediments to Marriage: 'I Could Do Bad By Myself'

The women's own interpretations concerning changes in household and family formation patterns are consistent with the structural explanation of poverty. Economic factors, according to women, played a prominent role in their decisions to forego marriage, bear children outside of marriage, and, in some cases, head households.

Iesha described how economic factors influenced her decisions. She said:

> I had a chance to get married when I first had my two [children]. We had planned the date and everything, go down to City Hall. . . .When the day came along, I changed my mind. Right today I'm glad I did not marry him because he still ain't got no job. He still staying with his sister and look where I am. Ever since I done had a baby I been on my own. I haven't lived with no one but myself. I been paying bills now. . . .

Other qualitative and ethnographic studies also describe the depressing effect that economic pressures have on marriage among poor women and men (Aschenbrenner 1975; Liebow 1967; Hannerz 1969; Rainwater 1970; Stack 1974; Sullivan 1985). The absence of legal marriage or economically stable partnerships, however, did not preclude the formation of strong and stable male-female relationships. Many of the women were involved in a variety of unions. As previously describe, some of these relationships were indeed conflictual. Others were remarkably stable, considering the economic constraints that both women and men faced. Several women described long-term relationships, some of which had endured for over a decade.

One said:

> I'm not married. I got three kids. But their father is there with the kids. He been there since I was 16. . . . I been with the same guy since I was 16 years old and I'm still with him now. I only had really one man in my life.

Another one echoed:

> We been together for so many years; I really think we could work it out. . . . I go over his house, me and the kids, and stay for weeks. Then we come back home. . . .

These comments are important because they identify the existence of strong alternative relationships that are not detected in demographic profiles that recognize only legal marriages. They also confirm the results of earlier ethnographic studies that identify a variety of male-female arrangements that exist outside of marriage (Aschenbrenner 1975; Jarrett 1992; Liebow 1967; Rainwater 1970; Schulz 1969; Stack 1974; Sullivan 1985). Such arrangements varied from casual friendships to fully committed partnerships. . . . The prospective mates of the women interviewed were generally unemployed, underemployed, or relegated to the most insecure jobs in the secondary labor market. Within the context of the larger discussion on perceptions of social and economic opportunities, women described the types of jobs their male companions and friends assumed. They included: car wash attendants; drug dealers; fast food clerks; grocery store stock and bag clerks; hustlers; informal car repairmen; lawn workers; street peddlers; and street salvage workers.

The focus group data thus confirm the structural explanation of poverty and its emphasis on economic factors, such as joblessness. But they also go beyond the primary concentration on the economic instability of men and its consequences for family maintenance. The focus group interviews indicate that women also considered their own resources in addition to these of the men. They assessed their own educational backgrounds, job experiences, welfare resources, and childcare arrangements. For example, women reviewed their educational qualifications and assessed their potential for economic independence.

Educational Attainment:

As far as working, I have to be serious. I don't have any skills and I prefer to go to school . . . do something progressive, you know, to try to get off of [welfare.]
Now I'm trying to go back to school 'cause when I dropped out . . . I was in the 11th grade and was pregnant. . . . I was pregnant with her then, so I had to leave school. . . .Now I'm trying to go back to school for nursing assistant, so I can get off all public aid: find somethin' else to do 'stead of being on welfare all my life. . . .

Work Experiences:

Contrary to common stereotypes, many of the women had worked. Women's past work experiences served to clarify the limitations of using the types of jobs available to them as a strategy of mobility.

Low Wages:
It don't make sense to go to McDonald's to make 3.35 an hour when you know you got to pay 4 dollars an hour to baby-sit and you got to have bus fare.

If you going to get something, you need something that's going to pay something, that's going to make a difference and not take away from it. And you know when they had that discussion like that on Oprah [Winfrey talk show], they don't really see that. They tell you you get out there. One girl get on there talking about she'll scrub the floor for 3.50 [an hour], but what it's going to do for you? You still losing out. You not bringing in as much as you get if you were at home. . . .

Welfare Experiences:

Welfare, like low-wage jobs, also represented an institutionalized impediment to mobility. The women's comments highlighted the need for benefits, the stigma of public aid, welfare regulations, and their need for childcare.

Need for Benefits:
. . . One reason, seriously . . . that I do not want [public aid] to take my check [is] because I need my medical card. They can take the money, but I need that medical card and I need those food stamps.

Stigma of Public Aid:
You got to go out there on your own not using [your] public aid background . . . because a lot of companies not going to hire you because you coming from public aid.

Welfare Regulations:
They give you the runaround for nothing. . . . This money not coming out . . . their pocketbooks. . . . [I]t's not like it's coming out they paycheck every week. . . . It's coming from your parents paying they state taxes. . . . You trying to take care of your children the best way you can and this is one of the ways that you can take care of your children. . . .

Childcare Needs:

Women, unlike men, had to factor childcare into their work schedules.

Well, I want to wait until my kids get up about 5 (to work), so if something's going on [at the babysitter's] they can tell me. I don't want to be worried. I don't have nobody. I keep my own kids.

If I want to go out and get a job, I ain't going to pick any daycare in the city, because they ain't so safe either. . . .

As a result of their limited educational attainment, low-paying jobs, welfare disincentives, and childcare needs, most women came to perceive their economic options as severely limited. Consequently, when women sought other opportunities, they took both men's economic limitations and their own into account.

Alternatives to Conventional Marriage: 'You Can Depend on Your Mama'

The focus group interviews expand on the structural explanation of poverty in yet another way. They serve to identify the strategic processes and sequences of events that follow women's decisions to forego marriage, bear children as single mothers, and in some cases, head households. Women responded to their poverty in three ways: they extended domestic and childcare responsibilities to multiple individuals; they relaxed paternal role expectations; and they assumed a flexible maternal role.

Domestic Kin Networks:

The extension of domestic and childcare responsibilities beyond the nuclear family represented a primary response to economic marginality. Extended kin networks that centered around women provided assistance to single mothers and their children. For example, LaDawn, whose unintended pregnancy interrupted her plans to leave home, attend college, and get "real wild," described how living with her mother provides valuable support for her:

When your money is gone and you at home with your mama, you don't have to worry about where you getting your next meal from because mama is always going to figure out a way how you can get your next meal. . . . And your mama would be there to depend on; you can depend on your mama. . . .

Ebony, who now lives alone, described the childcare benefits of living with her mother:

I'm on my own. . . . I wish my mother would come stay with me to help me out. Because when I was at home it was things that she knew that I didn't know nothing about. Why the baby crying so much. Well, you had it outside [the blanket] with no covers on. Letting me know so when the next [child] came I knew not to do this.

Diane also described the childcare benefits of living with her mother. She further hinted how her mother's assistance facilitates Diane's role as the primary caregiver:

My mother gives me good advice . . . if something's wrong. [My twins] had the chicken pox. What am I gonna do? . . . They itching. What should I put on them? She helps me out that way. And I stays with my mother. Me and my mother sit down and talk. We don't have no kind of problems as far as her trying to raise [my kids].

The women's accounts in these focus group interviews are paralleled in similar ethnographic studies. Aschenbrenner (1975), Jarrett (1992), and Sullivan (1985), in their works, highlight the importance of grandmothers, as well as other women kin, in the lives of poor women and children. Grandmothers provide money on loan, childcare on a daily basis, and help with cooking and cleaning. These services allow some young mothers to finish school and get a job, staying off public assistance. . . .

Expansion of the Paternal Role:

. . . A second type of strategy concentrated on paternal role performance. Women lowered their expectations of men and extended the paternal role to non-biological fathers as ways of facilitating the involvement of men in childcare. Evaluations of paternal role performance that hinged on providing for the family economically were replaced by assessments that centered on men's efforts to find work and assist with day-to-day child welfare (see also Rainwater 1970). For example, Jaleesa, an ebullient mother of one child, said of her daughter's father:

Even though he don't have a job, sometimes what counts is he spends time with his child. That child will think about that: "Well, my father's here when my mother's not here." [That child will] have someone else to turn to. And the father say: "Well I ain't got no job. I ain't going to be around a child." That's not all to it.

Anna, who openly proclaimed her strength the face of many obstacles, echoed leesa's sentiments:

I got three kids all by him and he try to help out when he can. He's not working now but [he] did try to help. And . . . he be going out looking for a job. I don't try to pressure. [Men] care about their kids. They wanna try to help. . . .

Additionally, women extended the paternal le to men other than the biological fathers of eir children. This strategy ensured that there as a male who provided nurturance and disci- ine, as well as economic support. For example, isha asserted:

It's not a father, but a male image. . . . My daughter will mind my brother better than she do me. I will tell her to sit down, whereas I would probably have to tell her four or five times; whereas my brother will come in with that manly image and will say sit down one time and she be sitting down.

Several ethnographic studies also provide ex- mples of how non-biological fathers supply pport for poor African-American children schenbrenner 1975; Burton 1991; Holloman d Lewis 1978; Liebow 1967; Schulz 1969; ack 1974; Sullivan 1985). These studies iden- y an array of male figures, such as uncles, andfathers, neighbors, fictive kin, and male mpanions who played significant roles in the es of many children.

Expansion of the Maternal Role:

A third strategy used by women to facilitate care of children entailed the expansion of the aternal role. . . .
Ethnographic research has consistently nd that strong and competent mothers are atly admired in low-income African-Ameri- n communities (Aschenbrenner 1975; Ladner 71; Rainwater 1970; Stack 1974). The focus up interviews provided corroboration.

Women's comments illustrated their strength and competence as mothers.

Crystal, Sharon, and Shelly, who currently were not living with male companions, individu- ally asserted:

I can discipline [my children] myself. I have that bass in my voice. . . . I raise my voice and they'll . . . sit down. They'll mind me; they'll mind my mother.

I think a father should be around. But it can't always be. I'm raising my children by myself.

[My daughter] is well taken care of and I feel good about myself that I can give her everything she needs without his help.

In addition to describing how poor African- American women respond to conditions of pov- erty, the interviews highlighted the meanings that women attributed to the alternative family roles that they assumed. Motherhood, irrespec- tive of women's single marital status, conferred them with a valued role. Moreover, women's ability to garner scarce resources, provide care for children, and in some cases, maintain house- holds under stark conditions of poverty led to en- hanced self-esteem. For example, Diane, mother of twin daughters, expressed her views on moth- erhood:

It's some fun parts in it and then you got some down parts when you got to do this and got to do that. But I enjoy my daugh- ters. . . . They make me happy. . . . They're what get me up in the morning.

Lois, who cared for her children as well as her sister's, gave a similar view:

People compliment [me]: "You really take time [with your kids]." Just because . . . I got three kids and not married, that don't mean I'm running the streets all the time. I'm at home helping my children. . . .

Discussion: 'Bringing People Back In'

As I got to know and to absorb a great deal about the daily routines and the physical and social contexts of the lives of many par- ents and children, the logic of many of the choices and much of the behavior of these low-income families became clearer. (Jef- fers 1967:117)

The primary goal of this paper is to expand on the structural explanation of poverty. The structural perspective correctly documents changes in household and family formation patterns and the relationship of these changes to economic factors. Nevertheless, it ignores alternative family arrangements and omits the role of personal agency in understanding poverty among the poor. The focus group data address these two limitations by concentrating on African-American women's first-hand accounts of their lives. Women's narratives describe family arrangements that were, indeed, different from mainstream patterns but that were viable, nonetheless. Significantly, these differences in household and family formation patterns do not represent abandonment of conventional aspirations (see also Rainwater 1987; Staples 1985; Williams 1992b). Further, women's accounts highlight the active roles that they played in caring for children and maintaining households. Women do not mechanistically respond to economic forces. Rather, they assess their options and make choices that allow them to forge meaningful lives despite the harsh economic conditions in which they and their children find themselves. . . .

The data derived from this study suggest several directions for future research. First, researchers should look seriously at alternative family arrangements and cease to assume the superiority of mainstream family patterns. Certainly it is conceivable that a two-parent household with adequate economic resources provides more opportunities for its children than an impoverished family with inadequate resources. However, researchers should not automatically assume that *all* middle-class families are stable and that *all* low-income families are unstable (see, for example, Coontz 1992).

Second, researchers should explore issues of coping and adaptation among poor families, rather than just document female headship and its demographic correlates. We need to identify more precisely the family dynamics that allow poor African-American families to cope (or fail to cope) with economic marginality. We know from past ethnographic research that a variety of family and household strategies can exist under the same social and economic conditions (see, for example, Clark 1983; Jarrett in press; di Leonardo 1984). Thus, the most theoretically compelling studies will be those that identify variations in coping strategies and seek explanations for these differences.

References

Anderson, Elijah. 1976. *A Place on the Corner.* Chicago: University of Chicago Press.

Aschenbrenner, Joyce. 1975. *Lifelines: Black Families in Chicago.* New York: Holt, Rinehart and Winston.

Auletta, Ken. 1982. *The Underclass.* New York: Random House.

Baca Zinn, Maxine. 1989. "Family, race, and poverty in the eighties." *Signs: Journal of Women in Culture and Society* 14:856–874.

——. 1990a. "Family, feminism, and race in America." *Gender & Society* 4:68–82.

——. 1990b. "Minority families in crisis: The public discussion." In *Women, Class, and the Feminist Imagination: A Socialist-Feminist Reader,* eds. Karen Hansen and Ilene J. Phillipson, pp. 363–379. Philadelphia: Temple University Press.

Baca Zinn, Maxine, and D. Stanley Eitzen. 1992. *Diversity in Families.* New York: Harper and Row.

Burton, Linda M. 1991. "Caring for children." *The American Enterprise* May/June:34–37.

Calder, Bobby J. 1977. "Focus groups and the nature of qualitative marketing research." *Journal of Marketing Research* 24:353–364.

Cerullo, Margaret, and Marla Erlien. 1986. "Beyond the 'normal family': A cultural critique of women's poverty." In *For Crying Out Loud: Women and Poverty in the United States,* eds. Rochelle Lefkowitz and Ann Withorn, pp. 248–261. New York: The Pilgrim Press.

Clark, Reginald M. 1983. *Family Life and School Achievement: Why Poor Black Children Succeed or Fail.* Chicago: University of Chicago Press.

Cook, Thomas D., and Thomas Curtin. 1987. "The mainstream and the underclass: Why are the differences so salient and the similarities so unobtrusive?" In *Social Comparison, Social Justice, and Relative Deprivation: Theoretical, Empirical, and Policy Perspectives,* eds. John C. Masters and William P. Smith, pp. 218–264. Hillsdale, NJ: Erlbaum Associates.

Coontz, Stephanie. 1992. *The Way We Never Were: American Families and the Nostalgia Trap.* New York: Basic Books.

Darity, William A., and Samuel L. Meyers. 1984. "Does welfare dependency cause female headship? The case of the black family." *Journal of Marriage and the Family* 46:765–779.

di Leonardo, Micaela. 1984. *The Varieties of Ethnic Experience: Kinship, Class, and Gender Among California Italian-Americans.* Ithaca, NY: Cornell University Press.

Franklin, Donna L. 1988. "Race, class, and adolescent pregnancy: An ecological analysis." *American Journal of Orthopsychiatry* 58:339–354.

Glasgow, David. G. 1980. *The Black Underclass: Poverty, Unemployment, and Entrapment of Ghetto Youth.* San Francisco: Jossey-Bass.

Hannerz, Ulf. 1969. *Soulside: Inquiries into Ghetto Culture and Community.* New York: Columbia University Press.

Hedges, Alan. 1985. "Group interviewing." In *Applied Qualitative Research*, ed. Robert Walker, pp. 71–91. Vermont: Gower Publishing Co.

Holloman, Regina, and Fannie E. Lewis. 1978. "The 'clan': Case study of a black extended family in Chicago." In *The Extended Family in Black Societies*, eds. Dimitri Shimkin, Edith Shimkin, and Dennis A. Frate, pp. 201–238. The Hague: Mouton.

Jarrett, Robin L. 1992. "A family case study: An examination of the underclass debate." In *Qualitative Methods in Family Research*, eds. Jane Gilgun, Gerald Handel, and Kerry Daly, pp. 172–197. Newbury Park, CA: Sage.

———. 1993. "Focus groups interviewing with low-income minority populations: A research experience." In *Conducting Successful Focus Groups*, ed. David Morgan, pp. 184–201. Newbury Park, CA: Sage.

———. In press. "Community context, intrafamilial processes, and social mobility outcomes: Ethnographic contributions to the study of African-American families and children in poverty." In *Ethnicity and Diversity*, eds. Geraldine K. Brookings and Margaret B. Spencer. Hillsdale, NJ: Erlbaum.

Jeffers, Camille. 1967. *Living Poor: A Participant Observer Study of Choices and Priorities.* Ann Arbor, MI: Ann Arbor Publishers.

Joe, Tom. 1984. *The 'Flip Side' of Black Families Headed by Women: The Economic Status of Men.* Center for the Study of a Social Policy, Washington, DC.

Katz, Michael. 1989. *The Undeserving Poor: From the War on Poverty to the War on Welfare.* New York: Pantheon Books.

Ladner, Joyce. 1971. *Tomorrow's Tomorrow: The Black Woman.* New York: Anchor Books.

Lemann, Nicholas. 1986. "The origins of the underclass." *Atlantic Monthly* 258:31–55.

Liebow, Elliot. 1967. *Tally's Corner: A Study of Negro Street Corner Men.* Boston: Little, Brown.

Marks, Carol. 1991. "The urban underclass." *Annual Review of Sociology* 17:445–466.

Mead, Lawrence. 1986. *Beyond Entitlement: The Social Obligations of Citizenship.* New York: Free Press.

Moen, Phyllis, and Elaine Wethington. 1992. "The concept of family adaptive strategies." *Annual Review of Sociology* 18:233–251.

Moynihan, Daniel P. 1965. "The Negro family: The case for national action." Washington, DC: Office of Policy Planning and Research. U.S. Department of Labor.

Murray, Charles. 1984. *Losing Ground: American Social Policy, 1950–1980.* New York: Basic Books.

Patterson, James. T. 1981. *American's Struggle Against Poverty, 1900–1980.* Cambridge, MA: Harvard University Press.

Piven, Frances F., Barbara Ehrenreich, Richard Cloward, and Richard F. Block. 1987. *The Mean Season.* New York: Pantheon Books.

Rainwater, Lee. 1970. *Behind Ghetto Walls: Black Families in a Federal Slum.* Chicago: Aldine Publishing Company.

———. 1987. *Class, Culture, Poverty, and Welfare.* Unpublished manuscript.

Reed, Adolph Jr. 1988. "The liberal technocrat." *The Nation* 246:167–170.

Ricketts, Erol R., and Isabel V. Sawhill. 1988. "Defining and measuring the underclass." *Journal of Policy Analysis and Management* 7:316–25.

Schulz, David. 1969. *Coming Up Black: Patterns of Ghetto Socialization.* Englewood Cliffs, NJ: Prentice Hall.

Stack, Carol. 1974. *All Our Kin: Strategies for Survival in a Black Community.* New York: Harper and Row.

Staples, Robert. 1985. "Changes in black family structure: The conflict between family ideology and structural conditions." *Journal of Marriage and the Family* 47:1005–1013.

Sullivan, Mercer. 1985. *Teen Fathers in the Inner-City.* New York: Ford Foundation.

Testa, Mark, Nan Marie Astone, Marilyn Krogh, and Kathryn M. Neckerman. 1989. "Employment and marriage among inner-city fathers." *Annals of the American Academy of Political and Social Sciences* 501:79–91.

Thorne, Barrie, and Marilyn Yalom. 1982. *Rethinking the Family: Some Feminist Questions.* New York: Longman.

Williams, Brett. 1992. "Us and them." *The Nation* 255:371–372.

Wilson, William J. 1987. *The Truly Disadvantaged: The Inner City, the Underclass, and Public Policy.* Chicago: University of Chicago Press.

Wilson, William J., and Robert Aponte. 1985. "Urban poverty." *Annual Review of Sociology* 11:231–258.

5

Black Leadership and Racial Integration:

Army Lessons for American Society

Charles C. Moskos
John Sibley Butler

Success Story—With Caveats

Two tendencies dominate the way race is talked about in America. One emphasizes the ways blacks and whites exist in nearly complete isolation from each other, even inhabiting "two nations."[1] The other is to subsume the issue of race into the less sensitive realm of class. Underlying both ways of discussing race is the paradigm of black failure. That commentators attribute this failure to a diverse array of causes—white racism, black family breakdown, cultural differences, economic changes, public policy, and so on— does not change the relentlessly negative picture of black America that is the premise for most racial discussion in these waning years of the twentieth century.

One major American institution, however, contradicts the prevailing race paradigm. It is an organization unmatched in its level of racial integration. It is an institution unmatched in its broad record of black achievement.[2] It is a world in which the Afro-American heritage is part and parcel of the institutional culture. It is the only place in American life where whites are routinely bossed around by blacks. The institution is the U.S. Army. . . .

As a rule of thumb, the more military the environment, the more complete the integration. Interracial comity is stronger in the field than in garrison, stronger on duty than off, stronger on post than in the world beyond the base. Even in the grueling conditions of deployments to the Persian Gulf, Somalia, or Haiti, not a single racial incident occurred that was severe enough to come to the attention of the military police—not one.

Even off duty and off post, far more interracial mingling is noticeable around military bases than in civilian life. Most striking, the racial integration of military life has some carryover into the civilian sphere. The most racially integrated communities in America are towns with large military installations.[3]. . .

Good Race Relations, Not Perfect

In noting and celebrating the success of good race relations in the Army, we are not blind to real and serious problems that persist. The Army is not a racial utopia. Black and white soldiers are susceptible to the same kinds of interracial suspicion and resentment that exist in civilian society. Although the Army stands in sharp and favorable contrast to nonmilitary institutions, it is not immune to the demons that haunt race relations in America. . . .

The presence in the Army of white racist "skinheads," even if only a few, points to a profound and counterintuitive lesson. The Army has focused foremost on avenues that promote black achievement rather than on the rhetoric of nonracism, the aim being to maximize the avenues of opportunity as well as to combat overt and covert racism. But when these two goals come into conflict, the Army has deemed it better to have blacks in substantial numbers and in leadership positions in an organization with some white racists than to have an organization with few blacks and fewer black leaders where racial bigots are absent (or, more likely, invisible).

If a trade-off must be made between, on one side, black advancement coexisting with white racists and, on the other, few blacks in a putatively nonracial setting, the Army firmly comes down on the side of the former—in contrast to the state of affairs at most elite universities, where antiracism is promulgated but where the Afro-American presence is limited. The absence of white racists thus is not considered a precondition for black achievement. . . .

In a very revealing pattern, a study of military veterans found that almost twice as many black veterans (69 percent) as white (37 percent) wished they had stayed in the Army.[4]. . .

[W]hatever its racial tensions, the Army stands out, even among governmental agencies, as an organization in which blacks often do better than their white counterparts. Here is a surprising statistic. Despite the federal government's strong commitment to establishing a good environment for racial minorities, black civil service employees are nearly two and a half times more likely to be fired than whites.[5] In the Army black soldiers are 20 percent less likely to be fired ("involuntarily separated") than white soldiers.[6]. . .

Why Study the Army?

We focus on the Army because it is the largest of the services and the one with by far the highest proportion of blacks. As of 1995, the 145,000 blacks in the Army constitute about half of all blacks in military uniform. Afro-Americans make up 27 percent of all Army personnel on active duty—about double the proportion in the Navy, Air Force, or Marine Corps. By rank, the number of blacks in the Army divides as follows: 24 percent of the lower enlisted levels, 35 percent of noncommissioned officers, and 12 percent of commissioned officers. Relative to the other military services, the Army stands out in the absolute and proportionate numbers of blacks at all levels, especially in the senior noncommissioned officer (NCO) and officer levels. . . .

[W]e examine some of the ways in which the Army's experience—and the Army's core principles—in the area of race relations can be transferred to the civilian sector, despite some obvious and important differences between the Army and nonmilitary organizations. One key difference between the way the Army and many civilian organizations reflect racial climate is that an officer's failure to maintain a bias-free environment is an absolute impediment to advancement in a military career. Most soldiers we have spoken to could not conceive of an officer who expressed racist views being promoted. We know of many civilian organizations in which this is not true.

Another, perhaps more important, distinction is that the Army does not lower its standards in order to assure an acceptable racial mix. When necessary, the Army makes an effort to compensate for educational or skill deficiencies by providing specialized, remedial training. Affirmative action exists, but without timetables or quotas governing promotions. What goals do exist are pegged to the proportion of blacks in the service promotion pool. Even then, these goals can be bypassed if the candidates do not meet standards.

In this regard, compared to most private organizations, the Army has an obvious advantage. The Army can maintain standards while still promoting Afro-Americans at all levels because of the large number of black personnel within the organization. The Army's experience with a plenitude of qualified black personnel illuminates an important lesson. When not marginalized, Afro-American cultural patterns can mesh with and add to the effectiveness of mainstream organizations. The overarching point is that the most effective and fairest way to achieve racial equality of opportunity in the United States is to increase the number of qualified Afro-Americans available to fill positions. Doing so is no small task. But as an objective and basic principle, it is infinitely superior to a system under which blacks in visible positions of authority are presumed to have benefitted from relaxed standards, a perception that stokes white resentment. . . .

Can We Really Draw Lessons from the Army?

Even if we grant that racial integration and black achievement have progressed further in the Army than in any other institution, can any lessons be drawn for civilian life? Surely the differences in formal organization and culture are so great, say the doubters, that little can be applied from the Army to the larger society. Critics might make three arguments to disqualify the Army as a model:

- The Army commands methods of surveillance and coercion unavailable to civilian institutions.

- Every individual in the Army has a modicum of economic security as well as decent housing and medical benefits for his or her family.

- Soldiers come from a segment of society that excludes the very bottom rungs; thus, they do not bring the most severe social problems into the Army.

In responding to these objections, we do not deny the significant differences between military and civilian life. instead, we argue that the Army's ability to change its own way of doing things has broadly applicable implications for overcoming racism in America.

The Army is not a democracy—but neither are most other organizations. To be sure, the Army relies more strongly on round-the-clock accountability than most civilian organizations, but accountability and control cannot in and of themselves force good race relations. The racial situation is far worse in prisons, where coercive authority weighs much more heavily than in the military. Moreover, racist norms and behavior can prevail in any large organization, including those with quasi-military structures. . . .

A more definitive rejoinder can be made to critics who state that the unique hierarchical conditions of military service account for its positive race relations. We must remember that the same authority structure existed in the Army of the 1970s, when racial turbulence was endemic. Something other than submersion of individual rights must have been involved in the Army's move from a racially tense situation to the relative harmony of the present period.

Concerning the second objection, it is true that soldiers enjoy some modicum of economic well-being. Once in the Army, not even the lowest soldier is "underclass." A private receives base pay of $10,000 a year, in addition to room and board, medical care, and other benefits. A master sergeant earns about $40,000 plus medical benefits for himself and his family, and is eligible for a pension of half of base pay after twenty years' service. A mid-level officer has similar benefits with base pay of about $55,000 a year. Again, however, we must ask why the Army of the 1970s was so torn by racial strife, when real earnings

and benefits were practically identical to what they are today. Likewise, why are race relations generally better in the Army than in the other services, which all have nearly identical systems of authority and compensation?

The solid economic status of most soldiers does not explain the dynamics of race relations in the Army. After all, racial tensions have sharpened in society at large at all income levels. Indeed, the "rage" of the black middle class in a racist American society is an increasingly dominant theme in the current literature.[7]

The most salient objection to the Army as a model for race relations is the one least likely to be mentioned: the Army, while excluding the very bottom rungs of American society, does not recruit from America's elite youths either. Perhaps the reason for the silence on a broadly based sharing of duty is that it raises the specter of restoring the draft. In any event, as measured by test scores and school credentials, the Army effectively excludes the bottom third of black youths and the bottom fourth of white youths. This is a valid point and must be addressed seriously. After all, if it is simply the quality of youth that matters, then all the Army's racial experiences and equal opportunity programs are largely irrelevant.

The rebuttal to this argument is that race relations are better in the armed forces than in institutions that presumably recruit the highest-quality youths in America—our colleges and universities. By conventional standards, the quality of young people entering these leading universities far surpasses that of the Army recruits. Yet today, precisely when the U.S. Army is held up as a model of race relations, our campuses are divided by mutual racial isolation and, too often, by racial hostility. . . .

In fact, anyone could easily trot out arguments to show why race relations should be worse in the Army than on campus. The Army, after all, is populated overwhelmingly by young males, the most trouble-prone group. The Army enforces constrained living conditions, with little outlet for private expression. Also, it sends young people into harm's way, a likelihood that should aggravate rather than reduce social tensions. How these negatives become positives are the key to the Army model.

What then can be learned? We suggest a broad lesson. Race relations can best be transformed by an absolute commitment to nondiscrimination, coupled with uncompromising standards of performance. To maintain standards, however, paths of opportunity must be created—through education, training, and mentoring—for individuals who otherwise would be at a disadvantage. We suggest another lesson as well: there must be enough blacks in the system. We do not know what the magic number is, but the lower range is probably close to the national ratio of one black for every nine Americans. This condition guarantees a sufficient pool from which to recruit black leaders, allows for the acceptance of features of Afro-American culture that enhance the organizational climate, and ensures that whites recognize the diversity among blacks. . . .

Overcoming Race: A Primer

How, then, do we transfer the Army's successes to nonmilitary settings? Differences between military and civilian settings preclude exact analogies, but we can articulate the key principles of the Army experience. . . .

Lesson One: Blacks and Whites Will Not View Opportunities and Race Relations the Same Way.

Even in the Army, the most successfully racially integrated institution in American society, blacks and whites still have disparate views of equal opportunity. Blacks consistently take a dimmer view of racial matters than whites. This cuts across gender and rank. In no foreseeable situation in any American institution, much less in society as a whole, is this likely to change soon. Nevertheless, the Army shows that black and white social attitudes can become significantly closer in egalitarian settings with shared experiences. It also shows that blacks and whites do not have to hold identical views of the racial situation in order to succeed together.

Lesson Two: Focus on Black Opportunity, Not on Prohibiting Racist Expression.

Civilian organizations, especially universities, try to improve the racial climate by eradicating racist statements and symbols. Such efforts are meaningful only when accompanied by concrete steps to expand the pool of qualified black students and faculty. Likewise, in governmental and corporate structures, the emphasis must continually be on opening avenues of opportunity for black participation and movement into leadership roles. Lamentable as the presence of white racists may be, it is not the core issue. Indeed, Afro-American history testifies eloquently that black accomplishment can occur despite pervasive white racism. It would be foolhardy to consider the absence of white racists as a precondition for black achievement. This is one of the most significant morals of the Army experience.

Lesson Three: Be Ruthless Against Discrimination.

Formal efforts to prohibit racist expressions can be a way of avoiding a genuine opening up of channels for black advancement, but this realization does not imply that any retreat from antidiscrimination should be made. Racist behavior cannot be tolerated within the leadership of an organization. Individuals who display racist tendencies must not be promoted to positions of responsibility. In the Army, racist behavior ends a person's career. That racial remarks are rarely heard among Army NCOs and officers, even in all-white groups, reflects how strictly this norm is adhered to. Whether formal or informal, promotion criteria must include sensitivity on racial matters. Shelby Steele's proposal to criminalize racial discrimination (though not his proposal to do away with affirmative action) has, in a manner of speaking, been accomplished de facto in the military.[8]

Lesson Four: Create Conditions so That White and Black Youth Can Serve on an Equal Basis to Improve Their Social and Civic Opportunities.

The intense cooperation required to meet military goals has a democratizing effect in the Army. Gordon W. Allport's long-standing and hard-wearing "equal contact" statement four decades ago remains a classic:

> Prejudice . . . may be reduced by equal status contact between majority and minority groups in the pursuit of common goals. The effect is greatly enhanced if this contact is sanctioned by institutional supports . . . and provided it is of the sort that leads to the perception of common interests and common humanity between members of the two groups.[9]

Some form of civilian national service is the only likely means of restoring the opportunities for young people that were reduced by the end of conscription and further limited by the military drawdown. The connection between the demise of the draft and the growth of an underclass is a plausible hypothesis and deserves examination. The critical point is that sharing the obligations of citizenship will act as a solvent for many of the differences among national servers. That all participants will live at not much more than subsistence levels and that all will be equally eligible for postservice educational benefits underscore the egalitarianism of the national service proposal. We encourage a public debate about the merits of youth service in either civilian or military capacities, whether compulsory, voluntary, or benefit-contingent.

The GI Bill following World War II was a remarkable success, a social experiment that led to a broad, lasting, and most positive impact in America. National service linked to a GI Bill principle—benefits premised on service, not need—would result in much the same democratizing effect that has traditionally occurred among military members. Precisely because many young people from across the social spectrum would participate—if not shoulder to shoulder, then at least under one large umbrella—invidious stereotyping would be kept to a minimum. As in the military, the emphasis must be on the service performed and not on the server. The GI Bill continues to serve as the best model to engender true equality of opportunity. A comprehensive sociological study completed in 1996 shows that an "away from home" experience, as traditionally accompanies military service, coupled with generous GI Bill benefits, dramatically improves the life chances of the youths who were most

disadvantaged prior to entering the armed forces.[10]

Lesson Five: Install Qualified Black Leaders as Soon as Possible.

The quickest way to dispel stereotypes of black incapacity is to bring white people into contact with highly qualified Afro-American leaders. In the Army, this contact is likely to occur on the first day and to continue throughout the term of service. Again, we stress that only in the Army are whites routinely bossed by blacks.

Historically black colleges and universities (HBCUs) play a large but underappreciated role in forming Afro-American leaders in a variety of fields. These institutions of higher education produce close to half of all black officers in the U.S. Army. In a sociological context, HBCUs show how two seemingly opposing goals—racial integration and strengthening black institutions—reflect the same movement toward an inclusive, shared American national identity.

Without a critical mass of blacks, as exists in the Army, the beneficial effects of equal opportunity for leadership roles are difficult to realize. Although the number that constitutes a critical mass cannot be specified with exactitude, the lower range probably approximates the number of blacks in the American population—around one in nine. It may be time to rethink the advisability of historically white and elite colleges' competing against each other for qualified black students and faculty.[11] Better, perhaps, would be policies for such blacks to accumulate in greater numbers in fewer selected institutions, thus building the critical mass that has allowed historically black schools to produce a disproportionate share of high achievers. We view affirmative action in college admissions as one of society's mechanisms to equalize opportunity, not as part of the reward system for achievement.

Lesson Six: Affirmative Action Must Be Linked to Standards and Pools of Qualified Candidates.

The Army eschews promotion quotas, but it does set goals. These goals are based on the racial composition of the relevant pool of qualified candidates, not on the proportion of blacks in the entire organization, much less on general population figures. Failure to meet goals must be explained, but "timetables" do not exist. This "soft" affirmative action contrasts with the quota-driven programs that have characterized federal agencies.[12] Indeed, the earlier noted promotion lag of blacks compared to whites at certain levels, especially from captain to major, indicates that Army promotions are not bound to goals.

Maintenance of common standards for promotion may cause short-term turmoil, as it did in the Army of the 1970s, but it also means that individuals who attain senior positions are fully qualified. Any set of standards must also take into account, as does the Army, such "whole-person" qualities as initiative, perseverance, leadership, and commitment to organizational goals. That the Army contained few putative liberals willing to rationalize an initial drop in standards allowed blacks who were promoted in the early days to become the strongest defenders of standards for their own black subordinates. An organization that promotes the less qualified to buy temporary peace only invites long-term disaffection.

Lesson Seven: Affirmative Action Must Follow a 'Supply-side' Model, Not a 'Demand-side' Model.

In practical terms, the Army has developed an affirmative action program based on "supply." This contrasts with the typical "demand" version of affirmative action, where goals and quotas are set before attempting to enlarge the pool of qualified people.

The Army shows that youths with deficient backgrounds can meet demanding academic as well as physical standards. The Army's internal programs bring young people up to enlistment standards, enlisted soldiers to noncommissioned officer standards, undergraduates to officer-commissioning standards, and high school graduates to West Point-admission standards. These programs are not targeted exclusively to minority soldiers, but the participants are disproportionately Afro-American. Here we interject an object lesson on an affirmative action program—one based on the demand-side

model—that seems destined not to work. In 1995, the Navy announced a "12/12/5" goal for the year 2000. By that date, the Navy wants to attain an officer accession that is at least 12 percent black, 12 percent Hispanic, and 5 percent Asian or Pacific Islander.[13] (In time, that figure is supposed to become the standard for the total officer composition.) Reaching that goal means the percentage of officer accessions in the designated racial categories would have to triple within five years. Asked about the origin of the "12/12/5" figure, a very senior Navy official told us it was the projected racial composition of the United States and the "Navy should look like America." Toward this goal, the Navy has introduced initiatives that allow recruiters some leeway in offering Navy ROTC scholarships to minority applicants.[14] Yet the Navy goals are untenable unless accompanied by new programs to expand the pool of minorities who could be raised to meet commissioning standards. Unlike the Army, for example, the Navy has a small presence in the ROTC programs in historically black colleges.[15] In the light of the Navy's insistence that standards "will not be dropped," the Navy's "12/12/5" goals appear unrealistic.

The lesson here is simple: diversity in and of itself is not a rationale for affirmative action. Indeed, under the 1995 Supreme Court ruling in *Adarand Construction v. Peña*, affirmative action for the purpose of reflecting racial and ethnic diversity for its own sake is unconstitutional. It is much better to build up avenues of equal opportunity than to concoct numbers to correspond with notions of diversity based on gross population numbers.

Lesson Eight: A Level Playing Field Is Not Always Enough.

The evaluation of programs to boost academic skills and test scores is fraught with difficulty. But "intelligence"—as measured by achievement tests—can be raised impressively through programs that are well staffed, have motivated participants, and use a military regimen. Residential programs away from the participants' home area seem to be the most effective way to resocialize young people toward productive goals. As in the Army, skill-boosting programs should emphasize mathematics, reading, and writing. These programs cost money and require a big commitment of resources; they also visibly pay off for those who complete them.

Good affirmative action acknowledges that members of disadvantaged groups may need compensatory action to meet the standards of competition. Bad affirmative action suspends those standards. Always, the objective should be to prepare members of a historically disadvantaged population to compete on an equal footing with the more privileged. Sometimes, as in the Army's remedial programs, "throwing money" at a social problem does solve it.

Lesson Nine: Affirmative Action Should Be Focused on Afro-Americans.

The Army's racial affirmative action is geared de facto to blacks. This principle should be generalized throughout our society. The basic social dichotomy in our society is black versus white and, increasingly, black versus nonblack. The core reality is that blacks have a dual sense of identity and grievance with America, one that is unique and far stronger than any other ethnic group's sense of belonging or not belonging. The confluence of race, slavery, and segregation has created a social reality that in the American experience is unparalleled. (Perhaps the Native American Indian story comes closest.) Multiculturalism ultimately trivializes the distinct history and predicament of black Americans. The Afro-American story is singular and of such magnitude that it cannot be compared to the experiences of other American ethnic groups, especially immigrant groups.[16] American blacks resemble neither the immigrants of yesterday nor the ones of today.

Likewise, affirmative action based on class or income is a chimera.[17] Not only is it much more difficult to implement than affirmative action based on race, ethnicity, or gender, but the nonblack poor would soon displace blacks in affirmative action procedures. More to the point, we argue that race overrides class as a source of ingrained prejudice in our country. (Ask yourself: Would the child of a white ditchdigger or that of a black physician cause more strain by marrying into a white family?) Affirmative action based on class or income, paradoxically, would work against black Americans, the very group for which it is most justified. Afro-Americans already are increasingly apprehensive that the "wide net" approach to affirmative action is another way of excluding blacks from channels of opportunity. A policy of class-based affirmative action would confirm these apprehensions.

Terminology on affirmative action is instructive. When the issue was defined originally as focusing on Afro-Americans, the preferred term was "equal opportunity." "Multiculturalism" and "diversity" as affirmative action concepts entered the vocabulary only after nonblack groups came to be included in the programs. The decline of Afro-Americans in affirmative action priorities corresponded directly with replacement of equal opportunity with the rhetoric of multiculturalism and diversity.

Lesson Ten: Recognize Afro-Anglo Culture as the Core American Culture.

American history needs a reconstruction to stress how much our nation's culture and moral vision derive from the Afro-American experience. White Americans must recognize the Afro-American elements in our bedrock culture; equally, black Americans must recognize their contributions to the common American culture and resist the lure of an Afrocentric curriculum that too easily obscures the contribution of Afro-Americans to our national heritage. In black thought, a duality persists on whether blacks are essentially outsiders with strong African connections or are quintessential Americans.[18] To the question, "Are blacks Americans?" the Army experience offers a resounding "Yes." This also means, in the sense of shared culture, that "Americans are part black." This may be the only way to lance the boil of a black "oppositional" culture. Just as we came to recognize our shared American religious culture as Judeo-Christian in origin, we hope for an acknowledgment of our common Afro-Anglo heritage.

We must abandon the mindset that being "black" and being "American" are mutually exclusive. This is a false dichotomy, though held by many black nationalists and most whites. Being black and being American is not an "either-or" dichotomy but a "both-and" relationship. The titles of the only two autobiographies by black generals are informative: *American* by Benjamin O. Davis, Jr., and *My American Journey* by Colin L. Powell.[19]

Lesson Eleven: Enhancing Black Participation Is Good for Organizational Effectiveness.

The blunt truth is that the way most Americans see it, the greater the black proportion in an organization, the poorer its effectiveness. The armed forces (along with historically black educational institutions) are the welcome exceptions. Two plain facts have profound meaning: first, the disproportionately black Army stands out as one of the most respected organizations in American society; and second, General Colin L. Powell occupies the pinnacle of American esteem. Not only has the military played a central role as an avenue of black achievement but it has also shown that a large Afro-American presence has been conducive to the smooth operation of a major American institution.

Indeed, the increase in the proportion of blacks has corresponded with an increase in the standing and effectiveness of the Army. Other variables also contributed to this improved state of affairs, but the military's early implementation of affirmative action and its enhancement of black achievement were necessary preconditions. Ultimately, any race-relations program must pass a single test. In the not-so-long run, does it improve organizational performance?

Lesson Twelve: If We Do Not Overcome Race, American Society May Unravel.

The final lesson of the Army experience is political. A society no longer united by foreign threats may discover that its own internal racial divisions are deeper and more intractable than anyone realized. The growing centrifugal tensions in America could easily make national unity the issue of the twenty-first century.

The military of the 1970s recognized that its race problem was so critical that it was on the verge of self-destruction. That realization set in motion the steps that have led to today's relatively positive state of affairs. As racial division grows in American society at large, will we come to the same realization?

Endnotes

1. Andrew Hacker, *Two Nations: Black and White, Separate, Hostile, Unequal* (New York: Charles Scribner's Sons, 1992). Hacker's account of race relations is much more pessimistic than the Kerner Report assessment a generation earlier. See National Advisory Commission on Civil Disorders, *Report of the National Advisory Commission on Civil Disorders* (New York: Bantam Books, 1968). An excellent compilation on the state of sociological knowledge of Afro-Americans is Gerald Jaynes and Robin N. Williams, Jr., eds., *A Common Destiny: Blacks and American Society* (Washington, D.C.: National Academy Press, 1989).

2. Even in areas of American life where blacks have visibly succeeded in large numbers, such as the entertainment industry and professional sports, these achievements have been narrow, limited to exceedingly talented people, and rarely reflected among the organizational leadership of these endeavors.

3. Reynolds Farley and William H. Frey, "Changes in the Segregation of Whites from Blacks during the 1980s," *American Sociological Review*, vol. 59 (February 1994), pp. 23–45. This study of residential segregation is based on the 1990 census.

4. Janice H. Laurence, *The Military: Purveyors of Fine Skills and Comportment For a Few Good Men* (Philadelphia: National Center on the Educational Quality of the Workforce, [University of Pennsylvania, 1994), p. 14.

5. *Washington Post* (April 10, 1995), p.1.

6. For a discussion of why the black attrition rate is lower than that of whites, see Andrew Moskos, "Black Exceptionalism: Making It in the Military," *Black Issues in Higher Education*, vol. 7, no. 4 (April 26, 1990), p. 76.

7. Ellis Cose, *The Rage of a Privileged Class* (New York: HarperCollins, 1993). The manner in which race persists in defining relations within middle-class and professional circles has a growing, if recent, literature. See also Derrick Bell, *Faces at the Bottom of the Well* (New York: Basic Books, 1992); Lois Benjamin, *The Black Elite* (Chicago, Ill.: Nelson-Hall, 1992); Jill Nelson, *Volunteer Slavery*

(Chicago, Ill.: Noble Press, 1993); Nathan McCall, *Makes Me Wanna Holler* (New York: Random House, 1994); and Brent Staples, *Parallel Time* (New York: Pantheon, 1994). Sardonic and enlightening observations of the treatment of upper-middle-class blacks in public settings are in Lawrence Otis Graham's *Member of the Club: Reflections on Life in a Racially Polarized World* (New York: Harper-Collins, 1995). For a sociological context, see Bart Landry, *The New Black Middle Class* (Berkeley: University of California Press, 1987).

8. Shelby Steele, "Affirmative Action Must Go," *New York Times* (March 1, 1995), p. A13.

9. Gordon W. Allport, *The Nature of Prejudice* (Garden City, N.Y.: 1958), p. 263.

10. Robert J. Sampson and John H. Laub, "Socio-economic Achievement in the Life Course of Disadvantaged Men: Military Service as a Turning Point, Circa 1940–1965," *American Sociological Review*, vol. 61, no. 3 (June 1996), pp. 347–67.

11. For a thoughtful piece on the effects on Afro-American achievement of a thin representation of blacks at elites schools, see Steve Sailer, "Where the Races Relate," *National Review* (November 27, 1995), pp. 41–44.

12. See the story on the Office of Federal Contract Compliance Programs by Steven A. Holmes, "Once-Tough Chief of Affirmative-Action Agency Is Forced to Change Tack," *New York Times* (August 6, 1995), p. A13.

13. *Navy Times* (May 1, 1995), p. 14.

14. Starting in 1995, Navy recruiters have been authorized to make an Immediate Selection Decision (ISD) to offer a minority student a Navy ROTC scholarship. In the first year, not a single black had been placed in the program because eligibility requires a minimum SAT score of 600 in mathematics.

15. In 1995, the number of Reserve Officer Training Corps (ROTC) units at historically black colleges by service was Army 27, Air Force 6, and Navy 5.

16. On the noncomparability of black Americans and other ethnic groups , we follow Stanley Lieberson, *A Piece of the Pie: Black and White Immigrants Since 1880* (Berkeley: University of California Press, 1980); and Nathan Irving Huggins, "Ethnic Americans," in his *Revelations: American History, American Myths* (New York: Oxford University Press, 1995), pp. 148–57. For a summary of studies on how whites treat blacks differently, see Thomas F. Pettigrew and Joanne Martin, "Shaping the Organizational Contexts for Black American Inclusion," *Journal of Social Issues*, vol. 43. no. 1 (1987), pp. 41–78. See also Orlando Patterson and Chris Winship, "White Poor, Black Poor," *New York Times* (May 3, 1992), p. 17; and Orlando Patterson, "Affirmative Action on the Merit System," *New York Times* (August 7, 1995), p. A11.

17. One of the most sophisticated arguments for class-based affirmative action is Richard Kahlenberg, "Class, Not Race," *New Republic* (April 3, 1995), pp. 21–27; and Kahlenberg, "Equal Opportunity Critics," *New Republic* (July 17, 24, 1995), pp. 20–25. For a formulation of affirmative action that comes closer to our position, see Jeffrey Rosen, "Affirmative Action: A Solution," *New Republic* (May 8, 1995), pp. 20–25; and Will Marshall, *From Preferences to Empowerment: A New Bargain on Affirmative Action* (Washington D.C.: Progressive Policy Institute, August 1995).

18. John Sibley Butler, "Multiple Identities," *Society* (May/June 1990), pp. 8–13. Michael Lind goes further, arguing that black Americans are more American than most white Americans. See his *The Next American Nation* (New York: Free Press, 1995), pp. 274–76.

19. Benjamin O. Davis, Jr., *American* (Washington, D.C.: Smithsonian Institute Press, 1991); Colin L. Powell, *My American Journey* (New York: Random House, 1995).

Latino/a Americans

Latino/a (or Hispanic) Americans constitute the second largest ethnic minority population in the U.S., and this population continues to increase rapidly. Using U.S. Census Bureau definitions, which have evolved over time, the Latino/a population has grown from 4.5 percent of the total U.S. population in 1970, to 6.4 percent in 1980, to 9 percent in 1990, to approximately 11 percent by 1996 (Valdivieso and Davis 1991; del Pinal and Singer 1997). These figures may be low estimates, and may not adequately count undocumented immigrants from Mexico, Central America, and Caribbean nations. Given the high levels of Latino/a immigration in recent years, the youthful age structure of the Latino/a population in the U.S., and the comparatively high fertility rates among Latinos/as as a whole, it is widely estimated that they will outstrip African Americans to become the largest minority population in the U.S. during the early years of the twenty-first century (del Pinal and Singer 1997).

The labels "Latino/a" and "Hispanic" generally refer to U.S. residents whose cultural heritage traces back to a Spanish-speaking country in Latin America, but it also includes individuals with links to Spain and many of those from areas of the southwestern U.S. that were once under Spanish or Mexican control (Valdivieso and Davis 1991). The use of these omnibus labels is appropriate in one sense, because many Latinos/as face similar issues and problems (e.g., high poverty rates, school dropout rates, bilingualism, prejudice, discrimination, and others), which warrant the attention of policymakers. Yet these labels remain controversial in many quarters, because they can also mask the considerable diversity of cultures and experiences within the Latino/a population (Gimenez 1992; Oboler, this volume). According to U.S. Census data, approximately 64 percent of Latinos in the U.S. are of Mexican descent, while 11 percent are Puerto Rican (this number does not include residents of the island of Puerto Rico), 5 percent are Cuban American, and 14 percent trace their origins to other Central or South American countries (del Pinal and Singer 1997). Although Latinos/as reside in every state of the union, there are clear pockets of Hispanic geographical concentration; nearly 85 percent of the Latino/a population in the U.S. lives in eight of the 50 states. California contains the largest number of Latinos of any state, more than 7.6 million, or 34 percent of the Latino/a population in the U.S. Texas ranks second, home to roughly 20 percent of all U.S. Latinos, followed by New York (10 percent), Florida (7 percent), Illinois (4 percent), and Arizona, New Jersey, and New Mexico (3 percent each) (Chapa and Valencia 1993).

We can glimpse the diversity among various Latino/a nationality groups by briefly examining the experiences of three segments of the Latino/a population: Mexican Americans, Puerto Ricans, and Cuban Americans. These three groups today occupy very different positions within the socioeconomic hierarchy of the U.S. To understand these major differences among segments of the Latino/a population, it is crucial to understand, among other factors: (a) the timing, circumstances, and permanence of entry for each group; (b) the human capital (e.g., work experience and skills, education) and English-language facility among the members of each group; (c) the structure of economic opportunities in the communities in which they settle; and (d) the popular and political responses of the host population (i.e., native-born U.S. citizens) to the arrival of each group.

As a group, Mexican Americans—by far the largest Latino/a population group—suffer from high rates of poverty and unemployment, and relatively low levels of education and occupational attainment. In 1992 the median family income for Mexican-origin families was only 59 percent that of European-origin families ($23,700 vs. $42,400). Approximately 26 percent of Mexican American families lived below the poverty line, compared with only 7 percent of non-Latino/a white families (U.S. Bureau of the Census 1994). These disparities in income levels and poverty rates are partly due to the high unemployment rates among Mexican Americans—nearly 12 percent, far higher than the 6 percent figure for non-Latino/a whites. In addition, those Mexican Americans who are in the labor force are concentrated in low-wage job categories. For instance, fewer than 9 percent of Mexican-origin males were employed in professional and managerial occupations in 1993, as compared with nearly 30 percent of their European American counterparts. On the other hand, approximately 46 percent of all employed Mexican-origin males worked as operators or laborers, or in service occupations; this figure was only around 26 percent for European-origin males (U.S. Bureau of the Census 1994). Low average education levels, high dropout rates among native-born Mexican Americans, and subpar English language facility among many recent immigrants, also contribute to these patterns. So, too, do the higher-than-average fertility rates that are common among Mexican-origin families, especially recent entrants (Chapa and Valencia 1993).

Mexican Americans are heavily concentrated in the southwestern U.S., especially in the metro areas of California and Texas and in borderland communities. A small proportion of the Mexican American population is descended from Spanish-speaking residents of these areas, who were subjugated—through political and economic means, and by brute force in a series of battles—by the "Anglos" (European Americans) who settled Texas and the other southwestern areas

(Montejano 1987). However, the vast majority of Mexican Americans in the U.S. today are native-born descendents of immigrants (del Pinal and Singer 1997). Indeed, throughout much of the 20th century, Mexican immigration has been encouraged by southwestern business interests seeking a steady flow of cheap labor for agriculture, mining, and other enterprises. Even when the U.S. virtually ended most immigration with the sweeping reforms of the 1920s, an exception was made for Mexican entrants. However, after the Great Depression produced high unemployment among Anglo workers, hostility toward Mexican Americans increased, and large numbers of Mexican-origin persons, including many U.S. citizens, were deported (or "repatriated") by authorities. When World War II led to new labor shortages, Mexican labor was once again welcome, leading to the Bracero program, which permitted guest workers from Mexico to work for specified terms in certain economic sectors. But animosity from European American labor subsequently led again to forced deportations—including forced relocations of many Latino/a citizens—during the infamous "Operation Wetback" from 1953–54. Not surprisingly, many observers regard the ongoing contemporary debates over immigration reform (see section 12, this volume) as merely the latest chapter in a sad but familiar story.

Today Mexican Americans in some parts of California and Texas continue to perform much of the agricultural labor, picking fruits and vegetables, although their wages and working conditions have improved in recent years due to unionization efforts and political mobilization. In cities like Los Angeles and San Antonio, residents of Mexican origin are heavily concentrated in other types of working-class jobs in the low-wage service sector (e.g., food service, janitorial services), construction, and manufacturing (Cardenas et al. 1993). Indeed, some observers attribute much of California's economic growth in the 1980s to Latino/a labor, which supplied the muscle for the construction boom of that period, as well as the garment and semiconductor industries. In some parts of the southwestern U.S., Mexican-origin women have also been deeply involved in domestic services, such as housework and child care, although there is evidence that recent immigrants from Central America may be displacing African Americans and Mexican Americans from these jobs in the region.

While the statistics for the Mexican-origin population as a whole are sobering, especially for recent immigrants, the Mexican American middle class is also expanding. In enclaves and barrios (e.g., the West side of San Antonio), one finds a large and growing number of businesses owned by Mexican Americans—shops, restaurants, small-scale service providers, and so on. In Los Angeles, while the Latino/a population doubled between 1983 and 1993, the number of licensed Latino/a enterprises—most of them owned by Mexican Americans—increased sevenfold during the same period (Feagin and Feagin 1996: 308). Mexican-origin women are increasingly moving into clerical and secretarial occupations, as well as sales positions (Segura, this volume). In addition, there is a growing Mexican American business, professional, and managerial class, benefiting from enhanced access to higher education, and in some cases from affirmative action programs in the public sector (e.g., minority contract set-asides by city, state, and federal governments) and private businesses.

The experience of Puerto Ricans differs from that of Mexican Americans in several respects. The Puerto Rican population on the mainland was quite small prior to World War II, numbering only around 70,000 in 1940. However, due partly to the labor shortages created by the war, recruiters from steel, electronics, garment, and other industries lured some Puerto Ricans to northeastern and midwestern cities. Then, beginning in the late 1940s, the island government—at U.S. prodding—implemented a new economic development strategy ("Operation Bootstraps") that emphasized the creation of infrastructure (e.g., roads, communications) and the recruitment of light manufacturing industries with generous tax breaks at the expense of agriculture. This strategy resulted in large-scale displacement of agricultural labor and high levels of rural-to-urban migration. Dwindling economic prospects on the island paved the way for significant migration to the mainland (Falcon 1991). Such migration became more attractive after Puerto Rico became a U.S. commonwealth in 1952, especially given the affordable airfares to the New York City area, and the rosy popular and media images of the U.S. as a land of opportunity, where hard work and sacrifice would be amply rewarded. By 1970, some 1.5 million Puerto Ricans resided on the mainland; this figure had grown to 2.7 million by 1990.

Compared with other segments of the Latino/a population, the socioeconomic position of Puerto Ricans is somewhat precarious. Despite the fact that average education levels are slightly higher for Puerto Ricans than for Mexican Americans, roughly two in every five Puerto Rican families live below the poverty line, as compared with one-fourth of Mexican-origin families. Puerto Rican families are twice as likely as Mexican-origin families to be headed by a female householder (40 percent vs. 20 percent), and for them the news is even worse: Approximately two-thirds of these female-headed Puerto Rican households live in poverty (U.S. Bureau of the Census 1994). Further, the percentages of households receiving public assistance and including children born out-of-wedlock are higher for Puerto Ricans than for other Latino/a groups. Consequently, while rich cultural traditions, social institutions, and extended kin ties seem to have limited the emergence of an "underclass" within most Latino/a communities (Moore and Vigil 1993), there is widespread concern about the possible emergence of a Puerto Rican "underclass" in some urban neighborhoods (Lemann, this volume).

What might account for Puerto Ricans' relatively disadvantaged position on the mainland? While there are significant Puerto Rican communities in several midwestern cities (e.g., Chicago, Cleveland), as well as recent migration to Sunbelt areas like Central Florida (Rohter 1994), approximately 50 percent of the Puerto Ricans living on the mainland reside in New York and New Jersey. In the 1950s and 1960s, large numbers of Puerto Ricans initially came to the New York area and took jobs in the garment, electronics, and other manufacturing industries, as well as in low-skilled service occupations (Falcon 1991;

Rodriguez 1991). However, most of these manufacturing jobs were lost to the Sunbelt states and overseas (to Asia and the Caribbean) during the 1960s and 1970s. Technological innovations also displaced many low-wage, low-skilled workers. These processes—well beyond the control of individuals, families, or local communities—had devastating effects on many Puerto Ricans (Torres and Bonilla 1993). While some degree of un(der)employment can be absorbed in neighborhoods where most residents have steady jobs (Sullivan 1993), the results of industrial restructuring trapped many Puerto Rican migrants in ghettos like the South Bronx area described by Lemann (this volume). The middle-class Puerto Rican community in New York is relatively small, partly due to the underrepresentation of Puerto Ricans in public sector employment (Torres and Bonilla 1993).

In addition, Puerto Rican migration to the mainland—particularly to the New York area—has tended to involve significant numbers of young singles, and fewer couples and extended families. Because of (a) the close cultural and family ties of many Puerto Ricans to the island; (b) financial hardship on the mainland; and (c) the proximity of the island, Puerto Ricans have tended to engage in circular migration over time. Taken together, these factors may have limited the ability of Puerto Rican communities on the mainland to nurture small-scale business enterprises or to mobilize family resources in crafting strategies for upward mobility (Waldinger et al. 1990).

Moreover, there is compelling evidence that Puerto Ricans experience high levels of discrimination in employment and other arenas at the hands of European Americans. Because many Puerto Ricans are of mixed racial background, they tend to have darker skin tone than the members of most other Latino/a groups (Rodriguez 1991). Trade unions, especially those representing skilled and craft workers, have sometimes excluded or restricted the access of Puerto Ricans. Even among relatively well-educated or highly skilled Puerto Ricans, their economic returns to human capital are lower than among other Latinos (Tienda 1989). Further, because

Puerto Ricans are relatively poor and often lack sufficient capital to buy homes in middle-class neighborhoods, many are vulnerable to discrimination by landlords, police, and others (Rodriguez 1991).

Many of these issues also confront the rapidly-growing Dominican immigrant population, which is also heavily centered in New York. Approximately one-half of all Dominican immigrants have entered the U.S. during the last decade—not counting the unknown numbers of undocumented Dominican entrants, who sometimes overstay their tourist visas. Although recent Dominican immigrants have included some of the more urban, youthful, and skilled members of that island's population, their average levels of socioeconomic status, education, and English language facility remain somewhat low compared with most other Latino/a groups. Most knowledgeable observers agree that the processes of industrial restructuring and economic decline in the New York area have adversely impacted the Dominican community there. In addition, as with Puerto Ricans, there are signs that darker-skinned Dominicans encounter considerable discrimination in employment, housing, and other arenas (Grasmuck and Pessar 1996).

The experience of Cuban Americans contrasts starkly in many respects with the experiences of other Latino/a groups. Cuban Americans are often portrayed as a "success story" because of their relatively high average incomes and education levels, which approach those of native-born European Americans and far surpass those of other segments of the Latino/a population (U.S. Bureau of the Census 1994). Cuban Americans are more likely to be self-employed or employed as business owners or proprietors than Mexican Americans or Puerto Ricans. Overall fertility rates are lower among Cuban Americans, as are rates of out-of-wedlock births, unemployment, and poverty. Indeed, only approximately 16 percent of Cuban-origin persons live below the poverty line, as compared with 26–40 percent of individuals from other Latino/a groups (U.S. Bureau of the Census 1994).

Why have Cuban Americans fared so much better as a group than other Latinos in the U.S.? As Perez-Stable and Uriarte (this volume) point out, their distinctive history helps to explain these contemporary patterns. Although Cuban elites had longstanding business and cultural ties with the U.S., the Cuban-origin population on the mainland numbered fewer than 75,000 until the Cuban Revolution of 1959–60, in which insurgent forces led by Fidel Castro ousted the rightist, pro-U.S. regime of Fulgencia Batista. As Castro's socialist government moved to nationalize foreign businesses and implemented extensive agrarian reform, a growing wave of Cuban business elites, wealthy landowners, and professionals emigrated to the U.S. The 1961 Bay of Pigs debacle, in which a poorly-designed invasion of Cuba led by anti-Castro emigres (with U.S. support) failed miserably, marked an important turning point in the development of the Cuban American community. Whereas most exiles to that early point had intended to live in the U.S. only briefly, until Castro could be deposed, many subsequently came to view their stay as long-term, perhaps even permanent (Portes and Bach 1985).

This initial wave of elite emigres was expanded and diversified somewhat in the mid-1960s, to include middle-level managers and professionals, merchants, landlords, and some skilled unionized workers. During the 1965–74 period, the official U.S. policy welcomed refugees from communism, and under this banner large numbers of employees and workers, independent craftsmen, small merchants, and others (the petite bourgeoisie) entered the country. An estimated 41 percent of Cubans who emigrated after the revolution came during this period (Pedraza 1996). Despite initial U.S. attempts to disperse Cuban refugees as part of the resettlement plan, most Cuban emigres relocated to the Miami area within several years of entry, and this quickly became the center of Cuban American society in the U.S.

The early exiles included persons with significant human capital—work skills and expertise, business knowledge and experience, and higher education—and, in some cases, financial capital as well (Portes and Bach 1985). Many also came with a strong work ethic and intact family structures, in some cases including extended kin ties. Due to their status as political refugees, many early Cuban emigres received unprecedented re-settlement assistance. For instance, the U.S. government provided low-interest guaranteed loans for business startups, housing assistance, and help with recertification for some professionals who emigrated (Perez-Stable and Uriarte, this volume). These and other initial advantages aided in these industrious emigres in establishing an enormous array of small and large enterprises during the following decade, in diverse economic sectors ranging from modest retail and service businesses to construction, banking and insurance, manufacturing, and others. The number of Cuban-owned firms exploded, growing from approximately 800 in 1967 to over 21,000 in 1979 (Waldinger et al. 1990). The dynamic "enclave economy" has been characterized by high levels of horizontal and vertical integration among firms; Cuban-owned firms often buy from and sell to one another, and they also employ large numbers of Cuban-origin workers. The economic "multiplier" effects of the enclave economy have been felt throughout the Greater Miami area, and have helped the community to absorb and accomodate successive waves of less-advantaged immigrants from Cuba—and, to a lesser extent, refugees from various Central American countries during the 1980s.

However, it would be a mistake to conclude that all Cuban Americans have been economically successful. From the 1979 to 1981 period, the Castro regime arranged the Mariel Boatlift, in which large numbers of lower working-class and unemployed Cubans, and some who were released from prisons, entered the U.S. To be sure, despite the disparaging claims of the Cuban government, most of the "criminals" among these entrants were guilty only of political protest or black market participation, which would not be considered crimes in the U.S., and many of the Marielitos brought valuable work skills with them. Nevertheless, while only 8.5 percent of Cubans who entered in the 1960–64 period were living below the poverty line in 1990, this figure was nearly 30 percent among those who came between 1975 and 1981. Poverty rates were even higher—a stark

38.7 percent—for Cubans who came to the U.S. during the 1987–90 period (Pedraza 1996). Many of these arrived on makeshift "balsas" or rafts, surviving great risks at sea only to confront inconsistent and vacillating U.S. policies toward refugees.

The diversity of experiences notwithstanding, there are several major issues confronting most Latino/a communities in the U.S. One key set of issues involves educational quality and access. Latino/a Americans, with the partial exception of Cuban-origin students, have substantial high school dropout rates; for most Latino/a population groups, these rates are higher than those of African Americans. Critical analyses suggest that these high dropout rates (indeed, some even call them "pushout" rates) may result partly from unresponsive teachers and administrators; efforts to cultivate more engaging forms of pedagogy and a greater sense of belonging and community in the schools could yield academic benefits for Latino/a students (Romo and Falbo 1996; Gonzalez and Padilla 1997). However, many additional factors contribute to high Latino/a dropout rates including: the high rates of pregnancy and childbearing among Mexican American and Puerto Rican teens; the poor quality and underfunding of primary and secondary schools in many Latino/a areas; lower average rates of academic achievement among Latino/a youths; and high rates of family poverty that may lead some Latino/a youths to seek employment rather than continuing with school. Further, many Latino/a students, especially recent immigrants, often lack proficiency in English, leading to poor school performance, discouragement, and low self-confidence. While bilingual education programs (i.e., those conducted in both English and Spanish) have traditionally been viewed as a remedy for this problem, these programs have been unevenly implemented, and are now under fire from political conservatives, some of whom also propose establishing English as the "official" U.S. language. Some Latino/a parents also worry that bilingual education hinders, rather than improves, students' English language ability. In May 1998, by a wide margin, Californians—including significant numbers of Latino/a

voters—passed Proposition 229, which curtails the use of bilingual education in that state's public schools.

According to recent research, Latino Americans (males) with good English language ability and high school education (or beyond) earn approximately as much money as European American males with similar credentials. On the other hand, Latinos lacking English facility and/or high school diplomas fare markedly worse in the labor market than than their counterparts (Stolzenberg and Tienda 1997). There is mounting evidence that high dropout rates are linked with the development of oppositional youth cultures, including a rejection of "Anglo" values of achievement and upward mobility (Portes and Zhou, this volume). Thus, the future social and economic prospects of Latino/a Americans depend heavily on finding ways to enhance educational performance, high school graduation rates, and job training for youths who leave school and for adults who are displaced from the labor force. In addition, only 6 percent of Mexican-origin adults over age 24 and only 8 percent of Puerto Rican (mainland) adults over 24 have attained college degrees; the comparable figure among European American adults is roughly 24 percent (U.S. Bureau of the Census 1994). Thus, many policy specialists argue that further steps (e.g., increased financial aid, affirmative action, mentorship and other programs) are also needed to bolster access and achievement in these settings (de los Santos and Rigual 1994).

Another major issue is the continuing need to combat prejudice and discrimination, mainly at the hands of European Americans. As we noted above, darker-skinned persons of Hispanic descent (e.g., emigres from the Caribbean) appear to suffer both ethnic and racial discrimination. But persistent discrimination against Latinos/as of varying skin tone has also been well-documented in various domains—housing, employment, and treatment by authorities (e.g., police, government officials). In employment tests, when matching pairs of European Americans and equally- or better-qualified Latino/a Americans applied for jobs, substantial percentages of the Latinos/as (20 percent or more in several cities) encountered discrimination. This was most common in hiring for white-collar positions that involve high levels of customer contact, but at least some discrimination was found in a wide range of job types (Feagin and Feagin 1996: 303–05). There are also numerous cases of employer discrimination against Latino/a workers who speak Spanish in the workplace (e.g., to Latino/a coworkers). In addition, negative European American stereotypes of Latinos also surface repeatedly in recent public opinion polls such as the NORC General Social Survey, in which Hispanics were widely viewed as less intelligent, lazier, less patriotic, and more violence-prone than European Americans (Davis and Smith 1996).

Much has been said about the political clout that Latino/a Americans may wield as their population grows in absolute numbers and as a percentage of the total U.S. population. However, scholars and activists wonder about the impact of Latino/a diversity on (pan-)ethnic identity and unity, and on the ability of Latino/a organizations and leaders to advance a coherent social and political agenda for the future. For decades, Mexican Americans and Puerto Ricans on the mainland have tended to endorse policies aimed at increasing opportunities for minority populations and promoting more equal distribution of wealth and resources. In practice, this has usually meant supporting Democratic candidates for public office. By contrast, because of their anti-communist roots, Cuban Americans have leaned toward conservative politics, heavily supporting the Republican party. However, these political winds may be shifting, albeit slowly. On the one hand, Mexican Americans tend to be quite traditional in their core values (de la Garza et al. 1996), and conservative political views are gaining favor among at least some members of the expanding Mexican-origin middle class (Chavez 1991). On the other hand, approximately 30 percent of the Cuban American population was born in the U.S. (Pedraza 1996); for them, domestic policy concerns may take precedence over traditional anti-Castro fervor, perhaps creating new opportunities for the Democratic party.

Latino/a leaders face two additional important challenges in the political arena. First, they confront the task of engaging and mobilizing newly naturalized Latino/a citizens, who are much less inclined to vote or to participate in other forms of political activity than their second- or third-generation counterparts (Diaz 1996). Second, particularly at the local level, high levels of immigration—along with the out-migration of European Americans—mean increased competition between Latino/a and African American (and in several cities, Asian American) residents for economic opportunities and political power (see section 11, this volume). Forging strategic alliances for cooperation among minority populations can have an important, and potentially positive, impact on the development of these major urban centers, and on the quality of life their citizens can enjoy in the twenty-first century.

References

Cardenas, Gilberto, Jorge Chapa, and Susan Burck. 1993. "The Changing Economic Position of Mexican Americans in San Antonio." Pp. 160–183 in *Latinos in a Changing U.S. Economy: Comparative Perspectives on Growing Inequality*, edited by R. Morales and F. Bonilla. Thousand Oaks, CA: Sage.

Chapa, Jorge, and Richard R. Valencia. 1993. "Latino Population Growth, Demographic Characteristics, and Educational Stagnation: An Examination of Recent Trends." *Hispanic Journal of Behavioral Sciences* 15: 165–187.

Chavez, Linda. 1991. *Out of the Barrio: Toward a New Politics of Hispanic Assimilation*. New York: Basic Books.

Davis, James A., and Tom W. Smith. 1996. *The NORC General Social Surveys: Cumulative Codebook, 1972–1996*. Chicago: National Opinion Research Center.

de la Garza, Rodolfo O., Angelo Falcon, and F. Chris Garcia. 1996. "Will the Real Americans Please Stand Up: Mexican American Support of Core American Political Values." *American Journal of Political Science* 40: 335–350.

de los Santos, Alfredo, Jr., and Anthony Rigual. 1994. "Progress of Hispanics in American Higher Education." Pp. 173–194 in *Minorities in Higher Education*, edited by Manuel J. Justiz, Reginald Wilson, and Lars G. Bjork. Phoenix: Oryx Press/American Council on Education.

del Pinal, Jorge and Audrey Singer. 1997. "Generations of Diversity: Latinos in the Unites States." *Population Bulletin* 52(3) October: 2–47.

Diaz, William A. 1996. "Latino Participation in America: Associational and Political Roles." *Hispanic Journal of Behavioral Sciences* 18: 154–174.

Falcon, Luis. 1991. "Migration and Development: The Case of Puerto Rico." Pp. 146–181 in *Determinants of Emigration from Mexico, Central America, and the Caribbean*, edited by S. Diaz-Briquets and S. Weintraub. Boulder, CO: Westview Press.

Feagin, Joe R., and Clairece Booher Feagin. 1996. *Racial and Ethnic Relations*, 5th ed. Englewood Cliffs, NJ: Prentice Hall.

Fernandez, Roberto M., Ronnelle Paulsen, and Marsha Hirano-Nakanishi. 1989. "Dropping Out Among Hispanic Youth." *Social Science Research* 18: 21–52.

Gimenez, Martha E. 1992. "U.S. Ethnic Politics: Implications for Latin Americans." *Latin American Perspectives* 19: 7–17.

Gonzalez, Rosemary, and Amado Padilla. 1997. "The Academic Resilience of Mexican American High School Students." *Hispanic Journal of Behavioral Sciences* 19: 301–317.

Grasmuck, Sherri, and Patricia Pessar. 1996. "Dominicans in the United States: First- and Second-Generation Settlement, 1960–1990." Pp. 280–292 in *Origins and Destinies: Immigration, Race, and Ethnicity in America*, edited by S. Pedraza and R. Rumbaut. Belmont, CA: Wadsworth.

Montejano, David. 1987. *Anglos and Mexicans in the Making of Texas, 1836–1986*. Austin: University of Texas Press.

Moore, Joan, and James Diego Vigil. 1993. "Barrios in Transition." Pp. 27–50 in *In the Barrios: Latinos and the Underclass Debate*, edited by J. Moore and R. Pinderhughes. New York: Russell Sage Foundation.

Pedraza, Silvia. 1996. "Cuba's Refugees: Manifold Migrations." Pp. 263–279 in *Origins and Destinies: Immigration, Race, and Ethnicity in America*, edited by S. Pedraza and R. Rumbaut. Belmont, CA: Wadsworth.

Portes, Alejandro, and Robert L. Bach. 1985. *Latin Journey: Cuban and Mexican Immigrants in the United States*. Berkeley: University of California Press.

Rodriguez, Clara. 1991. *Puerto Ricans: Born in the U.S.A.* Boulder, CO: Westview Press.

Rohter, Larry. 1994. "A Puerto Rican Boom for Florida." *New York Times*, January 31: A6.

Romo, Harriett D., and Toni Falbo. 1996. *Latino High School Graduation: Defying the Odds.* Austin: University of Texas Press.

Stolzenberg, Ross M., and Marta Tienda. 1997. "English Proficiency, Educational Experience, and the Conditional Assimilation of Hispanic and Asian Origin Men." *Social Science Research* 26: 25–51.

Sullivan, Mercer L. 1993. "Puerto Ricans in Sunset Park, Brooklyn: Poverty Amidst Ethnic and Economic Diversity." Pp. 1–26 in *In the Barrios: Latinos and the Underclass Debate*, edited by J. Moore and R. Pinderhughes. New York: Russell Sage Foundation.

Tienda, Marta. 1989. "Puerto Ricans and the Underclass Debate." *Annals of the American Academy of Political and Social Science* 501: 105–119.

Torres, Andres, and Frank Bonilla. 1993. "Decline Within Decline: The New York Perspective." Pp. 85–108 in *Latinos in a Changing U.S. Economy: Comparative Perspectives on Growing Inequality*, edited by R. Morales and F. Bonilla. Thousand Oaks, CA: Sage.

U.S. Bureau of the Census. 1994. *The Hispanic Population of the United States: March, 1993. Current Population Reports P20–475.* Washington: U.S. Government Printing Office.

Valdivieso, Rafael, and Cary Davis. 1991. *U.S. Hispanics: Challenging Issues for the 1990s.* Washington: Population Reference Bureau.

Waldinger, Roger, Howard Aldrich, Robin Ward, et al. 1990. *Ethnic Entrepreneurs.* Newbury Park, CA: Sage.

6

Cubans and the Changing Economy of Miami

Marifeli Pérez-Stable
Miren Uriarte

The experience of Cubans in Miami appears to stand apart from the Latino inequalities elsewhere in the U.S. economy. However mythical the "golden exile" . . . might have been, the perception of the successful Cuban is deeply ingrained among Cubans, other Latinos, and the general population. In important ways, the data back up these perceptions. Cubans earn higher incomes, have higher educational levels, and register lower poverty rates than other Latinos. Most Cubans in the United States, moreover, arrived as political exiles after the revolution of 1959. Thus, their migration differed markedly from that of Mexicans and Puerto Ricans.

Nonetheless, the "success story" has been "dysfunctional" for the characterization of Cuban communities, especially for those among them who do not quite live up to the prevailing image. The other side of the Cuban story, particularly in South Florida where most Cubans in the United States live, has clearly not received adequate attention. In this chapter we do not dismiss the predominant view of Cubans in U.S. society, but an analysis of their labor market participation in Miami over four decades delineates their profile in ways that allow for more meaningful comparisons with other groups. . . .

In this chapter we use the 1950, 1970, and 1980 U.S. Census Public Use Micro Data Sample and the 1988 Current Population Survey for the Miami SMSA to describe the effect of economic transformation on the insertion of Cubans into the economy of Miami. . . .

Miami and Havana: Development Trends Before 1959

An often-ignored aspect of the Cuban experience in Miami is the complementarity in the patterns of development between the sending and receiving economies of the immigrants: those of Havana and Miami during the 1950s. These patterns and their aborted prospects constitute an important structural context for the entrance of Cubans into Miami after 1959. In Miami, Cubans, especially *habaneros*, stepped into familiar terrain. Their human capital and their know-how tapped the potential in the socioeconomic context of Miami, and consequently, their skills found their market match. . . .

One of the consequences of the social revolution of 1959 was the migration of more than one-half million Cubans during the 1960s. The earliest exiles were especially unrepresentative of the Cuban population during the 1950s. They came from the wealthier, predominantly white, better educated, more urban, higher status occupational sectors of prerevolutionary society. Some arrived with little except a few personal belongings. Many managed to transfer some assets to the United States. A few had investments outside of Cuba well before the revolution. All came with substantial human capital, and just as important, with the insight that belonging to the Cuban middle class gave them into U.S. culture. During the 1950s, Cuba, particularly Havana, experienced substantial U.S. influence. At the time, no other group of Latin Americans could have entered the United States as prepared to succeed as middle-class Cubans were during the early 1960s. That Miami and Havana had been undergoing transformations that augured complementarity and competition, moreover, allowed the exiles to step into familiar territory.

Since the 1920s, tourism, real estate, construction, trade, and financial services had brought considerable expansion to Miami. The trade sectors were the most important employer. Services, especially the unskilled type supportive of tourism, were the second leading source of employment. Construction and transportation each accounted for about 7%-10% of Miami earners (Ballinger, 1936; Muir, 1953). Although manufacturing represented less than 10% of total employment, the city nonetheless had one of the fastest rates of industrial growth in the United States during the 1940s and 1950s. Largely because of tourism, links to the Caribbean were growing. Miami was often the first stop before traveling farther south. But these expanding ties were also rooted in the developing importance of Miami as a financial center for foreign trade, particularly to Latin America. . . . On the surface, Miami might have seemed not much more than a hard-pressed resort town. Underneath, however, longer term trends pointed to emerging transformations that the early influx of mostly upper- and middle-class Cubans undoubtedly encouraged.

During the 1950s, Havana was more decisively experiencing rapid changes. The capital was the motor behind the incipient transformation of dependent Cuban capitalism. With about 25% of the total population, Havana had . . . 54% of all professionals, 40% of all managers, nearly 60% of all office workers, about 40% of all skilled workers, and 54% of all service workers (Officina Nacional de los Censos Demografico y Electoral, 1955, pp. 1, 183, 196). Havana was the principal site for the expanding industrialization then taking place in Cuba. . . . During the 1950s, total wages in Havana province as those of all other provinces, especially Camaguey and Oriente, declined (R. C. Bonilla, 1983, pp. 416–417; Banco Nacional de Cuba, 1960, pp. 151–153). . . . Imports of consumer durables were growing significantly and most were destined for the *habanero* public (Banco Nacional de Cuba, 1960, p. 190). Moreover, *habaneros* were increasingly using credit to maintain their life-style. . . .

The Miami Economy, 1950–1988

Between 1950 and 1988, Miami underwent profound economic and demographic transformations. The restructuring process in the Miami SMSA entailed prodigious growth in the service sector, particularly in the high-end services, and the stagnation of the small manufacturing sector. . . .

Figure 6.1
Occupational Distribution of Earners, Miami Metropolitan Area, 1950-1988 (in percent).

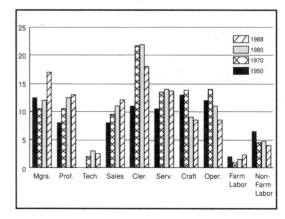

Source: U.S. Census PUMS 1950-1980; CPS 1988.

Two major trends mark the changes in the occupational structure of Miami during these four decades (Figure 6.1). First, there has been a marked increase in the managerial and professional occupations at the expense of those occupations requiring lesser skills. Miami's share of workers in more highly skilled occupations has increased steadily from 20% in 1950 to 31% in 1988. By comparison, the share of earners in clerical and other low-end services appears to have stabilized after rising sharply during the 1960s. Craft, operative, and laborer occupations have undergone a significant relative decline. Second, the occupational opportunities for low-skilled workers have narrowed. By 1988, the Miami profile appears to have consolidated: Clerical occupations still accounted for the largest number of workers, with the sum of managers and professionals/technical personnel representing one third of earners in Dade County. Crafters, operatives, and laborers continued to decline.

Demographic changes, especially in racial/ethnic makeup, are even more significant. . . . Between 1950 and 1990, the population of Miami nearly quadrupled from 495,084 to 1,937,094. In 1950, 83% of the population was non-Hispanic white, 13% black, and 4% Latino. . . . After 1970, non-Hispanic whites continued to decline, representing only 32% of the Miami SMSA population in 1990, while blacks increased their share to 19%. By 1990, Latinos had become the largest group, accounting for 49% of the population. . . . Diversification of the Latino population also characterizes the period. . . .During the 1960s and 1970s, Cubans constituted about 70% of the Latino population. . . . By 1990, however, the Cuban share of the Latino population had decreased to 59% and that of Central/South Americans and Dominicans had increased to 31%. Puerto Ricans remained at 8% [of the Latino/a population of the Miami SMSA].

With the change in population came a transformation in the region's labor force. As the Latinization of Miami went forward . . . Latino gains were particularly salient in manufacturing and high- and low-end services, all ascending sectors of the economy during the 1970s, and excepting manufacturing, during the 1980s as well. The black share of earners across sectors has largely remained constant. . . . A clear racial/ethnic order emerged where non-Hispanic whites dominated the higher salaried and more prestigious occupations with Latinos beginning to make modest inroads. But both Latinos and blacks were more likely to be employed in occupations of lower socioeconomic status. During the 1970s and 1980s, these trends consolidated. By 1988, non-Hispanic whites were solidly ensconced in the expanding high-level management and professional/technical occupations. Blacks and Latinos, although increasing their share of earners in these sectors, continued to be underrepresented.

The Differential Effect of Economic Transformation: Non-Hispanic Whites, Blacks, and Cubans in Miami

How the three main racial/ethnic groups have fared in the restructuring of the regional economy is an important aspect of the recent history of Miami. According to industrial and occupational distributions by racial/ethnic groups as well as data on income and poverty, non-Hispanic white earners have fared the best. . . . By 1988, 41% were employed as managers, technicians, and professionals; 43% labored as low-status white-collar workers in service, sales, and clerical occupations. Only 6% were still employed as operatives and laborers.

Rising incomes and declining poverty rates among non-Hispanic whites have resulted from the increase of their participation in the higher status occupations and the expanding sectors of the economy. . . . [Overall] non-Hispanic white poverty rates—low to begin with—declined slightly. . . . Poverty rates among non-Hispanic white earners, however, rose from 4.5% in 1970 to 5.3% in 1988, a local manifestation of national trends of growing numbers of working poor.

In contrast, blacks have fared much worse. Although increasing numbers of blacks have penetrated the ascending sectors of the economy, they have done so primarily in the lower status occupations. Black earners have particularly suffered because sectors where they were strong and occupations they once dominated have declined [(e.g., construction)]. . . .

The changing economy of Miami has brought significant changes for black occupational opportunities. Black managers, technicians, and professionals increased sharply: More than one out of five black earners was employed in these occupations in 1988. . . . Between 1950 and 1980, black operatives and laborers declined from 50% to 24%, and those in clerical, sales, and service jobs increased from 20% to 52%. This reversal may partially explain the decline of 15 percentage points in the labor force participation of black males and the rise by 21 percentage points in that of black women.

Black gains in the high-status occupations have not translated into a higher mean income relative to non-Hispanic white and Cuban males. . . . Not surprising, between 1970 and 1980, poverty rates for working-age blacks remained high. Although declining slightly during the 1970s, poverty rates were rising again during the 1980s. . . . The relative absence of jobs available to young blacks and the availability of low-paying jobs for black women seem to be contributing factors to the profile of black poverty in Miami. Black poverty rates have been about three times those of non-Hispanic whites. . . .

The Cuban experience lies somewhere between that of blacks and non-Hispanic whites. . . . During the 1970s, Cubans rapidly entered the high-end service sectors. By 1988, high-end services employed more Cubans than any other sector, 23.6%. In many ways, the sectoral experience of Cubans resembles that of non-Hispanic whites.

Occupationally, however, Cubans have had a different experience. Although Cubans have made substantial inroads in the high-status occupations, a large percentage of Cubans are still in the lower paying jobs. . . . In 1970, 71% of Cuban workers worked in sales or as clerks, service workers, operatives, and laborers. By 1988, 59% continued to do so, whereas 49% of non-Hispanic whites and 62% of blacks did.

In many ways, Cubans have also had to make occupational shifts similar to those of blacks: from operatives and laborers to white- and pink-collar employment. In 1970, Cuban earners were about equally employed in low-paying white-collar and service sectors (33.6%) as in operative and laborer occupations (36.7%). By 1988, only 18% remained in the declining operative and laborer occupations whereas 41% now had jobs in the low-paying service occupations. The shift is more rapid than that experienced by blacks and cushioned by a significant representation in the ascending occupational sectors. . . .

Finally, the distribution shows that only about 20% of Cubans conformed to the profile of success: managers and professionals in manufacturing, construction, the high-end services, and wholesale and retail trade. Most Cuban earners had a rather different experience: They worked as operatives and laborers in manufacturing and as office clerks, service workers, and salespeople in the service sectors and wholesale and retail trade. Although varying by sector, the difference in earnings between the high- and low-paying occupations is substantial. The 1988 Current Population Survey data appear to underscore widening income differentials between these two types of occupation.

Income and poverty trends support the indications of growing polarization. Between 1970 and 1988, earnings for Cuban workers as well as the rate of poverty among the working-age population and among earners increased. While incomes of non-Hispanic whites stagnated and those of blacks declined, those of Cuban males rose sharply. The mean income of Cuban females similarly rose, surpassing that of black women in 1988 but remaining well below that of non-Hispanic white females. Paralleling rising incomes were increases in poverty among the working-age population. In 1970, 13% lived in a poor household; by 1988, that rate was 17%. . . .

Explaining the Experience of Cubans in Miami

The incorporation of Cubans into the Miami economy has been generally successful. Rising poverty levels and growing earnings polarization notwithstanding, the economic experience of Cubans differs radically from that of other Latinos in their cities of major concentration as well as from that of other minorities in Miami itself. Cubans have entered the ascending sectors of the regional economy at both higher and lower levels. Although there is a continued concentration of substantial numbers in the manufacturing sector and in low-level occupations, there is also evidence Cuban earners are making a steady transition to higher paying occupations throughout the economy.

Human capital explanations are the most prevalent. Educational attainment—higher for Cubans than for other Latinos—is often mentioned to explain their labor market success. However, in the context of Miami, the higher education levels do not appear to be as important as the earnings Cubans obtain at different levels of education in comparison with others in Miami. Between 1970 and 1988, the levels of educational attainment of Cuban earners have been closer to those of blacks than those of non-Hispanic whites. . . . In 1988, an equal percentage (67%) of black and Cuban earners had at least a high school degree; the rate for non-Hispanic whites was 88%. Cubans have a slightly higher percentage of college graduates (17%) than blacks (14%). The rate for non-Hispanic whites is 26%.

But, without doubt, Cuban earners are able to maximize the income potential of their educational attainment relative to other minorities. Across different educational levels, Cuban earnings are closer to those of non-Hispanic whites. For example, among earners with less than a high school education, Cuban earnings were more likely to approximate those of non-Hispanic whites whereas those of blacks tended to lag considerably. . . . The gains are even more marked for those with a college education. In 1988, Cuban college graduates earned incomes slightly below non-Hispanic whites and substantially higher than black college graduates. . . .

Human capital explanations also focus on the "business know-how" of Cubans as a factor in their higher rates of self-employment. Cubans have, in fact, higher rates of self-employment than other groups in Miami (Figure 6.2). In 1988, rates of self-employment among Cubans (8.5%) surpassed those of non-Hispanic whites (7.4%) and were well above those of blacks (2.9%). Similarly, the mean self-employment earnings of Cubans relative to non-Hispanic whites has increased steadily. More important, among Cubans and non-Hispanic whites mean earnings from self-employment are higher than income from wage and salaries, whereas for blacks the reverse is the case.

The enclave economy appears to have enhanced the effect of education and work experience for Cubans in the Miami labor market. Although the data used in this paper do not allow the measurement of the effect of ethnic-owned enterprises on the incorporation of Cubans into the Miami economy, they do suggest the strength of the enclave. The occupational shifts that all Miamians have undergone appear to have been buffered for Cubans as a result of the opportunities available to them, but not to others within the enclave. Although enclave earnings are lower than in the mainstream economy, the class diversity of the enclave has allowed Cubans across the occupational spectrum to exercise their human capital in a more protected en-

Figure 6.2
Self-Employment Rates, by Race and Ethnicity of Earners, Miami Metropolitan Area, 1970-1988.

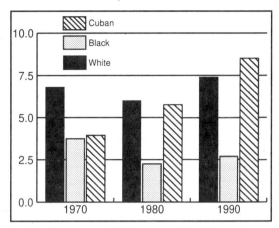

Source: U.S. Census PUMS 1970,1980; CPS 1988.

vironment. The enclave has thus facilitated the transition of Cubans into the mainstream sectors. During the 1980s, this transition appears to have accelerated and most likely explains the sustained increases in Cuban earnings.

Perhaps the most critical value of the enclave is the opportunity it affords for a mode of insertion that does not subject newcomers to the same degree of exploitation and discrimination as the primary and secondary labor markets. Enclave participation, even if exploitative, furnishes the immigrants with the opportunity to connect into a myriad of social networks, and consequently, gain more rapid social mobility. The high rates of self-employment for Cubans who left the island during the 1970s and the Mariel boat lift in 1980 point to the preeminence of structural factors. Although largely lacking the endowed human capital of earlier immigrants, the more recent entrants have nonetheless had better economic outcomes than Latino immigrants with comparable qualifications in other areas of the country (Portes & Bach, 1985, pp. 205–216; Portes & Jensen, 1989).

. . . Understanding how Cuban exiles founded the businesses and established the networks that produced the enclave is a central question. Answering it allows the model to transcend the notion of "Cuban exceptionality." Where the original capital that formed the enclave came from is perhaps its most crucial starting point. Portes (1987) gives us several answers. First, and perhaps most evident, the Cuban migration included many persons who already had investments and savings in the United States or brought substantial capital that allowed them to become rentiers or start new endeavors. Moreover, many Cuban exiles, because of their pre-1959 dealings with U.S. companies, had useful business connections that served them well when applying for credit and establishing new enterprises. Next, Portes mentions a South American bank in Miami that, when the first exiles arrived, employed Cuban bankers. These bankers proceeded to issue loans to their conationals on the basis of prior knowledge about the applicants' record and experience in Cuba. In the same vein, Portes points to wealthy South Americans who invested their capital in Miami because of political upheavals in their native countries. Primarily in commerce and construction, this venture capital allowed small Cuban distributors and contractors the opportunity to grow beyond the enclave. Its extent and weight are understandably difficult to determine, but drug-related capital accumulation is mentioned. Finally, he underscores the role of individual savings in the smaller, more ethnic-oriented enterprises characteristic of the later entrants who lacked previous business experience and capital from Cuba (Portes, 1987). . . .

[In addition to these factors,] the complementary development of Havana and Miami during the 1940s and 1950s allowed Cubans, especially the *habaneros*, to step into familiar territory—not unlike the ones they had left behind in the industrial belt around Havana—which came quickly to be controlled by Cubans at the top, and at the same time, offered a safe place for lower skilled Cubans to enter the labor market. The enclave also developed a service sector in which experienced entrepreneurs transplanted their business acumen from Havana to *la calle ocho* and provided entry level jobs for their compatriots.

[Moreover, there are a] host of political and ideological factors that, although not exclusively determinant in the origins of the enclave, should be included in the analysis. . . . The United States invested nearly $1 billion in assisting the Cubans because they were fleeing communism (Pedraza-Bailey 1985). In many ways, it was a multifaceted community development strategy. In its 12 years of existence, federal assistance to Cuban refugees encompassed direct cash assistance, food subsidies, and guaranteed health care for needy individuals as well as college loans for Cuban students, training and retooling programs for professionals, and English-language instruction and financial assistance for those establishing small businesses. State intervention reinforced the advantages of the Cubans, and in turn, enhanced the ability of the exiles to contribute to the transformation of the South Florida economy. No other Latino group or community has had the benefit of similar levels of targeted investment and state intervention sustained over a significant period of time.

. . .[In addition,] the geopolitics of the Caribbean after the Cuban revolution and the interplay of the U.S. state and exile counter-revolutionary movements articulated a political discourse that significantly contributed to the development of a Cuban collective identity. The role of the Central Intelligence Agency in providing some exiles with capital and business experience through the establishment of proprietary fronts should, for example, be mentioned, even if the full range of evidence is difficult to obtain (Argüelles, 1982; Forment, 1989). The downfall of Eastern European socialism, the disintegration of the Soviet Union, and current uncertainties about the future of Cuba itself, moreover, have reinforced the weight of ideological concerns in Cuban ethnic identity. . . .

Two important questions in relationship to the future of the Cuban enclave are, first, the role of second-generation Cubans in the enclave economy, and second, the effect of the enclave on growing diversity of the Latino population in Miami. There are indications from the data analyzed here that the retail enterprises in the enclave may serve as an entry point into the labor market for younger Cubans, particularly the retail trade sector. The question of whether they will fuel a second generation of the Cuban enclave, or as in other ethnic groups, the younger generation will immediately transcend it has not yet been answered. Similarly, there is evidence that "Other Hispanics" have very quickly attained even higher levels of self-employment than Cubans. Just a cursory observation of the main establishments of the enclave reveals that Central Americans (e.g., Nicaraguans) are easily penetrating it both as owners and as workers. . . .

Conclusions

In this chapter we bring out new facets of the images of Cubans in Miami. Although still impressive, the Cuban experience is considerably more complex than the success story would indicate. Miami developed very differently from the pattern anticipated during the 1930s and 1940s. As the U.S. gateway to Latin America was emerging, revolution convulsed Havana—Miami's Latin American counterpart. Consequently, many of the Cubans who were fueling the transformation of Havana during the 1950s made their way to Miami. Their presence in turn provided an added impetus to the development of Miami. During the 1960s, Miami and the exiles became an almost perfect match. Cubans thus look less like superachievers and more like a group intelligently transferring their skills to a propitious environment.

Our perspective allows underscoring some general lessons. First, the Cuban experience exemplifies successful state and private sector strategies on the adjustment and incorporation of immigrants. Encouraging the development of the enclave allowed Cubans the resources to control their own community. Far from the "social welfare" approach so characteristic of public and private sector policies toward other Latinos that so diminish and disempower individuals and communities, Cubans had the opportunity to exercise control over their community. Community development and community control, important pillars in the struggles of most Latino communities, have been critical factors in the attainments of Cubans in Miami. The fear of permanent separation from the mainstream that the independent development of Latino

and immigrant communities often raises, as well as the concern that strong ethnic identity retards economic advancement, did not materialize in the Cuban case.

A second important lesson is the breadth of the Cuban Refugee Program and other federal initiatives to support the adaptation of Cubans. The range of programs offered are the top items in any Latino community's wish list: educational opportunities; retraining programs; English-language instruction; small business loans; college loans independent of need; and nonstigmatized direct cash benefits, health care and food for those in need. Although these programs are not solely responsible for the Cuban success, they did provide a buffer against the initial, often traumatic experience of immigrants. No other Latino group has enjoyed similar favors. In this sense, the Cuban experience is indeed unique and needs to be underscored when comparing Cubans to other Latinos. . . .

During the 1980s, the increase in the [Miami] Latino population has been quite significant. Other Latinos, the principal contributors to that growth, appear to be taking advantage of the enclave. Not all, however, are doing so. Tensions between Cubans and Puerto Ricans may stem from the latter's lesser access to the protection of the enclave. For Cubans, now in titular control of the political structures, managing the demographic transition taking place in Miami is proving to be a more difficult task than achieving economic success. The future of group relations, indeed, depends on the economic and social development of the black and other Latino communities in Miami. Policies need to favor community-based economic development and employment and educational opportunities—policies similar to those that supported the successful incorporation of Cubans into the Miami economy.

References

Arguelles, L. 1982. "Cuban Miami: The Roots, Development, and Everyday Life of an Emigre Enclave in the US National Security State." *Contemporary Marxism* 5 (Summer): 27–43.

Ballinger, K. 1936. *Miami Millions: The Dance of the Dollars in the Great Florida Land Boom of 1925*. Miami: Franklin Press.

Banco Nacional de Cuba. 1960. *Memoria 1958–1959*. Havana: Editorial Lex.

Bonilla, R. C. 1983. *Escritos Economicos*. Havana: Editorial de Ciencias Sociales.

Forment, C. A. 1989. "Political Practice and the Rise of an Ethnic Enclave: The Cuban-American Case, 1959–1979." *Theory and Society* 18 (January): 47–81.

Muir, H. 1953. *Miami, U.S.A.* Coconut Grove, FL: Hurricane House.

Oficina Nacional de los Censos Demografico y Electoral. 1955. *Censos de Poblicacion, Viviendas y Electoral: Informe General*. La Habana: P. Fernandez y Cia, S. en C.

Pedraza-Bailey, S. 1985. *Political and Economic Migrants in America: Cubans and Mexicans*. Austin: University of Texas Press.

Portes, A. 1987. "The Social Origins of the Cuban Enclave Economy in Miami." *Sociological Perspectives* 30 (October): 340–372.

Portes, A., and R. L. Bach. 1985. *Latin Journey: Cuban and Mexican Immigrants in the United States*. Berkeley: University of California Press.

Portes, A., and L. Jensen. 1989. "The Enclave and the Entrants: Patterns of Ethnic Enterprise in Miami Before and After Mariel." *American Sociological Review* 54 (December): 929–949.

7

The Other Underclass

Nicholas Lemann

. . . Puerto Ricans are the second-largest Hispanic group—2.75 million people in the mainland United States. A third of them live in one city—New York.

As soon as the Hispanic category is broken down by group, what leaps out at anyone who takes even a casual look at the census data is that Puerto Ricans are the worst-off ethnic group in the United States. For a period in the mid-1980s nearly half of all Puerto Rican families were living in poverty. It seems commonsensical that for Hispanics poverty would be a function of their unfamiliarity with the mainland United States, inability to speak English, and lack of education. But Mexican-Americans, who are no more proficient in English than Puerto Ricans, less likely to have finished high school, and more likely to have arrived here very recently, have a much lower poverty rate. The *Journal of the American Medical Association* reported earlier this year that, as the newsletter of a leading Puerto Rican organization put it, "On almost every health indicator . . . Puerto Ricans fared worse" than Mexican-Americans or Cubans. Infant mortality was 50 percent higher than among Mexican-Americans, and nearly three times as high as among Cubans.

The statistics also show Puerto Ricans to be much more severely afflicted than Mexican-Americans by what might be called the secondary effects of poverty, such as family breakups, and not trying to find employment—which work to ensure that poverty will continue beyond one generation. In 1988 females headed 44 percent of Puerto Rican families, as opposed to 18 percent of Mexican-American families. Mexican-Americans had a slightly higher unemployment rate, but

Puerto Ricans had a substantially higher rate in the sociologically ominous category "labor force non-participation," meaning the percentage of people who haven't looked for a job in the previous month.

Practically everybody in America feels some kind of emotion about blacks, but Puerto Rican leaders are the only people I've ever run across for whom the emotion is pure envy. In New York City, black median family income is substantially higher than Puerto Rican, and is rising more rapidly. The black home-ownership rate is more than double the Puerto Rican rate. Puerto Rican families are more than twice as likely as black families to be on welfare, and are about 50 percent more likely to be poor. In the mainland United States, Puerto Ricans have nothing like the black institutional network of colleges, churches, and civil-rights organizations; there isn't a large cadre of visible Puerto Rican successes in nearly every field; black politicians are more powerful than Puerto Rican politicians in all the cities with big Puerto Rican populations; and there is a feeling that blacks have America's attention, whereas Puerto Ricans, after a brief flurry of publicity back in *West Side Story* days, have become invisible.

The question of why poverty is so widespread, and so persistent, among Puerto Ricans is an urgent one, not only for its own sake but also because the answer to it might prove to be a key to understanding the broader problem of the urban underclass. "Underclass" is a supposedly nonracial term, but by most definitions the underclass is mostly black, and discussions of it are full of racial undercurrents. To seek an explanation for poverty among Puerto Ricans rather than blacks may make possible a truly deracialized grasp of what most experts agree is a nonrace-specific problem. Although there is no clear or agreed-upon answer, the case of Puerto Ricans supports the view that being part of the underclass in the United States is the result of a one-two punch of economic factors, such as unemployment and welfare, and cultural ones, such as neighborhood ambience and ethnic history.

The First Emigration

. . . In [1898] an autonomous Puerto Rican government was set up, with Spain's blessing, but it functioned for only a few days; American troops invaded during the Spanish-American War and the island became a possession of the United States shortly thereafter. The U.S. conquest of Puerto Rico was not the bloody kind that resonates psychologically through the generations; there was little resistance, and the arrival of the troops was cheered in many places. In 1917 all Puerto Ricans were granted U.S. citizenship and allowed to elect a senate, but until after the Second World War the island was run by a series of colonial governors sent from Washington.

During this period Puerto Rico underwent an economic transformation, as big U.S. sugar companies came in and established plantations. Previously the island's main crops had been grown on small subsistence farms up in the hills. The sugar plantations induced thousands of people to move down to the coastal lowlands, where they became what the anthropologist Sidney Mintz calls a "rural proletariat," living in hastily constructed shantytowns and often paid in company scrip. The most salient feature of Puerto Rico throughout the first half of the twentieth century, at least in the minds of non-Puerto Ricans, was its extreme poverty and overpopulation. . . . [M]ore than half of Puerto Rican children of school age didn't go to school . . . the island had the highest infant-mortality rate in the world, and . . . it was the second most densely populated place on earth, after Java.

From such beginnings Puerto Rico became, after the Second World War, one of the great economic and political successes of the Latin American Third World. The hero of the story is Luis Muñoz Marín (the son of the most important Puerto Rican political leader of the early twentieth century), who founded the biggest Puerto Rican political party and, after the United States decided to allow the island to elect its own governor, was the first Puerto Rican to rule Puerto Rico, which he did from 1949 to 1964. Muñoz was the leading proponent of the idea of commonwealth status, as opposed to statehood or independence, for Puerto Rico. Under the system he helped to institute, Puerto Ricans forfeited some rights of U.S. citizenship, such as eligibility for certain federal social-welfare programs and the right to participate in national politics, and in return remained free of certain responsibilities, mainly that of paying federal income taxes. (Local taxes have always been high.). . .

In 1940 New York had 70,000 Puerto Rican residents, in 1950 it had 250,000, and in 1960 it had 613,000. In general, what brought people there was economic prospects vastly less dismal than those in Puerto Rico. Back home, at the outset of the migration, industrialization was still in its very early stages, sugar prices were depressed, and thousands of people who had moved from the hills to the lowlands a generation earlier now had to move again, to notorious slums on the outskirts of urban areas. . . . Among Muñoz's many works was the construction of high-rise housing projects to replace the slums, but during the peak years of Puerto Rican emigration little decent housing for the poor was available locally.

In particular what set off the migration was the institution of cheap air travel between San Juan and New York. During the 1940s and 1950s a one-way ticket from San Juan to New York could be bought for less than $50, and installment plans were available for those without enough cash on hand. Muñoz's government may not have invented the emigration, but it did do what it could to help it along—first by allowing small local airlines to drive down air fares, and second by opening, in 1948, a Migration Division in New York, which was supposed to help Puerto Ricans find jobs and calm any mainland fears about the migration which might lead to its being restricted, as had been every previous large-scale migration of an ethnic group in the twentieth century.

The South Bronx Becomes the South Bronx

At first the center of Puerto Rican New York was 116th Street and Third Avenue, in East Harlem. . . . By the end of the 1950s the Puerto Rican center had begun to shift two miles to the north, to 149th Street and Third

Avenue, in the Bronx, which is where it is today.

At the time, the South Bronx was not a recognized district. A series of neighborhoods at the southern tip of the Bronx—Mott Haven, Hunts Point, Melrose—were home to white ethnics who had moved there from the slums of Manhattan, as a step up the ladder. These neighborhoods were mostly Jewish, Italian, and Irish. Most of the housing stock consisted of tenement houses, but they were nicer tenements than the ones on the Lower East Side and in Hell's Kitchen. From there the next move was usually to the lower-middle-class northern and eastern Bronx, or to Queens. During the boom years after the Second World War whites were leaving the South Bronx in substantial numbers. Meanwhile, urban renewal was displacing many blacks and Puerto Ricans from Manhattan, and the city was building new high-rise public housing—much of it in the South Bronx. . . .

For most of the Puerto Ricans moving to the South Bronx, though, the neighborhood was just what it had been for the area's earlier occupants—a step up (usually from East Harlem). All through the 1950s and 1960s it was possible to see Puerto Ricans as a typical rising American immigrant group (rising more slowly than most, perhaps), and their relocation to the South Bronx was part of the evidence. The idea that New York was going to be continually inundated by starving Puerto Rican peasants for whom there was no livelihood at home had faded, because spectacular progress was being made back on the island: per capita income increased sixfold from 1940 to 1963; the percentage of children attending school rose to 90.

In a new preface for the 1970 edition of *Beyond the Melting Pot*, Nathan Glazer and Daniel Patrick Moynihan wrote, "Puerto Ricans are economically and occupationally worse off than Negroes, but one does find a substantial move in the second generation that seems to correspond to what we expected for new groups in the city." In keeping with the standard pattern for immigrants, Puerto Ricans were beginning to achieve political power commensurate with their numbers in the city. And the War on Poverty and the Model Cities program created a small but important new cache of jobs for Puerto Ricans which were more dignified and better-paying than jobs in the garment district and hotel dining rooms and on loading docks and vegetable farms.

But the 1970s were a nightmare decade in the South Bronx. The statistical evidence of Puerto Rican progress out of poverty evaporated. After rising in the 1960s, Puerto Rican median family income dropped during the 1970s. Family structure changed dramatically: the percentage of Puerto Ricans living in families headed by a single, unemployed parent went from 9.9 in 1960 and 10.1 in 1970 to 26.9 in 1980. The visible accompaniment to these numbers was the extraordinary physical deterioration of the South Bronx, mainly through arson. Jill Jonnes, in *We're Still Here: The Rise, Fall, and Resurrection of the South Bronx*, wrote:

> There was arson commissioned by landlords out for their insurance. . . . Arson was set by welfare recipients who wanted out of their apartments. . . . Many fires were deliberately set by junkies—and by that new breed of professional, the strippers of buildings, who wanted to clear a building so they could ransack the valuable copper and brass pipes, fixtures, and hardware. . . . Fires were set by firebugs who enjoyed a good blaze and by kids out for kicks. And some were set by those who got their revenge with fire, jilted lovers returning with a can of gasoline and a match. . . .

Exact numbers are difficult to come by, but it seems safe to say that the South Bronx lost somewhere between 50,000 and 100,000 housing units during the 1970s, and this produced the vistas of vacant, rubble-strewn city blocks by which the outside world knows the South Bronx. . . . Theories abound about why, exactly, the South Bronx burned: the excessive strictness of rent control in New York, the dispiriting effects of welfare and unemployment, the depredations of drugs. It is not necessary to choose among them to be able to say that the burning took place because most parties had abandoned any commitment to maintaining a functional society there. . . .

By virtue of the presidential visits and its location in New York City (and its prominence in *Bonfire of the Vanities*), the South Bronx has become the most famous slum in America. To visit it today is to be amazed by how much less completely devastated it is than we've been led to expect. The area around 149th Street and Third Avenue, which is known as the Hub, is a thriving retail district, complete with department stores and the usual *bodegas* (corner stores) and *botanicas* (shops selling religious items and magic potions). . . .

What accounts for the signs of progress is, first, a decision during the prosperous 1980s . . . to commit a sum in the low billions to the construction and rehabilitation of housing in the South Bronx. This has led to the opening of many thousands of new housing units. Some of them are very unpopular in the neighborhood, because they are earmarked to house homeless people who are being moved out of welfare hotels in Manhattan. Community leaders in the Bronx grumble that there's a master plan to export Manhattan's problems to their neighborhood.

Several impressive community-development groups, including the Mid-Bronx Desperadoes, Bronx Venture Corporation, and Banana Kelly, have played a part in the rehabilitation of the neighborhood, by using funds from the city and foundations to fix up and then manage apartment buildings. Nationally, a generation's worth of efforts to redevelop urban slums haven't worked well on the whole. The lesson of the community groups' success in the Bronx seems to be that if the focus of redevelopment is on housing rather than job creation, and if there is money available to renovate the housing, and if the groups are permitted to function as tough-minded landlords, then living conditions in poor neighborhoods can be made much more decent.

The biggest community-development organization in the South Bronx is the South East Bronx Community Organization, which is run by Father Louis Gigante. . . . The area surrounding St. Athanasius [Gigante's parish, in Hunts Point] is an oasis of clean streets and well-kept housing, which Gigante runs in the manner of a benevolent dictator. He is known for his tough tenant-screening policy. "You've got to house a base of people with economic strength," he told me recently. "We look at family structure—how do they live? We visit everyone. We look in their background and see if there are extensive social problems, like drugs or a criminal record. Back in the late seventies, I'd only take ten or twelve percent of people on some government subsidy—including pensions. I was looking for working-class people. You cannot put a whole massive group of social problems all together in one place. They're going to kill you. They're going to destroy you. They're going to eat you up with their problems.". . .

A different group—Dominicans—is now streaming into New York (mainly Washington Heights, in Manhattan, but also the South Bronx) but is too recently arrived to have produced the kind of leaders whose names are widely recognized. A common Dominican route to the United States is to pay a smuggler $800 or $1,000 for boat passage from the Dominican Republic to Puerto Rico, and then to buy a plane ticket from San Juan to New York. Estimates of the number of Dominicans who have moved to New York City in the past decade run between a half million and a million. Dominicans are known for their industriousness, and many of them are illegal aliens ineligible for any kind of social-welfare program; they have gone into the undesirable, illegal, or disorganized end of the labor market, working in sweatshops, driving gypsy cabs, dealing drugs, and operating nightclubs and other perilous small businesses. In New York City, according to Ramon Velez, 6,500 "Puerto Rican Judases" have sold their *bodegas* to Dominicans. Gigante says that many of his tenants are now Dominican. Partly because the Dominican migration is predominantly male and the Puerto Rican family in the South Bronx is predominantly female-headed, Dominican-Puerto Rican marriages and liaisons are becoming common. Surely the Dominican migration is partly responsible for the increased vitality that the South Bronx has begun to display.

I don't mean to make the South Bronx sound happier than it is. Only a block and a half from the Hub, at the corner of 148th

Street and Bergen Avenue, is an outdoor drug market, one of many in the area. There is still a great deal of deteriorated housing and vacant land where housing used to be. I spent a couple of mornings recently at Bronx Venture Corporation, a job-placement and community-development organization in the Hub, talking to Puerto Ricans who had come in to get help finding work. Without exception they wanted to leave the South Bronx. They complained about absent fathers, angry mothers, brothers in jail, sisters on welfare; about ruthless competition with the Dominicans for jobs, shoot-outs between drug dealers, high schools where nobody learns, domestic violence, alcoholism, a constant sense of danger. Something is badly wrong there.

Why Is There a Puerto Rican Underclass?

There is no one-factor explanation of exactly what it is that's wrong. In fact, most of the leading theorists of the underclass could find support for their divergent positions in the Puerto Rican experience.

One theory, which fits well with William Julius Wilson's argument that the underclass was created by the severe contraction of the unskilled-labor market in the big northeastern and Midwestern cities, is that Puerto Ricans who moved to the mainland during the peak years of the migration were unlucky in where they went. New York City lost hundreds of thousands of jobs during the 1970s. Particularly unfortunate for Puerto Ricans was the exodus of much of the garment industry to the South. "What I see is a community that came here and put all its eggs in one basket, namely the garment industry and manufacturing," says Angelo Falcón, the president of the Institute for Puerto Rican Policy. When the unskilled jobs in New York began to disappear, Puerto Ricans, who had little education and so were not well prepared to find other kinds of work, began to fall into drugs, street crime, and family dissolution.

The ill effects of unemployment have been exacerbated by the nature of Puerto Rican sex roles and family life. The tradition on the island is one of strong extended-family networks. These deteriorated in New York. "You find the extended family in Puerto Rico and the nuclear family here," says Olga Mendez, a Puerto Rican state senator in New York. The presence of relatives in the home would make it easier for Puerto Rican mothers to work; their absence tends to keep mothers at home, and so does the island ethic that women shouldn't work. In 1980 in New York City, 49 percent of black women and 53 percent of white women were out of the labor force—and 66 percent of Puerto Rican women. Even this low rate of labor-force participation is much higher than the rate for Puerto Rican women on the island. In the United States today the two-income family is a great generator of economic upward mobility, but it is a rare institution among poor Puerto Ricans, whose men are often casualties of the streets, addicted or imprisoned or drifting or dead. Also rare is the female-headed family in which the woman works. "That poverty rates soared for Puerto Rican families while they have declined for black families largely can be traced to the greater success of black women in the labor market," says a 1987 paper by Marta Tienda and Leif Jensen, two of the leading experts on Puerto Ricans.

Conservatives who emphasize the role of the welfare system in creating the underclass would say that since other Hispanic groups have labor-force participation rates and family structures markedly different from those of Puerto Ricans, the real issue must be the availability of government checks, not jobs. Other than Cubans, Puerto Ricans are the only Spanish-speaking ethnic group for whom full U.S. citizenship (and therefore welfare eligibility) in the immigrant generation is the rule rather than the exception. "What should be an advantage for Puerto Ricans—namely, citizenship—has turned into a liability in the welfare state," Linda Chavez writes in *Out of the Barrio: Toward a New Politics of Hispanic Assimilation*. "They have been smothered by entitlements."

In the community of underclass experts the role of pure skin-color prejudice is not much stressed these days, but the case can be made that it has contributed to the woes of poor Puerto Ricans. A staple of Puerto Rican reminiscence, written and oral, is the shock and hurt that dark-skinned Puerto Ricans feel when they come here and experience color prejudice for the first time. Blacks were enslaved on Puerto Rico for centuries—emancipation took place later there than here—but the structure of race relations was different from what it was in the American South. Plantations were relatively unimportant in pre-emancipation Puerto Rico, blacks were always a minority of the island's population, and there was a much higher proportion of free blacks than in the United States. Puerto Rico never developed the kind of rigid racial caste system that characterized places with plantation economies and black majorities. Intermarriage was common, and there was no bright legal and social line between those having African blood and whites. (The U.S. Census Bureau no longer asks Puerto Ricans to identify themselves by race.) In Puerto Rico the prosperous classes tend to be lighter-skinned, but dark-skinned people who acquire money don't find the same difficulty in being accepted in neighborhoods and social clubs that they do here.

On the mainland racial prejudice may play a role in shutting Puerto Ricans out of jobs, in ensuring that they live in ghettos, and in instilling an internalized, defeatist version of the wider society's racial judgments. But what's striking about the racial consciousness of Puerto Ricans as against that of African-Americans is the much lower quotient of anger at society. The whole question of who is at fault for the widespread poverty—the poor people or the United States—seems to preoccupy people much less when the subject is Puerto Ricans. For example, conservatives now commonly attribute the persistent poverty of the black underclass to the "victim mentality" expressed by black professors and leadership organizations. I think that the victim mentality among blacks is much more a part of the life of the upper-middle class than of the poor. But even if we grant the premise that ethnic groups are ideologically monolithic, the Puerto Rican case would indicate that the victim mentality doesn't have anything to do with persistent poverty: the Puerto Rican leadership does not have a victim mentality, but persistent poverty is much more severe among Puerto Ricans than

among blacks. The National Puerto Rican Coalition publishes first-rate studies about Puerto Rican poverty that take different sides on the question of whether or not it's completely society's fault—something it's difficult to imagine of the NAACP. . . .

A final theory about why Puerto Ricans are so poor as a group has to do with migration patterns. During the peak years of migration from Puerto Rico to the mainland, the people who migrated were apparently worse off than the people who didn't. A paper by Vilma Ortiz, of the Educational Testing Service, cites figures showing that in 1960 a group of recent Puerto Rican immigrants had a lower percentage of high school and college graduates than a control group on the island. Ortiz's view that it was not a migration of the most ambitious and capable—that people with less education and lower-status occupations were likelier to move—fits with the idea that for Muñoz emigration was a way to reduce the crush of destitute former peasants on the island. Since about 1970, most experts believe, the pattern has been changing and better-educated Puerto Ricans have become more likely to leave the island, because of a shortage of middle-class jobs there. Oscar Lewis wrote in *La Vida*, his 1965 book about Puerto Rican poverty, "The majority of migrants in the New York sample had made a three-step migration—from a rural birthplace in Puerto Rico to a San Juan slum to New York.". . .

The consequent isolation of the Puerto Rican poor seems to be even more pronounced than the isolation of the black poor. Churches in black ghettos are all-black institutions often dominated by middle-class blacks; the major churches in the South Bronx are Catholic and aren't run by Puerto Ricans. The work force of the New York City government is a third black and only a tenth Puerto Rican, meaning that middle-class blacks are much more likely than middle-class Puerto Ricans to return to the slums during the workday to perform professional social-service functions. The most common form of upward mobility in the South Bronx is supposed to be military service (South Bronx soldiers were often in the news during the Gulf War), but that makes people more successful by taking them thousands of miles away from the neighborhood.

The leaders of the South Bronx often don't live there. . . . When middle-class blacks move out of black ghettos, they usually relocate to more prosperous black neighborhoods, which form a nonblighted locus of the ethnic culture. Puerto Ricans who leave the South Bronx for other parts of the New York area tend to melt into more integrated neighborhoods, where it's much harder to maintain the fierce concern with "the race" that has historically existed in the black middle class. Ramon Daubon, of the National Puerto Rican Coalition, goes so far as to say, "There is no distinctive middle-class Puerto Rican neighborhood in the United States."

There *is* a Levittown for Puerto Ricans who are pursuing the standard dream of escape to suburban comfort—just outside San Juan. "If a Puerto Rican makes fifty or sixty thousand a year here, he wants to move back," says Ramon Velez. "He wants to buy land, build a house." Black middle-class emigrants from ghettos tend to remain in the same metropolitan area. Middle-class Puerto Ricans who move back to Puerto Rico can hardly function as role models, political leaders, counselors, or enlargers of the economic pie for the people in the South Bronx. "Look around in Puerto Rico," Velez says. "The legislature, all the influential people—they're all from New York. Two of my former employees are in the state senate. Those who are able to achieve something here and make money, they go back."

When young middle-class Puerto Ricans leave the island for the mainland because they can't find work as doctors or engineers at home, they often gravitate not to New York but to Sun Belt destinations like Orlando and Houston. The Puerto Rican population of Florida rose by 160 percent in the 1980s. New York now has a reputation on the island as the place that poor people move to, and later leave if they make any money. The percentage of mainland Puerto Ricans who live in New York has dropped steadily over the years, and if you exclude Nuyoricans from the social and economic statistics, Puerto Ricans look much less like an underclass.

Douglas Gurak and Luis Falcón, in a 1990 paper on Puerto Rican migration patterns, argue that poverty, non-participation in the labor force, and unstable marriages were often characteristic of the Puerto Ricans who are now poor here, rather than resulting from the economic and social conditions of New York. They write,

> It is clear that the selectivity of the migration process . . . results in an overrepresentation of women in the New York region who are characterized by traits associated with poverty. Those with less labor force experience, less education, more children, and more marital instability are the ones most likely to migrate to the mainland. Those with more stable unions, fewer children and more education are more likely to return to the island.

In Puerto Rico, especially rural Puerto Rico, common-law marriage and out-of-wedlock childbearing are long-established customs. Before Muñoz's modernization efforts brought the rates down, a quarter of all marriages on the island were consensual, and one-third of all births were out of wedlock. (Muñoz himself had two daughters out of wedlock, and married their mother only when he was about to assume the governorship of Puerto Rico.) Female immigrants to New York, Gurak and Falcón say, tend to come out of this tradition, and they are more likely than those who don't emigrate to have recently gone through the breakup of a marriage or a serious relationship. Other Hispanic emigrants, such as Dominicans and Colombians, tend to rank higher than nonemigrants on "human capital" measures like education, family structure, and work history; and Puerto Rican immigrants who settle outside New York aren't generally more disadvantaged than people who remain in Puerto Rico. The overall picture is one of entrenched Puerto Rican poverty becoming increasingly a problem in New York City rather than nationwide.

Although their explanations vary, experts on Puerto Rican poverty tend to agree on how to ameliorate it: both Marta Tienda and Douglas Gurak, for example, call for special educational and job-training efforts. There is something about black-white race relations in America that leads people in all camps to dismiss those kinds of anti-poverty efforts in behalf of blacks as unimaginative, old-fashioned, vague, unworkable, or doomed to failure. The self-defeating view that the problem is so severe that it could be solved only through some step too radical for the political system ever to take seems to evaporate when the subject is Puerto Ricans rather than blacks. . . .

8

Chicanas in White-Collar Jobs:

'You Have to Prove Yourself More'

Denise A. Segura

... When Chicanas secure white-collar jobs, they tend to find work in female-dominated clerical occupations. These jobs, often dismissed by labor-market researchers as a low-wage ghetto, nevertheless represent a considerable step upward for Chicana workers, particularly when they are in large, stable organizations (Pesquera 1985; Segura 1986, 1989).

Approximately half of all Chicana labor-force participants work in female-dominated white-collar jobs, mostly clerical (Malveaux and Wallace 1987; Dill, Cannon, and Vanneman 1987). While this is an impressive growth from 1980 levels, substantially lower proportions of Chicanas than non-Hispanic women work in professional/managerial white-collar occupations (14.1% and 28%, respectively) (U.S. Bureau of the Census 1991).

Chicanas' movement into white-collar jobs contributes to growing heterogeneity in the work force, although it has eroded neither occupational segregation nor inequality at work and in the family. This paper explores how 152 Chicana white-collar workers in a major public university view their employment experiences and family responsibilities in ways that contribute to the production of gender and gender-race/ethnicity in the labor market and in the larger ethnic community. ...

Reproducing Gender and Chicano Ethnicity

The theoretical reference point for this paper is the perspective originally developed by West and Zimmerman (1987), and usefully applied to other empirical data on women's work (Berk 1985). This framework views gender and race-ethnicity not just as categorical statuses, but as dynamic, interactional accomplishments. It presumes that in the course of daily affairs—work, for example—we present, reaffirm, and reproduce ourselves as belonging to, and competently representative of, gender and racial-ethnic categories. Thus, the worker not only *is* Chicana, she also "does" Chicana. And, work activities provide ample opportunities for the reaffirmation of membership in good standing of that group.

Female-dominated jobs offer unique occasions for women to "do gender," or enact and thus reaffirm what we take to be the "essential nature" of women (West and Zimmerman 1987; West and Fenstermaker n.d.). When an occupation involves "helping others," or "serving men," etc., women can simultaneously affirm themselves as competent workers, and also reinforce social conceptualizations of their "essential" femininity within the organization, for the clientele, and among themselves.

Fenstermaker, West, and Zimmerman observe: "The demands of gender do not *compete* for attention on the job; together they form *one of the dimensions of the job* that is daily enacted by participants" (1991:301, emphasis added). Hochschild's (1983) study of what she terms "emotional labor" in two occupations—flight attendants and bill collectors—details the different expectations for male and female workers required by the employer, clients, and among the workers themselves. Unlike female flight attendants, males were not sought by customers (or trained by the organization) for nurturance or gentleness, nor were they expected to display constant cheerfulness. Male flight attendants also tended to be promoted more quickly than women. Hochschild's study offers one instance of how both institutions and workers are held accountable for the "doing of gender" and affirms Fenstermaker et al.'s contention that, "regardless of position, the *practice* of gender and its complex relation to the practice of work will support inequality on the job" (1991:299).

The notion of gender as an accomplishment acquires other nuances when women have children and families to care for. In the United States, women continue to do the vast majority of household labor even when they are employed full-time (Berk 1985; Hochschild 1989). Moreover, most household members view the typical asymmetric division of household labor as "fair" (Berk 1985). One explanation for the tenacity of this attitude among men and women is that such judgments concerning equity involve many more considerations than efficiency or effort. Berk (1985:204) argues that, when women engage in housework and child care, one social product is "a reaffirmation of one's *gendered* relation to the work and to the world. In short, the 'shoulds' of gender ideals are fused with the 'musts' of efficient household production." The result is what we have in the past thought of as "irrational" and "unfair" household arrangements.

The notion of gender as a situated accomplishment allows for real interaction between gender and variations in women's material conditions or circumstances, including race-ethnicity. . . . Ethnicity is marked by a set of norms, customs, and behaviors different from the dominant or majority ethnic group as well as "a shared feeling of peoplehood" (Gordon 1964; Keefe and Padilla 1987). Chicano race-ethnicity encompasses both psychological processes of group attachment (identity, attitudinal orientation, and preferences) and behavioral manifestations (cultural knowledge, language, use, and traditions) (Garcia 1982:296). While no single reason can account for the persistence of Chicano culture and the racial-ethnic community, causal factors stem from treatment by the majority group and the racial-ethnic minority group and from the interaction between them that occurs within social institutions (e.g., the labor market and the family) (Keefe and Padilla 1987; Zinn 1980). This suggests that, like gender, Chicano race-ethnicity is socially constructed through interaction and dynamically maintained by both institutions and individuals. Thus, within this framework, we can pose not just the "intersection" of race-ethnic and gender categories, but an *interaction* in the true sense of the term. Chicanas become not just female *Chicanos*, nor just women workers. And, their experiences at work—as they simultaneously produce both worker *and* Chicana—are unique (Fenstermaker, personal communication). . . .

Within the labor market, Chicano race-ethnicity is reinforced by discrimination (both objective and perceived) and social exclusion from the dominant group (Barrera 1979; Nelson and Tienda 1985). In addition, there are other, less obvious ways that Chicano race-ethnicity may be affirmed. Even as occupations contain a dimension of "doing gender," there may be a dimension of "doing Chicano race-ethnicity" as well. That is, organizations may structure jobs in ways that reaffirm Chicanos' sense of themselves as members of a unique racial-ethnic group (e.g., using bilingual workers as interpreters without additional pay). Or, Chicanos may themselves act in ways that either consciously or unconsciously serve the Chicano community. As one example of the first possibility, Chicanos who work in jobs structured to "serve" a racial-ethnic clientele (e.g., minority students) may encounter a reward system that affirms their racial-ethnic identification while doing their job. In the second case, Chicanos who work in jobs that are not overtly structured to accomplish race-ethnicity may nonetheless reaffirm their racial-ethnic identity. They often remain in white-collar jobs despite experiencing social isolation or discomfort because they feel that such "success" indirectly enlarges the options for others in the racial-ethnic community.

For Chicanas, accomplishing race-ethnicity is even more complex since their social identity involves gender and embraces the family and the labor market in ways that may have profound implications for Chicano culture. That is, insofar as women's employment is typically viewed as "for the family," such employment may not offer a dynamic avenue for challenging gender inequality or male privilege at home (Zavella 1987; Segura 1989a). This possibility is strengthened when

Chicanas work in jobs that affirm both their traditional gender and/or gender-race-ethnic sense of themselves. Also militating against a forceful challenge to gender inequality is women's household work, often eulogized as part of a distinct cultural heritage under assault by outside social pressures (Mirande and Enriquez 1979; Zinn 1982, 1979, 1975; Segura 1989a). For Chicanas to challenge traditional patterns involves integrating personal empowerment with the politically charged issue of culture-ethnic maintenance. Thus, the need or motivation to continue "traditional" patterns may be more complex for Mexican women inasmuch as doing housework or child care is the site of accomplishing not only gender, but culture-race/ethnicity as well. This dilemma adds another dimension to our understanding of the tenacity of Chicana inequality. The following section explores the ways gender and gender-race/ethnicity are affirmed in the lives of Chicana white-collar workers.

Method and Sample

In Fall 1989/Winter 1990, in collaboration with Beatriz Pesquera of the University of California, Davis, I administered a 20-page questionnaire on "women and work issues" to all Hispanic-identified women employed at a large public university in California. The questionnaire included a battery of closed-ended questions concerning work, the intersection of family and work, gender ideology, feminism, ethnicity, and political ideology. One hundred and fifty-two women completed the questionnaire, representing a response rate of 47.5 percent. In addition, we conducted follow-up interviews with 35 randomly selected informants. The purpose of the interviews was to explore in greater depth the meanings of work, gender, and ethnicity for this group of women. This paper is an exploratory analysis of these survey and interview data for their implications for the reproduction of gender, race-ethnicity, and labor-market stratification.

Background Characteristics

Most of the survey respondents are of Mexican (Chicano) descent (85%) with the rest either Latin American or Spanish (Hispanic) origin. All but fifteen women were born in the United States. All of the women express a great deal of pride in their ethnicity and a majority also feel that maintaining Chicano culture is important. Sixty percent of the respondents are bilingual in Spanish and English.

All but three women received high school diplomas; 118 have educations beyond high school; 43 have a B.A. degree or above. Their educational levels are much higher than the California norm for Chicanas (11th grade)....

Occupations

Chicanas' employment profiles and my textual analysis of their interviews reveals that their experiences at work—their social experiences, discrimination, harassment, or acceptance—all took on gendered and/or racial-ethnic features. By and large, the women work in environments that are both homogeneous in terms of gender (59.2% report all-female coworkers); race-ethnicity (80% report all-Anglo coworkers); and reproduce gender/race-ethnic hierarchies (only 29 women have minority women supervisors).

Of the 152 respondents, 41.4 percent ($n = 63$) work in jobs we classified as "lower-level clerical"; 28.9 percent ($n = 44$) are "upper-level clerical workers"; 5.9 percent are "technical aides and service workers" ($n = 9$); while 19.7 percent are "professional/managerial workers" ($n = 30$). Six women declined to provide information about their occupations. The mean income of the respondents is $23,288 annually....

Findings

Job Satisfaction

Exploring what Chicanas like and dislike about their jobs offers one way to gain insight into how labor-market mechanisms maintain occupational segregation. When jobs with limited opportunities offer certain subjective rewards (e.g., quality personal interaction, "helping others") or help meet instrumental needs (e.g., economic subsistence), they provide important reasons for women to stay in them, thereby reinforcing existing labor-market boundaries (Segura 1989b; Zavella 1987;

Pesquera 1985). The job characteristics valued by Chicanas may also provide insight into ways in which they accomplish gender and/or race-ethnicity. That is, when a Chicana indicates pleasure or displeasure with a specific job characteristic, she engages in self-reflection—a process that involves interaction with herself and the larger group to which she holds herself accountable. Insofar as a Chicana connects her job to a larger group, she may be affirming her gendered relation to the world and reinforce her racial-ethnic sense of self.

Contradictory accounts exist regarding the role gender plays in workers' evaluations of their jobs (see England and Browne 1992 for a review of this topic). Some argue that women value social aspects of their jobs more than men and also place less emphasis on pay and career-related values (Crewley, Levitan, and Quinn 1973). Other research finds no significant gender difference in what workers value about their jobs when occupation and organizational level are taken into account (Brief and Aldag 1975). Using similar control variables, still other investigators find that women are more likely than men to emphasize competence to do the job and good personal relations on the job (Neil and Snizek 1987; Agassi 1979). Whether women and men like or dislike different aspects of their jobs overlooks one critical possibility: what workers do at work may reaffirm their gender and/or their race-ethnicity. It is equally possible that the intrinsic reward of ably "doing gender and/or race-ethnicity" may provide them with an additional incentive to stay on the job. . . .

The in-depth interviews provide insight into the meanings women attach to social aspects of work as well as job features that make them "feel good." Women's accounts of their jobs reveal two major patterns. First, women discuss job features and job satisfaction in terms that affirm social conceptualizations of femininity. Second, their accounts reveal a sense of affinity or connection with Chicano ethnicity. For example, when I asked an upper clerical worker what she valued about her job, she replied:

I need to do that because for your self-esteem to feel that you're doing something and you're helping other people accomplish themselves [is important]. In that sense it's good for my health and also for my kids. I think if they see that you're involved with something, it helps them reach beyond their own world to see that there is an outside world there. And, that there's things that they can pursue that they enjoy. [upper clerical worker #64a]

This informant values her job for allowing her to "help others," a trait socially ascribed to the "feminine nature." Her commitment to affirm the feminine is captured by her insistence that helping others is "good" for her health and is maternally nurturant. Her subsequent opinion that her job to "reach beyond their own world" demonstrates solidarity with her racial-ethnic group's politicized view that Chicano youth have limited options (Ogbu 1978; Garcia 1981; Keefe and Padilla 1987). Moreover, gainfully employed in an upper clerical job, she sees herself as a role model for the larger Chicano community. Finally, her words underscore the centrality of "family" among the respondents—a dynamic consistent with the politics of Chicano cultural maintenance (Williams 1990; Keefe and Padilla 1987).

Other respondents worked in jobs structured to do "gender and race-ethnicity," or "help" racial-ethnic minority students or staff. One Chicana professional worker employed in this type of job stated:

It is very satisfying when you're working with a Chicano student or with a black student who really wants to become a veterinarian. To see them being admitted to a Vet school is really very satisfying and to see them graduate is just incredible. I just graduated my second class, and every year they'll say, "Thanks!" And, God—the parents will say, "We never thought we'd have a doctor in the family!" So, that's really neat to feel that way, but I'm still limited in that I'm not doing enough. [professional worker #10]

This informant, like others employed in jobs structured to "help" racial-ethnic minority students or staff is satisfied when she is able to do the job competently. Critical here is that the gendered act associated with women—that of "helping others"—intersects with bettering the racial-ethnic community, thereby allowing the respondent to simultaneously accomplish gender-and-race-ethnicity.

Many of the respondents (60.3%) reported they liked feeling "in control" of their job. When I explored what this meant, I found that Chicanas filtered their evaluation of their jobs through a gender and/or race-ethnic lens. That is, they valued job control as a means to better help others (a value associated with women) and also expand the job range of Mexican American women (a value associated with the ethnic community and women). As one lower clerical worker (#4) succinctly stated: "You're helping in some ways helping people in helping make a difference." In this way, the preference for on-the-job "control" implies a politicized sense of themselves as racial-ethnic women striving for social change.

About one-fifth of the respondents are dissatisfied with their jobs. Women with children tended to dislike their jobs if their supervisors were inflexible about taking time off and making up work. Since women bore the major responsibility for taking children to doctor appointments or caring for them when they were sick or on vacation, women valued jobs that offered them a degree of flextime. Women employed in lower-level clerical jobs tended to be unhappy with their pay. In general, women disliked their jobs when they felt they were not doing anything they perceived as "helpful" or "useful.". . .

Chicanas who "feel good" about helping minority students obtain information about financial aid or other resources are actually performing tasks essential to their jobs. In helping others, Chicanas affirm their gender and their race-ethnicity. The organization structures this enactment (e.g., specifications of the job description) and they are held accountable for it by their coworkers and clients (e.g., through performance evaluations). Chicanas' impetus to continue this process is intertwined with the process of identity as well as the larger politic of accessing jobs outside the purview of most Chicana workers in the state.

Sexual Harassment and Race-Ethnic Discrimination

Women's gendered and race-ethnic sense of themselves is reinforced by other, unrewarding features of the job. In this study, about one-third of the respondents reported experiencing sexual harassment (n = 50), while nearly 44 percent (n = 67) said they had encountered discrimination based on gender and/or race-ethnicity. Sexual harassment and discrimination reinforces Chicanas' sense of on-the-job vulnerability and their social inequality. In addition, the way in which women describe sexual harassment and employment discrimination reveals how gender and gender-race-ethnic boundaries are maintained in the organizational setting. While maintaining these boundaries is not the same as the accomplishment of gender on the job, it provides a context in which it occurs. . . .

Sixty percent of the women who indicated having experienced sexual harassment reported "doing something about it." Usually this meant, "telling the person to stop," "talking with friends and family," or "complaining to the appropriate personnel officer." Eleven women did "nothing" and another nine women acted as though nothing had happened.

Chicanas voiced outrage when women (especially themselves) were cast in the role of instigators rather than victims by coworkers and/or supervisors:

> Everyone likes to pretend it [sexual harassment] doesn't happen. When you go from one position to the next in this university it's so small that bosses know each other and say, "Hey, this woman—watch out for her." So, you get blackmailed that way. And so you sort of have to be careful in how you handle it—you don't want to give that person a chance to get out of it. So, if you really want to nail him, you'd better go through the channels and make sure that when you do it you do it well. [professional worker #102a]

Implicit in this informant's words is the sense that women who assert themselves in ways that directly confront men risk retaliation by those participating in the interpersonal networks of supervisors and other workers.

Bosses warn each other. In her assertiveness, the Chicana worker violates *all* relevant expectations of the group: as a worker, as a woman, and as a Chicana; she becomes a threat to the organization, and especially vulnerable to informal workplace sanctions. . . .

A problem of equal or greater magnitude is discrimination based on Chicanas' combined gender-race/ethnicity. It is noteworthy that with few exceptions ($n = 9$), survey respondents did not privilege one form of discrimination over the other. Rather, they felt their experiences reflected *both* gender and race-ethnicity.

During their interviews, Chicanas spoke passionately of their firsthand experiences with on-the-job discrimination. Almost to a woman, they argued that employers, coworkers, the organization, and society itself maintain pejorative, stereotyped images of Chicana and Hispanic women:

When people look at us they don't *see us* [her emphasis]. They just see the stereotypes that they have gotten from the movies or somewhere . . . they think we are all uneducated. They have this "indito" under the cactus plant idea. I've had people say, "I didn't know that there were any educated people in Mexico that have a graduate degree." I think we stumble against the wall because they're looking at us across a barrier that is their imagination. [professional worker #212a]

. . . [One] informant told me that she had resisted interpreting her experience as evidence of gender/racial-ethnic discrimination. In this regard, she is very similar to the majority of the women interviewed. Survey respondents typically tried to downplay the salience of gender/racial-ethnic discrimination in their personal lives although most (70%) considered it a feature of the organization and society at large. All the women interviewed believe that women of Mexican descent have a "harder time" getting good jobs than either Anglo men, Anglo women, or Latino men.

Women who believed they had experienced discrimination condemned it and described its nuances at length. Several told of "subtle discrimination," i.e., comments that devalue their culture and/or features of their combined gender/race-ethnicity:

. . . it's subtle discrimination. I haven't gotten a job because of, or I don't know if I have gotten a job because of my color. You know, subtle stuff—that subtle baloney that people pass you over because they think that women of color aren't as brilliant as they [Anglos] are. That sort of thing. Actually, they can be condescending to me. [upper clerical worker #155a]

. . . Interestingly, many of the women reporting that they had not personally experienced job discrimination (although they were careful to note their belief in its importance), attributed it to their fair, or light complexions:

Maybe I haven't felt as much discrimination because I'm not—I'm kind of fair complected. So, a lot of people don't know, or don't even assume that I'm Mexican. They're real surprised when I say, "Yeah, I'm Mexican." [professional worker #5]

Many women also offered analyses of the consequences of gender-race-ethnicity for Chicana employment inequality. Some women argue that discrimination is the primary reason Chicanas are overrepresented in lower-level positions in the organization. Other women assert that the organization often "punishes" Chicanas who try to "push" their way into a promotion either by denying them the job or actually downgrading it. . . . Few women, however, felt able to officially challenge job discrimination within the organization. Integral to their reluctance is their sense that they lack credibility in the institution due, in part, to pejorative stereotypes that symbolize essential parts of the gendered and raced expectations that are constantly being played out in social interaction and, ultimately, situate Chicanas in a socially subordinate position. . . .

Discrimination at work plays an important role in reinforcing gender and/or race-ethnic boundaries in the organization. Research on ethnicity indicates that individual and institution-level discrimination help maintain a "sense of peoplehood" among the group. Chicanas interpret their personal experiences of discrimination as part of the shared experiences of the larger racial-ethnic community. While most of the Chicanas in this study assert that maintaining their culture is important to them, discrimination within an institution serves to hold them accountable to this resolution. In this way, the organization reinforces Chicanas' gender-race-ethnic sense of themselves.

Chicanas' racial-ethnic identity is not only maintained by negative events such as discrimination or by intrinsic rewards on the job. Women in the present study also affirm their race-ethnicity by organizing and/or participating in a variety of cultural activities in the community. In addition, one-third of the survey respondents belonged to an Hispanic Workers Advocacy group at their worksite. Women feel this group promotes a positive image of Chicanos/Latinos and will help erode the power wielded by negative cultural stereotypes currently embedded in the institution.

The Intersection of Family and Work

An analysis of social dynamics that contextualize Chicanas' options and maintain their social inequality would be incomplete without considering the family (Smith 1987, Zavella, 1987). Motherhood is simultaneously a source of joy and a powerful constraint on employment and occupational mobility. Coltrane argues that "the routine care of home and children . . . provide opportunities for women to express and reaffirm their gendered relation to men and to the world" (1989:473). Among the 111 Chicana respondents with children, family caretaking constrains their chances for mobility in the world of work. It also forms one way they accomplish gender and culture.

One way Chicanas strive to manage the contradictions of overwork is to try carving out two separate worlds where, in reality, there is but one world and one woman trying to meet the expectations of children, coworkers, supervisors, and her own ambitions. As one woman said:

For the most part, my job doesn't interfere too much with home. When I leave work, I leave my work. I switch stations to do whatever I need to do for the family. But, there are times when, yes, work does tend to tire you out and you do carry it

home with you in terms of less energy and not having the energy to deal with the family. That's really hard, especially when both of you come in very tired and you sort of want the other one to do something because you're too tired to deal with it. Then it's hard. The poor kids, they don't understand. They just know that they're hungry and "how come you guys won't feed us?" [professional worker #102a]

This woman speaks to the dilemma of reconciling what Hochschild refers to as the "competing urgencies" of family and work. Interestingly, women in this study downplayed the spillover between work and family. In the surveys and in their interviews, women consistently reported that their jobs "almost never" (27%) or only "occasionally" (47.7%) interfered with their abilities to manage their family responsibilities. Yet, their discussions of the intersection of family and work reveal they are experiencing considerable tension and stress in this relationship.

Ironically, ideological changes that have expanded the domain of women's competencies may impede women's articulation of their stress meeting family and work responsibilities. As one woman argues:

I think as women, maybe the progress has been kind of negative in some aspects. You know, we go out and say that we can do this—we can work, we can raise a family, and all that. And yet at the same time, I feel like maybe we've hurt ourselves because we can't do it all. I don't believe there is super-woman. [professional/managerial worker #5a]

An additional constraint felt by many of the Chicana workers is their responsibility to maintain Chicano cultural traditions and forms. One woman said:

In order to be valued we have to be wives and mothers first. That cultural pressure is the most difficult to overcome. [professional worker #10]

This informant struck a chord that resonated throughout the study: Mexican/Latina women take on much of the caretaking work in the household as an expression of Mexican culture. Charged with cultural socialization of offspring, Chicanas often avoid debating their partners about the household division of labor. . . . Yet, when asked about the actual division of labor, women reported doing most of the housework and wished their husbands/partners would do more.

Traditional gender roles and gender ideologies are particularly resistant to change when they are framed within what Caufield (1974) terms a "culture of resistance." Consistently, Chicanas refuse to engage in sustained struggle with husbands/partners over the division of household labor even though they admit they are, as one Chicana professional worker (#6) said, "too stressed and torn between career and family responsibilities to feel good about the accomplishments!" Rather, Chicanas conform to their community's gendered expectations reaffirming both their womanhood and their culture:

> I'm just happy [about] who I am and where I come from. Our women, Latino women, do things just a little bit differently because of who we are and where we came from. There are certain things that we do . . . for our husbands that I know that other women, white women have problems doing . . . for instance—and I've seen it because my brother-in-law was married to a white woman. You're eating and you go to the stove to maybe serve yourself a little more. It's just normal, I think. You're brought up with that real nurturing with, "honey, do you want some more?" . . . And her comment was, "well, he can get up by himself." Just the real independence on their side, and I think we're brought up a little more nurturing to our male counterparts. Maybe there's more machismo there too—whatever. It's the way you're brought up. [upper clerical worker #64a]

The desire to affirm their gender and their race-ethnic culture is strengthened in those cases where women work in jobs that value services to other women and/or Chicanos on the campus. . . .

Summary and Conclusion

This study has demonstrated ways in which gender and race-ethnicity are affirmed in the labor market among selected Chicana white-collar workers. By considering both the features of jobs that Chicanas value and dislike and the perceived barriers to success at work that they encounter in the organization, I have identified mechanisms that reinforce occupational segregation by gender and gender-race-ethnicity.

There is, however, another outcome of Chicana employment. Chicanas' job performances and their concurrent fulfillment of family responsibilities mutually reinforce the accomplishment of culture and ethnicity. Whereas traditional Marxist and feminist analyses view market labor as potentially "liberatory" by increasing women's economic clout (e.g., Engels [1884] 1968; Smith 1987; Moore and Sawhill 1978; Hartmann 1981; Ferree 1987), this study finds the opposite. That is, while women usually enjoy their jobs, work is not so much "liberatory" as intensifying their accomplishment of gender both in the tasks they do at work as well as the sex-typed tasks they continue to do at home. Moreover, their attachment to family is linked ideologically to the survival of the culture, rendering their accomplishment of gender an overt act of racial-ethnic and cultural politics. This particular finding may well be a neglected truth in many women's lives. . . .

Chicana workers in this study have a clear sense of their socially imposed limits, but struggle to survive and wrest meaning from worlds where their multidimensional experiences and constraints defy easy solutions and answers. The complexity of their struggle is captured by an informant's observation that became the subtitle of this paper: "You have to prove yourself more." But, while Chicanas prove their competence at work and in the family, they not only reproduce gendered social relations but simultaneously affirm their culture and racial-ethnic identity as well.

References

Agassi, Judith B. 1979. *Women on the Job: The Attitudes of Women to their Work*. Lexington, MA: Lexington Books.

Barrera, Mario. 1979. *Race and Class in the Southwest: A Theory of Racial Inequality*. South Bend, IN: University of Notre Dame Press.

Berk, Sarah Fenstermaker. 1985. *The Gender Factory: The Apportionment of Work in American Households*. New York: Plenum.

Brief, A.P., and R.J. Aldag. 1975. "Male-Female Differences in Occupational Attitudes within Minority Groups." *Journal of Vocational Behavior* 6:305–314.

Caufield, Mina Davis. 1974. "Imperialism, the Family, and Cultures of Resistance." *Socialist Revolution* 2:67–85.

Coltrane, Scott. 1989. "Household Labor and the Routine Production of Gender." *Social Problems* 36:473–491.

Crewley, Joan F., Teresa E. Levitan, and Robert Quinn. 1973. "Facts and Fiction about the American Working Woman." Ann Arbor: Survey Research Center, University of Michigan.

Dill, Bonnie Thornton, Lynn Weber Cannon, and Reeve Vanneman. 1987. "Pay Equity: An Issue of Race, Ethnicity and Sex." Washington, DC: National Commission on Pay Equity.

Engels, Frederick. [1884] 1968. *Origin of the Family, Private Property, and the State*. Moscow: International Publishing.

England, Paula, and Irene Browne. 1992. "Trends in Women's Economic Status." *Sociological Perspectives* 35:17–51.

Fenstermaker, Sarah, Candace West, and Don H. Zimmerman. 1991. "Gender Inequality: New Conceptual Terrain." Pp. 289–305 in *Gender, Family, and Economy: The Triple Overlap*, edited by R. Lesser-Blumberg. Newbury Park, CA: Sage.

Ferree, Myra Marx. 1987. "The Struggles of Super-woman." Pp. 161–180 in *Hidden Aspects of Women's Work*, edited by Christine Bose, Roslyn Feldberg, and Natalie Sokoloff. New York: Praeger.

Garcia, John A. 1981. "Yo Soy Mexicano . . .: Self-Identity among the Mexican Origin Population." *Social Science Quarterly* 62:88–98.

———. 1982. "Ethnicity and Chicanos: Measurement of Ethnic Identification, Identity, and Consciousness." *Hispanic Journal of Behavioral Science* 4:295–314.

Gordon, Milton M. 1964. *Assimilation in American Life: The Role of Race, Religion, and National Origin*. New York: Oxford University Press.

Hartmann, Heidi. 1981. "The Family as the Locus of Gender, Class, and Political Struggle: The Example of Housework." *Signs: Journal of Women in Culture and Society* 6:366–394.

Hochschild, Arlie R. 1983. *The Managed Heart: Commercialization of Human Feeling*. Berkeley: University of California Press.

Hochschild, Arlie R. [with Anne Machung]. 1989. *The Second Shift, Working Parents and the Revolution at Home*. New York: Viking.

Keefe, Susan E., and Amado M. Padilla. 1987. *Chicano Ethnicity*. Albuquerque: University of New Mexico Press.

Malveaux, Julianne, and Phyllis Wallace. 1987. "Minority Women in the Workplace." Pp. 265–298 in *Women and Work: Industrial Relations Research Association Research Volume*, edited by K.S. Koziara, M. Moskow, and L. Dewey Tanner. Washington, DC: Bureau of National Affairs.

Mirande, Alfredo, and Evangelina Enriquez. 1979. *La Chicana*. Chicago: University of Chicago Press.

Moore, Kristin A., and Isabel U. Sawhill. 1978. "Implications of Women's Employment for Home and Family Life." Pp. 201–255 in *Working Women: Theories and Facts in Perspective*, edited by Ann H. Stromberg and Shirley Harkess. Palo Alto: Mayfield.

Neil, Cecily C., and William E. Snizek. 1987. "Work Values, Job Characteristics, and Gender." *Sociological Perspectives* 30:245–265.

Nelson, Candace, and Marta Tienda. 1985. "The Structuring of Hispanic Ethnicity: Historical and Contemporary Perspectives." *Ethnic and Racial Studies* 8:49–74.

Ogbu, John U. 1978. *Minority Education and Caste: The American System in Cross-Cultural Perspective*. New York: Academic.

Pesquera, Beatriz M. 1985. "Work and Family: A Comparative Analysis of Professional, Clerical and Blue-Collar Chicana Workers." Ph.D diss. University of California, Berkeley.

Segura, Denise A. 1986. "Chicana and Mexican Immigrant Women in the Labor Market: A Study of Occupational Mobility and Stratification." Ph.D diss. University of California, Berkeley.

———. 1989a. "The Interplay of Familism and Patriarchy on the Employment of Chicana and Mexican Immigrant Women." Pp. 35–53 in *Renato Rosaldo Lecture Series Monograph*, vol. 5. Tucson: Mexican American Studies and Research Center, University of Arizona.

———. 1989b. "Chicana and Mexican Immigrant Women at Work: The Impact of Class, Race, and Gender on Occupational Mobility." *Society* 3:37–52.

Smith, Dorothy E. 1987. "Women's Inequality and the Family." Pp. 23–54 in *Families and Work*, edited by N. Gerstel and H. E. Gross. Philadelphia: Temple University Press.

U.S. Bureau of the Census. 1991b. "The Hispanic Population in the United States: March 1990."

Current Population Report, Series P–20, No. 449. Washington, DC: U.S. Government Printing Office.

West, Candace, and Sarah Fenstermaker. n. d. "Power, Inequality and the Accomplishment of Gender: An Ethnomethodological View." In *Theory on Gender/Feminism on Theory*, edited by Paula England. New York: Aldine. Forthcoming.

West, Candace, and Don H. Zimmerman. 1987. "Doing Gender." *Gender and Society* 1:125–151.

Williams, Norma. 1990. *The Mexican American Family, Tradition and Change*. New York: General Hall.

Zavella, Patricia. 1987. *Women's Work and Chicano Families: Cannery Workers of the Santa Clara Valley*. Ithaca, NY: Cornell University Press.

Zinn, Maxine Baca. 1975. "Chicanas: Power and Control in the Domestic Sphere." *De Colores, Journal of Emerging Raza Philosophies* 2:19–31.

——. 1979. "Chicano Family Research: Conceptual Distortions and Alternative Directions." *Journal of Ethnic Studies* 7:59–71.

——. 1980. "Gender and Ethnic Identity among Chicanos." *Frontiers* 5:18–23.

——. 1982. "Mexican-American Women in the Social Sciences." *Signs: Journal of Women in Culture and Society* 8:259–272.

9

Decision Making Within the Working Class

Norma Williams

. . . Two contradictory conclusions regarding decision making between [Mexican American] husbands and wives are expressed in the social science literature. One is the importance of "machismo" as an all-encompassing form of male domination. The other is the egalitarian nature of the relationship between husbands and wives.

A number of ethnographic studies have portrayed the Mexican American family structure as strongly patriarchal (Madsen 1964; Rubel 1966), a view that continues to be perpetuated by well-known social scientists (Queen et al. 1985). Mexican American men have been described as adhering to an ideal in which manliness (machismo) is equated with authority, strength, honor, bravery, and sexual prowess. It is the husband who makes all the important decisions in the family. The wife defers to him, and by implication she gains her identity through being married and through being a mother.

In contrast, a recent body of literature on decision making in the Mexican American family argues the opposite: Decision making in the Mexican American family has been seen as increasingly egalitarian in nature according to Hawkes and Taylor (1975), Cromwell et al. (1973), and Ybarra (1977, 1982). These studies have relied heavily on the theoretical orientation and research procedures of Blood and Wolfe (1960), who contended that decision making between husbands and wives results from their differential control of strategic resources (in effect, this is a variant of "exchange theory"). Blood and Wolfe,

and others utilizing their orientation, have collected their data through closed-ended questionnaires. Such a research procedure does not enable us to uncover the processual nature of decision making. . . .

Herein I examine the orientations of both husbands and wives beginning with the family setting and moving out to the workplace and the community, in an attempt to determine how this broader setting affects conjugal relationships [among working-class Mexican American couples in three Texas cities]. . . .

Sex-role Expectations

Sex-role expectations are relevant for understanding power relations in the family. What a wife or husband is expected to do may have some effect on the manner in which power is exerted. Scanzoni and Szinovacz (1980:42) contend that "traditional sex roles—roles that are sharply different and rigid—tend to make family decision making 'unnecessary' or else quite simple." From this perspective, there are a great many implied understandings between husbands and wives as to what each is supposed to do, and both take these expectations for granted. Although no human interaction is so fixed as to exclude shifting interpretations of these normative expectations, nonetheless, traditional role expectations set broad constraints on how wives and husbands relate to each other—though, as we observe, we must be careful in how we interpret these kinds of data.

What exists among working-class husbands and wives is that they reply in rather traditional terms to questions regarding gender (or sex) role expectations or definitions of their own or their spouse's role. Thus, in the abstract, tradition is a meaningful aspect of the lives of working-class couples. But, in this instance, what they say does not correspond to what they do. . . .

Among working-class couples, the wife is expected to care for the children and perform household duties such as cooking, washing, and housecleaning. The husband is perceived as the provider for the family. . . . The women constantly stressed taking care of the home and being a good wife.

A few women did not adhere to the traditional ideal expectations. "I have to have food on the stove for him. He expects me to get up to cook when he gets home. I did it for years. I spoiled him. The last two years I have backed off.". . .

As far as women were concerned, it is quite apparent that men should work, provide for the family, and love their children. In discussing ideal expectations concerning their role, working-class wives gave little, if any, attention to how they should be treated by their husbands.

When we look at the role expectations from the male perspective, we see that these are in keeping with those of their wives. Two major themes emerge with respect to the wife's role. "Bringing up the children is the number one priority." The husband cannot spend a great deal of time with the children because he must work. In addition to caring for children the wife should "prepare the meals, clean the house, do the dishes, and have the clothes ready." One man spoke of his wife as providing "maid services."

With respect to male expectations for themselves, the husbands reiterated many of the views that their wives held. . . . The emphasis was definitely upon the good provider role; it was the number-one consideration. Yet, some men observed that they should teach their children discipline as well as love. And, in some instances, they spoke of providing spiritual guidance for the children.

Only a few men deviated from these ideal expectations. One man conceded that he helped his wife because she worked, but he then justified his action when he said, "We have an agreement—she takes care of the inside and I take care of the outside. She helps me outside and I help her inside."

While the ideal expectations are useful background information, they do not tell us a great deal about how persons come to remake their roles and how they actually reach certain kinds of decisions. Taken at face values, the ideals expressed suggest little, if any, change in traditional sex roles. . . .

Specific Role-making Patterns

. . . Husbands and wives were very aware that fundamental changes in their relationship with each other had occurred over time. This was particularly true for those who had been married for a number of years. A number of women took the view that the men were not as dominant today as in the early years of marriage. This pattern is highlighted in the comments of one wife who, in discussing her changing relationship with her husband, indicated:

> Whatever he said went like that. I'm not so timid now. I have some say. If I don't like what he does, I'll tell him so. Before we did not communicate with each other. He was a very dominating person, and even my friends noticed this pattern.

The men replayed the themes of the wives. In the early years of marriage, "I said something and that was it." Today, the husbands stress that there is more discussion with their wives.

While changes in the roles of husbands and wives were apparent to the participants, the couples were unable to define just what was going on. Only after a rather extended period in the field did I sort out the fundamental role-making pattern that is taking place among working-class women. Essentially the women are striving to attain a new personal, as well as social, identity for themselves. . . . The issue is not equality but the search for a separate identity on the part of the wives.

The wives' newfound personal and social identity sets them apart from traditional Mexican American women. Strikingly, none of the working-class women in Austin and Corpus Christi (and Kingsville as well) expected to follow the traditional mourning patterns if they became widowed. That women no longer sustain a symbolic social identity with their husbands after the latter's death certainly reflects a major change from the past. Moreover, the husbands did not expect them to follow this traditional pattern.

A somewhat separate identity is essential today if a woman is to carry out certain activities within the public sphere after her husband's death. In view of the fragmentation of the traditional extended family, a widow can no longer rely on relatives to shop for groceries or carry out basic tasks for herself and her family. Also, the demands of the workplace do not permit these women to engage in extended mourning rites. Thus they have had to do more than take the roles of others; they have had to reshape, often in a reflective manner, their own roles in the light of the major structural changes that have been occurring in modern urban communities. . . .

Type I. A Personal (but Limited Social) Identity

A very few of the women have achieved a personal identity apart from that of their husbands, but they have been unable to translate this into a meaningful social (i.e., public) identity. In their own private way they view themselves as separate from their husbands. But the lack of a broader network of family, friends, or fellow workers has made it impossible for them to establish the kind of social identity they long for, one that would provide public support for their personal identity.

The experiences of one Mexican American woman serve to illustrate this pattern. During the interviews, she complained that she did not have an ID card issued by the Department of Public Safety. She had heard that she could obtain one, but her husband was unwilling to assist her in this endeavor, and she lacked a network of friends or a kinship system that could help her. She needed transportation as well as assistance in filling out the proper papers. Her lack of social identity had been embarrassing; for instance, she had at times mistakenly been identified as a Mexican national, although she was born in the United States and is a Mexican American.

After a couple of interviews, she asked me to help her secure an ID, and I agreed to assist her. Her husband did not object, in part because I was an "outsider" and in part because of my educational status. After she obtained her ID, she was able, for example, to cash checks, and she was therefore elated with her newfound social identity. The ID dramatizes the need for a separate identity if one is to carry out even minimal activities, such as cashing checks, within the impersonal, public sphere of a contemporary urban setting. College-educated women take these matters for granted.

Type II. An Emerging Personal and Social Identity

Most of the working-class married women I interviewed or encountered in my fieldwork were in the process of attaining a degree of personal and social identity (i.e., autonomy) apart from that of their husbands. This identity has come to be achieved, and is expressed, in a variety of ways. It typically involves support by relatives, friends, or persons in the workplace. Moreover, it may involve personal achievements outside the home that reinforce the fact that the woman in question does indeed command special skills and knowledge that make her different from her husband. Also, it involves the learning of social skills, including negotiation and image management, that make it possible for a wife to cope more effectively with her husband's resistance to her emerging identity.

First, as to the support system, one of the most crucial kinds consists of older children, especially daughters. . . . [D]aughters who become better educated than their mothers play a role in socializing the latter into creating a new identity, and at times they are able to intervene with their fathers and persuade them to become less rigid in their expectations. . . .

The newfound identity of these working-class women is given credibility by their special knowledge or achievements in the public sphere. One woman had taken the lead in helping some of her fellow workers obtain their general equivalency diploma (GED). She proved to herself that she could act independently of her husband, and that she could do so in an effective manner. In addition, a number of women took pride in their ability to budget effectively and shop for bargains. This practical knowledge provided their families, especially the children, with opportunities they might otherwise lack. As a result of this situation, many respondents were reflectively aware of having created a personal and social identity that differed greatly from that of their mothers and grandmothers. This permitted them to cope with a variety of demands associated with everyday urban life.

. . . [N]ew social skills are important in helping women build a personal and social identity apart from that of their husbands.

Working-class women must learn how to negotiate with their spouses, and they may also learn how to use impression management (Goffman 1959). They are reflectively aware of the fact that they may have to act differently at work than at home in order to cope with the tensions that develop between their husbands' more traditional expectations and the new expectations that arise at work. Therefore, some women conceal certain information about their activities in the workplace from their husbands. For example, one working-class woman had baked a cake for a party on the job, but her husband ate part of it. She had not told him what the cake was for because he would have disapproved of her "partying" at work, and she feared that he would have insisted that she quit her job.

Another pattern that emerged was that these women learned to modify their husbands' positions through effecting incremental, rather than drastic, changes. One woman indicated that she purposely makes small changes in the way she does things. Her husband "yells about it," but then he gets used to it, and then she makes other little changes. He tends to forget some of what occurred, and though he resists each change, after a time he comes to accept the reality that new expectations have arisen.

Many of these wives are aware of the need for "strategies" that will permit them to attain a greater degree of personal and social identity. They know they have not achieved the identity they aspire to, but they also realize that they have made strides in modifying their husband's actions. And most of the husbands are cognizant of the new social relationship that is emerging and begrudgingly accept many of the changes.

Type III. A Personal and Social Identity (with Reservations)

. . . One married woman, who was over 40, indicated that she was ready to do something different with her life. She conceded that it would be easier for her than for other women her age to make a change because she had greater financial security than other women she knew. And there were few constraints on her. She was not working and had time to think about what to do with her life.

Yet another woman in this category speaks for herself:

I have the financial security now and I am braver. I still have more to do. I am 44, I've got money, a good car and my kids are behind me. Now, if I am not home in time to make dinner, he can make a sandwich. We've been together a long time and he knows how to make a sandwich. I have had to stand my ground. Two years ago I wanted to go to school to study for a radiologist. He didn't let me. He said I didn't have to. I got my GED. Recently . . . I made a stand that I'm going out and I do. I go out during the day with friends to go out to eat. Not at night. I guess I was scared to go out. I always felt the obligation that I had to come home to cook.

These women stand apart from the typical working-class women I encountered. Because of their relative financial security, and convinced that they have played a major role in helping their husbands to achieve success, these women have developed a personal and social identity that brings them somewhat closer to the identity that college-educated women . . . take for granted. . . .

Specific Decision-making Areas

We shall look at five major decision-making areas, [which] provide us with a basis for evaluating the nature of decision making within the Mexican American family.

I have used my interview data as a starting point for my analysis. Moreover, I have greatly supplemented this information with data collected through participant observation. As the research progressed the participant observation assumed increased importance, for it provided a context within which to place some of the responses to questions in the in-depth interviews.

In general, there was considerable agreement between husbands and wives with respect to many decision-making practices. Still, some differences emerged; these are taken account of below.

Management of Finances

I wanted to know who is responsible for paying the bills and managing the family's income. In the interviews, I posed the general question "Who controls the finances?" and then proceeded to probe in a variety of ways regarding just what meanings are attached to this realm of decision making by both husband and wife. . . .

The comments of some of the wives are revealing of the typical (or dominant) pattern.

> I pay the bills. He doesn't have the patience. He never knows what goes in and out. I do the matching and mismatching.

> I do it all. I deposit his check and mine. He doesn't know anything about the bills. But if I end up in the hospital, he can do it. . . .

Although the aforementioned type of decision making is the dominant one, a relatively small group of working-class couples indicated that they assumed almost equal responsibility in taking care of weekly or monthly bills. One woman avowed, "We both take care of the finances. He reminds me, but I write the checks." Another said, "I make out the budget, but he looks at it."

Within a still smaller group of couples, the husbands paid the bills. In the words of one wife, "He does everything. I don't have to worry." And the same point was made by the husbands. Thus,

> I do everything. I pay the bills, make the checks, mail the checks. I give her the spending money she needs . . . but not because I am the man.

Just what are we to make of these observations regarding control over everyday finances? If we take the traditional husband/wife expectations as a baseline, it is clear that some changes have occurred over the past few decades. Apparently, bill paying has come to be viewed increasingly as part of the wife's "private sphere" wherein she has always had considerable influence. This has resulted in part from the fact that role making by working-class women has enabled them to acquire knowledge about the public sphere—paying bills, dealing with credit, and the like—knowledge that has permitted them to function in a somewhat independent manner.

Purchase of a Car

"Who determines what kind of car to buy?" was another question I sought to answer. Most working-class persons, both husbands and wives, stated that the husband makes the decisions on all the criteria—model, color, and price—whether the car is for the family or for himself. Here [one wife expresses herself:]

> He goes out on his own to buy the truck and Mustang too. He gets a good deal and buys it. Then he tells me about it and I co-sign.

. . . [W]omen rationalized their actions with the statement, "He picks out the car because I don't know too much about it." Or,

> We will go out and look at a car and if I don't like it, he will tell me the good things about the car—for example, it doesn't use too much gas—and of course I say yes.
> He will have the final word. Most of the time I'd rather he make the big decisions. I could go out and buy a car but I don't want to. He will.

. . . The observations of the husbands were in keeping with those of the wives. Thus,

> I wanted a truck and I bought it—color, model, everything. I don't ask her. If she doesn't like it, she doesn't drive it.

> I bought her a used car. She didn't want it. It had only 18,000 miles. We argued over it. She wanted a new car. We reasoned it out. We got it. Now she likes it.

There were, to be sure, exceptions to this overall pattern. . . . A small subgroup of women had much greater influence over the decisions about buying a car. One of the husbands said, "I am the leader of the home, but I share my decisions about buying a car. I don't see why we have to fight over it. We talk." A very few women said that they had purchased their own car. Thus,

> After the last two cars, I said, hey, I'm going to pay for it. I'm going to choose it. It shocked him but he went along with it. I pay for the car from my own checking account.

As I interpret these patterns, the husband's influence in the public sphere carries over to the purchase of a car. It has been an area of traditional male control, and on the whole the women do not view this issue as a major one. They don't interpret the fact that the man buys the car as having serious relevance for how they define their own power with respect to that of their husbands.

Responsibility for House Repairs

Decisions in this realm seem to be much in line with those relating to the purchase of an automobile. The well-defined pattern for working-class couples was that the husband is responsible for the house repairs.

> He does it all. He paints; he just put in new tiles; and he refinished the cabinets. He can do just about everything.

> He is very handy. I'm not a nagging wife. He kind of oversees the repairs.

Some of the wives, while indicating that their husbands do the repairs around the house, said that they have to remind their husbands about which repairs are needed. "I tell him what needs to be done. When something breaks, I fuss at him until he does it."

As for the husbands, almost all of them noted that they make the repairs.

> I do them. I do the painting and put in the appliances myself. I did the roofing and built the shelves. I try to save money by buying my own materials. She picked the color of the paneling.

. . . In only a small number of instances did I encounter working-class women who insisted that both spouses were responsible for getting the house repaired. One wife spoke about the problem as follows: "He does the minor repairs around the house. However, I do the math and measuring to figure out what he needs. I get the lumber and paint and clean the yard."

Only a few persons did not do their own repairs. Concerning working-class persons, we must recognize that they have relatively modest resources, and paying for house repairs can be a costly venture. That the husbands should make the repairs is not surprising. Many of these men have during some part of their lives held jobs that required some skills as laborers. Thus, not only are they required to make house repairs through economic necessity, but they tend to have the skills necessary to carry out these tasks. And, of course, certain kinds of house repairs require considerable physical strength.

Purchase of Furniture

Another question I asked in my in-depth interviews was, "Who decides what kind of furniture to buy?" I was interested in who makes the decisions regarding the purchase of specific items of furniture, such as a living-room suite, a bedroom suite, or a television set. I also inquired about other items of furniture, such as recliners, stereos, or videotape recorders.

Unlike the situation with respect to the diversity in the decisions about house repairs, there is considerable diversity in the responses regarding the buying of furniture. Originally I had assumed that the women would have control over such items as the bedroom or living-room furniture and the men would most likely purchase the TV set. But the patterns were by no means as well defined as I had anticipated.

On the matter of the living-room and bedroom furniture two main decision-making patterns emerged. One involves wives making the major decisions; the other involves a joint decision by the couples.

In one major form of decision making—that wherein the wife purchased the furniture—the women averred:

> I bought the washer and dryer. Anything I use, I buy it. It's my decision.

. . . Their husbands lent support to these statements.

> I leave it up to the women to buy that [referring to the living-room and bedroom suites].

In one case, the wife was consciously aware of her own role making as she engaged in the purchase of furniture.

> I like to buy furniture. I go with my daughter. I finally got this family to realize that I want to do things without asking permission.

Within the other major type—that wherein the couples saw themselves as purchasing furniture together—the wives said, "We shop together for all the furniture." The husbands supported the statements of their wives.

In only a small number of instances was the husband the main purchaser of household items. When we consider the TV set as a separate item, however, complexities arise. Few wives seem to have made the decision concerning it—either the husband alone chose the TV set or the couple did it together. Even so, some women insisted that they look for sales. Nevertheless, husbands more than wives had a major role in purchasing the TV set, "*La señora se encarga de comprar* (my wife is in charge of buying). She bought the living room and bedroom furniture. I like to watch TV. *A mí se me puso que quería un TV* (I decided I wanted a TV)."

. . . The purchase of furniture illustrates several aspects of this social activity. First, husbands and wives may attach different meanings to different items in the home. Some pieces are more important to the wife, others to the husband. This situation leads to greater variation than when one is dealing with the purchase of a single item, such as an automobile.

Second, in many instances, subtle forms of negotiation seem to take place between spouses (cf. Strauss 1978). These persons cannot (and do not) take large purchases lightly, for they have limited financial resources. They thus come to an agreement through a variety of comments and discussions over time. This makes it difficult to identify the chief purchaser or decision maker concerning particular household items.

Third, some of the decisions were apparently the product of habitual action. At times, couples, when asked how they arrived at decisions, stated that they "came to an agreement" with respect to a particular purchase. I sought to probe as to the nature of this process. But some respondents simply insisted that they had "come to an agreement." In some instances I became convinced, based on the context of their comments, that this agreement had been achieved because of habitual ways of responding to each other. Cou-ples, after living together for years, are accustomed to making decisions in particular ways. From their point of view, they make the decision together and arrive at an agreement, not through self-conscious negotiation but through habitual action (Baldwin 1988). Although the respondents were reflective about many aspects of their life, one cannot ignore the place of habit in the forming of certain decisions. . . .

Disciplining of Children

In order to uncover another dimension of decision making, I inquired as to "Who disciplines (or punishes) the children—you or your spouse?" I gave this problem area special attention in my field observations. In general, the first reaction is that both husbands and wives are responsible for the disciplining of children. But it did not take long for more subtle patterns to emerge. Two kinds of decision making appear. In the first type, both spouses are responsible for the disciplining process, but the data suggest that the husband is much stricter than the wife. But strictness is not equivalent to dominance. Despite the general male dominance that prevails, women play a salient role in the disciplining of children.

In this type, husbands and wives define themselves as sharing in the disciplining process, but with a difference. In the second type, however, the wife is the chief disciplinarian, although the husband is more demanding of conformity in the behavior of the children. Under the first type, the wives made the following observations:

My husband spanks them. I talk to them. My husband carries most of the weight. He is the law. Sometimes he tells the kids that I am too lenient. He is stricter. I discipline the children, but they listen to him.

I can scream all day and no one listens. He can say one word and they behave.

As for the husbands,

I think I do most of the disciplining, but then she does her share. Sometimes, she will say to one of the children, "I'll spank you," but she doesn't do it.

We both do. I think my wife does a lot of the minor [disciplining]. For bigger things, I do it too.

In the second type, the wife is defined as the main disciplinarian; however, the husbands make their presence felt. Within this group, the wives noted:

Since I am at home, I do the disciplining. He will sometimes help, mainly with the boys. But I do it.

I never said, "We'll wait until Dad gets home," I dealt with it right then and there. [Yet] the children knew he was the head.

The husbands agreed that the wives discipline the children. "When they were little, only my wife did it." *"Bueno cuando ella está ocupada me toca a mi"* (Well, when she is busy, it's my job). Several added that if their wives could not control the children, they stepped in and took care of it themselves.

We don't believe in spanking unless they really deserve it. But when she needs help, she gets me to talk to them.

Again, the two groups, if taken together, reflect the typical pattern within the working class in Austin and Corpus Christi. (It also seems to be the prevailing pattern in Kingsville.) Although the groups are theoretically different, empirically they shade into each other. One group of couples stressed that they share somewhat equally in the disciplining of children but that the husband is stricter.

The other group saw the wife as the main disciplinarian; however, even here the husband does some disciplining of the children and tends to be stricter.

Within both types, the wives tend to conceive of their husbands as too stern and rigid as disciplinarians, and the latter are generally aware that their wives do not always approve of this.

For example, it was not uncommon for women to say, as one mother did, "He wants to hit them. But I don't let him." Or another, "I don't intervene in front of them. A couple of times I did and this aggravated the situation." Another said, "We never agree" [over the disciplining of the children]. . . .

In practice, the wives at times intervened directly or indirectly, in protecting the children from any harsh discipline. This seems to reflect to some degree the emerging sense of personal and social identity on the part of these women. . . .

Conclusions

. . . Certainly, working-class couples in Austin and Corpus Christi (as well as Kingsville) view their marital relationship as being very different from that of their parents. Yet they hold to rather traditional expectations regarding how wives and husbands should act. The men are to be the providers, the women the carriers of the expressive care of the children and the home.

But these traditional expectations mask fundamental role-making processes among working-class couples, especially the women. We delineated three role-making patterns. In the most prevalent type, working-class women are striving to establish a personal and social identity somewhat apart from that of their husbands. . . . In some realms, decision making appears to be quite traditional in nature; in others, major changes seem to have occurred—the latter primarily because women are in the process of remaking their roles.

References

Baldwin, J. D. 1988. "Habit, Emotion, and Self-Conscious Action." *Sociological Perspectives* 31: 35–58.

Blood, R. and D. M. Wolfe. 1960. *Husbands and Wives*. Glencoe, IL: Free Press.

Cromwell, R. E., R. Corrales, and P. M. Torsiello. 1973. "Normative Patterns of Marital Decision-Making Power and Influence in Mexico and the United States: A Partial Test of Resource and Ideology of Theory." *Journal of Comparative Family Studies* 4: 177–196.

Goffman, E. 1959. *The Presentation of Self in Everyday Life*. Garden City, NY: Doubleday.

Hawkes, G. R., and M. Taylor. 1975. "Power Structure in Mexican and Mexican-American Farm Labor Families." *Journal of Marriage and the Family* 37: 807–811.

Madsen, W. 1964. *The Mexican-Americans of South Texas*. New York: Holt, Rinehart, and Winston.

Queen, S. A., R. W. Habenstein, and J. S. Quadagno. 1985. *The Family in Various Cultures.* New York: Harper and Row.

Rubel, A. 1966. *Across the Tracks: Mexican-Americans in a Texas City.* Austin: University of Texas Press.

Scanzoni, J., and M. Szinovacz. 1980. *Family Decision-Making.* Beverly Hills: Sage.

Strauss, A. 1978. *Negotiations: Varieties, Contexts, Processes, and Social Order.* San Francisco: Jossey-Bass.

Ybarra, L. 1977. "Conjugal Role Relationships in the Chicano Family." Unpublished Ph.D. dissertation, University of California, Berkeley.

———. 1982. "When Wives Work: The Impact on the Chicano Family." *Journal of Marriage and the Family* 44: 169–178.

10

Language, National Identity, and the Ethnic Label 'Hispanic'

Suzanne Oboler

. . . In this chapter I discuss the extent to which the past social positions and immigration experiences of the people I interviewed differentially affect their perceptions of themselves once in the United States. I also explore their views of "Americans" and of the treatment they encounter in this country. Both their acquired self-perceptions and their perceptions of Americans are relevant to their interpretation of the label Hispanic. Using this information as background data, the chapter then explores the meanings and values they attributed to the term Hispanic in their lives.

The self-assessment in the context of U.S. society of the people I interviewed points to the recognition of their previous social class backgrounds in shaping both their expectations and the ways they perceive how far they've come in this society. . . .

Yet, insofar as racial and ethnic distinctions in Latin America are not attributed the same significance as class, Latin Americans' "discovery" of the salience of race and ethnicity as a form of social classification in this country is particularly significant to explore. While the men and women in this study could easily describe their perceptions of their situation in relation to their own past, most of them—particularly those with a working-class background—found it more difficult to articulate their position in the hierarchy of racial and ethnic classification and distinc-

tions that they encountered in the United States. While some of the Latin American immigrants I interviewed tried to understand its rationale, others viewed it as an unresolved given. . . .

[Many women with whom I spoke] are critical of the fact that Hispanics are differentiated from "whites." At the same time, this exchange points to the fact that Latin Americans filter the racial categories in this country through their own racial categorizations. In so doing, however, they implicitly acknowledge that perceptions in their societies do indeed adhere to the same type of racial criteria that prevails in the United States, although it is important to emphasize that these perceptions are interpreted in a different light in the dominant Latin American discourse. Nevertheless, any similarities or comparisons should be drawn with caution, for in Latin America, race-related value judgments are publicly articulated in a different way than they are in U.S. society.

Indeed, every attempt is made to minimize the recognition of the effect of race in the organization of daily life in Latin America. . . . In this sense, one can say that although Latin Americans may find the emphasis of racial categorizations in the United States perplexing, this does not mean that awareness of racial differences are passed over in their perceptions. . . .

Similarly, confusion about ethnic or racial classification doesn't mean that racial prejudices are absent from the ways that Latin Americans perceive African American people in the United States. . . .

To a large extent the meaning this group of immigrants attributed to the use of racial or ethnic forms of classification in this society was also influenced by the values stemming from their class positions in their own countries. These included not only class-based values but also the *culturally specific* racial prejudices that accompanied them in Latin America, given the close and gradated correlations between class and race there. Thus, for example, when asked to comment on whether his life had changed in the United States, Francisco, formerly a middle-class hearing specialist in his own country and now working in the garment industry, first established his class background, pointing out that there was considerable social distance between him and the other Latin Americans with whom he worked in the factory:

> They [Americans] exploit us with very low salaries, and they delude us into thinking that life is owning a car. Here it's common for people to have a car—you can get one dirt cheap; there's no status in it. You see, having an acceptable car, a good house does bring you status in any South American country. They delude people who could never have had a car in their own country. But the comforts of a good kitchen, of being able to wash your plates, of having a dishwasher, a refrigerator, a good sound system, a television: none of that is really life. *There is no pride in acquiring any of it for anyone who comes here with an education.* (Francisco, Colombia; my emphasis)

In Latin America, having an "education" is one of the euphemisms for being middle class. . . . [A]lthough in our discussion Francisco constantly separated himself socially from the other Latin Americans in the factory, he was also very conscious of the ways in which racial and ethnic categories in the United States obviate his own use of social class distinctions:

> My eyes have been opened in relation to Europeans here. I've found out that a lot of Europeans are illiterate. The problem is that we Latin Americans are not appreciated. We are considered the lowest race here. We are only here to work at the bottom. Because there's a bad policy here in the U.S. There are around 32 or 33 million of us and yet we are considered a minority. The percentage of Greeks, Germans, Poles, is very low, yet they have special privileges which we don't have. (Francisco, Colombia)

In the above statement, Francisco does not talk about the "special privileges" accorded to *all* Americans: Instead, he refers to "privileged" white European ethnic groups, whom he perceives as sharing his social, racial, and educational background, and excludes African Americans and other

nonwhite citizens. Thus he believes his own trajectory in this country should emulate "Greeks, Germans, Poles," because in his country, he shared what he perceives to be their white, middle-class values. He does not take into account their national origins or the specific immigrant history of their respective groups in this country.

Indeed a comparison between the ways that the previous class backgrounds of Francisco and Maria have shaped how they perceive their position in this society are quite telling. Maria discusses her successful position today in terms of a past situation that she identifies negatively:

> It's hard, life is really hard there [in the Dominican Republic]. . . . I've gone up in life here. I can't complain about this country. It's helped me a lot. (Maria, Dominican Republic)

Francisco, on the other hand, speaks of his past in glowing terms, and does "complain about this country." Moreover, whereas Maria looks to the past in assessing her current situation, Francisco projects himself into the future, comparing his (low) status as a Latin American with "Greeks, Germans, Poles"—that is, with Americans who, as he states, "have special privileges which we don't have." In other words, Francisco has adopted the ethnic-racial discourse prevailing in this society as a strategy that, on one hand, differentiates him from other Latin American workers and, on the other, claims the same rights accorded to middle-class, assimilated Americans. In order to preserve his previous (higher) class position, he adopts ethnic and racial categories of discourse prevalent in the United States to articulate his position in his new society.

Both Maria's satisfaction with what she has achieved here and Francisco's evaluation of his situation in this society are linked to their respective past lived experiences. Francisco's demand for equal and full rights is in accordance with his class position in his old society and his desire to attain it once again in his new society. Maria's discourse, on the other hand, appears to be grounded more in her accommodation or resignation to a particular social status, which she perceives more positively here in the United States. In her words, "After paying all the bills, it's almost the same here [as the Dominican Republic], but you are more comfortable here." In contrast to Francisco, Maria identifies and compares her current status in relation to her home country rather than to United States society. Indeed, Maria's discourse—which includes the bringing of her family to this country—contrasts with Francisco's in that it emphasizes her successes: her expectations in terms of achieving a better life for herself and her family at least appear to have been fulfilled. As she put it, "Everything I used to think about [coming to the United States] when I was a little girl has become a reality for me. I achieved it on the basis of sacrifice and effort."

Francisco's aspirations, on the other hand, are far from fulfilled. His references to the past serve primarily to point out how much better off he was in his old country. His discourse, unlike Maria's, includes a desire for incorporation into U.S. society, albeit projected into the future and defined by him in terms of equal access to the rights and privileges of the (white) middle classes in the United States.

Indeed, for poorer Latin Americans like Maria, accustomed as they are to perceive class belonging as the determinant of social mobility and status, social mobility in the United States may indeed be enhanced, at least potentially, whether or not they are "lumped" together with nonwhites and regardless of nationality. However, for those who, like Francisco, were better off before they immigrated, the road to incorporation into American society may be more costly, at least in terms of cultural perceptions. Once in the United States, all Latin Americans are "Hispanics," and thus all have to come to terms with this ethnic label assigned to them by the host society. At the same time, those like Francisco confront discrimination often for the first time and are further forced to recognize, through their own individual experience, the significance of racial and social prejudices, stereotypes, and labels that their own country's social organization historically allowed them to bypass, by virtue of their previous higher social status in their society's hierarchy.

Where the Personal Meets the Political: Issues of Latino Unity

These distinctions should by no means be interpreted as implying that all the men and women in this study, regardless of their class backgrounds, did not also acknowledge the cultural and particularly linguistic commonalities that emerge in the context of the presence of other ethnic groups and that might thus unify Latinos in particular situations. . . .

Yet, as some authors have asserted, these very real shared linguistic and cultural commonalities should not be confused with automatic adherence to political and ideological panethnicism. . . . [T]he possibility that Americans and Latinos may at times have more in common than upper-and lower-class Latinos is noteworthy . . . and requires closer examination. . . . [T]he men and women of this study as a whole often homogenized Americans in defining their Latino or Latina self and culture in relation to the U.S. context. In this respect, it is important to note that the extent to which people will emphasize their perception of the differences of "the other" from themselves—whether those differences are between Latinos and Americans or are internal to the Latino community—may depend on how socially and culturally distant "the other" is from the self. For many people of Latin American descent, for example, "the American"—as the "external" referential other—may be perceived as much more distant from the cultural experience of a Latino than another Latin American national. But closer distinctions (the internal boundaries) are also essential in forging the cultural horizon of the Latino self within the group. Hence many of the people in this study were prone to erase the differences among those they designated as Americans while stressing the subtle distinctions between self and other within the Latino population. In specifying this strategic internal boundary, national differences and prejudices like class, gender, and race variations and biases within each national-origin group will also be easily identifiable. . . .

The Impact of Social Class in Defining the Label Hispanic

The Middle-Class Response

The culturally derived importance of establishing one's identity and position in social terms in Latin American society can lead middle-class immigrants to use U.S. categories about their origins to define their group's social position in the United States. In her interview, Soledad, the other middle-class, college-educated person in this study, insisted that each individual should be identified by her or his nationality. Nevertheless, like Francisco, she also immediately adopted the U.S. ethnic category, Hispanic, rather than that of her nationality to refer to Latin Americans in this country. Her perception of both its positive and negative value emerged in the following discussion among Soledad and three other Latin American women concerning the census questionnaire:

> I'm Colombian, but I wrote down that I was Hispanic. (Soledad, Colombian)

> I think they wanted you to write it so that they know who speaks Spanish. (Veronica, Dominican Republic)

> Yes, but it's also to send more help to the Hispanic communities, like for bilingual schools and things like that. (Soledad) . . .

> Well I know that they separate Puerto Ricans. (Delores, Guatemala)

> . . . It's because they're undecided about Puerto Ricans. They don't really know if they're American or if they're Puerto Rican. See, they have a problem with Puerto Ricans because they can't believe that they can be Americans and still speak Spanish. So they catalogue them as Americans for some things, but for others they're Puerto Ricans. When they count for something they're Americans, but when they don't need them to count for anything they're *boricuas*. But in different ways, they do that with all of us who speak Spanish. You know, if an American is running, he's just doing exercise; but if

one of us is running, we've just committed a robbery. (Soledad)

In the above conversation, Soledad first identified herself as Colombian but insofar as she recognized the discussion was within the context of the U.S. census, she then immediately translated her identity into the U.S. terminology, Hispanic. ("I'm Colombian, but I wrote down that I was Hispanic.") Her discussion of the greater social benefit to be derived from grouping all Latin American nationalities together as Hispanics—in terms of resource allocations for services such as bilingual schools and so on—shows that she is aware of the government's policies and the relationship between formal ethnic identification and the distribution of resources. However, while Soledad recognizes the social value of the term Hispanic, she is also aware of the stereotypes associated with it: first by implicitly alluding to her understanding of its source—the unresolved political condition and ambivalent position of Puerto Ricans in the United States—and then by attributing to language much of their difficulties ("They can't believe that they can be Americans and still speak Spanish"). Soledad ends her statement by extending her allusions to the prejudice she perceives against Puerto Ricans to encompass "all of us who speak Spanish" and provides an example of her perception of the prejudice against Hispanics as committing crimes in the United States.

Like Soledad, Francisco did not hesitate to include himself in the category of Hispanic as he discussed his position *as a Hispanic* relative to the rest of the population in this society. . . . [H]e too seems to be aware of the importance of ethnicity in the organization of U.S. society and discusses the term itself, referring primarily to its negative attributes in this context:

> They invented the word Hispanic to discriminate against us.
> It is used to separate us from a cultural point of view. It is used to separate us from a religious point of view. It is used to separate us from an economic point of view. It is used to separate us from an intellectual point of view. They do not recognize our merits. We have several Nobel prize winners. . . . But in this country,

they don't acknowledge our achievements. (Francisco, Colombia)

Both Francisco and Soledad perceive the term Hispanic as signifying discrimination against Latin Americans and hence identify it as a term of segregation of "all of us" from mainstream U.S. society. Nevertheless, they use it to identify themselves within the U.S. context, thus accepting the ethnic and racial categories in the country. At the same time, they both discussed the position of all Hispanics in the United States in broader sociological rather than personal terms, commenting on the negative implications of the term and comparing the position of Hispanics to that of other groups in this society. . . .

The Working-Class Response

Unlike either of the middle-class people discussed above, the rest of the men and women in this study were not as prone to identify themselves explicitly as Hispanics. Like that of their middle-class counterparts, the point of departure in establishing their identity in this country stemmed from their past social status and position in their country of origin. But unlike Francisco and Soledad, the working-class immigrants measured their progress in the United States in terms of their society of origin, where . . . many of them would be considered . . . second- and third-class citizens. In this sense, they would view themselves as better off in this country—as the case of Maria exemplifies—and hence would be applying the categories reserved for measuring incorporation into their previous society, rather than this one. . . .

While several explained the term Hispanic as reflecting language use, others made statements whose meaning in one way or another reflected the following comment by one informant: "Hispanic? Oh, yes, that's what *they* call us" (Dolores, Guatemala). However, the majority were reluctant to self-identify as Hispanics and hesitated to discuss the term, perceiving it as identifying a group of people whose negative attributes had absolutely no correspondence to themselves. . . . In trying to evade these negative connotations, it is not surprising that many find reasons to simply distance themselves from the term. . . . In so doing, they signaled their deep disapproval of those they conceive of as Hispanics in this society. . . . Indeed, sometimes the discussion on the negative meaning attributed to the term Hispanics brings out prejudices that one national group might have about another:

I don't want to mention specific nationalities but it is true that there are people who put music on really loud; they drink beer and throw the cans out on the street. (Rosa, El Salvador)

. . . Refusing to identify herself as a Hispanic, she thus negatively assesses its social value. . . . Rosa, like others in this study, shows her fear of having the connotations of the label imposed on her sense of self and life and, in so doing, openly distances herself from the label in personal rather than in the broad sociological terms adopted by Francisco and Soledad.

Culture, Language, and Discrimination

Regardless of their social class, all of the men and women in this study emphasized the importance of learning the English language. No matter how difficult it was to learn, they simultaneously struggled to maintain their own language and customs. . . . Indeed, knowing several languages was viewed by many in very positive terms. . . . Not surprisingly, bilingualism was also the ideal expressed by the informants in relation to their own children's upbringing:

I've always liked languages. I think that the more languages people know, the more opportunities they'll have to develop themselves. My language is Spanish. I want my children to speak it so that they'll know their culture and so that they'll never be ashamed of being Latin American. Because I know a lot of families here who are ashamed of being Colombian. (Alicia, Colombia)

Many noted either explicitly or implicitly, as in Alicia's comment, their awareness of the effects of the existing prejudice against Hispanics in their daily lives. It is interesting to observe in this respect that several theorists have noted the link Alicia established between language and culture as a significant approach to staving off the effects of prejudice on children. . . .

Most of the workers interviewed in this study perceived bilingualism as valuable in people's lives. For them, learning English was as essential as maintaining Spanish. Most emphasized the importance of learning English, and for many the reason was self-evident. As Jaime (Honduras) put it, "I have to learn English because in this country, people speak English." Ofelia (Colombia) said, "I'm studying English because I live in a country in which speaking English is a necessity." Others explicitly associated learning English with getting a better job and hence improving their social positions. . . . Several commented on the value of speaking English for establishing better communications with English-language speakers. . . .

[L]earning English is perceived as a ticket of entry into U.S. society. And this access in turn is perceived primarily in terms of material advancement. . . . At the same time, learning English is also perceived as a means for improving relations between Spanish and English speakers. These findings, of course, contradict the claims about Hispanics made by organizations such as U.S. English who are lobbying to add an English Language Amendment to the Constitution of the United States.

Some people in this study believed that because Americans "read about Latin America and the Caribbean," as Julieta (Mexico) noted, they do understand their cultures. . . . Others sought to give balanced views on Americans' perceptions of Latinos:

> It's true that most of them don't know our culture. But I think Americans who have relations with us and know us do understand us; but most of us don't relate to them because we don't know their language and we don't have any American friends. (Veronica, Dominican Republic)

But the more common statements made in the interviews related to the importance of communicating with Americans because "most of them" (Americans) seemed to have such limited understanding of the cultures of Latin America. In general terms, they ex-

pressed their perception of this as resulting from a "lack of interest in our cultures" (Dolores, Guatemala). . . .

To a certain extent, the working-class people in this study also tended to attribute some of the cause of this prejudice to their own lack of knowledge of English. The perception of the prejudice against Latin Americans as resulting from lack of language skills led many, like Veronica and Alicia, quoted earlier, to suggest that learning the language would certainly help to bridge the gap between Americans and Latin Americans in the United States. In fact, several believed that their going to school to learn English would solve the problem of prejudice against them once and for all. . . .

Almost all of the people I interviewed noted that the best thing about life in the United States was, as Teresa (Puerto Rico) put it, "that you're always working," or in the words of Veronica (Dominican Republic), it is easier "to achieve what you want here." For Julieta (Mexico), who preferred life in her country because it was "more peaceful," living in the United States was better in terms of its "better employment opportunities" and thus "economically." Yet she too noted that the worst thing about this country was "the racism." Indeed, their positive views about the economic possibilities opened to them in the United States was weighed against the prejudice they experienced as Spanish-speaking Latin Americans in this country. Many, particularly among the working-class immigrants, could point to some incident in their daily life experiences that exemplified prejudice against Latinos. . . .

Although some understood the existing prejudice against them as stemming from simplistic generalizations about "those two or three families," as Rosa put it, the ambivalence expressed by most also reflected their belief that, nevertheless, the prejudice of Americans toward Hispanics was unwarranted and the result of the *social and class* distance they perceived between Hispanics and "Americans." Maria, for example, noted that prejudice begins early in children's lives at schools. She commented that parents like herself have to fight hard against American teachers' reinforcement of the negative connotations associated with the label Hispanic, which invariably affect the self-image of second-generation Latinos growing up in this country. . . . Given their awareness of the stereotypes associated with the Spanish language, it is not surprising that many of the working-class men and women shunned the term Hispanic as a means of self-identification. . . .

Reimagining the American Continent

. . . Like most of the people interviewed, Rosa defines herself in terms of her nationality, Salvadorean. Her reluctance to use the term Hispanic was at least partly due to the negative connotations that others associated with the term and her consequent perception of the stigma attached to it.

Indeed, in many ways, the "Hispanic" was the external other. At the same time, through its negation, the label Hispanic became the basis on which the sense of one's self and identity was being constructed in the new context. For the people in this study, the root of the problem with the term Hispanic was the stigmatizing stereotypes resulting from reducing all Spanish-speaking people to one homogenizing idea. In addition, most were aware that along with showing Americans' lack of knowledge about the other countries in the hemisphere, labels such as this also efface what are for them obvious national, ethnic, and social distinctions:

Neither Americans or Europeans know much about geography. In this respect they are very ignorant. That's why they group us all together. They don't know the difference, because they don't know their geography. Because for example, just because you speak Spanish, they immediately ask, "You Puerto Rican?" And I tell them, "No, I'm South American or Colombian but I speak Spanish and the Puerto Rican people do too." Because they think that everyone who speaks Spanish is Puerto Rican . . . or, for example, the Dominicans will say, "We are Caribbeans," because they identify with the Caribbean, and the Americans can't relate to that because culturally they only know about themselves. (Soledad, Colombia)

The extent to which Latin Americans resented what they perceived as Americans' lack of knowledge about their respective cultures can be seen in the ways they defined their identity in the U.S. context—"We are all of us Americans," as Julian (Peru) put it. It is also clear in the relationship they established between people's self-identification and their insistence on specifying the continent's geography:

. . . I only know one America. Its geographical position may be North America, Central America, or South America. But we're all American. Colombia isn't located in Europe, it isn't located in Asia, and it isn't in Africa either. So, if they take the name of the entire continent for their country, what is left for ours? What is the name of the continent that Colombia is on? (Alicia, Colombia)

Like Alicia, many of the men and women in this study stressed the fact that they are as American as U.S. citizens. The use of the term Latin American in this sense becomes simply the counterweight of the term North American. . . . It was clear that for Juan, a U.S.-born Puerto Rican, the tensions had specific political and historical antecedents:

I'm American only by accident, because Puerto Rico's a territory of the United States. I don't think that's by choice, because they've got American bases there. (Juan, Puerto Rico, U.S.-born)

. . . Although he acknowledges that he is Americanized, however, Juan refuses the identity of "American," recognizing it as having been imposed on Puerto Ricans as much as the word Hispanics had been. As he explained, "Puerto Ricans never call each other Hispanics," just as "they never called each other spics.". . .

[P]articularly in the process of defining the group's internal boundaries and their own identity within it, this study's Latin American population affirmed the significance of specifying their respective national origins among themselves. Veronica told me:

If I introduce you to someone I would say "This is my friend, she's from Peru." Or else, I'd say, "She's South American, or Peruvian." (Veronica, Dominican Republic)

Regardless of social class, while the men and women clearly understood the implications of the label Hispanic and their own reasons for its existence, they did not necessarily see the purpose in their personal lives of homogenizing the various nationalities under the label Hispanic. . . .

The Weight of Race, Class, National Origins, and Language in the Label 'Hispanic'

In defining the meaning that the term Hispanic in the United States has for themselves, the men and women in this study showed that they were conscious of the differences among the various Latin American nationalities. Yet they were also aware of the effects that the assumptions and prejudices stemming from the indiscriminate grouping of Hispanics in the United States had on their lives. . . .

A certain cynicism was also not absent from the sometimes lengthy explanations of the origins and meaning of the term:

> . . . They just count all Latin people in one bunch. They do it to the blacks, too. I mean, come on, they're more than just blacks. You got your American blacks, you got your African, your Jamaican; then you got your Puerto Rican blacks; some guys are darker than me. Then you got your Dominican blacks, you got white people that are dark skinned. And it's just that they clump 'em all together just so they can generalize everybody. . . .
>
> So you got your Hispanics over here which includes whatever race you want to put in it south of the border. Then you got your blacks, anything from the Congo down. Then you got your whites which is Americans. (Juan, Puerto Rico, U.S.-born)

In view of the prevalence of race-related representations in New York City, where he grew up, it is not surprising that a New York-born Puerto Rican discussed the meaning of Hispanic in strictly racial-ethnic terms. Although Juan recognized the diversity within the various groups, he also had a firm perception of a two-tiered racial hierarchy made up of "whites" and "everybody else" in the United States. He defined Hispanics as including "whatever race you want to put in it south of the border," while singling out "whites" as "Americans": his interpretation, then, clearly recognizes that in this country race and nationality are conflated. . . .

Interpreting the weight of the various components of the term Hispanic—race, class, national origins, and language—becomes an essential part of people's self definition. . . . To a large extent, their choice of identity expresses their expectations of and strategies for incorporation into the U.S. social structure. While, as Latin Americans, they may insist that they are as American as the "gringos," their confrontation with race and class representations in U.S. society forces them to incorporate these dimensions both in the way they imagine the "American community" and in their own lived experience as Hispanics in the United States.

Asian Americans*

Asian Americans represent a diverse cross section of ethnic groups originating from East and South Asia. Socially and culturally these ethnic groups are very different from one another, yet throughout their history in the United States, Asian American groups have experienced similar forms of discrimination and prejudice. The diversity in the Asian American population reflects the realities of global transmigration and complex relationships between Asian countries and the United States. This introduction gives a brief historical overview of the experiences of Asian Americans and the four articles in this section that discuss some of the issues facing Asian Americans today.

We begin with some basic demographic information about the current Asian American and Pacific Islander population of the U.S. According to data from the decennial U.S. censuses, this segment of the population has grown rapidly over the past two decades. As of 1990, there were approximately 7.27 million Asian Americans and Pacific Islanders in the U.S.—6.9 million people identifying with various Asian population groups, along with 365,000 Pacific Islanders. Thus, Asian Americans and Pacific Islanders constituted 2.9 percent of the total U.S. population in 1990, up from 1.5 percent in 1980 (Kitano and Daniels 1995). By March, 1996, the U.S. Bureau of the Census estimated that there were roughly 9.65 million Asian Americans and Pacific Islanders, around 3.6 percent of the total U.S. population (U.S. Bureau of the Census 1997), and many experts predict that Asian Americans and Pacific Islanders may account for more than 4 percent of the U.S.

population by century's end (O'Hare and Felt 1991).

The Asian American/Pacific Islander label actually includes a large number of quite heterogeneous national origin groups. According to data from the 1990 U.S. Census, the largest Asian American population segment is Chinese Americans, a term which refers to people who trace their origins to mainland China, Taiwan, and Hong Kong. This population numbered roughly 1.65 million in 1990, accounting for nearly 24 percent of the total Asian American/Pacific Islander population in the U.S. As of 1990, Filipino Americans were the second-largest Asian-origin group, totalling 1.4 million (20.4 percent of the Asian total). They were followed, in order, by Japanese (847,500; 12.3 percent), Asian Indian (815,500; 11.8 percent), Korean (799,000; 11.6 percent), and Vietnamese (614,500; 8.9 percent). In addition, there were over 200,000 self-identified Hawaiians; Laotian- and Cambodian-origin groups each totalling nearly 150,000, and Thai and Hmong populations in the U.S. were approaching 100,000 in 1990 (Kitano and Daniels 1995).

Although there are Asian-origin persons living in every state, and in virtually every city and town in the U.S., the Asian American/Pacific Islander population remains heavily urbanized. California is home to more members of this population group than any other state—approximately 2.85 million in 1990. Most of these persons reside in two major metropolitan areas, Los Angeles/Anaheim/Riverside and San Francisco/Oakland/San Jose. Large Asian-origin populations can also be

---

* This introduction was written by Wendy Ng of San Jose State University.

found in the New York/northern New Jersey/Long Island area (875,000) and in Honolulu (525,000). Not all Asian Americans and Pacific Islanders live in coastal states, however; Texas (320,000) and Illinois (285,000) also have substantial numbers of Asian-origin residents (O'Hare and Felt 1991; Kitano and Daniels 1995).

Immigration from Asia beginning in the second half of the nineteenth century brought over one million people from China, Japan, Korea, India, and the Philippines (Chan 1991). The first Asian immigrants came from China, and were followed by successive waves of immigration from Japan, Korea, the Indian subcontinent, and the Philippines. Most of the first immigrants were men and came from poor rural backgrounds. Those who came to the United States experienced various forms of institutional discrimination, prejudice, and racism. Similar to European immigrants, their motivation for migrating was due to both internal conditions of their home countries as well as external global conditions which encouraged international migration from abroad to the United States. However, once in the United States, they were treated as strangers, foreigners, and aliens. Asians were denied rights to citizenship, to own land, to marry outside their racial group, and to testify in courts of law. While individually, Chinese, Japanese, Koreans, Filipinos, and Asian Indians viewed themselves as different from one another, their treatment by the majority group did not always acknowledge these differences. Further, Asian Americans do not fit the model of "forced" migration, as experienced by African Americans, and were not subjected to "colonization" as were Native Americans and Latinos. Because Asian American migration is perceived as similar to European migration most analyses of their adaptation use assimilation to explain their adaptation and incorporation into American society. But assimilation models have failed to address the persistence of racism directed toward Asian Americans.

Historically, Asian American groups first encountered discrimination in immigration laws. Beginning with the Chinese Exclusion Act of 1882, the U.S. government sought to control the numbers of Chinese laborers entering the United States. Following the Exclusion Act, other legislation further restricted immigration of other Asian ethnic groups: the 1907 Gentlemen's Agreement and later the Immigration Act of 1924 affected the Japanese, the 1917 Barred Zone Act affected Asian Indians, and the 1934 Tydings-McDuffie Act limited Filipino migration to the United States (Chan 1991). Despite these restrictions, Asian Americans found ways to enter the United States. The use of false documents in which Chinese men became "paper sons" was the most common for the Chinese. Japanese men arranged marriages with "picture brides" which allowed them to bring wives to America. Because of restrictive immigration laws, it was difficult for some Asian communities to form because of the lack of women. For example, some Sikh Asian Indian men never returned to India, instead making lives in America intermarrying with native born European and Mexican women (Leonard 1991). Filipino men who immigrated were subjected to antimiscegenation laws which prevented their marriage with white women, which they successfully challenged in California's courts. They argued that they were not "mongoloid," as ethnologists had classified them (Chan 1991).

Asian Americans also experienced institutional racism in the form of discriminatory citizenship laws. The Naturalization Act of 1790 guaranteed the right of citizenship to "free white persons." Congress granted naturalization privileges to "persons of African nativity or descent" after the Civil War and American Indians were granted citizenship in 1924. Immigrant Asians were denied the right of citizenship by naturalization, thus affecting their political enfranchisement through voting. The ability of Asians to own land was affected by alien land laws in at least 13 states, most on the West Coast. These laws targeted Chinese, Japanese, Korean, and Asian Indian immigrants who were considered aliens ineligible for citizenship (Chan 1991).

The treatment of Asian Americans has often depended on global conditions in relation to Asia. This is most clearly illustrated when the United States entered World War II in 1942. President Franklin Roosevelt signed Executive Order 9066 which empowered the military to make decisions excluding any persons from certain military areas on the West Coast. Over 120,000 persons of Japanese ancestry, both citizens and noncitizens, were sent to isolated internment camps throughout the United States. While the relocation is often attributed to war hysteria, it was also influenced by long-standing anti-Asian sentiment in the United States.

The Civil Rights Movement of the 1950s and 1960s brought sweeping changes resulting in social changes in institutional discrimination directed toward African Americans. As a result, Asian Americans benefited as protected class members from institutional reforms resulting in nondiscriminatory practices in state and federal governments. Due in part to the Civil Rights Movement and to raised national awareness of race relations issues, overt practices of discrimination have virtually disappeared. Still, there are occasions in which blatant practices of racism and racial violence appear. Incidents of overt racism are often initiated in response to problems within the U.S. economy, foreign trade deficits or increased economic competition with Asian countries. It is often assumed that Asian Americans are immune from overt discriminatory practices, especially given their "model minority" image, but they still do experience hostility because of their race.

In 1982, Vincent Chin, a Chinese American, was brutally murdered by two white autoworkers. They called Chin a "Japanese" and blamed him for their being out of work. Chin's two assailants, Ronald Ebens and Michael Nitz, were allowed to plead guilty to manslaughter and were sentenced to three years probation and fined $3,780 each (Takaki 1989). For many Asian Americans, Chin's murder and the light sentence of his murderers are testimony to the inequality of the justice system and the continued racism directed toward Asians. After Chin's death, Asian Americans realized how much race relations depended on the relations between Asia and the United States. Chin was treated as a foreigner because he did not "look the part" of an American, and the fact that Chin was Chinese but was misidentified as being Japanese points to the fact that many members of the majority group in America do not perceive the differences among Asian groups and view Asians as a single category.

Several factors have contributed to the rise in hate crimes toward Asian Americans. The increase in the urban Asian population increases the likelihood of interaction between non-Asians and Asians. Many are not familiar with the differences among Asian American groups and are unfamiliar with particular cultural customs. For example, Asian Indians have been harassed for their style of dress, speech accents, and religion. Some of the harassment includes racial taunts and slurs, but there have been more serious incidents like that in which Navroze Mody, an Indian professional, was killed by a gang in New Jersey in 1987 (Sheth 1995). More often than not, problems in the economy are accompanied by a rise in anti-Asian or anti-immigrant sentiment. The period of Southeast Asian refugee resettlement in the mid-1970s coincided with an economic recession and many Americans, both black and white, felt that Asian immigrants took their jobs and businesses (Min 1995).

The dynamics of race relations in the United States has focused on black-white relations. Because Asian Americans make up such a small percentage of the overall population, they are not seen as affecting much of the racial dynamic. Yet, as evidenced by the events in Los Angeles in 1992, race relations have become a more complex interplay between and among racial minority groups. Economic differences play a primary role in perpetuating intraracial conflict and theoretical models have not sufficiently addressed this. The Los Angeles uprising and riots drew attention to the complexities of intraracial relations between African Americans, Asians, and Latinos in Southern California. Following the acquittal of the policeman accused of beating motorist Rodney King, protests throughout South Central Los Angeles involved looting and vandalism of stores owned by African and Korean Americans. Among the events leading to the 1992 uprising was the earlier trial of Soon Ja Du, a Korean storeowner who was convicted of voluntary manslaughter in the death of Latasha Harlins, a teenage African American girl. Du was sentenced to probation and community service. The leniency of her sentence was viewed with outrage by many in the African American community and in response, many Korean American businesses were boycotted in the Los Angeles area (Marable 1994).

The presence of Korean-owned businesses in predominantly black neighborhoods has sparked discussion over structural factors and availability of resources for Asian immigrant groups. Ethnic enterprise models of adaptation have been used to explain what becomes of immigrant groups in America (Bonacich and Light 1985; Portes and Manning 1986; Portes and Rumbaut 1990). These models suggest that Latino and Asian immigrants use small businesses catering to ethnic markets within their own groups and to other ethnic groups to combat discriminatory practices in mainstream job markets. Certain Asian ethnic groups have historically occupied certain job markets, like Chinese laundry workers and Japanese farmers, but today Asian Americans fill a variety of economic niches, including Korean dry cleaners, Cambodian donut shops proprietors, and South Asian Indian motel owners. Some theoretical models have suggested that in advanced capitalist societies, Asian Americans serve as "middleman" minorities: located between black and white, they are a social and economic buffer between the white majority group and the mostly racial minority working class and underclass (Bonacich 1973).

Among the more recent immigrants have been Vietnamese, Cambodian, and Lao refugees. After the fall of Saigon in 1975, over 130,000 sought refugee status in the United States (Rumbaut 1995). This first wave of refugees consisted of South Vietnamese military personnel, former employees who worked for the U.S., and many of the country's upper- and middle-class elite. The U.S. government's policy toward refugee resettlement was to disperse the population so that no one community would be burdened with the social welfare needs of the population. It was believed that dispersion would encourage assimilation because refugees would be forced to conform to their host communities to achieve self-sufficiency as quickly as possible. The idea that assimilation and adjustment would be achieved through this method of resettlement ignored the fact that other Asian American groups had not been absorbed by the majority community and that Vietnamese and other Southeast Asian groups might potentially face problems in resettlement among a largely non-Asian, white population. The social problems facing the refugee population ranged from second language acquisition, psychological trauma such as depression, and anti-Asian hostility.

In the late 1970s and early 1980s a second group of Southeast Asian refugees arrived in the United States. Commonly called "second wave refugees," this group was comprised of ethnic Chinese from Vietnam ("boat people"), Hmong and Mien tribal groups from Laos, and Cambodians (Khmer) who had survived Pol Pot's killing fields. In all, it is estimated that over one million refugees from Southeast Asia have resettled in the United States, with over 750,000 in other western countries (Rumbaut 1995). Studies of refugees tend to focus on the social service aspects of refugee resettlement. Refugees arrived when inflation and unemployment were high and the unpopularity of the Vietnam War was still fresh in many people's memories. They encountered a change in their social and economic status, and sometimes, hostility in their new communities. The arrival of the second wave refugees also coincided with secondary migration of first wave refugees so that large populations of refugees were now concentrated in urban and suburban areas such as San Jose and Orange County, California, and Houston, Texas.

It is often assumed that Southeast Asian refugees share similar cultural patterns, but this is simply untrue. They have different modes of adaptation and adjustment which depend on cultural factors, life views, and internal and external resources that refugees bring with them to the United States. In an ethnographic study of Vietnamese and Cambodian (Khmer) refugees, Freeman and Welaratna (1993) found that each group had different adaptations to life in America. Studies comparing Vietnamese and Cambodian refugees compare their different levels of achieving economic self sufficiency. Vietnamese have been "successful" refugees partly due to their longer time in America and to an hierarchical, individualistic family structure (Rumbaut 1995). Cambodians, on the other hand, have been found to have less success in establishing economic self-sufficiency. Freeman and Welaratna argue that the success of these refugees must be understood within the context of Cambodian culture, which places greater value on mutual cooperation, the nature of the job, and its value to human society. Therefore, what is often viewed as low-status positions occupied by Cambodia may actually be high-status positions from their perspective, especially if these jobs help others (Freeman and Welaratna 1993). This study recognizes the individual differences in refugee experience based upon cultural modes of adaptation as well as differing definitions of "self-sufficiency" and success, frequently ignored by social science researchers.

Two other Asian ethnic groups whose numbers in the United States have grown in recent years are Filipinos and Asian Indians. Both groups have a high number of professionals, particularly in the medical field. Filipinos have had a unique relationship with the United States which has affected the composition and rate of immigration. Because the Philippines was a colony of the United States following the Spanish-American war, Filipinos have been exposed to American society and culture. During the early part of this century the first Filipino immigrants were largely men from rural backgrounds. Following Philippine independence in 1946, restrictive quotas limited Filipino immigration. It was not until the liberalization of immigration laws in 1965 that contemporary immigration grew dramatically. Today's Filipino immigrants are largely comprised of college-educated professionals. As a group they are very diverse, and there are numerous subcultures within the Filipino American population based upon dialect, regional origins, and kinship ties. Differences in occupational and economic achievement for Filipinos occur between native-born and foreign-born groups,

where foreign-born Filipinos hold the top occupational categories. Overall, Filipinos are similar to other Asian ethnic groups in that they receive low returns for their educational investments (Agbayani-Siewert and Revilla 1995).

Contemporary Asian Indian immigrants also have high levels of educational and professional achievement. Many immigrated to the United States under a special preference category reserved for professionals, and many came as foreign students, completed their master's degrees or Ph.D.s, and later changed their status to become permanent residents. The adjustment of Asian Indians to American society is smoother because they do not have serious language barriers and are able to work in occupations for which they have already been trained (Sheth 1995). Asian Indians have also entered into new occupations to work independently from the majority group. Large numbers of Indians and Pakistanis have developed franchises as taxi drivers in large metropolitan areas, and one Indian ethnic group, the Gujarati, dominate the hotel and motel industry in many areas. These types of ethnic enterprises work well as a structural solution to the discrimination Asian Indians might face in the mainstream labor market.

In the area of education, Asian Americans have had substantial success in the United States. Yet, those gains are tempered by a backlash toward minority special admissions at many highly selective universities. Takagi's (1992) analysis of college and university admissions procedures show that there has been discrimination against Asian American students. When Asian and white students compete for limited admissions slots, selective criteria are used to eliminate Asian students or lower their chances for admission. Those against affirmative action argue that universities use mythical quotas against Asian American students to allow less qualified minority students into universities. On the other hand, Asian American educators and leaders argue against comparing Asian American admissions with affirmative action because these students are not competing with one another for admissions slots (Min 1995). Overall, the issue of Asian American admissions into highly selective colleges and universities raises questions as to what happens when an ethnic group begins to reach parity, as Asian Americans have in education, and what happens if their numbers begin to exceed a hypothetical ceiling. Education has become the testing ground for such decisions, and the conflict surrounding educational admissions indicates that there is still concern over racial representativeness.

The four articles in this section address some of the contemporary dynamics of the Asian American population and the historical basis for these dynamics. Won Moo Hurh and Kwang Chung Kim analyze the implications of the "model minority" stereotype of Asian Americans. They note that Asian Americans have experienced institutional discrimination in the form of immigration and citizenship laws compounded with stereotypes of Asians as the "yellow peril" and other demeaning images supporting anti-Asian sentiment. When looking at Asian Americans' occupations and income, they are above the national median. However, Hurh and Kim's findings show that both foreign-born and native-born Asian men and women are underemployed. In other words, Asian Americans pay a higher cost for their training and education by not being rewarded in terms of occupation and income. They suggest that the "model minority" stereotype of Asian Americans is detrimental in two ways: first, it may deny Asians access to programs to combat social problems within the community; second, the stereotype implies that Asians are a "model" that other minorities should be held up to as a standard. Such comparisons negatively affect relations between Asians and other groups, and are especially inaccurate given the actual social and economic diversity within the Asian community.

In-Jin Yoon discusses the development of Korean business activity in several Chicago communities. Korean immigration has grown considerably since the change in immigration law in 1965. Compared to earlier Chinese and Japanese immigration which was largely from a rural peasant background, contemporary Korean immigrants are from urban, educated backgrounds. As noted by Portes and Manning (1986), immigrant groups must often develop their own resources and ethnic enclaves to combat exclusion and discrimination upon entering a new society. Korean immigrants come with little capital, but often pool their resources in order to start small businesses, and rely upon family networks in order to maintain and run these businesses. Korean immigrants often develop businesses in two different areas: one serving the Korean ethnic market, the second serving the non-Korean market. Yoon points to how these markets are economically intertwined, showing that success and failure within the non-Korean, predominantly African American markets also affect the economics of the Korean ethnic markets.

Min Zhou explores the economic roles of contemporary immigrant Chinese women in New York City's Chinatown. Historically, the Chinese population in America has had a skewed sex ratio because most Chinese immigration at the beginning of this century consisted of men. With the repeal of the Chinese Exclusion Act in 1943 and the liberalization of immigration quotas through the 1965 Immigration Act, Chinese female immigration has increased. As a result, Chinatown communities have grown and Chinese women have entered into productive labor in the ethnic enclave market. Chinese women however, are disadvantaged by their gender and immigrant status and have limited job opportunities. Despite this, Min points out that Chinese women's labor is needed to economically contribute to their families.

In this section's final article, Yen Le Espiritu analyzes the formation of a pan-Asian ethnic identity. Asian American ethnic groups have thought of themselves as having a singular ethnic identity as Chinese, Japanese, Korean, or Filipino. The move toward pan-Asian consciousness was sparked by the Civil Rights Movement and college ethnic and racial movements in which Asian Americans began to see the similarities in their historical experiences. Thus, over time, the distinctions between different Asian ethnic groups have become less important and pan-Asian identity has come to provide a greater social and political base. This social movement for ethnic inclusion presents a stronger argument for political and social power based upon the similarity of experiences, rather than differences in culture.

Many Asian Americans have attained measurable social and economic status in American society, but these gains have been mitigated by continued anti-Asian sentiment. As Hurh and Kim argue, despite the model minority image, Asian Americans often pay a higher cost for their social and economic status; their rewards are still not as great as those of Americans of European background. Socioeconomically, Asian Americans are distributed in bipolar fashion, with far more individuals at both the upper and lower ends of income brackets, and at higher and lower ends of occupational hierarchies. The class polarization within the Asian American population tends to mask the needs of the most recent immigrants at the low end of the socioeconomic scale. Not all Asian groups have been able to succeed. The most recent immigrants, particularly refugees, have a much more difficult adjustment process and suffer social and economic hardship which is often unrecognized by society in general. Asian Americans face structural barriers in the labor market, similar to those that confront women and other minorities. Those Asian Americans who have been able to successfully achieve middle- and upper- class status may find their advancements hindered by a "glass ceiling" limiting their movement into higher occupational levels. It is suggested that Asian Americans are unassertive and do not possess the leadership skills necessary to occupy high-level management positions, or positions requiring authority. Simply put, Asian Americans continue to be negatively stereotyped with respect to certain forms of gains (i.e., occupational mobility), but positively stereotyped (i.e., as a model minority) when it benefits institutions and dominant groups.

Perhaps the future of Asian ethnic groups in America lies in the formation of new identities and concepts of what constitutes the ethnic group. To be sure, it is not likely that Asian Americans will disappear as a racial category as one might expect with the classic European model of assimilation. As suggested by Espiritu, the discrete ethnic categories of Chinese, Japanese, Filipino, Korean, Vietnamese, and Asian Indian may blend to a pan-Asian identity, as long as there is a movement propelling the groups together. However, with new immigration from Asia, pan-Asian American unity might be difficult to achieve since many immigrants' identities are tied to a home country national identity. The future of Asian Americans will depend on how this new Asian American identity is constructed, how social institutions respond to Asian Americans as a group rather than individual ethnic groups, and how Asian Americans voice their political power in their overall incorporation into American society.

References

Agbayani-Siewert, Paula and Linda A. Revilla. (1995). "Filipino Americans." In Pyong Gap Min, ed., *Asian Americans: Contemporary Trends and Issues*. Thousand Oaks: Sage. Pp. 134–168.

Bonacich, Edna. 1973. "A Theory of Middleman Minorities." *American Sociological Review*. 38:583–594.

Bonacich, Edna and Ivan Light. 1988. *Immigrant Entrepreneurs: Koreans in Los Angeles, 1965-1982*. Berkeley: University of California Press.

Bonacich, Edna and John Modell. 1980. *The Economic Basis of Ethnic Solidarity: Small Business in the Japanese American Community*. Berkeley: University of California Press.

Chan, Sucheng. 1991. *Asian Americans: An Interpretive History*. Boston: Twayne.

Freeman, James M. and Usha Welaratna. 1993. "Success and Failures: Vietnamese and Cambodian Views of Adjustment in America." In Linda A. Revilla et al., eds., *Bearing Dreams, Shaping Visions*. Pullman, Washington: Washington State University Press. Pp. 93–100.

Kitano, Harry H.L., and Roger Daniels. 1995. *Asian Americans: Emerging Minorities*. Englewood Cliffs, NJ: Prentice Hall.

Leonard, Karen. 1991. *Making Ethnic Choices: California's Punjabi-Mexican Americans*. Philadelphia: Temple University Press.

Marable, Manning. 1994. "Beyond Racial Identity Politics: Toward a Liberation Theory for Multicultural Democracy." In Gary Y. Okihiro et. al., eds., *Privileging Positions The Sites of Asian American Studies*. Pullman, Washington: Washington State University Press. Pp. 315–334.

Min, Pyong Gap, ed. 1995. *Asian Americans: Contemporary Trends and Issues*. Thousand Oaks: Sage.

O'Hare, William P., and Judy Felt. 1991. "Asian Americans: America's Fastest Growing Minority." *Population Trends and Public Policy*, paper no. 19. Washington: Population Reference Bureau.

Portes, Alejandro and Robert D. Manning. 1986. "The Immigrant Enclave; Theory and Empirical Examples." In Susan Olzak and Joane Nagel, eds., *Comparative Ethnic Relations*. New York: Academic Press. Pp. 47–68.

Portes, Alejandro and Ruben G. Rumbaut. 1990. *Immigrant America: A Portrait*. Berkeley: University of California Press.

Rumbaut, Ruben G. 1995. "Vietnamese, Laotian, and Cambodian Americans." In Pyong Gap Min, ed., *Asian Americans: Contempo-rary Trends and Issues*. Thousand Oaks: Sage. Pp. 232–270.

Sheth, Manju. 1995. "Asian Indian Americans." In Pyong Gap Min, ed., *Asian Americans: Contemporary Trends and Issues*. Thousand Oaks: Sage. Pp. 169–198.

Takagi, Dana Y. 1992. *The Retreat From Race: Asian-American Admissions and Racial Politics*. New Brunswick, New Jersey: Rutgers University Press.

Takaki, Ronald. 1989. *Strangers From a Different Shore: A History of Asian Americans*. Boston: Little, Brown.

US Bureau of the Census. 1997. Current Population Survey: Selected Social Characteristics of the Population, March 1996. Released 12/9/97. Internet site: www.Census.gov/population/estimates/nation/intfile 3-1.txt. (Filenames: PE-10/PPL-57 and E9798 RMP.TXT).

11

The 'Success' Image of Asian Americans:

Its Validity, and Its Practical and Theoretical Implications

Won Moo Hurh
Kwang Chung Kim

Introduction

In an effort to lessen the spectre of the "Yellow Peril," the U.S. Congress passed the Chinese Exclusion Act and President Chester A. Arthur signed the bill on 6 May 1882. This law, which prohibited Chinese immigration to the United States until 1943, was an actual consequence of the negative Chinese image held by a majority of Americans (Isaacs 1962). These negative images, such as "Chinese deceit, cunning, idolatry, despotism, xenophobia, cruelty, infanticide, and intellectual and sexual perversity," were already reflected in the public media prior to the arrival of the first wave of Chinese labourers to California in 1848 (Miller 1969, p. 201). The early Chinese immigrants were initially received as "exotic curiosities" but this soon changed to "unassimilable, immoral, treacherous heathens" who would take away whites' jobs and possibly also their women (Lyman 1970; Sue and Kitano 1973). This unfavourable perception of Chinese immigrants was later extended to Japanese, Korean, and Filipino immigrants and then persisted for a century with little modification.

However, in 1982, the centennial year of the Chinese Exclusion Act of 1882, *Newsweek* published an article entitled, "Asian-Americans: A 'Model Minority,'" conveying a posi-

tive image of Chinese, Japanese, Koreans, and Vietnamese in the United States:

> Despite years of discrimination—much of it enforced by the federal government—the difficulties of acculturation and a recent backlash against their burgeoning numbers, Asian-Americans now enjoy the nation's highest median family income: $22,075 a year compared with $20,840 for whites. The Chinese have a term for it—"gung-ho"—and the industrious Asians believe they are contributing a needed shot of some vanishing American values: thrift, strong family ties, sacrifice for the children. (*Newsweek*, 6 December 1982, p. 39)

The dominant group's perception of racial and ethnic minorities usually fluctuates over time depending on the vicissitudes of international relations, the national socio-economic structure, the dominant group's cultural values, and the minority's adaptive capacities. However, the amplitude of recent changes in majority Americans' perception of Asian Americans has certainly been dramatic.

What factors would account for this change? To what extent is the success image of Asian Americans true? How would such a model-minority image affect Asian Americans, the other minorities (black and Mexican Americans), and majority Americans themselves?

The debate on the success image of Asian Americans is certainly not a new issue. Since the mid-1960s a considerable number of scholarly works have been published, either supporting or rejecting the validity of the success image (for details on this polemic issue, see Chun 1980; Kim and Hurh 1983). Beyond the question of the validity, however, this article purports to explore practical and theoretical implications of the dominant group's positive labelling of a racial/ethnic minority.

Majority Americans' Image of Asian Americans: An Historical Overview

. . . Asian Americans have . . . been a target for severe prejudice and discrimination. Ironically, much of the past discriminatory practices have been legitimized by the U.S.

Congress and federal government (institutional racism). Anti-Asian legislation was, however, largely a consequence of majority Americans' negative stereotypes of Asians. For example, the Immigration Act of 1924 grew out of the anti-Oriental image held by whites, especially by those who resided on the west coast. This law has thus been commonly known as the Oriental Exclusion Act. In other words, Anglo-Americans' negative images (stereotypes) of Chinese and Japanese were largely confirmed by national and state institutions.

In general, ethnic stereotypes are exaggerated images of the characteristics of a particular ethnic group (Schaefer 1984, p. 63; cf. Brigham 1971). In Walter Lippmann's terms, stereotypes are "pictures in our heads" which may be either negative or positive, or relatively true or false (Lippmann 1922; Ogawa 1971, pp. 2-3). They are simplified, time-saving, and convenient devices often used by the dominant group to sort out "bad guys" from "good guys" or vice versa, and in so doing one can label, isolate, confine, or exclude a particular defenseless minority group. In this respect, verbalized stereotypes anticipate and often bring actual consequences: a typical case of self-fulfilling prophecy. . . .

The majority of Americans' image of "Orientals" has fluctuated over time, reflecting the changes in international relations and in socio-economic and political conditions of the United States. As Sue and Kitano (1973) observe, the early negative image of Chinese reflects America's economic problems and unemployment in the late 1800s. The negative image which was extended later to Japanese became worse in 1940, reflecting the U.S. involvement in World War II. During that war the Chinese image was somewhat improved as China was an American ally, but soon after the war the image became ambivalent due to the establishment of the Peoples' Republic of China in 1949 (Lyman 1974, pp. 119-133). As Yee (1973, p. 103) put it, American perception of Chinese fluctuated back and forth; but generally, the past negative image of the Asian population in the United States has been transformed into a positive one, especially in the 1960s.

The change in the majority Americans' image of Asian Americans may largely be attributed to the professionalization and upward social mobility of young Chinese and Japanese Americans who were generally American-born and college-educated (Lyman 1974, p. 119). Moreover, the influx of college-educated immigrants from Korea, the Philippines, Taiwan, Hong Kong and India since the revision of the U.S. immigration law in 1965 reinforced the positive image of Asian Americans. Another significant factor in accentuating the success image of Asian Americans was the Civil Rights movement in the 1960s. As Chun (1980, p. 2) correctly observes, "at that time [in the sixties], when the nation was still groping for solutions to its racial unrest, the portrayal of Asian Americans as a successful minority seemed to serve a need": the need to blame blacks and other disadvantaged minorities for their own failure and the nation's "race problems." In 1966, the success image of Japanese and Chinese Americans was conveyed to the American public by *New York Times Magazine* (January 9) and *U.S. News & World Report* (December 26). Nowadays, the success image is extended to other Asians, such as Koreans, Filipinos, Vietnamese and Asian Indians (*Newsweek* 1982; *Time* 1985). Thus "unassimilable heathens" became "successful model minorities" in about 100 years. . . . The validity and implications of the success image of Asian Americans will be examined next.

Validity of the Asian-American 'Success' Image

As mentioned earlier, Asian Americans' success stories began to appear in the American popular press in the mid-1960s. . . . Although the success theme includes a stereotype about the Asian American problem-free family and community life, most of the past studies on Asian Americans focused their attention on the socio-economic status that Asian Americans achieved in comparison with that of the dominant group (particularly white males). In such a conceptual framework, Asian Americans would be considered "successful," if the level of their socio-economic achievement reached or exceeded that of whites. The socio-economic achievement is then empirically measured by the following indices: (1) education (the mean or median years of schooling or the proportion of those who completed high school or college education); (2) occupation (the mean occupational prestige or the proportion of those who are employed in technical or professional occupations or in white collar occupations as a whole); and (3) earnings (family or individual).

By the above measures, Asian Americans are generally found to have been successful. Japanese Americans have achieved a level of education similar to that of whites since the early 1940s (Fogel 1966). Since 1960, both native- and foreign-born Chinese Americans have achieved the level of education equal to, or even higher than, that of whites (Hirschman and Wong 1981). According to the 1980 census data, both native- and foreign-born Filipinos and the immigrants from Korea and India also exhibit a high level of education. . . .

In terms of economic achievement, prior to World War II, a high proportion of Japanese and Chinese Americans were in small business. The small business tradition had changed little during the war, although the wartime relocation reduced the number of Japanese small businesses. In the post-war period, a high proportion of young Japanese and Chinese Americans gained access to technical or professional occupations through their higher education. Due to such an increased access to technical or professional occupations and continued participation in small business, a higher proportion of Japanese and Chinese Americans have been employed in white collar occupations than have whites (Hirschman and Wong 1981). Today Koreans and other Asian immigrants tend to show a similar occupational distribution. In these conditions, our sample estimation from the 1980 census reveals that the occupational prestige scores of many Asian male groups are on the average higher than those of white males (cf. Stevens and Cho 1985).

The high proportion of Asian Americans in white collar occupations and their high rate of labour-force participation resulted in a relatively high family income in the past (Urban Associates 1974; Wu 1980). The 1980 census confirms this point again. . . . [F]our of the six largest Asian ethnic groups (Japanese, Chinese, Filipinos and Asian Indians) maintain a higher mean annual family income than white families. Another Asian group (Koreans) is very close to whites in their family income. Even in their annual mean individual earnings, three Asian ethnic groups (Japanese, Chinese and Asian Indians) exceed those of whites. . . .

[However,] minority members may pay a higher price than whites for achieving a given level of status. It is, therefore, necessary to examine additionally the relative amount of investment made or price paid by minority members, when the nature of their socio-economic achievement is empirically tested.

Family income eloquently illustrates this point. As already reviewed, many Asian Americans have higher family incomes than whites; however, the Asian families are likely to pay a disproportionately higher price for it. Chun (1980, p. 4) states this issue as follows:

> [Asian Americans'] high income may be the result of longer work hours or sacrificed weekends. It follows that for the household income to be a usable index for purposes of group comparison, one has to make adjustments for the number of wage earners and the number of hours worked. In addition, since education is known to be a substantial contributor to occupational mobility as well as higher income, the level of wage income should be adjusted at least for wage earner's education.

. . . Asian Americans can be considered as "successful," only if (1) they pay a price equal to that paid by whites for the same level of achievement, or (2) Asian Americans achieve a higher level of status than whites with a proportionally higher level of price paid by Asian Americans. Conversely, Asian Americans cannot be considered "successful" under the following conditions: . . . (a) the level of Asian achievement is equal to that of whites, but Asians pay a higher price than whites; (b) whites and Asians are equal in the price paid, but Asians achieve less than whites; (c) Asians achieve a higher level of status, but Asians pay disproportionately a higher price than whites; and (d) Asians achieve less than whites, but Asians pay a higher price than whites. In all of these cases the reward (achievement) rate per unit of cost (investment) is smaller for Asian Americans than for whites. The existence of such a differential rate of reward would demonstrate that Asian Americans experience disadvantaged discrimination or inequality in the achievement of socio-economic status. As long as they are disadvantaged or discriminated against, they cannot be considered successful regardless of the level of their achievement. Chun (1980, p. 3) expresses this point succinctly as follows:

> If members of a minority group view education as the only means of social mobility and invest heavily in their children's college education at a disproportionate sacrifice to family finances, should that college education be regarded necessarily as a sign of success of this group?

. . . [When adjusted for variations in education, occupational prestige, weeks worked, etc.,] the earnings ratio of foreign-born Asian males in general (except Japanese) ranges from .68 to .89, revealing the fact that they earn less than white males under the equivalent condition of investment. Moreover, the earnings ratio of foreign-born Asian males is not generally better than that of non-Asian minorities, such as black and Mexican Americans. At this point we must also emphasize the fact that foreign-born Asian males are found to be placed in the American labour market quite differently from other minority (non-Asian) males—the former's original earnings are greater than their adjusted earnings, whereas the reverse is true for the latter. This means, for foreign-born Asian males, their earnings inequity problems largely derive from the discriminatory mechanism of the American labour market; whereas for non-Asian minority males, their earnings problems involve both labour market barriers and a relative lack of human capital.

A surprisingly high earnings ratio of foreign-born Japanese males may indicate that they are occupationally more associated with the export-oriented Japanese economy than the U.S. economy (Nee and Sanders 1985). . . .

The investment factors important to American workers do not seem to explain effectively the earnings of these Japanese foreign-born workers.

The earnings ratio of native-born Japanese, Chinese and Filipino males is higher than that of foreign-born males in their own ethnic groups; however, these native-born Asian males still earn less than white males under the equivalent condition of investment. This finding concurs with the observation made by Hirschman and Wong (1981, p. 507).

> . . . native-born Japanese, Chinese and Filipino men . . . have average earnings roughly equivalent to or higher than white men. However, since the backgrounds of Asian American men (education and occupation) are generally higher than that of whites, parity of earnings does not indicate similarity of the earnings determination process.

Regardless of their racial or ethnic status, the earnings ratio of female workers is uniformly lower than that of their male counterparts in their respective racial or ethnic group. This pattern suggests that female workers' problems of severe earnings inequity derive from their gender status rather than from their racial or ethnic status. No wonder the earnings ratio of white females is no better than that of other females. Therefore these facts do not support the contention that minority female workers are doubly disadvantaged.

The preceding findings concerning Asian Americans are hardly surprising, when their labour market experiences are reviewed. In spite of their high education, Asian Americans are repeatedly found to have experienced a great deal of difficulty in getting jobs commensurate with their education. . . . Under these circumstances, overqualification for their jobs or underutilization of their education (underemployment) has been the most persistent and serious occupational problem for both native- and foreign-born Asian Americans (Kim 1982; Li 1980). We thus observe from the 1980 census data that Asian Americans still earn less than whites despite an additional year of schooling.

Due to such problems of underemployment and other labour market barriers, Asian Americans are generally employed in relatively unfavourable conditions. Our study of Korean immigrants in the Los Angeles area (Hurh and Kim 1984) shows that Korean immigrants are clustered into the following three types of occupations: (1) self-employed small business; (2) other white-collar occupations; and (3) low-skilled manual or service occupations. Korean small businesses are heavily concentrated in their own ethnic community or in the difficult markets of other minority communities (Bonacich and Jung 1982). In this situation, the owner-operators of small business and their family members work for unusually long hours under an intensive competitive pressure (Hurh and Kim 1984; Kim and Hurh 1985). For business survival, they are also forced to take a variety of physical and economic risks.

Those Koreans in the other two types of occupations indicate that the majority of their work colleagues are minority workers, including Koreans or a combination of minority and white workers. The Korean workers employed in such a situation are found to be paid less than those who work mainly with white workers. What this study reveals is that the majority of Korean immigrants either hold inferior occupations and/or work in unfavourable conditions. . . .

Chinese Americans are highly polarized into two types of occupations: (1) those in low-skilled manual or service occupations and (2) those in technical or professional occupations (Ng 1977; Tsai 1980; Wu 1980). Workers in the first type suffer from a variety of severe labour market disadvantages. Even those in the second type are found to face serious career problems as stated below:

> That is to say, although education may have enabled Chinese Americans to enter certain professional and technical occupations that require special and often lengthy training, they tend to be paid less once in these occupations. Because the ceiling of their potential attainment seems to be fixed at a lower level over their entire careers, they are on the whole "underutilized." One might say that they

run less risk of "rising to their level of incompetence." (Wu 1980, p. 54)

Such career problems are not unique to Chinese Americans. In general, Asian Americans are excluded from positions of power and influence, and are thus concentrated in low-ranked positions (Kuo 1979). . . .

Three important conclusions may be drawn from the preceding analysis of the labour market experiences of Asian Americans. First, the common measurement of the Asian Americans' "success" which does not test the investment aspect of Asian Americans' socioeconomic status is conceptually too simplistic and thus distorts the complex reality of Asian Americans' labour market experiences. As a result, this simplistic approach remains blind to Asians' experience of disadvantage, discrimination or inequity, while it promotes the Asian success image.

Second, the success theme has been indiscriminately applied to both native- and foreign-born Asian Americans. It has been observed, however, that the two groups of Asians are subject to different processes of earnings allocation. They should therefore be separately treated in future research, especially when the majority of certain Asian groups are foreign born, such as Koreans, Indo-Chinese, and Asian Indians. Third, regardless of their ethnic status, the native-born Asian males are still relatively more disadvantaged than white males. . . .

Implication of the Success Stereotype

Practical Consequence

. . . In contrast to the rosy picture portrayed in the success literature, the cost of being a model minority seems to be higher than the benefit for the following reasons. First, Asian Americans are considered by the dominant group as "successful" and "problem free" and not in need of social programmes designed to benefit disadvantaged minorities such as black and Mexican Americans. As the U.S. Commission on Civil Rights (1980, p. 19) aptly put it: "If a minority group is viewed as successful, it is unlikely that its members will be included in programmes designed to alleviate problems they encounter as minorities." A number of cases of official inattention to the problems and needs of Asian Americans have already been reported in public documents and scholarly publications (U.S. Commission on Civil Rights 1977, 1979, and 1980; Kim, Bok-Lim 1973, 1978; Kim, E. H. 1975; Kitano and Sue 1973). . . .

Suffice to say that the success image serves a negative function which is to ignore the real problems and needs of Asian Americans, such as unemployment, poverty and mental illness among the elderly, and increasing rates of divorce and juvenile delinquency (Kim, Bok-Lim 1973, 1978). . . .

Another negative function of the success image deals with disguised underemployment and the development of a "false consciousness" among Asian Americans. We have already discussed the problem of disguised underemployment which gives not only a false image of Asian Americans' success to the dominant group but also develops an illusion of status attainment among Asian Americans themselves. Despite underemployment, Asian Americans tend to accept the dominant group's definition of success in order to minimize their feelings of relative deprivation and discontentment. As the feminine stereotype "normalizes" women's underemployment in the American society (institutional sexism), the "hardwork/success" image about Asian Americans has routinized their underemployment (institutional racism). In other words, underemployment is a "normal" or "usual" price Asian Americans have been paying for their "success"—the attainment of the middle-class status. . . . For example, our study of the Korean immigrants in the Los Angeles area reveals that the general level of Korean immigrants' life satisfaction is rather high in spite of their pervasive underemployment (Hurh and Kim 1984). The American social structure of ethnic confinement (social and occupational) limits the range of the immigrants' socio-economic opportunities, and the immigrants' perception of such structural limitations (including their own cultural handicap) would tend to lower the levels of their aspirations. As a consequence, they may feel relatively satisfied with their immigrant life in spite of an objectively

apparent status inconsistency in the new country (Hurh and Kim 1980, 1984: 138–55). . . .

The dominant group's stereotype of Asian Americans as a model minority also affects negatively other minorities. Since the Asian Americans' "success" may be considered by the dominant group as a proof of openness in the American opportunity structure, there is a constant danger that other less successful minorities could be regarded as "inferior" and/or "lazy." These less achieving minorities may be blamed for their own failure and become victims of scapegoating ("Japanese have made it. Why can't they?"). Such effects of the Asian American success image on other minorities have not been studied empirically. The probable effects may be summarized as follows: (1) incorrect perception of Asian Americans' upward mobility; (2) an increased sense of relative deprivation; and (3) a feeling of *ressentiment* against Asian Americans (Yu, 1980). The last aspect has recently become increasingly problematic since a large number of Asian Americans, especially Korean immigrants, are engaged in small businesses in black and Mexican American communities. . . . Moreover, there seems to be a resurgence in anti-Asian sentiment and activities among whites—across the nation in the form of violence, vandalism, harassment and intimidation. The evidence collected by the U.S. Commission on Civil Rights (1986, p. 58) suggests that "one factor contributing to anti-Asian activity is economic competition between recent refugees and immigrants and other persons in the same community."

Finally, the practical consequences of the Asian success image on the dominant group encompass all the afore-mentioned functions of the stereotype: (1) exclusion of Asian Americans from social programmes supported by public and private agencies (benefit-denying/fund-saving function); (2) disguise of Asian Americans' underemployment (institutional racism promoting function); (3) justification of the American open social system (system preserving function); (4) displacement of the system's fault to less-achieving minorities (victim blaming function); and (5) anti-Asian sentiment and activities (*res-

sentiment reinforcing function). Most of these functions may not have been intended . . . nevertheless the consequences are real. . . .

References

Bonacich, Edna, and Tae Hwan Jung. 1982. "A portrait of Korean small business in Los Angeles, 1977," in Eui-Young Yu, Earl H. Phillip and Eun Sik Yang (eds.), *Koreans in Los Angeles: Prospects and Promises*, Los Angeles: Koryo Research Institute and Center for Korean-American and Korean Studies, California State University, pp. 75–98.

Brigham, John C. 1971. "Ethnic stereotypes," *Psychological Bulletin*, vol. 76, no. 1, pp. 15–38.

Chun, Ki-Taek. 1980. "The myth of Asian American success and its educational ramifications," *IRCD Bulletin* (A Publication of the Institute for Urban and Minority Education, Teachers College, Columbia University), vol. 15, no. 1, pp. 1–12.

Fogel, Walter. 1966. "The effects of low educational attainment on income: A comparative study of selected ethnic groups," *Journal of Human Resources*, vol. 1, no. 2, pp. 22–40.

Hirschman, Charles, and Morrison G. Wong. 1981. "Trends in socio-economic achievement among immigrant and native-born Asian Americans," *Sociological Quarterly*, vol. 22, no. 4, pp. 495–514.

Hurh, Won Moo, and Kwang Chung Kim. 1980. "The process of Korean immigrants' adaptation in the U.S.: Length of residence and life satisfaction," a paper presented at the annual meeting, American Sociological Association, New York, August 27–31.

——. 1984. *Korean Immigrants in America: A Structural Analysis of Ethnic Confinement and Adhesive Adaptation*, Madison, NJ: Fairleigh Dickinson University Press.

Isaacs, Harold R. 1962. *Images of Asia: American view of China and India*, New York: Capricorn Books.

Kim, Bok-Lim. 1973. "Asian Americans: no model minority," *Social Work*, vol. 18, no. 2, pp. 44–53.

——. 1978. *The Asian Americans: Changing Patterns, Changing Needs*, Montclair, NJ: Association for Korean Christian Scholars in North America.

Kim, Elaine H. 1975. "The myth of Asian American success," *Asian American Review*, vol. 2, no. 1, pp. 122–49.

Kim, Kwang Chung, and Won Moo Hurh. 1983. "Korean Americans and the 'success' image: a critique," *Amerasia*, vol. 10, no. 2, pp. 3–21.

——. 1985. "Ethnic resources utilization of Korean immigrant entrepreneurs in the Chicago minority area," *International Migration Review*, vol. 19, no. 1, pp. 82–111.

Kim, Sukja Paik. 1982. "Underemployment of recent Asian immigrants: Koreans in Los Angeles," unpublished Ph.D. dissertation, Virginia Commonwealth University, Richmond, Virginia.

Kitano, Harry H. L., and Stanley Sue. 1973. "The model minorities," *Journal of Social Issues*, vol. 29, no. 2, pp. 1–9.

Kuo, Wen H. 1979. "On the study of Asian Americans: Its current state and agenda," *Sociological Quarterly*, vol. 20, no. 2, pp. 279–90.

Li, Angelina H. 1980. *Labor Utilization and the Assimilation of Asian Americans*, Springfield, VA: National Technical Information Service, U.S. Department of Commerce.

Lippmann, Walter. 1922. *Public Opinion*, New York: Harcourt, Brace.

Lyman, Stanford M. 1970. *The Asians in the West*, Reno, NV: Desert Research Institute.

——. 1974. *Chinese Americans*, New York: Random House.

Miller, Stuart C. 1969. *The Unwelcome Immigrant: The American Image of the Chinese, 1885–1982*, Berkeley, California: University of California Press.

Nee, Victor, and Jimy Sanders. 1985. "The road to parity: determinants of the socio-economic achievements of Asian Americans," *Ethnic and Racial Studies*, vol. 8, no. 1, pp. 75–93.

New York Times Magazine. 1966. "Success story, Japanese American style," January 9: 38.

Newsweek. 1982. "Asian-Americans: A 'model minority,'" December 6, pp. 39–51.

Ng, Wing-Cheung. 1977. "An evaluation of the labor market status of Chinese Americans," *Amerasia*, vol. 4, no. 1, pp. 101–22.

Ogawa, Dennis M. 1971. *From Japs to Japanese: The Evolution of Japanese American Stereotypes*, Berkeley: McCutchan Publishing Co.

Schaefer, Richard T. 1984. *Racial and Ethnic Groups*, 2nd ed., Boston, MA: Little, Brown.

Stevens, Gillian, and Joo Hyun Cho. 1985. "Socioeconomic indexes and the new 1980 census occupational classification scheme," *Social Science Research*, vol. 14, no. 2, pp. 142–68.

Sue, Stanley and Harry H. Kitano. 1973. "Stereotypes as a measure of success," *Journal of Social Issues*, vol. 29, no. 2, pp. 83–98.

Time. 1985. "To America with skills: a wave of arrivals from the Far East enriches the country's talent pool," July 8, pp. 43–6.

Tsai, Frank Wen-Hui. 1980. "Diversity and conflict between old and new Chinese immigrants in the United States," in Roy Simon Bryce-Laporte (ed.) *Sourcebook on the New Immigration*, New Brunswick, NJ: Transaction Books, pp. 329–37.

Urban Associates, Inc. 1974. *A Study of Selected Socio-Economic Characteristics of Ethnic Minorities Based on the 1970 Census, vol. 11. Asian Americans*, Arlington, VA: Urban Associates, Inc.

U.S. Commission On Civil Rights. 1977. *The Forgotten Minority: Asian Americans in New York City*, Washington, DC: U.S. Government Printing Office.

——. 1979. *Civil Rights Issues of Asian and Pacific Americans: Myths and Realities*, Washington, DC: U.S. Government Printing Office.

——. 1980. *Success of Asian Americans: Fact or Fiction?* Washington, DC: U.S. Government Printing Office.

——. 1986. *Recent Activities Against Citizens and Residents of Asian Descent*, Washington, DC: U.S. Government Printing Office.

U.S. News & World Report. 1966. "Success Story of one minority group in U.S.," December 26, p. 73. York: Basic Books.

Wu, Yuan-Li (ed.). 1980. *The Economic Condition of Chinese Americans*, Chicago: Pacific/Asian American Mental Health Center.

Yee, Albert H. 1973. "Myopic perceptions and textbooks: Chinese Americans' search for identity," *Journal of Social Issues*, vol, 29, no, 2. pp. 99–113.

Yu, Jin H. 1980. *The Korean Merchants in the Black Community*, Elkins Park, PA: Philip Jaisohn Foundation.

Reprinted from: Won Moo Hurh and Kwang Chung Kim, "The 'Success' Image of Asian Americans: Its Validity, and Its Practical and Theoretical Implications." In *Ethnic and Racial Studies*, Volume 12, Number 4, pp. 512–538. Copyright © 1989 by Routledge. Reprinted by permission.

12

The Growth of Korean Immigrant Entrepreneurship in Chicago

In-Jin Yoon

Introduction

Contemporary Korean immigrant entrepreneurship departs from the traditional patterns of immigrant entrepreneurship in several important respects. First, unlike previous immigrant groups (for example, the Chinese at the turn of the century), who were mostly uneducated, and from rural and low-class origins, recent Korean immigrants are mostly well educated, urban, and of middle-class backgrounds. Because of their greater human capital compared with that of their predecessors, recent Korean immigrants are likely to take a more individualistic approach to establishing and maintaining businesses (Light 1984). Second, traditional social relations based on extended kinship and region of origin have little influence on Korean immigrant businesses. Instead, modern ethnic institutions such as Korean immigrant newspapers, Korean Christian churches, and business associations play important roles in Korean immigrant businesses (I. Kim 1981). Third, economic development in South Korea and international trade between the United States and South Korea provided the initial business opportunities for Korean immigrants (I. Kim 1981; Min 1988).

From 1962 on, South Korea started an export-oriented economic development that was highly dependent on foreign markets, especially those of the United States and Japan. In the early period, cheap consumer goods such as clothing, footwear, wigs and travel bags were the major export items. Korean immigrants imported Korean-made products and distributed them to Korean retailers in minority areas of large cities. This international trade linkage among Korean manufacturers, importers and retailers provided Korean immigrants with a competitive edge over other ethnic members who did not have similar advantages. Fourth, unlike previous immigrant groups who started businesses from their protected ethnic markets and then expanded into open markets servicing the non-ethnic population, Korean immigrants started businesses in minority areas from the outset. As will be explained, Korean immigrant businesses developed both in Korean ethnic markets and in non-ethnic minority markets almost simultaneously.

In this article, I shall first explain how Korean immigrant entrepreneurship has evolved in Chicago. Second, I shall describe an ethnic succession of businesses in Chicago's minority areas to explain how changes in urban patterns of U.S. cities have facilitated the entrance of Korean businesses into minority areas. Finally, I shall explain how Korean immigrants mobilize class, family and ethnicity in establishing and maintaining small businesses.

Review of the Literature

. . . Three factors are singled out as key variables in explaining why certain immigrant and ethnic groups participate in small businesses at high rates while others do not: (1) employment opportunity structures in the general labour market; (2) business opportunity structures; and (3) the relative organizing capacity of members of an immigrant or ethnic group to mobilize resources (Kim, Hurh, and Fernandez 1989; Waldinger, Aldrich, and Ward 1990; Yoon 1991). . . .

In this interactive model of immigrant and ethnic entrepreneurship, each factor is a necessary condition of business participation, but is not sufficient in its own right. For example, business opportunities have little relevance to an individual who does not possess resources to take advantage of available business opportunities. By the same token, resources increase a person's likelihood of being self-employed only when self-employment is a desired goal for that person. The desirability of self-employment is, in turn, largely determined by a person's employment opportunities in the general labour market. For that reason, immigrants, who are often more disadvantaged than U.S.-born citizens in the labour market, have stronger incentives of becoming independent business owners.

The types of resources and the ways in which immigrants and ethnic members mobilize them in relation to business opportunities depend in part on their individual background characteristics and in part on their cultural heritage (for example, rotating credit associations). For theoretical purposes, I divide these resources into three types, "ethnic resources," "class resources" and "family resources."

Ethnic resources are defined as "resources and forms of aid preferentially available from members of one's own ethnic group or derived from the ethnic group's heritage" (Min and Jaret 1984, p. 432). Ethnic resources are roughly equally available to all members of an ethnic group who share a common origin and culture and actively participate in shared activities where common origin and culture are important ingredients. Ethnic resources may be material (for example, financial aid), informative (for example, business advice), or experiential (for example, job training). Ethnic customers, ethnic employees and suppliers, ethnic media and publications and ethnic social organizations can all be considered ethnic resources.

In contrast, class resources are "private property in the means of production and distribution, wealth, and investments in human capital" (Light 1985, p. 173). Class resources are available only to members of an ethnic group whose social and economic position in society enabled them to invest in human capital or to be endowed with these resources from their parents. Class resources may include education, wealth and occupational skills and experiences.

Finally, family resources are defined as resources and any forms of support from one's immediate family members who are related to the individual by birth, marriage or family lineage. Financial aid, business advice, or labour from immediate family members can be considered family resources. Thus, theoreti-

---

Table 12.1
Typology of Korean Businesses

Origin of supply	Ethnicity of customers	
	Korean	Other
	I	II
South Korea	**Korean-oriented business** Korean food and gift stores; travel agencies; newspapers and book stores; Korean video rental stores.	**Minority-oriented business** Wig stores; clothing stores; footwear stores; miscellaneous general merchandise stores.
	III	V
United States	**Ethnic professional business** Accounting, legal, and health services; real estate and insurance brokers; auto repairs and auto dealers.	**Majority-oriented business** Fruit and vegetable stores; dry-cleaning and laundry stores; snack shops; gas stations; garment subcontractors.

Note: Adopted from I. Kim, *The New Urban Immigrants*, 1981, p. 105, and modified to fit Korean businesses in Chicago.

cally we can distinguish three types of resources: (1) ethnic resources from the non-kin members of one's co-ethnic groups; (2) class resources from individual human capital; and (3) family resources from immediate family members.

The distinction of the three types of resources is not clear-cut and is subject to judgment, but the distinction is still useful in analyzing how immigrant and ethnic businesses are organized and how their organizational patterns differ from one group to another. If groups differ in the types and magnitudes of resources, this fact may provide us with a key to understanding why certain groups are successful in entrepreneurial careers while others are not.

Data and Methodology

The primary data for this case-study came from field observations and interviews with 103 Korean business owners in black neighbourhoods in the west and south of Chicago and with ninety-six Korean business owners in the northwest of Chicago, which is usually called "Koreatown of Chicago." Interviews with the former group were completed between September and October 1987, and with the latter group between November 1987 and May 1988.

A Historical Overview of Korean Immigrant Businesses in Chicago

Korean businesses in Chicago can be broadly classified as four types of cells by interrelating the following two factors: (1) whether the customers are Koreans or members of other ethnic groups; (2) whether the products and services originate in South Korea or in the United States. [See Table 12.1]

The businesses in the first cell developed from the demand of Korean immigrants for their cultural products (for example, Korean food and Korean movies). These businesses concentrate on the Korean community and offer fast and convenient service for the needs of Koreans. I call these businesses "Korean-oriented businesses." The businesses in the third cell developed from the international trade between the United States and

Figure 12.1
Korean Business Concentration Areas in Chicago

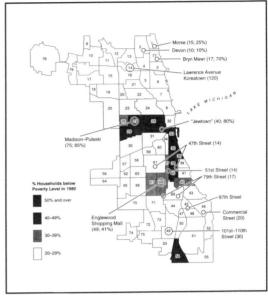

Source: The *Korean Times of Chicago*, 1986. The Chicago community poverty areas map was adopted from William J. Wilson, *The Truly Disadvantaged*, 1987, 52.

Note: In parentheses are the number (and sometimes the percentage) of Korean stores in each KBCA.

South Korea. These businesses sell Korean-made consumer goods in minority areas of large cities. Low-income blacks and Hispanics are the major customers of these businesses. I call these businesses "minority-oriented businesses."

The above two types of Korean businesses were the first Korean businesses to be established in Chicago and continue to be the backbone of Korean businesses. The same pattern is generally true in other large cities such as Los Angeles and New York where Koreans are concentrated (I. Kim 1981; Kim and Hurh 1985; Light and Bonacich 1988; Min 1988).

The businesses in the second cell developed from the demand of Korean immigrants for professional and technical service. These businesses are usually run by Korean immigrants who came to study at American universities and earned professional licenses in their specialty. I call these businesses "ethnic professional businesses." The businesses in the fourth cell do not have any economic connection with either Korean customers or South Korea. Instead, they cater for the general, non-Korean population, providing them with products and services at low cost. I call these businesses "majority-oriented businesses."

In this study I shall focus on the businesses in the first and third cells, "Korean-oriented businesses" and "minority-oriented businesses," because they were the entry points of Korean immigrants into small businesses in Chicago.

Ethnic Succession of Businesses in Minority Areas

Areas of Korean business concentration in Chicago's west and south sides had been dominated by Jewish and Italian business owners until the early 1970s. The process of ethnic succession of businesses well illustrated in the following case-studies of three Korean business concentration areas: "Madison-Pulaski Shopping District," "Englewood Shopping Mall" and "Jewtown" [see Figure 12.1 for geographic locations of Korean business concentration areas in Chicago].

The "Madison-Pulaski Shopping District," located at the intersection of Madison and Pulaski Roads, is the biggest Korean business concentration area in Chicago's black areas. In 1986 there were 75 Korean stores in the area, accounting for [77] percent of a total of 98 stores. The shopping district, which used to be called "the downtown of blacks," had been dominated by Italian and Jewish business owners until Korean immigrants came into the area in the early 1970s. The exploding demand of blacks for wigs at that time, however, enabled Korean business to enter the area and flourish. One former wig store owner in the area recalled that he made money as though he were grabbing leaves scattered on the ground. Because business was so good, he did not have time to count his takings at the site. He dumped the money into a laundry bag and spent the night counting all the money he had earned during the day. As the demand for wigs declined in the mid-1970s, however, Korean business owners changed their wig business to one of clothing or general merchandise. As a result, by 1986 clothing (thirty-one), general merchandise (thirty), and footwear (eight) constituted the majority of Korean businesses in the area.

The "Englewood Shopping Mall," located at 63rd and Halsted Streets, was constructed as part of the Chicago South Areas Redevelopment Project in 1966. Shortly after the construction of the Mall, businesses in the Mall were almost monopolized by the Jews. In 1968 a Korean wig dealer opened a wig store in black areas. He made huge profits in the wig business during the late 1960s and early 1970s and his success attracted into the Mall a growing number of Korean business owners in the mid-1970s and early 1980s. In 1986 there were twenty clothing stores, seventeen general merchandise stores, ten footwear stores, and two snack shops, accounting for 40 percent of the 120 stores in the Mall.

"Jewtown," located at Halsted and Maxwell Streets, is the Korean business concentration area nearest to downtown Chicago. "Jewtown" was the centre of the Jewish business community at the turn of the century. Jewish business owners dominated the area in the late 1960s even though it had become a residential area for blacks, Hispanics and Italians by the 1940s. In 1971 a Korean immigrant opened the first Korean wig and clothing store in the area. From the mid-1970s, Koreans began to take over Jewish stores, and by 1986 the number of Korean businesses increased to thirty-seven, accounting for 80 percent of a total of forty-six in the area.

The above three black areas had been residential areas for various ethnic groups: Germans, Irish and Scandinavians had occupied those areas between the early 1850s and late 1890s. Italians and Russian Jews replaced the older immigrant groups in the late 1890s. As early as the 1900s, the three areas became the centre of Jewish and Italian businesses. For example, the Englewood shopping area was the second busiest commercial area in Chicago at that time (Chicago Fact Book Consortium 1984).

Blacks began to move into the areas in the 1950s and by 1980 constituted more than 90 percent of the population. The migration of blacks into the areas coincided with a series of events that eventually led to a decline in the prosperity of the areas. Racial changes there led to the exodus of white residents in the 1960s. Out-migration of whites naturally gave rise to the interethnic succession of businesses from the early 1970s. However, the business succession was slower than the residential succession, because Jewish and Italian business owners remained in these racially transient areas even after their ethnic groups had moved to the north and northwest parts of Chicago.

Most of the Jewish and Italian business owners in black areas were said to be first-generation immigrants, and were not replaced by their children or subsequent co-ethnic immigrants. As Waldinger (1986) points out, children of first-generation Jewish or Italian immigrants, who often receive a college education, tend to establish themselves as professional and white-collar workers. As European ethnics seek out salaried employment, they set up a vacancy chain.

In addition to the interethnic residential succession, civil disorders of the 1960s in black areas were responsible for the exodus of white businesses from black areas (Aldrich and Reiss, Jr. 1970). Faced with a rising crime rate, decreasing profitability, and surrounded by blacks who were hostile to white businesses, white business owners had a strong desire to move to another location. Thus, before Korean immigrants entered black areas to open their businesses, the combination of the changing ethnic composition and civil disorder left a vacancy in business opportunities in black areas.

Korean immigrants as a recent immigrant group did not meet severe discrimination and resistance from local black residents—at least initially. In fact, one of the important reasons for Koreans to site their businesses in black areas was the lower level of discrimination and hostility against Koreans in those areas compared with white areas. Blacks were perceived by Koreans to be simple and easy to please, whereas whites were seen to look down on Koreans. Some of the respondents of this study attributed the mild attitudes of blacks towards Koreans to the sharing of the common minority status in a white-dominated society. The mild reception of Koreans by blacks might also be due to the uncertainty among blacks of how to react to these new immigrants. Thus, although the attitude of blacks towards Koreans has deteriorated in recent years, Koreans—at least when they first entered black areas—were not subject to the same level of antipathy and rejection as Jewish and Italian business owners faced.

While the most competitive, lower-status fields were abandoned, the higher-profit, more difficult-to-enter lines often retained their previous ethnic entrepreneurs. By the 1970s Jews and Italians remaining in businesses became building owners, wholesalers or importers. Many Korean retailers in black areas now depend on Jewish wholesalers, especially in the shoe-repairing and the dry-cleaning and laundry businesses. In 1985 there were 170 Korean shoe-repair stores in Chicago, accounting for a third of all shoe-repair stores in the city. However, there was only one Korean supplier in the shoe-repair business at that time, so Korean shoe-repair stores had to depend on Jewish suppliers (*Korea Times of Chicago*, 22 July 1987).

Likewise, almost all the Korean dry-cleaning and laundry stores in Chicago are dependent on Jewish suppliers. In 1991 there were 2,000 Korean dry-cleaning and laundry stores in Chicago, accounting for 66 percent of all laundry stores in the city (*Korea Times of Chicago*, 14 July 1990). By 1991, however, there was only one Korean supplier in the dry-cleaning and laundry business. To make matters even worse, Korean laundry store owners prefer Jewish suppliers to the Korean supplier because of the larger stock and the more professional service offered by the Jewish supply stores.

Business Formation and Management

While structural factors, such as the interethnic succession of business and the export-import trade between the United States and South Korea, have provided initial business opportunities to Korean immigrants, the underlying cause of Koreans' high rates of business participation was limited job opportunities congruent with their class backgrounds.

The majority of Korean immigrants were the middle class and white-collar workers in South Korea prior to their immigration to the United States. Seventy percent of the respondents of this study received four years or more of college education, and 43 percent were professional, managerial, and other white-collar workers in Korea. Despite their highly selective class backgrounds, more than half of the respondents started as manual, service or sales workers after their arrival in the United States. Lack of competence in the English language and the less transferable Korean education and occupational skills in the American labour market were the primary causes of their inability to find white-collar wage employment, for which they had been trained.

Thus, being restricted to limited opportunities in the general labor market, Korean immigrants turned to small businesses to make more money by working for themselves rather than for other people, even though this meant their putting in longer working hours and running the risk of constant threats and violence in high-crime areas. Driven by an urge for material success, Koreans put in extremely long hours, usually even on Sundays and holidays, with members of the family all working in the stores. The average working hours of the respondents were sixty-two hours a week and about sixty percent of them had family members working in their stores at least part time. Unpaid family members, if available, provided, on average, forty-five hours per week.

Long working hours and unpaid family labour were not at all strange to Koreans, because they came from a society where long working hours and family labour are the norm. In addition, in Korean society, Koreans have to support themselves as best they can because there are virtually no meaningful government welfare programmes for the poor and unemployed. As a result, peddling is still regarded as a quick and easy way to make a living in Korea, one that allows a disadvantaged person to begin with limited capital. Although the proportions of self-employed workers and unpaid family workers among all Korean workers have been declining during the last three decades, in 1988 more than 40 percent of Koreans were still engaged in small businesses either as the owners or as unpaid family workers (Korean Ministry of Labor 1975–1989). Having grown up in this highly *self-help*-oriented society, it is not surprising that large numbers of Korean immigrants have ventured into *self-employed* small businesses when they experienced limited opportunities in the general labour market.

As self-employed businesses became the most attractive alternative to their limited job opportunities, their advantageous class, family, and ethnic resources enabled them to realize their goal of becoming independent business owners. As Table 12.2 shows, a ma-

Table 12.2
Financial Resources Utilized to Capitalize the Current Business

Source	Total N	Total %	Black Areas N	Black Areas %	Koreatown N	Koreatown %
Personal savings	122	61.3	60.2	60	6	2.5
Loans from kin	69	34.7	40	38.8	29	30.2
Loans from friends	39	19.6	21	20.4	18	18.8
Kye	55	27.6	32	31.1	23	24.0
Bank loans	54	27.1	25	24.3	29	30.2
Money from Korea	35	17.6	21	20.4	1	4
Partnership	9	4.5	6	5.8	3	3.1
Others	8	4.0	5	4.9	3	3.1
N	1	9	9	10	39	6

Note: The total percentage is over 100 because each respondent utilized one or more financial resources.

jority of the respondents accumulated capital through personal savings (61 percent), but still a sizeable proportion obtained loans from kin (35 percent), friends (20 percent), banks (27 percent), and *"kyes"* (28 percent) (in English—"contract"), Korean rotating credit associations, to capitalize their businesses.

Financial resources are only one aspect of resources for business development. Information, training opportunity, patronage by co-ethnic members and ethnic solidarity are other important dimensions of resources. Korean immigrants built a complex web of social networks in the U.S. by combining kinship, friendship, church membership, and school ties. Because an overwhelming majority of Korean immigrants came to the United States through family networks, Korean immigrants were able to establish an extensive social support network based on kinship ties (two-thirds of the respondents of this study came to the United States by invitation of their family members in the United States).

Non-kinship networks were also extensively utilized by Korean immigrants to cope with individual crises. The husbands' or wives' common schooling, occupational experience, and church membership in the new or old land provided the basis of non-kinship networks. For those who lacked kinship networks in the United States, these non-kinship networks served as substitutes for the extended family for the exchange of material and emotional support (I. Kim 1981). By combining both kinship and non-kinship networks in an opportunistic manner, Korean immigrants managed to construct a complex web of social ties in the new land. Such a wide range of social networks provided potential Korean business owners with access to resources offered by family members, friends, and co-ethnic members, thereby increasing their chances of becoming independent business owners.

One of the by-products of social networks among Korean immigrants is the concentration of Korean businesses in select industries. Because of kinship-centred chain migration, many Korean immigrants tend to find their first employment in their sponsors' businesses. As they learn business skills and build networks with clientele and suppliers while employed in their sponsors' businesses, they tend to follow the same line of business as that of their sponsors.

The clustering of Korean businesses is also encouraged by the change of ownership between Korean owners and employees. Korean employees often receive some financial assistance from their previous owners in a form of the owners' finance. Store rent and stock can be paid on a long-term basis at low interest. Such favours definitely lower the initial financial burden for potential business owners. This kind of intra-ethnic succession of businesses is often facilitated by the personal relationships and ethnocentric bonds between Korean owners and Korean employees.

The intra-ethnic succession of businesses is particularly noteworthy in the Korean dry-cleaning and laundry business. According to the Korean Dry Cleaners Association, as of June 1990, there were 8,802 Korean dry-cleaning and laundry stores in the United States (excluding Hawaii and Alaska), accounting for 48 percent of the U.S. total of 18,350 dry-cleaning and laundry stores (*Korea Times of Chicago*, 8 November 1990). In Chicago, Koreans owned 2,000 dry-cleaning and laundry establishments, accounting for 66 percent of a total of 3,000 laundry establishments.

Korean immigrants began to enter Chicago's dry-cleaning and laundry business in the early 1970s by taking over the Jewish immigrants' laundry stores. Once a Jewish laundry store was purchased by a Korean, subsequent business transactions tended to occur exclusively between Koreans. Such an intra-ethnic succession of business was aided by Korean-language immigrant newspapers where all business opportunities relevant to Korean immigrants were advertised in the classified advertisements section. Korean buyers and sellers had earlier access to such information than non-Koreans, therefore keeping business opportunities within the Korean community.

The vertical integration between Korean retailers and suppliers is another strong feature of Korean immigrant businesses. When we classify suppliers by ethnicity, 63 percent of the respondents have one or more Korean suppliers. Korean retailers say that they receive some benefits or special services from Korean suppliers. For example, extended credit terms, lower prices and easy access to information are the main benefits gained from having Korean suppliers. Since Korean suppliers dominate general merchandise, clothing, footwear, and wig trades, Korean retailers' can get early information about which items have recently arrived and which ones are "hot." Korean retailers who feel uncomfortable in dealing with American suppliers because of language and cultural barriers can deal freely and comfortably with Korean suppliers.

The popular items in the general merchandise trades are toys, dolls, handbags, accessories, jewelry and cheap electronics that are made in several Asian countries such as South Korea, Taiwan, Hong Kong and the People's Republic of China. In recent years, Taiwan-made general merchandise items have become the most favoured among Korean retailers because of their low price. Korean-made products are said to be of better quality than Taiwanese products, but they cannot compete with the latter in price. The rising wages in South Korea increase the price of Korean-made merchandise, reducing their competitive advantages in the international commodity market. To meet the growing demand of Korean retailers for cheaper products, an increasing number of Korean importers have changed their supply sources from South Korea to Taiwan and Mainland China.

The close interdependence between Korean wholesalers and retailers is similar to the food chain in ecology. Korean retailers in minority areas are heavily dependent on the economic conditions of blacks and Hispanics. Korean retailers in Koreatown are, in turn, affected by the business sales of Korean retailers in minority areas, because Korean retailers in minority areas and their family members are an important consumer group of the Korean retail stores in Koreatown. Sluggish business sales in minority areas mean reductions in spending in Koreatown. Likewise, Korean wholesalers are affected by the business sales of Korean retailers in minority areas. During economic recessions, Korean wholesalers have difficulty in collecting delayed payments for their supplies from Korean retailers. Thus, deteriorating economic conditions of blacks and Hispanics hurt, first, Korean retailers in minority areas, then Korean retailers in Koreatown, and finally Korean wholesalers.

References

Aldrich, Howard, and Albert J. Reiss, Jr. 1970. "The effects of civil disorders on small business in the inner city," *Journal of Social Issues*, vol. 26, pp. 187–206.

Chicago Fact Book Consortium. 1984. *Local Community Fact Book Chicago Metropolitan Area Based on the 1970 and 1980 Censuses*, Chicago: Chicago Review Press.

Chin, Ku-Sup, In-Jin Yoon, and David Smith. "Immigrant small business and international economic linkage: A case of the Korean wig industry in Los Angeles, 1968–1977," forthcoming in *International Migration Review*.

Kim, Illsoo. 1981. *New Urban Immigrants: The Korean Community in New York*, Princeton, NJ: Princeton University Press.

Kim, Kwang Chung, and Won Moo Hurh. 1985. "Ethnic resource utilization of Korean immigrant entrepreneurs in the Chicago minority area," *International Migration Review*, vol. 19, pp. 82–111.

Kim, Kwang Chung, Won Moo Hurh, and Marilyn Fernandez. 1989. "Intragroup differences in business participation: Three Asian immigrant groups," *International Migration Review*, vol. 23, pp. 73–95.

Korea Central Daily Of Chicago. 1991. *1991 Korean Business Directory*. Chicago: Korea Central Daily of Chicago.

Korean Ministry of Labor. 1975–1989. *Yearbook of Labor Statistics*, Seoul, Korea.

Light, Ivan. 1984. "Immigrant and ethnic enterprise in North America," *Ethnic and Racial Studies*, vol. 7, no. 2, pp. 195–216.

——. 1985. "Immigrant entrepreneurs in America: Koreans in Los Angeles," in Nathan Glazer (ed.), *Clamor at the Gates*, San Francisco: Institute for Contemporary Studies Press.

Light, Ivan, and Edna Bonacich. 1988. *Immigrant Entrepreneurs: Koreans in Los Angeles, 1965–1982*, Berkeley: University of California Press.

Min, Pyong Gap. 1988. *Ethnic Business Enterprise: Korean Small Business In Atlanta*, New York: Center for Migration Studies.

Min, Pyong Gap, and Charles Jaret. 1984. "Ethnic business success: The case of Korean small business in Atlanta,". *Sociology and Social Research*, vol. 69, pp. 412–35.

Waldinger, Roger. 1986. *Through the Eye of the Needle: Immigrants and Enterprise in New York's Garment Trades*, New York: New York University Press.

Waldinger, Roger, Howard Aldrich, and Robin Ward. 1990. *Ethnic Entrepreneurship: Immigrant Business in Industrial Societies*, Newbury Park, CA: Sage Publications.

Wilson, William. 1987. *The Truly Disadvantaged: The Inner City, The Underclass and Public Policy*, Chicago, IL: University of Chicago Press.

Yoon, In-Jin. 1991. "Self-employment in business: Chinese-, Japanese-, Korean-Americans, Blacks, and Whites," unpublished PhD dissertation, Department of Sociology, University of Chicago.

13

The Other Half of the Sky:

Socioeconomic Adaptation of Immigrant Women

Min Zhou

"Women hold up half of the sky." This saying describes what is true of Chinatown's enclave labor force. More often than not, when people think of the Chinese in the United States, they imagine railroad workers, hand laundrymen, or restaurant waiters. Women are seldom seen, or heard of, in Old Chinatown. Past studies of Chinese immigration and immigrant incorporation have often depicted female immigrants as invisible or stereotyped, even after 1965 when women began to come in large numbers. These studies have emphasized the experience of men or examined the research with little recognition that the experience of immigrant women may be different from that of men. More recently, studies of the enclaves of Cubans in Miami and Chinese and Koreans in New York and Los Angeles have begun to show interest in women's position in enclave labor markets (Bonacich, Light, and Wong 1977; Perez 1986; Bonacich and Light 1988; Portes and Jensen 1989; Zhou and Logan 1989; Portes amd Rumbaut 1990). Some researchers consider the ethnic enclave highly exploitative of women (Bonacich, Light, and Wong 1977; Phizacklea 1983; Bonacich 1984). Others perceive it not simply as an adaptive response to the new environment but also as a continuation of ethnic social and cultural patterns (Perez 1986; Haines 1986; Zhou and Logan 1989; Portes and Jensen 1989; Portes and Rumbaut 1990). Contrasting arguments highlight the exploitative aspects of the enclave and the cooperative family orientation of ethnic entrepreneurship.

In Chinatown, women constitute a major share of the ethnic labor force, and their position in the labor market is not the same as men's. Thus, patterns of socioeconomic adaptation of men are not applicable to women. . . .

Immigrant Chinese Women in New York

The Impact of Female Chinese Immigration

New York's Chinatown was a bachelors' society for the greater part of this century. Not until after 1965, when U.S. immigration policies were revised to favor family reunification, did Chinese women enter New York in large numbers, changing the Chinatown bachelors' society forever. Now the community is bustling with young families. In the 1940s, there were six times as many Chinese men as women in New York State; and in the 1950s, Chinese men still outnumbered women by nearly 300 percent. Now the ratio is nearly balanced. Immigration statistics show that from 1982 to 1985 more Chinese women than men entered the United States—53 percent women and 47 percent men from mainland China; 53 percent and 47 percent from Taiwan; and about 50 percent and 50 percent from Hong Kong. In fact, women immigrants have outnumbered men almost every year since then, especially since the mid-1970s, when China finally opened itself up to the West. Not only do women dominate the immigration trend, but the majority (65 percent) are in the working ages of twenty to fifty-nine (67 percent for immigrants from China, 50 percent for those from Hong Kong, and 68 percent for those from Taiwan). By the 1980s, 79 percent of the Chinese households in New York were family-type households, and 87 percent of the Chinese families were married-couple families (compared to the state's average of 70 percent family-type households and 78 percent married-couple families). The average number of persons per family was 3.73 for the Chinese, a little higher than the state average (3.30).

As Chinatown's social nature has changed, the pressure on the community's physical capacity has become enormous. Chinatown's limited housing, aging and deteriorated, is simply not capable of accommodating the demands of the incoming families. In fact, this strategic piece of turf has become a battlefield on which investors and businessmen compete for economic opportunities, and it is no longer primarily a residence for new immigrants. Consequently, families are spread out in other areas of the city, depending on easy subway access to Chinatown. . . .

Residential out-migration of the Chinese population in recent years can be partially attributed to the entry of women. . . . Large-scale immigration of women has two major effects on Chinatown's economy: First, through sheer numbers and by promoting a family-centered society in which most adults are living with a spouse, it has expanded the market for Chinese goods and services that are inaccessible in the larger society, thus developing the enclave protected sector. Second, by providing a large additional pool of cheap and low-skilled labor at a critical time in the city's overall economic restructuring, it has promoted the rapid development of a Chinese garment industry, which serves as a backbone of the enclave export sector in Chinatown. Women's concentration in the garment industry is extraordinary: more than 55 percent of all immigrant Chinese women who worked at least 160 hours and earned over five hundred dollars in 1979 were employed in the garment industry.

Characteristics of Immigrant Chinese Women in New York

. . . In 1980 the foreign born composed nearly three-fourths (74 percent) of the total female Chinese population in New York State. The age distribution shows that more than half of the female Chinese were between twenty-five and sixty-four years old, with a much smaller group on both ends—7 percent aged under five years and 8 percent aged sixty-five or over. On the average, as compared to New York State's non-Hispanic white women, Chinese women were younger. They were more likely to be married (60 percent versus 52 percent) and less likely to be divorced or separated (3.2 percent versus 7.9 percent). The educational achievement of Chinese women went to both extremes. On one end, they constituted a fairly large per-

centage of the illiterate or semiliterate (21 percent, as compared to only 3 percent for non-Hispanic white women); on the other end, they had a higher percentage of college education compared to white women (21 percent versus 15 percent). Chinese women had a much higher rate of labor-force participation (59 percent versus 45 percent and for immigrant Chinese women the rate was much higher). Occupationally, female Chinese were very segregated. They were disproportionately concentrated in positions as operators and laborers and fewer of them were administrators, managers, and technicians than was the case among non-Hispanic whites. They were underrepresented in administrative-support jobs, which were regarded as female-dominated occupations.

Data on immigrants' socioeconomic status upon arrival were not broken down by sex, and statistics were not available to show the socioeconomic characteristics of women before immigration. Yet ethnographic data indicated that the majority of the adult immigrant women came from rural areas in south China, and the rest came from cities all over China. They were from various socioeconomic backgrounds. Many young adult women aged twenty to thirty-five from mainland China immigrated through marriage, taking advantage of the 1965 immigration laws.

In China, particularly in villages around the Pearl River delta in the south, where emigration originated, many young women tend to prefer marriage abroad as a way to come to America. They perceive immigration as the only way to upgrade their socioeconomic status and that of their families. Marriage abroad is possible because many Chinese immigrant men, already in the United States, have difficulty finding a Chinese wife in Chinatown. They often depend on the ethnic or kinship networks in their home villages in seeking a wife. For example, Mei Chao's husband, Mr. Cheng, originally immigrated from Hong Kong with his family and became a naturalized citizen. For him, the primary purpose for getting married was to carry on the family name. Since he had limited choice in finding a Chinese wife here, he decided to "import" one, as many of his coworkers did.

He met Mei Chao in Taishan through a relative and managed to get her out a few months after their wedding in China.

Younger women from rural China, particularly those who married into the country, usually had limited education, English-language ability, and marketable skills. They did not have very high aspirations for themselves; rather, they tended to work for the benefit of the family as a whole. Despite these initial disadvantages, they seem to have had fewer adjustment problems than older or better-educated women. First, life in America was regarded as absolutely better than life in the backward villages in China. Long before immigration they knew that, if they were willing to work just as hard as in China, they could make a lot of money in the Gold Mountain. So they were ready and eager to work, either to save money to send back to their natal families or to help bring in additional income and accumulate capital for their own families. Second, they were accustomed to working outside the home. The low-wage jobs and long working hours in Chinatown did not seem to bother them at all, for these rural women were used to doing backbreaking menial farmwork in the fields for very little pay. Third, despite the fact that they were uneducated and unskilled, they could quickly learn the minimum skills required to operate a sewing machine. Therefore, the initial disadvantages, on the one hand, kept women dependent on Chinatown's economy and, on the other hand, helped them withstand the social and psychological pressures associated with immigration.

Middle-aged women made up another portion of the incoming female population. Most of these immigrant women are wives and mothers who had immigrated with children under twenty-one to reunite their families. After 1943 wives of the Chinatown sojourners began to immigrate. Some of these middle-aged women, who could have come years earlier, in the 1940s and 1950s, delayed their American trip primarily because of the need to take care of their families and small children or their parents-in-law, who were too old to immigrate. This group of women is the most altruistic. They came mainly for their children, not for themselves. They did not re-ally immigrate for the comfort and freedom of the American life, for they often look on themselves as too slow to adjust to the new country and too old to learn English and to establish a career of any sort. All they wish for is the success of their children. Without knowing English, without comparable skills and training, and without youth their options in the labor market are limited. Jobs in Chinatown become their only option. (This is true even for some women who had a higher level of education and professional skills because of both ethnic and gender discrimination.) Some choose to stay home to help with the housework and to care for their small grandchildren. Those who work outside the home are almost uniformly employed in private household service and the garment industry. Even if most know they will not go back to China, their mentality is still based in China. They do not seem to have socioeconomic aspirations for themselves.

Yet another portion of the female immigrant population is composed of well-educated and professional women. Many women from this group also immigrated under relative-preference categories. Some were students who attended U.S. colleges and decided to stay after completing their education. The American-trained women tend to refuse to identify themselves with Chinatown. They are more likely to find jobs in the mainstream economy. In contrast, those not educated in the United States mostly depend on the economic enclave because of their poor English ability (and, for some, lack of transferable skills). However, the better-educated and professional immigrant women do not seem to benefit from the enclave as much as immigrant men with similar socioeconomic backgrounds. Most of the jobs commensurable with their past professional experience and education are taken by men. Therefore, the human-capital characteristics of women do not seem to generate as great economic returns as those of men. The male supremacy that dominates the Chinese culture also reinforces gender discrimination in the enclave labor market—good jobs are simply not open to women in Chinatown. Thus, some of these female immigrants often feel more disadvantaged, disappointed, and deprived than other immigrant women.

However, those who are ambitious and motivated can often succeed through self-employment. In many cases, their efforts are combined with their husbands' in family economic pursuits. In Chinatown, female entrepreneurs are more likely to run businesses with their husbands. . . .

From whatever background, all Chinatown women share a common characteristic: They are all, in one way or another, performing multiple roles as daughters, wives, mothers, and wage earners. As immigrants, Chinese women (like men) bear all sorts of disadvantages associated with immigrant status—ethnic visibility, weaker educational credentials, poorer English and occupational skills. In addition, they also carry with them a set of traditional roles that have been internalized into their value system at an early stage of life. They continue to assume these roles when uprooted from their country of origin because Chinatown, though surrounded by the world's most advanced civilization, has long maintained the most traditional Chinese culture and values. However, what is special about these women is that they have a strong work ethic and family commitment. They believe that, together with their family members, they can "make it" in America. The high rate of labor-force participation for immigrant women indicates that they are committed to work outside the home. Although the economic contribution of women has enhanced their status in the family and the community, there is still a long way to go before women can achieve equal rights with men in Chinatown. As wage earners, they are limited to jobs in the low-wage sector of the economic enclave.

Labor Market Performance

Women made up nearly half of the Chinese immigrant labor force in New York. . . . Occupationally, immigrant women in the city leaned toward jobs at the lower end of the occupational scale, and close to 60 percent of them were garment workers. Immigrant Chinese women living outside New York City fared much better. They had much better

knowledge of English, and their educational achievement was remarkable, not better than that of immigrant Chinese men but much better than their female white counterparts. They showed higher proportions in better occupations.

Immigrant Chinese women in or out of New York City tend to be full-time workers, but marked differences in individual income exist between Chinese men and women workers . . . reflecting the effects of lower educational attainment, lower English skills, and also gender discrimination. However, women living outside the city earned only half as much as their male counterparts, despite their much-improved human-capital characteristics and occupational attainment. It seems that, relatively, immigrant women were better off in the city.

Education, Occupation, and Earnings

. . . U.S.-born Chinese women with at least some high school education had incomes higher than those of non-Hispanic white women, and those with college education had incomes similar to their counterparts'. They seem to have fared better relative to white women than the rest of the group.

Chinese women who had lower income returns on their education may be in occupations that generally pay less. According to the 1980 census, almost half of the U.S.-born Chinese women occupied the top-ranking white-collar occupations (49 percent as compared to 37 percent of their white counterparts). Immigrant Chinese women, however, did not fare quite as well. Only 15 percent were in the top-ranking occupations, while more than half were concentrated in the entry-level menial jobs typical of enclave economies. . . . U.S.-born Chinese women did much better than their white counterparts in white-collar professional occupations, and immigrant Chinese women did just as well as whites in those occupations. However, Chinese women were disadvantaged at managerial positions as well as on menial jobs.

Returns on Human Capital in the Enclave

The majority of immigrant women participate in the enclave labor market. A major part of Chinatown's economy depends on the availability of female immigrant labor. While the enclave seems to take advantage of women, it also creates jobs for these women, who otherwise would not be able to find work or would have to go back to China. The specific question here is whether participation in the enclave economy affects immigrant women's ability to reap earnings returns on human capital, as hypothesized for men.

. . . Generally, occupational success should be closely related to higher earnings return. If human capital did not bring a significant return in income, as is the case for the Chinese female workers in the enclave economy, we should expect that it would not bring a return in occupational attainment. Nevertheless, in New York, I found that Chinese immigrant women within the enclave have no measurable earnings returns on previous human capital but that human capital has helped them achieve higher occupational prestige. These results did not stem in any obvious way from the personal characteristics of these women; they are not unusually low in education, nor are they predominantly part-time workers.

What accounts for the fact that the earnings of immigrant Chinese women are unrelated to their experience, education, English-language ability, and citizenship? In Chinatown, women workers face two sorts of disadvantages. The first, which they share with men, is the set of disadvantages associated with immigrant status. The second is a set of cultural obstacles within the enclave: occupational segregation by gender (particularly in the garment industry) and the traditional multiple roles of daughters, wives, mothers, and wage workers. Data on the census and fieldwork research on women in the garment industry provide more insight.

Chinatown's Garment Workers

Chinatown's garment industry took root and grew [during the 1970s,] at a time when New York City's manufacturing sector was declining. . . . Chinatown's garment industry sprang up basically in response to a new wave of immigration, which supplied not only a large pool of cheap female labor but also a group of entrepreneurs who were willing to invest in and manage the garment trade. Moreover, declining manufacturing left vacant many loft buildings in which the garment industry could develop. Between 1975 and 1980, the number of Chinese-owned garment factories grew by an average of 36 a year, reaching a peak of 430 in 1980. In that year Chinatown contained one-third of all the jobs in Manhattan's women's outerwear industry and a much larger share of the production jobs (ILGWU 1983). As a result, Chinatown's garment industry has grown into one of the two basic sectors (the restaurant industry being the other) of the enclave economy. Immigrant women have played a crucial role in the community's economic development.

Female workers are not different from men in regard to their immigrant status— poor English-language ability, lack of transferable work skills, and limited information concerning the larger employment market. They are forced to take low-paying, long-hour, menial jobs in Chinatown. However, as women, female workers have encountered more barriers than men in their new country. Gender discrimination both in and out of Chinatown; the traditional roles of women as daughters, wives, and mothers; the denial of equal educational opportunities to women in the Chinese culture; and their dependent status as immigrant wives leave women almost nothing but one option—to work in the garment industry.

The large number of women who have flooded the ethnic labor market in Chinatown has exacerbated the effect of the rigid gender division, turning the entire garment industry into a female occupation. In Chinatown's garment industry, more than 80 percent of the Chinese immigrant workers are women. . . . Comparing characteristics of all female workers in the industry, the Chinese were more likely to be married and live with children (86 percent of them were married, and 78 percent had at least two children). They arrived more recently (86 percent entered the United States after 1965). About 41 percent of them were naturalized U.S. citizens. Furthermore, they displayed relatively lower human-capital characteristics. Most were poorly educated (the mean years of school completed was only eight); only a few of them (2–4 percent) had some college education. They knew very little English (less than 15 percent of them spoke English well). But most of them took up full-time jobs. . . . Ninety-five percent of the Chinese in the garment industry were sewing machine operators.

Chinese female garment workers were extremely low paid. Their average annual salary in 1979 was only a little more than five thousand dollars, at an average hourly pay of only $2.80, far below minimum wage (though it is also possible that many of the workers underreported their income). Interviews with the garment workers revealed that most of the factories set the hourly rate according to experience. For new hands, it was below or about minimum wage. For more skilled workers, the rate varied from $4.00 to $5.50. But many workers, mostly older women, who did miscellaneous work in the factory (e.g., cleaning, cutting thread, wrapping) were paid between $2.50 and $3.00 per hour.

Why should Chinese women be so disproportionately engaged in the garment industry? Some may think that women are particularly good at certain jobs, which are hence defined as women's jobs. Our society has always taken for granted the common assumption that the gender division of labor is natural and generally beneficial for women. The reality is that jobs that are defined as women's work invariably entail lower rates of pay, status, and skill, whereas higher-paid skilled jobs tend to be the preserve of men (Stone 1983; Blau and Ferber 1986). The making of garments has been traditionally accepted as women's work because of the rigid gender divisions within the labor market. The garment industry, long before the Chinese entered it, was supported by a large pool of cheap female labor from the European immigrant groups—the Jews, Italians, Greeks, and others. Nowadays, as immigrants of European origin are gradually being accepted into the American mainstream, the industry has been taken over by the newer immigrant groups, particularly the Chinese and the Hispanics.

According to the common assumption, women enter the garment trade because they are good at it. However, history shows that men once held those jobs. Chinese men used to dominate laundry work, and the coat and suit industry used to be dependent on male European immigrants. Why then does the gender division of labor remain so rigid? It is not because of the particular skills that women or men possess but because of the association of the occupation with women's principal roles and their subordinate status.

As immigrants, both men and women experience racial or cultural subordination, which acts to confine them to certain types of work and reinforces their disadvantaged status as wage workers. But for immigrant women, immigrant disadvantages are shaped in a particular way because they share with all women subordination as a gender. Thus, wherever a woman comes from, whether she works or not, whether she is married or has children, her principal role in life is defined not as a wage worker first but as a wife or mother. It is this definition that is replicated and reinforced through the creation of whole sectors of low-paid, low-skilled women's work (Phizacklea 1983).

The negative consequences of the stereotyped definition of women's role can also be understood from another perspective. Confinement to the low-wage, labor-intensive sector implies that women can afford to take such jobs because their paid work is only "secondary" or "supplementary." Their role is still defined as an actual, or potential, wife or mother; they still have to depend, economically and socially, on a male breadwinner.

In Chinatown, women are disproportionately engaged in the garment industry while men are concentrated in restaurants. This gender division is closely associated with women's traditional roles. First, as a principal breadwinner, a man is expected to have a stable full-time job; as a dependent and a wife, a woman is expected to perform her principal role as wife and mother, and a stable job is not her primary concern. Chinatown's restaurant industry is relatively more stable, in the sense that it is basically supported year-round by an ethnic market, whereas Chinatown's garment industry is highly seasonal and unstable. Because of rising labor costs, a lot of apparel manufacturing, particularly for the standardized portion of the demand, has been transferred to the Third World—Southeast Asia, particularly Hong Kong, Taiwan, and even China—where the cost of labor is low. New York's manufacturing sector retains only that portion of the demand that is transient, unstandardized, and susceptible to the quick-changing vagaries of fashion. This portion of the demand is unpredictable. Chinatown's apparel orders are mostly for lower-priced women's sportswear and the stylish products that are made to fill in mass-consumption lines that stores leave open to take advantage of unpredictable and late changes in demand (ILGWU 1983; Sassen-Koob 1984; Weiner and Green 1984). The uncertainty and unpredictability make Chinatown's garment work highly seasonal.

Unlike the restaurant business, which is more independent, the garment industry falls into the export sector of the enclave economy, and it depends largely on the fluctuating demand of the larger consumer market and the production decisions of apparel manufacturers who are not Chinatown insiders. Lack of control over the consumer market and production renders Chinatown's garment industry vulnerable to competition from producers of low-priced standardized lines that are located abroad and to market changes. When demand declines, fewer orders are contracted into Chinatown, and more workers have to be laid off. Thus, a man, as the head of the family, tends to head for the relatively more stable restaurant jobs, leaving the garment jobs for women. An interview with a restaurant waiter provides support for this point. Asked whether he would like to work in the garment factory, he answered: "No, I would not want to work in the garment factory. You know, in Chinatown, the garment job is a woman's job. How could one support his family with a woman's job? I have a couple of kids to raise. What would happen to my family if the factory did not get enough orders and I got laid off?" Apparently, this waiter was implying that a man did not work in the garment factory because he was the breadwinner. Men, thus, are less likely to enter the sweatshop.

Another reason that women flock to the garment industry is that it offers full-time and part-time jobs to them, regardless of their prior labor-market experience. Although most of the women have not worked in the job before immigration, they learn as they work because the required skills are minimal. Within a short period of time, many become experienced sewing machine operators.

. . . [W]ages for sewing machine operators are generally lower than the wages and tips waiters can earn. Chinatown's garment industry is highly competitive. In order to survive the competition, the Chinese garment contractors have to offer low prices for orders and make marginal profits by pushing wages down as low as possible. Half of the garment workers earned less than $5,000 in 1979. As for men, about 42 percent of all male workers were in the restaurant business, and more than 70 percent of them were waiters. In 1979, male restaurant workers earned an average of $1,200 more than female garment workers; and men who were in the garment industry earned an average of $2,000 more than women.

Moreover, because women are still given total responsibility for the household work, the working wives or mothers tend to prefer jobs that leave them time for taking care of their housework and children. Thus, they are not suitable for restaurant jobs, which require a rigid work schedule, particularly the evening shift. Garment work does not need to be done on a fixed schedule, and many Chinese garment contractors offer flexible work hours and favorable locations to their workers, in part as a way to compensate for the low wages. Workers can take the time off during the day to drop off and pick up their children at school or to nurse their babies. They are even allowed to bring their babies to the workshop.

Most of the garment factories are firmly anchored in the extended Chinatown area despite the increasingly tight commercial space, rising rent, and Chinatown's residential dispersion. The main reason is that Chinatown has a large pool of cheap female immigrant labor. Many garment workers live in the enclave and walk to work, but even those who live in Queens or Brooklyn still prefer to go back to Chinatown to work, because there they can fulfill some of their household duties at the same time—shopping and picking up groceries and ready-cooked food on their way home. It would not be as convenient for women to work in factories in outer boroughs, because they would still need to go back to Chinatown to shop and therefore would have to spend more time outside the home. Many women commute to Chinatown to work at the jobs available to them, therefore. Even if their families move out of the area, they must continue to work, for their contributions to the family's income are essential to fulfill the goals of self-employment and home ownership.

But the farther the families move away from the garment center, the longer the journey to work, and the greater the pressure on women in performing all the expected roles. . . .

In Chinatown garment workers must rely on family members and others in the community for child care. The majority of the Chinatown garment workers are mothers of small children, desperately juggling work with the household chores, shopping, cooking, and arranging for baby-sitters. Child care is an especially burning issue for many of these working women. In Chinatown in 1988 there was only one subsidized day-care center for garment workers and a few home day-care services that were sponsored by the city government and some of the quasi-governmental organizations. Miss Kwan, a union activist, said that the immigrant mothers "cannot believe that when they get here, there is nobody to take care of their kids." In China many workplaces had day-care facilities for their own employees, or some women could leave the kids with the grandparents. Here in Chinatown only a few young mothers can ask their parents to take care of their children. The rest have to take their small children along to work or leave them with paid baby-sitters.

The New York City Chinatown Daycare Center, located at 115 Chrystie Street, was opened in 1983 in a unique cooperative effort involving the ILGWU, the Great Blouse, Skirt, and Undergarment Association, individual manufacturers, and the Agency for Child Development, Human Resources Ad-

ministration of New York City. The center had space for about eighty children and always had a full enrollment. . . . However, the formal means of support and the subsidized day-care services were not sufficient to meet the pressing needs of the garment workers. Many working women had to turn to family or private day-care services to solve their problem. In Chinatown a lot of older, retired women take care of their grandchildren as older women are traditionally expected to do. Women in Chinatown usually find their baby-sitter through kinship networks, and baby-sitters do not have to put up ads to get a job. Also, some mothers choose not to work, to stay home with their children instead. Many of these women usually baby-sit two or three more children, in addition to their own, in order to make some extra money and to provide playmates for their own children. . . .

Private day care is available in individual homes. The costs ranged from fourteen to twenty dollars per day in 1988, and the services were reliable and flexible. These places became an effective means to solve the childcare problem. The working mothers usually spent half of their wages on child care. They also needed support from their bosses, who would allow children to come to the garment shop to wait for their mothers. Younger children could be left in private care all day, but older kids had shorter school hours. Mothers usually dropped them off at school before they went to work. If kids went to schools in Chinatown, they simply walked to the garment shops and stood by the sewing machines while their mothers worked. Older children might help their mothers hang up finished garments, turn belts, or prepare garments for sewing, but the young ones generally just stood by waiting (Sung 1987). But if children were not in Chinatown schools, mothers had to arrange pickup and extended day care for their children.

The garment industry thrives, taking advantage of women's willing acceptance of low wages. The stiff competition in the industry also leads to poor working conditions. In Chinatown there is evidence of growing numbers of garment shops with many fire and safety hazards, paying wages below the federal minimum. The U.S. Labor Department has repeatedly raided and filed charges against some of the Chinatown garment factories over the past ten years. However, these actions are only a minimal deterrent to garment owners intent on keeping wages low and paying their workers off the books. For these employers, as Ms. Fung, a staff attorney for the Asian-American Legal and Education Fund, pointed out, such actions—imposition of fines and closing of factories—were considered only a routine business expense; most shop owners quickly reopened their shops, knowing that the Labor Department officers would not be returning soon after their press conferences. In Ms. Fung's opinion, shared by many Chinatown leaders, such raids on the garment industry would hurt only Chinese garment workers (*New York Times* 1981). These were primarily poor immigrant women with limited education and restricted occupational options. Many of them were willing to work long hours at low wages and without overtime pay, so long as they had some sort of job that could bring in income to support themselves and their families. These workers would simply lose their jobs following a raid. They then blamed the government, rather than the law-breaking employers, for depriving them of a livelihood. Unaware of their rights and taking a different stance toward this work, these women would try to obtain jobs in other garment factories that might also engage in illegal practices. In Chinatown today, the garment industry provides jobs to immigrant women who would otherwise not be able to work. As a result, three out of five women workers are low-wage garment workers. . . .

The garment industry may appear highly exploitative of women, but from the point of view of these women workers, the industry is their only opportunity. They all seem to be satisfied that they have a job at all, whatever it may be. As Mrs. Chen put it, "I would have to go back to China if there wasn't a garment industry in Chinatown." The willingness of immigrant women to accept substandard working conditions and wages is certainly a problem in that it can exert pressure on other enclave workers to reduce what they are willing to work for. However, for these women, getting a job and being paid fairly still remain two separate issues. They are more concerned about having a job of some sort to help their families move ahead than about their own rights. Some people would argue that it is all right for a woman to take a low-wage job, since she only works for pin money and her husband is supporting them. Others expect a woman's work and earnings to affect household norms and behavior. Chinatown's reality is that a woman works out of economic necessity, and her income is added to her husband's as a family income. However, her employment and income do not seem to change household behavior and norms. This pattern is also evident for non-Hispanic white working women in the larger economy (Hunter and Spitze 1983). A woman's expected duties as a wife and a mother do not change much when she becomes a wage earner; rather, they hinder her from seeking higher-paying jobs. As a result, women's equal rights with men remain as distant as they were before immigration. However, the roles women play are indispensable for the social mobility of the family as whole, and this state of affairs is taken for granted by women workers in Chinatown. . . .

References

Blau, F.D. and M.A. Ferber. 1986. *The Economics of Women, Men, and Work*. Englewood Cliffs, NJ: Prentice-Hall.

Bonacich, E. 1984. "United States Capitalist Development: A Background to Asian Immigration." Pp. 79–129 in *Labor Immigration Under Capitalism: Asian Workers in the United States Before World War II*, edited by L. Cheng and E. Bonacich. Berkeley: University of California Press.

Bonacich, E., and I. Light. 1988. *Immigrant Entrepreneurs: Koreans in Los Angeles, 1965–1982*. Berkeley: University of California Press.

Bonacich, E., I. Light, and C.C. Wong. 1977. "Koreans in Small Business." Society 14: 54–59.

Haines, D.W. 1986. "Vietnamese Refugee Women in the US Labor Force: Continuity or Change?" Pp. 62–75 in *International Migration: The Female Experience*, edited by R.J. Simon and C.B. Brettell. Totowa, NJ: Rowman and Allanheld.

Huber, J., and G. Spitze. 1983. *Sex Stratification: Children, Housework, and Jobs*. New York: Academic Press.

ILGWU (International Ladies Garment Workers' Union, Local 23–25) and the New York Skirt and Sportswear Association. 1983. *The Chinatown Garment Industry Study*. New York: Abeles, Schwartz, Haeckel, and Silverblatt.

Perez, L. 1986. "Immigrant Economic Adjustment and Family Organization: The Cuban Success Story Reexamined." *International Migration Review* 20: 4–20.

Phizacklea, A. (ed.). 1983. *One-Way Ticket: Migration and Female Labor*. London: Routledge and Kegan Paul.

Portes, A., and L. Jensen. 1989. "The Enclave and the Entrants: Patterns of Ethnic Enterprise in Miami Before and After Mariel." *American Sociological Review* 54: 929–949.

Portes, A., and R. Rumbaut. 1990. *Immigrant America: A Portrait*. Berkeley: University of California Press.

Sassen-Koob, S. 1984. "Notes on the Incorporation of Third World Women Into Wage Labor Through Immigration and Off-Shore Production." *International Migration Review* 28: 1144–1167.

Stone, K. 1983. "Motherhood and Waged Work: West Indian, Asian, and White Mothers Compared." Pp. 33–52 in *One-Way Ticket: Migration and Female Labor*, edited by A. Phizacklea. London: Routledge and Kegan Paul.

Sung, B.L. 1987. *The Adjustment Experience of Chinese Immigrant Children in New York City*. New York: Center for Migration Studies.

Weiner, E. and H. Green. 1984. "A Stitch in Our Times: New York's Hispanic Garment Workers in the 1980s." Pp. 278–296 in *A Needle, A Bobbin, A Strike: Women Needleworkers in America*, edited by J.M. Jensen and S. Davidson. Philadelphia: Temple University Press.

Zhou, M., and J.R. Logan. 1989. "Returns on Human Capital in Ethnic Enclaves: New York City's Chinatown." *American Sociological Review* 54: 809–820.

14

Coming Together:

The Asian American Movement

Yen Espiritu

Arriving in the United States, nineteenth-century immigrants from Asian countries did not think of themselves as "Asians." Coming from specific districts in provinces in different nations, Asian immigrant groups did not even consider themselves Chinese, Japanese, Korean, and so forth, but rather people from Toisan, Hoiping, or some other district in Guandong Province in China or from Hiroshima, Yamaguchi, or some other prefecture in Japan. Members of each group considered themselves culturally and politically distinct. Historical enmities between their mother countries further separated the groups even after their arrival in the United States. . . . However, non-Asians had little understanding or appreciation of these distinctions. For the most part, outsiders accorded to Asian peoples certain common characteristics and traits that were essentially supranational (Browne 1985: 8–9). Indeed, the exclusion acts and quotas limiting Asian immigration to the United States relied upon racialist constructions of Asians as homogeneous (Lowe 1991: 28).

Mindful that whites generally lump all Asians together, early Asian immigrant communities sought to "keep their images discrete and were not above denigrating, or at least approving the denigration of, other Asian groups" (Daniels 1988: 113). It was not until the late 1960s, with the advent of the Asian American movement, that a pan-Asian consciousness and constituency were first formed. To build political unity, college students of Asian ancestry heralded their common fate—the similarity of experiences and treatment that Asian groups endured in the

United States (Omi and Winant 1986: 105). In other words, the pan-Asian concept, originally imposed by non-Asians, became a symbol of pride and a rallying point for mass mobilization by later generations. This chapter examines the social, political, and demographic factors that allowed pan-Asianism to take root in the 1960s and not earlier.

Ethnic 'Disidentification'

Before the 1960s, Asians in this country frequently practiced ethnic disidentification, the act of distancing one's group from another group so as not to be mistaken and suffer the blame for the presumed misdeeds of that group (Hayano 1981: 162). Faced with external threats, group members can either intensify their solidarity or they can distance themselves from the stigmatized segment. Instead of uniting to fight anti-Asian forces, early Asian immigrant communities often disassociated themselves from the targeted group so as not to be mistaken for members of it and suffer any possible negative consequences (Hayano 1981: 161; Daniels 1988: 113).

Social and Demographic Changes: Setting the Context

Although Asians in the United States have long been engaged in political action, their efforts never drew public attention until the 1960s (Chan 1991: 171). Prompted by broader political struggles and internal demographic changes, college students of Asian ancestry spearheaded the Asian American movement. Critical to its development was the mobilization of American blacks. Besides offering tactical lessons, the civil rights and the Black Power movements had a profound impact on the consciousness of Asian Americans, sensitizing them to racial issues (Uyematsu 1971). The anticolonial nationalist movements in Asia also stirred racial and cultural pride and provided a context for the emergence of the Yellow Power movement (P. Wong 1972). Influenced by these broader political struggles, Americans of Asian ancestry united to denounce racist institutional structures, demand new or unattended rights, and assert their cultural and racial distinctiveness. Normal urban issues such as housing, education, and social welfare began to take on ethnic coloration.

From an Immigrant to a Native Population

Before 1940, the Asian population in the United States was primarily an immigrant population. . . . Immigrant Asians faced practical barriers to pan-Asian unity. Foremost was their lack of a common language. Old national rivalries were another obstacle, as many early Asian immigrants carried the political memories and outlook of their homelands. . . .

During the postwar period, due to immigration restrictions and the growing dominance of the second and third generations, American-born Asians outnumbered immigrants. . . . By 1960, approximately two-thirds of the Asian population in California had been born in the United States (Ong 1989: 5–8). As the Asian population became a native-born community, linguistic and cultural differences began to blur. Although they had attended Asian-language schools, most American-born Asians possessed only a limited knowledge of their ethnic language (Chan 1991: 115). By 1960, with English as the common language, persons from different Asian backgrounds were able to communicate with one another (Ling 1984: 73), and in so doing create a common identity associated with the United States.

Moreover, unlike their immigrant parents, native-born and American-educated Asians could muster only scant loyalties to old world ties. Historical antagonisms between their mother countries thus receded in importance (P. Wong 1972: 34). . . .

As national differences receded in subjective importance, generational differences widened. For the most part, American-born Asians considered themselves to have more in common with other American-born Asians than they did with foreign-born compatriots. According to a third-generation Japanese American who is married to a Chinese American, "As far as our experiences in America, I have more things in common than differences with a Chinese American. Being born and raised here gives us something in common. We have more in common with each other than with a Japanese from Japan, or a Chinese from China" (Ichioka interview). Much to their parents' dismay, young Asian Americans began to choose their friends and spouses from other Asian groups. . . . This muting of cultural and historical divisions distressed their parents, who, more often than not, had supported these divisions for most of their lives. . . .

The Watershed of World War II

Before World War II, Asian immigrant communities were quite distinct entities, isolated from one another and from the larger society. Because of language difficulties, prejudice, and lack of business opportunities elsewhere, there was little chance for Asians in the United States to live outside their ethnic enclaves (Yuan 1966: 331). Shut out of the mainstream of American society, the various immigrant groups struggled separately in their respective Chinatowns, Little Tokyos, or Manilatowns. . . . Although statistical data do not exist, ethnographic accounts confirm the ethnic homogeneity of each early Asian immigrant community. . . . Within these enclaves, diversity among Asian nationalities was more salient than commonality.

Economic and residential barriers began to crumble after World War II. The war against Nazism called attention to racism at home and discredited the notions of white superiority. The fifteen years after the war was a period of largely positive change as civil rights statutes outlawed racial discrimination in employment as well as housing (Daniels 1988: ch. 7). Popular attitudes were also changing. Polls taken during World War II showed a distinct hostility toward Japan: 74 percent of the respondents favored either killing off all Japanese, destroying Japan as a political entity, or supervising it. On the West Coast, 97 percent of the people polled approved of the relocation of Japanese Americans. In contrast, by 1949, 64 percent of those polled were either friendly or neutral toward Japan (Feraru 1950).

During the postwar years, Asian American residential patterns changed significantly. Because of the lack of statistical data, a longitudinal study of the changing residential patterns of Asian Americans cannot be made.

However, descriptive accounts of Asian American communities indicate that these enclaves declined in the postwar years. . . .

Although single-ethnic communities were still the norm, residential segregation between Asian nationalities declined in the postwar years. Formerly homogeneous, the ethnic enclaves started to house other Asian groups—as well as non-Asian groups. . . . Multigroup urban centers also emerged. Paul Wong (1972: 34) reported that since the early 1960s, Asian Americans of diverse national origins have moved into the suburbs outside the major Asian communities such as Berkeley or San Mateo, California. Although a small proportion of the local population, these Asian Americans tended to congregate in pockets; consequently, in some residential blocks a majority of the residents were Asian Americans.

Moreover, recent research on suburban segregation indicates that the level of segregation between certain Asian American groups [as shown by indices computed for 822 U.S. suburbs] is often less than that between them and non-Asians. . . . [F]rom 1960 to 1980 the level of segregation between Chinese and Japanese Americans was much less than that between these two groups and blacks and, in one case, less than that between these groups and whites. . . . [Further,] from 1960 to 1980, Chinese segregation from the Japanese shows a more pronounced decline (-14.14) than that of Chinese or Japanese from whites (-10.61 and -7.23 respectively) and from blacks (-4.59 and -2.65 respectively). Though not comprehensive, these studies together suggest that Asian residential segregation declined in the postwar years.

As various Asian groups in the United States interacted, they became aware of common problems and goals that transcended parochial interests and historical antagonisms. One recurrent problem was employment discrimination. . . . Moreover, although the postwar period marked the first time that well-trained Chinese and Japanese Americans could find suitable employment with relative ease, they continued to be passed over for promotion to administrative and supervisory positions (Kitano and Daniels 1988: 47). Asians in the United States began to see themselves as a group that shared important common experiences: exploitation, oppression, and discrimination (Uyematsu 1971).

Because inter-Asian contact and communication were greatest on college campuses, pan-Asianism was strongest there (P. Wong 1972: 33-34). Exposure to one another and to the mainstream society led some young Asian Americans to feel that they were fundamentally different from whites. Disillusioned with the white society and alienated from their traditional communities, many Asian American student activists turned to the alternative strategy of pan-Asian unification (Weiss 1974: 69–70).

The Construction of Pan-Asian Ethnicity

Although broader social struggles and internal demographic changes provided the impetus for the Asian American movement, it was the group's politics—confrontational and explicitly pan-Asian—that shaped the movement's content. Influenced by the internal colonial model, which stresses the commonalities among "colonized groups," college students of Asian ancestry declared solidarity with fellow Asian Americans—and with other Third World minorities (Blauner 1972: ch. 2). Rejecting the label "Oriental," they proclaimed themselves "Asian American." Through pan-Asian organizations, publications, and Asian American studies programs, Asian American activists built pan-Asian solidarity by pointing out their common fate in American society. The pan-Asian concept enabled diverse Asian American groups to understand their "unequal circumstances and histories as being related" (Lowe 1991: 301).

From 'Yellow' to 'Asian American'

Following the example of the Black Power movement, Asian American activists spearheaded their own Yellow Power movement to seek "freedom from racial oppression through the power of a consolidated yellow people" (Uyematsu 1971: 12). In the summer of 1968, more than one hundred students of diverse Asian backgrounds attended an "Are You Yellow?" conference at UCLA to discuss issues of Yellow Power, identity, and the war in Vietnam (Ling 1989: 53). In 1970, a new pan-Asian organization in northern California called itself the "Yellow Seed" because "Yellow [is] the common bond between Asian-Americans and Seed symboliz[es] growth as an individual and as an alliance" (Masada 1970). This "yellow" reference was dropped when Filipino Americans rejected the term, claiming that they were brown, not yellow (Rabaya 1971: 110; Ignacio 1976: 84). . . .

Other community organizers used the term "Oriental" to define their organizations and service centers. In Southern California, the Council of Oriental Organizations (COO) became the political base for the diverse Asian American communities. . . . But Asian American activists also rejected *Oriental* because the term conjures up images of "the sexy Susie Wong, the wily Charlie Chan, and the evil Fu Manchu" (Weiss 1974: 234). It is also a term that smacks of European colonialism and imperialism: *Oriental* means "East"; Asia is "east" only in relationship to Europe, which was taken as the point of reference (Browne 1985). To define their own image and to claim an *American* identity, college students of Asian ancestry coined the term *Asian American* to "stand for all of us Americans of Asian descent" (Ichioka interview). While *Oriental* suggests passivity and acquiescence, *Asian Americans* connotes political activism because an Asian American "gives a damn about his life, his work, his beliefs, and is willing to do almost anything to help Orientals become Asian Americans" (cited in Weiss 1974: 234).

The account above suggests that the creation of a new name is a significant symbolic move in constructing an ethnic identity. In their attempt to forge a pan-Asian identity, Asian American activists first had to coin a composite term that would unify and encompass the constituent groups. Filipino Americans' rejection of the term "yellow" and the activists' objection to the cliché-ridden *Oriental* forced the group to change its name to Asian American. . . . [But,] while *Yellow*, *Oriental*, and *Asian American* connote different ideologies, all three terms signify panethnicity.

Pan-Asian Organizations

. . . In 1968, activists at the University of California, Berkeley, founded one of the first pan-Asian political organizations: the Asian American Political Alliance (AAPA). According to a co-founder of the organization, its establishment marked the first time that the term "Asian American" was used nationally to mobilize people of Asian descent (Ichioka interview). AAPA was formed to increase the political visibility and effectiveness of Asian American activists. . . .

AAPA differed from the traditional Asian cultural groups on most college campuses in two primary ways: its political activism and its pan-Asian emphasis. Reflecting the various political movements from which its members had come, AAPA took progressive stands against the war in Vietnam and in support of other Third World movements (Ichioka interview). Espousing a pan-Asian framework, AAPA brought together young Chinese, Japanese, and Filipino American activists (Nishio 1982: 37). . . . AAPA's influence spread to Southern California as Asian American students formed similar organizations on the UCLA and California State University, Long Beach campuses (Ling 1984; Yoshimura 1989).

Pan-Asian organizations also mushroomed in other parts of the country. In 1969, through the initiative of West Coast students, Asian American organizations began to form on East Coast campuses. . . . Similarly, in the Midwest, the civil rights, antiwar, and United Farm Workers movements drew Asian Americans together. Out of these political gatherings emerged a group of Asian American activists who subsequently formed Madison's Asian Union, Illinois' Asian American Alliance, and Minneapolis' Asian American Political Alliance (*Rice Paper* 1975).

Not only did pan-Asian organizations reinforce the cohesiveness of already existing networks, but they also expanded these networks. By the mid-1970s, *Asian American* had become a familiar term (Lott 1976: 30). Although first coined by college activists, the pan-Asian concept began to be used extensively by professional and community spokespersons to lobby for the health and welfare of Americans of Asian descent. In addition to the local and single-ethnic organizations of an earlier era, Asian American professionals and community activists formed national and pan-Asian organizations such as the Pacific/Asian Coalition and the Asian American Social Workers (Ignacio 1976: 162; Kuo 1979: 283–284). Also, Asian American caucuses could be found in national professional organizations such as the American Public Health Association, the American Sociological Association, the American Psychological Association, the American Psychiatric Association, and the American Librarians Association (Lott 1976: 31). Commenting on the "literally scores of pan-Asian organizations" in the mid-1970s, William Liu (1976: 6) asserted that "the idea of pan-Asian cooperation [was] viable and ripe for development."

Asian American Studies

On college and university campuses, the most important legacy of the Asian American movement was the institutionalization of Asian American studies. Beginning in 1968, under the slogan of self-determination, Asian American and other U.S. Third World students fought for an education more relevant and accessible to their communities. Reflecting the larger national struggle over cultural hegemony, these students demanded the right to control their educational agenda, to design their own programs, and to evaluate their instructors (Umemoto 1989: 3–4). In 1968, after the most prolonged and violent campus struggles in this country's history, Asian American studies programs were established at San Francisco State College (now University) and at the University of California at Berkeley. These campus struggles emboldened students at other colleges to fight for ethnic studies courses, programs, and departments and forced college administrations to heed such demands (Murase 1976a: 205–209). In succeeding years, Asian American Studies programs were established on major campuses throughout the country. . . .

Although varied in their curriculum development and course offerings, Asian American Studies programs built, and continue to build, an Asian American heritage, putting courses and reading selections together and expounding similarities—as well as differences—in the experiences of Asian peoples in the United States. Indeed, the curriculum was designed to help students "know who they are as Asian Americans" (Contemporary Asian Studies Division 1973: 38). Clearly part of the heritage being created hinges on Asian Americans' shared history of racial discrimination. Many courses stress an Asian American identity and experience, yielding highly emotional discussions on subjects dealing with discrimination, alienation, and racism (Weiss 1974: 241). . . .

Also, Asian American scholars began to reinterpret Asian history in the United States to bring out what is common to all Asian Americans. These histories highlight a record of violence against Asians, who were denied the rights of citizenship, forbidden to own land, interned in relocation camps, and forced to live in poverty-stricken enclaves (Jensen and Abeyta 1987: 406). For example, in discussing discriminatory laws and informal acts perpetrated against Chinese, Korean, Filipino, and Japanese immigrants, Lowell Chun-Hoon (1975: 47) concluded that "what is significant [about this exploitation] is that all of these varied Asian groups, each representing a separate country and unique culture, encountered a similar or identical pattern of racial oppression and economic exploitation." Also, Asian Americans were treated increasingly as a single unit of analysis in academic studies. . . .

Along the same lines, in addition to explaining specific group experiences, Asian American writers have turned their attention to those experiences shared by the various Asian peoples. In the 1971 publication *Roots: An Asian American Reader*, the autobiographies and poems that appear in the "Identity" section "express the increasing commitment of Asian Americans to redefine and articulate their individual and collective identity. While they reflect a wide range of backgrounds and responses to American society, there can be found a common level of experience with which all Asians in America can identify" (Tachiki 1971: 4). This new direction enlarged the context of Asian American writing, and led to the use of the term "Asian American literature" (E. Kim 1982). As Jesse Hiraoka (1986: 95) stated, the overriding objective "became that of establishing an Asian American heritage in terms of the arrival and stay of the Asians in the United States, and the changes that occurred as they consolidated their presence in American society."

In sum, Asian American Studies provides an institutional means to reach more Asian American students and to create "an Asian American awareness expressing a unity of all Asians, Chinese, Japanese, Filipino, Korean, Samoan, and Hawaiian" (E. Wong 1988: 248). Its by-products—the Association for Asian American Studies, national conferences, research centers, and publications—further stimulate pan-Asian solidarity because they provide a forum for Asian Americans to discuss common problems and experiences." In these settings, "the experiences of different Asian groups were compared and recognized as historically intertwined" (Ling 1989: 73).

Asian American News Media

The 1960s and 1970s also saw the rapid growth of a pan-Asian news medium directed toward the largest possible Asian audience, covering both ethnic and panethnic developments and concerns. . . . Ethnic publications are important because they promote ethnic ideology and keep alive ethnic symbols and values, heroes, and historical achievements. It is the very business of the ethnic media to be concerned with the events and progress of the ethnic group (Breton 1964: 201). Until the late 1960s, most of the Asian newspapers and periodicals were concerned primarily with local and single-ethnic issues.

Pan-Asian periodicals came out of the Asian American movement, the efforts of Asian American student organizations on university campuses across the country. In fact, "these newspapers, pamphlets, and magazines were the lifeblood of the movement" (Quinsaat 1976: 267). While the traditional ethnic press continued to be important, its neglect and disdain of such political issues as civil rights, the Vietnam war, and ethnic studies prompted young dissidents to launch their own publications. Much of their journalism was committed to the empowerment of the Asian American people.

Although not always successful, some publications attempted to formulate a pan-Asian perspective rather than any singular ethnic outlook (Quinsaat 1976). In 1969, five UCLA students put up $100 each to launch the monthly publication *Gidra*, the first and most widely circulated pan-Asian publication. In all, during its five years of publication, about two hundred individuals participated in producing *Gidra* (Murase 1976b). On the East Coast, *Getting Together*, a New York Chinatown newspaper, expounded Asian American issues from a militant orientation; its stated purpose was to "further advance the just causes of Asian people in this country" (Chin 1971: 30; *Getting Together* 1972: 1). These movement periodicals covered both ethnic and panethnic concerns. . . . Initiated in 1971 by the Yale Asian American Students, *Amerasia Journal* (now housed at UCLA) became the only national scholarly publication devoted exclusively to the study of the experience of Asians in America.

Besides functioning as a source of news for young Asian American activists, these media efforts also forged pan-Asian consciousness. Through articles, poetry, and photographs in a variety of publications, and by meeting together, these young Asian Americans across the country began to communicate with one another and to share their frustrations and their dreams. From these efforts, they began "to formulate their own values, establish their own identities and sense of pride, and create a new 'culture' which they can truly call Asian American" (Chin 1971: 29). . . .

By the mid-1970s, due to inadequate manpower and funding, many of the movement publications had folded. In their place came slicker and more business-minded publications. The transition from radical to "bourgeois" journalism reflects broader changes in pan-Asian political consciousness in the last two decades—from the confrontational to the more orthodox. For example, founded in the late 1980s, both *Rice* and *AsiAm* were nationally distributed magazines geared toward young and upper-income Asian-American professionals. Among the pan-Asian newspapers,

Asian Week, published in San Francisco since 1979, has been the most stable. According to the weekly's managing editor, the management team decided to name the newspaper *Asian Week* instead of the proposed *Chinese Week* to "reflect the widespread acceptance of the pan-Asian concept" (Andersen interview). In recent years, some single-ethnic newspapers have also broadened their scope to cover additional Asian communities. For example, in the mid-1980s, *East/West* dropped its subtitle "A Chinese American Newspaper" and devoted more space to national Asian American issues. A content analysis of the longstanding Japanese American publication *Pacific Citizen* indicates that, from 1955 to 1985, the newspaper became more pan-Asian. . . . [T]he surge in Asian articles coincided with the Asian American movement of the late 1960s.

Although varied in their successes, these pan-Asian journals testify to the salience of a generalized Asian American readership. They are also important because they bring the news of the entire Asian American population to the various Asian American subgroups. In so doing, they enlarge the scope of Asian American awareness and dialogue beyond the boundaries of province and nationality. . . .

Conclusion

The development of a pan-Asian consciousness and constituency reflected broader societal developments and demographic changes, as well as the group's political agenda. By the late 1960s, pan-Asianism was possible because of the more amicable relationships among the Asian countries, the declining residential segregation among diverse Asian groups in America, and the large number of native-born, American-educated political actors. Disillusioned with the larger society and estranged from their traditional communities, third- and fourth-generation Asian Americans turned to the alternative strategy of pan-Asian unification. Through pan-Asian organizations, media, and Asian American Studies programs, these political activists assumed the role of "cultural entrepreneurs" consciously creating a community

of culture out of diverse Asian peoples." This process of pan-Asian consolidation did not proceed smoothly nor did it encompass all Asian Americans. Ethnic chauvinism, competition for scarce resources, and class cleavages continued to divide the subgroups. However, once established, the pan-Asian structure not only reinforced the cohesiveness of already existing networks but also expanded these networks. . . . [A]lthough first conceived by young Asian American activists, the pan-Asian concept was subsequently institutionalized by professionals and community groups, as well as government agencies. The confrontational politics of the activists eventually gave way to the conventional and electoral politics of the politicians, lobbyists, and professionals, as Asian Americans continued to rely on the pan-Asian framework to enlarge their political capacities.

References

Anderson, Patrick. 1990b. "Demos Hire Nguyen to Lure Asians." 9 March.

Blauner, Robert. 1972. *Racial Oppression in America*. New York: Harper & Row.

Breton, Raymond. 1964. "Institutional Completeness of Ethnic Communities and the Personal Relations of Immigrants." *American Journal of Sociology* 70: 193–205.

Browne, Blaine T. 1985. "A Common Thread: American Images of the Chinese and Japanese, 1930–1960." Ph.D. dissertation, University of Oklahoma.

Chan, Sucheng. 1991. *Asian Americans: An Interpretive History*. Boston: Twayne.

Chin, Rocky. 1971. "Getting Beyond Vol. 1, No. 1: Asian American Periodicals." *Bridge* 1(2): 29–32.

Chun-Hoon, Lowell. 1975. "Teaching the Asian-American Experience: Alternative to the Neglect and Racism in Textbooks." *Amerasia Journal* 3(1): 40–59.

Contemporary Asian Studies Division, University of California, Berkeley. 1973. "Curriculum Philosophy for Asian American Studies." *Amerasia Journal* 2(1): 35–46.

Daniels, Roger. 1988. *Asian America: Chinese and Japanese in the United States Since 1850*. Seattle: University of Washington Press.

Feraru, Arthur N. 1950. "Public Opinion Polls on Japan." *Far Eastern Survey* 19(10): 101–103.

Getting Together. 1972. 3–17 March, p. 1.

Hayano, David M. 1981. "Ethnic Identification and Disidentification: Japanese-American Views of Chinese-Americans." *Ethnic Groups* 3(2): 157–171.

Hiraoka, Jesse. 1986. "Asian American Literature." Pp. 93–97 in *Dictionary of Asian American History*, edited by Hyung-Chan Kim. New York: Greenwood Press.

Ignacio, Lemuel F. 1976. *Asian Americans and Pacific Islanders (Is There Such an Ethnic Group?)* San Jose: Pilipino Development Associates.

Jensen, Richard J., and Cara J. Abeyta. 1987. "The Minority in the Middle: Asian-American Dissent in the 1960s and 1970s." *Western Journal of Speech Communications* 51: 402–416.

Kim, Elaine H. 1982. *Asian American Literature: An Introduction to the Writings and Their Social Context*. Philadelphia: Temple University Press.

Kitano, Harry H. L., and Roger Daniels. 1988. *Asian Americans: Emerging Minorities*. Englewood Cliffs, NJ: Prentice-Hall.

Kuo, Wen H. 1979. "On the Study of Asian-Americans: Its Current State and Agenda." *Sociological Quarterly* 20 (Spring): 279–290.

Ling, Susie Hsiuhan. 1984. "The Mountain Movers: Asian American Women's Movement in Los Angeles." M.A. thesis, University of California, Los Angeles.

——. 1989. "The Mountain Movers: Asian American Women's Movement in Los Angeles." *Amerasia Journal* 15(1): 51–67.

Liu, William. 1976. "Asian American Research: Views of a Sociologist." *Asian Studies Occasional Report*, no. 2.

Lott, Juanita Tamayo. 1976. "The Asian American Concept: In Quest of Identity." *Bridge*, November, pp. 30–34.

Lowe, Lisa. 1991. "Heterogeneity, Hybridity, Multiplicity: Marking Asian American Differences." *Diaspora* 1: 24–44.

Masada, Saburo. 1970. "Stockton's Yellow Seed." *Pacific Citizen*, 9 October.

Murase, Mike. 1976a. "Ethnic Studies and Higher Education for Asian Americans." Pp. 205–223 in *Counterpoint: Perspectives on Asian America*, edited by Emma Gee. Los Angeles: UCLA Asian American Studies Center.

——. 1976b. "Toward Barefoot Journalism." Pp. 307–319 in *Counterpoint: Perspectives on Asian America*, edited by Emma Gee. Los Angeles: UCLA Asian American Studies Center.

Nishio, Alan. 1982. "Personal Reflections on the Asian National Movements." *East Wind*, Spring/Summer, pp. 36–38.

Omi, Michael, and Howard Winant. 1986. *Racial Formation in the United States: From the 1960s to the 1980s*. New York: Routledge and Kegan Paul.

Ong, Paul. 1989. "California's Asian Population: Past Trends and Projections for the Year 2000." Los Angeles: Graduate School of Architecture and Urban Planning.

Quinsaat, Jesse. 1976. "Asians in the Media: The Shadows in the Spotlight." Pp. 264–268 in *Counterpoint: Perspectives on Asian America*, edited by Emma Gee. Los Angeles: UCLA Asian American Studies Center.

Rabaya, Violet. 1971. "I Am Curious (Yellow?)." Pp. 110–111 in *Roots: An Asian American Reader*, edited by Emma Gee. Los Angeles: UCLA Asian American Studies Center.

Rice Paper. 1975. 1(2): (whole issue).

Tachiki, Amy. 1971. "Introduction." Pp. 1–5 in *Roots: An Asian American Reader*, edited by Amy Tachiki, Eddie Wong, and Franklin Odo. Los Angeles: UCLA Asian American Studies Center.

Umemoto, Karen. 1989. " 'On Strike!' San Francisco State College Strike, 1968–69: The Roots of Asian American Students." *Amerasia Journal* 15(1): 3–41.

Uyematsu, Amy. 1971. "The Emergence of Yellow Power in America." Pp. 9–13 in *Roots: An Asian American Reader*, edited by Amy Tachiki, Eddie Wong, and Franklin Odo. Los Angeles: UCLA Asian American Studies Center.

Weiss, Melford S. 1974. *Valley City: A Chinese Community in America*. Cambridge, MA: Schenkman.

Wong, Elaine. 1988. "UCLA Denies Any Policy of Limiting Asian Admissions." *Los Angeles Times*, 19 November.

Wong, Paul. 1972. "The Emergence of the Asian-American Movement." *Bridge* 2(1): 33–39.

Yoshimura, Evelyn. 1989. "How I Became an Activist and What It All Means to Me." *Amerasia Journal* 15(1): 106–109.

Yuan, D. Y. 1966. "Chinatown and Beyond: The Chinese Population in Metropolitan New York." *Phylon* 23(4): 321–332.

Native Americans

At the time that Christopher Columbus "discovered" America, the Native population numbered in the millions (Thornton 1987; Snipp 1989). Indeed, while scholarly estimates differ significantly, some revisionist accounts put the figure as high as 10 million. By 1900, this number had declined to less than 250,000. However, according to 1990 census figures, a striking reversal of Native American numbers has apparently taken place: Approximately 2 million persons now identify themselves as Native Americans (Eschbach 1993). The dynamics underlying the rising numbers of self-identified Native Americans in recent years are complex and multifaceted, and are discussed at greater length by Nagel (this volume). Most Native American tribes today are small, and only four of these report more than 100,000 members. The two largest tribes today are Cherokee (308,000) and Navajo (219,000); together they account for more than one-fourth of all Native Americans. According to recent estimates (U.S. Bureau of the Census 1993), most Native Americans live in states that are west of the Mississippi River; Oklahoma has the largest Native American population, followed by California and Arizona. Only a small minority of the Native American population today (20 percent or so) lives on reservations and trust lands. The largest single concentration of urban-dwelling Native Americans can be found in the Los Angeles metropolitan area, where it is estimated that approximately 58,000 Native Americans from 117 different groups reside. Of all urban settings, Oklahoma City has the largest percentage of Native Americans; they account for roughly 4 percent of the population of that metropolitan area (Feagin and Feagin 1996: 219).

The long history of subordination and genocide of Native peoples began prior to the formal establishment of the Republic (Thornton 1987). Dutch and English settlers seized land from several of the East Coast tribes that relied mainly on hunting, farming, and fishing, and initiated a pattern of violent subjugation that was later replicated in other areas. In addition, the early English settlers enslaved significant numbers of Natives, subsequently coming to rely heavily on African slaves because of the persistent risk of escape by Natives. After the founding of the Republic, federal officials facilitated the theft of Native lands. Despite declarations of good faith, government officials negotiated treaties with various tribes through threat, fraud, and deception, and then repeatedly failed to honor their agreements (McNickle 1962). Settlers in frontier areas were permitted to ignore boundary rights, and to encroach constantly onto tribal lands, pushing Native peoples steadily into western frontier territories. Some high-ranking leaders, including President Andrew Jackson, supported or condoned these activities, and opposed the establishment or enforcement of treaties with Native peoples.

In addition to this ongoing pattern of land seizure by settlers, Natives were also subjected to large-scale forced relocation through the Indian Removal Act of 1830. Cherokees and other tribes migrated in large numbers at gunpoint along the "Trail of Tears" to lands west of the Mississippi River (McNickle 1962). While many Natives died en route, the survivors faced the threat of starvation and illness at the conclusion of the long march, as well as formidable problems of adaptation to unfamiliar territory. Further, throughout the 19th century westward migrants encroached with increasing regularity on the territories of various Plains tribes, who had adopted nomadic hunting lifestyles. Contrary to the prevailing Hollywood imagery, violent clashes between settlers and Natives were relatively infrequent, and claimed far fewer casualties on either side than is popularly believed (Unruh 1979). Much of the violence during this era involved attacks by federal troops against the Sioux, Comanches, and other tribes, whose attempts to fight back were met with massive retribution.

Throughout most of the 19th century, the federal government pursued a two-track policy toward Native American tribes. On the one hand, tribes were forced onto reservations, where they were treated as "wards" of the state. Those tribes that resisted were tracked by federal troops and targeted for extermination. The Bureau of Indian Affairs (BIA)—established in 1824—was charged with the administration of reservation life, the provision of supplies, the organization of lands, and other aspects of relations between the federal government and reservation Natives. While the BIA was responsible for aiding and protecting Native Americans, its activities also included suppressing Native cultures and religions and ensuring that tribal political leaders were malleable to the interests of the federal government and land-hungry European Americans.

An array of shifting, and often contradictory, government policies over the past century has contributed to the current marginalization of Native Americans (Thornton 1987). In the late 19th century, federal policy attempted to force the assimilation of tribal members by providing land to Native Americans in small allotments (40-160 acres), distributed to family units and individuals rather than tribal collectivities. The goal was to turn Native Americans into farming entrepreneurs, distancing them from traditional tribal cultures. When the courts ruled that Native Americans were technically not U.S. citizens, and hence could not vote in elections, the 1887 Dawes Act provided that those who demonstrated competence in managing their allotments would be granted citizenship. This assimilationist policy was widely deemed a failure, and its citizenship provision was superceded by the Indian Citizenship Act of 1924, which granted citizenship to all Native Americans.

Federal policy toward Native Americans underwent an abrupt change with the Indian Reorganization Act (IRA), a piece of New Deal legislation passed in 1934 and developed by the liberal commissioner of Indian affairs, John Collier (Spicer 1962). Under the IRA, Native Americans were granted an array of cultural and civil rights; the land allotment programs begun in the 1880s were ended. The IRA also provided for the establishment of semi-autonomous tribal governments, as well as measures to stimulate the economic development of reservations, and new oversight designed to curb the exploitative transfer of tribal lands to European American interests. Despite a number of such progressive steps, the IRA was criticized for excluding the Oklahoma tribes and for granting too much power to the Secretary of the Interior. In addition, critics opposed provisions designed to replace tribal governance structures with new councils, which resembled corporate boards of directors more than traditional structures, and which required federal approval (Jaimes, this volume). As an outgrowth of the IRA, however, a number of tribes began the process of self-government, managing their own reservation affairs under federal supervision.

During the post-World War II era, federal policy toward Native Americans has undergone several additional changes (Snipp 1989). During the 1950s, there was a clear turn away from the liberalizing provisions of the IRA. Indeed, legislation was aimed at terminating federal supervision of tribes. This initiative was pressed by fiscal conservatives, who hoped to save the costs of administering reservation affairs and providing social assistance to Native Americans, as well as by European Americans seeking greater access to tribal lands. In more recent years, however, there has been another broad policy turn away from termination and toward Native American autonomy and development. Since the 1970s, legislation has allowed for the devolution of some functions (e.g., education, some social programs) to local reservations, and also increased access to credit for entrepreneurial ventures involving Native Americans. Nevertheless, the BIA has maintained control over federal policies governing tribal recognition, as well as regulations defining which individuals can claim Native American status (Jaimes, this volume). The BIA also continues to supervise tribal government, banking, highways, utilities, and millions of dollars in tribal trust funds. Although the BIA has traditionally afforded at least some protection against corporate interests and others seeking to exploit Native American lands and resources, there is a growing push for tribal autonomy from BIA supervision.

As we prepare to enter the 21st century, a number of significant issues and challenges face the Native American population. Despite some improvement in recent decades, Native Americans continue to experience high unemployment rates (U.S. Bureau of the Census 1993). According to 1990 census data, Native American men overall suffered from 15 percent unemployment—a rate roughly three times higher than that for whites (European Americans). For those Native Americans residing on reservations, the unemployment rate was much higher—over 25 percent—and on some reservations more than 50 percent of the adults were unemployed. Further, these figures do not take into account the undoubtedly large numbers of Native Americans who have grown discouraged and have stopped looking for work. Native American poverty rates are also comparatively high. Approximately 30 percent of all Native American families lived below the poverty line in 1990; among reservation-dwelling families, this figure was nearly 50 percent. The median income of non-reservation Native Americans was only 62 percent of that of the U.S. population as a whole; for Native American families on reservations, this figure was an appalling 38 percent (U.S. Bureau of the Census 1993). Not surprisingly, these economic conditions are associated with higher than average rates of various health problems, comparatively high mortality rates, and above-average rates of alcoholism and various other social problems among Native Americans, especially on reservations (Snipp 1992).

Although reservations tend to have high rates of poverty and unemployment (Moore, this volume), there are significant variations across reservations. Some gaps have widened since the 1970s, when federal policies shifted to provide greater tribal autonomy over economic development and other reservation affairs. A few comparisons illustrate these differences (Cornell and Kalt 1992): In 1989, the unemployment rate among adults on the Rosebud Sioux reservation was estimated by the Bureau of Labor Statistics (BLS) at 90 percent, and fewer than 5 percent of adults had annual incomes above the BIA-determined poverty line. Further, poverty rates among the Rosebud Sioux actually rose by 10 percent between 1977-89. Similar deterioration was observed on various other Native American reservations during this period. In contrast, among the Kootenai residents on the Flathead reservation, poverty rates dropped by double-digit percentages over the same period; similar declines in poverty were noted among the White Mountain Apache, Cochiti Pueblo, and other reservation populations (Cornell and Kalt 1992).

What accounts for such divergent experiences? Despite the plethora of factors traditionally thought to impede development on reservations, including federal government domination and European American exploitation, data compiled by the Harvard Project on American Indian Economic Development underscore the capacity of many tribes to craft innovative development approaches. Increasing autonomy from federal agencies is permitting some tribes to pursue development that is "successful" on their terms, promoting economic security while preserving cultural integrity and political sovereignty. Clearly some factors associated with reservation development (e.g., natural resource endowments, distance from markets) are virtually immutable, and others (e.g., tribal cultural orientations, human capital) can be changed only slowly. However, Cornell and Kalt (1992) point out that tribal institutions can also have a major impact (for good or ill) on reservation development, and often tribal governance structures are open to reform. In general, they argue that tribes are better able to promote development when there is a match between cultural standards of government legitimacy and the formal structure of tribes' current government. Further, they find that it is extremely important for tribes: (1) to establish clear separation of powers among branches of the governance structure, with a viable system of checks and balances; and (2) to insulate the day-to-day administration of tribal enterprises from political pressures (e.g., for nepotism, cronyism, or misappropriation of wealth).

In recent years, tribes have pursued a range of development activities, with varying degrees of success. A number of tribes are attempting to capitalize on their unique legal and political status, which gives them access to market niches and resources not readily available to competitors (Snipp 1992). For instance, tribes have developed vigorous gaming industries (e.g., high stakes bingo, racing, casinos) on tribal lands, largely beyond the reach of state regulators (Cordeiro 1992). Other tribes have established duty-free stores that are exempt from state taxes. Some tribes have profited from the prudent investment of proceeds from treaty rights settlements (White 1990). Bordewich (this volume) discusses the interesting case of the Mississippi Choctaw, who have used corporate investment in light manufacturing industries as a strategic device to accumulate capital, to enhance human capital among the Choctaw, and to stimulate infrastructure development and further economic diversification.

One of the pressing problems that limits reservation development is the low average level of education (Cornell and Kalt 1992; Snipp 1992). Moreover, some studies indicate that human capital deficits, rather than discrimination, are mainly responsible for the relatively low earnings and negative labor market experiences of many Native Americans (U.S. Bureau of the Census 1993). Only around 60 percent of Native Americans over the age of 25 have completed high school, as compared with around 75 percent of all Americans in that age range. The Native American figure may be deceptively high, since it almost certainly includes a large number of GEDs (Snipp 1992). High school

dropout rates among Native Americans are alarmingly high; a 1991 Department of Education task force report estimated this figure at 36 percent, which is substantially higher than the figures for other racial and ethnic populations in the U.S. (U.S. Department of Education 1991). This report severely criticized both federal and local educational systems for their resistance to Native American cultures, and for their failure to meet the needs of Native American students. Moreover, fewer than 10 percent of Native Americans over the age of 25 have a college degree (U.S. Bureau of the Census 1995), and Native American enrollment in higher education remains quite low, despite increases in the size of the college-age population. Since the late 1960s, approximately two dozen tribally controlled colleges have formed; while most of these are two-year community colleges that emphasize mainly vocational education, a few offer bachelor's and advanced degrees (Snipp 1992). Improving educational opportunities among Native Americans is critical for future economic development and prosperity.

Native Americans confront other significant issues as well. For instance, a range of struggles continue over water and fishing rights, especially involving tribal lands in the Pacific Northwest (Olson and Wilson 1984). While the substantial natural resource endowments located on some tribal lands, especially in the western U.S., offer potential development advantages, there are also concerns about exploitation of tribes by corporate interests eager to mine the rich mineral reserves. To reduce this risk, nearly 60 Native American groups now belong to the Council of Energy Resources Tribes (CERT), which was formed in the 1970s to assist tribes in negotiating more favorable contracts with mining and energy corporations (Feagin and Feagin 1996: 217).

Further, some types of natural resource extraction raise concerns about environmental justice for Native Americans. In particular, radioactive materials have long plagued western reservations. The largest and most productive uranium (and vanadium) mines in the U.S. are in the four-corners area, and roughly two-thirds of all uranium mines in

North America are located on Native lands. For two decades uranium mining on the reservations proceeded with minimal regulation, leaving radioactive debris that threatened water supplies of many communities. In recent years, some tribes have allowed construction of hazardous waste facilities on tribal lands, including the mammoth Yucca Mountain Project, a permanent radioactive waste storage facility in Nevada. The federal government encouraged acceptance of this project with the enticement of money (royalties and jobs) and with the understanding that tribes could develop and implement appropriate environmental safeguards. But many critics suspect that the far-reaching costs of such projects will far outweigh any financial benefits that accrue to Native Americans.

To many observers, these and other episodes exemplify the two faces of power that constitute the essence of internal colonialism: (1) exploitation, or the active extraction of resources and labor; and (2) neglect, or the passive reluctance to return benefits to affected areas or address the human consequences of exploitation. But internal colonialism also has important cultural dimensions, which Native American groups are increasingly mobilizing to protest. European American exploiters of sacred lands and artifacts have rarely worked to preserve or return them. Native American religious rituals, dress, and artistic traditions (including performing arts) are commonly misrepresented by European American institutions (Snipp 1989). Key aspects of Native history are also widely misreported, and Native Americans are the focus of unflattering stereotypes in media, film, and popular culture. Further, the (mis)appropriation of Native American cultural artifacts and expressions has become extremely popular and chic. Pictoral art and crafts are cravenly mass-produced. "Sweat lodges" have gained popularity as New Age reinterpretations of sacred Native American rituals, amid scattered protests from Native tribes. These insulting misappropriations also extend to sporting events, where depictions of maniacal Washington "Redskins" and the Atlanta Braves' "tomahawk chop" have been widely criticized (Davis 1993).

As the 21st century rapidly approaches, Native American populations confront a number of difficult challenges. While improving the economic fortunes and futures of all Natives, and especially those on reservations, is a major concern, other complex issues also loom large. For instance, debates will continue over matters of identity—over who can legitimately claim the label "Native American," and about the consequences of the long history of federal policies using "blood quanta" to define who is (and is not) Native American (Jaimes, this volume). Moreover, in the wake of the contemporary political awakening among Native Americans, many leaders and commentators wonder how to build on "pan-Indian" identity and consciousness (Nagel, this volume) to articulate a coherent public agenda and enhance Native American political influence.

References

Cordeiro, E.E. 1992. "The Economics of Bingo: Factors Influencing the Success of Bingo Operations on American Indian Reservations." Pp. 205-238 in *What Can Tribes Do? Strategies and Institutions in American Indian Economic Development*, edited by S. Cornell and J.P. Kalt. Los Angeles: American Indian Studies Center, UCLA.

Cornell, S., and J.P. Kalt. 1992. "Reloading the Dice: Improving the Chances for Economic Development on American Indian Reservations." Pp. 1-59 in *What Can Tribes Do? Strategies and Institutions in American Indian Economic Development*, edited by S. Cornell and J.P. Kalt. Los Angeles: American Indian Studies Center, UCLA.

Davis, L.R. 1993. "Protest Against the Use of Native American Mascots: A Challenge to Traditional American Identity." *Journal of Sport and Social Issues* 17 (April): 9-22.

Eschbach, K. 1993. "Changing Identification Among American Indians and Alaskan Natives." *Demography* 30: 635-652.

Feagin, J.R., and C.B. Feagin. 1996. *Racial and Ethnic Relations*, 5th ed. Englewood Cliffs, NJ: Prentice-Hall.

McNickle, D.A. 1962. *The Indian Tribes of the United States*. London: Oxford University Press.

Olson, J.S., and R. Wilson. 1984. *Native Americans in the Twentieth Century*. Provo, UT: Brigham Young University Press.

Snipp, C.M. 1989. *American Indians: The First of This Land*. New York: Russell Sage Foundation.

———. 1992. "Sociological Perspectives on American Indians." *Annual Review of Sociology* 18: 351-372.

Spicer, E.H. 1962. *Cycles of Conquest*. Tucson: University of Arizona Press.

Thornton, R. 1987. *American Indian Holocaust and Survival*. Norman, OK: University of Oklahoma Press.

Unruh, J.D. 1979. *The Plains Across*. Urbana: University of Illinois Press.

U.S. Bureau of the Census 1993. *We the First Americans*. Washington: U.S. Government Printing Office.

———. 1995. *Statistical Abstract of the United States: 1995* (115th ed.). Washington: U.S. Government Printing Office.

U.S. Department of Education. 1991. *Indian Nations at Risk: An Educational Strategy for Change*. Washington: U.S. Government Printing Office.

White, R.H. 1990. *Tribal Assets*. New York: Henry Holt.

15

Federal Indian Identification Policy:

A Usurpation of Indigenous Sovereignty in North America

M. Annette Jaimes

By all accepted standards of international jurisprudence and human decency, American Indian peoples whose territory lies within the borders of the United States hold compelling legal and moral rights to be treated as fully sovereign nations. It is axiomatic that any such national entity is inherently entitled to exercise the prerogative of determining for itself the criteria by which its citizenry, or "membership," is to be recognized by other sovereign nations. This is a principle that applies equally to superpowers such as the U.S. and to non-powers such as Grenada and Monaco. In fact, it is a tenet so widely understood and imbedded in international law, custom, and convention that it bears no particular elaboration here.

Contrary to virtually universal practice, the United States has opted to preempt unilaterally the rights of many North American indigenous nations to engage in this most fundamental level of internal decisionmaking. Instead, in pursuit of the interests of their own state rather than those of the nations that are thereby affected, federal policymakers have increasingly imposed "Indian identification standards" of their own design. Typically centering upon a notion of "blood quantum"—not especially different in its conception from the eugenics code once adopted by nazi Germany in its effort to achieve "racial purity" . . .—this aspect of U.S. policy has increasingly wrought havoc with the American Indian sense of nation-hood (and often the individual sense of self) over the past century. This chapter offers a brief analysis of the motivations underlying this federal usurpation of the American Indian expression of sovereignty and points out certain implications of it.

Federal Obligations

The more than 370 formally ratified treaties entered into by the United States with various Indian nations represent the basic real estate documents by which the federal government now claims legal title to most of its land base. In exchange for the lands ceded by Indians, the United States committed itself to the permanent provision of a range of services to Indian populations (i.e., the citizens of the Indian nations with which the treaty agreements were reached), which would assist them in adjusting their economies and ways of life to their newly constricted territories. . . . As Evelyn C. Adams frames it:

> Treaties with the Indians varied widely, stipulating cash annuities to be paid over a specified period of time or perpetually; rations and clothing, farming implements and domestic animals, and instruction in agriculture along with other educational opportunities . . . [And eventually] the school supplemented the Federal program of practical teaching.[1]

The reciprocal nature of such agreements received considerable reinforcement when it was determined, early in the 19th century, that "the enlightenment and civilization of the Indian" might yield—quite aside from any need on the part of the United States to honor its international obligations—a certain utility in terms of subordinating North America's indigenous peoples to Euroamerican domination. Secretary of War John C. Calhoun articulated this quite clearly in 1818:

> By a proper combination of force and persuasion, of punishment and rewards, they [the Indians] ought to be brought within the pales of law and civilization. Left to themselves, they will never reach that desirable condition. Before the slow operation of reason and experience can

convince them of its superior advantages, they must be overwhelmed by the mighty torrent of our population. Such small bodies, with savage customs and character, cannot, and ought not, to be allowed to exist in an independent society. Our laws and manners ought to supersede their present savage manners and customs . . . their [treaty] annuities would constitute an ample school fund; and education, comprehending as well as the common arts of life, reading, writing, and arithmetic, ought not to be left discretionary with the parents. . . . When sufficiently advanced in civilization, they would be permitted to participate in such civil and political rights as the respective States.[2]

The utter cynicism involved in Calhoun's position—that of intentionally using the treaty instruments by which the United States conveyed recognition of Indian sovereignty as the vehicle with which to destroy that same sovereignty—speaks for itself. The more important point for purposes of this study, however, is that by 1820 U.S. strategic interests had congealed around the notion of extending federal obligations to Indians. The tactic was therefore continued throughout the entirety of the period of U.S. internal territorial conquest and consolidation.[3] By 1900, the federal obligations to Indian nations were therefore quite extensive.

Financial Factors

. . . The situation was compounded by the fact that the era of Indian population decline engendered by war and disease had also come to an end; the population eligible for per capita benefits, which had been reduced to a quarter-million by the 1890s, could be expected to rebound steadily in the 20th century. With its land base secured, the United States was casting about for a satisfactory mechanism to avoid paying the ongoing costs associated with its acquisition.

The most obvious route to this end, of course, lay in simply and overtly refusing to comply with the terms of the treaties, thus abrogating them.[4] The problems in this regard were, however, both two-fold and extreme. First, the deliberate invalidation of the U.S. treaties with the Indians would (obviously) tend to simultaneously invalidate the legitimacy which the country attributed to its occupancy of much of North America. Second, such a move would immediately negate the useful and carefully nurtured image the U.S. had cultivated of itself as a country of progressive laws rather than raw force. The federal government had to appear to continue to meet its commitments, while at the same time avoiding them, or at least containing them at some acceptable level. A devious approach to the issue was needed.

This was found in the so-called "blood quantum" or "degree of Indian blood" standard of American Indian identification which had been adopted by Congress in 1887 as part of the General Allotment Act. The function of this piece of legislation was to expedite the process of Indian "civilization" by unilaterally dissolving their collectively (i.e., nationally) held reservation land holdings. Reservation lands were reallocated in accordance with the "superior" (i.e., Euroamerican) concept of property: *individually* deeded land parcels, usually of 160 acres each. Each Indian, identified as being those documentably of *one-half or more Indian blood*, was entitled to receive title in fee of such a parcel; all others were simply disenfranchised altogether. Reserved Indian land which remained unallotted after all "blooded" Indians had received their individual parcels was to be declared "surplus" and opened up for non-Indian use and occupancy.

Needless to say, there were nowhere near enough Indians meeting the Act's genetic requirements to absorb by individual parcel the quantity of acreage involved in the formerly reserved land areas. Consequently, between 1887 and 1934, the aggregate Indian land base within the U.S. was "legally" reduced from about 138 million acres to about 48 million.[5] Moreover, the allotment process itself had been manipulated in such a way that the worst reservation acreage tended to be parceled out to Indians, while the best was opened to non-Indian homesteading and corporate use; nearly 20 million of the acres remaining in Indian hands by the latter year were arid or semi-arid, and thus marginal or useless for agricultural purposes.[6]

By the early 1900s, then, the eugenics mechanism of the blood quantum had already proven itself such a boon in the federal management of its Indian affairs that it was generally adapted as the "eligibility factor," triggering entitlement to any federal service from the issuance of commodity rations to health care, annuity payments, and educational benefits. If the government could not repeal its obligations to Indians, it could at least act to limit their number, thereby diminishing the cost associated with underwriting their entitlements on a per capita basis. Concomitantly, it must have seemed logical that if the overall number of Indians could be kept small, the administrative expenses involved in their service programs might also be held to a minimum. Much of the original impetus toward the federal preemption of the sovereign Indian prerogative of defining "who's Indian," and the standardization of the racist degree-of-blood method of Indian identification, derived from the budgetary considerations of a federal government anxious to avoid paying its bills.

Other Economic Factors

As the example of the General Allotment Act clearly demonstrates, economic determinants other than the mere outflow of cash from the federal treasury figure into the federal utilization of the blood quantum. The huge windfall of land expropriated by the United States as a result of the act was only the tip of the iceberg. For instance, in constricting the acknowledged size of Indian populations, the government could technically meet its obligations to reserve "first rights" to water usage for Indians while simultaneously siphoning off artificial "surpluses" to non-Indian agricultural, ranching, municipal, and industrial use in the arid west[7]. The same principle pertains to the assignment of fishing quotas in the Pacific Northwest, a matter directly related to the development of a lucrative non-Indian fishing industry there.[8]

By the 1920s, it was also becoming increasingly apparent that much of the agriculturally worthless terrain left to Indians after allotment lay astride rich deposits of natural resources such as coal, copper, oil, and natural gas; later in the century, it was revealed that some 60 percent of all "domestic" uranium reserves also lay beneath reservation lands. It was therefore becoming imperative, from the viewpoint of federal and corporate economic planners, to gain unhindered access to these assets. Given that it would have been just as problematic to simply seize the resources as it would have been to abrogate the treaties, another expedient was required. This assumed the form of legislation unilaterally extending the responsibilities of citizenship (though not all the rights; Indians are still regulated by about 5,000 more laws than other citizens) over all American Indians within the United States.

> Approximately two-thirds of the Indian population had citizenship conferred upon them under the 1877 Allotment Act, as a condition of the allotment of their holdings.... [In 1924] an act of Congress [8 U.S.C.A. 1402 (a) (2)] declared all Indians to be citizens of the United States and of the states in which they resided.[9]...

The Indian Citizenship Act greatly confused the circumstances even of many of the blooded and federally certified Indians insofar as it was held to bear legal force, and to carry legal obligations, whether or not any given Indian or group of Indians wished to be a U.S. citizen. As for the host of non-certified, mixed-blood people residing in the U.S., their status was finally "clarified"; they had been definitionally absorbed into the American mainstream at the stroke of the congressional pen. And, despite the fact that the act technically left certified Indians occupying the status of citizenship in their own indigenous nation as well as in the U.S. (a "dual form" of citizenship so awkward as to be sublime), the juridical door had been opened by which the weight of Indian obligations would begin to accrue more to the U.S. than to themselves. Resource negotiations would henceforth be conducted between "American citizens" rather than between representatives of separate nations, a context in which federal and corporate arguments "for the greater good" could be predicted to prevail.

In 1934, the effects of the citizenship act were augmented by the passage of the Indian Reorganization Act [(IRA)]. The expressed purpose of this law was finally and completely to usurp the traditional mechanisms of American Indian governance (e.g., the traditional chiefs, council of elders, etc.), replacing them with a system of federally approved and regulated "tribal councils." . . .

. . . [T]here has been very little for the IRA form of Indian government to do *but* sign off on leasing and other business arrangements with external interests. The situation was and is compounded by the fact that grassroots Indian resistance to the act's "acceptance" on many reservations was overcome by federal manipulation of local referenda.[10] This has left the IRA governments in the position of owing Washington rather than their supposed constituents for whatever legitimacy they may possess. All in all, it was and is a situation made to order for the rubber-stamping of plans integral to U.S. economic development at the direct expense of Indian nations and individual Indian people. This is readily borne out by the fact that, as of 1984, American Indians received, on the average, less than 20 percent of the market royalty rates (i.e., the rates paid to non-Indians) for the extraction of minerals from their land. As Winona LaDuke observes:

> By official census counts, there are only about 1 1/2 million Indians in the United States. By conservative estimates a quarter of all the low sulphur coal in the United States lies under our reservation land. About 15 percent of all the oil and natural gas lies there, as well as two-thirds of the uranium. One hundred percent of all U.S. uranium production since 1955 has been on Indian land. And we have a lot of copper, timber, water rights and other resources too. By any reasonable estimation, with this small number of people and vast amount of resources, we should be the richest group in the United States. But we are the poorest. Indians have the lowest per capita income of any population group in the U.S. We have the highest rate of unemployment and the lowest level of educational attainment. We have the highest rates of malnutrition, plague disease, death by expo-

sure and infant mortality. On the other hand, we have the shortest life-span. Now, I think this says it all. Indian wealth is going somewhere, and that somewhere is definitely not to Indians. I don't know your definition of colonialism, but this certainly fits into mine.[11]

In sum, the financial advantages incurred by the United States in its appropriation of the definition of Indian identity have been neatly joined to even more powerful economic motivators during this century. The previously noted reluctance of the federal government to pay its bills cannot be uncoupled from its desire to profit from the resources of others.

Contemporary Political Factors

. . . Today, the function of the Indian identity question appears to reside at the less rarified level of maintaining the status quo. First, it goes to the matter of keeping the aggregate number of Indians at less than 1 percent of the overall U.S. population and thus devoid of any potential electoral power. Second, and perhaps of equal importance, it goes to the classic "divide and conquer" strategy of keeping Indians at odds with one another, even within their own communities. As Tim Giago, conservative editor of the *Lakota Times*, asks:

> Don't we have enough problems trying to unite without . . . additional headaches? Why must people be categorized as full-bloods, mixed-bloods, etc? Many years ago, the Bureau of Indian Affairs decided to establish blood quanta for the purpose of [tribal] enrollment. At that time, blood quantum was set at one-fourth degree for enrollment. Unfortunately, through the years this caused many people on the reservation to be categorized and labeled. . . . [The] situation [is] created solely by the BIA, with the able assistance of the Department of Interior.[12]

What has occurred is that the limitation of federal resources allocated to meeting U.S. obligations to American Indians has become so severe that Indians themselves have increasingly begun to enforce the race codes excluding the genetically marginalized from both identification as Indian citizens and consequent entitlements. In theory, such a posture leaves greater per capita shares for all remaining "bona fide" Indians. But, as American Indian Movement activist Russell Means has pointed out:

> The situation is absurd. Our treaties say nothing about your having to be such-and-such a degree of blood in order to be covered. . . when the federal government made its guarantees to our nations in exchange for our land, it committed to provide certain services to us as we defined ourselves. As nations, and as a *people*. This seems to have been forgotten. Now we have Indian people who spend most of their time trying to prevent other Indian people from being recognized as such, just so that a few more crumbs— crumbs from the federal table—may be available to them, personally. I don't have to tell you that this isn't the Indian way of doing things. The Indian way would be to get together and demand what is coming to each and every one of us, instead of trying to cancel each other out. We are acting like colonized peoples, like subject peoples. . . .[13]

The nature of the dispute has followed the classic formulation of Frantz Fanon, wherein the colonizer contrives issues which pit the colonized against one another, fighting viciously for some presumed status within the colonial structure, never having time or audacity enough to confront their oppressors.[14] In the words of Stella Pretty Sounding Flute, a member of the Crow Creek band of Lakota, "My grandmother used to say that Indian blood was getting all mixed up, and some day there would be a terrible mess. . . . [Now] no matter which way we turn, the white man has taken over."[15]

The problem, of course, has been conscientiously exacerbated by the government through its policies of leasing individual reservation land parcels to non-Indians, increasingly "checkerboarding" tribal holdings since 1900. Immediate economic consequences aside, this has virtually ensured that a sufficient number of non-Indians would be residents in reservations, and that intermarriage would steadily result. During the 1950s, the federal relocation program—in which reservation-based Indians were subsidized to move to cities, where they might be anticipated as being subsumed within vastly larger non-Indian populations—accelerated the process of "biological hybridization." Taken in combination with the ongoing federal insistence that "Indianness" could be measured only by degree of blood, these policies tend to speak for themselves. Even in 1972 when, through the Indian Education Act (86 *Stat.* 334), the government seemed finally to be abandoning the blood quantum, there was a hidden agenda. As Lorelei DeCora (Means), a former Indian education program coordinator, put it:

> The question was really one of control, whether Indians would ever be allowed to control the identification of their own group members or citizens. First there was this strict blood quantum thing, and it was enforced for a hundred years, over the strong objections of a lot of Indians. Then, when things were sufficiently screwed up because of that, the feds suddenly reverse themselves completely, saying it's all a matter of self-identification. Almost anybody who wants to can just walk in and announce that he or she is Indian—no familiarity with tribal history, or Indian affairs, community recognition, or anything else really required— and, under the law, there's not a lot that Indians can do about it. The whole thing is suddenly just . . . really out of control. At that point, you really did have a lot of people showing up claiming that one of their ancestors, seven steps removed, had been some sort of "Cherokee princess." And we were obliged to accept that, and provide services. Hell, if all of that was real, there are more Cherokees in the world than there are Chinese.[16]

Predictably, Indians of all perspectives on the identity question reacted strongly against such gratuitous dilution of themselves. The result was a broad rejection of what was perceived as "the federal attempt to convert us from being the citizens of our own sovereign nations into benign members of some sort of all-purpose U.S. 'minority group,' without sovereign rights."[17] For its part, the government, without so much as a pause to consider the connotations of the word "sovereign" in this connection, elected to view such statements as an Indian demand for resumption of the universal application of the blood-quantum standard. Consequently, the Reagan administration, during the 1980s, set out to gut the Indian Education Act[18] and to enforce degree-of-blood requirements for federal services, such as those of the Indian Health Service.[19]

An even clearer example of the contemporary reassertion of eugenics principles in federal Indian identification policies came under the Bush administration. On November 30, 1990, Public Law 101-644 (104 *Stat.* 4662) went into effect. Grotesquely described as "an Act to promote development of Indian arts and crafts," the statute legally restricts definition of American Indian artists to those possessing a federally issued "Certificate of Degree of Indian Blood"—derogatorily referred to as "pedigree slips" by opponents—or those certified as such by "federally recognized tribes" or the "Alaska Native Corporation." Excluded are not only those who fall below blood-quantum requirements, but anyone who has, for politico-philosophical reasons, refused to cooperate with federal pretensions to define for itself who will and who will not be considered a member and citizen of a recognized indigenous nation. Further, the entire populations of federally unrecognized nations such as the populous Lumbees of North Carolina, Abenakis of Vermont, and more than 200 others, are simply written out of existence even in terms of their internal membership identification as Indians.

In order to put "teeth" into the legislation, Congress imposed penalties of up to $1 million in fines and as much as fifteen years in a federal prison for anyone not meeting its definition to "offer to display for sale or to sell any good, with or without a Government trademark, which . . . suggests it is Indian produced." For galleries, museums, and other private concerns to display as "Indian arts or crafts" the work of any person not meeting the federal definition of Indianness, a fine of up to $5 million is imposed. Under such conditions, the Cherokee National Museum in Muskogee, Oklahoma was forced to close its doors when it was discovered that even the late Willard Stone—a talented sculptor, creator of the Great Seal of the Cherokee

Nation, and a probable "full blood"—had never registered himself as a bona fide Indian according to federal standards.[20] At this juncture, things have become such a welter of confusion that:

> The Federal government, State governments and the census Bureau all have different criteria for defining "Indians" for statistical purposes, and even Federal criteria are not consistent among Federal agencies. For example, a State desiring financial aid to assist Indian education receives the aid only for the number of people with one-quarter or more Indian blood. For preference in hiring, enrollment records from a Federally recognized tribe are required. Under regulations for law and order, anyone of "Indian descent" is counted as an Indian. If the Federal criteria are inconsistent, State guidelines are [at this point] even more chaotic. In the course of preparing this report, the Commission contacted several States with large Indian populations to determine their criteria. Two States accept the individual's own determination. Four accept individuals as Indian if they were "recognized in the community" as Native Americans. Five use residence on a reservation as criteria. One requires one-quarter blood, and still another uses the Census Bureau definition that Indians are who they say they are.[21]

This, without doubt, is a situation made to order for conflict, among Indians more than anyone else. Somehow, it is exceedingly difficult to imagine that the government would wish to see things turn out any other way.

Implications

The eventual outcome of federal blood-quantum policies can be described as little other than genocidal in their final implications. As historian Patricia Nelson Limerick recently summarized the process:

> Set the blood quantum at one-quarter, hold to it as a rigid definition of Indians, let intermarriage proceed as it had for centuries, and eventually Indians will be defined out of existence. When that happens, the federal government will be freed of its persistent "Indian problem."[22]

Already, this conclusion receives considerable validation in the experience of the Indians of California, such as the Juaneño. Pursuant to the "Pit River Consolidated Land Settlement" of the 1970s, in which the government purported to "compensate" many of the small California bands for lands expropriated during the course of non-Indian "settlement" in that state (at less than 50 cents per acre), the Juaneño and a number of other "Mission Indians" were simply declared to be "extinct." This policy was pursed despite the fact that substantial numbers of such Indians were known to exist, and that the government was at the time issuing settlement checks to them. The tribal rolls were simply ordered closed to *any* new additions, despite the fact that many of the people involved were still bearing children, and their population might well have been expanding. . . .

American Indian Response

Of late, there have been encouraging signs that American Indians of many perspectives and political persuasions have begun to arrive at common conclusions regarding the use to which the federal government had been putting their identity and the compelling need for Indians to finally reassert complete control over this vital aspect of their lives. For instance, Dr. Frank Ryan, a liberal and rather establishmentarian Indian who has served as the director of the federal Office of Indian Education, began during the early 1980s to reach some rather hard conclusions about the policies of his employers. Describing the federal blood-quantum criteria for benefits eligibility in the educational arena as "a racist policy," Ryan went on to term it nothing more than "a shorthand method for denying Indian children admission to federal schools [and other programs]."[23] He concluded that, "The power to determine tribal membership has always been an essential attribute of inherent tribal sovereignty," and called for abolition of federal guidelines on the question of Indian identity without *any* lessening of federal obligations to the individuals and groups affected.[24] The question of the (re)adoption of blood-quantum standards by the Indian Health Service, proposed during the '80s by the Reagan administration, has served as even more of a catalyst. The National Congress of American Indians, never a bastion of radicalism, took up the issue at its 43rd Annual Convention, in October 1986. The NCAI produced a sharply worded statement rejecting federal identification policy:

> [T]he federal government, in an effort to erode tribal sovereignty and reduce the number of Indians to the point where they are politically, economically and culturally insignificant, [is being censured by] many of the more than 500 Indian leaders [attending the convention].[25]

The statement went on to condemn:

> . . . a proposal by the Indian Health Service to establish blood quotas for Indians, thus allowing the federal government to determine who is Indian and who is not, for the purpose of health care. Tribal leaders argue that *only* the individual tribe, not the federal government, should have this right, and many are concerned that this debate will overlap [as it has, long since] into Indian education and its regulation as well. . . . [Emphasis added.][26]

Conclusion

The history of the U.S. imposition of its standards of identification upon American Indians is particularly ugly. Its cost to Indians has involved millions of acres of land, the water by which to make much of this land agriculturally useful, control over vast mineral resources that might have afforded them a comfortable standard of living, and the ability to form themselves into viable and meaningful political blocks at any level. Worse, it has played a prominent role in bringing about their generalized psychic disempowerment; if one is not allowed even to determine for one's self, or within one's peer group, the answer to the all-important question "Who am I?" what possible personal power can one feel s/he possesses? The negative impact, both physically and psychologically, of this process upon succeeding generations of Native Americans in the United States is simply incalculable. . . .

The restriction of federal entitlement funds to cover only the relatively few Indians who meet quantum requirements, essentially a cost-cutting policy at its inception, has served to exacerbate tensions over the identity issue among Indians. It has established a scenario in which it has been perceived as profitable for one Indian to cancel the identity of her/his neighbor as means of receiving her/his entitlement. Thus, a bitter divisiveness has been built into Indian communities and national policies, sufficient to preclude our achieving the internal unity necessary to offer any serious challenge to the status quo. At every turn, U.S. practice vis-a-vis American Indians is indicative of an advanced and extremely successful system of colonialism. . . .

Endnotes

1. Adams, Evelyn C., *American Indian Education: Government Schools and Economic Progress*, King's Crown Press, New York, 1946, pp. 30–31.

2. Calhoun is quoted in *American State Papers: Indian Affairs* (Volume II), Wilmington, Delaware, 1972, pp. 183–4.

3. The bulk of the obligations in question were established prior to Congress' 1871 suspension of treaty-making with "the tribes" (Title 25, Section 71, U.S. Code). Additional obligations were undertaken by the federal government thereafter by "agreement" and as part of its ongoing agenda of completing the socio-political subordination of Indians, with an eye toward their eventual "assimilation" into the dominant culture and polity.

4. This strategy was actually tried in the wake of the passage of the House Concurrent Resolution 108 in June 1953. Predictably, the federal dissolution of American Indian nations such as the Klamath and Menominee so tarnished the U.S. image that implementation of the policy was shortly suspended (albeit the law remains on the books).

5. Collier, John, *Memorandum, Hearings on H.R. 7902 Before the House Committee on Indian Affairs*, (73rd Cong., 2d Sess.), U.S. Department of the interior, Washington, D.C., 1934, pp. 16–18.

6. Deloria, Vine, Jr., and Clifford M. Lytle, *American Indians, American Justice*, University of Texas Press, Austin, 1983, p. 10.

7. See Hundley, Norris C. Jr., "The Dark and Bloody Ground of Indian Water Rights," in Roxanne Dunbar Ortiz and Larry Emerson, eds., *Economic Development in Indian Reservations*, University of New Mexico Press, Albuquerque, 1979.

8. See American Friends Service Committee, *Uncommon Controversy. Fishing Rights of the Muckleshoot, Puyallup, and Nisqually Indians*, University of Washington Press, Seattle, 1970. Also see Cohen, Fay G., *Treaties on Trial: The Continuing Controversy over Northwest Indian Fishing Rights*, University of Washington Press, Seattle, 1986.

9. League of Women Voters, *Indian Country*, Publication No. 605, Washington, D.C., 1977, p. 24.

10. Probably the best overview of the IRA process may be found in Deloria, Vine Jr., and Clifford M. Lytle, *The Nations Within: The Past and Future of American Indian Sovereignty*, Pantheon Press, New York, 1984; on referenda fraud, see Chapter ii.

11. LaDuke,Winona, presentation at International Women's Week activities, University of Colorado at Boulder, March 13, 1984; tape on file.

12. Giago, Tim, "Blood Quantum Is a Degree of Discrimination," *Notes From Indian Country*, Vol. 1, State Publishing Co., Pierre, SD, 1984 p. 337.

13. Means, Russell, speech at the law school of the University of Colorado at Boulder, April 19, 1985; tape on file.

14. See Fanon, Frantz, *The Wretched of the Earth*, Grove Press, New York, 1966.

15. Quoted in Martz, Ron, "Indians decry verification plan for federally-funded health care," *Cox News Service*, Pierre, SD, October 7, 1986.

16. DeCora (Means), Lorelei, statement on radio station KILI, Porcupine, SD, October 12, 1986.

17. Means, Ted, statement before the South Dakota Indian Education Association, Pierre, SD, November 16, 1975.

18. See Jones, Richard, *American Indian Policy. Selected Major Issues in the 98th Congress*, Issue Brief No. lB83083, Library of Congress, Government Division, Washington, D.C. (updated version, February 6, 1984), pp. 3–4.

19. Martz, op. cit.

20. Nichols, Lyn, "New Indian Art Regulations Shut Down Muskogee Museum," *San Francisco Examiner*, December 3,1990.

21. American Indian Policy Review Commission, *Final Report*, Vol. 1, May 17,1977, U.S. Government Printing Office, Washington, D.C., 1977, p. 89.

22. Limerick, Patricia Nelson, *The Legacy of Conquest: The Unbroken Post of the American West*, W. W. Norton and Co., New York, 1987, p. 338.

23. Ryan, Frank A., *A Working Paper Prepared for the National Advisory Committee on Indian Education*, Paper No. 071279, Harvard American Indian Education Program, Harvard University Graduate School of Education, Cambridge, MA, July 18, 1979, p. 3.

24. Ibid., pp. 41–44.

25. Quoted in Martz, Ron, "Indians maintain U.S. trying to erode tribal sovereignty: cultural insignificance said to be goal," *Cox News Service*, Pierre, SD, October 26, 1986.

26. Quoted in Martz, Ron, "Indians decry verification plan for federally-funded health care," *Cox New Service*, Pierre, SD, October 26, 1986.

16

American Indian Ethnic Renewal:

Politics and the Resurgence of Identity

Joane Nagel

... Between 1960 and 1990, the number of Americans reporting American Indian as their race in the U.S. Census more than tripled, growing from 523,591 to 1,878,285. This increase cannot be accounted for by the usual explanations of population growth (e.g., increased births, decreased deaths). Researchers have concluded that much of this population growth must have resulted from "ethnic switching," where individuals who identified their race as non-Indian (e.g., White) in an earlier census, switched to "Indian" race in a later census. Why are more and more Americans reporting their race as American Indian?

My research draws on historical analyses and interview data, and combines a social constructionist model of ethnic identity with a social structural approach to ethnic change. I argue that the increase in American Indian ethnic identification reflected in the U.S. Census is an instance of "ethnic renewal." Ethnic renewal refers to both individual and collective processes. *Individual ethnic renewal* occurs when an individual acquires or asserts a new ethnic identity by reclaiming a discarded identity, replacing or amending an identity in an existing ethnic repertoire, or filling a personal ethnic void. Reclaiming a discarded identity might entail resuming religious observances or "retraditionalization" (e.g., the return to orthodoxy by American Jews). Replacing an identity in an existing ethnic repertoire might involve religious conversion (e.g., the conversion to Islam by Christian African Americans); amending an

existing ethnic repertoire might involve exploring a new side of one's family tree and including that nationality or ethnicity among one's working ethnic identities (e.g., the taking on of Armenian ethnicity by an Irish Armenian American already involved in Irish American ethnic life). Filling a personal ethnic void might entail adopting a new ethnic identity for the first time (e.g., Americans reconnecting with their ethnic "roots" and joining ethnic social, political, or religious organizations). *Collective ethnic renewal* involves the reconstruction of an ethnic community by current or new community members who build or rebuild institutions, culture, history, and traditions (Nagel 1994; forthcoming).

My thesis is that ethnic renewal among the American Indian population has been brought about by three political forces: (1) federal Indian policy; (2) American ethnic politics; and (3) American Indian political activism. Federal Indian policies have contributed to the creation of an urban, intermarried, bicultural American Indian population that lives outside traditional American Indian geographic and cultural regions. For these individuals, American Indian ethnicity has been more optional than for those living on reservations. Changes in American political culture brought about by the ethnic politics of the civil rights movement created an atmosphere that increased ethnic consciousness, ethnic pride, and ethnic mobilization among all ethnic groups, including American Indians. The resulting "Red Power" Indian political activist movement of the 1960s and 1970s started a tidal wave of ethnic renewal that surged across reservation and urban Indian communities, instilling ethnic pride and encouraging individuals to claim and assert their "Indianness." ...

Background

Negotiating and Changing Individual and Collective Identities

In the past 30 years, our understanding of ethnicity has increasingly stressed the socially constructed character of ethnicity. The pioneering work of Fredrik Barth (1969) shows ethnicity to be situational and variable. Many studies have followed that have found ethnicity to be more emergent than primordial, ethnic group boundaries to be more fluid than fixed, ethnic conflicts to arise more from clashes of contemporary interests than from ancient animosities, ethnic history and culture to be routinely revised and even invented, and the central essence of ethnicity—ethnic identity—to be multifaceted, negotiable, and changeable (see Conzen, Gerber, Morawska, Pozzetta, and Vecoli 1992; Sollors 1989). . . .

Opportunities for individual ethnic change vary. Certainly some people, for instance, American Whites, have a wide menu of "ethnic options" from which they are free to choose (Waters 1990). It is more difficult for members of other racial or ethnic groups to change their ethnicity, particularly communities of color. This is because in the United States such groups confront a world of "hypodescent," where one drop of particular blood (African, Asian) dictates a specific ethnic group membership, leaving limited options for individual members (see Harris 1964; Davis 1991). European Americans and African Americans represent two ends of an ethnic ascription continuum, in which Whites are always free to remember their ancestry and Blacks are never free to forget theirs. These ethnic boundaries are maintained and policed by both Blacks and Whites, although their content and location can change over time (see Collas 1994 for a discussion of "transgressing racial boundaries").

Despite such strict racial regimes, and perhaps because of their constructed character, there is constant flux at the edges of individual ethnic identity and ethnic group boundaries. For instance, despite the "one drop rule," Davis (1991) describes centuries of defining and redefining "Blackness" in the United States (also see Stein 1989), and discusses divisions among Americans of African descent based on national origin and skin tone (also see Keith and Herring 1991; Waters 1994). . . .

Individuals change their ethnic identity often, singly and *en masse*. Perhaps the most common form of ethnic switching is religious conversion. This sort of ethnic change is most likely to occur when a particular religion-based ethnicity is especially stigmatizing. Schermerhorn (1978) reports a common form of ethnic switching in India, where Hindu Untouchables convert to Islam to escape untouchability.

Another instance of mass ethnic change occurred in the former Yugoslavia during Ottoman rule, when Christian conversions to Islam created a permanent ethnic boundary. . . .

American Indian Ethnicity: Opting for an Indian Identity

American Indians reside at the intersection of two racial regimes: hypodescent and self-identification. In some portions of the United States Indianness is strongly socially ascribed and often mandatory (e.g., in the Southwest or the Northern Plains). In these settings Indian ethnicity is regulated in two ways. The first is informal and external to Indian communities, and involves ascription mainly, though not exclusively, by non-Indians. In this instance of classic hypodescent, any visible "Indianness" labels an individual as "Indian." The second, more formal way American Indian ethnicity is regulated can be both internal and external to native communities, and involves official membership in Indian tribes. In this case, tribal, state, and/or federal governments recognize an individual as an "enrolled" member or not.

In much of the United States, however, American Indian ethnicity is largely a matter of individual choice; "Indian" ethnicity is an ethnic option that an individual can choose or not. This is *not* to say that *anyone* can choose to be an Indian or that all observers will unanimously confirm the validity of that choice. Indeed, there is enormous controversy among native people about who should be considered an Indian for purposes of receiving tribal services, federal benefits, affirmative action consideration, or rights to participate in tribal governments (Larimore and Waters 1993; Reynolds 1993; Snipp 1993).

An important point to make here about supratribal "American Indian" ethnicity is that it is purely a social construction. That is, the Native American population is comprised of many linguistic, cultural, and religious groups, more than 300 of which are separately recognized by federal or state governments in the lower 48 states (with many more in Alaska and Hawaii); each group has its own political, legal, and police system, economy, land base, and sovereign authority. Around two-thirds of American Indians identified in the U.S. Censuses are official members of these recognized communities (Snipp 1989). Thus, when we speak of an "American Indian" race or ethnicity, we are of necessity referring to a group of individuals from various tribal backgrounds, some of whom speak native languages, most of whom converse in English, some of whom live on or regularly visit reservation "homelands," most of whom live off-reservation, some of whom participate in tribal community life, most of whom live in urban areas.

Despite this diversity, researchers assert that, indeed, there are "Indians," and this all-encompassing category can be seen as an "ethnic group." For instance, Deloria (1992a) argues that as American Indians became increasingly involved in off-reservation political and economic life after World War II, they came to see themselves as minority group members and as part of the larger American ethnic mosaic. In fact, many Native Americans carry within their portfolio of ethnic identities (which may include identities based on kin or clan lineage, tribe, reservation, language, and religion) a supratribal or pan-Indian "Indian" identity, which is often reserved for use when interacting with non-Indians. Finally, as further evidence of the existence of an "American Indian" ethnic group, in recent decades increasing percentages of Americans who identify their race as "Indian" fail to specify a tribal affiliation, suggesting that their primary ethnic identity is supratribal or "Indian" (Masumura and Berman 1987).

Patterns of American Indian Identification, 1960–1990

The U.S. Census provides data for examining both ethnic choice and ethnic ascription in American society. Beginning in 1960, the Census Bureau moved from a system where enumerators assigned each person a race to a system that permitted individual racial self-identification. This move from ascription to racial choice opened the door to individual racial "switching," especially for those ethnic categories not strongly governed by social conventions of hypodescent. . . .

Between 1970 and 1980, the American Indian population increased the most: The population grew from 792,730 in 1970 to 1,364,033 in 1980, an increase of 72 percent. Researchers wondered what accounted for this growth. They searched for the usual explanations: increased birthrates, decreased death rates, immigration, changes in census coding procedures. As these explanations were examined one by one and each failed to account for Indian population growth, researchers looked to alternative, more sociological explanations. For instance, Passel and Berman (1986) and Deloria (1986) argue that the unexplained percentage of Indian population growth is the result of "recruitment, i.e., changes in self-definition" by individuals from non-Indian in one census to Indian in the next (Passel and Berman 1986:164). Thornton (1987) suggests that such increases are the result of "biological migration": the migration of non-Indian genes into the American Indian population" (p. 174), the offspring of whom identify themselves as Indian. Steiner (1967) characterizes individuals likely to be included in the ranks of the unaccounted for Indian population as "new Indians"—urban, educated, and multicultural—people whom Snipp (1989) describes as "individuals who in an earlier era of American history would have 'passed' unrecognized into white society" (p. 57). Eschbach (1992) depicts the Indian population explosion as the result of "new identification" by Americans of varying degrees of Indian ancestry who formerly reported a non-Indian race, but who changed their race to "Indian" in a later census. And, finally, there is the somewhat unkind, informal description of newly identified census Indians as "wannabes," non-Indian individuals who want to be American Indian and thus identify themselves as such (Deloria 1981:140; Giago 1991; Taliman 1993:10).

Describing the 'New' Indian Population

Although researchers seem to agree that individual ethnic change is an important factor in the recent growth of the American Indian population, the reasons remain unclear. Phrased as research questions, we might ask: Who are these "new" Indians? And, what motivates them to change their ethnicity?

A survey of U.S. Census data and demographic research on the characteristics of the American Indian population provides some answers to the first question. Demographers calculate "natural increases" in the population by subtracting deaths from births; when population growth exceeds this number, the difference is referred to as the "error of closure" (Passel and Berman 1986:164; Harris 1994). The largest growing segments of the population are those likely to have the highest "errors of closure," and hence the most likely influx of new members. Thus, by examining the fastest growing segments of the Indian population we can infer some of the social characteristics of the "new" Indians. . . .

During the 1960–1990 period, the urban Indian population increased 720 percent compared to a 218 percent increase in rural areas (Sorkin 1978:10; U.S. Bureau of the Census 1989:150, 1992). Thus, *the "new" Indians are much more likely to live in urban areas than rural areas.* There are also regional differences in Indian population growth. Passel and Berman (1986) compared 1970–1980 population growth rates in "Indian states" with those in "non-Indian states," and found that the Indian population was growing twice as fast in non-Indian states: A 114 percent increase occurred in non-Indian states compared to only a 56 percent increase in Indian states. Eschbach (1995:103) examined population growth rates in regions of the country with states containing historically small Indian populations similar to Passel and Berman's "non-Indian states." He found that population growth in these regions during the period from 1960 to 1990 was six times greater than in the regions containing states with historical Indian populations. These two studies strongly suggest that *the "new" Indians are much more likely to be from states with historically small Indian populations.*

Researchers have also found that Indian population growth is associated with racial intermarriage. American Indians have very high intermarriage rates compared to other racial groups. For instance, Snipp (1989:157) compared rates of intermarriage of Blacks, Whites, and Indians in the 1980 Census and found that nearly half of Indians were intermarried (48 percent) compared to only 2 percent of Blacks and 1 percent of Whites. Sandefur and McKinnell (1986:348) report that Indian intermarriage has been increasing, rising from approximately 15 percent in 1960 to 33 percent in 1970, and Eschbach (1995:93) reported that in 1990, 59 percent of married Indians had a non-Indian spouse. . . . Eschbach (1995:95) also found that rates of intermarriage varied by the "Indianness" of a region, with intermarriage ranging from 16 to 64 percent in Indian regions, and from 72 to 82 percent in non-Indian regions. Eschbach also noted that population growth was greatest in those regions with the highest intermarriage rates, increasing from approximately 151,000 in 1960 to 928,000 in 1990—a 500 percent increase (1995:103). The implication of this research on Indian intermarriage is that *the "new" Indians in the 1970, 1980, and 1990 Censuses are more likely to be intermarried.*

The race assigned to children in mixed marriages provides another important piece of information about the characteristics of the fastest growing segment of the American Indian population. Where hypodescent does not dictate the race of mixed race children, parents may choose their child's race. . . . Eschbach (1992, 1995) reported that in the 1980 Census, 47.4 percent of children from Indian-non-Indian parents were assigned an Indian race (1992:150); that proportion fell slightly in 1990 to 46.7 percent (Eschbach 1995:97). Region mattered in such racial decision-making. Eschbach (1995:97) found that in non-Indian regions the proportion of children given an Indian race in 1990 ranged from 33 to 45 percent; in comparison, in historically Indian regions, 36 to 73 percent of mixed race children were assigned an Indian race. Further, those regions with the greatest Indian population growth were areas where children of mixed marriages were *less likely* to be classified by their parents as Indians. These findings suggest that *the "new" Indians are more likely to assign a non-Indian race to their mixed offspring.*

Finally, we come to that major indicator of assimilation—native language loss. Indian language usage has declined dramatically in the past century. . . . [In] 1980, 74 percent of American Indians spoke only English in their homes (U.S. Bureau of the Census 1989:203); by 1990, the percentage had risen to 77 percent (U.S. Bureau of the Census 1992:66). Snipp (1989) found, not surprisingly, that native language usage varies by region, with Native Americans from regions with historically large Indian populations much more likely to speak an Indian language than are those from historically non-Indian regions. As Indian population growth is highest in these non-Indian regions, we can conclude that *the "new" Indians are quite likely to speak only English.*

Adding the above data together, a picture emerges of the fastest growing segment of the Native American population: Compared to the total American Indian population, these Indians are more urban, more concentrated in non-Indian states without reservation communities, more often intermarried, less likely to assign their mixed offspring an Indian race, and more likely to speak only English. These characteristics are all descriptive of a population more "blended" into the American demographic and cultural mainstream than their reservation coethnics, more likely to have more flexible conceptions of self, residing in parts of the country that permit a wide range of ethnic options. In other words, under the proper conditions, the fastest growing portions of the American Indian population are available for ethnic renewal.

Accounting for American Indian Ethnic Renewal

What *are* the conditions that promote American Indian ethnic renewal? Restated, what has motivated these new Indians to change their ethnicity? The answers to this question can be found in policy and politics: federal Indian policy, American ethnic politics, and Native American political activism.

Federal Indian Policy

Beginning in the nineteenth century, federal Indian policy was designed to assimilate American Indians into the Euro-American cultural mainstream (e.g., through forced English language acquisition, Anglo-centric education in Indian boarding and day schools, and reservation land reduction programs). Despite a brief pause in federal assimilation programs during the "New Deal" era, the net result of decades of federal Indian policy was the creation of an English-speaking, bicultural, multi-tribal American Indian population living in U.S. cities. World War II also spurred the urbanization and acculturation of the Native American population, as Indians volunteered and were drafted into the military and non-enlisted native workers left reservations for wartime industrial jobs in urban areas. Many of these Indian veterans and workers never returned to the reservation (Nash 1985; Bernstein 1986). Post-World War II programs for job training and urban relocation were specifically designed to reduce reservation populations during the "termination" era of federal Indian policy, and provided a further push in the reservation-urban Indian population stream. . . .

Not only did federal Indian policy help urbanize the Indian population, many programs had a major impact on the organizational fabric of urban Indian life. For instance, relocation programs directly funded the creation and operation of a number of Indian centers in both relocation target cities and cities near large reservation populations (Ablon 1965). These centers were established to provide services and meeting places for burgeoning urban Indian populations. Further, as an indirect consequence of relocation efforts, other urban Indian organizations blossomed: intertribal clubs, bars, athletic leagues, beauty contests, powwows, and dance groups, as well as Indian newspapers and newsletters, social service agencies, political organizations, and Christian churches (Hertzberg 1971; Guillemin 1975; Steele 1975; Mucha 1983; Weibel-Orlando 1991).

In a few urban areas, some of these organizations had a specific tribal character and were frequented only by members of a particular tribe (Hodge 1971). However, the vast majority of urban Indian organizations were intertribal and had names reflecting their inclusionary character: the Cleveland American Indian Center, the *Inter-Tribal Tribune* (newsletter of the Heart of America Indian Center, Kansas City), the Los Angeles American Indian Bowling League, [and so on.] . . . [The diverse organizations that populated the urban Indian organizational landscape formed the core of an intertribal network and informal communication system in urban Indian communities. They were important building blocks in the development of a supratribal level of Indian identity and the emergence of a pan-Indian culture, both of which were essential ingredients in the Red Power political mobilization of the 1960s.]

American Ethnic Politics

Two forces converged in the 1960s to end the assimilationist thrust of federal Indian policy and to set in motion the contemporary period of American Indian ethnic renewal. One was the civil rights movement and the shifts in American social and political culture that followed in its wake. The other was President Lyndon Johnson's solution to the problem of race in America—the Great Society, the War on Poverty, and the civil rights legislation of the 1960s. The fluctuating currents of cultural change and reform politics that marked the 1960s were responded to by increasingly cosmopolitan and sophisticated American Indians who lobbied successfully to send federal War on Poverty and community development resources into impoverished urban and reservation communities (Witt 1968:68; Deloria 1978:88).

This mix of volatile ethnic politics and an explosion of federal resources, many earmarked for minority programs, combined with earlier federal Indian policies, which had concentrated large numbers of tribally diverse, educated, acculturated, and organizationally connected Indians in American cities. The result: a large-scale mobilization of urban Indians marked by a rapid growth of political organizations, newspapers, and community programs. . . . The demographic changes that underlay the rise of Black militancy in American cities, namely, the "great Black migration" from the rural south to the urban north (Cloward and Piven 1975; Edsall and Edsall 1991; Lemann (1991), were paralleled by the movement of American Indians

off the reservations. The federal response to Black protest—civil rights legislation and the War on Poverty—spilled over into other minority communities, including America Indian communities, which were quickly mobilizing in the wake of Black insurgency. The ethnic militancy of the 1960s redefined mainstream America as "White" and exposed and challenged its racial hegemony. For America's ethnic minorities it was a time to cast off negative stereotypes, to reinvent ethnic and racial social meanings and self-definitions, and to embrace ethnic pride. For American Indians it marked the emergence of supratribal identification, the rise of Indian activism, and a period of increased Indian ethnic pride. Despite their often brutal treatment by United States' authorities and citizens throughout American history, American Indians have ironically, but consistently, occupied a romanticized niche in the American popular media and imagination (Berkhofer 1978). The durable symbolic value of the American Indian as a cultural icon was further enhanced by the increased ethnic pride characterizing the civil rights era. The result increased the appeal of Indian ethnicity for many individuals, and no doubt contributed to the resurgence of Indian self-identification. . . .

American Indians indeed were able to navigate the changing currents of American ethnic politics, and their successes resulted in increased federal spending on Indian affairs, making American Indian identification a more attractive ethnic option for many Americans of Indian descent. The settlement of land claims by the Indian Claims Commission and the U.S. federal court system during the 1970s and 1980s was another important source of funds for Indian communities. . . .

Increased federal spending in general and land claim awards in particular, along with the inclusion of Indians in many affirmative action and minority set-aside programs, contributed to the American Indian ethnic resurgence in part because they increased both the symbolic and the potential material value of Indian ethnicity. Individuals of Indian ancestry became more willing to identify themselves as Indians, whether or not such identification was a strategy to acquire a share of real or putative land claims awards or other possible ethnically allocated rewards (such as scholarships, mineral royalties, employment preference). It was in this atmosphere of increased resources, ethnic grievances, ethnic pride, and civil rights activism that Red Power burst on the scene in the late 1960s and galvanized a generation of Native Americans. The rest of the country watched as the media covered such events as the occupation of Alcatraz Island, the takeover of the Bureau of Indian Affairs headquarters in Washington, D.C., and the siege at Wounded Knee.

American Indian Activism: Red Power

. . . Red Power played an important symbolic role in motivating individual ethnic renewal on the part of Indian participants and observers; this ethnic renewal took two forms, and both forms are relevant to the argument I present here.

The first type of individual ethnic renewal involves individuals who most likely would have identified themselves as Indians in earlier censuses, and thus is best summarized as a resurgence in ethnic pride which did not involve taking on a new ethnic identity (e.g., does not involve racial switching). Instead, this type of individual ethnic renewal involved a reaffirmation, reconstruction, or redefinition of an individual's ethnicity. For example, the slogan, "I'm Black and I'm proud" reflected such a redefinition of "Negro" in the U.S. in the 1960s. These individuals did not change their race, rather they changed the *meaning* of their race. This parallels the resurgence of Native American ethnic pride among individuals who already identified themselves as "Indian."

The second type of individual ethnic renewal involves individuals who would *not* have identified themselves as Indian in earlier censuses, but rather would have "passed" into the non-Indian race categories. For these individuals, a resurgence of ethnic pride meant not only redefining the worth and meaning of their ancestry, but also involved laying a new claim to that ancestry by switching their race on the census form from non-Indian to Indian. This type of individual ethnic renewal is, I believe, reflected in census data. . . .

Activism and Identity: Reversing the Causal Connection

The traditionally understood relationship between identity and activism is that identity precedes activism, making particular individuals more likely than others to engage in protest activities (for a review of this literature see McAdam 1988 and Tarrow 1992). Much recent research on social movements questions this assumption, exploring more fully the interrelationships among activism, identity, and culture. Fantasia (1988) points out the capacity of both spontaneous and planned protest action to reshape conceptions of personal and collective identity, redefine notions of fairness and justice, and build community consensus and solidarity. Benford and Hunt (1992), Hunt and Benford (1994), and Snow and Anderson (1993) document the emergence of collective ideologies and identities in social movement organizations and movements, and the interplay between movement-sited interpretative frames and rhetoric and larger political and cultural themes in the emergence of collective identity. Taylor and Whittier (1992) and Groch (1994) focus on the importance of group boundaries and collectively negotiated and defined meaning systems in the emergence of oppositional consciousness among movement participants and constituents.

The resurgence of American Indian ethnic identity in the 1970s and 1980s is consistent with these findings and illustrates the power of activism to inspire individual and collective ethnic pride and to raise ethnic consciousness. My interviews most strongly support the notion that activism has its biggest impact on individuals who themselves personally witness or become directly involved in protest action. The narrative accounts of both activists and nonactivists, however, also suggest that social movements exert a wider impact, affecting the attitudes of nonparticipants as well, though to a lesser extent. . . .

Activism as a Crucible for Ethnic Pride and Identity

The occupation of Alcatraz Island was followed by dozens of protest actions around the country throughout most of the 1970s. During this and the following decade, many individuals of native ancestry were motivated to reconnect with their ethnic roots. . . .

The personal journeys described by many Native Americans involve a seeming contradiction: they go forward by going back; or as one native person characterized it to me, "We become what we were." This process of becoming often involves a spiritual component that for many Indians, perhaps for most, represents the symbolic core of Indianness and is a central part of the ethnic renewal process. Deloria (1992b) acknowledges the cardinal importance of spiritual matters in native life and identifies an underlying spiritual agenda in Indian activism. Indeed, activist Frances Wise noted the direct importance of Red Power activism in changing policies and creating a climate that permitted and supported individual ethnic renewal through traditional dress and spiritual practices. In the early 1970s she was involved in organizing a successful challenge to an Oklahoma school board's restriction on men's hair length. She noted the changes that resulted:

> It had a big impact. People now wear long hair, people who said back then, "Are you sure you know what you're doing with this [protest]?" Now they can wear their hair long—and they do. . . . Another outcome is we have greater numbers of people who have both traditional Indian educations and are also educated in white ways. (Telephone interview with Frances Wise, Oklahoma City, OK, August 25, 1993)

During and since the Red Power period, the religious and spiritual dimension of tribal life has become a focal concern among many of the Indian people with whom I spoke. Many reported becoming Sun Dancers for the first time as adults, many spent time with tribal elders seeking instruction in tribal history and traditions, many learned more of their tribal language, many abandoned Christian religions and turned to native spiritual traditions, and some have returned to their home reservations. In recounting his decision to return to the reservation, Horse Capture (1991) believes that he is not the only one embarked on such a journey back to what he was:

> Originally I thought I was alone on this quest. But as time has passed, a whole generation and more were influenced by these same forces, and we traveled the same course. (p. 203)

Conclusion

The rise in American Indian ethnic identification during the last three decades has resulted from a combination of factors in American politics. Assimilationist federal Indian policies helped to create a bicultural, intermarried, mixed race, urban Indian population living in regions of the country where ethnic options were most numerous; this was a group "poised" for individual ethnic renewal. The ethnic politics of the civil rights era encouraged ethnic identification, the return to ethnic roots, ethnic activism, and provided resources for mobilizing ethnic communities; thus, the climate and policies of civil rights provided individuals of native ancestry (and others as well) symbolic and material incentives to claim or reclaim Indian ethnicity. Red Power activism during the 1960s and 1970s further raised Indian ethnic consciousness by dramatizing long held grievances, communicating an empowered and empowering image of Indianness, and providing Native Americans, particularly native youth, opportunities for action and participation in the larger Indian cause. Together then, federal Indian policies, ethnic politics, and American Indian activism provided the rationale and motivation for individual ethnic renewal.

The overall explanation of the resurgence of American Indian ethnicity I offer here can be seen as part of a general model of ethnic renewal. The impact of federal Indian policies on American Indian ethnic renewal represents an instance of the political construction of ethnicity (i.e., the ways in which political policy, the structure of political opportunity, and patterns of political culture shape ethnic boundaries in society). The impact of events in this larger political arena on Indian ethnic activism and identity illustrates the role of politics and political culture in ethnic mobilization (i.e., the power of political *zeitgeist* and shifting political definitions to open windows of opportunity for ethnic activists and to affirm and render meaningful their grievances and claims). The impact of Red Power on American Indian ethnic consciousness reveals the role of human agency in individual and collective redefinition and empowerment (i.e., the power of activism to challenge prevailing policies, to encourage ethnic awareness, and to foster ethnic community-building). This model of ethnic renewal suggests that, given the capacity of individuals to reinvent themselves and their communities, ethnicity occupies an enduring place in modern societies.

References

Ablon, Joan. 1965. "American Indian Relocation: Problems of Dependency and Management in the City." *Phylon* 66:362–71.

Barth, Fredrik. 1969. *Ethnic Groups and Boundaries.* Boston, MA: Little, Brown.

Benford, Robert D., and Scott A. Hunt. 1992. "Dramaturgy and Social Movements: The Social Construction and Communication of Power." *Sociological Inquiry* 62:36–55.

Berkhofer, Robert F. 1978. *The White Man's Indian: Images of the American Indian from Columbus to the Present.* New York: Alfred A. Knopf.

Bernstein, Alison Ricky. 1986. "Walking in Two Worlds: American Indians and World War Two." Ph.D. dissertation, Department of History, Columbia University, New York.

Cloward, Richard A., and Frances Fox Piven. 1975. *The Politics of Turmoil: Poverty, Race, and the Urban Crisis.* New York: Vintage Books.

Collas, Sara. 1994. "Transgressing Racial Boundaries: The Maintenance of the Racial Order." Paper presented at the annual meeting of the American Sociological Association, August 8, Los Angeles, CA.

Conzen, Kathleen N., David A. Gerber, Ewa Morawska, George E. Pozzetta, and Rudolph J. Vecoli. 1992. "The Invention of Ethnicity: A Perspective from the U.S.A." *Journal of American Ethnic History* 12:3–41.

Davis, James F. 1991. *Who Is Black? One Nation's Definition.* University Park, PA: Pennsylvania State University.

Deloria, Vine, Jr. 1978. "Legislation and Litigation Concerning American Indians." *The Annals of the American Academy of Political and Social Science* 436:88–96.

———. 1981. "Native Americans: The American Indian Today." *The Annals of the American Academy of Political and Social Sciences* 454:139–49.

———. 1986. "The New Indian Recruits: The Popularity of Being Indian." *Americans Before Columbus* 14:3, 6–8.

———. 1992a. "American Indians." Pp. 31–52 in *Multiculturalism in the United States: A Comparative Guide to Acculturation and Ethnicity,* edited by J. D. Buenker and L. A. Ratner. Westport, CT: Greenwood Press.

———. 1992b. *God Is Red: A Native View of Religion.* 2d ed. Golden, CO: North American Press.

Edsall, Thomas B., and Mary D. Edsall. 1991. *Chain Reaction: The Impact of Race, Rights, and Taxes on American Politics.* New York: W. W. Norton.

Eschbach, Karl. 1992. "Shifting Boundaries: Regional Variation in Patterns of Identification as American Indians." Ph.D. dissertation, Department of Sociology, Harvard University, Cambridge, MA.

———. 1995. "The Enduring and Vanishing American Indian: American Indian Population Growth and Intermarriage in 1990." *Ethnic and Racial Studies* 18:89–108.

Fantasia, Rick. 1988. *Cultures of Solidarity.* Berkeley, CA: University of California Press.

Giago, Tim. 1991. "Big Increases in 1990 Census not Necessarily Good for Tribes." *Lakota Times,* March 12, p. 3.

Groch, Sharon A. 1994. "Oppositional Consciousness: Its Manifestations and Development: A Case Study of People with Disabilities." *Sociological Inquiry* 64:369–95.

Guillemin, Jeanne. 1975. *Urban Renegades: The Cultural Strategy of American Indians.* New York: Columbia University Press.

Harris, David. 1994. "The 1990 Census Count of American Indians: What Do the Numbers Really Mean?" *Social Science Quarterly* 75:580–93.

Harris, Marvin. 1964. *Patterns of Race in the Americas.* New York: Norton.

Hertzberg, Hazel. 1971. *The Search for an American Indian Identity: Modern Pan-Indian Movements.* Syracuse, NY: Syracuse University Press.

Hodge, William H. 1971. "Navajo Urban Migration: An Analysis from the Perspective of the Family." Pp. 346–92 in *The American Indian in Urban Society,* edited by J. O. Waddell and O. M. Watson. Boston, MA: Little, Brown and Company.

Horse Capture, George P. 1991. "An American Indian Perspective." Pp. 186–207 in *Seeds of Change,* edited by H. J. Viola and C. Margolis. Washington, DC: Smithsonian Institution Press.

Hunt, Scott A., and Robert D. Benford. 1994. "Identity Talk in the Peace and Justice Movement." *Journal of Contemporary Ethnography* 22:488–517.

Keith, Verna M., and Cedric Herring. 1991. "Skin Tone and Stratification in the Black Community." *American Journal of Sociology* 97:760–78.

Larimore, Jim, and Rick Waters. 1993. "American Indians Speak Out Against Ethnic Fraud in College Admissions." Paper presented at a conference sponsored by the American Council on Education: "Educating One-Third of a Nation IV: Making Our Reality Match our Rhetoric," October 22, Houston, TX.

Lemann, Nicholas. 1991. *The Promised Land: The Great Black Migration and How It Changed America.* New York: A. A. Knopf.

Masumura, William, and Patricia Berman. 1987. "American Indians and the Census." Unpublished manuscript.

McAdam, Doug. 1988. *Freedom Summer.* New York: Oxford University Press.

Mucha, Janosz. 1983. "From Prairie to the City: Transformation of Chicago's American Indian Community." *Urban Anthropology* 12:337–71.

Nagel, Joane. 1994. "Constructing Ethnicity: Creating and Recreating Ethnic Identity and Culture." *Social Problems* 41:1001–26.

——. Forthcoming. *American Indian Ethnic Renewal: Red Power and the Resurgence of Identity and Culture.* New York: Oxford University Press.

Nash, Gerald D. 1985. *The American West Transformed: The Impact of the Second World War.* Bloomington, IN: Indiana University Press.

Passel, Jeffrey S., and Patricia A. Berman. 1986. "Quality of 1980 Census Data for American Indians." *Social Biology* 33:163–82.

Reynolds, Jerry. 1993. "Indian Writers: Real or Imagined." *Indian Country Today*, September 8, pp. A1, A3.

Sandefur, Gary D., and Trudy McKinnell. 1986. "American Indian Intermarriage." *Social Science Research* 15:347–71.

Schermerhorn, Richard A. 1978. *Ethnic Plurality in India.* Tucson, AZ: University of Arizona Press.

Snipp, C. Matthew. 1989. *American Indians: The First of This Land.* New York: Russell Sage Foundation.

——. 1993. "Some Observations about the Racial Boundaries and the Experiences of American Indians." Paper presented at the University of Washington, April 22, Seattle, WA.

Snow, David A., and Leon Anderson. 1993. *Down on Their Luck: A Study of Homeless Street People.* Berkeley, CA: University of California Press.

Sollors, Werner, ed. 1989. *The Invention of Ethnicity.* New York: Oxford University Press, 1989.

Sorkin, Alan L. 1978. *The Urban American Indian.* Lexington, MA: Lexington Books.

Steele, C. Hoy. 1975. "Urban Indian Identity in Kansas: Some Implications for Research." Pp. 167–78 in *The New Ethnicity: Perspectives from Ethnology*, edited by J. W. Bennett. St. Paul, MN: West Publishing Company.

Stein, Judith. 1989. "Defining the Race, 1890–1930." Pp. 77–104 in *The Invention of Ethnicity*, edited by W. Sollers. New York: Oxford University Press.

Steiner, Stanley. 1967. *The New Indians.* New York: Harper and Row.

Taliman, Valorie. 1993. "Lakota Declaration of War." *News from Indian Country* 7:10.

Tarrow, Sidney. 1992. "Mentalities, Political Cultures, and Collective Action Frames." Pp. 174–202 in *Frontiers in Social Movement Theory*, edited by A. D. Morris and C. M. Mueller. New Haven, CT: Yale University Press.

Taylor, Verta, and Nancy E. Whittier. 1992. "Collective Identity in Social Movement Communities: Lesbian Feminist Mobilization." Pp. 104–20 in *Frontiers in Social Movement Theory*, edited by A. D. Morris and C. M. Mueller. New Haven, CT: Yale University Press.

Thornton, Russell. 1987. *American Indian Holocaust and Survival.* Norman, OK: University of Oklahoma Press.

U.S. Bureau of the Census. 1989. *Census of Population, Subject Reports, Characteristics of American Indians by Tribes and Selected Areas, 1980.* Washington, DC: Government Printing Office.

——. 1992. *Census of the Population, General Population Characteristics, American Indian and Alaskan Native Areas, 1990.* Washington, DC: Government Printing Office.

Waters, Mary C. 1990. *Ethnic Options: Choosing Identities in America.* Berkeley, CA: University of California Press.

——. 1994. "Ethnic and Racial Identities of Second Generation Blacks in New York City." *International Migration Review* 28:795–820.

Weibel-Orlando, Joan. 1991. *Indian Country, L.A.: Maintaining Ethnic Community in Complex Society.* Champaign, IL: University of Illinois Press.

Witt, Shirley Hill. 1968. "Nationalistic Trends among American Indians." Pp. 53–75 in *The American Indian Today*, edited by S. Levine and N. O. Lurie. Deland, FL: Everett/Edwards, Inc.

Reprinted from: Joane Nagel, "American Indian Ethnic Renewal: Politics and the Resurgence of Identity." In *American Sociological Review*, Volume 60, pp. 945–965. Copyright © 1995 by American Sociological Association. Reprinted by permission.

17

How Giveaways and Pow-Wows Redistribute the Means of Subsistence

John H. Moore

In the state of Oklahoma each year about 300 Indian pow-wows and memorials of various kinds are announced by flyers, in newspapers, and at public meetings. In addition, many other small giveaways are held without public announcement, totalling altogether perhaps a thousand events. . . .

In this article I wish to emphasize small-town events and behavior away from the pow-wow ground among people whom Kehoe (1980) has recognized as a "social network." By reference to socioeconomic data, I will argue that in Oklahoma this network facilitates a system of exchange and redistribution which is crucially important for Indian people, providing needy Native American families with the "means of subsistence." The means of subsistence I define formally as "the goods and services necessary to sustain life"—food, clothing, heating oil, and health care. I argue that pow-wows and giveaways were invented by Indian people to fill the gaps in an uncertain local economy and to compensate for government social services that often are erratic and arbitrary in their effect on Indian families.

Although giveaways and pow-wows are best known from the cultures of Plains Indians, there are similar traditional practices among many of the other native peoples of North America (Grobsmith 1979:123–24). . . .

The practices to be described in this paper, then, are predominantly those which are common, if not universal, among Oklahoma tribes of Plains origin—Plains Apaches, Southern Arapahoes, Caddos, Southern Cheyennes, Comanches, Kiowas, Pawnees, and Wichitas, as well as the Chiwere or Dhegiha Sioux—Ioways, Kaws, Osages, Otoes, and Poncas. In addition, these practices are increasingly found among some Central Algonkian tribes in Oklahoma that have adopted certain important aspects of pow-wow culture—Delawares, Sacs, Foxes, Kickapoos, Potawatomis, and Shawnees. The particular focus of this paper will be the Southern Cheyennes and Southern Arapahoes, who are . . .the most active of the pow-wow tribes of Oklahoma. . . . I will emphasize here those practices which I believe are very general among southern Plains Indians. Whether this analysis is also valid for the northern groups I cannot say, since I have attended only a very few northern Plains pow-wows. . . .

Especially interesting for future work is the opportunity to compare Southern Cheyenne and Northern Cheyenne giveaways, since the two groups are ethnically similar and somewhat intermarried (Weist 1973). Grobsmith's analysis seems to indicate that the northern Plains Indian groups are different from the southerners, since she argues for a ritual rather than economic interpretation of giveaways (1981:75–76). One basic difference might be that while many northern Plains Indians live on discrete, bounded reservations in areas of low total population, Oklahoma Indians tend to constitute minority communities within areas of greater non-Indian population.

Diverse kinds of events have been called "pow-wows," and they have a multitude of functions. Best known are the large urban pow-wows which are alleged to endorse pan-Indian values (Young 1981). These large affairs provide entertainment for Indians and visitors, offer cash prizes to dancers, and present opportunities to local organizations, craftspeople, and traders for selling food and craftwork. But I will argue here that these big urban pow-wows are atypical, and in Oklahoma they are decidedly in the minority both in terms of the number of events and the number of Indian people in attendance. More typical are the rural and small-town events attended by local residents who are well acquainted with one another.

. . . [I]t is rural areas, not urban ones, which are more important for pow-wow culture. Also, these rural and small-town pow-wows tend not to be "pan-Indian" in the sense of having many different tribes in attendance. Rather, the gatherings reflect the ethnicity of the sponsoring community (Ashworth 1986:92–115).

To people not familiar with Plains Indian values, several aspects of the giveaways and "specials" which are incorporated into pow-wow programs might seem unusual. Firstly, in the noncommercial pow-wows, there is no admission, and food is free. Visitors are invited to the head of the line when dinner is served, and they are given big portions of food, with many jokes about carrying a second plate or going around again. Non-Indians, accustomed to Euro-American notions of purchase and exchange, are often uncomfortable as the guests of strangers, and sometimes they seek to pay for the food, which embarrasses everyone. To compound their discomfort, such visitors are sometimes given lavish gifts during giveaways, the standard gifts being a blanket for a man and a shawl for a woman. Often I have heard visitors remark, "What's the catch?" There is no catch for visitors; they have simply been the objects of Indian hospitality.

Another mystery to visitors is that persons honored by a giveaway . . . do not themselves receive gifts, but are merely observers as their sponsors give away blankets, shawls, baskets of groceries, money, clothing, dishes, furniture, and even horses and automobiles to other people in attendance at the event. But in Euro-America, it is the honoree who receives the plaque, the trophy, or the gold watch. By contrast, Plains Indian values require that the honoree gets nothing but the privilege of shaking the hands of the gift recipients, who are required by etiquette just to compliment the gift, and not say "thank you."

The Simple Giveaway

Simple giveaways, which are typical of the small Indian communities in central and western Oklahoma, are most frequently held to commemorate such occasions as (1) the death of a member of the family, after the wake and before the funeral; (2) the end of the mourning period, one year after the death of a loved one, so that the family can once again appear at public functions; (3) the return of a son from the armed services, often sponsored by the local "war mothers"; or (4) a graduation from high school or college. . . .

Simple giveaways are usually held at noon or six in the evening (both are called "dinner" in local English dialect) and begin with a "feed." Members of the extended family work several days to prepare an elaborate meal of traditional foods such as boiled beef, fry bread, corn soup, and sweet rice. . . . The simple giveaway is usually held in some local meeting place, such as the many "community halls" built with federal money since the 1950s, or increasingly in the tribal "multi-purpose centers" . . . or local halls rented from the American Legion, Elks Club, Moose Lodge or similar non-Indian organizations. In summer, giveaways are often held outside, at the home of the host family. . . .

The free food itself constitutes the most direct means for providing subsistence to needy people in the community. Such people usually wait until last to eat and show by their posture and demeanor that they are in need, standing aside as the others file through the food line, eyes downcast, often with sacks or pots they have brought. These people, usually younger men and women, are colloquially said to be from families that are "hard up." At an event attended by 150 people, there might be two to five such people, representing several families.

After everyone has been served, the needy people pass through the line, receiving extra-generous portions. For them, there are no jokes about food. Sometimes they are weeping. After they have passed through the line, the servers take their sacks and pots and fill them with the surplus food. There is always an abundance of food, or else the host family is embarrassed. The surplus has been prepared in the expectation that needy people will be present. In some communities, there is so much food and so many feeds that it is possible for hungry families to subsist for some time just from the food distributed at giveaways, pow-wows, and memorials. In Geary, Watonga, and Clinton, Oklahoma, for example, there is an event with dinner nearly every weekend, and sometimes two or three events.

After the dinner the host family cleans up the hall and then brings out the goods to be distributed at the giveaway. Most often the gifts are laid out on the floor in front of the chairs of the family or on the ground in front of the family. At the better-organized events there are slips of paper with the names of the intended recipients pinned to the shawls and blankets. The giveaway begins with a welcome and usually a prayer in the native language from a senior man of the family or from a well-known man who has been honored by being invited to serve as master of ceremonies (MC). He states the reason for the giveaway, and makes other appropriate remarks. For the giveaway, the guests have physically arranged themselves into extended families. . . . It is usually incumbent on the most senior members of an extended family in the community to attend, along with a few younger relatives. Attendance at the giveaway, of itself, implies the existence of friendship and alliance between the host and guest families. Who will attend is almost perfectly predictable from the standpoint of the hosts. Problems arise when families attend who were thought to be out of town, or who were perhaps not expected because of disputes among some members of the two families. Often there is a frantic rearrangement of name slips or the finding of additional gifts while dinner is being served.

At funerals, especially, the host family makes decisions about gifts while the guests are eating. Since deaths are most often unexpected, the family may not have an adequate supply of blankets and shawls to give everyone at the funeral. Most people, then, bring both a blanket and a shawl when they come to the funeral, going home with a blanket and a shawl which someone else has brought. Most often, it is only the senior members of

the extended family, usually a married couple, who receive high-status gifts like blankets and shawls, while the junior members of the family, especially children, receive small gifts of beadwork, toys, or candy which are distributed around the circle from baskets and boxes while the elders are being called out formally for the giveaway.

The giveaway begins when a man and woman from the host family step forward with a blanket and shawl, respectively, while the master of ceremonies calls out the name of a person or couple who will receive the gifts. If the giveaway is in honor of a person who is present, for example a new high school graduate, that person also stands in front next to the people distributing the gifts.

Although the most senior and most respected guests are usually called out first this is not always the case. Also singled out for early attention and important gifts are people who have travelled a long way to the event or people who are strangers. Especially if an honored guest at the event has brought a friend, that friend is honored lavishly, even if unacquainted with the host family. If the event is a funeral or memorial which has required an all-night meeting of the Native American Church, these members of the peyote lodge are called out early to receive gifts. Also receiving early attention are friends who have cooked and otherwise helped prepare the event but who are not members of the extended family.

Etiquette requires that hosts not give to members of their own families, but here we have some variability among Oklahoma tribes. Comanche hosts, for example, will give to their own elderly grandparents, but Cheyennes normally will not. Such differences largely reflect significant differences in the kinship systems and kin behavior of the different tribes, and in particular differences in avoidance/respect relationships. One would not call out a relative who is avoided, since the giveaway requires that the host shake the hand of the recipient. . . .

There is much variability, not only among tribes but among families, about the propriety of giving to one's own kin. But generally, my impression is that one does not give away to people who are already in the daily sharing network, however this network is defined by the tribe or family.

A simple giveaway usually lasts less than an hour, as gifts are handed forward to the presenters by junior members of the family and people are called out to receive their gifts. The recipients exhibit a great deal of modesty in their behavior. They are slow to answer the call, and some quiet discussion and shuffling of feet usually precedes the entrance of the recipients into the open area. Often the recipient holds the hand of the presenter for a while and compliments the honoree, recalls the name of some shared relative now dead, or remarks on the beauty of the gift.

Toward the end of the giveaway the hosts can tell if they have sufficient gifts for the assembled guests. If there are surplus gifts, honored guests can be called out again. If there are not enough gifts, there is a kind of pleasant embarrassment, as the MC notes the large number of people who have come unexpectedly to honor the family and the occasion. Often cash gifts are made discreetly to the last guests to be called out, folded into a handshake. If the money runs out, the last people are called out and given a handshake or a hug, while the MC comments on the embarrassment of the family. On several occasions I have noted that when an honored elder of the community comes late to the giveaway, everything stops while the elder is called out, given gifts, and complimented publicly by the MC or members of the family. The compliments are very indirect. Most often it is sufficient to note that an elder "was a close friend of my grandmother," that he or she "has lived his whole life in the community" or that she "was a founder of the war mothers." To end the giveaway the MC simply announces that the event is over and thanks everyone for attending, sometimes adding another prayer in the native language. . . .

Significance of Giveaways

If one only observed behavior at the giveaway itself, it might seem an empty exercise. People bring blankets and shawls to a central place where they are redistributed. Over the course of a year a family will give as many gifts as they receive. These gifts are usually not sold or even used, they just continually circulate. It would appear that everything in the course of a year comes out even, blanket for blanket and shawl for shawl. This view, however, is very superficial and does not consider the concrete economic behavior of which the giveaway is merely the social symbol.

If one explores behavior in modern Plains Indian communities on a day-to-day basis through the year, as an ethnographer, it is clear that there is a real material system for distributing the means of subsistence which underlies and parallels the symbolic system exhibited at the simple giveaway. That is, the same people that an extended family might "call out" at a giveaway are the people "called upon" for help through the year when the family is in need. These allied families are called upon only when the resources of the extended family are completely exhausted. The adult members of an extended family share among themselves casually and constantly. But when the cash is gone and the refrigerator is empty, other families must be solicited for help. . . .

I am arguing here that the people called out at simple giveaways are not being honored for some abstract "status" which they enjoy in the community, but in gratitude for actual, necessary, and sometimes crucially important help in time of need. By giving gifts publicly in a ceremony, the host family is acknowledging the gifts received privately and quietly during the year. Sometimes these times of need are alluded to when the public gift is given. Here are two examples of the kinds of very indirect allusions which can be announced during a giveaway: "Sometimes people get in difficulties, and there are some who are always ready to help." "Last winter we had a situation in our family that we don't like to talk about, and we're glad to see our friends here today.". . .

Drums, Dancers and Sponsors

If a family wishes to make an event more significant, it invites a "drum" to provide traditional music. This addition makes the event a "pow-wow" rather than a simple giveaway.

A "drum" comprises an experienced group of singers who sit around a large bass drum, or a traditional one with leather stretched over a cylinder of wood, keeping time by beating on the drum and singing appropriate traditional songs. Each singer has his own drumstick and is usually a relative of the leader. The leader is responsible for conducting practice sessions, recruiting new members, and keeping the drum's calendar. For performing at a pow-wow the drum must be paid in money and gifts, and in modern times there are enough events in Oklahoma for some groups to be fully professional, supported by their work at pow-wows.

In addition to a drum, the family must invite a "head staff" to lead the dancers who will participate. On pow-wow flyers . . . these staff members have titles which are most often abbreviated. A complete head staff for an average-sized pow-wow might consist of the following: HS, Head Singer; AD, Arena Director; MC, Master of Ceremonies; HMD, Head Man Dancer; HLD, Head Lady Dancer; HLBD, Head Little Boy Dancer; HLGD, Head Little Girl Dancer; and WB, Water Boy. In addition, other more specialized staff members might include such people as HMGD, Head Man Gourd Dancer or HLBD, Head Lady Buckskin Dancer.

The families who would undertake to sponsor a large pow-wow are usually members of a local pow-wow club. And here we begin to see an exhibition of the extent of sharing networks, since a local club represents the core of a local familial network. The people who pow-wow together are the same ones who can be found together during the week. . . .

The rationales for the chartering of the clubs are several. Many are gourd dance clubs, whose focal members are older men who wear distinctive sashes and carry unique fans as they dance. Among the various Plains tribes, gourd dance clubs can be more or less religious, and more or less social/secular, and they are not entirely distinct from the veterans clubs, which require past service in the armed forces for full membership. Veterans clubs might comprise only gourd dancers, or they might also include people who do not dance at all. Among sponsoring groups, espe-cially interesting are the war mothers clubs, which first were organized after World War I to honor sons in military service (Schweitzer 1983). Large communities sometimes have several pow-wow clubs formed from the same large network of families, but under different rationales and comprising people of different age or sex. For example, the older men of a sharing network might form a gourd clan, the younger men a veterans group, and the women a war mothers group. . . .

When a family giving a pow-wow gets the sponsorship of an established pow-wow group, attendance at the event is much higher. Attendance can be increased even more by seeking additional cosponsoring groups or a cosponsoring nuclear or extended family which also seeks to honor some family member or conduct a memorial giveaway. The same effect comes from strategically inviting a head staff. In each case, accepting the invitation implies that you will bring your extended family, and perhaps your pow-wow club or other social group, and that you will urge other families and groups to attend also. Consequently, all these invitations are extremely sensitive and delicate, since there are intimate relationships of alliance and hostility among all the different dancers and their families, as well as among the pow-wow groups, and one must be careful to invite groups who are compatible with one another. In all cases, the group or person being invited wants to know who else has been invited. . . .

As part of a pow-wow, a giveaway becomes more complex. Not only must the sponsoring family give to the senior people present, but also to the drum, the head staff, and the officers and members of other sponsoring organizations. But the advantage of a pow-wow over a simple giveaway is that it makes possible the distribution of gifts within a much larger network, increasing the number of people who might be called upon in time of need. That is, although the "cost" of sponsoring a pow-wow is much greater than for a simple giveaway, so are the potential benefits.

As with the simple giveaway, a pow-wow gift implies either thanks for some past favor or the obligation to help in the future, or both. Prominent men are sometimes reluctant to attend pow-wows where they have no established alliances, since it is understood that the presentation of a gift implies a serious obligation. (Perhaps that is why most gift recipients don't say "thank you.")

In Oklahoma there are perhaps a hundred or more families who are prominent participants in pow-wows all around the state—as singers, staff, sponsors, or recipients of gifts. These are the "pow-wow people." They represent all the Plains tribes in Oklahoma as well as other tribes from the central part of the state, especially Algonkians and Dhegiha Sioux, and they can be found anywhere in the state on a given weekend. The presence of a few of these families at a small pow-wow ensures its success. Most often they receive several important gifts, and they are singled out at an event for more than their equitable share of attention. But they also have enormous obligations. During a normal week at home, they are likely to be solicited by people from anywhere in pow-wow country for some favor. And having made a long trip, the solicitants sometimes expect a *big* favor—an air fare, a hundred dollars, the loan of a car. . . .

The Political Economy of Pow-Wows and Giveaways

. . . In this section I will argue that redistribution of the means of subsistence is one of the primary functions of the events described above. I will argue this by reference to social and economic data derived from the Oklahoma counties which constitute "pow-wow country." In evaluating this thesis we must first consider why it is necessary for subsistence to be redistributed at all among American Indians. That is, why would each person in the pow-wow area not just keep their own goods and income within the extended family, instead of going to the great bother of redistributing it? There are two reasons why subsistence must be redistributed: first, because it is *scarce*, and second, because it is *erratic*.

Ashworth has already suggested the general relationship between pow-wow frequency and poverty level (Ashworth 1986:137). Looking at fifty-seven communities in pow-wow country, he correlated the number of pow-wows over a two-year period with the percent of Indian population living under the official poverty level. His results are reproduced as follows:

Pow-wow frequency over 24-month period	Average percentage of Indian population below poverty level
1–9	21.5
10–19	26.2
20–29	31.9
30–52	43.7

. . . Concerning employment, a special difficulty is posed for Indian people when they do manage to find a job. Often this means that another member of the family, a spouse, a sibling, or a parent, loses some kind of public assistance payments. If after a few months the job is lost, considerable paperwork is required to re-enroll a relative in state and federal programs of assistance. These transition periods between employment and assistance are exceptionally troublesome to families, and it is during these periods that the family is most likely to need help from others in the community.

One frequent source of help for families in need is the men and women who have recently retired to their childhood home in a rural community or returned from a stint of work in some distant city—Chicago or Los Angeles. Such people frequently sponsor a pow-wow, working through their family or pow-wow club, thereby securing a recognizable place in the community. Men and women retired from the armed forces are especially noticeable in this regard, as they often have some retirement bonus to distribute to family, friends, and solicitants. In the case of servicemen, the war mothers organizations can be called upon as sponsors.

During the days of the military draft, the war mothers were much more active than they are now, sponsoring events on two prominent occasions in the career of a draftee—his shipment overseas and his discharge. The former took place after basic and advanced training, with the family and the war mothers giving away in honor of the serviceman. At discharge, however, it is the serviceman who sponsors, singling out those who were generous to him a few years before. He is also generous privately, helping out all who ask until his money is gone. These recipients then become the people he calls on to help him make an adjustment to civilian life. Although this is perhaps the most clear-cut case of redistributive behavior, the cycle was acted out over about two years, the term of obligation under the draft. Nowadays there is necessarily a longer time from distribution to reciprocity, since the current terms of enlistment are usually from three to six years. The Persian Gulf War was handled as a special event in the pow-wow network, like a graduation, and did not seem to affect the established pattern for military service.

Although many Indian people receive lease and royalty money from ownership of trust land or from subsurface rights to land that has been sold, the form of the payments is erratic and confounds any attempt to develop a regular, dependable income. Farming and grazing leases, "surface leases," are contracted through the Bureau of Indian Affairs for a three- to five-year period and are paid annually, usually in January. As with finding a job, the receipt of a grass lease check can cause a family to lose their public assistance payments. To reestablish eligibility for some of these programs, one must demonstrate that one has no assets, and so good reasons exist for the family to quickly sponsor a pow-wow and dispose of money and property. Not surprisingly, Ashworth's data show that most benefits and memorials are held from February to May, just after the checks are received (1986:111). . . .

During calendar 1980, a high point of the oil boom in western Oklahoma, the Anadarko Area Office, which administers the major Plains tribes in western Oklahoma, disbursed over $8 million in oil and gas royalties to individual Indian people. Abject poverty nonetheless remained in the population, but those who had money gave it away lavishly, rewarding those who had helped them over the years and hedging against hard times to come. Embarrassed by their quick fortunes and under heavy social pressure to share with others, some Indian people began to engage in "wretched excess." A Kiowa pow-wow man publicly gave a prominent Osage man a horse with its mane and tail braided with $100 bills. A Cheyenne woman gave each of her three close woman friends a new pickup truck, the model General Motors already had dubbed the "Chevy Cheyenne." In these cases, the gifts were not merely symbolic, but constituted real, usable wealth. But these were unusual times.

During normal years things are not so flush for a typical Indian extended family. Usually, there might be a person or two in the extended family who is employed, perhaps someone else who is on public assistance, and also someone who gets occasional lease or royalty money. The point of the giveaway and pow-wow system is that it also allows a family to have "money in the bank" in the form of help given in the past to other families, symbolized by exchanges at giveaways and pow-wows. As long as possible the family will redistribute its own resources to survive, but there often comes a time when other families must be called upon to "help out." They do so willingly, not only because of friendship and respect but also in the knowledge that sometime soon they might be in the same situation, looking for a family that has just received its lease money or some other modest bonanza. And while the timing of these bonanzas is not always predictable, it is certain that they will come. The whole giveaway complex is predicated on this expectation.

Conclusion

At the most abstract level, how one interprets giveaway behavior within the context of ethnological theory depends on the tribe under discussion; each has a somewhat different socioeconomic structure. For the Comanches, the best model might be that of a "big man" actively looking out for his community's welfare, accumulating goods, and raising his personal prestige in accordance with his success as a leader, organizer, and redistributor (Sahlins 1963). With the Cheyennes a different model is required. Although a traditional chief has high status, he has no property, taking a passive role as tribal members shower him with public and private gifts, while supplicants constantly denude him of what he has been given. The pattern seems to be some kind of "levelling," as with the potlatch of the Northwest Coast (Codere 1950). For Kiowas and Osages, ascribed status seems to be important, since personal ancestry is constantly recited at their giveaways and pow-wows (Linton 1936:113-31).

Among those Central Algonkians and Dhegiha Sioux who participate in pow-wows, the focus seems to be on the drum and on the pow-wow activities, rather than on traditional tribal roles. It is relevant that the people of these tribes are heavily intermarried with one another, so that "full-blood" Ioways or Shawnees, for example, are hard to find. That is, a community in north central Oklahoma is likely to be of mixed tribes: individuals do not owe respect to the institutions of one single tribe, but to several. With tribal institutions diluted, social attention falls on the giveaway and pow-wow, pan-Indian institutions which are universally understood and which transcend the leadership traditions of any particular tribe.

Comparing Southern Cheyenne with Northern Cheyenne giveaway practices as reported by K. Weist, there seem to be several significant differences. First of all, "tables" of goods representing horses are not ordinarily given away in Oklahoma. Also, there are no Oklahoma Cheyenne giveaways which can rival the huge presentations of goods witnessed by Weist. However, the main argument of this article, that public gifts imply private sharing arrangements, might also be valid for the Montana Cheyennes. . . .

In closing, I must argue that in the cases of Oklahoma tribes, the most significant and most fundamental aspect of the giveaway and pow-wow complex is the redistributive function. It is fundamental because it keeps people alive, providing them with the means of subsistence—food, money, heat, medical care. Sociologically, the perspective of redistribution is important because it ties the formal aspect of the pow-wow, the ceremony, directly to the causal variable, the economy. In different ways, Ashworth and I have shown that poverty level is the independent variable, pow-wow frequency the dependent variable.

In the course of organizing economic redistribution, the pow-wow system allows the emergence of a new kind of community leader, the pow-wow man, with intensive and extensive networks of influence which reach across community and tribal boundaries. The need for an expansion of such networks is especially severe among the small Dhegiha and Algonkian tribes in north central Oklahoma. How these pow-wow leaders and their functions are integrated into the total social and political structure of a tribe, however, varies from group to group.

References

Ashworth, Kenneth. 1986. *The Contemporary Oklahoma Pow-wow.* Ph.D. dissertation, University of Oklahoma.

Codere, Helen. 1950. *Fighting with Property.* New York: J. J. Augustin.

Grobsmith, Elizabeth S. 1979. "The Lakota Giveaway: A System of Social Reciprocity." *Plains Anthropologist* 24: 123–131.

———. 1981. "The Changing Role of the Giveaway Ceremony in Contemporary Lakota Life." *Plains Anthropologist* 26: 75–79.

Kahoe, Alice B. 1980. "The Giveaway Ceremony of Blackfoot and Plains Cree." *Plains Anthropologist* 25:17–26.

Linton, Ralph. 1936. *The Study of Man.* New York: D. Appleton-Century.

Sahlins, Marshall. 1963. "Poor Man, Rich Man, Big Man, Chief. *Comparative Studies in Society and History* 5: 295–303.

Schweitzer, Marjorie M. 1983. "The War Mothers: Reflections of Space and Time." *Papers in Anthropology* 24: 157–171.

Weist, Katherine M. 1973. "Giving Away: The Ceremonial Distribution of Goods Among the Northern Cheyenne of Southeastern Montana." *Plains Anthropologist* 18: 97–103.

Young, Gloria A. 1981. *Pow-wow Power: Perspectives on Historic and Contemporary Intertribalism.* Ph.D. dissertation, Indiana University, Bloomington.

18

How to Succeed in Business:

Follow the Choctaws' Lead

Fergus M. Bordewich

Philadelphia, Mississippi, is the kind of place that seemed to survive more from habit than reason after the timber economy that was its mainstay petered out in the 1950s. There is a scruffy, frayed-at-the-edges look to the empty shop fronts and the discount stores where more vibrant businesses used to be, but by the standards of rural Mississippi, Philadelphia counts itself lucky. "Kosciusko and Louisville, they have to wait to buy a tractor or, sometimes, even to meet their payrolls," boasts the mayor, an amiable former postman by the name of Harlan Majors. "And they don't have a fire department worth a hoot. I have 16 full-time firemen."

Philadelphia's trump, the thing that those other towns will never have, is Indians. "Our best industry by far is the Choctaw Nation," Majors says. "They're our expansion and upkeep. They employ not only their own people, but ours too. It has never been as good as it is now. Our economy depends on them. If the tribe went bankrupt, we'd go into a depression."

For generations the Choctaws were a virtual textbook example of the futility of reservation life. Over the last quarter-century, however, the 8,000-member tribe has defied even its own modest expectations by transforming itself from a stagnant welfare culture into an economic dynamo, and one of the largest employers in Mississippi. Choctaw factories assemble wire harnesses for Ford and Navistar, telephones for AT&T, and audio speakers for Chrysler, Harley-Davidson and Boeing. The tribe's greeting card plant hand-finishes 83 million cards each year. Since 1991, the tribe has operated one of the largest printing plants for direct-mail advertising in the South. Sales from the tribe's industries have increased to more than $100 million annually from less than $1 million in 1979. As recently as 15 years ago, 80 percent of the tribe was unemployed; now, having achieved full employment for its members, nearly half the tribe's employees are white or black Mississippians. Says William Richardson, the tribe's economic development director, "We're running out of Indians."

The quality of life for the great majority of Choctaws has measurably improved. The average income of a family of four is about $22,000 per year, a sevenfold increase since 1980. Brick ranch houses have largely supplanted the sagging government-built bungalows amid the jungle of kudzu-shrouded oaks and pines that forms the heart of the Choctaws' 22,000-acre reservation. The Choctaw Health Center is among the best clinics in Mississippi, while teachers' salaries at the tribal elementary schools are 25 percent higher than at public schools in neighboring, non-Indian towns. "They're willing to buy the best," says a non-Indian teacher who formerly taught in Philadelphia. The tribal television station, the primary local channel for the region, broadcasts an eclectic daily menu that includes thrice-daily newscasts and Choctaw-language public service shows on such diverse topics as home-financing and microwave cooking.

The Choctaws are also a national leader in transferring the administration of federal programs from the Bureau of Indian Affairs (BIA) to the tribes. Virtually everything once carried out by the bureau—law enforcement, schooling, health care, social services, forestry, credit and finance—is now performed by Choctaw tribal bureaucrats. "We're pretty well gone," says Robert Benn, a courtly Choctaw who was the BIA's local superintendent until his recent retirement.

His sepulchral office was one of the last still occupied in the bureau's red-brick headquarters in Philadelphia. "We've seen our heyday. The tribe is doing an exemplary job. They're a more professional outfit than we ever were."

Throughout the sprawling archipelago of reservations that makes up modern Indian country, tribes like the Choctaws are demolishing the worn-out stereotype of Indians as permanent losers and victims, and effectively killing, perhaps with finality, what historian Robert J. Berkhofer Jr. aptly termed the "white man's Indian," the mythologized figure whose image, whether confected by racism or romance, has obscured the complex realities of real Native Americans, from *The Last of the Mohicans* to *Dances With Wolves.* For the first time in generations, Indian tribes are beginning to shape their own destinies largely beyond the control of whites: revitalizing tribal governments, creating modern economies, reinventing Indian education, resuscitating traditional religions and collectively remaking the relationship between the United States and the more than 300 federally recognized tribes.

To be sure, in terms of overall statistics, Indian country continues to present a formidable landscape of poverty and social pathologies. On some reservations, unemployment surpasses 80 percent. Rates of alcoholism commonly range higher than 50 percent. Indians are twice as likely as other Americans to be murdered or to commit suicide, and five times more likely to die from cirrhosis of the liver. In spite of increased access to education, 50 percent of Indian young people drop out of high school. There is no cure-all for these problems, but for the first time since the closing of the frontier, responsibility for finding solutions rests increasingly in Indian hands.

Without viable tribal economies, however, self-determination is likely to remain little more than a pipe dream. A few Indian communities have reaped astonishing profits from legalized tribal gambling, which has grown into a $6 billion industry, accounting for about 2 percent of the $330 billion that Americans legally bet each year. By 1994, more than 160 tribes were operating some form of gambling activity, including 40 full-fledged casinos, in 20 states. The tiny Mashantucket Pequot Tribe, whose Connecticut casino grosses about $800 million annually, half again as much as Donald Trump's Taj Mahal, has repurchased tribal land and provided scholarships and medical coverage for members. The tribe has also contributed $10 million to the Smithsonian's National Museum of the American Indian.

Tribal "gaming," as it is rather delicately known, is not a panacea, however. Although rumors of mob involvement have been largely disproved, some tribes have squandered their earnings. Moreover, it is likely that gambling will taper off as an important source of tribal revenue by the end of the decade, as states grant gambling licenses to other groups.

Other tribes have been blessed with abundant natural resources, which they are now able to exploit in their own interest for the first time. Between 50 percent and 80 percent of all the uranium, between 5 percent and 10 percent of all the oil and gas reserves, and 30 percent of all the coal in the United States lie on Indian lands. Many tribes own rights to water whose value is dramatically increasing. More than 90 tribes have land that is densely forested, while millions of acres of leased tribal grassland provide pasturage for ranchers, and millions of acres more are leased to farmers.

Today, the Navajos of Arizona and the Jicarilla Apaches of New Mexico, among others, operate their own tribal oil and gas commissions to regulate production on their lands. The Southern Ute tribe of Colorado has set up its own oil production firm. One of the most innovative tribes, the Confederated Tribes of Warm Springs, in Oregon, operates three commercial hydroelectric dams and an extensive forestry industry, as well as a textile plant that has produced sportswear for Nike and Jantzen and beadwork for export to Europe, a luxury vacation lodge, and a factory that recently began manufacturing fireproof doors from diatomaceous earth—or fossilized sea creatures.

However, the experience of the Mississippi Choctaws has made clear that even the most poorly endowed tribes, with able and determined tribal leadership, a pragmatic willingness to cooperate with non-Indians, some federal support and the ability to raise capital, can hope to remake themselves into viable communities able to compete in the modern American economy.

The origin of the Choctaws is mysterious. Some say that they arose pristine from the earth at Nanih Waiya, the Mother Mound of the Choctaws, a man-made hill north of the modern reservation, in Winston County. "After coming forth from the mound, the freshly made Choctaws were very wet and moist, and the Great Spirit stacked them along the rampart, as on a clothesline, so that the sun could dry them," as one story has it.

Throughout documented times, the Choctaws were mainly an agricultural people, raising corn, beans, pumpkins and melons in small plots. However, exhibiting an instinct for business that was probably far more prevalent among Native Americans than history records, they raised more corn and beans than they needed for their own use and sold the surplus to their neighbors. Like their neighbors and sometime enemies, the Cherokees, Chickasaws, Crees and Seminoles, the Choctaws gradually adopted European consumer goods, styles of agriculture and schooling, as well as less-savory practices, such as the exploitation of African slaves. By the early 19th century the Choctaws and these neighboring tribes became known collectively as the "Five Civilized Tribes" of the Southeast.

However, the relentless pressure of settlement steadily whittled away at the Choctaws' lands until, in 1830, in the poignantly named Treaty of Dancing Rabbit Creek, the tribe reluctantly relinquished what remained of its land in the East, most members agreeing to remove themselves to the Indian Territories, where their descendants still inhabit the Choctaw Nation of Oklahoma.

Originally, about one-third of Mississippi's Neshoba County was allotted to those Choctaws who chose to remain in the East. By mid-century, however, virtually all of it had passed out of Choctaw hands, sometimes legally, but often through fraud and extortion. Virtually without exception, the Choctaws were reduced to an impoverished life of sharecropping, living scattered among the forests of oak and pine. In time, their numbers were swelled by others who drifted back from the Indian Territories, disillusioned by the anarchy of tribal politics there and the difficulties of life on the frontier.

Ironically, the tripartite racial segregation that deepened as the 19th century progressed only strengthened the Choctaws in their traditions, language and determination to be Indian in a part of America where, for all intents and purposes, Indians had simply ceased to exist. Rather than send their children to schools with blacks, the Choctaws refused to send them to school at all. In 1918, when the federal government winkled out enough land from private owners to establish the present-day Choctaw reservation, nearly 90 percent of the tribe were full-bloods. Most spoke no English at all.

The story of the Choctaw revival is inseparable from that of Phillip Martin, the remarkable chief who has guided the tribe's development for most of the past 30 years. Martin is a physically unimposing man, short and thick-bodied, with small, opaque eyes and thinning hair that he likes to wear slicked back over his forehead. Beneath a grits-and-eggs plainness of manner, he combines acute political instincts with unflagging tenacity and a devotion to the destiny of his people. "He's like a bulldog at the postman—he just won't go away," says Lester Dalme, a former General Motors executive who has managed the tribe's flagship plant, Chahta Enterprise, since 1980. "At the same time, he'll give you the shirt off his back whether you appreciate it or not. He truly loves his people. He can't stand even one of his enemies to be without a job."

By all rights, Martin's fate should have been as gloomy as that of any Choctaw born in the Mississippi of 1926. "Everybody was poor in those days. The Choctaws were a bit worse," he recalls.

As a boy, he cut pulpwood, herded cows and picked cotton for 50 cents per 100 pounds. In those days, Choctaw homes had no windows, electricity or running water. Alcoholism and tuberculosis were endemic. Few Choctaws had traveled outside Neshoba County, and many had never even been to Philadelphia, only seven miles away. The etiquette of racial segregation was finely modulated. Although Choctaws were not expected to address whites as "sir" and "ma'am" or to step off the sidewalk when whites passed, they were required to sit with blacks in movie houses and restaurants. "But we never had enough money to eat in a restaurant anyway,"

Martin says, with irony, in his porridge-thick drawl.

Martin earned a high school diploma, rare among Choctaws of that time, at the BIA boarding school in Cherokee, North Carolina. His first experience of the larger world came in the Air Force at the end of World War II. Arriving in Europe in 1946, he was stunned by the sight of starving French and Germans foraging in garbage cans for food. White people, he realized for the first time, could be as helpless as Indians.

At the same time, he was profoundly impressed by their refusal to behave like defeated people and by their determination to rebuild their lives and nations from the wreckage of war. He wondered, if Europeans could lift themselves back up out of poverty, why couldn't the Choctaws? When he returned to Mississippi, he quickly learned that no one was willing to hire an Indian. Even on the reservation, the only jobs open to Indians were as maintenance workers for the BIA, and they were already filled. Martin recalls, "I saw that whoever had the jobs had the control, and I thought, if we want jobs here we're going to have to create them ourselves."

He eventually found work as a clerk at the Naval Air Station in Meridian. He began to take an interest in tribal affairs, and in 1962 he became chairman of the Tribal Council at a salary of $2.50 per hour. In keeping with the paternalistic style of the era, the BIA superintendent presided over the council's meetings. He also decided when tribal officials would travel to Washington and chaperoned their visits there, as Indian agents had since the early 19th century. Says Martin, "I finally said to myself, 'I've been all over the world. I guess I know how to go to Washington and back. From now on, we don't need the superintendent.' So after that we just up and went." Martin became a fixture in the Interior Department and the halls of Congress, buttonholing agency heads and begging for money to replace obsolescent schools and decrepit homes, and to pave the reservation's corrugated red-dirt roads.

The tribe's first experience managing money came during the War on Poverty in the late 1960s, when the Office of Economic Opportunity allowed the Choctaws to supervise a unit of the Neighborhood Youth Corps that was assigned to build new homes on the reservation; soon afterward, the tribe obtained one of the first Community Action grants in Mississippi, for $15,000. "That $15,000 was the key to all the changes that came afterward," says Martin. "We used it to plan a management structure so that we could go after other federal agency programs. I felt that if we were going to handle money, we had to have a system of accountability and control, so we developed a finance office. Then we won another grant that enabled us to hire accountants, bookkeepers, personnel managers and planners."

The Choctaws remained calculatedly aloof from both the civil rights movement of the 1960s and the Indian radicalism of the 1970s. Martin says, "We didn't want to shake things up. Where does it get you to attack the system? It don't get the dollars rolling—it gets you on welfare. Instead, I thought, we've got to find out how this system works." Eighty percent of the tribe's members were on public assistance and receiving their food from government commodity lines. "It was pathetic. We had all these federal programs, but that wasn't going to hold us together forever. I knew that we had better start looking for a more permanent source of income." It would have to be conjured from thin air: the reservation was devoid of valuable natural resources, and casino gambling was an option that lay far in the future.

In key respects, Martin's plan resembled the approach of East Asian states like Singapore and Taiwan, which recognized, at a time when most developing countries were embracing socialism as the wave of the future, that corporate investment could serve as the driving force of economic development. Martin understood that corporations wanted cheap and reliable labor, low taxes and honest and cooperative government. He was convinced that if the tribe built a modern industrial park, the Choctaws could join the international competition for low-skill manufacturing work. In 1973, the tribe obtained $150,000 from the federal Economic Development Administration to install water, electricity and sewer lines in a 20-acre plot cut from the scrub just off Route 7. "It will attract somebody," Martin promised. For once, he was dead wrong. The site sat vacant for five years.

With his characteristic tenacity, Martin began writing to manufacturers from one end of the United States to the other. He kept on writing, to 150 companies in all, until one, Packard Electric, a division of General Motors, offered to train Choctaws to assemble wired parts for its cars and trucks; Packard would sell materials to Chahta Enterprise, as the tribe called its new company, and buy them back once they had been assembled. On the basis of Packard's commitment, the tribe obtained a $346,000 grant from the Economic Development Administration and then used a Bureau of Indian Affairs loan guarantee to obtain $1 million from the Bank of Philadelphia.

It seemed, briefly, as if the Choctaws' problems had been solved. Within a year, however, Chahta Enterprise had a debt of $1 million and was near bankruptcy. Production was plagued by the kinds of problems that undermine tribal enterprises almost everywhere. Many of them were rooted in the fact that, for most of the tribe, employment was an alien concept. Workers would abruptly take a day off for a family function and not show up for a week. Some spoke no English. Others drank on the job. Many were unmarried women with small children and had no reliable way to get to work. The tribe's accountants had already recommended selling everything off for 10 cents on the dollar.

The man to whom Martin turned was Lester Dalme, who was then a general supervisor for GM and who had been raised in rural Louisiana with a virtually evangelical attitude toward work. "My mom taught us that God gave you life and that what you're supposed to do is give Him back your success," says Dalme, a trim man now in his 50s whose office at Chahta Enterprise is as plain as his ethics. Dalme remembers facing the plant's demoralized workers. "They had no idea how a business was run, that loans had to be paid. None of them, none of their fathers, and none of their grandfathers had ever worked in a factory before. They had no idea what quality control or on-time delivery meant. They thought there was a big funnel up there somewhere that money came down. They thought profit meant some kind of plunder, something someone was stealing." Dalme told them, "Profit isn't a dirty word. The only way you stay in business and create jobs is to make a profit. Profit is what will finance your future."

Dalme cut back on waste, abolished some managerial perks and put supervisors to work on the assembly line. Day care was set up for workers with small children; old diesel buses were organized to pick up those without cars. Dalme told employees that he would tolerate no alcohol or hangovers in the plant. He kept an average of three of every ten people he hired, but those who survived were dependable workers. He saw people who had been totally destitute begin to show up in new shoes and clothes without holes, and eventually in cars. After six or seven months, he saw them begin to become hopeful, and then self-confident.

Workers speak with an almost redemptive thrill of meeting deadlines for the first time. Wayne Gibson, a Choctaw in his mid-30s who became a management trainee after several years on the assembly line, recalls, "Factory work taught us the meaning of dependability and punctuality. You clock in, you clock out. It also instilled a consciousness of quality in people. You're proud of what you do. When I was on the production line and I had rejects, it really bothered me. I had to explain it the next day. We're proud of coming in here and getting that '100 percent zero defects' rating."

Chahta Enterprise has grown steadily from 57 employees in 1979 to more than 900 today. Once the tribe had established a track record with lenders, financing for several more assembly plants and for a modern shopping center followed. In 1994 the Choctaws inaugurated Mississippi's first inland casino as part of a resort complex that will include a golf course and a 520-room hotel. "Now we're more into profit centers," says William Richardson, a former venture capitalist from Jackson who was hired by Martin to function as a sort of resident deal-maker for the tribe. "We're as aggressive as hell and we take risks."

And so, today, the Choctaws have achieved virtually full employment. Increasingly, the jobs that the tribe has to offer its members are technical and intellectual, as engineers, business managers, teachers and statisticians; the tribe is, in short, creating for the first time in history a Choctaw middle class.

The scene at the Choctaw Manufacturing Enterprise, just outside Carthage, Mississippi, is typical enough at first glance. Although the building is architecturally undistinguished—just a low, white-painted rectangle hard by cow pastures and pinewoods—it is modern and spacious, and well-ventilated against the withering summer heat. Inside, workers perch at long tables, weaving wires onto color-coded boards that will become part of Xerox photocopiers. It is slow work; as many as 300 wires must go into some of the harnesses and be attached to up to 57 different terminals. Painstakingly, in deft and efficient hands, the brown and green wires are made to join and bifurcate, recombine and intertwine again in runic combinations. As they work, the long rows of mostly women listen, as do factory hands in similar plants anywhere in America, to the thumping beat of piped-in radio, and swap gossip and news of children, and menus for dinner. Across the floor, at similar tables, others are assembling telephones and putting together circuit boards for computers and audio speakers, and motors for windshield wipers.

But in another sense, the factory floor is remarkable and profound. The faces bent over the wires and phones and speakers record a transformation that no one in Mississippi could have envisioned 40 years ago when Phillip Martin came home from the military looking for any kind of job. The faces are mostly Choctaw, but among them are white and black faces, too, scores of them, all side by side in what was once one of the poorest backwaters of a state that to many seemed second to none in its determination to keep races and classes apart.

"I don't like what this country did to the Indians: it was all ignorance based on more ignorance based on greed," Martin says, in his meditative drawl. "But I don't believe that you have to do what others did to you. Ignorance is what kept us apart. We'd never have accomplished what we did if we'd taken the same attitude. I don't condemn anyone by race. What kept us down was our own lack of education, economy, health care—we had no way of making a living. I believe that if we're going to fit in this country, we'd better try our best to do it on our own terms. But we also have to live with our neighbors and with our community. We all have a common cause here: the lack of jobs and opportunities has kept everyone poor and ignorant. If we can help local non-Indian communities in the process, we do it. We all depend on one another, whether we realize it or not."

For the Choctaws especially, the mere fact of work is a revolutionary thing in a place where there was no work before. In 1989, there were four Choctaws in the Carthage plant's management; now there are 13. "The next generation will be able to manage their own businesses," says Sam Schisler, the plant's CEO, a freckled Ohioan in mauve trousers and a navy blue polo shirt who, like Lester Dalme, joined the Choctaws after running plants for Packard Electric. "I'm happy to manage myself out of a job."

There is something more. The audio speakers whose parts have been imported from Thailand and the circuit boards that have come from Shreveport are not glamorous, but they are symbolic: the children of the share-croppers for whom a visit to Philadelphia, Mississippi, was a major undertaking have begun to become part of the larger world. "We'll be building the circuit boards ourselves at some point," Schisler says.

The plant, the humid pastures and the pinewoods lack the topographical drama of the rolling prairie and sagebrush desert that are the more familiar landscapes of Indian country. But the red clay of Neshoba County has endured a history no different in its essentials from that of the homelands of the Iroquois, the Sioux, the Paiutes or the Apaches. It too was fought over and mostly lost and, until a few years ago, was equally, even ineradicably one might have said, stained with hopelessness. It is today a land of redemption; not the exotic redemption of evangelical traditionalists who would lead Indians in search of an ephemeral golden age that never was, but a more prosaic and sustainable redemption of a particularly American kind that comes with the opportunity to work a decent job, and with knowing that one's children will be decently educated and that the future will, all things being equal, probably be better than the past.

Indian history is, after all, not only a story of wars, removals, and death, but also one of compromises and creative reinventions of Indian communities continually remaking themselves in order to survive. In the course of the past five centuries, Indian life has been utterly transformed by the impact of European horses and firearms, by imported diseases and modern medicine, by missionary zeal and Christian morality, by iron cookware, sheepherding, pickup trucks, rodeos and schools, by rum and by welfare offices, and by elections, alphabets and Jeffersonian idealism, by MTV and *The Simpsons*, not to mention the rich mingling of Indian bloodlines with those of Europe, Africa and the Hispanic Southwest. In many ways, the Choctaw revolution, like the larger transformation of Indian country in the 1990s, is yet another process of adaptation, as Native Americans, freed from the lockstep stewardship of Washington, search for new ways to live in the modern world.

European Americans

European Americans constitute a large and diverse segment of the American mosaic. Although several European-origin groups (e.g., Irish, Italian) confronted prejudice and even outright hostility upon immigrating to the United States, subsequent generations have experienced considerable social and economic mobility. In sharp contrast to persons of color, most European American population groups today face scant discrimination and few meaningful ethnic barriers to success. Despite compelling evidence of many forms of assimilation among European-origin groups, however, ethnic identities retain significance for some European Americans. We briefly discuss the current status of European American identities, noting signs of possible transformation as well as the continuing importance of religio-ethnic and regional identities among some European-origin Americans.

The distinct European migrations to the United States led to groupings of whites who saw other white groups as different and sometimes threatening (this issue is discussed again in the section on migration). The first great migratory stream surged after 1820 and diminished to a trickle by the beginning of the Civil War. Those northern and western European migrants came from similar locations as the colonists who arrived before the Revolutionary War. The second great stream of migrants (1880s–1924), the "new migrants," came mainly from Southern and Eastern Europe and they are still sometimes called "ethnics." The earlier migrants from Northern and Western Europe often viewed these new migrants with suspicion because of their religions, languages, heritages, and even their complexions. Some of these differences are still perceptible today, and some people attach importance to them.

Among the earliest European migrants to the United States were those from England and other parts of the British Isles. The British migrations, like those of other Europeans and most all migrations to the United States, were point specific. The Puritans and others from eastern England came to New England, migrants from the Midlands of England came to areas a bit farther west, many of the Scots headed to the Appalachian area, and many of the southwest English came to the American South.

The English Americans of urban New England established control early. They became dominant in business, commerce, government, and education, and English became the primary language. As other groups of the old migration from Northern and Western Europe worked at integrating themselves into society, they came to see a need to slow the entry of Southern and Eastern Europeans. Old country memories may have been the wellspring, but the main American tension was competition over the ever-present need for jobs and housing. The quest for jobs led immigrants to particular cities and industries which resulted in their concentrations in certain neighborhoods. First generation Irish workers started off as unskilled laborers, but by the second generation many had moved into city jobs in police and fire departments, and by the 1860s Irish were prominent in city politics in New York City and Boston (see Chapter 12 in Kitano 1997). Poles moved into the steel industry in Pittsburgh and Cleveland. With high demand for jobs and housing, the established groups were raising barriers against the newcomers. Barriers took the form of trade unions and restrictionist laws against contract labor migration in 1880s. These new migrants found themselves in "defended neighborhoods," drawing in upon and reinforcing ethnic ties.

Many of the community studies of the United States show in detail the ways ethnic communities kept alive traditions from the old country, fighting politically, culturally, economically, and physically against other ethnic groups that seemed to threaten their space, power, and ways of life. These pre-1970 studies concentrated on European ethnic neighborhoods. In Whyte's (1943) *Street Corner Society* we see how Italian immigrants invaded an Irish immigrant area. Whyte shows that "Cornerville" became a highly organized community with its own code of values, a complex social pattern with a distinctive culture. Gans' (1962) study of the West End of Boston and Suttles' (1968) examination of the Addams Area of Chicago investigated sociocultural ecology of the neighborhood change process. Both Gans and Suttles show how Italian communities tried to retain old patterns but had to adapt to other European and non-European ethnic groups. The general picture of European ethnic neighborhoods in urban America was one of a reluctant but continual changing, moving, and blending into the larger society. The post-1970 studies usually present the painful end of old ethnic communities (Levine and Harmon 1992) or focus on contemporary immigrant (Kim 1981; Gold 1992) or African American (Anderson 1990; Davis 1991) communities.

For most whites the allegiances and the memories of the old country and the old neighborhood have faded. Suburbanization and internal migration generally have pulled European Americans away from the ethnic concentrations that once held the group and the culture together. It is increasingly difficult to see the residue of the European immigration streams of earlier periods. Although there are still identifiable European American ethnic communities in most northeastern and midwestern cities, as well as ethnic concentrations in the suburbs that ring those cities (e.g., Alba et al. 1997), social distance among European American ethnic populations has decreased throughout the latter decades of the twentieth century, and the signs of structural and cultural assimilation are widely apparent. Education, occupation, and income levels among most European American national-origin groups have diminished sharply (Jiobu 1991). Rates of intermarriage have also increased (Lieberson and Waters 1988), as education seems to have supplanted ethnicity and religion as the major basis of homogamy among European Americans (Kalmijn 1993).

Alba (1990) notes that there is "a paradoxical divergence between the long-running and seemingly irreversible decline of objective ethnic differences—in education and work, family and community—and the continuing subjective importance of ethnic origins to many white Americans" (p. 290). Alba finds that "no more than one-fifth of native-born whites . . . hold intensely to an ethnic identity" but for "a large group . . . ethnic identity is of middling salience" (p. 294). With the overwhelming rates of intermarriage and blending of European Americans, "ethnic identity is a choice" for most whites, but "it is a meaningful choice" (p. 296).

In a landmark investigation of contemporary European American ethnicity, Waters (1990) used data on ancestry and ethnic self-identification from the U.S. Census to show that many individuals choose their identities from a complex array of possibilities in their background, and that some identities are far more likely to be emphasized than chance or ancestry alone would predict. To explore the dynamics of these and other ethnic choices, Waters conducted approximately 200 in-depth interviews with non-Jewish European Americans in suburban communities in the Northeast and on the Pacific coast. She uncovered a number of factors that influence the ethnic choices of European Americans; of particular significance are surnames (and confusion about the origins of surnames), intermarriage, and the "rankings" of ethnic groups. Due perhaps to media treatments, some groups (e.g., Italian Americans) enjoy positive images such as interesting cultural traditions, romantic sounding languages, good food and drink; while others (e.g., Scottish Americans) seemingly do not.

Several other findings from the Waters (1990) study are quite important. First, she found that European American identities carried few consequences and placed few limitations on the lifestyles or personal freedoms of the individuals whom she interviewed. Virtually no one could recall any incident in which they were discriminated against because of ethnic reasons. Few of her respondents indicated that they would object to a close relative marrying someone who identified with another European American group, or that they would object to having neighbors from other European American backgrounds, although they raised strong objections to interracial marriages and neighborhoods. Further, while Waters' respondents reported a wide array of "ethnic" cultural practices (e.g., holidays, wedding and funerary customs, foods), on close inspection many of these were actually idiosyncratic family practices not recognized or shared by self-identified co-ethnics. And while many respondents reported feeling a strong psychological bond with their ethnic groups and extolled their values, these respondents were notably vague about what distinguished their ethnic community from other groups.

A clear picture of the evolving nature of suburban, non-Jewish European American ethnicity emerges from this research. According to Waters (1990 and this volume), specific European American ethnic identities are largely voluntary; while many respondents report strong feelings on this issue, conventional ethnic labels hold little meaning for others, who prefer simply to be "American." Further, contemporary European American identities are situational. Although they are psychologically important, the content of these identities is surprisingly fluid. They can be emphasized when ethnicity is salient (e.g., on holidays) or on social occasions when they may be advantageous (e.g., when they make an individual seem interesting or attractive), but they can be shed as irrelevant on most other occasions without fear of sanction from co-ethnics or others. White ethnic identities can be voluntary because the remaining differences have become so minor. Alba (1985) finds that Italian Americans are nearly identical to Protestants from Northern and Western Europe in a range of values, attitudes, and lifestyle choices. Since the distinctions among most white ancestry groups are so blurred, Waters (1990) found that:

> having an ethnic identity was for the most part something that brought pleasure to the individual. Rather than being a handicap to full participation in American society, it was seen as giving one a feeling of community and special status as an interesting or unique individual. This symbolic ethnicity makes no claims or demands on individuals whatsoever. In fact these ethnic groups never have to meet in any meaningful sense, unless you call a Saint Patrick's Day parade a meeting, and yet there is a collectivity with which one can identify and yet feel a part of in an individualistic and often atomistic society." (p. 92)

While most European American national-origin groups have experienced considerable assimilation, certain religio-ethnic groups have maintained distinctive identities. Perhaps the best example is Jewish Americans (Zenner, this volume). One powerful impetus for the maintenance of ethnic identity has been the need for solidarity and vigilance in the face of centuries of persecution. Religio-ethnic prejudice and discrimination have impacted Jewish immigrants to America as well, and according to some observers, anti-Semitism may even be on the rise in the contemporary US. Indeed, the percentage of Jews believing that anti-Semitism is "a serious problem in America today" increased sharply during the 1980s, from 45 percent in 1983 to 85 percent in 1990 (cited in Goldberg 1993). There are examples of ongoing discrimination against Jews; for example, some private clubs continue to exclude Jews from membership. Currents of anti-Semitic opinion within some segments of the African American community also remain a point of concern (Morris and Rubin, this volume). Anti-Semitism continues to occupy a central position in the rhetoric of far-right organizations (e.g., militia, "patriot," and white supremacist groups). The number of reported hate crimes against Jews (e.g., personal assaults, vandalism of Jewish synagogues and cemetaries) increased during in the 1980s before levelling off and declining slightly in the early 1990s (Horowitz 1993). And some right-wing figures and organizations in the U.S. and abroad challenge even the historical accuracy of the Holocaust.

Upon reviewing the evidence, however, many observers doubt that anti-Semitism poses a significant threat to American Jews today (Goldberg 1993). For instance, a comparison of findings from three national surveys conducted by the National Opinion Research Center indicates that anti-Semitic attitudes have declined sharply since the 1960s (Smith 1993). Most Americans seem to hold positive images of Jews (e.g., as hardworking and intelligent), and only small percentages of Americans (15 percent or fewer) would oppose living in mostly Jewish neighborhoods, or having a close relative marry a Jew (Davis and Smith 1996). In addition, while the percentage of Americans in surveys who doubt that the Holocaust occurred varies depending on question wording, this percentage tends to be small (under 20 percent), and the doubts seemingly have more to do with ignorance of history than with anti-Semitic ideology (Smith 1995).

Despite the legacy of prejudice and discrimination, by most indicators Jews in the US have attained considerable success (Gold and Phillips 1996). Although many community surveys of Jews have been conducted over the years, perhaps the best single data source is the National Jewish Population Survey (NJPS), a large cross-sectional survey of American Jews first conducted in 1971, and then replicated in 1990 (Kosmin et al. 1991). According to these data, despite the history of quotas designed to limit Jewish access to higher education and employment, Jewish Americans in the 1990s tend to be much better educated and more affluent than other American adults (Kosmin et al. 1991; US Bureau of the Census 1992). Only 6 percent of Jews have less than a high school education (compared with nearly 25 percent of the total US population). At the other end of the educational spectrum, nearly one-fourth of Jewish women and one-third of Jewish men held advanced degrees; the comparable figures for the total US population were 6 per-

cent and 11 percent. According to 1990 NJPS data, the median household income among Jewish Americans was approximately 28 percent higher than the median income for all white households in the US. Most Jewish Americans held salaried white-collar jobs, and roughly 16 percent were self-employed; both figures were much higher than in the overall US population (cited in Feagin and Feagin 1996: 176).

The American Jewish population is extremely heterogeneous, across a number of different dimensions. Once heavily concentrated in the urban Northeast, Jews now reside in significant numbers in various Sunbelt states, particularly Florida, California, and Texas (Kosmin et al. 1991). In recent years, the Jewish population in the US has also been expanded and enriched through the immigration of refugees from Russia and other parts of the former Soviet Union. Whereas Jewish Americans traditionally voted overwhelming for Democratic candidates, increasing numbers now support the GOP. While many Jews continue to participate actively in religious institutions, and there is some evidence that the more conservative variants of Judaism may be prospering (Davidman 1991), much of the focus of Jewish collective life is secular, centering on Jewish institutions, philanthropy, and support for the state of Israel (Gold and Phillips 1996). With each successive generation, a growing percentage of American Jews eschew religious participation and other forms of communal involvement. According to NJPS data, the rate of Jewish intermarriage increased roughly four-fold between 1971 and 1990 (Lazerwitz 1995). Taken together, these and other developments have sparked lively and ongoing debates about the future of Jewish religio-ethnic community in the contemporary US (Abrams 1997; Dershowitz 1997).

The case of white Southerners is especially interesting. European American ethnic identity has arguably been less salient in the South than in other regions of the U.S., such as the urban Northeast and Midwest. One reason for this may be the relatively homogeneous ethnic environment that has traditionally characterized the South. While diverse ethnic groups have long been scattered throughout the region (e.g., French-speaking Cajuns of southern Louisiana, German and Czech communities in central Texas), much of the Southeast was settled by immigrants from the poorer and more remote parts of the British Isles, especially persons of Scots/Irish origin (Fischer 1989). Other cleavages have long been more important than ethnicity; these include race first, social class, religion—and region itself. From the inception of the Republic, white Southerners harbored a rich and distinctive regional culture, originating partly around notions of honor (Nisbett and Cohen 1995). The Civil War and the conflicts over slavery and state and regional autonomy fostered a strong historical antipathy toward the North—a sense of grievance nurtured by subsequent decades of (perceived) economic exploitation and anti-Southern stereotyping.

Sociologist John Shelton Reed (1982) suggests that white Southerners' sense of regional identity (feelings of closeness to other white southerners) and regional consciousness (sense of common-fate solidarity shared among white Southerners) may parallel the ethnic sentiments found in other parts of the U.S. To be sure, dramatic changes such as economic growth and in-migration are sweeping the region (Applebome 1996). Nevertheless, the South retains a degree of cultural distinctiveness—exemplified by regional norms supporting political and economic conservatism, Protestant fundamentalism, and sanctions regarding the appropriateness of violence (Ellison 1991)—and many Southerners continue to identify strongly with the region (Reed, this volume). As outward marks of Southernness such as regional dialects are reduced through education and increased exposure to non-natives, one wonders whether southern regional identity will, like European American identities in other regions, become increasingly voluntary and situational. If this occurs, then southern identity may remain psychologically important, but the content may become more fluid. Among well-educated suburbanites, in particular, regional identity may be organized less around collective memory and grievance, and more around taste cultures (e.g. music, food), interpersonal styles, and broader cultural values.

Americans of various European-origin backgrounds have long dominated the economic, political, and cultural landscape of the US. By the mid-twenty-first century, however, European Americans will no longer constitute a numerical majority, according to most demographic estimates. As is discussed elsewhere in this volume, this shift is due to high levels of recent immigration from non-European nations, especially from Latin America and Asia, and the higher fertility rates and younger age structures of non-European-origin groups. As the demographic profile of the US is changing, the articles in this section indicate that the identities of most European American ethnic groups are also in a state of flux. Despite undeniable and extensive evidence of ethnic assimilation, for at least some segments of this population ethnic identities (or analogous identities) retain social and psychological significance, even as they are being reconsidered and reconstructed on the eve of a new century.

References

Abrams, Elliott. 1997. *Faith or Fear: How Jews Can Survive in a Christian America*. New York: Free Press.

Alba, Richard. 1985. *Italian Americans*. Englewood Cliffs, N. J.: Prentice Hall.

——. 1990. *Ethnic Identity: The Transformation of White America*. New Haven: Yale University Press.

Albe, Richard D., John R. Logan, and Kyle Crowder. 1997. "White Ethnic Neighborhoods and Assimilation: The Greater New York Region, 1980–1990." Social Forces 75: 883–912.

Anderson, Elijah. 1990. *Street Wise: Race, Class, and Change in an Urban Community*. Chicago: University of Chicago Press.

Applebome, Peter. 1996. *Dixie Rising: How the South Is Shaping American Values, Politics, and Culture*. New York: Times Books/Random House.

Davidman, Lynn. 1991. *Tradition in a Rootless World*. Berkeley: University of California Press.

Davis, James A., and Tom W. Smith. 1996. *The General Social Surveys: Cumulative Codebook, 1972–1996*. Chicago: National Opinion Research Center.

Davis, John E. 1991. *Contested Ground: Collective Action and the Urban Neighborhood*. Ithaca, NY: Cornell University Press.

Dershowitz, Alan M. 1997. *The Vanishing Jew: In Search of Jewish Identity for the Next Century*. Boston: Little, Brown, and Co.

Ellison, Christopher G. 1991 "An Eye for an Eye? A Note on the Southern Subculture of Violence Thesis." *Social Forces* 69: 1223–1239.

Feagin, Joe R., and Clairece Booher Feagin. 1996. *Racial and Ethnic Relations*, 5th ed. Englewood Cliffs, NJ: Prentice Hall.

Fischer, David H. 1989. *Albion's Seed*. Oxford: Oxford University Press.

Gans, Herbert J. 1962. *The Urban Villagers: Group and Class in the Life of Italian-Americans*. New York: The Free Press.

Gold, Steven J. 1992. *Refugee Communities: A Comparative Field Study*. Newbury Park, CA: Sage Publications, Inc.

Gold, Steven J., and Bruce Phillips. 1996. "Mobility and Continuity Among Eastern European Jews." Pp. 182–194 in *Origins and Destinies: Immigration, Race, and Ethnicity in America*, edited by S. Pedraza and R. Rumbaut. Belmont, CA Wadsworth.

Goldberg, J.L. 1993. "Scaring the Jews." *New Republic*, May 17.

Horowitz, Craig. 1993. "The New Anti-Semitism." *New York magazine*, January 11.

Jiobu, Robert M. 1991. *Ethnicity and Inequality*. Albany: SUNY Press.

Kalmijn, Matthijs. 1993. "Spouse Selection Among the Children of European Immigrants: A Comparison of Marriage Cohorts in the 1960 Census." *International Migration Review* 27: 51–78.

Kim, Illsoo. 1981. *New Urban Immigrants: The Korean Community in New York*. Princeton, NJ: Princeton University Press.

Kitano, Harry H.L. 1997. *Race Relations*, 5th edition. Upper Saddle River, N.J.: Prentice Hall.

Kosmin, Barry, et al. 1991. *Highlights from the CJF 1990 National Jewish Population Survey*. New York: Council of Jewish Federations.

Lazerwitz, Bernard. 1995. "Jewish-Christian Marriage and Conversions: 1971 and 1990." *Sociology of Religion* 56: 432–443.

Levine, Hillel and Lawrence Harmon. 1992. *The Death of an American-Jewish Community*. New York: Free Press.

Lieberson, Stanley and Mary Waters. 1988. *From Many Strands*. New York: Russell Sage Foundation.

Nisbett, Richard and Dov Cohen. 1995. *Cultures of Honor*. Boulder, CO: Westview Press.

Reed, John Shelton. 1982. *One South: An Ethnic Approach to Regional Culture*. Baton Rouge: Louisiana State University Press.

Smith, Tom W. 1993. "The Polls—A Review: Actual Trends or Artifacts: A Review of Three Studies of Anti-Semitism." *Public Opinion Quarterly* 57: 380– 393.

——1995. "The Polls—A Review: The Holocaust Denial Controversy." Public Opinion Quarterly 59: 269–295.

Suttles, Gerald D. 1968. *The Social Order of the Slum: Ethnicity and Territory in the Inner City*. Chicago: University of Chicago Press.

U.S. Bureau of the Census. 1992. *Statistical Abstract of the United States, 1991*. Washington: Government Printing Office.

Waters, Mary C. 1990. *Ethnic Options*. Berkeley: University of California Press.

Whyte, William Foote. 1943. *Street Corner Society: The Social Structure of an Italian Slum*. Chicago: University of Chicago Press.

19

The Costs of a Costless Community

Mary C. Waters

What does claiming an ethnic label mean for a white, middle-class American? Census data and my interviews suggest that ethnicity is increasingly a personal choice of whether to be ethnic at all, and, for an increasing majority of people, of which ethnicity to be. An ethnic identity is something that does not affect much in everyday life. It does not, for the most part, limit choice of marriage partner (except in almost all cases to exclude non-whites). It does not determine where you will live, who your friends will be, what job you will have, or whether you will be subject to discrimination. It matters only in voluntary ways—in celebrating holidays with a special twist, cooking a special ethnic meal (or at least calling a meal by a special ethnic name), remembering a special phrase or two in a foreign language. However, in spite of all the ways in which it does not matter, people cling tenaciously to their ethnic identities: they value having an ethnicity and make sure their children know "where they come from."

In this chapter I suggest two reasons for the curious paradox posed by symbolic ethnicity. First, I believe it stems from two contradictory desires in the American character: a quest for community on the one hand and a desire for individuality on the other. Second, symbolic ethnicity persists because of its ideological "fit" with racist beliefs.

American Values and Symbolic Ethnicity

Analysts of American culture have long noticed the fundamental tension between the high values Americans place on both individuality and conformity. Writing over 100 years ago on the American psyche and character, Alexis de Tocqueville developed a theme that has been a recurrent observation of all students of the nature of American character—the tension between the conflicting values of individualism and conformity, or between self-reliance and cooperation. In fact, Tocqueville coined the term *individualism* to describe the particular way in which people in America "turned in on themselves" all of their feelings and beliefs. . . .

Tocqueville noticed that while individualism led people to find their own beliefs within themselves, this isolation was at the same time compatible with conformity, because people are constantly looking for affirmation of those beliefs in the people around them. Contrasting democratic societies with aristocratic ones, Tocqueville argues that while "knowing your place" in an aristocratic society binds individuals to their ancestors and descendants, the peculiar effect of democracy is to isolate individuals from one another and from the generations that precede and follow them. . . .

Tocqueville saw the uniquely American proclivity for joining voluntary groups—associations of all different kinds—as a necessary moderating influence on this individualism. By participation in these small groups—local government and communities—Americans would find the sense of connection to others that would inoculate them from the dangers of despotism. Without these communities, the danger of a mass society of isolated individuals is that they are easy prey to despots taking advantage of a democratic system.

Since Tocqueville first noticed this tension between individualism and conformity, it has been a central theme in discussions of the nature of American culture and character. Rupert Wilkinson, in *The Pursuit of American Character* (1988), a review of writing on American character between 1940 and 1980, argues that the dual attraction of Americans to individualism and community is the overriding theme of all accounts of American character in this period. He argues that the course from the 1940s to the 1980s was full circle, starting with a renewed interest in Toc-queville's concern with individualism, pro-ceeding through a period of concern with so-cial pressure and conformity . . . and then re-turning to a concern with unstable, isolating egoism. . . .

Describing the situation in the 1980s and the most recent books examining the elusive "American character," Wilkinson focuses on the concern of these authors with the conflict "between modern American culture and deep yearnings for community," and a renewed stress on the problems caused for people by social atomism, rather than conformity.

Wilkinson asks the interesting question of whether this shift reflects merely a change in writers' sensibilities or an actual change in American behavior and values. He suggests that the massive suburbanization that has oc-curred since the 1940s may have led to this move on the part of most Americans away from extensive involvement in community. . . .

[My research centers on] the families that live in these suburbs and live these lives, and it is possible that [this] isolation . . . is in part responsible for [their] expressed wishes . . . for more "community." Symbolic ethnicity fulfills this particularly American need to be "from somewhere." Having an ethnic identity is something that makes you both special and simultaneously part of a community. It is something that comes to you involuntarily through heredity, and at the same time it is a personal choice. And it allows you to express your individuality in a way that does not make you stand out as in any way different from all kinds of other people. In short, sym-bolic ethnic identity is the answer to a di-lemma that has deep roots in American cul-ture.

The Element of Choice

Symbolic ethnicity [is] appealing . . . for another reason as well—the element of choice involved. . . . Even among those who have a homogeneous background and do not need to choose an ancestry to identify with, it is clear that people do choose to keep an ethnic identity. And until recently many so-cial scientists who have attempted to under-stand this persistence of ethnic identity have looked at the nature of the particular ethnic groups—extolling the virtue of particular strands of the ethnic culture worth preserv-ing. Yet if one looks at ethnicity almost as though it were a product one would purchase in the marketplace—Stein and Hill's "dime store" ethnics—one can see that symbolic ethnic identity is an attractive product.

The choice to have a symbolic ethnicity—in all the ways I have described—is an attrac-tive and widespread one despite its lack of demonstrable content, because having a symbolic ethnicity combines individuality with feelings both of community and of con-formity through an exercise of personal choice. . . .

Part of the reason that ethnicity is so ap-pealing to people is evident in the reasons people give to the question of *why* they "like being ethnic." Being ethnic makes them feel unique and special and not just "vanilla," as one respondent put it. They are not like every-one else. At the same time, being ethnic gives them a sense of belonging to a collectivity. It is the best of all worlds: they can claim to be unique and special while simultaneously finding the community and conformity with others that they also crave. But that "commu-nity" is of a type that will not interfere with a person's individuality. The closest this type of ethnic identity brings a person to "group ac-tivity" is something like a Saint Patrick's Day parade. It is not as if these people belong to ethnic voluntary organizations or gather as a group in churches or neighborhood or union halls. They work and reside within the main-stream of American middle-class life, yet they retain the interesting benefits—the "special-ness" of ethnic allegiance.

An exaggerated way of examining the rea-sons behind these choices is through a ques-tion I asked that freed respondents from any constraint based on the belief that ethnicity is inherited. I asked people, "if you could be a member of any ethnic group you wanted, which one would you choose?" It is clear from the answers that having an ethnic iden-tity gives people a feeling of "specialness" and fulfills a longing for community. . . .

. . . [E]ven those who hunger for a roman-ticized version of an all-encompassing ethnic community realize that they only want the positive aspects of that community. [They want] the warmth of a close community without the restrictions that . . . usually accompany such a community. But while [they] fantasize that the warmth and familial ties missing from [their] own life would be present if they were American Indian or a gypsy, in fact, the situation they describe is precisely what a symbolic ethnic identity gives to middle-class Americans—a sense of rich culture through a community with no cost to the other contradictory values we also crave: individuality, flexibility, and openness to new ideas.

In fact the very idea that Americans have of "community" is very much tied up in their minds with ethnicity. Ethnicity is sometimes defined as family writ large. The image that people conjure up of "community" is in part one based on common origins and interests. The concrete nature of those images in America is likely to be something like a small town or an ethnic ghetto, while in many other parts of the world this sense of peoplehood or community might be realized through nationalist feelings. . . . [T]he idea of being "American" does not give people a sense of one large family, the way that being French does for people in France. In America, rather than conjuring up an image of nationhood to meet this desire, ethnic images are called forth.

. . . [P]recisely what we crave about community and tradition is also tied to things we don't crave—conformity, lack of change, and rigidity. The maintenance of boundaries around a community involves costs to the individuals inside as well as providing the benefits of nurturance and security. Community seen one way is warm and nurturing; seen another, it is stifling and constricting.

This is the essential contradiction in American culture between individuality and community. . . . And I think this is the best way to understand the symbolic ethnicity I have described—it gives middle-class Americans at least the appearance of both: conformity with individuality; community with social change. And as an added bonus—which almost ensures its appeal to Americans—the element of choice is also there. Ethnicity has a built-in sense of appeal for Americans that should make Coke and Pepsi

envious. Madison Avenue could not have conspired to make a better and more appealing product. This partly explains the patterns in the choices people make about their ethnic identities. When given a choice, whites will choose the most "ethnic" of the ancestries in their backgrounds.

Over and over again people told me that they liked keeping an ethnic identity because it gave them a sense of who they were, where they had come from, and, as one respondent said, made them "more interesting." And the more unusual your ancestry sounds, the more "interesting" you are. . . .

Those who don't have a strong ethnic identity or who don't have an ancestry in their past that makes them feel special or interesting feel as though they should at least hold on to what they do have. . . . You have to have something you can identify with. If it is a "special" ethnicity, you can be interesting or elite, but nevertheless you must have something. . . . Symbolic ethnicity is thus not something that will easily or quickly disappear, while at the same time it does not need very much to sustain it. The choice itself—a community without cost and a specialness that comes to you just by virtue of being born—is a potent combination.

Symbolic Ethnicity and Race

But what of the consequences of this symbolic ethnicity? Is it a harmless way for Saturday suburban ethnics to feel connected and special? Is it a useful way to unite Americans by reminding us that we are all descended from immigrants who had a hard time and sacrificed a bit? Is it a lovely way to show that all cultures can coexist and that the pluralist values of diversity and tolerance are alive and well in the United States?

The answer is yes and maybe no. Because aside from all of the positive, amusing, and creative aspects to this celebration of roots and ethnicity, there is a subtle way in which this ethnicity has consequences for American race relations. After all, in much of this discussion the implicit and sometimes explicit comparison for this symbolic ethnicity has been the social reality of racial and ethnic identities of America's minority groups. For the ways in which ethnicity is flexible and symbolic and voluntary for white middle-class Americans are the very ways in which it is not so for non-white and Hispanic Americans. . . .

So for all of the ways in which I have shown that ethnicity does not matter for white Americans, I could show how it does still matter very much for non-whites. Who your ancestors are does affect your choice of spouse, where you live, what job you have, who your friends are, and what your chances are for success in American society, if those ancestors happen not to have been from Europe. Whether this is a temporary situation, and the experience of non-whites in America will follow the same progression as the experience of these white ethnic groups, has been one of the central questions in American social science writing on this subject. The question, then, of whether ethnic groups such as Italians and Poles are in some way the same as minority groups such as Chicanos and blacks is a complicated one. . . . Stephen Steinberg (1981) and others writing on the ethnic revival of the 1970s argue quite strongly that the self-conscious organization of white ethnics on the basis of their ethnicity was a racist response to the civil rights movement of the 1960s and 1970s and to celebrations of racial and ethnic identities by non-white groups.

Michael Novak, author of *The Rise of the Unmeltable Ethnics*, was the conservative leader of the white ethnic movement of the 1970s. He tries to answer the criticism that white ethnics are anti-black and "going back to their ethnicity" in order to oppose the black power movement. He writes: "The new ethnicity is the nation's best hope for confronting racial hatred. A Pole who knows he is a Pole, who is proud to be a Pole, who knows the social costs and possibilities of being a Polish worker in America, who knows where he stands in power, status and integrity—such a Pole can face a black militant eye to eye" (Novak 1973, 294). Novak really could not have been more wrong here, but not only for the most obvious reason. In the context of the content of the rest of his book and the debates of the early 1970s, Novak was wrong because the "new white ethnics" *were* in op-

position to the black power movement, and various other developments that came out of the civil rights movement. And Novak's own work was read then and can be read now as fanning the flames of racial division at the time.

But the other sense in which Novak is wrong in this passage is in part a result of some of the developments of the new ethnicity movement of the 1970s. A Polish-American who "knows he is a Pole, who is proud to be a Pole, who knows the social costs and possibilities of being a Polish worker" is less able to understand the experience of being black in America precisely because of being "in touch with his own ethnicity." That is because the nature of being a Pole in America is as I have described it throughout this book—lacking in social costs, providing enjoyment, and chosen voluntarily.

One . . . major . . . [concern] has been the disparity between the idea and the reality of ethnicity for white ethnics. The reality is that white ethnics have a lot more choice and room for maneuver than they themselves think they do. The situation is very different for members of racial minorities, whose lives are strongly influenced by their race or national origin regardless of how much they may choose not to identify themselves in ethnic or racial terms. Yet my respondents did not make a distinction between their own experience of ethnicity as a personal choice and the experience of being a member of a racial minority.

People who assert a symbolic ethnicity do not give much attention to the ease with which they are able to slip in and out of their ethnic roles. It is quite natural to them that in the greater part of their lives, their ethnicity does not matter. They also take for granted that when it does matter, it is largely a matter of personal choice and a source of pleasure.

The fact that ethnicity is something that is enjoyed and will not cause problems for the individual is something people just accept. This also leads to the belief that all ancestries are equal—more or less interchangeable, but that you should be proud of and enjoy the one you have. . . .

The sentiment among my respondents was that people should be proud of their heritage, whatever it is. And because they happened to be Irish or Polish or Italian, they were proud to be Irish or Italian or Polish. But they could just as easily have been something different. . . .

This approach to their own ethnicity leads to a situation where whites with a symbolic ethnicity are unable to understand the everyday influence and importance of skin color and racial minority status for members of minority groups in the United States. . . .

The people I interviewed were not involved in ethnic organizations and were not self-consciously organized on the basis of their ethnicity. However, I do think that the way they experience their ethnicity creates a climate leading to a lack of understanding of the ethnic or racial experience of others. People equated their European ancestral background with the backgrounds of people from minority groups and saw them as interchangeable.

Thus respondents told me they just did not see why blacks and Mexican-Americans were always blaming things on their race or their ethnicity. For instance, Bill McGowan:

A lot of people have problems that they bring on themselves. I don't care what religion or what nationality they are. The Mexicans, a lot of times they will say, "Well, it is because I am Mexican that it is much harder." But if they were Irish they might have the same problems. People are people.

Barbara Richter:

I think black people still do face discrimination to a point. But when other people come to this country with half a brain in their head and some industrious energy and they make it on their own after a while, I just think the opportunities are there for everyone.

Sean O'Brien:

I think everybody has the same opportunity. It doesn't matter what their background is. The education is there and if they have the gumption to go after it, they can do anything they damn well please. It doesn't make any difference if they are Irish, German, Jewish, Italian, or black. There are all different groups who are

multi-millionaires. They have the same opportunities. I think a black kid has the same opportunity as one of my own. . . .

Others denied, especially, that blacks were experiencing discrimination, citing examples of when affirmative action policies had hurt them or their families as "reverse discrimination." Megan O'Keefe:

I never saw blacks being discriminated against at all. Now whether they are or not, maybe it is true. But I have seen a lot of the reverse. I have seen a lot of reverse discrimination.

Part of the tradition handed down as part of an ethnic ancestry are the family stories about ancestors having faced discrimination in the past. In fact, a large part of what people want to pass on to their children is the history of discrimination and struggle that ancestors faced when first arriving in the United States. All of my respondents were sure that their ancestors had faced discrimination when they first came to the United States. Many had heard stories about it within their families, some had read about it in history books, but all were sure it had happened. It was also one of the most important things mentioned to me by parents when they talked about what they wanted their children to know about their ethnic ancestry. . . .

People were all aware of the fact that their ancestors had come here as immigrants to make a better life and that they had faced adversity to do it—and they often pointed to the similarities between the experience of their ancestors and the discrimination experienced by non-whites now. Carol Davis's image of what it used to be like for the Irish is perhaps the most affected by being seen through the prism of the civil rights movement:

Q: Did your ancestors face discrimination when they first came here?

A: Yes, from what I was told they were. I know that Irish people were treated almost like blacks for a while. They weren't allowed in certain buildings. They were discriminated against. From what my mother says there were even signs in Philadelphia for Irish people not to come into the restaurants. I think they were even forced to ride in the back of the bus for a while there.

This type of interpretation of history contributes to the problems middle-class Americans of European origin have in understanding the experiences of their contemporary non-white fellow citizens. The idea that the Irish were forced to sit at the back of a bus (when, in 1840?) in a sense could be seen to bring people together. The message of such a belief is that all ethnicities are similar and all will eventually end up successful. If the Irish had to sit at the back of the bus sometime in the past, and now being Irish just means having fun at funerals, then there is hope for all groups facing discrimination now. But, of course, if the Irish did not need legislation to allow them into the front of the bus, then why do blacks? If the Irish could triumph over hardships and discrimination through individual initiative and hard work, then why the need for affirmative action and civil rights legislation?

It is clear that people have a sense that being an immigrant was hard, that society did not accept their groups, and that now discrimination and prejudice is much less than it was before. People also believe that blacks, Hispanics, and Asians are still in a somewhat earlier stage. But, on the other hand, beliefs that the discrimination faced by Irish, Italians, and Serbs was the same both in degree and in kind as that faced by non-whites sets the stage for resentment of any policies that single out racial minorities.

The way in which they think about their own ethnicity—the voluntary, enjoyable aspects of it—makes it difficult to understand the contemporary position of non-whites. Thus some people made it a point to assert their ethnic identity on forms or in situations where forms or institutions were trying to determine minority status. . . .

[T]he process and content of symbolic ethnicity tend to reinforce one another. If invoking an ethnic background is increasingly a voluntary, individual decision, and if it is understood that invoking that background is done for the enjoyment of the personality traits or rituals that one associates with one's ethnicity, then ethnicity itself takes on certain individual and positive connotations. The process and content of a symbolic ethnicity then make it increasingly difficult for white ethnics to sympathize with or understand the experience of a non-symbolic ethnicity—the experience of racial minorities in the United States.

The Future of Symbolic Ethnicity

. . . Given the fact that the structural conditions and trends that give rise to symbolic ethnicity are continuing, I would expect that symbolic ethnicity will continue to characterize the ethnicity of later generation whites. The individual and familial construction of the substance of that ethnicity, along with increasing intermarriage, means that the shared content of any one ethnicity will become even more diluted. Consequently there will be increased dependence on the mass media, ethnic stereotypes, and popular culture to tell people how to be Irish or Italian or Polish.

But that dilution of the content of ethnicity does not necessarily mean that there will be a decline in the personal satisfaction associated with having a symbolic ethnicity. Partly this is because the contentless nature of this ethnicity enables it to provide the feeling of community with no cost to the individuality we Americans value so highly. But it is also because this ethnicity is associated by people with close and intimate ties in their nuclear families, in fragments of their extended families, and with close friends and neighbors. The Saint Patrick's Day parties I attended with my respondents may not have had too much to do with being Irish, and the people giving them may have had very little Irish in their complicated family trees, but the parties were warm and rich celebrations, which embody traditions for the people who gather each year. The "community" that gathers for these celebrations is not necessarily illusory, but it is a voluntary, personally constructed, American creation.

The paradox of symbolic ethnicity is that it depends upon the ultimate goal of a pluralist society and at the same time makes it more difficult to achieve that ultimate goal. It is dependent upon the concept that all ethnicities mean the same thing—that enjoying the traditions of one's heritage is an option available to a group or individual—but that such a heritage should not have any social costs associated with it. The options of symbolic ethnicity involve choosing among elements in one's ancestry and choosing when and if voluntarily to enjoy the traditions of that ancestry. However . . . the individuals who enjoy a symbolic ethnicity for themselves do not always recognize the options they enjoy or the ways in which their own concepts of ethnicity and uses of those concepts constrain and deny choice to others.

Americans who have a symbolic ethnicity continue to think of ethnicity—as well as race—as being biologically rooted. They enjoy many choices themselves, but they continue to ascribe identities to others—especially those they can identify by skin color. Thus a person with a black skin who had some Irish ancestry would have to work very hard to decide to present him or herself as Irish—and in many important ways he/she would be denied that option. The discussion of racial intermarriage makes this point clearly—racial identity is understood by these respondents as an inherited physical aspect of an individual, not as a social construct. Thus respondents exhibit contradictory ideas about minorities in American society—they are clear that there is a fundamental difference between a white ethnic and a black person when the issue is intermarriage in their own families. On the other hand, they do not understand why blacks seem to make such a big deal about their ethnicity. They see an equivalence between the African-American and, say, Polish-American heritages.

So symbolic ethnicity only works for some ancestries—the pluralist ideal of an equality of heritages is far from a reality in American life. But at the same time, as I have argued, the legacy of symbolic ethnicity is to imply that this equality exists. The political result of that ideological legacy is a backlash against affirmative action programs that rec-ognize and try to redress the inequalities in our society.

The ultimate goal of a pluralist society should be a situation of symbolic ethnicity for all Americans. If all Americans were free to exercise their "ethnic option" with the certainty that there would be no costs associated with it, we could all enjoy the voluntary, pleasurable aspects of ethnic traditions in the way my respondents describe their own enjoyments. It is important not to romanticize the traditional white ethnic group. In addition to its positive aspects, it was experienced as extremely constricting and narrow by many people. There are parts of these past ethnic traditions that are sexist, racist, clannish, and narrow-minded. With a symbolic ethnic identity an individual can choose to celebrate an ethnic holiday and refuse to perpetuate a sexist tradition that values boys over girls or that channels girls into domestic roles without their consent. The selective aspects of a symbolic ethnicity are in part what make it so enjoyable to so many individuals. . . . It is a sad irony that the enjoyment and individual character of their own ethnicity contributes to the thinking that makes these middle-class whites oppose the very programs designed to achieve that reality.

References

Novak, M. 1973. *The Rise of the Unmeltable Ethnics: Politics and Culture in the Seventies.* New York: MacMillan Co.

Steinberg, S. 1981. *The Ethnic Myth: Race, Ethnicity, and Class in America.* Boston: Beacon Press.

Tocqueville, A. de. 1835–39. *Democracy in America.* Translated by George Lawrence. Garden City, NY: Doubleday, 1969.

Wilkinson, R. 1988. *The Pursuit of American Character.* New York: Harper and Row.

20

Jewishness in America:

Ascription and Choice

Walter Zenner

Introduction

. . . In this paper, the changing nature of what it means to be Jewish in America will be discussed. Rather than speaking of Jewish ethnicity, the term "Jewishness" is preferred because of the importance of the religious component of Jewish identity which makes it quite different from other identities like "Black" or "Italian" or "Native American" (Amerind). At the same time, the ancestral elements are also present, which makes "Jewishness" different from Protestant and even Catholic definitions of being a "Christian." . . . While Judaism generally does not proselytize actively, converts are accepted into the fold. Most Jews are members of the group on account of their ancestry, but proselytes, beginning with the Biblical Ruth, have been significant in Jewish history. Since sociology of religion is segregated from sociology of ethnic relations, this facet is often neglected. With regard to Jewish ethnicity in particular it cannot be ignored.

Here I will argue that in present-day America, Jewishness has ceased to be a given for many of those who are born Jews nor is it excluded as an alternative for Gentiles. While the vast majority of those who are born Jews still see themselves as Jewish in terms of an ancestral heritage, their Jewishness is being transformed into a preference, rather than an ascribed status, *à la* caste or race. This transformation follows certain general patterns present in American life. American Protestantism, with its roots in the competition between various established churches and dissenting sects, developed a viewpoint whereby membership in a church was a matter of individual faith, rather than an imposition from parents or the surrounding society. The spirit of capitalism which permeated economics, politics, and the arts made the metaphor of the marketplace applicable to ideas, both religious and secular. . . .

Citizenship and nationality in the United States is conceived in the same terms as religion—as a matter of choice, while the American-born are automatically citizens, no regard is given to their ancestry. Even the children of illegal aliens are automatically citizens. . . . Becoming an American is achieving a position in the world. Stressing this ideal should not blind us to the opposing ideologies of racism, anti-Semitism, and anti-Catholicism which present an opposite ideal and which continue to exist with varying degrees of manifestation and latency.

This idea of becoming an American by choice fits in very well with urban American values today. Freedom in choosing occupations, neighborhoods, clothing, foods, and sexual partners are highly valued, especially in those places where most American Jews reside. In fact, the great debates of contemporary America are often phrased in terms of conflicts of rights and freedoms, such as the abortion controversy.

The transformation of Jewishness will be described and explained in a number of ways. First, the general trends discerned by social scientific research dealing with American Jewry will be reported. The historical dimensions of the changes will be briefly outlined, in terms of both the European and American backgrounds. Then attention will be turned to certain influences of American culture, particularly those relating to the value of individuality. Next, the manner in which widely accepted retentions and elaborations of Jewish culture themselves illustrate this transformation will be examined. Jewishness in America is also exemplified by those on the margins of the community, either Jews moving out of the Jewish community or trying to combine Judaism and other religions or non-Jews wholly or partially adopting Judaism.

The existence of several categories of the marginal in itself tells us about Jewish identity in this period. While most of the studies and reports on which this paper is based demonstrate the erosion of traditional Judaism, it is necessary to remind ourselves that within this general entropy there are regenerative processes. While these also are often products of individuality, they illustrate the complexity of the processes involved in ethnic and religious identifications in America today.

General Trends

There are a number of general social trends marking American Jewry as it enters the last fifteen years of the twentieth century. There are approximately 5.5 million Jews in the U.S. today. . . .

1. Jews are increasingly attracted to those professions accessible through higher education. Many now work for large corporate entities including the government and universities, although considerable self-employment persists. Jewish participation in the old small business sector, exemplified by mom-and-pop stores, has declined. In part, this is because this sector as a whole has declined; in part, it has been abandoned by Jews for more prestigious enterprises. There are, of course, new small businesses such as financial advising and consultancy (see Elazar 1976: 33–6; Cohen 1983: 76–97; Kuznets 1972; Zenner 1980, forthcoming).

2. As the majority of American Jews enter what are the third and fourth generations since immigration from Eastern Europe, one finds a decline in institutional affiliation, both with synagogues and with the philanthropic and defense organizations. More and more later-generational Jews have more and more Gentile friends and spouses, although predominantly Jewish familial and friendship circles continue to have importance.

3. There has been a decline in ritual observance, connected especially with more and more higher education and entry into the professions. This is less true of those who continue in the small business/self-employment sector.

4. Jews have moved away from their early inner-city and Northeastern metropolitan concentrations. Increasing numbers have moved to newer sunbelt communities and new university centers and other areas where the traditional communal structures are "underdeveloped." Even there, however, they have formed new synagogues and other communal structures. As in other areas this follows a general trend.

5. The Jewish family has followed general trends in American society. The average age of marriage among Jews has risen and the fertility rate has declined. Divorces have risen and so has the tendency towards intermarriage. The latter two continue to be below the national averages for other groups but the general curves follow national trends. Communal affiliation among the single, the divorced, and the intermarried is lower than for those in conventional families.

6. Politically Jews have been associated with the Democratic party, at least since the 1930s, and have generally been characterized by left-liberal sympathies. There have always been, however, Jews who were conservative and Republican. . . .

7. As more and more Jews have moved out of the core of the community and become less affiliated with it, the more orthopraxic Jews have gained in confidence and prominence. Occupationally, educationally, and even behaviorally—outside of areas of ritual practice, these "integral Jews," as Elazar (1976: 71) calls them, are similar to their "assimilating" counterparts. Among them as among the Conservative, Reform, and unaffiliated, one finds increasing divorce and alcoholism—although the extent to which this is true may be less. Even intermarriage (although here inevitably accompanied by conversion) is found among orthodox Jews. . . . The existence of the orthodox group among American Jews, is important in that it provides an important core and an alternative for others. By its persistence, adaptability, and rise to prominence, it provides a model.

These trends indicate the general conformity of American Jews to others in the United States, albeit with some twists which are uniquely Jewish.

Historical Dimensions

The special characteristics of Jewishness today must be understood in the light of Diaspora Jewish history. While technically open to converts, for the better part of two millennia Jews under Christendom and Islam were forbidden to accept proselytes. While Jews could convert to the majority religion, such conversion involved a total break with one's family and kin, unless they also converted. Since Jews were specialized economically, this often entailed a drastic change in occupation. During this period Jews were subject to rabbinic and secular authorities of the Jewish community. The community in both Europe and the Middle East was a recognized corporate body which collected taxes for itself and the state. Members could be disciplined by fines, ostracism, and other sanctions. Jewish atheists and "non-Jewish Jews" did not exist in this period.

This pattern was broken in Western Europe during the eighteenth century. . . . In this process, Jewishness was transformed from having a close connection with a corporate body in a particular place and with similar communities elsewhere to something vague and ill-defined. Jews could opt out of the organized community, even when it was state-supported, without conversion. They could ignore Jewish institutions in their everyday lives. Now a whole range of people were recognized as Jews from near-converts to Christianity who had not been baptized, and unbelievers, through the inter-married, moderate Reform, Conservative, to ultra-Orthodox Jews who segregated themselves from the others. Increasing numbers of Jews went to school and worked side-by-side with Gentiles though their social lives were often segregated (Sharot 1976: 63–100; Katz 1973: 104–222).

In North America, informal and flexible patterns of communal organization developed early on. Judaism was not an established religion. The rigid division between Central European and Spanish-Portugu[ese] Jews was not maintained. American Jews [fol]lowed the Protestant pattern of organizing [along] congregational lines. There was nothing [to] prevent secession, if a faction disapproved [of] a rabbi on personal, political or religi[ous] lines. In the nineteenth century, Ameri[can] Jewry was split between the Reform and [the] more traditional Conservative-Ortho[dox] groupings. The massive East European [immi]gration at the end of that century was it[self] divided by a variety of ideologies, includ[ing] socialist, nationalist, Yiddishist, Hebraist, [Or]thodox and atheist. Efforts at forming an u[m]brella communal structure failed at both [the] national level and in New York City (H[owe] 1976). Only when some of the ideological [di]visions lessened in importance and the se[nse] of outside danger during the Second W[orld] War increased could some successful coo[rdi]nation of effort occur. Still, each organizat[ion] to this day maintains its autonomy. In ad[di]tion, any Jew in America can defy the wis[hes] of the community and can probably f[ind] some other Jews who will sympathize w[ith] him/her. Of course, some issues, such as [as]sertive opposition to the State of Israel, [will] still call forth a measure of ostracism.

The Impact of American Individualism and Conformity

In dealing with American Jewry, one m[ust] weigh the impact of general United Sta[tes] culture. Much of this culture is shared w[ith] other countries of West European origin, [al]though the degree of competitive individu[al]ism is considered more extreme here th[an] even in Canada. Paradoxically the pressu[re] to conform to American ways is also stron[g.] This is explained by the shared criteria of s[uc]cess found in American society. This in[di]vidualism has been accepted by Americ[an] Jews. . . .

Anglo-conformity which marked Am[eri]can cultural policies until recently was [par]ticularly successful because it was not [im]posed by the federal government but thro[ugh] the zeal of English-speaking Americans [at] every level of society. Immigrants were [en]couraged to speak English, adopt Ameri[can] dress, and American ways. Even new im[mi] grants within two or three years of arrival found themselves going to public school, eating turkey with dressing on Thanksgiving, and becoming spiritual descendants of the Mayflower Pilgrims. Compulsory education and universal conscription during the two World Wars speeded this process. The public schools and more recently the mass media encouraged conformity in other areas as well, such as the adoption of American dating patterns. The trend towards "sexual liberation" which became so clear during the 1960s was, in fact, a logical consequence of premarital patterns of dating and the choice of marital partners on the basis of sexual attraction, characteristic of America since the 1920s. Except for the Hasidim and, to a lesser extent, among Middle Eastern Jews, such mores have been accepted by most segments of American Jewry.

American individualism is often expressed by everyone wanting to do their own thing with the least amount of restriction possible, even though it may mean conforming to what one's neighbor is doing. There is also fierce competition on both an individual and collective level. . . . This individual competitiveness fits very well into the vocabulary of freedom and rights.

From 1840 to 1950, there was intense competition by Jews in forming congregations, philanthropic groups and communal organizations. Often these groups worked at cross-purposes, even during the tragic period of the Second World War. Since 1950, the competition has abated though the old organizations persist. New groups continue to be formed. These include the radically separatist and militantly rightwing Jewish Defense League, the formation of gay synagogues, the various moderate and radical leftwing groups, the havurot, feminist circles, and organizations which attempt to assert a departure from the Establishment like the Committee for a Safe Israel, Breira, Friends of Peace Now, and the New Jewish Agenda. Many such groups are ephemeral but they may form the cutting edge of a new establishment (e.g., Maibaum 1971).

The competitiveness of individual entrepreneurship has also entered into the regulation and observance of the dietary laws among traditional orthopraxic Jews. In the traditional community, the rabbi served as judge of the community, not for a voluntarily organized association. Supervision of the slaughter of kosher animals for eating was equally communal; indeed, in most larger communities, the shohet or ritual slaughterer was considered a communal functionary and the proceeds from the sale of kosher meat went into the community's treasury (Baron 1942: 107–10 and 256–60). A quite different situation prevails in the United States. There is no official communal or governmental supervision, except insofar as the government may provide some protection against fraud. In addition, new complications have arisen. One is the fact of long-distance slaughter and shipment of meat, so that butchers in community X must depend upon slaughterhouses far away. Another is that people rely more and more upon previously prepared foods and only obtain information about ingredients and the presumed propriety of the food from labels.

While local kashrut councils still exist, individuals may choose to buy kosher or non-kosher meat. Those who observe the dietary laws may either buy locally butchered meat or meat prepared hundreds of miles away under the supervision of rabbis whom they trust. There is competition between different orthodox factions for which group has the most trustworthy supervision. This is especially the case with regard to products for the Passover when the strictest laws apply and when many who are indifferent to kashrut during the rest of the year buy prepared foods which are proper for that holiday (Shenker 1979).

In the realm of food there have been other influences as well. The possibility of synthetic foods which look like what they are not and the introduction of new tastes have left their mark on the orthopraxic. As far as the former is concerned there are now products which appear to be dairy but which can be served with meat, like Dairy Cream, and the reverse, such as artificial bacon bits. The international styles which mark American cuisine today can be found in a kosher form, such as French, Italian and Chinese.

Traditional Jewish Retentions and Their Elaborations

. . . Jewish ritual even in the attenuated form practiced by large numbers of American Jews is a retention. The services in a Reform synagogue, for instance, still are structurally based on the same prayers as that of the Orthodox synagogues and the text of the prayers, albeit altered, abridged and reinterpreted is recognizably from the same source.

Priorities in observance have changed. Previously minor rituals and ceremonies have been given much wider observance. So Hanukkah, a once minor holiday, has become a visible sign of Jewishness, obviously because it is parallel to Christmas and it is suited to Zionism and American ideas of religious liberty. The Bar Mitzvah ceremony which only developed during the late Middle Ages and its half-century old companion, the Bat Mitzvah ceremony, now mark a crucial rite between childhood and adolescence for American Jewish youth. These ceremonies have even replaced the once widely observed Confirmation ritual of the Reform which was based on a Lutheran model. Yom Kippur and the Passover Seder remain central observances. Other ceremonies and holidays have declined in importance and are often not observed by the multitudes of non-orthodox Jews, such as Sukkot (the Feast of Tabernacles, which comes five days after Yom Kippur).

The synagogue, home observances of festivals, Jewish community centers and the like help demarcate a Jewish symbolic arena in both time and space. While many, if not most, Jews only move in and out of the arena a few times a year, others remain in the arena for a wide range of activities. While there is no corporate Jewish body, the activities within the arena and the movements through it indicate that American Jewry retains its vitality.

One important activity within the arena has been fundraising. The importance of fundraising and giving has been related to the traditional Jewish value of *sedaqah* or charity (Elazar 1976: 86–95; S. Cohen 1983: 46–75, 56–75, 61–2, 128–9, 144, 156). Fundraising shows the overlap of Jewish and American values and norms. In addition to the value of *sedaqah* or charity, Jewish communal life has often been marked by intense competition for having the honor of giving large sums of money for synagogues, burial societies and the poor. . . . In the United States, such traditional patterns of giving have been utilized by the highly professional and sophisticated fundraisers of the United Jewish Appeal and other organizations.

So far our concern has been with central symbols and values which transcend specific Jewish culture areas and speech communities. Jewishness in America, however, has an association with the former Yiddish-speaking Ashkenazic Jews from Eastern Europe, who form the vast majority of American Jews. Some identifiable art-forms and styles representing this culture persist. [For example,] in recent years, there has been a revival of *klezmer*, an improvisational form of music from Eastern Europe, albeit performed today primarily for Jewish audiences. Generally, however, American Jews increasingly share the tastes of other Americans. Bagels are becoming as American as pizza, frankfurters, chop suey and apple pie, while younger Jews are often giving up corned beef for alfalfa sprouts. The differences in styles and tastes between Jews and their neighbors are diminishing, as the East European influence becomes more and more diluted.

The Marginally Jewish

In America today, the boundary between Jew and non-Jew is not a clear one. There are those who identify as Jews who would be excluded by Jewish law. These include the children of Jewish men by non-Jewish women (now accepted as Jews by the Reform), judaizing Christians who observe Jewish ritual, and members of Black sects which define themselves as Hebrews or Israelites but are not necessarily accepted as such by Jews. There are also people born as Jews but excluded from the community because of their conversion and participation in other religions, both Christian and non-Christian. Finally there are Jews who do not consider themselves Jews because of their lack of belief in Judaism and their non-participation in the Jewish community. These may include the children of Jewish women by non-Jewish men. Several of these categories deserve further discussion.

The intermarried and their children are obviously the largest and most important category here, whether we are dealing with Jewish men marrying non-Jewish women, or Jewish women who marry non-Jewish men. Conversions may occur in either direction or no religious conversion or affiliation may be the result. There has been a steady and inexorable increase in intermarriage which has undergone sociological scrutiny, although the study of the children of the intermarried has only recently begun to receive the attention it deserves. . . .

In terms of outcome, the increasing secularization of society has possibly resulted in less concern with religious conversion altogether, but rather with an accommodation. For the non-religious Jew and non-Jew, this may result in a compromise of general non-observance, possibly including both Christmas and Hanukkah. Thus a child may light the Hanukkah candles and get a visit from Santa Claus. Even the converted may have double religious experiences. In one large American metropolitan area, a Greek woman married a Sephardic Jew and converted to Judaism. She participates in the activities of an orthodox synagogue, sends her children to a Hebrew day school, but on Sundays her children attend Greek school at the local Orthodox church. A Jew who agreed to raise his children as Catholics goes with his family each year to his parents' Passover Seder. . . .

A recent study of the children of intermarriage show that those whose non-Jewish parent converted have a stronger identity as Jews than those whose parents did not. However, for both categories Jewishness is seen as an individual religious preference; they do not perceive it as a primordial non-contingent commitment (Mayer 1980, 1983; Lazerwitz 1971). All this leads to a diminution of the Jewish community as one built on kinship and descent.

As indicated above, the "non-Jewish Jews" are an important component of modern Jewry, even though they lie outside the organized community for the most part. They certainly overlap with the intermarried and often provide recruits for other religions.

Many Jews have been attracted to Asian religions, including Hare Krishna, the Maharishi movement, and groups linked to other gurus, as well as to the Unification Church. The interaction between Judaism and Christianity continues to be the most significant one for Americans.

The shifting boundaries between "Christian Jews" and "judaizing Christians" involve small numbers in a religiously sincere form, but are significant for their possible ramifications. . . .

While the "Christianity" and apostasy of those who joined established churches has always been clearly recognized by both Christian and Jew, it is common for converts to Christianity to assert that for them Christianity is the highest form of Judaism (K. Stern 1951). Most of these converts, still, throw off the practice of Jewish ritual with their conversion to Catholicism and Protestantism. Since the nineteenth century, however, a number of organizations, often under missionary auspices have sprung up which have combined Christian doctrine with the use of Hebrew and of Jewish ritual. The "Jews for Jesus" who preach what they call "Messianic Judaism" are a recent variety. Most Jews see such organizations as mere fronts for Protestant missionary activity and are not ready to accept such "Messianic Jews" as members in good standing in the community. Still students who are members of evangelical Jews for Jesus groups may return home to attend their families' Seders at Passover. Bob Dylan has gone through phases of Zionism and a born-again Christianity, thus exemplifying these trends. . . .

In America, one finds the mainstream churches being more open to Jewish influences than in the past. Both Protestants and Roman Catholics today acknowledge the Jewish roots of Christianity. This has been symbolized in particular by Christian celebrations of the Passover Seder prior to Easter. There have also been judaizers. A few years ago, a group of Lutheran ministers were accused of subordinating Christian doctrine to Jewish practice. These Lutheran ministers and their followers on Long Island adopted Jewish practices, including a strict observance of the Sabbath and dietary laws.

In fact, the main service was held on Sunday night, so members did not have to drive their cars on the Sabbath. Yet they were still believers in the divinity of Christ and came from Gentile families (Molotsky 1977). More recently, they have reformed their congregations into a kind of Christian synagogue with a Hebrew name (*New York Times* 1983). While coming from a different direction, such groups can be seen as merging with the "messianic Jews." . . .

[These and other] cases indicate a blurring of formerly clear ethnic/religious boundaries. Many different kinds of choices regarding religion and ethnic identity are being made. Simultaneously the central organizations are unable to control these choices, whether it is conservative congregations which permit the intermarried to participate in the congregation or the Reform rabbinical organization which cannot discipline rabbis who conduct mixed marriages without conversion of the Gentile party. Thus boundary maintenance, often seen as an essential quality of ethnicity (Barth 1969), becomes extremely difficult.

Regenerative Processes

Most of the emphasis here has been on how individualism has contributed to assimilation and the erosion of Jewish ethnicity and religiosity. Few social processes are clearly unidirectional. The emphasis has been on those processes indicating disintegration. There are also aspects, however, which indicate that American Jewry has the ability to maintain and reproduce Jewish cultural forms, particularly but not solely in the religious sphere.

Scholars and rabbis are now trained in North America as well as being imported. The Reform and the Conservative no longer rely on defectors from orthodox families for congregational rabbis. Jewish day schools have grown in numbers since the 1940s and exist in small and peripheral communities such as Dayton, Ohio, and Bangor, Maine, as well as in large metropolitan areas. They serve non-orthodox as well as orthodox Jews for a variety of reasons, but one of the motives must be the continued desire of Jewish parents for a Jewish schooling for their children. The orthodox day schools have contributed to the maintenance and growth of orthodox Judaism in the past two decades.

The continuing desire of Jews to express themselves as Jews persists. This is as true of leftist radicals as of neo-conservatives and mainstream liberals. Thus, an atheist rabbi in the 1970s founded a Society for Humanistic Judaism, whereas in the nineteenth century a rabbi had formed the non-ethnic Society for Ethical Culture. Jewish feminists organized their own circles and their own journal, *Lilith*. There are Jewish organizations which have combined left-liberal and radical programs, often critical of Israel and the American Jewish community, such as the New Jewish Agenda. The organizers of these groups include both religious and secular Jews. In addition, many *havurot*, or informal prayer and discussion groups, have been formed by non-orthodox religious Jews. . . .

There are . . . revivalist efforts within the Jewish community, which utilize various forms of missionary activity to attract Jews to more traditional forms of Judaism. . . . Most of these approaches, however, are individualistic. They bear on separate persons, not on the groups. As Sheingold has pointed out, they often involve intra-familial tensions. A "return to Judaism" whether of an orthodox or non-orthodox variety is often difficult to sustain without a family or traditional support group (Handelman 1984; Sheingold 1981).

Jewishness and Ethnicity in America

. . . . If we consider the Jews in America, in contradistinction to other ethnic groups of similar vintage, such as the Irish, the Italians, and the Poles, we find that they, unlike the latter, have a mechanism for accepting new members. It is conversion; yet only religions convert, ethnic groups do not. Thus one may see a possible course which Jewishness in America is likely to follow and in which it may persist. This was, of course, the dominant form of Jewish identity for a long time in America, outside of New York City. Now, however, it may be based more on choice by individuals of both Jewish and non-Jewish origin than it was in the past.

The religious forms of Judaism, whether traditionalist or modernist, will, however, have to compete with each other and with alternative claimants. These may include secularism and "Hebrew Christianity." If ethnic identity is a matter of ascription, then Jewish identity as a choice will have lost much of its ethnic character. Such a transformation requires many radical changes, but they are within the realm of possibility against the background of American individualism. The content of Jewishness in America combines retentions with forms and meanings which are infused with North American values. This, of course, replicates a process which has recurred in many places throughout Jewish history. What makes this process different today is that while there are many Jewish arenas, it is often hard to pinpoint real communities in a structural sense. Again it is permeated by individual activity. . . .

References

Baron, Salo W. 1942. *The Jewish Community.* Philadelphia: Jewish Publication Society of America.

Barth, Fredrik. 1969. *Ethnic Groups and Boundaries.* Boston: Little, Brown.

Cohen, Steven. 1983. *American Modernity and Jewish Identity.* New York and London: Tavistock.

Elazar, Daniel. 1976 *Community and Polity.* Philadelphia: Jewish Publication Society.

Handelman, Susan. 1984. "The Honeymoon is Over: Ba'alei Teshuvah after Ten Years." *Melton Journal,* No. 18 (Summer 1984): 6–8, 18.

Howe, Irving. 1976. *The World of Our Fathers.* New York: Harcourt Brace Jovanovich.

Katz, Jacob. 1973. *Out of the Ghetto.* Cambridge, Mass.: Harvard University Press.

Kuznets, Simon. 1972. *The Economic Structure of U.S. Jewry.* Jerusalem: Hebrew University Institute for Contemporary Jewry.

Lazerwitz, B. 1971. "Intermarriage and Conversion: A Guide for Future Research." *Jewish Journal of Sociology* 13(l): 41–64.

Maibaum, Matthew. 1971. "The Berkeley Hillel and the Union of Jewish Students: The History of a Conflict." *Jewish Journal of Sociology* 13: 153–72.

Mayer, Egon. 1980 "Processes and Outcomes: Marriages Between Jews and Non-Jews." *American Behavioral Scientist* 23: 487–518.

——. 1983. *Children of Intermarriage.* New York: American Jewish Committee.

Molotsky, J. 1977. "Two Long Island Churches Hold Christian and Jewish Services." *New York Times* (November 7): 1: 21.

New York Times. 1983. "Update on the News." November 13.

Sharot, S. 1976. *Judaism—A Sociology.* Newton Abbot: David & Charles.

Sheingold, Carl. 1981. "Jewish Rejuvenation." Paper presented at the Conference on the Evolving Jewish Family, New York, Queens College, June 21.

Shenker, Israel. 1979. "With Them It's Strictly Kosher." *New York Times Magazine* (April 15): 32–42.

Stern, Karl. 1951. *Pillar of Fire.* New York: Harcourt Brace.

Zenner, Walter. 1980. "American Jewry in Light of Middlemen Minority Theories." *Contemporary Jewry* 5(1): 11-30.

Zenner, Walter. 1991. *Minorities in the Middle: A Cross-National Analysis.* Albany: SUNY Press.

21

What Is a Southerner?

Regional Consciousness

John Shelton Reed

... [T]he question "Are you a Southerner?" can give people difficulty for two very different reasons. On the one hand, someone may have a perfectly adequate mental representation of the group but still not know whether it includes him, because he is genuinely a borderline case. His regional consciousness may be high but his location is marginal. This is, in fact, a relatively frequent combination: as we shall see, marginality often *produces* high consciousness.

On the other hand, someone may have no cognitive representation of the category "Southerner," or one too vague and ill-defined for him to know who is and is not in the category. . . . [For] some North Carolinians [in my studies] . . . the concepts "South" and "Southerner" had little or no meaning: the concepts were simply not part of their cognitive apparatus.

But I should emphasize again that most Americans and nearly all Southerners have some mental construction labeled "Southerner," some degree of regional consciousness. Only a small minority of our sample had difficulty telling us whether they were Southerners, and only a minority of that minority had difficulty because they did not understand the question. Among those who displayed enough regional consciousness to answer the question, however, there was a considerable degree of variation in how *much* regional consciousness they possessed.

At the other extreme from those for whom regional concepts have no meaning are people for whom the construct "Southerner" is very salient, people who often think in regional terms and for whom regional categories are an important way to divide up the world of their experience.

What background factors and experiences produce regional consciousness? How does someone come to hold a cognitive construct labeled "Southerner" and to believe it is useful? If certain conditions are met, this sort of "knowledge" can be obtained either first hand, through experience with other regional groups, or second hand, from others in one's family or community or from the mass media. That is, one can learn that regional groups exist and something about their characteristics either by being told about them or by observing and generalizing on one's own.

To some extent, American regions and regional groups are cultural products, at large in American culture, part of its folklore. Like other culturally given distinctions, this one is learned more or less unthinkingly as one grows into that culture. Regional concepts are part of the vocabulary of the national discourse, and those who wish or are obliged to follow that discourse will acquire the vocabulary. [Those] who [are] least likely to be able to think in these terms [are] people isolated from the national culture—by poverty, rurality, lack of education, and the like. We can surmise that high degrees of regional consciousness will be found among those most attuned to supralocal culture, whether by education, exposure to the mass media, or living and working in a relatively cosmopolitan setting. It is not merely that such people are more likely to think in terms of generalizations and abstractions in the first place, although certainly education, in particular, is often supposed to have that effect. It is, rather, that such people are more likely to have come into contact with regional concepts, to have found them useful, and to have had them "stick."

Determinants of Regional Consciousness

An index of regional consciousness will help us to explore these ideas. We asked respondents who said they thought of themselves as Southerners: "How often do you think of yourself as a Southerner? Very often, sometimes, or hardly at all?" At the end of the interview, to minimize "spillover," we returned to the subject: "How much thought would you say you have given to the South and to Southerners before today? Quite a lot, some, only a little, or almost none?" Each of these questions was scored zero, one, or two, according to how much regional consciousness the answer displayed, and the two scores were simply added to give an index score ranging from zero to four. Thirty-six percent of the white respondents who defined themselves as Southerners scored three or four, displaying high regional consciousness, if we take that to mean that they said they (1) often think of themselves as Southerners and had given at least some thought to the subject before the interview or (2) think of themselves as Southerners at least sometimes and had given quite a lot of thought to the subject in the past.

. . . [This] index is related to a number of items that it seemingly *ought* to be related to. One's "interest in how [other group members] as a whole are getting along" has been used in the past as a measure of group identification, but it seems to have more to do with what we are calling "consciousness" here. Certainly it is strongly related to our index: 81 percent of those with high scores on the index indicated a good deal of interest, compared to only 36 percent of those with the lowest score. . . .

[Regional] consciousness is most acute among educated, urban, white-collar, well-informed respondents—among the types of Southerners one is increasingly likely to encounter. This may seem puzzling if the precise meaning of "consciousness" is not kept in mind: here it means simply thinking about and in terms of regions. It is not a form of parochialism: on the contrary, since "region" is by its nature a *contrast* concept, emphasizing the distinction between the region and its surroundings, those who most often encounter the region's surroundings should be most likely to find regional concepts useful in dealing with their experience—assuming that the concepts are useful ones in the first place.

The Effects of Experience Outside the South

This brings us to the second way of developing or maintaining such concepts: not vi-cariously but directly, through experience and observation of one's own. . . . [E]xposure to non-Southerners is a potent "consciousness-raising experience" for Southerners. The level of regional consciousness is substantially higher among Southerners who have lived outside the South than among those who have not. A majority (50 percent) of those born outside the South show high consciousness, compared to 38 percent of the Southern-born. Thirty-seven percent of those who have never lived outside the South show high consciousness; 47 percent of those who have lived outside the region do so. Even traveling outside the South appears to have some effect: those who have traveled more than five hundred miles from home (which may include some who have never left the South) show higher levels of regional consciousness than those who have not, particularly those few respondents who have never been more than two hundred miles from their homes. . . .

[To be sure,] exposure is related to education, occupation, and . . . other variables. . . . [But] at every level of education, those with higher levels of exposure show higher levels of consciousness, and at each level of exposure, education seems to produce at least a slight increase in consciousness (although the effects of exposure are stronger). The lowest level of regional consciousness is found among respondents who have never been outside the South and are not high school graduates: only 18 percent display high consciousness. It appears that education can substitute to some extent for firsthand experience, serving perhaps as a sort of vicarious "exposure." College graduates who have only traveled in the North display about the same level of regional consciousness as those who have lived in the North but did not finish high school.

These findings should not come as a surprise to students of ethnic and racial groups, who have seen analogous findings for other groups. Among blacks, for instance, racial consciousness is highest, not among lower-class blacks in all-black neighborhoods, but among middle-class blacks whose occupations and housing patterns place them in frequent contact with whites. In an all-black situation, race is not salient, just as region is seldom salient for Southerners who never leave the South, nor water, ordinarily, for fish.

Exposure to non-Southerners can raise the regional consciousness of Southerners in two rather different ways. In the first place . . . being treated as a member of a category rather than as an individual can heighten one's awareness of the category and the process of categorization. Realizing that one's sex, race, ethnic group, or regional origin is salient to others, that it structures at least their initial responses to oneself, can certainly produce *self*-consciousness about attributes that may not previously have been considered very important. . . . Relations across group boundaries are socially important in part because they reinforce those very boundaries by reminding the participants that the groups exist and that they are members of them.

It is not necessary that the categorical treatment be invidious, that it be what we usually call "discrimination" (although that probably helps), merely that it be categorical. Although there is evidence of occasional discrimination against Southerners . . . most Southerners can also attest to the fact that some non-Southerners have extremely flattering views of them. That is not the point. Whether one is admired or despised, favored or mistreated, is less important in the generation of group consciousness than the fact that the different treatment is based on group membership. . . .

One frequent example—innocuous and neutral, on the face of it—is what might be called the "spokesman phenomenon." The question "What do you people think about . . . ?" and its variants imply that the questioner sees "you people" as a socially significant group and his respondent as a representative member. In some ways the form of the question is more telling than its content, or the nature of an accurate answer. No one would ask such a question with "you people" referring to left-handers, but if people did so often enough, we would certainly begin to see more self-conscious southpaws. . . .

The Nature of Regional Stereotypes

But regional consciousness is not related just to *others'* stereotypes. The other way in which interaction with non-Southerners can raise the regional consciousness of Southerners is by exposing them to regional differences and leading them to generalize about those differences: in other words, by generating regional stereotypes in Southerners. Those with high regional consciousness, we saw, are more likely than others to believe that "the Southern way of life" actually is different from that elsewhere in the United States. We can call their beliefs about that difference "stereotypes," if we define the term carefully.

By stereotype, I mean here simply someone's cognitive representation of a group or category ("image" would be as good a word), a type of generalization that is virtually prerequisite for thinking about a group at all. Someone with high regional consciousness is, by definition, someone who thinks about regions and regional groups: presumably that thought has some content and such a person therefore holds regional stereotypes of some sort. . . .

Although some [of our respondents] complained about heat, humidity, insects, and the like when asked for "the worst thing about the South," most respondents seemed to like the physical environment of their region. When we asked what the *best* thing is, two-thirds mentioned the South's climate, its forests, mountains, or coast, its lack of crowding and pollution, the opportunities it offers for outdoor recreation. In general, they seemed to agree with William Faulkner's view that the South is fortunate that God has done so much for it, and man so little. . . .

Unlike the South's attractions, its disadvantages are mostly man-made. Although a substantial minority (about one in five) responded to the question concerning the worst thing about the South by saying that there is *nothing* bad about it, the most frequent response to that question mentioned aspects of Southern society—its race relations, politics, or economy. There were more than occasional references to "backward" government or laws . . . to poor schools, roads, or public transportation. Far and away the most frequent complaint, however, was economic. As one respondent put it, "I can't think of anything bad about it [the South], other than we don't make too much money down here." ...

But our respondents clearly have images not just of the South but of *Southerners*. In other words, they have regional stereotypes. When we asked for the best thing about the South we did not limit respondents to one answer, and half volunteered that the best thing about the South is its people. The question about the most important difference between South and North produced even more responses that referred to the character and culture of Southerners (and a handful of respondents mentioned Southerners when asked to indicate the worst thing about the South).

Southerners are, by their own reckoning, slower, more traditional, and more polite and friendly than other Americans—a constellation of traits that, as some studies have shown, other Americans are generally prepared to grant them.

Some mentioned the South's "slower pace" with approval. ... A few shared much the same perception but evidently had their doubts about whether the comparison was to the South's advantage. ...

The same ambivalence was evident in comments on Southern conservatism or traditionalism, which was mentioned by some respondents as the best thing about the South, by others as the worst. Southerners, some told us, are "too slow to change," "narrow-minded," or "a little backward in [their] thinking." Others approved of Southern religiosity, the strength of family ties, and other values that might fairly be viewed as conservative. ...

Far and away the most frequent characterization of Southerners (by these Southerners) was an elaboration on the theme that Southerners are *good people*, as several said in so many words. "Good," to our respondents, meant primarily pleasant to be around: "considerate," "friendly," "hospitable," "polite," "gentle," "gracious," "cordial," "genteel," "courteous," "congenial," "nice"— all of these our respondents' words, many of them used often. Dissenting opinions were rare and were almost entirely voiced by migrants from the North. One said the worst thing about the South is "the attitude of Southerners ... especially if you're from New York state." ... However, some migrants felt the same as natives ("They've been very nice to me"), and most Southerners were unstinting in their praise of each other. ...

Learning About Regional Differences

At this point, we will make a distinction that may look somewhat artificial at first. To the extent that these warm feelings and this high regard indicate *identification* with one's fellow Southerners. ... To the extent that these feelings represent attempts to generalize about actual regional differences in attitudes and behavior, they tell us something about the content of Southerners' regional *stereotypes;* and that subject concerns us here.

Not all of our respondents shared the conventional view of what differentiates Southerners from other Americans, and some had no idea at all. Where do these views come from? What kinds of background and experience produce these perceptions? Certainly they are learned somehow, and one possibility suggested by the analysis of the antecedents of regional consciousness is that they are learned through exposure to non-Southerners. Such exposure increases the regional consciousness of Southerners. Does it also increase their readiness to generalize about the differences between non-Southerners and themselves in conventional ways? If there are cultural differences between Southerners and other Americans (and a substantial body of literature indicates that there certainly are), is it possible that the effect of interregional interaction is to produce stereotypes where none existed before or to strengthen existing ones (to the extent that they are accurate)?

It appears that it is possible. We constructed an index of stereotyping from adjectives presented to respondents as follows: "Now I'm going to read some words that people use to describe other people. I'm going to ask you whether each word applies more to Northerners or to Southerners. Do you think _____ applies more to Northerners or to Southerners?" The ten adjectives were chosen on the basis of pretesting that showed widespread perceptions of regional differences in those respects. "Courteous," "religious," "patriotic," "slow," "generous," and "loyal to family" are often seen as Southern traits, their opposites being, by implication at least, Northern traits. "Aggressive," "industrious," "materialistic," and "sophisticated" are traits likely to be ascribed by Southerners to Northerners. . . .

Figure 21.1 shows the relation between an index that measures the likelihood of thinking about regional differences in these conventional terms and exposure to the non-South. . . . A majority (57 percent) of those who have lived outside the South for up to six years score high on the index, more than twice the proportion (27 percent) of those who have never been outside the South. However, those with a great deal of experience outside the South are somewhat *less* likely to generalize in these terms than those with only an intermediate amount, a result giving additional support for the idea that although some people may know too little to stereotype, others seem to know too much.

This reversal at the upper end of the exposure continuum replicates the more usual finding about the effects of interaction across group boundaries on stereotyping: at the extreme end of the continuum, the so-called contact hypothesis works as specified and exposure reduces stereotyping. But before interaction can break down stereotypes, there must be stereotypes to break down. Our data suggest that many Southerners do not have stereotypes of Northerners before they actually encounter them, presumably because their regional status is simply not salient, because, that is, their regional consciousness is too low. This interpretation is supported by the results of a study by Gail Wood (1973), who, with a sample of college students and rather different measures of both stereotyping and exposure, found exactly the same inverse-U-shaped relation as that reported here. The Southern students in her study reported that their principal source of information about Northerners was "personal contact," unlike the Northern students, who more often said they formed their impressions from books and especially from movies. (For the Northern students, inciden-

tally, the relation between exposure and stereotyping was straightforwardly negative, as might be expected if books and movies had already brought Southerners to their attention.)

Figure 21.1
Relation of Stereotyping to Exposure.

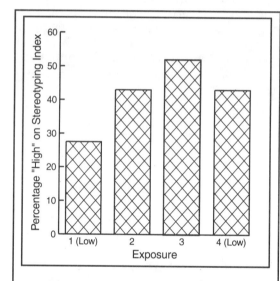

SOURCE: John Shelton Reed, "Getting to Know You: The Contact Hypothesis Applied to the Sectional Beliefs and Attitudes of White Southerners," *Social Forces* 59, no. I (September 1980): 129, fig. 1.
1. Never been outside South: Southern-born, never lived outside South (eleven Confederate states, Kentucky, and Oklahoma), longest distance traveled from present home is less than 500 miles.
2. Traveled in North: Southern-born, never lived outside South, longest distance traveled is over 500 miles. (Note: For some respondents, this travel may have been entirely in the South. It is impossible to tell from the survey items available.)
3. Lived in North: Southern-born or border state-born, lived up to six years outside South (unless included in 4 below).
4. Extensive Exposure to North: Northern-born, or one or more years of schooling in North, or lived in North more than six years.

Regional Consciousness and the 'Traditional Value Orientation'

There is an interesting paradox here. If we ask what Southerners are most conscious of their Southernness, most likely to be aware of regional differences and prepared to generalize about them, most likely to have well-defined ideas about their regional group and their place in it, the answer appears to be that these properties are most common among "New Southerners"—educated, well-traveled, fairly "sophisticated," urban folks. Since more and more Southerners fit this description, it would seem that at least the short-run consequences of the South's economic development, urbanization, and general modernization will be to *raise* the level of regional consciousness and regional stereotyping among Southerners, not to lower it.

If there is a sense in which educated, mobile, urban Southerners are more "Southern" than before, however, there are also ways in which they are less so. Southerners, by and large, have been and still are set off from other Americans by a distinctive set of attitudes and values. But some of these regional differences are decreasing and may indeed be disappearing. Many aspects of Southern culture have reflected a rural economy and society, poor education and little of it, and isolation from the outside world: in those respects, Southerners are becoming more "American" with each passing decade.

Harold Grasmick (1973) . . . identified a cluster of these variables and labeled them *the* "traditional value orientation," not just of the South but of folk and peasant societies in general (which is what the South has been, in the American context, until quite recently). He developed measures of familism, localism, fatalism, resistance to innovation, traditional sex-role ideology, racism, some aspects of authoritarianism, and suspicion and dislike of "outsiders" (in the Southern case, some aspects of sectionalism). . . . In particular, he showed that the traditional value orientation is strongly related to three factors: growing up on a farm, the absence of education, and the absence of a cluster of variables he called "late socialization experiences"— urban residence, travel and residence outside the South, and exposure to the mass media. (He found that old people were more likely to hold traditional values than young people, and women more likely than men, but he was able to demonstrate that these differences were entirely due to differences in back-

ground and experience between old and young people and between men and women.)

He also found that all of the components of the traditional value orientation tended to vary together: for instance, someone who displayed a high level of fatalism was also likely to hold racist attitudes, and vice versa. All of the traits that make up the traditional value orientation were concentrated in the same elements of the population and appeared to have the same correlates: immersion in the traditional rural culture of the South and isolation from the influences of education, city life, travel, and the mass media.

Using the items that Grasmick identified as indicators of this value orientation (excluding those that asked about the South per se) . . . I constructed an index similar to his. . . . The index was dichotomized: the top 58 percent of white Southern respondents were considered to show high traditionalism. . . . Although these values have not been the only ones that, on the average, have distinguished Southerners from other Americans, they certainly have made up a large part of the historic stereotype of Southerners and a conspicuous and often politically significant component of the actual regional difference. In this sample, the index clearly distinguishes the Northern-born respondents. Despite the fact that the base is restricted to those who say that they think of themselves as Southerners, only 11 percent of them score high on the index, compared to three out of five of the Southern-born. Presumably other Northern-born residents of the South (and non-Southerners in general) also display low levels of these traditional values.

. . . [Just] as Grasmick reported . . . traditionalism is inversely related to education, income, urban residence, media exposure, experience outside the South, and so forth. In other words, *the very same factors that increase regional consciousness decrease the likelihood that one will subscribe to "Southern" values*—if we take those values to be racism, localism, authoritarianism, and the other components of Grasmick's traditional value orientation.

The fact that the same social forces that heighten Southerners' regional consciousness also chip away at the traditional value orientation may help to account for the otherwise puzzling fact that regional consciousness is essentially uncorrelated with those traditional values. . . . That is, those who are most traditional are no more likely than others to display high regional consciousness, or, put the other way around, those Southerners who are most self-conscious have no more to be self-conscious about than other Southerners. . . .

Four Types of Southerners

. . . The typology in Figure 21.2 is of course an oversimplification, since both regional consciousness and the value dimension are continual rather than dichotomies, but it may help to clarify some implications of the fact that the two variables are uncorrelated. (The labels for the quadrants are perhaps too precious as well, but they will serve to identify the types.) Since the two variables that define the typology are virtually uncorrelated, if we define "high" and "low" in the figure to mean "above the median" and "below the median" respectively, then all four types exist in roughly equal numbers in the population.

Figure 21.2
Southern Types, Defined by Level of Regional Consciousness and Adherence to Traditional Value Orientation.

Traditional Value Orientation	Regional Consciousness	
	High	Low
High	"Fire-eater"	"Local" ("Peasant")
Low	"New Southerner"	"Cosmopolitan"

We can speculate about the nature of the long-term shifts from one quadrant to another. A plausible sequence, on the face of it, would be for economic and demographic change in the South—more education, cities, money, travel, mass media, and so forth—to move the bulk of the Southern population inexorably from the upper-left quadrant to the lower-right, from "fire-eaters" who espouse traditional values and think of themselves parochially as Southerners to "cosmopolitan" moderns who are not distinctively Southern in any of the important respects Grasmick identified and for whom the South is nothing but a place to live.

The data, however, do not allow this simple evolutionary picture. For many, the starting place is not the "fire-eater" quadrant but the "local" one: although these people possess the "peasant" characteristics that Grasmick enumerated, they also share with peasants elsewhere in the world the characteristic of narrow horizons, horizons too narrow for them to give much attention to a concept as abstract as "the South" or to think of themselves often as part of it. Those who lack regional consciousness may not be cosmopolitans at all, far from it. The starting point for many Southerners, it appears, is "localism"—in Robert Merton's definition, "an orientation to local social structures." This orientation produces adherence to local values, the traditional value orientation of the South, but at the same time it works against a more cosmopolitan recognition that these are *Southern* values, that is, against regional consciousness.

What forces are at work to move people out of the "local" quadrant in our typology? Historically, we can identify two distinct processes, one intermittent and operating in the short run, and the other long-term and more lasting in its effects, but neither leading directly to cosmopolitanism. In the first place, the sectional conflict that has been a frequent characteristic of American life—most notably, of course, during the Civil War and its aftermath, but off and on before and since—must operate to heighten regional consciousness. When the South as a whole is seen to be a contestant on the national stage, when Southerners collectively have (or are seen to have) common interests in need of expression or defense, the salience of the regional group—that is, regional consciousness—will be increased for its members. . . .

But the effects of sectional conflict are presumably temporary. We may suppose that there is a sociological equivalent of the Second Law of Thermodynamics that leads groups (including regional groups) to dissolve in the absence of at least intermittent reinforcement. When sectional conflict abates (as it always has, eventually), individuals forget; if individuals do not forget, new generations come along who never knew. Without the recurrent stimulus of regional conflict, one important element in the matrix of regional consciousness will be lacking. . . .

Our earlier analysis suggests, however, that there is another process by which the regional consciousness of Southerners is heightened, both for many individuals within their lifetimes and for succeeding generations. It depends less on the relations between sections at the national level than on the experiences and circumstances of individual Southerners. Urbanization, education, the prevalence of the mass media, and social and geographical mobility—all increasingly widespread among Southerners—can heighten regional consciousness at the same time that they undermine the traditional value orientation. More and more, these experiences are moving Southerners from the "local" quadrant of the table and making "New Southerners" of them; one must also assume that Southern children are increasingly *born* in that quadrant.

The changes produced by modernization will probably prove to be irreversible. To revert to a lost traditional value orientation is difficult, if not impossible. . . . It remains to be seen whether the awkward age represented by the "New Southerner" quadrant—heightened consciousness with diminished differences—is a terminus or merely a way station on the route to cosmopolitanism. However, it does appear to be at least a necessary intermediate step. It is this condition—not deracination but a sort of marginality—that is the characteristic modern predicament, and not just in the "New South."

References

Grasmick, Harold. 1973. "Social Change and the Wallace Movement in the South." Ph.D. dissertation, Department of Sociology, University of North Carolina, Chapel Hill.

Wood, Gail. 1973. "The Images of Southern Males and Females." Senior honors paper, Department of Sociology, University of North Carolina, Chapel Hill.

Part II

Current Issues in Racial and Ethnic Relations

The Changing Face of Prejudice

In the wake of the civil rights era, many Americans of diverse racial and ethnic backgrounds believed and expected that entrenched patterns of prejudice and discrimination would gradually disappear from the social landscape. In retrospect, as we prepare to enter the twenty-first century, such giddy optimism seems painfully naive. National polls document huge racial and ethnic divisions in life experiences, and in public opinion concerning virtually every topic, ranging from welfare reform to criminal justice issues and the death penalty to affirmative action. Experimental studies indicate that discrimination against African Americans and other racial and ethnic groups persists at alarming levels in housing, law enforcement, retail sales, and many other contexts (e.g., Turner 1992; Feagin, this volume). In several recent high-profile cases, major corporations have been sued successfully by minority employees or customers alleging a broad array of discriminatory practices in hiring and promotions, compensation, other personnel practices, and customer services. A plethora of white supremacist and separatist groups seem to enjoy new visibility and popularity as they promote hatred and violence against persons of color. Vicious hate crimes, such as the recent "dragging" murder of a popular African American man in East Texas, continue to plague our communities. Perhaps not surprisingly, there are abundant signs of distrust and alienation among persons of color: the credence given to various conspiracy theories as explanations of the social problems confronted by many African American communities (e.g., drugs, AIDS, poverty); and the popularity of separatist sentiments, among many other indicators. These and other developments raise troubling questions about the present and future of intergroup relations in the United States. In this introduction, we review several of the key issues in this complicated area of study

While the term "stereotype" has been used in several different ways, it often refers to the images (typically exaggerated or false, and usually unflattering) that people may hold regarding certain racial and ethnic groups. Although studies have examined stereotypes of a wide range of groups, much of the research over the years has focused on European Americans' (whites') images of African Americans. Research conducted on college students suggests that the content of such stereotypes—i.e., the traits attributed to African Americans by whites—has changed significantly in recent decades. In the classic Princeton studies of the 1930s, large majorities of white students labelled African Americans as superstitious and lazy, with smaller percentages also viewing blacks as happy-go-lucky, ignorant, and musical. More recent studies suggest that white students today have fewer well-defined stereotypes of African Americans; only one trait—"lazy"—remains from the Princeton list, and this image is a much less popular choice today than in earlier decades. However, significant numbers of European American (white) students today tend to view their African American counterparts as obnoxious, and even menacing, rather than benign; traits like "loud," "ag-

223

gressive," and "quick-tempered" lead one recent list of such stereotypes (Wood and Chesser 1994).

Negative images of African Americans also prevail among many European American (white) adults. One recent California survey shows that whites are viewed most favorably and African Americans most negatively on a number of traits—including intelligence, laziness, and congeniality—with Latino and Asian Americans receiving intermediate evaluations (Bobo and Zubrinsky 1996). Data from the General Social Surveys conducted by the National Opinion Research Center (NORC) tend to confirm this (Davis and Smith 1996). African Americans, and to a lesser extent Latino Americans, were seen as preferring to live off welfare, lazy, violent, and unintelligent, particularly when compared to whites and Asian Americans. Other studies also show that such negative group images are shared by African Americans themselves (Sniderman and Piazza, this volume). While NORC data demonstrate the persistence of negative images of African Americans and Latinos, they also show that anti-Jewish stereotypes have faded sharply as compared with earlier surveys.

One of the major trends in racial and ethnic attitudes in the United States has been the dramatic increase in white support for principles of racial integration and equality since the heyday of the civil rights movement, as indicated by responses to survey items on this topic (Schuman, Steeh, and Bobo 1988). Several questions gauging support for nondiscrimination and desegregation in major areas of social life have been asked repeatedly in surveys over the years, allowing us to compare responses across time periods. Virtually all of these items show similar increases in support for principles of racial equality. For example, one common survey question asks: "Do you think blacks should have as good a chance as white people to get any kind of job, or do you think white people should have the first chance at any kind of job?" Whereas in the 1940s more than half of European Americans (whites) openly endorsed anti-black discrimination in hiring, by the early 1970s white support for the principle of equal opportunity employment was almost unani-

mous, and major surveys stopped asking this question altogether. Another popular item asked: "Do you think white students and black students should go to the same school or to separate schools?" Although only 32 percent of whites nationwide expressed support for the "same school" option in 1942, this figure had climbed to 70 percent by 1965, and to 90 percent by 1982 (Schuman, Steeh, and Bobo 1988). Again, pollsters dropped this question from their surveys shortly thereafter. Support for the principle of residential desegregation is also strong. A common survey item on this subject inquires about (dis)agreement with the following statement: "White people have a right to keep blacks out of their neighborhoods if they want to and blacks should respect that right." When this item was first posed in 1963, only 39 percent of European Americans (whites) disagreed with the statement; disagreement had risen to 80 percent by 1991 (Gallup and Newport 1991; Schuman and Steeh 1996). In the 1996 NORC General Social Survey, nearly 90 percent of respondents disagreed with this statement, and more than two-thirds disagreed strongly (Davis and Smith 1996). Many other items dealing with principles of equality and desegregation have shown similar trends over time.

Several careful trend analyses have suggested that much of this contemporary change in racial attitudes has resulted from processes of cohort replacement, as older whites, who were socialized in an era of racial segregation, have now died, and have been replaced by younger cohorts with apparently more enlightened outlooks on racial equality (Firebaugh and Davis 1988; Kluegel 1990). However, not all dimensions of racial equality and integration meet with overwhelming endorsement from European Americans (whites). Of particular interest here are items on interracial marriage. When the Gallup organization first began to ask about whites' approval of this idea in the late 1950s, support for interracial unions was under 5 percent. To be sure, white support has increased, but in 1991 only 44 percent of whites approved of interracial marriage. Clearly many whites prefer to maintain this racial boundary within their families (Waters 1990). Still, while they may be uncomfortable with inter-racial marriage, very few Americans today (fewer than 15 percent) would ban the practice, whereas as late as the 1960s, a majority of whites in some polls endorsed laws against intermarriage (Schuman, Steeh, and Bobo 1988; Davis and Smith 1996).

Where do racial and ethnic attitudes and biases come from? Several types of explanations can be found in the work of social and behavioral scientists. Some suggest that the basic tendency to draw and maintain in-group versus out-group distinctions may have biological, perhaps even genetic, roots—that we are "hard-wired" for prejudice, because the tendency to prefer members of one's in-group and to be wary of others has proven critical for species survival and reproduction. This sociobiological perspective suggests that it may be unrealistic to attempt to eliminate prejudice per se; policies aimed at limiting the negative effects of discriminatory behavior may be more effective.

Others suggest that prejudice and discrimination are rooted in intrapsychic processes. There is evidence that persons who were raised by domineering parents and subjected to excessive supervision and harsh punishment as children may develop authoritarian personalities as adults. That is, they exhibit a distinctive cluster of personality traits and behaviors, such as a preoccupation with power and hierarchy, ethnocentrism, and intolerance of members of out-groups, including (for whites) persons of color (Sniderman and Piazza, this volume). Another psychological theory suggests that prejudice is a form of aggression which results from an inability to deal with frustration. When the causes of frustration are too powerful (e.g., one's employer) or too complex (e.g., economic restructuring, cultural change) to attack directly, individuals may lash out at more convenient targets to vent their hostility, and may engage in scapegoating, or blaming less powerful groups for their plight.

While these perspectives may have much to offer, most sociologists emphasize the influence of cultural transmission and socialization in shaping racial and ethnic stereotypes and images, norms, and attitudes. Be-cause racism is deeply embedded in American life, we gain information (accurate or in-accurate) about racial and ethnic groups in the course of learning about our society and culture. Families are often important sources of racial and ethnic socialization (e.g., stocks of knowledge about out-groups), especially as it is transmitted across generations (from parents and grandparents to children). Social clubs, schools, and churches can also socialize dominant cultural norms regarding race and ethnicity. This may help to account for the sizeable age and educational differences in racial attitudes that are found in most polls and surveys. Typically, lower levels of prejudice and higher support for the ideals of non-discrimination and desegregation are found among younger cohorts—those raised in the post-civil rights era—and better-educated persons.

In recent years, scholars and activists have also become concerned about the racial and ethnic content of media products (TV, movies, and videos). African Americans and other persons of color are rarely involved in writing or producing these shows, and the images of minorities can be problematic. For instance, one current focus of attention is the police documentary, or so-called "cop doc" (e.g., *Cops, America's Most Wanted*), in which persons of color are often portrayed in unflattering ways (e.g., as violent criminals) (Oliver 1994).

Of course vicarious experience (e.g., through books, films, role-taking, and other modes of communication) can sometimes provide valuable information about other groups and result in greater understanding and positive attitudes. This central assumption underlies many contemporary innovations in multicultural education (Banks 1993). In addition, one key source of information about members of other racial and ethnic groups is direct interpersonal contact. Indeed, students of intergroup relations have long believed that contact, particularly close and sustained contact, with members of different racial and ethnic groups provides direct information regarding the values, lifestyles, behaviors, and experiences of those groups (Sigelman and Welch 1993; Ellison and Powers 1994). When information about other groups is gained through long-term interactions with coworkers, neighbors, and others, the acquired information is likely to be relatively accurate and largely favorable in content. This positive first-hand information can then be generalized into a positive perception of the group(s) as a whole, and may counter unfavorable impressions and stereotypes acquired from less direct sources. Some observers have asserted that interracial or interethnic contact may promote positive attitudes only under ideal conditions—e.g., when the contact occurs between persons of equal status, under cooperative and noncompetitive conditions, and with the encouragement of authorities. This suggests that policies which increase or decrease the opportunities for intergroup contact, or which alter the conditions under which that contact occurs, have implications for the long-term formation of racial and ethnic attitudes. Seen in this light, the *de facto* racial and ethnic resegregation of American school systems and the continuing segregation of most residential communities is worrisome to many observers.

While whites' support for the principles of racial equality and desegregation has increased in linear fashion in recent decades, their enthusiasm for policies and programs ostensibly designed to implement these principles remains tepid at best (Schuman, Steeh, and Bobo 1988; Schuman and Steeh 1996). Indeed, white support for some implementation strategies has plummeted in recent years. For example, one popular survey item asks respondents whether the government "should see to it" that black and white children attend the same schools. Whites' support for the affirmative response has never been overwhelming, declining from its highwater mark of 42 percent in 1970 to around 25 percent in 1992 (Schuman and Steeh 1996). Similarly large percentages (75–80 percent) of whites have steadily opposed bussing school children to achieve racial balance (Davis and Smith 1996). Although response patterns can vary somewhat depending on the wording of specific survey items, the use of racial and ethnic preferences in hiring and school admissions is consistently rejected by a large majority of whites (see section 8, this

volume). Most race-targeted government programs meet a similar fate in national surveys (Bobo and Kluegel 1993; Davis and Smith 1996). A large national survey conducted by the Joint Center for Political and Economic Studies in 1997 gauged (dis)agreement with the following general statement: "We should make every possible effort to improve the position of blacks and other minorities, even if it means giving them preferential treatment." A whopping 83 percent of white respondents disagreed, as compared with fewer than half of African Americans (Shepard 1997).

The evidence speaks clearly: While European Americans (whites) voice support for principles of racial equality, they reject virtually every policy measure designed to make those principles a reality (Schuman, Steeh, and Bobo 1988; Schuman and Steeh 1996). Nor does this apparent inconsistency surface only with regard to government programs or public policies. Although white Americans have repeatedly voiced support for equal housing laws and practices in polls and surveys, most residential communities across our nation remain highly segregated along racial lines, and many whites reject the prospect of living in a neighborhood that includes more than a very few African American residents (Farley et al. 1994 and this volume; see next section, this volume).

What might account for the disjuncture among European Americans (whites) between support for principles of racial and ethnic equality and support for their implementation? One possibility is that whites' resistance to implementation policies stems from principled conservatism, which has grown in popularity since the 1970s. According to this view, many whites are not racist, but simply object to government-imposed remedies for racial and ethnic inequalities because they see such efforts as overly bureaucratic and ineffective, and because these programs limit individual freedom and waste money. Some studies cast doubt on this explanation, however, noting that opposition to these government policies is not always highly correlated with other indicators of principled conservatism (e.g., Schuman and Bobo 1988). In other words, many whites who are not otherwise conservative (i.e., do not necessarily favor limited government involvement in other spheres) decline to endorse the implementation of racial equality.

Another potential explanation centers on the situational pressures posed by the post-1980 political and economic climate in the United States. It is conceivable that many whites do support racial and ethnic equality; however, they may have been influenced by strident political rhetoric, economic restructuring, the use of group (race, ethnic, and gender) preferences in hiring and promotion, and other factors. All of these dynamics may exacerbate feelings of European American (white) vulnerability, and competition and conflict among racial and ethnic groups.

Some observers note yet another complication: In many cases, individuals may resist some strategies for implementing racial equality only because they dislike the specific policies under consideration, and not because they truly reject the idea of implementation per se. While a large majority of whites oppose the use of bussing to achieve racial and ethnic balance in primary and secondary schools, a non-trivial percentage of African Americans also oppose this policy (Schuman, Steeh, and Bobo 1988). According to one investigation, African Americans who reject bussing tend to value school quality over racial integration; they are more likely than white opponents to believe that schools should mirror the surrounding community, and to reason that the money spent on buying, maintaining, and operating buses should be devoted to academic resources and school infrastructure. On the other hand, compared with African American opponents of bussing, whites who dislike this strategy tend to emphasize freedom of choice and voluntarism (Schuman, Steeh, and Bobo 1988: 154–58). More generally, African-American support for many of the implementation strategies often asked about in surveys has also declined in recent years, partly due to a fundamental rethinking of the virtues of desegregation. Attempts to explain the "principle-implementation gap" among European Americans (whites) should also address the widening gap among persons of color.

Some researchers contend that whites' opposition to implementation policies springs largely from self-interest (Schuman, Steeh, and Bobo 1988). In part, individuals may be reluctant to endorse bussing, affirmative action, or residential desegregation because they perceive negative effects on their own lifestyles and future prospects—lowered school quality, loss of jobs or promotions for themselves or others they know, reduced property values, threats to personal and family safety, and so on. Indeed, there is some evidence supporting this explanation (e.g., Schuman and Bobo 1988). In addition, others suggest that collective self-interest may be equally important in the calculations of many whites. Even if they do not feel immediately vulnerable because of implementation strategies, they may worry about the cumulative, long-term impact of policies which upset the established racial/ethnic hierarchy in which they are well-positioned. Many Americans operate from a deeply-ingrained "sense of group position," a set of beliefs about the positions in the social order that certain groups should rightfully occupy relative to other groups (Bobo and Hutchings 1996). Challenges to this structure often elicit hostility from dominant group members.

Another possibility is that many whites still harbor racist convictions and do not really endorse racial equality and desegregation after all; they may simply give socially desired, culturally appropriate responses to survey items on these principles. If this is the case, then whites' expressed views on policy or implementation matters might offer a more accurate glimpse of their "true" feelings than their answers to questions about principles. Although most observers doubt that this type of response bias can explain the patterns discussed earlier, some potential for reactivity clearly exists here, as suggested by the many studies showing that responses to survey items on racial and political issues can depend heavily on the race of the interviewer (Finkel, Guterbock, and Borg 1991).

A number of theorists and researchers argue that the principle-implementation gap reflects the emergence of a new and perhaps more pernicious form of racial prejudice, variously termed "modern," or "aversive" racism (Dovidio et al., this volume). One version of this argument runs as follows: European Americans (whites) are socialized from childhood to harbor negative feelings toward persons of color, through non-verbal cues that express fear and disgust toward African Americans, and other racial and ethnic minority groups, as well as formal socialization through media and other institutions. At the same time, they are aware of (and may feel some guilt for) the long history of slavery, prejudice and discrimination against persons of color, which they understand to violate core civic values (e.g., egalitarianism, individualism) and human rights. "Modern" or "aversive" racists do not endorse—indeed, usually reject emphatically—traditional expressions of racial and ethnic prejudice, because they are seen as culturally inappropriate. Instead, negative feelings about persons of color now are most likely to be expressed when they can be accounted for in non-racial terms.

Thus, according to these theorists, "modern" or "aversive" racists are especially likely to reject affirmative action and other implementation strategies. In this way, they can resolve their ambivalence and honor their impulses toward racial bias *and* egalitarianism simultaneously—endorsing the principles of equal treatment for everyone, and claiming that implementation strategies (e.g., affirmative action, government programs) violate these same principles because they amount to special treatment for persons of color. This tendency is abetted by the belief that discrimination is rarely a problem for persons of color these days, and the claim that the situation of African Americans and other minorities is rapidly improving. Such perceptions are widespread among whites (Shepard 1997), and may be exacerbated by the dearth of meaningful interracial and interethnic contact and dialogue in many communities (Sigelman et al., this volume).

Not surprisingly, claims about a "new" form of racism are highly controversial. Some scholars remain skeptical that "modern" or "aversive" racism accounts for the widening "principle-implementation" gap (Schuman, Steeh, and Bobo 1988; Sniderman and Piazza, this volume). Still other

commentators feel that this approach embodies an anti-conservative bias, and that it unnecessarily smears many thoughtful, well-meaning European Americans with the "racist" label.

As we near the end of the twentieth century, public officials, scholars, and citizens alike continue to grapple uneasily with how best to define and ameliorate intergroup prejudice and discrimination. The American public remains pessimistic about the prospects for racial reconciliation and healing, as evidenced by the mixed reviews that have greeted President Clinton's efforts to stimulate dialogue on these issues. Nevertheless, the search for constructive remedies for the problems of racial and ethnic prejudice and discrimination will—and must—be a high priority as America enters the twenty-first century.

References

Banks, James A. 1993. "Multicultural Education: Development, Dimensions, and Challenges." *Phi Delta Kappan*, 75(1): 22–28.

Bobo, Lawrence, and Vincent L. Hutchings. 1996. "Perceptions of Racial Group Competition: Extending Blumer's Theory of Group Position to a Multiracial Social Context." *American Sociological Review*, 61: 951–972.

Bobo, Lawrence, and James Kluegel. 1993. "Opposition to Race-Targeting: Self-Interest, Stratification Ideology, or Racial Attitudes?" *American Sociological Review*, 58: 443–464.

Bobo, Lawrence, and Camille L. Zubrinsky. 1996. "Attitudes on Residential Integration: Perceived Status Differences, Mere In-Group Preference, or Racial Prejudice?" *Social Forces*, 74: 883–909.

Cose, Ellis. June 30, 1997. "Dialogue of Dishonesty." *Newsweek*: 39.

Davis, James A., and Tom W. Smith. 1996. *The General Social Surveys: Cumulative Codebook, 1972–1996*. Chicago: National Opinion Research Center.

Ellison, Christopher G., and Daniel A. Powers. 1994. "The Contact Hypothesis and Racial Attitudes among Black Americans." *Social Science Quarterly*, 75: 385–400.

Farley, Reynolds, Charlotte Steeh, Maria Krysan, Tara Jackson, and Keith Reeves. 1994. "Stereotypes and Segregation: Neighborhoods in the Detroit Area." *American Journal of Sociology*, 100: 750–780.

Finkel, Steven E., Thomas M. Guterbock, and Marian J. Borg. 1991. "Race-of-Interviewer Effects in a Preelection Poll: Virginia 1989." *Public Opinion Quarterly*, 55: 313–330.

Firebaugh, Glenn, and Kenneth Davis. 1988. "Trends in Antiblack Prejudice, 1972–1984." *American Journal of Sociology* 94: 251–272.

Gallup, George, Jr., and Frank Newport. 1991. "Blacks and Whites Differ on Civil Rights Progress." *Gallup Poll Monthly*, (August): 54–62.

Kluegel, James R. 1990. "Trends in Whites' Explanations of the Black-White Gap in Socioeconomic Status, 1977–1989." *American Sociological Review* 55:512–525.

Oliver, M. 1994. "Portrayals of Crime, Race, and Aggression in 'Reality-Based' Police Shows: A Content Analysis." *Journal of Broadcasting and Electronic Media*, 5: 179–191.

Schuman, Howard, and Lawrence Bobo. 1988. "Survey-Based Experiments on White Racial Attitudes Toward Residential Integration." *American Journal of Sociology*, 94: 273–299.

Schuman, Howard, and Charlotte Steeh. 1996. "The Complexity of Racial Attitudes in America." Pp. 455–469 in *Origins and Destinies: Immigration, Race, and Ethnicity in America*, edited by Silvia Pedraza and Ruben G. Rumbaut. Belmont, CA: Wadsworth.

Schuman, Howard, Charlotte Steeh, and Lawrence Bobo. 1988. *Racial Attitudes in America: Trends and Interpretations, revised edition*. Cambridge, MA: Harvard University Press.

Shepard, Scott. 1997. "Poll Shows Split Beliefs on Racial Preferences." *Austin American-Statesman*, June 18, A1.

Sigelman, Lee, and Susan Welch. 1991. *Black Americans' Views of Racial Inequality: The Dream Deferred*. New York: Cambridge University Press.

——. 1993. "The Contact Hypothesis Revisited: Interracial Contact and Positive Racial Attitudes." *Social Forces*, 71: 781–795.

Turner, M. 1992. "Discrimination in Urban Housing Markets: Lessons from Fair Housing Audits." *Housing Policy Debate*, 3: 185–215.

Waters, Mary C. 1990. *Ethnic Options*. Berkeley: University of California Press.

Wood, Peter B., and Michele L. Chesser. 1994. "Black Stereotyping in a University Population." *Sociological Focus*, 27: 17–34.

22

Pictures in
the Mind

Paul M. Sniderman
Thomas Piazza

Negative Characterizations of Blacks

Do whites see blacks as hard-working, responsible, trustworthy, or as lazy, self-destructive, violent? How negative, how hostile, are white attitudes toward blacks? Questions like these, it is sometimes suggested, are out of reach. Racism, it is asserted, is no longer blatant: people nowadays are reluctant to express openly their dislike of and contempt for blacks, indeed, are not prepared to express publicly a sentiment that could be interpreted as racist. Racism, it is said, is "subtle": it is disguised, kept out of sight.

This line of argument has intuitive appeal: it fits our common-sense understanding that people tailor their words and deeds to their social circumstances, concealing ideas or attributes that would evoke disapproval, were others in a position to detect them. And systematic research complements common sense. . . .

Consider the logic underlying the notion of subtle racism. The assertion that racism nowadays cannot be expressed openly and overtly but must instead be disguised presupposes the existence of strong social norms against the expression of frankly negative evaluations of blacks. But how compelling, one must ask, is the presupposition of a problack societal norm?

To obtain some sense of the willingness of whites to make derogatory assertions about blacks, we presented respondents with a variety of negative characterizations of blacks. These included assertions that blacks were inherently inferior to whites, inclined to exploit welfare, unwilling to work hard, irresponsible, belligerent, and violent. To begin with the most encouraging result, consider whites' reactions to a suggestion that blacks are innately inferior to whites. As part of a series of questions directed at determining why the average black American is not as well off as the average white American, we asked if the reason is that:

- *Blacks are born with less ability.*

Only 6 percent of whites concur with the characterization of blacks as inherently less intelligent and able than whites. . . . [T]he contrast between American racial attitudes at the end of the 1940s, when assertions of the innate inferiority of blacks were commonplace, and at the end of the 1980s, when such views were mouthed by only a relative handful, is like the difference between night and day. But without minimizing the importance of this change, it by no means follows that negative characterizations of blacks have disappeared.

. . . [A]t the opposite extreme from the stereotype of innate black inferiority, which is rare, is the perception of blacks' taking advantage of government assistance, which is anything but rare. By way of getting a grip on this stereotype, we asked respondents if they agreed that:

- *Most blacks who are on welfare programs could get a job if they really tried.*

Notice that we did not ask if "some" blacks on welfare could find a job and support themselves; we asked instead whether "most" of them could get a job—a rather different proposition. Yet the response to this negative characterization of blacks is at the opposite end of the spectrum from the response to assertions of inherent black inferiority. Whereas only a tiny percentage endorse the view that blacks are born less able than whites, a clear-cut majority—61 percent—believe that most blacks on welfare could find work if they wanted to.

Moreover, the belief that blacks on welfare are taking advantage of the program is only one instance of a cluster of beliefs which accent a lack of effort, initiative, self-reliance, and responsibility on the part of blacks. . . .

A perception of a lack of effort and responsibility, of the absence of a willingness to do the best one can in an admittedly difficult situation, has arguably become the most prominent feature of negative perceptions of blacks now. But it is by no means the only instance of perceived black behavior to which substantial numbers of whites take exception. Another, for example, is a perception of blacks as belligerent. Consider the following characterization:

- *Most blacks have a chip on their shoulder.*

Granted that many young inner-city male blacks act tough, striking a belligerent, aggressive posture in the company of whites; to perceive them as having a chip on their shoulder is no more than to perceive reality as it actually is. But this characterization was not specifically aimed at "young male ghetto blacks," or at "young male blacks," or even at "young blacks." And however the behavior and demeanor of many young ghetto males should be characterized, it is a stretch to argue that *most* blacks—women as well as men, over sixty as well as under twenty, in the suburbs as well as in the cities—are conspicuously and distinctively truculent. All the same, 36 percent of all whites—approximately one in every three—agree (strongly or somewhat) that most blacks have a chip on their shoulder.

This perception of blacks as belligerent and resentful, though no doubt reflecting in part a belief that blacks are not managing the responsibility common to everyone to behave decently and exercise self-control even in trying circumstances, also betrays an uneasiness and concern for personal safety on the part of whites. Thus, we asked whether:

- *Blacks are more violent than whites.*

About one in every five whites agreed.

Does it follow that whites who agreed that blacks are more violent—or, for that matter, those who agreed blacks are taking advantage of welfare or are not trying as hard as they could to get ahead—are racial bigots? Is agreement with a negative characterization, in and of itself, proof of prejudice?

All of these negative characterizations of blacks are fed by prejudice, as we shall show.

But apart only from the characterization of blacks as inherently inferior to whites, they cannot be entirely reduced to bigotry, for these characterizations capture real features of everyday experience. For example, the perception of blacks as more violent than whites, and in particular the apprehension about young black males as more prone to criminal conduct, has an element of reality to it. Although blacks are only slightly more than one in every ten in the population as a whole, in 1990 they were responsible for one in every two murders, and in 1989 for more than six in every ten robberies. The common perception of the disintegration of the nuclear family among blacks is also rooted in reality. In 1988, 63.7 percent of black births were out of wedlock, the figure being higher still in urban areas, and in 1990, 56.2 percent of black households were headed by women, the majority of whom had never been married. Nor is the common perception that blacks do not do well at school without a kernel of truth. The average Scholastic Aptitude Test score of blacks, in 1990, was 737, compared with an average white score of 993; and still more disturbing, the picture does not materially brighten if differences in income are taken into account. Even black students from well-off homes do not do well on standardized tests of academic aptitude; indeed, as Andrew Hacker (1992) has remarked, blacks "whose parents earn between $50,000 and $60,000 barely match Asians from families in the $10,000 to $20,000 range."

A person who is concerned about racial intolerance and the injustices it has inspired has difficulty accepting the notion that a negative characterization, merely by virtue of being negative, is not a sign of prejudice, still more so accepting the suggestion that many of these negative characterizations have an element of truth to them. Examining the reactions of whites to blacks in isolation, which is the way it has always been done in the past, obscures the depth of the problem of race. What blacks think of blacks also needs to be taken into account.

Taking advantage of a national survey conducted in 1991, we are in a position to do this for the first time. Everyone interviewed in the course of this study, whether black or white, was asked to describe what blacks as a group are like. A number of adjectives were read—for example, aggressive or violent, boastful, and irresponsible—with respondents indicating how well each adjective described blacks by picking a number from 0 to 10, the higher the number, the better or more accurate the description. . . .

Plainly, large numbers of whites are perfectly willing to express frankly negative evaluations of blacks. At least one in every two perceives blacks as a group to be aggressive or violent, and nearly as many are ready to describe blacks as boastful and complaining. . . [moreover] in every case blacks are at least as likely as whites to hold a negative view of blacks. For example, 52 percent of white respondents describe blacks as aggressive or violent; for black respondents, the number is 59 percent. For white respondents, 34 percent describe blacks as lazy; the number among black respondents is 39 percent. Indeed, when it comes to judgments of whether blacks as a group exhibit socially undesirable characteristics, whenever there is a statistically significant difference between the views of blacks and whites, it *always* takes the form of blacks expressing a more negative evaluation of other blacks than do whites. It is not true that blacks have a more negative view of blacks in every respect than whites. Just as they are more likely to believe that a negative adjective describes blacks, they are also more likely to believe that a positive adjective—such as intelligent or hard-working—also describes blacks. But these results should make plain that the negative characterizations of blacks made by both blacks and whites are rooted in part in a common reality. . . .

Who Accepts Negative Stereotypes?

A substantial and distinguished body of research has developed the general argument that whatever factors put a person "in touch with people whose ideas and values are different from one's own" promotes tolerance (Stouffer 1955; Selznick and Steinberg 1969; Quinley and Glock 1979; Apostle et al. 1983). These factors may include the mix of people and points of view in a person's part of the country, or the mix he or she is exposed to through traveling, or by taking part in politics, or—and this was once a theme—through the process of education. The more schooling people have had, the greater the likelihood that they will be exposed to, and be able to understand, the core values and official norms of American culture—values and norms that centrally include the principle of tolerance itself. So far as this is true, then whatever moves a person toward the center of American society and away from its periphery should promote all the varieties of tolerance—political, religious, and racial, too.

Not that all aspects of a person's social standing are of equal importance in promoting tolerance. . . . Consider first the factors that turn out to be unimportant. Common sense might suggest that negative reactions to blacks are driven by anxiety and resentment and hence should be most common among the have-nots and have-littles. For that matter, it may seem obvious that a more negative perception of blacks is nearly a signature characteristic of older Americans, raised in a different climate of opinion. But . . . neither family income nor age has much to do with acceptance of negative racial stereotypes. In contrast with results from the 1950s and 1960s, which showed that young adults tended to be more open-minded than the older ones they were replacing, our results suggest that the process of increasing societal tolerance with each new generation has, at least for the moment, come to an end.

But if age and income do not matter, education manifestly does. The number of years of schooling a person has had is significantly related to the number of negative characterizations about blacks that he or she accepts: as schooling goes up, acceptance of negative characterizations goes down. In addition, ideological orientation also makes a difference. The more liberal people perceive themselves to be, the fewer negative racial characterizations they are likely to endorse, while the more conservative they perceive themselves to be, the more negative characterizations they are likely to accept.

But how, exactly, do education and ideology work together? And what difference does either, or both, make to the overall willingness of whites to accept the most common stereotypes about blacks? . . . [F]or nearly every combination of education and ideology, the majority belief among whites is that most blacks on welfare could get a job if they really tried. Among respondents with at most a high school degree, conservatives and liberals are both overwhelmingly likely to perceive blacks as taking advantage of welfare: 91 percent of the less-educated conservatives and 78 percent of less-educated liberals agree that most blacks on welfare are exploiting it. The overall proportion of whites perceiving blacks as exploitative steadily drops the more formal schooling whites have had—from approximately eight in ten among the least educated to six in ten among the moderately educated, to five in ten among the most. But describing the variation this way conceals as much as it reveals, for increases in formal schooling undercut popular support for this stereotype chiefly among people who see themselves as liberal in outlook. Among well-educated conservatives, 71 percent still perceive blacks as taking advantage of welfare, and for that matter nearly 50 percent of well-educated middle-of-the-roaders agree. Only in one group—well-educated liberals—does a clear majority *reject* the view of blacks as exploiting welfare.

A similar pattern holds for diffusion of the other negative stereotypes—for instance, that blacks are poor because they simply don't try hard enough. Among the less educated, liberals are statistically as likely as conservatives to believe that if blacks would only try harder, they would be just as well-off as whites. Once again, the higher a person's level of formal education, the lower his or her level of agreement. The same pattern of distribution holds also for the perception that blacks are irresponsible and do not take care of their neighborhoods, with the stereotype most common among the least educated (and among them, just as common among liberals as among conservatives) and least common among the most educated—certainly if they are liberal.

. . . [T]hree things are significant: (1) the less educated people are, the more negative are their images of blacks; (2) the more conservative, the more negative are their images of blacks; and (3) the images that less-educated liberals and conservatives have of blacks are much alike, while those of well-educated liberals and conservatives markedly differ.

What does this pattern of results signify? What does it reveal about the diffusion of negative racial stereotypes in contemporary American life? First, the cleavage over images of blacks is more, not less, pronounced among the more aware and better educated citizens. But the reason for this is not because educated conservatives have an especially negative view of blacks, but rather because educated liberals have an especially positive view. Second, with the exception only of citizens who are uncommonly well educated and uncommonly liberal, what is striking is the sheer pervasiveness throughout contemporary American society of negative characterizations of blacks—particularly the stereotype that most blacks on welfare could get a job. Perceptions of blacks as inferior were supposed to represent an archaic stock of beliefs that were in the process of dying out, and some indeed do appear to be fading out. But it completely misreads contemporary American culture to suppose that all negative characterizations of blacks are dwindling away. On the contrary, images of blacks as failing to make a genuine effort to work hard and to deal responsibly with their obligations is a standard belief throughout most of American society. Only among the relatively small segment characterized both by extensive education and a liberal outlook on politics is it rejected by large numbers. We read these results as suggesting that, notwithstanding the role of societal institutions like formal schooling in reducing the prevalence of negative racial stereotypes, negative stereotypes of blacks' character are widely diffused through contemporary American society. Indeed, for these stereotypes to be rejected may be more the exception than the rule. . . .

The Psychology of Prejudice

Consider a specific stereotype—say, that blacks are more violent than whites. Agreement with this characterization may be an expression of prejudice, but it need not be. Someone, having read the newspapers and watched television over a period of years, may agree because the stereotype of black violence fits consistently the stream of information from the mass media to which they have been exposed. Or a person may accept the negative characterization because it fits accurately his or her personal experience, or, yet again, because it fits with objective social indicators—for example, published rates on violent crime. Moreover, the attribution of a negative characteristic to blacks need not signal a negative feeling toward them. To acquiesce in a characterization of blacks as more violent than whites may be the handiwork of bigotry, but, alternatively, it may reflect a conviction that blacks continue to be victimized by a racist society, and the brutality that some blacks exhibit is itself the product of a society that has brutalized them. Everyone who accepts a negative stereotype about blacks is not prejudiced, and still more to the point, some who accept a negative stereotype about blacks are sympathetic, not hostile, to blacks and supportive of policies to help them. But acknowledging this, can we tell if prejudice plays, if not a completely determinative, then at any rate a manifestly important role in fostering stereotypes of blacks? . . .

The [seminal] argument of Adorno and his colleagues (1950) is complexly woven together from many threads of evidence, but its two principal strands can be succinctly set out. The first is the "personality" thesis. Prejudice, according to the personality thesis, is rooted in part in people's most deep-seated psychological needs and conflicts—rooted, that is, in basic and enduring aspects of their personality, established early in childhood, primarily in response to their parents, particularly in reaction to punitive fathers and overbearing mothers.

The second strand of the argument [is] . . . [t]he idea of ethnocentrism, reoriented by Adorno and his colleagues to deemphasize the idealization of a person's own group, in favor of accentuating the denigration of groups he considers inferior. Ethnocentrism, so conceived, refers to the systematic tendency on the part of prejudiced individuals to dislike and derogate other ethnic groups

across-the-board. Racial prejudice is thus, in a literal sense, a blind and irrational reaction against blacks, blind and irrational because it has nothing intrinsically to do with blacks and may just as well manifest itself against Jews, or Asians, or any of many outgroups.

Ethnocentrism, we want to suggest, offers a key to the irrationality of some current negative stereotypes about blacks. Adorno and his colleagues demonstrated the irrationality of anti-Semitism by showing that negative stereotypes about Jews are part of a larger syndrome of prejudice against blacks and others. Inverting their logic, we shall demonstrate the irrationality of prejudice against blacks by showing that negative stereotypes about blacks are part of a larger syndrome of prejudice, one element of which is anti-Semitism. . . .

A generation ago, negative stereotyping of blacks was decidedly an aspect of a broader ethnocentrism. Now, there is talk of a "new racism." What we shall demonstrate, on the contrary, is that racial prejudice remains the same old racism at its core, as evidenced by the fact that negative stereotyping of blacks now, just as before, is embedded in a larger pattern of ethnocentrism.

The crucial datum is the consistency of reactions to outgroups. We shall explore three negative stereotypes of Jews:

- Jews are more willing than others to use shady practices to get ahead.

- Most Jews don't care what happens to people who aren't Jewish.

- Most Jews are pushy.

In response to each of these negative characterizations of Jews, respondents were asked whether they agreed strongly, agreed somewhat, disagreed somewhat, or disagreed strongly. What is striking is that people's reactions to black stereotypes are highly predictable on the basis of their reactions to Jewish stereotypes, and vice versa. . . . The person who says that Jews are pushy is a good bet to say that blacks have a chip on their shoulder, and the one who says that Jews use shady practices is an excellent bet to believe that blacks don't take care of their neighborhoods. Simply put, a response to any given question about Jews allows us to predict the response to any given question about blacks very nearly as well as another question actually about blacks.

Consistency is the mark of prejudice; indeed, by prejudice we mean explicitly the tendency systematically to respond negatively to outgroups. Thus, although a large number of whites endorse a few negative characterizations of blacks, only a much smaller number agree with many of them, and most of them are the very same people who agree with a large number of negative characterizations of Jews. For example, 84 percent of whites who agree with all six negative stereotypes about blacks agree with at least two out of three anti-Semitic items; conversely, only 10 percent of those who agree with only one negative characterization of blacks agree with two out of three anti-Semitic items. . . .

[W]hether people have barely made it out of high school or have graduated from college, whether they are just starting out, in their thirties, or are more mature, say, in their fifties or older, they will tend to espouse antiblack stereotypes if they espouse anti-Jewish stereotypes, and vice versa. This suggests that the psychology of racial prejudice is not as socially malleable as is often supposed. The tendency to respond in a systematic way to outgroups is not inhibited by one's social circumstances or standing and is as marked among the most educated and best off as among the least educated and worst off.

These findings suggest strongly that racism today is the same old racism: ethnocentrism is its mark now as much as ever, and not only on average but across quite different parts of American society. But perhaps there is a new racism in a different sense, still benefiting from its customary sources of support but now given a new lease on life by virtue of tapping new reservoirs in American society and culture?

The New Racism

. . . The suggestion that race prejudice continues to thrive because it is built-in to the American ethos itself is the central plank in the argument that a new racism has been born. Its proponents, whatever other points on which they disagree, all agree that the new racism is rooted in a "conjunction" of antiblack feeling and the kind of traditional values embodied in the Protestant ethic, including "hard work, individualism, sexual repression, and delay of gratification, with large doses of patriotism and reverence for the past thrown in" (McConahay and Hough 1976:40). The overall thrust of the definition is clear, although the details may seem, on examination, to be less than compelling. . . .

A clear distinction can and ought to be made between the place of a value like individualism and a value like discipline in the American culture, or in broader terms, between individualistic values and authoritarian ones. Individualism can fairly be described in the American setting as a traditional value, but . . . as bound up with a liberal tradition. The second set of values—obedience and discipline—has an altogether different standing in American culture. Who ever supposed that obedience was a characteristic that Americans either exhibited to an uncommon degree or held in uncommon esteem? And what about discipline? . . . [N]early every observer has agreed that what marks the American culture is precisely a lack of regimentation, an openness to challenge, spontaneity, even unruliness.

By way of seeing whether negative characterizations of blacks are tied to either of these two sets of values, we shall examine first the relation between aspects of individualism and the perception of blacks as failing to make an effort, and then the relation between these same perceptions of blacks and measures of authoritarian values.

The notion of individualism can be construed in a manifold of ways. . . . To begin with, individualism surely finds expression in the idea of achievement as a value. Achievement can itself be variously construed, to be sure; but here we shall take it to refer to a person's commitment to excelling, to being the best at what he or she does. Individualism can also convey a special commitment to the idea of success, particularly material success; so one indicator we shall take of the place of individualism in a person's thinking is the importance he or she attaches to making a lot of money. Furthermore, and on a quite different plane, individualism is said to find expression in the striving of one person against others; so we shall take as yet another indicator of individualism the extent to which a person attaches a special measure of importance to competition. For that matter, individualism often carries with it a presumption of the place of self in society, a priority of the claims that one chooses to make on or in behalf of oneself, as against those that others make upon one to fit in, to conform, to follow the approved path. So we shall take as additional indicators of individualism the importance that people attach to their own judgments (as opposed to those of others) as to what they should do, plus the importance they assign to encouraging originality in ideas.

If the perception of blacks as failing to work hard is premised on individualism as a value—as the new racism researchers insist—then some or all of these indicators of individualism will have a marked association with a readiness to perceive blacks as failing to make an effort. But [our analyses show that] virtually no relation exists between characterizing blacks as failing to work hard and believing in the idea of individualism—however the idea of individualism is construed. . . . [In fact, regardless of which indicator of individuation we use, we find that] individualism is not relevant one way or the other to perceptions of blacks.

But the case is quite different for authoritarian values. An enormous body of research has demonstrated that people who attach an uncommon importance to obedience and discipline tend to be harsh and judgmental, to be relatively unempathetic and ungenerous, particularly in responding to others who are unfamiliar to them or different in background or belief or appear to deviate from conventional standards of morality and propriety. And it is not difficult to see how, in consequence, people who place an uncommon value on authoritarian values would be more likely to respond to blacks in a way that is more uncharitable, punitive, and judgmental, and hence more likely to perceive blacks as manifesting a number of negative characteristics, among them a lack of discipline, self-control, and willingness to work hard.

And this is exactly what our study confirms. When we asked the following question:

- Given the way things are these days, how important is it to strengthen law and order? Is it very important, somewhat important, or not important?

We found a marked relation between the importance people attach to authority as a value and acceptance of the stereotypes of blacks as failing to make an effort. . . . [T]he importance of people's orientations to authority emerges in other measures. For example, everyone was asked if they basically agree (or basically disagree) that:

- Respect for authority is one of the most important things that children should learn. . . .

- The sooner we all acquire similar values and ideals, the better off we'll be. . . .

[We also asked:]

- Now, thinking of the country as a whole, how important is it to maintain respect for America's power in the world, even if that means spending a lot of money on the military? Would you say that is very important, somewhat important, or not important?

. . . [In each instance, the more importance a person attaches to authoritarian values,] the more likely he or she is to perceive blacks as failing to make a genuine effort to work hard and to make it on their own.

We want now to turn from the attitudes of whites toward blacks to their attitudes toward policies dealing with blacks, in order to see if in the realm of public policy as well as in the realm of racial stereotypes the force at work is not individualistic values but authoritarian ones. As a representation of racial policy preferences we shall focus on a pair of issues—more government spending in behalf of blacks . . . and government efforts to ensure fair treatment in employment for blacks. . . . The relation between these policy preferences and the values associated with individualism is very small—indeed, as a rule, indistinguishable from zero. On the other hand, the relation between opposition to government help for blacks on both policy issues and authoritarian values is similar to what we observed with negative stereotypes of blacks, although weaker in strength.

In short, over a wide range of different conceptions of individualism, and regardless of whether the focus is on white attitudes toward blacks or on white attitudes toward public policies dealing with blacks, the suggestion that the classic American value of individualism is at the heart of the contemporary problem of race is simply, and flatly, wrong.

The Old Racism or New?

By way of summary, four points merit emphasis. First, substantial numbers of Americans are perfectly willing to express frankly negative characterizations of blacks, particularly as failing to try as hard as, they could or should to overcome their problems. Second, although racial stereotyping is more common in some parts of American society than in others (showing up more often, for example, among the poorly educated than among the well educated), it is nonetheless widely diffused, and indeed far from uncommon except in pockets of American society that are themselves relatively uncommon by virtue of having both a liberal orientation and an educational advantage. Third, negatively stereotyping blacks is part of a larger syndrome of negatively stereotyping outgroups in general now as before, suggesting that the nature of racism today is the same at its core as it was a generation ago. And fourth, racial stereotyping has very little to do with individualistic values but is instead closely tied up with authoritarian values. . . .

References

Adorno, T.W., et al. 1950. *The Authoritarian Personality*. New York: Harper.

Apostle, R.A., C.Y. Glock, T. Piazza, and M. Suelzle. 1983. *The Anatomy of Racial Attitudes*. Berkeley: University of California Press.

Hacker, A. 1992. *Two Nations: Black and White, Separate, Hostile, and Unequal*. New York: Charles Scribners Sons.

McConahay, J.B., and J.C. Hough, Jr. 1976. "Symbolic Racism." *Journal of Social Issues* 32: 23–29.

Quinley, H.E., and C.Y. Glock. 1979. *Anti-Semitism in America*. New York: Free Press.

Selznick, G., and S. Steinberg. 1969. *The Tenacity of Prejudice*. New York: Harper and Row.

Stouffer, S. 1955. *Communism, Conformity, and Civil Liberties*. New York: Doubleday.

23

Cognitive and Motivational Bases of Bias:

Implications of Aversive Racism for Attitudes Toward Hispanics

John Dovidio
Samuel Gaertner
Phyllis Anastasio
Rasyid Sanitioso

... Within the limits of the available research ... this chapter attempts to provide a framework for understanding and integrating evidence on attitudes, bias, and behaviors of non-Hispanic whites toward Hispanics. In particular we apply for the first time a model of contemporary prejudice and discrimination developed with respect to attitudes toward blacks to understand current attitudes toward Hispanics, and we consider the implications for the workplace.

In this chapter we propose, in contrast to the approaches that dominated the study of prejudice for the first half of this century, that prejudice is substantially rooted in *normal* processes and is thus widespread. This approach recognizes that the nature of prejudice directed toward any particular group (e.g., blacks, Hispanics, Jews, women) will be shaped by historical and contemporary pressures and therefore will be unique in many ways. Nevertheless this perspective focuses on the ways that fundamental processes contribute to bias; consequently we will emphasize the commonalities among attitudes toward diverse groups. It is important to note, however, that our proposal that bias is based

on normal processes does *not* suggest that prejudice is excusable, acceptable, or immutable.

In this chapter we consider the origins and consequences of prejudice. Prejudice is an attitude involving negative feelings, beliefs based on group characterization (a stereotype), and a behavioral disposition toward (e.g., tendency to avoid) members of a distinguishable group. We first discuss the historical view that stereotypes and prejudices are irrational beliefs and feelings. We then review the more recent perspective that emphasizes how normal biases in the ways people think can contribute to prejudice. Next, we examine how these cognitive biases interact with motivational and sociocultural factors to shape the nature of contemporary forms of bias. We present in some detail evidence on the existence of a modern, subtle form of bias—aversive racism. Then we examine evidence concerning patterns of bias and discrimination toward Hispanics. ...

The Bases of Prejudice

Traditional Psychological Approaches to Prejudice

The theories that historically have dominated the psychological study of the etiology of prejudice have generally pointed to some form of intrapersonal, interpersonal, or societal dysfunction. The equation that has implicitly guided this research has been as follows: Prejudice is bad; bad is abnormal; therefore, people who are prejudiced are abnormal. The psychodynamic orientation that guided the work on the authoritarian personality (Adorno, Frenkel-Brunswik, Levinson, and Sanford 1950), perhaps one of the best-known works on prejudice, provides a classic demonstration of how assumptions of psychopathology influence mainstream conceptions of prejudice. This research originally was sponsored by the American Jewish Committee to understand the rise of anti-Semitism in the 1930s and the psychological mechanisms that could permit the Nazi atrocities toward Jews. The central question of this work was, Who is prejudiced? The authoritarian personality, which was proposed to develop from experiencing harsh and punitive child-rearing practices, was characterized by (a) rigid adherence to conventional and conservative values; (b) a strong desire to identify with authority and to value hierarchical structure; (c) a low tolerance for ambiguity; (d) a strong desire to make categorical, particularly in-group/out-group, distinctions; (e) strong beliefs in mystical or supernatural control; and (f) generalized hostility that would be manifested in part by a general negative prejudice toward out-groups.

The legacy of this program and orientation has been a mixed one. One very positive aspect is that authoritarianism has consistently been found to correlate with general prejudice. The original work by Adorno et al. (1950), for example, showed close associations among authoritarianism, racial prejudice, anti-Semitism, and prejudices against Mexican Americans and the mentally ill; Weigel and Howes (1985) demonstrated that authoritarianism correlated with self-reported prejudice toward blacks, homosexuals, and the elderly. On the negative side, perhaps because of the robustness of its relation to prejudice, the authoritarian personality framework (along with scapegoat, relative deprivation, and negative self-concept orientations) led the field to focus on prejudice as psychopathology.

We do not deny the validity of the work on the authoritarian personality, but rather we suggest that the view of prejudice as psychopathology may represent a too narrow and thus misleading perspective. First, the orientation of prejudice as abnormality directs attention to a relatively small proportion of the population. The work of Adorno et al. (1950), for example, suggests that high authoritarians are at the root of most of the prejudice and discrimination in society and implies that programs for ameliorating racism should be targeted toward this particular population. Racism, however, can occur at the institutional and cultural level, as well as at the individual level (Jones 1986).

Second, and perhaps relatedly, traditional approaches to prejudice have distracted researchers from considering how normal cognitive and motivational processes can contribute to the development, maintenance, and perpetuation of prejudice and discrimination. If prejudice is based even in part on normal functional processes, then it may be more widespread than originally assumed and more resistant to change. Third, these traditional approaches address traditional, "old-fashioned" forms of bigotry but may not be sensitive to more subtle, contemporary forms of bias.

Perhaps because of the these limitations, much of the contemporary research on prejudice focuses on how *normal* cognitive processes can contribute to bias. The role of biases in the way people acquire, process, and store information about others is considered in the next section.

Cognitive Processes Underlying Bias and Prejudice

Cognitive psychologists have studied extensively how the external reality is perceived and experienced as modified by the subjective expectations one has about the stimulus environment. These expectations act as a filter and allow the perceiver to screen out irrelevant or sometimes inconsistent information. This selective process is based on a major assumption of cognitive psychology: The amount of attention available to experience the world is of finite quantity. To expend this finite amount of attention on objects and details that have no implications for the perceiver's well-being is inefficient and may in fact be detrimental by diverting attention away from perceiving what is essential for survival. This process is therefore thought to be an adaptive mechanism with evolutionary survival value. One implication, though, is that what people normally perceive is not an accurate representation of the objective world but rather a narrowed, selective, and often biased sampling from that world.

One of the fundamental strategies of selective processing is categorization. Categorization typically occurs spontaneously on the basis of physical similarity, proximity, or shared fate (Campbell 1958). Whereas the categorization of objects on the basis of color or of people on the basis of race or ethnic group is not in itself bias, it does form a foundation for the subsequent development of bias. Several consequences of social categorization have been well documented.

First, because of the centrality of the self-concept in all perception, social categorization is most often reduced to a distinction between the group containing the self, the in-group, and other groups, the out-groups. Although the authoritarian personality research indicates individual differences may exist in the salience or importance of this categorization, all people engage in this process.

Second, once people are categorized as members of groups, those in the out-groups are seen as more similar to and more interchangeable with one another (the out-group homogeneity effect; Mullen and Hu 1989) and as generally more *dis*similar to the in-group (McGarty and Penny 1988). These results can be obtained even if assignment to the group is arbitrary (e.g., random) and the group label is socially meaningless (e.g., the blue group). Categorization of others as members of the in-group, in contrast, increases perceptions of similarity to the self (Stein, Hardyck, and Smith 1965). Increases in the salience of the in-group boundary increase in-group members' perceived similarity to the self, particularly on dimensions central to group membership (Hogg and Turner 1987).

Third, the mere categorization of people into groups is sufficient to increase attraction to in-group members and may at times lead to a devaluation of people identified as out-group members (Brewer 1979). People behave more positively and helpfully to in-group than to out-group members (Piliavin, Dovidio, Gaertner, and Clark 1981); they also evaluate in-group members more favorably and associate more desirable personal and physical characteristics to in-group than to out-group members (e.g., Doise et al. 1972). In a recent demonstration of this effect (Dovidio 1991), we informed white, African American, and Hispanic (Latino) students that they either consistently overestimated or underestimated the number of dots on a card or that they had long or short lines on the palms of their hands. Although assignment to groups was actually random, these students consistently described others in their group

(e.g., over-estimators) more positively than others in another group (e.g., under-estimators). This in-group favoritism bias was equivalent for white, African American, and Latino students.

Fourth, people process and retain information about in-group and out-group members differentially. They process information in a more detailed fashion for in-group members than for out-group members (Park and Rothbart 1982), have better memory for information about ways in-group members are similar and out-group members are dissimilar to the self (Wilder 1981), and remember less positive information about out-group members (Howard and Rothbart 1980). Increasing the accessibility or salience of the out-group facilitates processing of stereotype-consistent traits (Smith and Branscombe 1986), of more negative characteristics (Dovidio, Evans, and Tyler 1986), and of prototypic physical characteristics (Klatzky, Martin, and Kane 1982).

Fifth, different explanations are made about the behaviors of in-group and of out-group members. Positive behaviors and successful outcomes are more likely to be attributed to internal, stable characteristics (the personality) of in-group than out-group members (Hewstone, Jaspers, and Lalljee 1982). Blame for an accident and other negative outcomes are more likely to be ascribed to the personality of out-group members than of in-group members (Hewstone, Bond, and Wan 1983). In general, behavior that disconfirms expectancies tends to be attributed to situational rather than internal causes (Crocker, Hannah, and Weber 1983; Kulik 1983).

Categorizing a person into a social group (e.g., women, Hispanics, accountants) therefore systematically influences how information about that person is processed, stored, interpreted, and recalled. The organized cognitive structures that guide perceptions and expectations of persons based on their category (e.g., ethnic group) membership are called *social schemata*. Stereotypes are a classic example of social schemata. Hispanics, for instance, are stereotypically depicted as aggressive, poor, friendly, and family oriented (Marin 1984). In general, information that is more consistent with a stereotype is processed more efficiently, recalled more accurately, and remembered longer (Hewstone 1989). These effects seem to occur at the initial stages of perception and processing, as well as at the later stage of retrieval (Rothbart, Evans, and Fulero 1979), and they can occur without conscious awareness (Devine 1989). In addition, people tend to seek out and prefer information about others that confirms their preconceptions (Bodenhausen and Wyer 1985; Skov and Sherman 1986) and behave in ways that support their stereotypes, even despite inconsistent evidence (Wilder and Shapiro 1984). Consequently stereotypic beliefs and inferences (for example, the presumption that Hispanics will not move long distances for jobs) often do not reflect the reality (Edwards, Thomas, Rosenfeld, and Bower 1989). As Fiske and Taylor (1984) observed, "People tend to make the data fit the schema rather than vice versa" (p. 177). Thus stereotypes are highly resistant to change.

Comparing Traditional and Cognitive Approaches

Traditional perspectives view stereotypes as the consequence of pathological needs that distort normal processing. In contrast, the cognitive framework explains stereotyping as one of the costs of the efficiency in information processing that schemata provide. In addition, within the cognitive framework the traditional distinction between stereotypes as beliefs and prejudice as attitudes involving cognitive, affective, and behavioral predispositional components breaks down. Not only do such social schemata as stereotypes guide perceptions of others, but these schemata can also trigger emotional reactions (Fiske 1982). In addition, expectancies associated with social stereotypes lead to self-fulfilling prophecies: When a schema is activated, people think and act in ways consistent with their stereotype, and then others respond in ways that confirm the stereotypic expectations (Sibicky and Dovidio 1986; Snyder, Tanke, and Berscheid 1977). . . . These theories, however, do not fully account for the consistent decline in expressed social prejudice that has been observed over the past 30 years.

Since the 1940s, perhaps as a consequence of Hitler's demonstration of the evils of prejudice, whites' attitudes toward blacks, for example, have become dramatically less negative. This impetus was reinforced by the civil rights legislation of the 1960s that made discrimination illegal rather than simply immoral. Nationwide polls have demonstrated that whites increasingly reject negative characterizations of African Americans (Schuman, Steeh, and Bobo 1985). . . How can these data be reconciled with either the psychopathological orientations or the cognitive perspective? Has racism actually declined, or has it taken a different form? In the next section we consider a framework, aversive racism, that considers both the overt expression of bias and underlying feelings and beliefs to account for the apparent decline in racism.

The Nature of Modern Bias: Aversive Racism

The Theoretical Framework

Aversive racism represents a modern, subtle form of bias. We use the term to describe the type of racial attitude that we believe characterizes many white Americans who possess strong egalitarian values. Many of these people also possess negative racial feelings and beliefs that they either are unaware of or try to dissociate from their nonprejudiced self-images. In contrast to aversive racism is the more traditional form of racism, *dominative* racism, which involves overt bigoted beliefs and racial hatred (Kovel 1970). It should be noted that while we believe that the prevalence of the old-fashioned, red-necked form of racism has been declining, we also recognize that the old-fashioned form continues to be a significant force in the United States. Indeed not all racists are subtle.

We conceive of aversive racism as an adaptation resulting from an assimilation of an egalitarian value system with (a) impressions derived from human cognitive mechanisms that contribute to the development of stereotypes and prejudice, and (b) feelings and beliefs derived from historical and contemporary cultural racist contexts. The aversive racism perspective assumes that cognitive and motivational biases and socialization into the historically racist culture of the United States with its contemporary legacy lead most white Americans to develop negative feelings and beliefs about relative superiority to blacks and other minorities. Because of current cultural values, however, most whites also have convictions concerning fairness, justice, and racial equality. The existence of both almost unavoidable racial and ethnic biases and the desire to be egalitarian forms the basis of an ambivalence that aversive racists experience.

The focus of our research has not been on who is biased—we assume that most people, because they are normal, have developed some racial and ethnic biases. Instead our focus is on systematically identifying the situational conditions that will prime the egalitarian portion of an aversive racist's attitude and reveal the contexts in which the negative feelings will be manifested. In general we propose that because aversive racists consciously recognize and endorse egalitarian values and ideals, they will *not* discriminate against blacks and other minorities in situations in which norms prescribing appropriate behavior are clear and unambiguous. Wrongdoing, which would directly threaten the egalitarian self-image, would be obvious in these situations. We further propose that when the normative structure within the situation is weak, ambiguous, or conflicting, or if a person can justify or rationalize a negative response on the basis of some factor other than race or ethnicity, negative feelings toward blacks and other minorities will be manifested. Here, blacks and other minorities may be treated unfavorably or in a manner that disadvantages them, yet whites can be spared the recognition that they behaved inappropriately. Thus an aversive racist can discriminate against minority group members without challenging his or her egalitarian self-image. Indeed, across a number of paradigms, we have found consistent support for this framework (see Gaertner and Dovidio 1986b).

Empirical Findings

The greater subtlety of aversive racism compared with traditional forms of racism suggests that conventional measures such as authoritarianism may not accurately assess bias. Aversive racism involves more indirect manifestations of prejudice, and thus it requires assessment methods that are different (and more subtle) from traditional questionnaire methods. In this section we review a number of studies that use different techniques and methodologies and demonstrate not only the existence but also the nature of aversive racism.

In one test of the aversive racism perspective, we investigated whether high- and low-prejudice-scoring white students would help black or white victims in emergency situations depending on the clarity of norms regarding intervention (Gaertner and Dovidio 1977). White subjects were led to believe that they were the only bystanders or were among three witnesses (all white) to an emergency involving a black or white victim. According to Darley and Latane (1968), the normatively appropriate behavior, helping, is clearly defined when a bystander is the only witness to an emergency. In contrast the appropriate response when other bystanders are believed to be present is less clear and obvious: The presumed presence of other bystanders allows bystanders to diffuse responsibility (Darley and Latane 1968), to relieve feelings of obligation to help by coming to the conclusion that someone else will act. Gaertner and Dovidio (1977) found that the white subjects who believed that they were the only witnesses to the emergency were as likely to help black victims as white victims. When other bystanders were present, however, whites were more likely to diffuse responsibility and less likely to intervene to aid the black victim than the white victim. Thus, in the situation in which socially appropriate behavior was clearly defined, white subjects behaved in accordance with their generally nonprejudiced self-images and did not discriminate against the black victim; when appropriate action was not clearly defined and witnesses could rationalize nonintervention, white bystanders discriminated against black victims. Whereas the situational context was a strong predictor of bias, traditional measures of racial attitudes were not. Neither self-report of prejudice nor authoritarianism correlated overall with responses to the black victim when bystanders were alone or in the presence of others.

The subtlety of aversive racism may commonly be manifested as in-group favoritism, as opposed to out-group derogation. Aversive racists do not describe blacks in more overtly negative terms than whites. Negative characterizations could be interpreted readily, by others or by oneself, as being racially biased. For example when Dovidio, Mann, and Gaertner (1989) asked subjects to evaluate black and white people on 7-point scales with positive and negative endpoints (for example, *good* [1] to *bad* [7]), no difference was found in evaluative ratings of blacks and whites. A biased response ("bad") is obvious, and subjects consistently rated others, both black and white, on the positive end. When the measurement instrument was varied slightly, however, by placing positive and negative characteristics in separate scales (e.g., *good:* 1 = "not at all" to 7 = "extremely"; *bad:* 1 = "not at all" to 7 = "extremely"), bias was expressed—but subtly. When the ratings of blacks and whites on the negative scales were examined, no racial bias appeared: Blacks were *not* rated more negatively than whites. The ratings on the positive scales, however, did reveal a significant difference. Whereas, blacks were not rated more negatively than whites, whites *were* evaluated more positively than were blacks (see also, Gaertner and McLaughlin 1983, Study 3). Note that this phenomenon is not the old-fashioned bias reflecting open and unqualified negative feelings and beliefs about black inferiority. White college students did not characterize blacks more negatively (e.g., more lazy) than whites—a response that could readily be interpreted as racial prejudice—but these respondents did systematically characterize whites more positively (e.g., as more ambitious) than blacks. Although more subtle and less overtly negative, it is still racial bias.

This pattern of subtle bias, we believe, has relevance to the types of evaluations that occur in personnel decisions. In the next part of our research, in particular, we examine how modern biases pertaining to the racial categories of black and white affect responses to a specific black or white person applying for college admission (Kline and Dovidio 1982). White college students were informed that the study involved input to admissions decisions and were asked to evaluate on several dimensions an applicant to their university. The credentials of the applicant, based on transcript information such as SAT scores, rank in class, and activities, were varied systematically: strongly qualified (which admissions officers reported merited a 90% chance of acceptance), moderately qualified (50% change for acceptance), and weakly qualified (10% chance for acceptance). The race of the applicant was manipulated by varying a photograph that accompanied the transcript.

The results demonstrated that when the applicant had weak qualifications, discrimination did not occur between black and white applicants: Both were rated low. When the applicant had moderate qualifications, whites were evaluated slightly, but not significantly, more positively than blacks. When the applicant had strong qualifications, both blacks and whites were evaluated well, but blacks were evaluated less positively than whites who had the same qualifications. Consistent with the previous research presented in this chapter, bias did not occur at all levels; it occurred only at the positive end. It was not that blacks were worse than whites, it was just that blacks were not as good as whites.

In addition to predicting the way white people behave toward blacks, we believe that the aversive racism framework has direct implications for the conceptualization of the nature of contemporary racial and ethnic attitudes. In general, because current racial and ethnic attitudes may be more subtle than traditional forms, conventional methods of assessing these attitudes may not be sufficiently sensitive. For example the survey procedures that have indicated that the racial attitudes of white Americans toward black Americans are currently positive, accepting, and supportive (e.g., Schuman et al. 1985) involve obtrusive measures and public and deliberate responses, and thus may be influenced by social desirability concerns. Because public norms of tolerance have changed for the better (which in itself may represent progress), many social scientists have argued that surveys overestimate the amount of racial tolerance and underestimate the amount of covert prejudice in America today (Dovidio and Gaertner 1986; Jackman and Muha 1984).

Because survey and questionnaire responses are susceptible to evaluative concerns and impression management motivations, we followed up our self-report studies with response latency experiments that may provide more social-desirability-free measures. Two different types of paradigms have been used. In one paradigm, a lexical decision task, the subject is presented simultaneously with two strings of letters and is asked to decide (yes or no) whether both strings are words. On "word" trials, faster responses are assumed to reflect greater association in memory between the two words. In classic work with this task, Meyer and Schvaneveldt (1971) demonstrated that highly associated words (e.g., doctor, nurse) produced faster responses than did unassociated words (nurse, apple). Using the lexical decision task to assess racial attitudes, Gaertner and McLaughlin (1983) paired the words *blacks* and *whites*, explicitly representing the racial categories, with positive and negative attributes. They found that subjects made their decisions about the letter strings faster when positive attributes were paired with *whites* than with *blacks*. Subjects, however, showed no difference in response latencies for negative attributes paired with *whites* and *blacks*.

In a second paradigm that has been employed, a priming task, the subject is presented with two words sequentially and is asked to decide whether the second word, a characteristic, could *ever* describe the first (prime) word, a social category. In a study of racial attitudes by Dovidio and Gaertner (1991), on each trial the subject was first presented with a prime of *black* or *white* and asked to think about the racial groups. Each prime was then followed by a positive trait (e.g., good) or a negative characteristic (e.g., bad). Note that subjects were not directly asked to make personal judgments concerning the appropriateness of characteristics to racial groups; the stimuli on the trials of interest were constructed so that the response would always be yes, the characteristic could *potentially* describe a member of the primed racial group.

The latency results paralleled those of Gaertner and McLaughlin (1983). Differences in response latencies between black and white primes occurred for positive but not for negative attributes. In both racial attitude studies, negative characteristics were not more associated with blacks than with whites; in both experiments, however, positive characteristics were more associated with whites than with blacks. In addition, other response latency research has supported our position that many of the biases involved in aversive racism may be based on normal processes, such as the categorization of people into in-groups and out-groups. Perdue, Dovidio, Gurtman, and Tyler (1990) found patterns of responses to in-group designators (e.g., we) and out-group designators (e.g., they) that closely matched the pattern of white subjects' response latencies to whites and blacks (Dovidio and Gaertner 1991). These results thus implicated normal processes such as in-group/out-group categorization as a basis for contemporary racism. . . .

Examining the Nature of Bias Toward Hispanics

We recognize that the aversive racism framework should be applied cautiously to groups other than African Americans. Historically the relationship between whites and blacks has been radically different from the relationship between whites and Hispanics (see Pettigrew, Frederickson, Knobel, Glazer, and Ueda 1982). Nevertheless some of our earlier findings suggest the utility of this perspective for other groups. For example Gaertner (1973) found that normative structure was useful for explaining anti-Semitism in New York City. When normative structure was clear, no discrimination occurred against Jews; when the norms for appropriate behavior were weaker and more ambiguous, discrimination against Jews occurred. In addition Dovidio and Gaertner (1983) reported that subjects interacting with male and female supervisors and workers of high and low ability responded identically to women as they did to African Americans in the study discussed in the previous section (Dovidio and Gaertner, 1981). Thus in the remainder of this section we examine the processes posited in the aversive racism framework with respect to bias toward Hispanics. The major expectations are that (a) public attitudes toward Hispanics will have become less negative and more accepting; (b) in situations in which appropriate behavior is clearly defined, non-Hispanic whites will not discriminate against Hispanics, but in situations in which a negative response can be justified or rationalized, they will show negative biases; and (c) more bias will be expressed toward higher status Hispanics.

Attitudes Toward Hispanics

As with most other groups, traditional characterizations of Hispanics by non-Hispanic whites have been negative. As Ramirez (1988) summarized, Mexican American values have been portrayed pejoratively and in opposition to European American values (Saunders 1954; Vaca 1970; Zintz 1969). Mexican Americans traditionally have been described by non-Hispanic whites as present oriented, motivated for immediate gratification, passive, unambitious, not goal or success directed, and external in locus of control. Non-Hispanic whites describe their own group as future oriented, able to defer gratification, active, ambitious, goal and success directed, and internal in locus of control.

With respect to mass media, Hispanics have been underrepresented on television, appearing as less than 2% of television characters from 1955 to 1986, compared with their 9% representation in the population. Only 10% of the Hispanic characters that did appear on television were depicted as executives or professionals (compared with 22% for non-Hispanic whites and 17% for blacks). Portrayals were largely negative (41%, compared with 31% for non-Hispanic whites and 24% for blacks) (Lichter, Lichter, Rothman, and Admundson 1987); Hispanic characters have appeared primarily on prime-time television as criminals or as victims of violence (Gerbner, Gross, Signorielli, and Morgan 1986). Furthermore virtually all of the Hispanic characters have been men; Hispanic women have been almost totally unrepresented (Greenberg and Baptista-Fernandez 1980; Liebert and Sprafkin 1988). With respect to television commercials, Hispanics appear more frequently, representing about 6% of the characters (compared with 26% for blacks), but they mainly appear in background roles (Wilkes and Valencia 1989).

In contrast to the traditional biases against Hispanics, self-reports of bias have declined dramatically. The trend toward expressions of egalitarianism toward blacks is reflected also in attitudes toward Hispanics. . . . Thus, paralleling the change that has occurred for blacks, most non-Hispanic whites do not currently express negative feelings toward Hispanics.

With respect to attitudes toward blacks, we demonstrated that the expression of bias is currently more subtle than in the past. Although whites do not express the belief that blacks are worse than whites, they report that whites are better than blacks. In addition, response latency measures indicate that despite their overt egalitarian responses, whites have less positive associations with blacks than with whites. Research bearing directly on this issue regarding Hispanics is sparse but consistent. In a study of attitudes toward Chicanos, Locci and Carranza (1990) employed the Scale of the Measurement of Attitude Toward Chicanos, which independently assesses negative and positive orientations. Consistent with the implications of our work, these authors found that Chicanos and non-Hispanic whites did not differ in their responses to Chicanos for the *unfavorable* items, but non-Hispanic whites did rate Chicanos less positively on the *favorable* items. In addition, using a lexical decision task similar to that used by Gaertner and McLaughlin (1983), Thompson, Stephan, and Schvaneveldt (1980) found in their response latency study that non-Hispanic subjects had more positive associations with non-Hispanic whites than with Chicanos. As we argued earlier, response latency tasks are not as susceptible to social desirability concerns as are traditional self-report measures. Thus despite overt expression of egalitarian sentiments, subtle bias toward Hispanics exists.

Normative Context and the Expression of Bias

A central prediction of the aversive racist framework is that bias will not be expressed when normatively appropriate behavior is clear, but it will appear when what is right or wrong is not clearly defined or when the person can justify or rationalize a negative response. Consistent with this framework, across two studies in which non-Hispanic subjects rated a person who was described in very positive terms, Chicanos were rated as positively as were non-Hispanic whites. Inconsistent with our hypothesis, however, Chicano target persons described in negative terms (a college student with no friends, interests, or plans for the future), a description that could permit a justifiable negative response, were not evaluated more unfavorably than were non-Hispanic white target persons (Carver, Gibbons, Stephan, Glass, and Katz 1979; Carver, Glass, Snyder, and Katz 1977). . . .

Other research that is either more involving or provides more salient justifications for negative responses, however, is more consistent with the aversive racism framework. In terms of involvement, White and Sedlacek (1987) found that bias toward Hispanics increased as situations required more personal contact. Additional research indicates that norms for appropriate behavior are still critical. Lipton (1983) created six-person student juries for a disciplinary hearing involving a non-Hispanic or Hispanic defendant and led subjects to believe that their decisions actually would affect defendants' outcomes. The responses of non-Hispanic white subjects were affected by the context, specifically the composition of the jury. These subjects were harsher on Hispanic defendants when they participated with only non-Hispanic jury members than with both Hispanic and non-Hispanic jury members. The presence of Hispanic jurors may have made egalitarian norms more salient and consequently reduced bias.

Additional research reveals that teachers also have demonstrated subtle bias in the classroom that can result in a self-fulfilling prophecy. In an observational study, teachers praised non-Hispanic children more often than Chicano children and gave Chicano students less attention. The participation rate of Chicano students, perhaps as a consequence of differential treatment, was lower than the

rate for non-Hispanic children (U.S. Commission on Civil Rights 1973).

In terms of salient justifications, although people may overtly deny their prejudice against a specific ethnic group, such as Hispanics, their biases may be expressed indirectly and symbolically in terms of negative reactions to language or cultural differences. Ramirez (1988) observed, "The Mexican-American's speaking of English with a Mexican accent has served as another rationalization for different treatment and for prejudice" (p. 143). Across a number of studies, speakers of standard English have been judged as more favorable, competent, successful, valuable, and acceptable than Spanish-accented speakers (Arthur, Farrar, and Bradford 1974; Giles and Powesland 1975; Ryan and Carranza 1975).

Modern forms of bias involve beliefs in cultural superiority, which despite overt denials of bias may be reflected in relatively unfavorable responses to critical aspects of Hispanic cultures (Jones 1986; Ramirez 1988). Thus use of Spanish itself may evoke bias. Recognizing this possibility, several legal scholars have been concerned about fair treatment of non-English-speaking persons (e.g., Chang and Araujo 1975). Stephan and Stephan (1986) obtained experimental evidence consistent with this concern. In a simulated jury study, the defendant in an assault case testified either in English or in Spanish, through a translator. Non-Hispanic jurors considered the defendant more guilty when he testified in Spanish than in English, except when the judge explicitly alerted jurors to the possibility of this cultural bias.

Huddy and Sears (1990) also found that cultural bias may be manifested as opposition to bilingual education that is rationalized on the basis of factors other than prejudice toward Hispanics.

According to the aversive racism framework, bias is unlikely to occur when it can be readily recognized, by others or oneself, as an indication of prejudice. Ferdman (1989) conducted a study, supportive of our framework, in which managers evaluated a Hispanic manager videotaped in four different situations. Before they saw the videotape, they received information that in one condition emphasized his individual qualities and in another condition his Puerto Rican identity. Non-Hispanic subjects showed no bias as a function of this manipulation; they did not discriminate solely because of his ethnic group membership. Ferdman (1989) also varied the manager's behavior in ways that reflected different cultural styles. Specifically Ferdman modeled the behaviors on the basis of preliminary work on Hispanic managers who "handled conflict and approached work tasks in a manner consistent with the norms of Hispanic culture" (p. 171) and on non-Hispanic managers who exhibited an "Anglo, normative" style. Although subjects' responses did not differ as a consequence of the salience of ethnicity, they did evaluate the manager significantly less favorably when he displayed a "Hispanic, non-normative managerial style" than when he exhibited an "Anglo, normative style." Thus discrimination was manifested indirectly, in response to non-normative behavior styles, and not directly, as the result of ethnic identification. Overall the studies reviewed in this chapter provide tentative support for the extension of aversive racism to understanding when bias will or will not occur toward Hispanics. . . .

Conclusion

In this chapter, we have proposed that prejudice may be rooted in normal processes and that to focus only on the psychopathology of prejudice obscures important practical and theoretical issues. In particular the tendency to categorize people and objects, the cognitive and evaluative differentiation that results, the persistence of stereotypes, and the consequent errors of omission and commission conspire to predispose even the most well-meaning of people to value other social groups less than their own.

Despite these basic processes that promote bias, current norms for egalitarianism provide a countervailing force. The simultaneous existence both of the positive desire to be nonprejudiced and the negative cognitive, motivational, and sociocultural forces that contribute to bias form the basis of the ambivalence that aversive racists experience. What determines whether it is the positive or negative aspect of the aversive racist's attitude that gets expressed is the nature of the situation. In situations in which appropriate behavior is clearly defined, aversive racists will not discriminate against traditionally underrepresented groups; discrimination in these situations would be obvious to others and to oneself and thus would directly challenge an aversive racist's nonprejudiced self-image. In situations in which appropriate behavior is not clearly defined or in which a negative response can be justified or rationalized on the basis of some factor other than race, sex, or ethnicity, the negative beliefs and feelings will be expressed; under these conditions, aversive racists will discriminate against traditionally disadvantaged groups but subtly and in ways that will not challenge their nonprejudiced self-concepts. We have developed this framework primarily with work on whites' responses to blacks, but in this chapter we tentatively extend this framework for understanding the nature of current attitudes to Hispanics, as well.

While the expression may be more subtle, the consequences of contemporary forms of bias are comparable to that of old-fashioned racism—the perpetuation of a system that provides whites advantaged status relative to Hispanics, blacks, and other minorities. In addition, aversive racists incorrectly identify themselves with the solution rather than the problem of prejudice and discrimination. Because of this subtle but insidious form of racism, people's good intentions cannot be relied on. Practical remedies and theoretical solutions must address the basic processes that underlie aversive racists' orientations to traditionally disadvantaged groups.

References

Adorno, T. W., E. Frenkel-Brunswik, D. J. Levinson, and R. N. Sanford. (1950). *The Authoritarian Personality.* New York: Harper.

Arthur, B., D. Farrar, and B. Bradford. (1974). Evaluation reactions of college students to dialect differences in the English of Mexican Americans. *Language and Speech, 17,* 255–270.

Bodenhausen, G. V., and R. S. Wyer, Jr. (1985). Effects of stereotypes on decision making and information processing strategies. *Journal of*

Personality and Social Psychology, 48, 267–282.

Brewer, M. B. (1979). In-group bias in the minimal intergroup situation: A cognitive motivational analysis. *Psychological Bulletin, 86,* 307–324.

Campbell, D. T. (1958). Common fate, similarity, and other indices of the status of aggregates of persons as social entities. *Behavioral Science, 3,* 14–25.

Carver, C. S., F. X. Gibbons, W. G. Stephan, D. C. Glass, and I. Katz. (1979). Ambivalence and evaluative response amplification. *Bulletin of the Psychonomic Society, 13,* 50–52.

Carver, C. S., D. C. Glass, M. L. Snyder, and I. Katz. (1977). Favorable evaluations of stigmatized others. *Personality and Social Psychology Bulletin, 3,* 232–235.

Chang, W. B. C., and M. U. Araujo. (1975). Interpreters for the defense: Due process for the non-English speaking defendant. *California Law Review, 63,* 801–823.

Crocker, J., D. B. Hannah, and R. Weber. (1983). Person memory and causal attributions. *Journal of Personality and Social Psychology, 44,* 55–66.

Darley, J. M., and B. Latane. (1968). Bystander intervention in emergencies: Diffusion of responsibility. *Journal of Personality and Social Psychology, 8,* 377–383.

Doise, W., G. Csepeli, H. Dann, C. Gouge, K. Larsen, and A. Ostell. (1972). An experimental investigation into the formation of intergroup relations. *European Journal of Social Psychology, 2,* 202–204.

Dovidio, J. F. (1991). *Bias in the minimal intergroup situation among African Americans, Latinos, and Non-Hispanic Whites.* Unpublished manuscript, Colgate University, Department of Psychology, Hamilton, NY.

Dovidio, J. F., N. Evans, and R. B. Tyler. (1986). Racial stereotypes: The contents of their cognitive representations. *Journal of Experimental Social Psychology, 22,* 22–37.

Dovidio, J. F., and S. L. Gaertner. (1981). The effects of race, status, and ability on helping behavior. *Social Psychology Quarterly, 44,* 192–203.

———. (1983). The effects of sex, status, and ability on helping behavior. *Journal of Applied Social Psychology, 13,* 191–205.

———. (1986). Prejudice, discrimination, and racism: Historical trends and contemporary approaches. In J. F. Dovidio and S. L. Gaertner (Eds.), *Prejudice, Discrimination, and Racism* (pp. 1–34). Orlando, FL: Academic Press.

———. (1991). Changes in the nature and expression of racial prejudice. In H. Knopke, J. Norrell, and R. Rogers (Eds.), *Opening Doors: An Appraisal of Race Relations in Contemporary America* (pp. 201–241). Tuscaloosa: University of Alabama Press.

Dovidio, J. F., Mann, J., and Gaertner, S. L. (1989). Resistance to affirmative action: The implications of aversive racism. In F. Blanchard and R. Crosby (Eds.), *Affirmative Action in Perspective* (pp. 81–102). New York or Berlin: Springer-Verlag.

Edwards, J. E., P. J. Thomas, P. Rosenfeld P, and J. L. Bower. (1989, August). *Moving for employment: Are Hispanics less geographically mobile than Anglos and Blacks?* Paper presented at the Annual Meeting of the Academy of Management, Washington, DC.

Ferdman, B. M. (1989). Affirmative action and the challenge of the color-blind perspective. In F. A. Blanchard and F. J. Crosby (Eds.), *Affirmative Action in Perspective* (pp. 169–176). New York or Berlin: Springer-Verlag.

Fiske, S. T. (1982). Schema-triggered affect: Applications to social perception. In M. S. Clark and S.T. Fiske (Eds.), *The Seventeenth Annual Carnegie Symposium Cognition* (pp. 55–78). Hillsdale, NJ: Lawrence Erlbaum.

Fiske, S. T., and S. E. Taylor. (1984). *Social Cognition.* Reading, MA: Addison-Wesley.

Gaertner, S. L. (1973, April). *Helping behavior and anti-Semitism among black and white communities.* Paper presented at the Annual Convention of the Eastern Psychological Association, Washington, DC.

———. (1976). Nonreactive measures in racial attitude research: A focus on "Liberals." In P. Katz (Ed.), *Toward the Elimination of Racism* (pp. 183–211). New York: Pergamon.

———. (1985, March). *When groups merge: Reducing the salience of group boundaries.* Paper presented at the American Educational Research Association Annual Meeting, Chicago.

Gaertner, S. L., and J. F. Dovidio. (1977). The subtlety of white racism, arousal, and helping behavior. *Journal of Personality and Social Psychology, 35,* 691–707.

———. (1986). The aversive form of racism. In J. F. Dovidio and S. L. Gaertner (Eds.), *Prejudice, Discrimination, and Racism* (pp. 61–89). Orlando, FL: Academic Press.

———. (1991). *Reducing Bias: The Common Ingroup Identity Model.* Unpublished manuscript, University of Delaware, Newark.

Gaertner, S. L., and J. R. McLaughlin. (1983). Racial stereotypes: Associations and ascriptions of positive and negative characteristics. *Social Psychology Quarterly, 46,* 23–30.

Gerbner, G., L. Gross, N. Signorielli, and M. Morgan. (1986). *Television's mean world: Violence Profile No. 14–15*. Philadelphia: University of Pennsylvania, Annenberg School of Communications.

Giles, H., and P. Powesland. (1975). *Speech Style and Social Evaluation*. New York: Academic Press.

Greenberg, B. S., and P. Baptista-Fernandez. (1980). Hispanic Americans: The new minority on television. In B. S. Greenberg (Ed.), *Life on Television: Content Analyses of U.S. TV Drama* (pp. 3–12). Norwood, NJ: Ablex.

Hewstone, M. (1989). Changing stereotypes with disconfirming information. In D. Dar-Tal, V. F. Graumann, A. W. Kruglanski, and W. Stroebe (Eds.), *Stereotyping and Prejudice* (pp. 207–233). New York or Berlin: Springer-Verlag.

Hewstone, M., M. H. Bond, and K. Wan. (1983). Social facts and social attributions: The explanation of intergroup differences in Hong Kong. *Social Cognition, 2*, 142–157.

Hewstone, M., J. Jaspers, and M. Lalljee. (1982). Social representations, social attribution, and social identity: The intergroup images of "public" and "comprehensive" schoolboys. *European Journal of Social Psychology, 12*, 241–269.

Hogg, M. A., and J. C. Turner. (1987). Intergroup behavior, self-stereotyping, and the salience of social categories. *British Journal of Social Psychology, 26*, 325–340.

Howard, J. M., and M. Rothbart. (1980). Social categorization for in-group and out-group behavior. *Journal of Personality and Social Psychology, 38*, 301–310.

Huddy, L., and D. O. Sears. (1990). Qualified support for bilingual education: Some policy implications. *Annals of the American Academy of Political and Social Science, 508*, 119–134.

Jackman, M. R., and M. J. Muha. (1984). Education and intergroup attitudes: Moral enlightenment, superficial democratic commitment, or ideological refinement? *American Sociological Review, 49*, 751–769.

Jones, J. M. (1986). Racism: A cultural analysis of the problem. In J. F. Dovidio and S. L. Gaertner *(Eds.), Prejudice, Discrimination, and Racism* (pp. 279–314). Orlando, FL: Academic Press.

Klatzky, R. L., G. L. Martin, and R. A. Kane. (1982). Increase in social-category activation on processing of visual information. *Social Cognition, 1*, 95–109.

Kline, B. B., and J. R. Dovidio. (1982, April). *Effects of race, sex, and qualifications on predictions of a college applicant's performance.*

Paper presented at the annual meeting of the Eastern Psychological Association, Baltimore.

Kovel, J. (1970). *White Racism: A Psychohistory*. New York: Pantheon.

Kulik, J. (1983). Confirmatory attribution and the perpetuation of social beliefs. *Journal of Personality and Social Psychology, 44*, 1171–1181.

Lichter, S. R., L. S. Lichter, S. Rothman, and D. Admundson. (1987). Prime-time prejudice: TV's images of blacks and Hispanics. *Public Opinion, 4*, 13–16.

Liebert, R. M., and J. Sprafkin. (1988). *The Early Window: Effects of Television on Children and Youth* (3rd ed.). Elmsford, NY: Pergamon.

Lipton, J. P. (1983). Racism in the jury box: The Hispanic defendant. *Hispanic Journal of the Behavioral Sciences, 5*, 275–290.

Locci, S. C., and E. L. Carranza. (1990). Attitudes toward Chicanos by students in Mexican American Studies classes: A research note. *Hispanic Journal of the Behavioral Sciences, 12*, 397–407.

Marin, G. (1984). Stereotyping Hispanics: The differential effect of research method, label, and degree of contact. *International Journal of Intercultural Relations, 8*, 17–27.

McGarty, C., and R. Penny. (1988). Categorization, accentuation, and social judgment. *British Journal of Social Psychology, 27*, 147–157.

Meyer, D. E., and R. W. Schvaneveldt. (1971). Facilitation in recognizing pairs of words: Evidence of dependence between retrieval operations. *Journal of Experimental Psychology, 90*, 227–234.

Mullen, B., and L. T. Hu. (1989). Perceptions of ingroup and outgroup variability: A meta-analytic integration. *Basic and Applied Social Psychology, 10*, 233–252.

Park, B., and M. Rothbart. (1982). Perception of outgroup homogeneity and levels of social categorization: Memory for the subordinate attributes of ingroup and outgroup members. *Journal of Personality and Social Psychology, 42*, 1050–1068.

Perdue, C. W., J. F. Dovidio, M. B. Gurtman, and R. B. Tyler. (1990). "Us" and "Them": Social categorization and the process of intergroup bias. *Journal of Personality and Social Psychology, 59*, 475–486.

Pettigrew, T. F., G. M. Frederickson, D. T. Knobel, N. Glazer, and R. Ueda. (1982). *Prejudice*. Cambridge, MA: Belknap.

Piliavin, J. A., J. F. Dovidio, S. L. Gaertner, and R. D. Clark, III. (1981). *Emergency intervention*. New York: Academic Press.

Ramirez, A. (1988). Racism toward Hispanics: A culturally monolithic society. In P. Katz and D. Taylor (Eds.), *Towards the elimination of racism: Profiles in controversy* (pp. 137–157). New York: Plenum.

Rothbart, M., M. Evans, and S. Fulero. (1979). Recall of confirming events: Memory processes and the maintenance of social stereotypes. *Journal of Experimental Social Psychology, 15*, 343–355.

Ryan, E. B., and M. A. Carranza. (1975). Evaluative reactions toward speakers of standard English and Mexican American accented English. *Journal of Personality and Social Psychology, 31*, 855–863.

Saunders, L. (1954). *Cultural Differences and Medical Care: The Case of Spanish-speaking People of the Southwest.* New York: Russell Sage.

Schuman, H., C. Steeh, and L. Bobo. (1985). *Racial Attitudes in America: Trends and Interpretations.* Cambridge, MA: Harvard University Press.

Sibicky, M., and J. F. Dovidio. (1986). Stigma of psychological therapy: Stereotypes, interpersonal reactions, and the self-fulfilling prophecy. *Journal of Counseling Psychology, 33*, 148–154.

Skov, R. B., and S. J. Sherman. (1986). Information-gathering processes: Diagnosticity, hypothesis confirmatory strategies, and perceived hypothesis confirmation. *Journal of Experimental Social Psychology, 22*, 93–121.

Smith, E. R., and N. R. Branscombe. (1986). *Stereotypes can be Processed Automatically.* Unpublished manuscript, Purdue University, Lafayette, IN.

Snyder, M., E. D. Tanke, and E. Berscheid. (1977). Social perception and interpersonal behavior: On the self-fulfilling nature of social stereotypes. *Journal of Personality and Social Psychology, 35*, 656–666.

Stein, D. D., J. A. Hardyck, and M. B. Smith. (1965). Race and belief. An open and shut case. *Journal of Personality and Social Psychology, 1*, 281–299.

Stephan, C. W., and W. G. Stephan. (1986). Habla ingles? The effects of language translation on simulated juror decisions. *Journal of Applied Social Psychology, 16*, 577–589.

Thompson, J. S., W. G. Stephan, and R. W. Schvaneveldt. (1980, March). *The organization of social stereotypes in semantic memory.* Paper presented at the Annual Meeting of the Rocky Mountain Psychological Association, Tucson, AZ.

U.S. Department of Labor, Bureau of Labor Statistics. (1988). *Employment and earnings* (Vol. 35, No. 7). Washington, DC: Government Printing Office.

Vaca, N. A. (1970). The Mexican American in the social sciences: II. 1936–1970. *El Grito, 4*, 17–51.

Weigel, R. H., and P. W. Howes. (1985). Conceptions of racial prejudice: Symbolic racism revisited. *Journal of Social Issues, 41*, 117–138.

White, T. J., and W. E. Sedlacek. (1987). White student attitudes toward blacks and Hispanics: Programming implications. *Journal of Multicultural Counseling and Development, 15*, 171–183.

Wilder, D. A. (1981). Perceiving persons as a group: Categorization and intergroup relations. In D. L. Hamilton (Ed.), *Cognitive processes in stereotyping and intergroup behavior* (pp. 213–257). Hillsdale, NJ: Lawrence Erlbaum.

Wilder, D. A., and P. N. Shapiro. (1984). Role of outgroup cues in determining social identity. *Journal of Personality and Social Psychology, 47*, 342–348.

Wilkes, R. E., and H. Valencia. (1989). Hispanics and blacks in television commercials. *Journal of Advertising, 18*, 19–25.

Zintz, M. V. (1969). *Education across cultures.* Dubuque, IA: Kendall/Hunt.

24

Cultural Differences and Discrimination:

Samoans Before a Public Housing Eviction Board

Richard Lempert
Karl Monsma

In the 1971 case, *Griggs v. Duke Power* (401 U.S. 424), the United States Supreme Court held that if an employment test (or other mechanism for screening job applicants) had a disparate impact on a group protected by Title VII of The Civil Rights Act of 1964, discrimination in violation of the Act would be presumed unless the employer could prove the "job-relatedness" of the test. (For details on the *Griggs* case, see England 1992 chap. 5.) The *Griggs* case represents a high-water mark in the Supreme Court's jurisprudence of discrimination, for it establishes proof rules that can catch both intentional and inadvertent discriminators in their net. Under the Fourteenth Amendment, discrimination ordinarily requires evidence of unequal treatment and not just a disparate impact; when the *Griggs* case was decided Title VII could have been interpreted in the same way.

What the *Griggs* test does not recognize is that the very concept of discrimination is contestable. In assuming that job-relatedness negates the discriminatory implications of proven disparate impacts, the Court ignores the possibility that accepted criteria of job performance (e.g., punctuality) in themselves may privilege the performance standards of one social group vis-à-vis another and may endure precisely because they embody a dominant group's understanding of proper behavior. It is not clear that in *Griggs*

the Justices perceived this issue; but if they did, one can sympathize with their reluctance to address it. For when one enters this realm, which we call *cultural discrimination*, the concept of discrimination becomes problematic, as discrimination can be situated as much in perspectives on behavior and outcomes as in behavior and outcomes themselves. For this reason the concept "discrimination" has long been contested political territory, even if in most debates about discrimination, the courts and other participants studiously ignore this fact.

Identifying Discrimination

We illustrate these points and elucidate the concept of cultural discrimination by examining the decisions made by an informal tribunal—the Hawaii Housing Authority's (HHA) eviction board.

. . . [Conventional empirical approaches] treat discrimination as a residual category. To use ethnic discrimination as an example, if a significant bivariate relationship exists between ethnicity and the likelihood of an adverse outcome, the conventional approach does not conclude that discrimination exists unless the relationship persists when other factors that might affect outcomes regardless of ethnicity are also taken into account. When, however, ethnicity adds significantly to the ability of other variables to predict adverse outcomes, we regard that as evidence of ethnic discrimination. The more adequately we have accounted for other variables that might have affected the outcome, the more certain we are that such discrimination has occurred.

This conventional approach does not, however, allow one to trace out all the disadvantaging implications of ethnicity, no matter how adequately other variables that might influence the decision-maker are identified and measured. First, there is the familiar problem of institutional discrimination. A sentencing judge, for example, may weigh a defendant's prior arrests the same, regardless of the ethnicity of the defendant. However, discriminatory decisions by police or complainants may result in more frequent or more serious prior arrests for the typical minority defendant than for the typical White defendant.

Second, there is what we call "cultural discrimination," a phenomenon typically ignored in studies of discrimination in legal decision-making. Decision-makers may value certain behaviors and devalue others, regardless of the ethnic identity of the person exhibiting them. But the decision-makers' values may reflect their cultural roots, and they may fail to respect or even to recognize the ways the behavior of others is part of a different cultural value system. For example, a state legislature may make it illegal for parents to withdraw children from school before age 16, and the state's judges may punish Amish parents who violate the law in the same way they would punish non-Amish parents. Not only does this law and its enforcement fail to respect the reasons why Amish beliefs counsel against schooling past the eighth grade (*Wisconsin v. Yoder*, 406 U.S. 205 [1972]), it also fails to recognize that schooling until at least age 16 came to seem "natural" to the state's citizens only when urbanization and the mechanization of agriculture reduced the value of child labor relative to that of more educated adults. Thus both the makers and enforcers of compulsory schooling laws have acted without considering that, if agricultural production statewide were technologically similar to that of the Amish, withdrawing children from school at age 14 might seem "natural."

While the legal system provides ready examples of cultural discrimination (Post 1988), the phenomenon is not limited to legal decision-makers. . . . [We are interested in] members of a particular ethnic group who, in comparison to others from the same social class, are disadvantaged by the application of apparently legitimate criteria in a universalistic fashion. The "legitimate criteria" reflect cultural understandings shared by the judges but not by all of those judged. . . .

Cultural discrimination has been most readily identified in education. Various authors have discussed how language and other culturally acquired characteristics children bring to school can affect their treatment, and ultimately their success, in educational institutions (Erickson and Mohatt

1982; Labov 1972; Lareau 1989; Philips 1983). . . . We illustrate the implications of culture for outcomes in a different setting—an informal legal tribunal—and add to the existing literature, not only by emphasizing the problematic and political nature of what counts as discrimination, but also in other important ways.

. . . [I]n most studies that show people are disadvantaged because of cultural traits, class is confounded with culture. Our study, however, deals only with low-income public housing tenants, all of whom would be conventionally categorized as lower class. This allows us to avoid culture-class confusion, because variation among our subjects cannot be due to class differences.

. . . [M]uch of the research on cultural disadvantages in school deals with such characteristics as accents, abilities brought to the classroom, game-playing patterns, and the like. These are noncognitive factors—students unthinkingly bring such disadvantaging characteristics with them—and members of the dominant culture are ordinarily unaware that such culturally conditioned characteristics elicit their negative responses. However the cultural behavior we examine, excuse making, is cognitive. Our subjects do think about what excuses to give and attempt to construct excuses that will be accepted. Judges responding to these excuses similarly consider—and indeed discuss—the validity of the excuses they hear. Thus, our example shows how cultural understandings can limit even conscious cognitive efforts to behave in ways acceptable to a dominant culture and can lead to considered decisions that reject another's cultural motivations, even while recognizing and on occasion appreciating them.

In examining how Samoans fare before the HHA's eviction board, we are observing an unfamiliar minority group before an unusual court. This situation, in fact, enhances our ability to identify and explore nuances of cultural discrimination, and what we learn contains important general lessons. The different layers we peel away in our search for discrimination caution against too readily accepting the conclusions of studies limited to data that are less rich. Moreover, cultural discrimination of the sort we identify is also likely to exist in other situations where members of one class or status group pass judgment on members of another. . . .

Data and Subjects

The Research Setting

We examine the legal decisions of the Hawaii Housing Authority's (HHA) eviction board from 1966 through 1985. This board consisted of a group of citizen-volunteers whose assent was required for the HHA to evict a tenant. . . .

Throughout the years 1966 to 1985, procedures before the eviction board were informal. Tenants usually appeared without lawyers. The HHA's case was briefly presented, usually by questioning the housing project manager, and the tenant could respond however he or she wanted. Almost always the HHA's charges were admitted. In three-quarters of the cases, the charge was nonpayment of rent, and the fact of nonpayment was almost always indisputable; but even when some other lease violation was charged, like fighting or keeping pets, the tenant usually admitted the violation and made excuses for it. Ordinarily, after the tenant presented explanations, promises, or excuses, board members, the HHA's prosecutor, and occasionally the project manager questioned the tenant. Throughout, the tone was informal, and there was considerable effort to ensure that the tenant understood what was being said. The typical hearing took between 20 and 30 minutes. . . .

Only some of the HHA's eviction files included information on ethnicity. Where this information was missing, we coded ethnicity into two categories, Samoan or non-Samoan, based on first and last names. Married couples were coded as Samoan if either partner had a Samoan first or last name. The coding was done by a sociology graduate student native to Hawaii and conversant with island culture. Since Samoan names are usually distinctive, we have confidence in this coding.

In addition to the data collected from the HHA's files, in 1987 we conducted semi-structured interviews, usually lasting 30 to 90 minutes, with the HHA's prosecutors, board members, and others who had been connected with the eviction process from 1966 on. This group includes the four people who prosecuted most of the cases in our sample, almost all eviction board members (including every chairperson), all the current housing project managers and many former ones, staff supervisors (including current and past Executive Directors), the two legal aid paralegals who most often appeared in eviction actions, and private and legal aid lawyers who served on occasion as defense counsel. The majority of those interviewed were not Caucasian, although Caucasians and people of Japanese ancestry were the most frequently represented ethnic groups. Other interviewees were of Chinese, Hawaiian, Filipino, Korean, Samoan, or mixed heritages. The board members were citizen-volunteers from a variety of backgrounds. Apart from the two public housing tenants on each panel, most were from the middle class. . . .

These interviews complement our file data with information about the observations and attitudes of those who, apart from the tenants, figured most prominently in the eviction process. In addition we attended and either recorded or took detailed notes on all eviction board hearings held during the summers of 1969 and 1987. . . .

About Samoans in Hawaii

Although our data only allow us to investigate discrimination against Samoans, we expected that if any group were discriminated against in the eviction process it would be the Samoans. In part we expected this because our interviewees often spontaneously described problems with Samoans. Only three other ethnic groups were similarly mentioned (Laotians, Vietnamese, and Tongans). Not only were there far more mentions of Samoans than of other groups, but when members of other groups were mentioned as troublemakers, the trouble often involved difficulties with Samoans.

More importantly, we thought Samoans were the likeliest victims of discrimination because Samoans in Hawaii are a particularly disadvantaged group. Their per capita income is the lowest of any ethnic group in Hawaii for which separate statistics are kept, (Kincaid and Yum 1987; U.S. Commission on

Civil Rights 1979). More than half of the Samoan adults in Hawaii have nine years of school or less (Baker 1986). Unemployment rates for Samoans are high (Hect, Orans, and Janes 1986). A disproportionate number of Hawaii's Samoans are in prison (Howard 1986), and Samoans in Hawaii are generally regarded as a violent and dangerous people (Howard 1986; Hect et al. 1986). Indeed, even among California's Samoan immigrants, it is recognized that "Samoans in Hawaii are stigmatized" (Janes 1990). This view is confirmed in a study of the opinions held of each other by five Hawaiian ethnic groups (Caucasians, Japanese Americans, and immigrant-generation Filipinos, Vietnamese, and Samoans) [Yum and Wang 1983]. . . .

Table 24.1
Percentage Distribution of Reason for Subpoena Among Samoans and Other Ethnic Groups: 1966 to 1985

Reason for Subpoena	Percentage Among Samoans	Percentage Among Other Ethnic Groups
Falsification, fraud	10.3	8.3
Nonpayment of rent	78.5	72.6
Guests	3.8	4.2
Pets	1.9	6.2
Other trouble	5.4	8.7
Total percent	99.9	100.0
Number of cases	261	1,000

Note: X^2 = 12.08, d.f. = 4

Overall Samoans account for about 21 percent of both the eviction actions the HHA commenced by subpoena and the cases in which the hearings were held. Because we have no information on the ethnic composition of the HHA's housing projects, we cannot say whether Samoans are disproportionately represented in these data. . . .

Reasons for Eviction

Samoans charged with violating HHA rules were somewhat more likely than other tenants to be subpoenaed for fraud or nonpayment of rent and less likely to be subpoenaed for pet violations and other kinds of troublesome behavior (see Table 24.1). The ethnic difference in subpoenas for fraud may

occur because many Samoan tenants spoke English poorly or not at all. Fraud usually involved accusations of concealing family income, and the tenant's defense was often that he or she didn't understand that certain income had to be reported.

The proportion of subpoenas issued for nonpayment of rent may be slightly higher among Samoans than among other ethnic groups because Samoans in the United States often face demands for money which they feel they cannot deny. Samoan families that help members emigrate to the United States often expect regular cash payments in return (Holmes 1974), and all Samoan families expect that even distant members will contribute cash toward special occasions, such as funerals and weddings (Ablon 1970, 1971). Churches, too, expect regular financial contributions, and churches are especially important institutions for many Samoan immigrants. Thus Samoans are more likely than tenants from other ethnic groups to experience strong social pressures to spend their rent money for other purposes. Alternatively, the high proportion of financial cases among Samoans may simply reflect the fact that they are less likely than other tenants to engage in nonfinancial troublesome behavior. This may be true in the case of pets, since Samoans seldom keep dogs, but if project managers and tenant board members can be believed, it is almost certainly *not* true of fighting, noisemaking, and similar offenses. Perhaps the underrepresentation of Samoans in such cases is because Samoans are reluctant to complain about each other or because non-Samoans are intimidated into keeping quiet.

The high proportion of Samoans subpoenaed for nonpayment of rent or for fraud is not explained by changes over time in the HHA's eviction process. The percentage of cases brought for financial reasons is higher among Samoans than among non-Samoans in all time periods we use to distinguish important changes in the eviction process.

Evidence for Discrimination

. . . [Analysis of quantitative data on HHA evictions indicates] that Samoans accused of financial violations fare worse in the eviction process than similarly situated non-Samoans. We may call this Samoan disadvantage "discrimination," but we should be aware of precisely what this means: Samoans threatened with eviction have a somewhat worse chance of remaining in project housing than tenants from other ethnic groups who are like them [in terms of case characteristics, tenant-authority history, and various household characteristics, such as income and financial resources, number of children, and other factors].

Qualitative Evidence From Interviews

. . . [It is certainly possible that] discrimination occurs; that is, that board decisions are motivated by prejudice against Samoans. Samoans are socioeconomically the least advantaged of the various ethnic groups that populate Hawaii and are apparently stigmatized on this account. In deciding whether to evict, the board members may be biased against Samoans, or the HHA's prosecutor or manager-complainants may push harder for eviction when Samoans are involved. Interviews with prosecutors, project managers, and board members indicate that some do hold negative stereotypes of Samoans.

For example, one prosecutor, talking generally about cases in which inoperative vehicles had been parked in project lots, said he would tell the owner of such a car:

> I don't care if it is up on blocks and you are going to have to have 50 Samoans come out and help you carry it away—two weeks from now the car is gone, or it is there, and that is what decides whether you are going to stay or not stay.

It is instructive that the prosecutor assumed that Samoans would be involved and that the solution might involve Samoan manual labor.

One board chairperson conveyed his image of Samoans in apologizing for the fact that a nonpayment case we observed was nothing special:

> This wasn't a very good case for you . . . it was one of our real rinky dink cases. We didn't have the Samoans, we didn't have the shouting, we didn't have the language barrier, we didn't have any witnesses. . . .

And, a longtime project manager, admired by tenants for his care and understanding, acknowledged the stereotype:

> Even I will say, "Ooo, that's a wild one," or "he's a Samoan," but really I had Japanese who were just as ornery in talking to me; yeah, like any other strains. You know, it is funny, as I recollect, prejudice is, I think, a matter of perception or you see . . . maybe a Black guy who gets hostile and there is [nothing] there, but if [you see] that, then I guess it exists.

The attitudes reflected in these remarks might suggest that managers and prosecutors push harder for eviction when Samoans are defendants, and that board members are more likely to hold against Samoans in close cases. But . . . in our interviews, board members and others were more likely to comment on the special situation of Samoans than they were to make remarks suggesting generalized prejudice. For example, a former board chairperson, when asked about her stance toward nonpayment of rent cases, said about Samoans and Micronesians:

> I felt there were cultural and language barriers often. I think some people used them as excuses, but I think in a lot of cases people were not used to the kinds of system that they needed to respond to in order to remain in public housing. . . . And that didn't mean that the Authority did not have the right to collect their rent, but it became real difficult for the board to often make that decision [to evict], because I honestly don't think that the person who was responsible [for] that rent understood the expectations from their cultural context.

A former board member, when asked whether any special accommodations were made for Samoans who had, in their own minds, good reasons for spending rent money on something other than their rent (e.g., contributing to a funeral in Samoa), commented:

> I think all of us had an empathy, and perhaps even a sympathy, for these folks [Samoans], because we realized that we always had to stop and think, well maybe they really don't understand. We always had to appreciate the cultural difference,

and I think all of us took that into consideration. However, we tried to end up judging them the same way we would anybody else [p. 901]. . . .

Cultural Discrimination

The three board members we have quoted, and others as well, all realized that Samoans faced substantial pressure to spend rent money to meet their cultural obligations. They had, in different degrees, sympathy for the Samoans' plight and saw their fellow board members as similarly understanding. However, ultimately all of them, with varying degrees of reluctance, concluded that if Samoans could not pay the rent by drawing on their "cultural situation" or in some other way, the board had to evict them.

If, as one board member said, the board ended up "judging [Samoans] the same way [it] would anybody else," the board did not discriminate within the meaning of the Fourteenth Amendment's Equal Protection Clause since this requires differential treatment on the basis of a protected characteristic, such as race. Yet if Samoans were not selected for harsh treatment because of their race, how can one explain the disadvantage that attaches to Samoans in quantitative [data on evictions]? We think the answer lies in the differing cultural logics of Samoan tenants and eviction board members: What seemed natural or appropriate to Samoans did not seem natural or appropriate to board members. In judging Samoans like anybody else, in failing to take for granted what Samoan tenants took for granted, the board produced a pattern of decisions similar to the pattern that might have resulted if Samoan ethnicity were intentionally treated as a factor weighing in favor of eviction. Our interviews and our knowledge of Samoan culture convince us that this pattern is primarily due to the unique ways Samoans were prone to excuse rent payment lapses.

The Quality of Excuses

The excuses most housing tenants give for skipping rent payments usually refer to factors beyond their control, such as illness, unemployment, thefts of wallets, and the like. The excuses Samoans offer, however, often

refer to sending money to relatives for weddings and funerals, traveling to Samoa for these purposes, and giving money to their church. To Westerners, these kinds of expenditures seem to be within a person's control; but to Samoans they may seem every bit as compelling as the need to pay doctors' bills.

Put simply, a good Samoan is a bad public housing tenant. Central in Samoan life are the *aiga* (extended family), the *matai* (family chief), and, especially in the United States, the church (Grattan [1948] 1985; Holmes 1974; Janes 1990). A Samoan achieves status through the *aiga* because Samoans share in the status of their *aigas* and because, in the case of males, the *aiga* chooses its own chiefs. As head of the family, the *matai* controls the family's property and allocates the family's wealth. While the degree of *matai* control over property has broken down in recent years as a cash economy has largely replaced the property-based subsistence economy in Samoa, a concomitant aspect of this change is that Samoans are expected to make cash contributions to their *matai* and *aiga*. Indeed, Samoan families often fund their relatives' emigration as an investment, with the return to the family taking the form of regular "remittances" once the relatives have gotten jobs (Ali'Ilima and Stover 1986). It is particularly important that cash gifts be sent in connection with certain ceremonial occasions, especially funerals and weddings (Ablon 1971). Not doing so dishonors both the individual (making it unlikely he will ever achieve chiefly status) and, if the family cannot make up the shortfall, the *aiga*. It may also mean that in a crisis situation the individual cannot count on the *aiga* for support.

Samoans in the United States often have relatives living near them, so the *aiga* can in part be reconstituted in this country. However, even when there are numbers of relatives in the United States, the larger part of the *aiga* and its *matai* are likely to live in Samoa. In these circumstances the church fills the gap and provides a general trans-family support network for its members. In return, however, Samoans are expected to support their church's needs in much the same way as they would support their *aiga's* requests. This means that Samoan churches in the

United States are another source of culturally-reinforced demands for funds. Facing such strong cultural pressures, Samoans may give rent money to the *aiga* or church. Board members treat rent payments as a primary obligation and can be particularly resentful if, as is often the case, the tenant's primary source of income comes from welfare. Thus, while board members may recognize the special pressures that Samoans face, most do not regard them as legitimate excuses for not paying the rent. . . . Another board member, who clearly recognized the cultural reasons for certain Samoan behavior patterns, similarly concluded:

> I think that many of the cultural things that have held up and have proven good in island countries cannot withstand the city. . . . [M]y feeling is . . . that if they come to this urban situation, nobody is forcing them, and they come to it; they must adjust to it. I am willing to take into consideration that [cultural reasons explain lease violations], but there comes a place where I think that they must adjust, and the two cultural patterns do not.

Another board member was less able to empathize. She commented that as a board member she had learned over time to be less sympathetic to tenants, and when asked how she had learned to overlook the "sob stories," she made it clear that for her, even the excuses got stale:

> Oh, well, from experience I guess. There are so many of them that come on and say, especially the Samoans; I mean they always say that they cannot pay their rent because they have to support the church and things like that. But after you get 10, 15 of them telling you the same things. . . .
> [Or funerals or things like that?]
> Yea, or they gotta go home; they gotta go back to Samoa because somebody is sick over there or things like that. But you know, when you come down to it, they are all on welfare, and they are using your money too—so you learn to become a little bit more, you know, you don't believe all the things that they tell you.

Sometimes, tenants' excuses may be hard to believe, but the excuses this board member mentions are credible within the context of Samoan culture, even if they are repeated by tenant after tenant. Perhaps if the excuse were that a wallet had been stolen or that a child had fallen ill, this board member, despite some skepticism, would have credited the reason.

Consider the following example of an excuse that worked for a tenant who at the time of the hearing owed $345.00 in rent. It was recorded in the summer of 1987, when the board had become quite strict, and virtually no excuses were effective.

> Prosecutor:
> How come you got behind in this?

> Tenant:
> Well, as I told them when they called that my boy had fell in the river and almost cut off his finger and I don't have medical for him because he is not my real son. It is her son, and I cannot get him under my medical until we sign more papers or get a lawyer to say he is going to be my son. So, I had to pay cash in order to get it done. They wouldn't let him go under my medical, and therefore the stitches and everything costs about $243.00 or something like that, and we were short already on the money.

The tenant then explained why, after three months, the debt still had not been paid up.

> Yeah, well that put us behind already right there, because rent was due, but then his finger was also due too. We had to save his finger, right? And then the following month when I got paid I had to cash my check, and I was in Waikiki, and I had to go to work. So when I had gotten to work and put all my things in my locker and locked it, somebody had broken into my locker and stole my money out of my locker. So, right there we were hurting for the whole month. I told them I would catch it up as soon as my next two pay checks, because I only get paid every two weeks. So there was no money or no way that I could get any money to pay it until I get paid.

Significantly, the chairperson began the board's private deliberations by saying that he believed the man's story with respect to both the injured finger and the stolen money. . . .

[A former] chairperson recognized the validity of Samoan excuses within a Samoan's cultural logic, but rather than do "as much as we possibly could" for these cases, he left what could be done strictly up to them:

> [W]e told [Samoans whose rent money had gone to meet *aiga* obligations] that they did help at one time and they helped someone in a period of need; now they are in a period of need. . . .
>
> And we would say, now it is your turn to go to the coalition in your time of need for them to help you. And if you can get that, fine. This is the parameters in which you have to deal. That's all.

As this chairperson's remarks indicate, even a willingness to credit Samoan excuses did not mean they would work. Indeed, some managers and board members went further and argued that the only way that Samoans could learn how to be "good" housing tenants was if particularly Samoan excuses were not tolerated. As one project manager said:

> We have a lot of Samoans at this project, and there is a Samoan custom that every time somebody dies, you give money to the family to help bring the family over from Samoa. I have the hardest time trying to change that custom, but little by little. [I tell them] you pay your rent first, then you help the family.

If this manager succeeds, he will be making his Samoans better public housing tenants, but worse Samoans. Ironically, he might also be depriving them of their ability to call upon church and family when, for good Western (or Samoan) reasons, the family falls behind on rent and needs a lump sum to clear its debt. Managers and board members report that once the crisis of eviction is real to them, Samoans are often able to acquire money from church or kinfolk to clear their debts. Samoans who have not contributed to the church or *aiga* cannot count on support from these sources.

Thus, despite some comments suggesting that some board members and HHA officials hold stereotypically negative views of Samoans, and despite data showing that, other measurable variables being equal, Samoans fare worse than other tenants in eviction hearings, it is difficult to say whether the HHA's eviction board discriminates against Samoans. The difficulty lies not in the opaqueness of the eviction process. . . . The difficulty exists because the Samoan example makes problematic what we mean by discrimination. There probably is no "legal" discrimination, for the board members are arguably responding in the same way to Samoans as they would to other tenants who made similar excuses. But other tenants seldom make similar excuses; they do not spend money as Samoans do, and their sense of appropriate excuses is different.

. . . The tools that Samoan culture provides are ill-suited to the end of persuading an eviction board to be lenient. Yet they are suited to other ends that Samoan tenants value, such as maintaining status within the *aiga*. Not only do Samoan tenants find themselves in a dilemma that other tenants need not confront, but often, because of the taken-for-granted nature of many cultural assumptions, they do not even recognize the dilemma they are in. Samoan excuses, real or made-up, do not move managers or board members who share a very different taken-for-granted world. For these reasons, Samoans are disadvantaged because of their ethnic heritage, just as surely as they would be if the board were peopled by bigots who would not give Samoans an even break. The Samoan disadvantage exists because Samoan tenants live where the rules of another culture dominate, and they must litigate cases before a board whose members, even while recognizing the distinctive features of Samoan culture, share the assumptions of the dominant culture and resist those of the dominated one. It is this form of cultural dominance that might be called *cultural discrimination*. . . .

Conclusion

We began our empirical analysis by noting that Samoans in Hawaii tend to be disadvantaged and stigmatized relative to other ethnic groups. Thus we thought they might be discriminated against in the housing eviction process. . . .

Instead a large part of the Samoan disadvantage seems to be related to how the board evaluated excuses. "Western" excuses like illness were accepted while "Samoan" excuses, like paying for an uncle's funeral, were not. Does this privileging of culturally familiar excuses over culturally unfamiliar ones constitute discrimination? From a broad sociological perspective one can answer yes. Consider Feagin and Eckberg's (1980) definition of racial or ethnic discrimination—"the practices and actions of dominant race-ethnic groups that have a differential and negative impact on subordinate race-ethnic groups" (p. 9). The Samoan disadvantage seems to fit this definition, except the practices that disadvantage Samoans are not so much those associated with a dominant ethnic group as they are those associated with a world view and values common across most assimilated ethnic groups in Western Europe and North America.

But what follows from defining the Samoan disadvantage as discrimination? Does it follow that we have identified an immoral practice that should be eliminated? Or is it reasonable to argue, as more than one board member did, that rejecting traditional Samoan excuses was fair because by moving to the United States and accepting welfare subsidies Samoans knowingly entered a social system that imposed constraints conflicting with their cultural obligations? Moreover, Samoans could learn the ways of the dominant culture, including how to formulate acceptable excuses. Thus, Samoan heritage is not the inescapable handicap it would be if the board were dominated by bigots. In these circumstances should Feagin and Eckberg's definition apply?

We may also ask whether legally remediable discrimination exists. The question is more complicated than it appears, for the law applies different tests of discrimination in different contexts. The most directly relevant case is *McCleskey v. Kemp* (481 U.S. 279 [1987]) which examined apparently discriminatory court decisions. In the *McCleskey* case the defendant argued that the Georgia death penalty statute was administered in a racially discriminatory fashion that violated the Eighth and the Fourteenth Amendments.

McCleskey presented the Supreme Court with statistics showing that in cases like his, murderers of White victims were more likely to receive the death penalty than murderers of Black victims. The Court held that the statistical evidence of discrimination did not help McCleskey, because it could not show that in his particular case there was an intent to discriminate on the basis of his victim's race. A similar attitude would mean that to show discrimination by the eviction board, Samoan tenants would have to show, not that they faced higher probabilities of eviction because they were Samoan, but that they were in fact evicted because they were Samoan rather than because of the lease provisions they violated. This is an almost impossible task, and the Court that decided the *McCleskey* case knew it.

A second approach is that taken by the Supreme Court in *Batson v. Kentucky* (476 U.S. 79 [1986]), the case which held that under the Equal Protection Clause of the Fourteenth Amendment a prosecutor could not base a peremptory challenge on a juror's race. This case, too, would be of little help to a Samoan claiming discrimination, because a *Batson* claim can be defeated if the prosecutor is able to give a plausible reason for challenging a juror. Reasons given for evicting Samoans are plausible so long as the board's cultural understandings are shared.

This brings us back to *Griggs v. Duke Power,* which we, called a "high-water mark" in the jurisprudence of discrimination. The *Griggs* test has the potential to condemn actions that reflect cultural discrimination, because it focuses on outcomes and makes intentions irrelevant. Nevertheless, even if we put aside the fact that *Griggs* was never intended to apply to court decisions but only to employment matters, the eviction board's decisions would be unlikely to be condemned. Suppose we regard HHA eviction board decisions as analogous to employment tests. Our data show that Samoans are disproportionately harmed by these decisions; thus the burden shifts to the HHA to show that the board's decisions were justified by some criterion that bears the same relationship to board decisions that job-relatedness has to employment decisions (i.e., it reflects the rationale for the test). What is this criterion? One obvious criterion is a tenant's ability to pay the rent owed if eviction is not ordered. By this criterion, Samoan tenants would prevail if the HHA could not show that tenants who gave "Samoan excuses" were worse risks for payment of rent owed than tenants who gave other excuses. Because Samoans faced with eviction might be able to mobilize aid from church or *aiga*, they might well be no worse risks.

The HHA, however, would point out that the law did not obligate them to give second chances to all who might succeed and would opt for a different criterion. They would argue that the board's commission—as is any court's—was to reach just decisions. Just court decisions ordinarily rest on past actions and excuses more than they focus on likely future performance. Thus, unless the conception of justice were disassociated from the evaluation of past behavior and redefined as accurate prediction, the *Griggs* standard, even if it applied, would not condemn the board's action as discriminatory. As far as justice is concerned, the law ordinarily partakes of dominant cultural understandings. A change in these understandings, at least among elite decision-makers, is a prerequisite to legal attacks on cultural discrimination in adjudicative settings.

Yet without changing its understandings, the HHA's eviction board appears to have eliminated the "cultural discrimination" we identified. By the time our 1987 fieldwork began, the board had retreated to formalism: The law allowed tenants to be evicted whenever they were behind in their rent, and the HHA, after years of trying, had persuaded the board to adopt the general policy of always evicting when rent was owed at the time of the hearing, regardless of the reason (Lempert 1989). Under this policy, Samoans are not disadvantaged vis-a-vis other tenants by the quality of their excuses—excuses do not count. But Samoans may still be disadvantaged in housing if their culture encourages them to give or lend money and consequently to owe rent when other tenants would not. Formalism, by silencing excuses, renders this disadvantage invisible. . . .

We are not the first to note disadvantages that people can suffer when judged by members of another culture. But the concern of most prior researchers, particularly those focusing on education, has been on situations where decision-makers do not realize the cultural roots of their taken-for-granted assumptions and thus misinterpret another's behavior. Indeed, some of this literature seems to carry the optimistic implication that, given people of good will, if cultural assumptions were obvious, problems of biased decision-making would disappear. Our research indicates that decision-makers may decide cases according to their own cultural understandings, even when they recognize, and to some extent respect, the cultural roots of others' actions. We suggest that when one culture's understandings dominate a decision-making arena, conflict with and the subordination of other cultures is inevitable, whether or not cultural differences are appreciated.

. . . [The processes studied here make] problematic the very label "discrimination." This is not to say that cultural discrimination is a misnomer, but in more ways than one discrimination is a matter of perspective. To perceive this is to realize that the definition of discrimination is an object of political struggle. Ultimately, it is power that will determine whether cultural discrimination becomes a legal as well as a sociological concept.

References

Ablon, Joan M. 1970. "The Samoan Funeral in Urban America." *Ethnology* 9:209–27.

——. 1971. "The Social Organization of an Urban Samoan Community." *Southwestern Journal of Anthropology* 27:75–96.

Ali'Ilima, Fay, and Mary Stover. 1986. "Life Histories," Pp. 123–45 in *The Changing Samoans: Behavior and Health in Transition*, edited by P. Baker, J. Hanna, and T. Baker. New York: Oxford University Press.

Baker, Thelma S. 1986. "Changing Socialization Patterns of Contemporary Samoans." Pp. 146–73 in *The Changing Samoans: Behavior and Health in Transition*, edited by P. Baker, J. Hanna, and T. Baker. New York: Oxford University Press.

England, Paula. 1992. *Comparable Worth: Theories and Evidence*. New York: Aldine de Guyter.

Erickson, Frederick, and Gerald Mohatt. 1982. "Cultural Organization of Participation Structures in Two Classrooms of Indian Students." Pp. 132–74 in *Doing the Ethnography of Schooling*, edited by G. Spindler. New York: Holt, Rinehart, and Winston.

Feagin, Joe R. and Douglas L. Eckberg. 1980. "Discrimination: Motivation, Action, Effects, and Context." *Annual Review of Sociology 6:* 1–20.

Grattan, F. J. H. [1948] 1985. *Introduction to Samoan Custom*. Papakura, New Zealand: R. McMillan.

Hect, Julia A., Martin Orans, and Craig R. Janes. 1986. "Social Settings of Contemporary Samoan." Pp. 39–62 in *The Changing Samoans: Behavior and Health in Transition*, edited by P. Baker, J. Hanna, and T. Baker. New York: Oxford University Press.

Holmes, Lowell. 1974. *Samoan Village*. New York: Holt, Rinehart, and Winston.

Holstein, James A. 1987. "Producing Gender Effects on Involuntary Mental Hospitalization." *Social Problems* 34:141–55.

Howard, Alan. 1986. "Samoan Coping Behavior," Pp. 394–418 in *The Changing Samoans: Behavior and Health in Transition*, edited by P. Baker, J. Hanna, and T. Baker. New York: Oxford University Press.

Janes, Craig R. 1990. *Migration, Social Change, and Health: A Samoan Community in Urban California*. Stanford, CA: Stanford University Press.

Kincaid, D. Lawrence, and Judy Ock Yum. 1987. "A Comparative Study of Korean, Filipino and Samoan Immigrants to Hawaii: Socioeconomic Consequences." *Human Organization* 46:70–77.

Labov, William. 1972. *Language in the Inner City*. Philadelphia, PA: University of Pennsylvania Press.

Lareau, Annette. 1989. *Home Advantage: Social Class and Parental Intervention in Elementary Education*. Philadelphia, PA: Falmer.

Lempert, Richard. 1989. "The Dynamics of Informal Procedure: The Case of a Public Housing Eviction Board." *Law and Society Review* 23:347–98.

Philips, Susan Urmston. 1983. *The Invisible Culture*. New York: Longman.

Post, Robert C. 1988. "Cultural Heterogeneity and Law: Pornography, Blasphemy, and the First Amendment." *California Law Review* 76:297–335.

U.S. Commission on Civil Rights, Hawaii Advisory Committee. 1979. "Immigration Issues in Hawaii: A Report of the Proceedings of a Consultation Conducted by the Hawaii Advisory Committee to the United States Commission on Civil Rights in Honolulu, Hawaii, 25 Aug. 1978." Washington, DC: Government Printing Office.

Yum, June Ock, and Georgette Wang. 1983. "Interethnic Perception and the Communication Behavior Among Five Ethnic Groups in Hawaii." *International Journal of Intercultural Relations* 7:285–308.

Reprinted from: Richard Lempert and Karl Monsma, "Cultural Differences and Discrimination: Samoans Before a Public Housing Eviction Board." In *American Sociological Association*, Volume 59, pp. 890–910. Copyright © 1994 by American Sociological Review. Reprinted by permission.

Sources and Consequences of Residential Segregation

One of the most persistent problems in American race and ethnic relations is the high level of residential segregation. In fact, sociologist Lawrence Bobo (1989) has termed residential segregation "the structural lynchpin" of contemporary U.S. racial inequality. Why is this issue so important? First, the location of real estate is strongly correlated with market value. Homes are the largest investment most Americans will ever make, and their value shapes the net worth of individuals and families. This, in turn, affects creditworthiness, helping or impairing the ability to take out loans to finance new businesses, children's college educations and other important activities. Further, residential location is also a marker of status and prestige with far-reaching implications in American society. The limited housing options of African Americans and other minorities both reflect and deepen patterns of racial inequality (Oliver and Shapiro 1995).

Residential location also shapes the quality of life in other ways. For instance, where one lives can determine the type and quality of education available for children as well as the social and cultural environment that families encounter. Recent studies show that neighborhood surroundings affect children's learning and development over and above household and school influences (Brooks-Gunn, Duncan, Klesanov, and Sealand 1993). In addition, neighborhoods differ sharply in levels of social pathology (e.g., crime rates), as well as in their proximity to recreation, shopping, and other amenities. Neighborhoods often vary in their access to municipal services and in their leverage to extract concessions from local governments. Some scholars, most notably Douglas Massey and his associates, have argued that residential segregation has helped to cause the growth of an urban African American "underclass" and the dissolution of minority community life (see Wacquant and Wilson, this volume) by concentrating the effects of job losses within a limited number of vulnerable neighborhoods (Massey and Denton 1993). Further, high levels of residential segregation also constrain opportunities for intergroup social contacts and impede the formation of interracial and interethnic friendships, limiting the chance that such relationships can break down stereotypes and change negative images of out-groups (Sigelman et al., this volume).

Researchers and community activists are increasingly concerned about race and ethnic differences in the exposure to environmental hazards such as industrial pollutants, noise, toxic wastes, and landfills, sometimes termed "locally undesirable land uses" (LU-LUs) (Been 1994). Such sites are not only aesthetically displeasing and can detract from the value of nearby properties but also present health risks, especially to children and the elderly. Some critics also contend that enforcement of environmental regulations is lax in minority neighborhoods (Bullard 1994). There are also concerns about hazards found within older homes and schools (e.g., lead-based paints and asbestos), which are inhabited disproportionately by African

Americans and Latino/a Americans (Ong and Blumenberg 1993).

Sociologists and policy-makers often measure segregation at the metropolitan level using a statistic called the "index of dissimilarity." This index is calculated to show the proportion of residents of a given racial or ethnic population who would have to relocate to other areas of the city in order to achieve racial or ethnic parity across Census tracts (combinations of neighborhoods). The index ranges from a minimum theoretical value of 0 to a maximum theoretical value of 100. Using U.S. Census data, Farley and Frey (1994) examined the changes in the levels of residential segregation for U.S. metropolitan areas between 1980 and 1990. Despite the passage of fair housing laws and the growing African American and Latino/a American middle classes, these researchers reported only slight overall changes in levels of metropolitan segregation during the 1980s. They calculated that the average metropolitan index of dissimilarity for African Americans dropped somewhat over this period, from 68.8 to 64.3. However, Latino/a Americans and Asian Americans actually became slightly more residentially concentrated in metropolitan America during this decade (Farley and Frey 1994).

Further, even during this period of modest overall improvement, some metropolitan areas actually experienced a rise in African American segregation. Worse yet, researchers like Massey, Farley, and others have documented a particularly ominous pattern, which is sometimes termed *hypersegregation*. This refers to situations in which African Americans are almost completely segregated, and where indices of dissimilarity approach the theoretical maximum of 100. According to Farley and Frey (1994), for example, the most segregated metropolitan area in the U.S. in 1990 was Gary, Indiana, with a score of 91. Gary was followed by Detroit with 89, Chicago with 87, and Cleveland with 86. Approximately 15 U.S. metropolitan areas had scores of 80 or above. The implications of this are staggering: in these cities, at least 80 percent of African American residents would have to relocate to other Census tracts in order to attain a proportional distribution.

In general, levels of segregation tend to be higher in the larger, older cities of the Northeast and upper Midwest. These urban settings have largely stagnant housing stocks, with long-settled neighborhoods populated by well-defined successions of ethnic groups. In addition, these cities have now experienced nearly three decades of white flight to the suburbs, and African Americans in inner-city Census tracts tend to have low average income levels, and therefore are often unable to relocate. Despite the vivid legacy of racial oppression in the South, average levels of residential segregation are somewhat lower in Sunbelt cities than in the North. And, interestingly, the most segregated Southern cities are not in the traditional Deep South; rather, they include the largely white retirement meccas of Florida, including Naples, Sarasota, and Fort Myers (Farley and Frey 1994).

The surprisingly low levels of segregation in Sunbelt cities result partly from historical regional differences in settlement and annexation patterns (Farley, Steeh, Jackson, Krysan, and Reeves 1994 and this volume). Rates of economic growth and the timing of housing construction are also important predictors of segregation, and these factors help to explain regional variations. Because discrimination was illegal in homes and apartments built after 1969, levels of segregation are especially low in metropolitan areas where growth rates are high and where much of the housing stock is of recent origin. These conditions accurately characterize many cities in the South and Southwest.

In addition, segregation levels tend to be relatively low in university communities. Given that education levels are linked with racial attitudes, white residents in these areas may have greater tolerance for African American or Latino American neighbors than residents of other metropolitan areas. Military-base communities also have low levels of racial segregation, because (a) base housing is often assigned; and (b) these cities have much greater population turnover and fewer long-settled neighborhoods that would be likely to resist racial integration (Farley and Frey 1994).

Historians tell us that at the beginning of the twentieth century, U.S. cities were less segregated than they are today. What processes produced the current high levels of racial segregation? Between 1900 and 1920 the first wave of the Great Migration from the South to northern cities of African Americans in search of jobs, especially in manufacturing industries, created new competition for affordable housing. In many cities, European Americans responded with campaigns of violence and intimidation; firebombing became a popular way to discourage African Americans from moving into white ethnic neighborhoods. Another common strategy of racial and ethnic exclusion was to add a restrictive covenant to a property deed; through such a covenant, African Americans (and other minorities) could be prohibited occupying a given property for a given period of time.

Ironically, the federal government—now a strong force for desegregation—actually played an important role in creating and sustaining segregated neighborhoods (Farley and Frey 1994). When the Federal Housing Administration (FHA) developed mortgages in the 1930s, they promoted the use of color-coded maps as a guide to the creditworthiness of local neighborhoods. FHA officials and financial institutions assumed that neighborhoods in racial transition—coded red on these maps—were downwardly mobile and hence posed risks for lenders and borrowers. For years thereafter, such discriminatory practices were endorsed by federal agencies, and by the banking and real-estate industries. Real-estate agents were encouraged to steer clients toward racially homogenous areas, and professional codes prohibited them from introducing minorities into white neighborhoods.

Although these practices were important causes of (hyper-)segregation, other developments also contributed to this problem (Farley et al. 1994). For instance, large-scale suburbanization following World War II, promoted by expanded mortgage lending and highway development, made it possible for many working- and middle-class European Americans to leave inner-city neighborhoods. These early developments also set the stage for a subsequent period of "white flight," which occurred in response to school busing and urban racial conflict during the 1960s. Although some African Americans made it to the suburbs, they tended to cluster in communities that were populated by other minorities. Predominantly white suburbs developed strategies aimed at restricting the access of African Americans, and suburban institutions—zoning commissions, schools, police, and so on—pursued policies that demonstrated insensitivity, and even outright hostility, toward minority group members. During the 1960s and 1970s, urban renewal projects razed substandard housing in many downtown areas. Later, public housing complexes were often built in these same urban tracts. Because minorities have disproportionately resided in public housing, the practice of concentrating such projects in inner-city areas only intensified the problem of segregation.

Since the 1960s, we have witnessed changes in federal housing and civil rights policies, positive shifts in white racial attitudes, and the substantial growth in the African American, Latino/a American, and Asian American middle classes. Yet despite these changes, residential segregation persists at high levels. Some critics attribute this to continuing institutional racism, and they point to studies suggesting discrimination in lending practices as well as other systemic mechanisms in banking and real estate that seem to treat minorities badly and which appear to work against neighborhood desegregation (Galster 1990; 1992; Oliver and Shapiro 1995). Other researchers, including Judith DeSena (this volume), call attention to informal mechanisms within white neighborhoods that pressure homeowners and landlords to avoid selling or renting to minorities.

Some skeptics, notably the geographer William Clark (1991), argue that to a large degree these contemporary patterns reflect preferences of minority group members themselves, particularly African Americans, for racially and ethnically homogeneous neighborhoods. However, Farley and colleagues (this volume) reject this argument. While agreeing that some African Americans may be weary of being "pioneers"—the first minorities to move into unfriendly white ter-ritory—Farley and associates present survey data showing that African Americans over-whelmingly prefer to live in racially mixed neighborhoods. Therefore, they conclude that white racial prejudice is largely respon-sible for the persistence of the status quo.

References

Been, Vicki. 1994. "Locally Undesirable Land Uses in Minority Neighborhoods: Dispropor-tionate Siting or Market Dynamics?" *Yale Law Journal* 103: 1383-1422.

Bobo, Lawrence. 1989. "Keeping the Lynchpin in Place: Testing the Multiple Sources of opposi-tion to Residential Integration." *Revue Inter-nationale de Psychologie Sociale* 2: 306–323.

Brooks-Gunn, Jeanne, Greg J. Duncan, Paula Kato Klabanov, and Naomi Sealand. 1993. "Do Neighborhoods Influence Child and Ado-lescent Development?" *American Journal of Sociology* 99: 353-395.

Bullard, Robert. 1994. "Overcoming Racism in Environmental Decision Making." *Environ-ment* 36(4):10-26.

Clark, William V.A. 1991. "Residential Prefer-ences and Neighborhood Racial Segregation: A Test of the Schelling Segregation Model." *Demography* 28: 1-19.

Farley, Reynolds, and William H. Frey. 1994. "Changes in the Segregation of Whites from Blacks During the 1980s: Small Steps Toward a More Integrated Society." *American Socio-logical Review* 59: 23–45.

Farley, Reynolds, Charlotte Steeh, Tara Jackson, Maria Krysan, and Keith Reeves. 1994. "The Causes of Continued Racial Residential Segre-gation: Chocolate City, Vanilla Suburbs Revis-ited." *Journal of Housing Research* 4: 1–38.

Galster, George. 1990. "Racial Steering by Real Estate Agents: Mechanisms and Motivation." *Review of Black Political Economy* 19: 39-63.

——. 1992. "Research on Discrimination in Housing and Mortgage Markets: Assessment and Further Directions." *Housing Policy De-bate* 3(2): 639-683.

Massey, Douglas S., and Nancy A. Denton. 1993. *American Apartheid: Segregation and the Mak-ing of the Underclass.* Cambridge, MA: Har-vard University Press.

Oliver, Melvin L. and Thomas M. Shapiro. 1995. *Black Wealth/White Wealth: A New Perspective on Racial Inequality.* New York: Routledge.

Ong, Paul M., and Evelyn Blumenberg. 1993. "An Unnatural Tradeoff: Latinos and Environ-mental Justice." Pp. 207–225 in *Latinos in a Changing US Economy*, edited by Rebecca Morales and Frank Bonilla. Newbury Park, CA: Sage.

25

Stereotypes and Segregation:

Neighborhoods in the Detroit Area

Reynolds Farley
Charlotte Steeh
Maria Krysan
Tara Jackson
Keith Reeves

Figure 25.1
Neighborhood Diagrams Used for White Respondents, DAS 1976 and 1992.

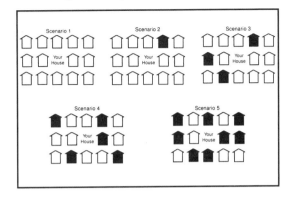

Racial Residential Attitudes of Whites, 1976 and 1992

Living with Blacks on the Block

Racial transition occurred in many neighborhoods within older metropolises such as Detroit after World War II (Hirsch 1983; Mayer 1960; Taeuber and Taeuber 1965, chap. 5). Whites resisted the entry of blacks to their neighborhoods, but eventually a few moved in. Shortly thereafter whites began to leave, often using federally backed loans to buy homes in exclusively white suburbs. After some years, the old neighborhood had a largely black population. This drastically altered the city of Detroit, whose white population fell by 86% as it changed from 16% black in 1950 to 76% black in 1990 (U.S. Bureau of the Census 1952, table 34; 1991, table 4). The number of whites in the city declined from 1,546,000 to 222,000.

To determine the preferences of *whites* in our 1976 and 1992 studies of the metropolis, [based on the Detroit Area Study, or DAS], we presented every respondent with five cards, each of which showed 15 homes (see Figure 25.1). With the first card, we asked them to imagine that they lived in an all-white neigh-borhood—a realistic assumption for most—using the center home as theirs. They were then shown a second card, which indicated one house occupied by blacks and 14 by whites. We asked how comfortable they would feel if their own neighborhood came to resemble that minimally integrated neighborhood. If they said "very comfortable" or "somewhat comfortable," they were shown cards with successively greater proportions of blacks until a card elicited a response of "somewhat uncomfortable" or "very uncomfortable," or they came to the fifth card showing a majority black neighborhood. (For summary of 1976 findings, see Farley et al. [1978].)

There are reasons for optimism about whites' changing attitudes. In 1976, three-quarters of our respondents said they would be comfortable living with one black family but, in 1992, this had increased to 84%. By 1992, seven out of 10 whites claimed they would feel comfortable if their neighborhood came to have the racial composition of the metropolis; that is, if it looked like card 3, which showed 12 white and three black households. This information is provided in Figure 25.2.

As the ratio of blacks to whites increased, the comfort of whites declined, and, quite clearly, most whites—in both 1976 and 1992—felt uncomfortable when they were the racial minority. Just 35% of whites in 1992 said they would be comfortable in an eight-households-black, seven-households-

Figure 25.2
Attractiveness of Neighborhoods Of Varying Racial Compositions for White Respondents, DAS 1976 and 1992.

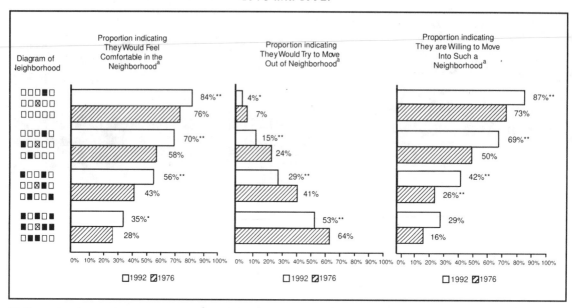

(Significance shown for change from 1976 to 1992); *p < .05; **p < .01; the denominator for % is the total white population.)

white neighborhood, but this is a significant increase from 28% in 1976.

Interracial neighborhoods will never be stable if there is extensive "white flight" when blacks move in. We sought to measure whether whites would leave if blacks moved into their neighborhoods. We took the first mixed-neighborhoods card that elicited a response of "uncomfortable" from a white respondent and asked if he or she would try to move away should their own neighborhood come to have the racial composition pictured. If the respondent said no, we presented a card showing the next highest representation of blacks and repeated the "moving away" question. Responses are shown in the middle panel of Figure 25.2. This question was posed to the 65% of white respondents who said they would feel uncomfortable if their neighborhood came to look like one of the mixed areas shown on the cards (the base for these percentages is the total white sample). We assume, for example, that a white who would try to move away from a three-households-black, 12-households-white neighborhood would certainly try to leave an area with

eight black households and seven white households.

Few whites would try to move away if one black entered their neighborhood. In 1992, only 4% would do so, a significant drop from the 7% who would have moved away in 1976. If Detroit-area residents selected their neighborhoods randomly, the typical neighborhood would resemble the three-black-, 12-white-households situation. In 1992 15% said they would try to move away from a neighborhood like this, suggesting that the overwhelming majority of whites would remain and meaning that whites are willing to accept a representation of blacks on their own block equal to that of the metropolis. Greater representations of blacks, however, led more whites to say they would try to leave, and in 1992, as in 1976, the majority of whites would move away from a majority-black neighborhood, although even here there was a significant liberalization of white responses.

Because integrated neighborhoods will remain racially mixed only if some whites replace those blacks and whites who move away from such locations every year, we also assessed the willingness of whites to move into mixed areas. Each respondent was presented with the same five cards and was asked if there were any of these neighborhoods they were willing to move into should they find an attractive home they could afford.

Are Detroit-area whites willing to move into neighborhoods that already have black residents? The answer is yes if there are just a few, but no if there are many. In 1992, almost 90% of whites said they *would* move into a neighborhood with one black and 14 white residents (see Figure 25.2). Considering the neighborhood resembling the racial composition of the metropolis—three black households and 12 white households—almost 70% would move in, but 30% would not. The racial tolerance of whites has a limit, and neighborhoods with five or eight black households were not attractive to whites in either 1976 or 1992. White demand for housing in an area is clearly affected by its racial composition.

How Widespread Were the Changes in White Attitudes About Residential Integration?

Were changes between 1976 and 1992 in attitudes widespread or were they restricted to younger whites or the extensively educated? We calculated scores indexing white attitudes concerning two dimensions of integration. Each had a minimum value of zero, which indicates the acceptance of residential integration, and a maximum of 100, which reports strong opposition.

First, if a white said he or she would be "very uncomfortable" should their neighborhood come to have one black resident, he or she received the maximum score of 100. If a person said they would be "very comfortable" in the eight-black-, seven-white-households neighborhood, he or she got the minimum score of zero on this index of *white discomfort* with black neighbors. Second, a white who said he or she *would not* consider moving into an attractive, affordable home should it be located in a neighborhood with a single black household received the maximum score of 100, while someone who said they *were willing to enter* the majority-black neighborhood shown on card 5 got a score of zero. Note that high scores indi-

cate a white rejection of residential integration, low scores an acceptance of it.

. . . The average [white] score on this discomfort index fell from 47 to 40 between 1976 and 1992. This means that, on average, the first card to produce an "uncomfortable" response from whites in 1976 was the five-black-, 10-white-households neighborhood while, in 1992, it was the eight-black-, seven-white-households neighborhood. The willingness of whites to move into racially mixed neighborhoods changed in a similar manner, and all of these changes were significant.

Two primary determinants of racial attitudes among whites are their birth cohort and their educational attainment. Younger persons report more liberal attitudes than older ones and people who spent many years as students typically espouse different attitudes than those who did not complete high school. . . . Younger whites said they were more comfortable with blacks on their block than did older whites, and they also reported more willingness to move into integrated neighborhoods. Educational attainment was strongly linked to attitudes about integration. On both of these measures, whites with college degrees were about one-half a standard deviation different from those who did not have a secondary school diploma.

We anticipated that family income would be related to these attitudes about residential integration in a fashion similar to education. Persons in prosperous families, we presumed, would be more tolerant of black neighbors since they possess the resources to move to a different neighborhood should that be desirable. But family income was not significantly linked to these attitudes. Gender differences were modest, but there is clear evidence that women, more than men, reported being comfortable with black neighbors.

For more than two decades, whites in the city of Detroit have lived in a majority-black municipality, although most of their close neighbors are whites. Many locations in the suburban ring have specific reputations with regard to racial integration. Dearborn and Livonia—just outside Detroit—have reputations for hostility toward blacks; Macomb County has a reputation for greater hostility toward blacks than does Oakland County. We hypothesized that individuals might be influenced by these reputations when they selected a suburban home and that living in particular locations would reinforce strongly held attitudes. However, we found that whites living in these locations. . .did not differ significantly in their attitudes about residential integration. We were not surprised that, by 1992, whites in the city of Detroit expressed the greatest comfort with black neighbors. They are, of course, the residual of whites who remain in a largely black central city.

The shift toward more liberal attitudes was not restricted to particular groups of whites. . . . The trend toward more liberal white attitudes will likely continue as older whites and their limited educations are replaced by younger more extensively educated whites.

While these results tell us about the neighborhood preferences of whites, they do not tell us anything about what constitutes those attitudes. Why do whites prefer neighborhoods with a certain racial composition? Why do they say they would leave a neighborhood with a particular composition? To go beyond the information from forced-choice questions, we laced the survey with open-ended questions, thereby securing insight into how respondents understood or explained racial residential segregation. Respondents who indicated in the "would move out" questions that they would try to leave a racially mixed area—53% of all white respondents—were asked to explain why, in their own terms.

Regardless of which particular neighborhood a person indicated they would move out of, the most frequently mentioned reason was a concern about declining property values. Approximately 40% of respondents who said they would move out gave this as their reason. As one respondent put it: "I'd like to feel I'm not racist, but as a homeowner, I'd be concerned that my property value would go down. That seems to be what happens. It's not the African American's fault, but the whites' reactions."

A respondent who would move out of a neighborhood with just one black family explained: "That would have a significant impact on the value of my property—which is the single biggest investment I have, and I wouldn't risk that." And a white who would move out if his neighborhood came to have five black families referred to "past experiences." When asked to explain, the respondent stated, "Values of houses go down when blacks move in. It's not right, but you have to go with what everybody else does. For Sale signs would pop up and I can't afford to lose on my house."

The second most common theme, mentioned by just under one in five respondents who would move out (or about 10% of all white respondents) was that the arrival of blacks would bring increases in crime, violence, and drug problems. They would move out, they said, because they feared for their safety. Two respondents who each stated they would move out of a neighborhood with three black families illustrate this theme: "Because the neighborhood is turning black—I assume crime rates would rise." And "When you get one black family, you get a whole bunch of them. A lot of drug addicts come in."

Whites in our survey gave many reasons for wanting to move out of certain neighborhoods, but the two most common were beliefs that property values would fall, and, to a lesser degree, the perception that crime rates would rise in such areas. These explanations give a different meaning to Clark's (1991) hypothesis that white and black preferences are the driving force behind residential segregation: the preferences do not reflect so much a desire to "live with my own kind" or to "be around people that are like myself" (a response given by fewer than 10% of respondents to this question) as they reflect a desire to maintain the property values and safety of their neighborhood.

Racial Residential Attitudes of Blacks, 1976 and 1992

Living with Whites on the Block

Few, if any, Detroit neighborhoods went from black to white, so it was pointless to ask African-Americans if they would be upset by the arrival of whites in their neighborhoods; thus, the residential preference questions for blacks differ from those for whites. We showed blacks five diagrams of neighborhoods varying in composition from all-black to all-white, as illustrated in Figure 25.3.

Figure 25.3
Neighborhood Diagrams Used for Black Respondents, DAS 1976 and 1992.

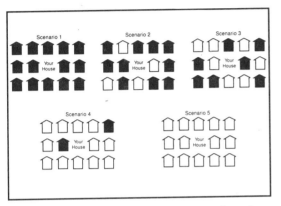

Blacks were asked to imagine that they were searching for a house and found a nice one they could afford. This home was desig-

nated at the center of each neighborhood. They were then given the cards and asked to rank the neighborhoods from the one most attractive to them to the one least attractive.

When the residential preferences of Detroit blacks in 1976 and 1992 are compared, we find little change. Figure 25.4 shows the percentage of black respondents who rated each neighborhood as their first or second choice. Most African Americans preferred areas that were racially mixed where there already was a substantial representation of blacks. The ideal neighborhood was one in which blacks comprised at least one-half the residents. Figure 25.4 illustrates that there have been statistically significant declines in the proportion of blacks who ranked the "3 black/12 white" or "8 black/7 white" neighborhood as their first or second choice and a significant increase in the percentage who highly rated the "11 black/4 white" area as the first or second choice. Shifts in the preferences of blacks were away from residential integration.

If the American apartheid system is to disappear, some blacks will move into largely or

Figure 25.4
Attractiveness of Neighborhoods of Varying Racial Compositions for Black Respondents, DAS 1976 and 1992.

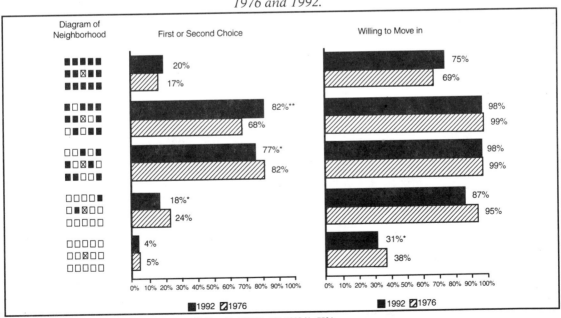

(Significance shown for change from 1976 to 1992); *p < .05; **p < .01; 1976 N = 404; 1992 N = 750.)

exclusively white neighborhoods. Are blacks willing to be the pioneers who change the racial composition of an area, or do they strongly prefer already integrated areas? We gave the cards to blacks, asked them to imagine that they had been searching for a home and had found an attractive one they could afford. It could be located in any of the areas shown on the cards ranging from all-black to all-white. We then asked them which neighborhoods they would be willing to enter.

There were no significant differences between 1976 and 1992 in the willingness of blacks to move where there already were black residents. Figure 25.4, however, shows that racially mixed neighborhoods are more popular with blacks than the all-black area, In 1976 31% of blacks said they *would not* enter an all black neighborhood; in 1992 that figure had declined to 25%.

In addition, most Detroit area blacks are reluctant to be the first of their race in a white neighborhood. Less than one-third of the 1992 respondents are willing to take this risk, a significant decrease from the 38% who were willing to move into an all-white area in 1976.

In order to understand the meaning of these percentages for blacks, we need to relate them to the similar percentages for whites. A careful comparison of the percentages of black and white respondents who would move into integrated neighborhoods reveals that opinions are asymmetrically distributed between the races across neighborhoods. In both 1976 and 1992, black respondents reject only the segregated alternatives. However, they are almost as willing to move into neighborhoods that reflect the overall racial composition of the Detroit metropolitan area (25% black, 75% white), as they are to move into neighborhoods that are more predominantly black (e.g., 50%–75% black). In other words, black willingness to move into a neighborhood does not increase monotonically with a rise in the percentage of black residents.

On the other hand, the responses of whites suggest that almost all would be willing to move to an all-white neighborhood and, we assume, they would reject becoming a white pioneer in one of Detroit's black neighborhoods. Thus, in both 1976 and 1992 white willingness to move to a neighborhood is quite monotonic with the degree of its whiteness. . . .

The contrast between blacks and whites is unmistakable. At least *some* African-Americans (close to one-third) would be willing to move into the segregated white neighborhood even though almost *no* whites would choose an all-black area. Furthermore, the racial mix that mirrors the composition of the metropolitan region commands much more approval among blacks (87%) than it does among whites (69%). . . . While it is true that neither blacks nor whites want to live in areas that are occupied solely by members of the other race, it is also true that blacks are much less opposed to being among large numbers of whites than whites are to being among large numbers of blacks. These data, in and of themselves, cast considerable doubt on the proposition that racial residential segregation continues to exist because each race prefers to live where it is numerically dominant. Instead, the results suggest that this attitude has been more prevalent among whites in the past and may only now be gaining some ground among blacks, a possibility we consider below.

How Widespread Were the Changes in Black Attitudes About Residential Integration?

Changes in the residential preferences of blacks were small, but they suggest a slight shift away from residential integration. We wished to investigate whether these changes typified all groups of blacks. . . .

We calculated a score indexing the preferences of blacks based upon their ratings of the five neighborhoods. If a respondent ranked the all-black area first and then ranked the others in order of their blackness such that the all-white area was least attractive, he or she received the maximum score of 100. On the other hand, a black respondent who ranked the all-white neighborhood as their first choice, and then rated the others by their racial composition such that the all-black area was last, received the minimum score of zero. High scores on this index report a preference for black areas, while low scores were associated with a preference for residentially integrated neighborhoods. . . .

Overall, the score for blacks on this index of residential preference increased between 1976 and 1992 by five points. This change was consistent among blacks in all birth cohorts, at all educational or income levels, and among both black men and women. The shift in residential preferences away from integration characterizes all components of Detroit's black population except those at the highest income and educational levels. Blacks who graduated from college or whose family income exceeded $60,000 (in 1991 dollars) favored residential more in 1992 than in 1976.

The percentage of blacks willing to pioneer in all-white neighborhoods fell significantly from 38% to 31%. A roughly similar change characterized all subgroups of the black population with the exception of those at the top of the educational or income distribution, who were more willing to pioneer in white neighborhoods in 1992. Blacks who graduated from college and who are now earning sizable incomes may frequently work with white peers and thus have the financial resources and social skills to live wherever they please. And they may be seen by their white neighbors as "acceptable" African-Americans. (See Feagin and Sikes [1994] for evidence of the discrimination and hostility these blacks endure, nevertheless; also see Cose [1993].)

The attitudes of Detroit-area whites and blacks changed in surprisingly different ways between 1976 and 1992: whites reported more liberal attitudes about neighborhood mixing, while blacks increasingly preferred largely black areas and were less willing to enter all-white ones.

As with our analysis of whites' residential preferences, our open-ended questions give us insight into why blacks hold the preferences they do. The interviewer pointed to the neighborhood the black respondent selected as his or her first choice and asked, "Could you tell me why you think that is the most attractive neighborhood?" Following Clark's (1991) argument, that residential segregation persists because blacks prefer to live with blacks and whites with whites, we were interested in understanding why blacks hold such

preferences, if, in fact, they do. We focus on the extreme case—those 14% of the 750 black respondents whose first choice was the all-black neighborhood.

Among these respondents, nearly one-half mentioned that they "wanted to live with blacks," they "had always lived with blacks," or they "wanted to live with their own kind." This response, however, is really just a restatement of their preference. The second most frequently mentioned reason provides more insight into why they hold this preference: nearly one-quarter of those who said they wanted to live in an all-black neighborhood indicated it was because they felt it was safer and more welcoming. For example, one respondent explained: "I'd rather live among my own people. . . . I feel more comfortable. . . . My people have told me how I would be treated living around all whites." Another respondent illustrates a related sentiment: "Because white people are prejudiced against us. . . . If they don't want me living in their neighborhood, then I don't want to be there."

Finally, another reason given for wanting to live in an all-black neighborhood was a desire to live around people with common interests and values and to be a part of a community. One respondent explained: "I love to live around black people because of a commonality of values. I don't have anything against living with whites either, but I prefer to live around blacks."

While blacks' residential preferences are complex and driven by a variety of forces, this analysis suggests one important factor underlying their preferences: many blacks feel that whites would not welcome them or that their lives would be less comfortable and perhaps endangered if they shared a neighborhood with whites.

It is difficult to assess the prevalence of these sentiments. Our data provide indirect evidence of this dynamic. When we asked all blacks to explain why residential segregation existed, they commonly reported that "whites don't want to live around us." Thus, it appears that part of blacks' residential preferences can be attributed to the perceived hostility of whites toward blacks. In addition, recent analyses of in-depth interviews with several hundred middle-class, black professionals indicate that some African-Americans recognize fully the personal disadvantages of living in integrated settings. These interviews reveal as well the determination of some highly educated and articulate African-Americans to face uncomfortable and discriminatory situations and claim for themselves the accoutrements of success—a nice house, good schools, a desirable neighborhood (Feagin and Sikes 1994, chap. 6). . . .

Conclusion

. . . We examined how the neighborhood preferences of Detroit-area residents changed since 1976 and what led to such preferences. [Our] results show a link between whites' racial attitudes and their residential preferences, but it is a complicated one. Whites' attitudes about neighborhood integration became significantly more liberal over the recent past, as reflected in their increasing reports that they would be comfortable in mixed neighborhoods and would remain should modest numbers of blacks come to their area. When we asked whites who said they would try to move away when blacks came about their motivation for flight, the majority *did not* invoke racial stereotypes.

Still, the overall aversion toward living among blacks remains strong, and a substantial minority of whites mention stereotypes when asked direct questions about living with blacks on their block. The more integrated the neighborhood, the fewer the whites who would remain. And, although almost all whites say they would move into a minimally integrated neighborhood, less than half express a willingness to move into neighborhoods with more than a token representation of African-Americans.

Black preferences for mixed neighborhoods have weakened. As was the case 16 years ago, the majority of blacks prefer neighborhoods that are more than minimally integrated. However, black preferences for integrated neighborhoods—in contrast to those of whites—declined except among the black elite. Whether this trend is attributable to an increasing ideological commitment to develop and live in largely black communities, to growing apprehensions about white hostil-

ity, or to the belief that integration offers few benefits is unclear. . . .

If the liberal shift in white attitudes is genuine and continues, cohort replacement and the continuing trend toward greater educational attainment assure a further liberalization of white racial attitudes and, we hope, attitudes about living in integrated neighborhoods. But it is unrealistic to expect that the slow process of cohort replacement will be sufficient to stem the tide of residential segregation in a metropolis as riven by race as Detroit. Indeed, even if there were no steering and no racial discrimination in the marketing of housing, segregation would likely persist at high levels. The "Chocolate City, Vanilla Suburbs" (see Malbix/Ricks 1976) pattern sung about two decades ago on soul music stations is alive and well in Detroit. If residential integration is to be achieved in Detroit, programs to encourage it will have to be implemented and strongly encouraged. Real estate brokers need to be aware of the liberalization of white attitudes and of the apparent willingness of most of their potential black clients to live in mixed neighborhoods, including overwhelmingly white ones. Homeowners need to be assured that neighborhood services and the flow of credit will be maintained should their area become integrated. A variety of successful prointegration strategies have been effective for several decades in Shaker Heights (near Cleveland), Oak Park (near Chicago), and many other areas (DeMarco and Galster 1993; Saltman 1990). These include community efforts to prevent white flight and welcome members of the minority race, programs to protect against sharp falls in property values and slight discounts in interest rates for first-time home buyers who purchase in a neighborhood where they are the racial minority. Federal housing agencies, lending institutions, and the real estate industry may be able to capitalize on both the liberalization of white attitudes and the willingness of most blacks to live in mixed areas.

References

Clark, William A. V. 1991. "Residential Preferences and Neighborhood Racial Segregation: A Test of the Schelling Segregation Model." *Demography* 28 (1): 1–10.

Cose, Ellis. 1993. *The Rage of a Privileged Class.* New York: Harper Collins.

DeMarco, Donald L., and George C. Galster. 1993. "Prointegrative Policy: Theory and Practice." *Journal of Urban Affairs* 15 (2): 141–60.

Farley, Reynolds, Howard Schuman, Suzanne Bianchi, Diane Colasanto, and Shirley Hatchett. 1978. "Chocolate City, Vanilla Suburbs: Will the Trend toward Racially Separate Communities Continue?" *Social Science Research* 7 (December): 319–44.

Feagin, Joe R., and Melvin P. Sikes. 1994. *Living with Racism: The Black Middle-Class Experience.* Boston: Beacon Press.

Hirsch, Arnold R. 1983. *Making the Second Ghetto: Race and Housing in Chicago.* New York: Cambridge University Press.

Malbix/Ricks Music, BMI. 1976. *Chocolate City.* Casablanca Records.

Mayer, Albert. 1960. "Russell Woods: Change without Conflict: A Case Study of Neighborhood Transition in Detroit." In *Studies in Housing and Minority Groups,* edited by Nathan Glazer and David McEntire. Berkeley: University of California Press.

Saltman, Juliet. 1990. *A Fragile Movement: The Struggle for Neighborhood Stabilization.* New York: Greenwood Press.

Taeuber, Karl E., and Alma F. Taeuber. 1965. *Negroes in Cities: Residential Segregation and Neighborhood Change.* Chicago: Aldine.

U.S. Bureau of the Census. 1952. *Census of Population: 1950,* vol. 2, pt. 22. Washington, DC: Government Printing Office.

———. 1991. *Census of Population and Housing: 1990,* CPH–1–24. Washington, DC: Government Printing Office.

26

Local Gatekeeping Practices and Residential Segregation

Judith N. DeSena

Research on the causes of residential segregation has focused on the "institutional web" and market forces to explain the dual housing market in the United States (Farley 1987; Foley 1973; Kain 1968; Kain and Quigley 1975; Pearce 1979). This article examines the informal practices of local residents in perpetuating residential segregation. It is a study of the strategies used by white non-Hispanic residents in Greenpoint, Brooklyn, to maintain the segregation of Hispanics and to discourage people of color from moving into the neighborhood. An informal housing network in which available rental apartments and houses for sale are advertised by word of mouth is reinforced by the functioning of local institutions, namely, the Roman Catholic church and electoral politics. I propose that such actions reflect an invisible link between the micro-level analyses of discrimination documented by studies of real estate steering (Pearce 1979; Wienk, Reid, Simonson and Eggers 1979) and macro-level analyses of patterns of residential segregation (Farley and Allen 1987; Lieberson 1980). . . .

On a neighborhood level, segregation has been conceptualized as ordered segmentation (Suttles 1968) and the defended neighborhood (Suttles 1972). In actual practice, attempts to maintain separation among people of different ethnic and racial groups have taken the form of restrictive covenants or zones (Krase 1982), acts of violence (Rieder 1985), and the use of local networks (DeSena 1990). This study connects the national and statistical data on segregation with the informal practices of ordinary people. It offers an additional dimension to research on segregation. The analysis presents how white non-Hispanic residents of Greenpoint, in their everyday life, contribute to the maintenance of residential segregation. This research indicates that to a large extent the "work" of segregation on a neighborhood level is done by women who serve as "gatekeepers and home-seekers" (Pearce 1979). The article begins with a description of Greenpoint followed by a discussion of the study's research design. The strategies used to accomplish residential segregation in Greenpoint will be presented, with a focus on an informal housing network and local institutional arrangements.

Description of Greenpoint

Geography

Greenpoint is a peninsula at the northernmost tip of Brooklyn bounded on the north and east by Newtown Creek and on the west by the East River. The Brooklyn-Queens Expressway (Meeker Avenue) and North 7th Street serve as Greenpoint's southern boundary (New York City Planning Commission 1969). The Brooklyn-Queens Expressway is an elevated structure as it extends through Greenpoint and breaks up the continuity of residential areas.

Population

Greenpoint is a working-class neighborhood. Since the early 1900s Greenpoint's population has been largely white ethnic, composed mostly of Irish, Italian, and Polish families. The Irish were the largest group through the 1920s. A significant influx of Polish immigration occurred in Greenpoint after World War II (Susser 1982). More recently there has been an additional wave of Polish refugees who fled martial law in Poland. The relocation efforts of these immigrants are aided by local Polish organizations and churches. Greenpoint is currently viewed as the largest Polish community in New York City.

In 1990, the population of Greenpoint was approximately 39,365. Of these, 73 percent were members of white non-Hispanic ethnic groups. Since 1950 northern Greenpoint has seen an influx of Hispanic residents. In 1990 Hispanics constituted 22 percent of the neighborhood's population; and Asian and Pacific Islanders totaled 4 percent and blacks 1 percent of the population. The average across ethnic groupings for median household income in 1989 was $29,121, approximately the median household income of New York City in 1989, which amounted to $29,823. In 1990, a majority of Greenpoint's residents 25 years and older had between an elementary and a high school education. Moreover, in 1990 Greenpoint's employed persons 16 years and older worked mostly in technical, sales, and administrative support occupations, as professionals and managers, and in service jobs.

Housing

A majority of Greenpoint's housing was built before 1939 and many structures were built before 1900. More than 60 percent of the residential buildings are frame dwellings (New York City Planning Commission 1974). There are a few blocks in Greenpoint that consist of brownstones and brick townhouses—remnants of Dutch settlement from the nineteenth century. These particular streets are presently part of a seven-block historic district bordered by Franklin Street, Manhattan Avenue, Calyer, and Kent Streets.

Residential structures in Greenpoint are six stories or less, and 71 percent contain four or fewer dwelling units (New York City Planning Commission 1974). In addition, "the percentage of owner-occupied buildings with rental units is usually high" (Wellisz 1982, p. R9). Most homeowners share their building with renters. In 1990 the average median rent in Greenpoint was $450, compared with $496 for New York City. Long-term residents may pay less than the median rent because of tenure and rent control laws. However, rents in Greenpoint have been escalating. Some residents report monthly rents as high as $750 to $1,000.

Religion

There are approximately twelve churches in Greenpoint. Those with the largest congregations are Roman Catholic; Catholic churches in Greenpoint are recognized by residents as the center of ethnic life. There are two types of Roman Catholic churches in Greenpoint: Diocesan churches lie within small territorial boundaries, or parishes, which in turn form, with other parishes, a larger territory, or diocese (the parishes of diocesan churches do not overlap). National churches are those that serve a particular ethnic group; they are usually located within the boundaries of a diocesan church. There are three national churches in Greenpoint: two Polish and one Italian. There is also one diocesan church that is reportedly dominated by Irish residents.

Research Methods

The findings reported here are part of a larger qualitative study in which I conducted fifty-five open-ended interviews with residents of Greenpoint for the purpose of ascertaining the strategies employed to maintain residential segregation. A technique in interviewing was used by which I asked residents to tell me about the practices of their neighbors. The respondents seemed comfortable with this approach, since the focus of discussion was not on their behavior, but on the habits of locals and the customs of the neighborhood. The respondents talked freely. Interviews lasted anywhere from one hour to 2.5 hours. They were recorded on tape.

The interviews were obtained by a snowball sampling technique. The sample was stratified for sex, ethnicity, and age. Since ethnicity was an important variable in this study, I began by identifying ethnic clusters through block, and block group, data from the 1980 Census.

Clusters were identified for four major ethnic groups in Greenpoint: Hispanics, Irish, Italians, and Polish. Once the boundaries of these ethnic enclaves were apparent, I contacted individuals residing in each of these clusters. These individuals became key informants, directing me to others of the same ethnic background. At the end of each interview I asked respondents to refer me to others.

I also used content analysis and reviewed written accounts of the events described in the interviews. In particular, I examined local newspapers, church bulletins, and various flyers advertising meetings in the community. This approach enabled me to use the information in subsequent interviews, to probe these matters more effectively, and to keep abreast of current issues and concerns. Data were collected between 1983 and 1990. The data collection focusing on the neighborhood dynamics presented here is ongoing.

Greenpoint: A Segregated Neighborhood

According to its residents, Greenpoint is divided into two areas: the north and the south. Northern Greenpoint is composed mainly of Poles and Hispanics. Southern Greenpoint is made up of Polish, Irish, Italian, and Hispanic groups. Because of the existence of an Hispanic community in northern Greenpoint, residents point to Greenpoint Avenue as the symbolic boundary that separates the north from the south. One northern Greenpoint resident commented: "Like I said, I've been here 29 years and after Greenpoint Avenue, to me, that's the white neighborhood, and this side is more Puerto Rican."

"The boundary," Greenpoint Avenue, is a major thoroughfare and includes a bus route, truck route, and subway station. However, in many ways and for many residents, particularly those who live in southern Greenpoint, it marks the end of the area's commercial strip and the end of the neighborhood. A couple of residents from southern Greenpoint reported the following:

We never really went down that end, we had St. Anthony [Church] and we never really associated with St. Alphonsus [Church], that was like the other territory or something.

I always remember, once you cross Greenpoint Avenue, except for a few white blocks, that wasn't the good section of Greenpoint.

The urban landscape reinforces residents' differential perceptions of north and south. No banks are located north of Greenpoint Avenue and the annual street fair, and outdoor Christmas lights provided by local merchants to the south stop there. As one crosses Greenpoint Avenue going north, the ground slopes downhill. Bodegas are numerous on street corners. During the summer salsa music plays in the streets. Buildings are larger and show signs of deterioration to a greater extent than those in the south; some have been condemned and only their shells remain. Houses in the north have a lower market value than those in the south, and it is more difficult to obtain mortgages and home improvement loans for housing in the north. As one resident noted "as long as I remember, that was the poorer end of the neighborhood."

Southern Greenpoint is different. It tends to be better-maintained. Homes are renovated and building deterioration is less visible than in northern Greenpoint. Ethnic specialty stores are typically Polish, and butcher shops, bakeries, and grocery stores dot each corner. All kinds of retail stores can be found in the southern area.

White non-Hispanic respondents see a causal relationship between people of color and deteriorated living conditions. One resident reported:

Most of the Spanish people that I've seen move into homes and let them deteriorate. Maybe because most of them rent, I really don't know. . . . But to me, it's just the way that everything is let to fall apart. They really don't care if the windows are hanging open. It's not a good feeling when you go through the blocks where the Spanish people live, and then the streets where white people live. There's no pride whatsoever.

Northern Greenpoint came to be viewed by long-term white non-Hispanic residents as the undesirable part of the community because of the clustering of Hispanic residents, and their perception that people of color create urban decay. Because of this view, non-Hispanic whites resist residence by people of color.

How Greenpoint's symbolic boundary and its attendant segregation are maintained is the focus of this study. I propose that it is through the process of an informal housing network.

Greenpoint's Informal Housing Network

It is difficult for an outsider to rent an apartment or purchase a house in southern Greenpoint. Local realtors have said that "there isn't one-, two- or three-family houses available." The local newspaper lists only a few apartments and houses for sale, while the lengths of its "Apts. Wanted" and "Houses Wanted" columns increase. Residents of southern Greenpoint are particularly cautious about renting their vacant apartments. Not only do they want to control rigidly the type of tenants they may get, but they also want to determine who will be informed about the availability of an apartment. All respondents in southern Greenpoint, regardless of ethnicity, claimed that available apartments are rented "by word of mouth."

> There are some ads in the local paper, but I think most of the time it's by word of mouth. I think they mostly don't put ads in the paper, because when you put an ad in the paper, you don't know who is gonna come.
> Yeh, definitely . . . when there's an apartment vacant, no one knows about it. They're very hush, or word of mouth. Even if they're not Hispanic, they still watch who they rent to.

Resident homeowners go about finding a tenant by an informal network through which they tell family, friends, and neighbors that an apartment is available. Consequently, a person who knows someone is "in the market" for an apartment will recommend the individual to the owner. In other words, individuals seeking apartments are "sponsored" by local informants to homeowners. According to residents:

> Recommendations, absolutely. You want rooms, I know that Mary has rooms. I'll say "Mary, I know so and so, she seems to be a nice person, why don't you give her the rooms?"
> You keep it to yourself and rent it word of mouth. If you're a friend of mine [and]

you hear of an apartment, you say, "Here I got a good friend," you guarantee him.

Those who are selected as informants are assumed to have similar social characteristics as the homeowner and to possess the same values. They are the gatekeepers of the community. Most informants are local women. It is therefore presumed by both parties that an informant would sponsor only a potential tenant who is the "type" of person the homeowner is seeking. Thus, it is expected that an informant would sponsor only an individual whom the homeowner would find acceptable. As one resident stated:

> What they do is, they don't want strangers that they don't know in their house. They want people to come who are recommended, or people who may be friends of people that they know. They're cautious because they're not necessarily anxious for the dollars that would be coming in. They want to have a family type of residence, people that they can get along with. They do that for their own security and for their own happiness, because sometimes you can rent to somebody and not know who they are. And, you know, they may be flamingo [sic] dancers and you're subject to this sort of stuff all the time.

The practice of sponsoring an individual as a potential tenant to a homeowner places the reputation of the sponsor "on the line." Their standing in the community could be spoiled if a tenant they sponsored turned out not to be the kind of person initially expected. One presumption is that people who are selected as informants will sponsor only white non-Hispanic ethnics, not people of color. When a neighbor is chosen as an informant by a homeowner, the homeowner does not need to list specific requirements. Informants know what homeowners expect. Likewise, homeowners select informants who they presume will know the characteristics expected in a tenant. Given this relationship between homeowners and their selected informants, most people of color are unable to gain access to apartments or houses in southern Greenpoint. One resident summed up this practice of sponsorship by saying, "They tell you because they know you're not gonna tell Spanish or black."

Intimidation is used within the informal housing network. According to respondents, neighbors sometimes pressure one another about potential tenants and homeowners. The major focus is for people of color to be unable to gain access to available apartments or houses.

> This house was almost bought by a Cuban gentleman, and the lady on this side of us told our landlord that they are not welcome here, in very choice words she used; and they almost threatened him, "Don't sell," and the sale did not go through.
>
> When the guy across the street was selling his house, somebody came out and said, "I hope you're not selling to blacks."

Other respondents indicated that applying pressure is unnecessary because there is an "unwritten agreement," analogous to a "pact" among neighbors. They agree that they will not rent or sell to minority individuals.

> It's a, how can I put it, it's an unwritten law. In other words, you know your family's gonna hear it if you rent to a black. . . . I know what they would go through; that's why I wouldn't really do it.

This response suggests that the "pact" operates without any overt coercion. It further suggests that residents who violate the pact will be confronted by their neighbors.

One respondent spoke about a friend who rehabilitates abandoned housing in southern Greenpoint. This developer was thinking about renting to blacks, but was advised by his friend and Greenpoint resident:

> I think it will hurt you tremendously and I don't see that you should do that. . . . because of their color. . . . It seems that the power brokers don't want any more minorities than they have already.

The developer was advised not to violate the pact in order to avoid unfavorable repercussions which might have caused his business to suffer.

Neighborhood Women

To a large extent, local women control who obtains housing in Greenpoint by serving as the primary gatekeepers of the community. They "pass along the word" regarding the availability of housing to family, friends, and neighbors. In this way, they have replaced local realtors. Their "work" is carried out through the maintenance of a local network in which they serve as informal brokers in the local housing market, and are involved in recruiting potential tenants. Information about available housing and "homeseekers" is conveyed orally through a network of women who interact in the street, at social and religious functions, and at civic meetings. Women's activities, to a large extent, are informal. As part of their daily routine, women will meet as they shop, walk children to and from school, go to and from work, and attend community meetings at night, or play bingo. It is during these informal occasions that matters concerning housing are discussed. A local woman's anecdote illustrates this point:

> I was in a butcher shop one day, and we were talking. I just happen to mention that my niece was looking for rooms. And this woman says, "Hello"; she told me who she was, and that she had rooms. So there right in the butcher shop, not that I ever got the rooms. But [if I wanted] rooms for a friend of mine or for anybody, I would spread the word around in the Society [a women's religious organization]. That would be the first place. I'd say, "Girls, anybody hears of rooms let me know." They would tell someone.

Although this research documents a housing network, the local women's network involves other aspects of neighborhood life as well. Women exchange local news. They discuss who is moving, what the implications are for friends and family seeking housing, where the best sales are, what the new priest is like, who has recently been robbed. Women's networks in communities have been trivialized as gossip and mistakenly viewed as having no purpose. Greenpoint's informal housing network is an example of the importance of women's networks in shaping communities.

In summary, by controlling accessibility to housing, residents of southern Greenpoint resist minority growth and maintain segregation. To a large extent, local women control who obtains housing, Most apartments are rented through an informal housing network by which residents sponsor individuals as tenants. Some houses are also sold this way, while others are sold through realtors who are trusted not to "blockbust" because many of the realtors are also residents. In most cases available housing never reaches the open market, but remains part of the neighborhood's "underlife" (Suttles 1972). Moreover, by keeping news of the availability of housing out of the open market, southern Greenpoint residents are not discriminating in the traditional sense (they are not turning people away). Instead, residents take an offensive position and prevent people of color from applying for housing.

Local Institutions

Local institutions also participate in making Greenpoint a segregated neighborhood. This section will focus particularly on the contributions of the Roman Catholic church and local politics.

The Church

As stated earlier, there are a number of Roman Catholic churches in Greenpoint, which are of two types: Some are national churches, while others are diocesan churches. In northern Greenpoint there is a national, Polish church called Sts. Cyril and Methodius, which is located in the heart of the Hispanic community. This church holds masses and other services in Polish and English. It does not accommodate the Spanish-speaking community. St. Anthony-St. Alphonsus, a diocesan church located near the boundary that divides Greenpoint's northern and southern areas, offers masses in English and Spanish, thereby ministering to the Spanish-speaking community. Hispanics are not assisted by any other church. However, the Spanish-speaking and English-speaking congregations are segregated. Hispanics and other ethnic groups are physically separated, not only by a different mass, but also because

Spanish masses take place in the lower church (basement) of St. Anthony's church building.

In addition, parish activities are also segregated.

> Whenever it is social, for example, they don't allow it. [The parish) is going to have a dance for St. Valentine's Day but we are all going to be Spanish there, not one English speaker is going to go. They don't cross lines. I am trying to do something in that respect. Not only to bring the Hispanics into the English community, but I want to do the opposite too, take the English speakers and invite them over to our activities. Otherwise you're going to continue on and on with this problem of segregation because it's real. You have two parishes in one and I don't like that. I would like for all the people to be one.

Moreover, it was reported that parish committees are dominated by white non-Hispanics, mostly Irish parishioners. Hence, local churches reinforce neighborhood segregation in two ways. They either block the participation of some ethnic groups, as in the case of national churches, or attend to ethnic groups separately. In northern Greenpoint, Sts. Cyril and Methodius is a Polish island in the midst of a Hispanic population. Even when all ethnic groups are aided by the local diocesan church, the Hispanic and non-Hispanic white congregations are spatially segregated in church services and activities.

Local Politics

Greenpoint has long been a stronghold for the regular Democratic party. Control of the countywide party through the years reflects the successive waves of immigrants and their assimilation. During the 1920s and 1930s, the Irish controlled the countywide party. This was also reflected in Greenpoint, where a man named Peter J. McGuinness was district leader (McGuinness had replaced Patrick McCarren). At that time in the history of New York politics, the district leader's position was a powerful one. It was a party position that carried a number of patronage "goodies" (such as jobs and dismissed traffic violations). On Thursday nights residents would line up at the clubhouse to ask for favors. The district leader, through his network of influence, would deliver these favors. McGuinness contributed to defending Greenpoint by speaking against the development of public housing in Greenpoint. McGuinness stated to the City Planning Commission, "It's nothing personal. We just don't want any of them things in Greenpoint. We're a community by ourselves." Public housing was not built in Greenpoint, but it was constructed in adjacent neighborhoods such as Williamsburg, in Brooklyn, and Long Island City, in Queens.

The use of scare tactics in local political campaigns is another way that the local party resists population growth and representation of people of color. In 1980 there was a primary election held for state senator. The candidates were Thomas Bartosiewicz, the incumbent and a Greenpoint resident (who indicates ethnic succession in politics), and Lucille Rose, a black woman from Bedford-Stuyvesant. At this time, the boundaries of the district for state senator included Greenpoint, Bedford-Stuyvesant, and other areas. In an attempt to increase voter turnout in Greenpoint (the idea being that these were Bartosiewicz supporters), the local newspaper ran a front page story, "Remember: Vote on Tuesday, Sept. 9th." This article began:

> The future of Greenpoint-Williamsburg is at stake on Tuesday, September 9 as Democrats must turn out to vote in all time record numbers to support our Senator in the Primary Election. Senator Bartosiewicz is fighting against all odds in a fierce election campaign battle against boss-backed Bedford-Stuyvesant candidate Lucille Rose. (*Greenpoint Gazette*, September 2, 1980, p. 1)

Also on the front page were pictures of Bartosiewicz and Rose, with a caption that stated, "The Choice Is Clear." The use of pictures along with the article attempted to encourage residents to "get out and vote" for Bartosiewicz out of fear that someone black would be elected to represent Greenpoint. Moreover, on the day of the election, flyers were left on the windshields of cars in Greenpoint that had a picture of Lucille Rose with the caption, "Our New State Senator?" This

was a last attempt to encourage people to vote through the use of racial overtones. Bartosiewicz won this primary and also won the general election.

These two examples demonstrate how the local political system is involved in promoting segregation. Political tactics play on residents' fears that the neighborhood will be overtaken by people of color. In this way, the red flags of public housing or public officials who are people of color enable local party leaders to easily organize residents against change.

Since 1990, Greenpoint has also been subjected to legislative reapportionment plans (mandated after every census) that have aligned Greenpoint with other white, non-Hispanic areas of Brooklyn. Rather than draw district lines that might place the community with areas like Bushwick and Bedford-Stuyvesant, which are composed largely of people of color, recent reapportionment plans have placed the neighborhood in districts with white non-Hispanic communities such as Brooklyn Heights, Park Slope, and Bay Ridge (reflecting a desire on the part of the state legislature that "safe" seats for people of color are created and to insure that Greenpoint and other white non-Hispanic communities in Brooklyn continue to be represented by European American officials).

A complication that Greenpoint faces in political defense is that as a political entity it is absorbed into larger geographic districts. In recent years, Greenpoint has remained a Democratic bastion, and has done so by joining forces with other residents in adjoining communities. For example, the dominant political club, the Seneca Club, is headed by a Jewish district leader who has managed to bridge the diverse communities of Greenpoint and Williamsburg in an electoral coalition (Orthodox Jews in Williamsburg being the other key constituency) to defeat efforts by Hispanics and blacks seeking to gain political dominance.

Local institutions of religion and politics have contributed to Greenpoint's success in remaining a defended neighborhood. Families and individual persons of color face difficulties in finding housing and running for public office, as well as in being accepted as residents in the community and as participants of local institutions. In both informal and formal areas of neighborhood life, people of color have been blocked from full integration.

Conclusions

. . . The basic question raised by this study is the extent to which the actions of individuals perpetuate residential segregation. Some neighborhoods, like Greenpoint, wish to maintain their local culture and therefore attempt to exclude people of color. Although the working class is sometimes accused of being racist, they in fact share this characteristic with other social classes. Affluent groups do not need to resist population growth of people of color and defend their neighborhoods in the same way as the working class. Affluent groups use their economic position to exclude others from their neighborhoods. Zoning laws and local covenants also work to the advantage of the affluent. If neighborhood change should occur, affluent groups have the economic wherewithal to move. Working-class people cannot use economics as a resource. They actively resist minority growth through the strategies described here and therefore may be more quickly accused of racism than other social classes. However, their activism is felt to be their only means of expressing control and power. They are reactive because of their limited economic position; to defend what they have, they answer most community events by actively organizing against population influx of people of color, city policy decisions, or public housing locations. When social scientists try to explain the persistence of residential segregation, the importance of everyday social exchange as a mechanism of information control should not be underestimated. Combined with the actions of institutional players such as the Roman Catholic church and political parties, what people say and don't say has the power to shape metropolitan-wide patterns of residential segregation.

References

DeSena, Judith N. 1990. *Protecting One's Turf: Social Strategies for Maintaining Urban Neighborhoods.* Lanham, MD: University Press of America.

Farley, John E. 1987. "Segregation in 1980: How Segregated Are America's Metropolitan Areas?" Pp. 95–114 in *Divided Neighborhoods,* edited by Gary A. Tobin. Newbury Park, CA: Sage.

Farley, Reynolds, and Walter R. Allen. 1987. *The Color Line and the Quality of Life in America.* New York: Russell Sage Foundation.

Foley, Donald L. 1973. "Institutional and Contextual Factors Affecting the Housing Choices of Minority Residents." Pp. 85–147 in *Segregation in Residential Areas,* edited by Amos H. Hawley and Vincent P. Rock. Washington, DC: National Academy of Sciences.

Kain, John F. 1968. "Housing Segregation, Negro Employment and Metropolitan Decentralization." *Quarterly Journal of Economics* 82:175–197.

Kain, John F., and J. M. Quigley. 1975. *Housing Markets and Racial Discrimination: A Micro-Economic Analysis.* New York: National Bureau of Economic Research.

Krase, Jerome. 1982. *Self and Community in the City.* Washington, DC: University Press of America.

Lieberson, Stanley. 1980. *A Piece of the Pie: Black and White Immigrants Since 1880.* Berkeley: University of California Press.

Massey, Douglas S., and Nancy A. Denton. 1987. "Trends in the Residential Segregation of Blacks, Hispanics, and Asians: 1970–1980." *American Sociological Review* 52:802–825.

Molotch, Harvey L. 1972. *Managed Integration.* Berkeley: University of California Press.

New York City Planning Commission. 1969. *Plan for New York City: A Proposal,* Part 3, *Brooklyn.* New York: Author.

New York City Planning Commission. 1974. *Greenpoint: Striking a Balance Between Industry and Housing.* New York: Author.

Pearce, Diana M. 1979. "Gatekeepers and Homeseekers." *Social Problems* 26:325–342.

Rieder, Jonathan. 1985. *Canarsie: The Jews and Italians of Brooklyn Against Liberalism.* Cambridge, MA: Harvard University Press.

Susser, Ida. 1982. *Norman Street.* New York: Oxford University Press.

Suttles, Gerald D. 1968. *The Social Order of the Slum.* Chicago: University of Chicago Press.

Suttles, Gerald D. 1972. *The Social Construction of Communities.* Chicago: University of Chicago Press.

Wellisz, Christopher. 1982. "If You're Thinking of Living in Greenpoint." *New York Times,* December 12, p. R9.

Wienk, Ronald E., Clifford E. Reid, John C. Simonson, and Frederick J. Eggers. 1979. *Measuring Racial Discrimination in American Housing Markets: The Housing Market Practices Survey.* Washington, DC: Department of Housing and Urban Development, Office of Policy Development and Research.

27

Making Contact?

Black-White Social Interaction in an Urban Setting

Lee Sigelman
Timothy Bledsoe
Susan Welch
Michael Combs

Black America and white America have been characterized as two separate, hostile, and unequal nations (Hacker 1992). Study after study of racial attitudes and the legal, economic, and social status of African-Americans has documented that the latter two adjectives—hostile and unequal—are appropriate, but far fewer studies have been made of racial separation. Although considerable research has focused on residential segregation (Massey and Denton 1993), the sheer proximity of the races to one another (Alba and Logan 1993) tells us little about personal interaction between blacks and whites. Fundamental questions remain unanswered about interracial contact in situations that range from casual encounters to intense relationships. . . . In this article, we intensively examine contact between blacks and whites in a major American metropolitan area, Detroit. Our purposes are to determine the prevalence of various sorts of contact between blacks and whites, contrasting the current situation with that of a quarter century ago, and to probe the conditions that facilitate or impede such contact.

The Changing Racial Environment

. . . Detroit offers an excellent setting in which to examine interracial contact, but our primary reason for selecting Detroit as a research site was the unique availability of survey data from the late 1960s—the 1968 and 1969 iterations of the Detroit Area Study.

In 1960, Detroit was less than 30% black. After riots ravaged the city in 1967, white flight to the suburbs turned into a panic-stricken stampede. Large portions of the city—especially the parts with heavy concentrations of blacks—were never rebuilt, and the area was dealt another harsh blow by the deterioration of the American auto industry. Unemployment soared, social pathologies multiplied, and blacks were hit hardest of all. The population of the city plummeted from over 1.5 million in 1970 to barely a million in 1995, while the suburbs grew by 7%. Blacks currently comprise about three-fourths of the city's population but only 6% of the suburbs'. In 1970, the income of the average family in the city was 75% of the income of the average suburban family, but by 1990 it was less than half.

The Detroit metropolitan area is one of 16 "hypersegregated" metropolitan areas in the United States (Massey and Denton 1993). In hypersegregated areas, the spatial separation of the races makes it unlikely that blacks or whites will encounter members of another race in their own neighborhood or in surrounding neighborhoods. The city has some white enclaves, but most whites live in the suburbs, which run the socioeconomic gamut from grimy downriver communities to exclusive Grosse Pointe. Suburban whites tend to make little use of the central city.

Trends in Interracial Contact

On the assumption that broad societal changes have facilitated social contact between blacks and whites (Blau 1977), we expected interracial contact to have increased over the past quarter century. The falling away of legal barriers to integration and the opening up of middle- and upper-echelon jobs to blacks both imply greater interracial contact, though continuing residential segregation limits such contact.

This expectation was confirmed. . . . [D]uring [the 1968/69–1992 period], the proportion of blacks who attended integrated schools more than doubled. As a consequence, the once-pronounced racial gap in the likelihood of having experienced segregated schooling vanished; almost four out of five adults under 70 years of age, black and white alike, attended school with at least one member of the other race.

Most blacks who attended school with whites had numerous white classmates. Indeed, almost 60% of those who went to grade school with whites and almost 70% of those who attended junior high and high school with whites had more than a few white classmates. By contrast, most whites who went to an integrated school had only a few black classmates: only 40% of those who had black classmates in grade school and only 30% of those who had black junior high and high school classmates recall having more than a few. Only 6% of whites were in the racial minority in either grade school or junior high and high school; 20% of blacks in grade school and 25% in junior high and high school were in the racial minority. In this respect, Detroit blacks are roughly similar to those throughout the Midwest, where 30% attended majority-white schools (Orfield 1993, p. 239).

Even in 1968, most blacks had some contact with whites on the job, and since then the trend has continued apace. For whites, job contact with blacks was still the exception in 1969, but by 1992 more than two whites in three had job-related contacts with blacks. . . .

Blacks are no more likely now than they were a quarter century ago to have white families living nearby, but the percentage of whites with at least one black family living in the neighborhood has almost tripled, from 22% to 61%. This is still well below the comparable figure for blacks, but it represents substantial change in a relatively brief period. It is an especially surprising figure in light of Detroit's hypersegregation. However, even though most blacks and whites now have some neighbors of the other race, only 26% of blacks and 13% of whites claim to have more than a few. . . .

Thus, over the last quarter century, Detroit-area blacks have become much more likely to have attended school with whites and to have job-related contacts. If anything, though, they have become somewhat less likely to have white neighbors. For whites,

every trend has been toward greater exposure to blacks, and yet such exposure may be superficial, for example, going to school with only a handful of black students or living near a single black family in a primarily white neighborhood. . . . Because blacks are more likely than whites to engage in neighboring (Lee, Campbell, and Miller 1991) and because in Detroit blacks are more likely to have white neighbors than whites are to have black neighbors, there is a black-white imbalance in visiting neighbors of the other race. That gap may have closed slightly between 1968–69 and 1992, but far more salient is the sheer infrequency of interracial neighboring. As we have seen, approximately one black in five and two whites in five have no neighbors of the other race. Of those who do, only about one in 10, black or white, claims to have the type of relationship in which visiting in one another's home plays any part; 57% of blacks and 66% of whites "hardly know" their neighbors of the other race. . . .

In general, then, whites in metropolitan Detroit have more personal contact with blacks than they did 25 years ago, but they do not have contact with many blacks. Blacks' daily exposure to whites has changed considerably less over the years, and blacks still find themselves, for the most part, interacting with whites in situations where whites are numerically predominant. Finally, close personal contact between blacks and whites, as indicated by having neighbors of the other race in one's home and as distinct from mere exposure or casual contact, has undergone little change. Rare in the late 1960s, it remains rare today.

This is as far as our trend analyses can take us, but it is not as far as we can go. Figure 27.1, based on questions from our 1992 survey about the frequency of conversations with members of the other race in various settings, conveys a more complete picture of personal contact between blacks and whites. Although in most instances blacks are involved in more interracial conversations than whites are, most of these differences are not large. There is exactly the same gradation among the settings for blacks and whites, ranging from settings where conversations between blacks and whites are most likely to those where they are least so. If we compare the totals of frequent and occasional ("sometimes") conversations, we see that conversations while shopping are most common, followed by conversations on the job, at sporting events, and at children's events. Least common are conversations in church or at other religious activities. If we examine only occasions where interracial conversation is frequent, then discussions on the job are by far the most common. Blacks and whites also talk frequently while shopping, but the other types of contact offer fewer opportunities for interracial conversation. . . .

Respondents in our 1992 Detroit survey were asked how many good friends they had of the other race. Forty-three percent of blacks said they have a good friend who is white, and 27% of whites said they have a good friend who is black. These are considerably higher than the proportions observed in a 1975 national survey that used the same definition (Jackman and Crane 1986); in that survey, only 21% of blacks claimed to have a close white friend. Unfortunately, there is no way to determine how much of the difference between the 1975 and 1992 estimates is attributable to the difference between Detroit and the rest of the country and how much stems from change over time. Surely some of it reflects the greater opportunities in Detroit than in the nation as a whole for whites to have black friends, since one-quarter of the Detroit metropolitan area population is black compared with only one-eighth of the nation as a whole. . . .

It is possible that a genuine change in the likelihood of interracial friendships has occurred since the mid-1970s, but we must treat this merely as a possibility. Even if we assume that genuine change has occurred, we must not exaggerate it. In 1992, 73% of whites in the Detroit area claimed to have no black friends at all, and, of those who had any, the great majority (89%) had "only a few"; among blacks, the counterpart figures were only slightly lower (57% and 84%).

Conditions of Interracial Contact

Now let us begin to consider the conditions that facilitate or impede both casual and close interracial contact. Drawing on Blau's (1977) structural analysis of heterogeneity, we probe the impacts of several aspects of the social structure—in particular, physical propinquity and socioeconomic attributes.

The Influence of Propinquity

A simple premise underlies this portion of the model: the greater the physical propinquity of two groups, the greater the likelihood of social interaction between them (Blau 1977, pp. 90–91). Being surrounded for most hours of the day and most days of the week primarily, or even exclusively, by members of one's own race limits one's opportunities for interracial contact, but spending substantial time in a racially heterogeneous environment increases the chances for such contact.

Sheer propinquity increases informal interaction and eventually promotes friendship (Blau 1977; Hallinan 1982; Hallinan and Williams 1989; Verbrugge 1983). People make friends with others who are available to be friends, and neighbors and coworkers generally fit that description better than anyone else (Berscheid and Walster 1969; Festinger, Schachter, and Back 1950; Vander Zanden 1984). Most people's primary daily activities occur within the neighborhood where they live and the place where they work. Almost everyone ventures outside his or her own neighborhood at least occasionally, but most people spend a great deal of their time at home, at work, or somewhere nearby. One study concluded that the two principal determinants of friendship patterns within neighborhoods were the distance between houses and the direction they face (Festinger et al. 1950), and casual contacts tend to be even more localized than close friendships.

How does propinquity affect contact between blacks and whites? Those who live in racially diverse areas have more opportunities to interact with members of the other race than do those who live in all-black or all-white areas, who are racially isolated for a major portion of each day. Accordingly, racially mixed neighborhoods are likely to stimulate interracial friendships and promote interracial contacts in church, school, and civic activities and in casual, everyday endeavors such as shopping (Jackman and

Crane 1986). According to one recent study, low-income blacks who move to white suburbs are just as likely to have friendly contacts with neighbors and are more likely to have white friends than low-income blacks who relocate inside the largely black inner city (Rosenbaum et al. 1991). Racially mixed neighborhoods are also more likely to have integrated schools, enabling interracial friendships to begin developing at an early age and promoting cooperative interactions between black and white parents (DuBois and Hirsch 1990).

Figure 27.1
Frequency of Interracial Conversations, 1992 (% Talking "Frequently" or "Sometimes").

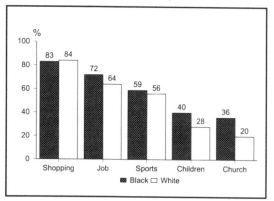

We also know, however, that white acceptance of blacks as neighbors becomes strained when blacks approach 50% of the population (Farley et al. 1994). On that basis, interracial contact might be expected to rise as a function of the percentage of blacks in the population only until that percentage reaches a tipping point, after which interracial contact might be expected to decline. Moreover, the simple likelihood of coming into contact with members of another group increases more rapidly as group numbers initially rise from zero than after the group has achieved substantial size. . . .

The likelihood of interracial contact is affected by where one works. For many white suburbanites and black city dwellers, work may be the main or even the only site of regular contact with members of the other race, whether as coworkers, customers, bosses, or employees. At the very least, having a job outside the home brings one into contact with more people than one encounters when one stays at home. Under certain conditions—as when a black city dweller makes the daily trek out from the predominantly black city to work in a predominantly white suburb, or when a white suburbanite commutes in the opposite direction—working outside the home can increase not only the number but also the variety of the people with whom one has regular contact (Fischer 1982). Moreover, work-based relationships can, over the course of time, be transformed into social relationships and even enduring friendships.

Another opportunity for interracial contact is provided by church attendance, especially if attendance is regular and generalized to other church-related activities. For many blacks and white ethnics, the church is the center of social and community life. Churches in the Detroit area have long crusaded for racial harmony, and several major churches in the city have multiracial congregations.

Nor is *present-day* physical propinquity to members of another race the only consideration, for having had contact as children with members of the other race could also affect current interracial contact. Those who grew up in a racially diverse environment might be expected to view black-white contact as normal and thus to have greater contact with members of the other race.

Indeed, many of the social policies of the 1960s were based on the assumption that race relations would improve if ways could be found to bring blacks and whites together as children. The movement to desegregate public schools was premised not only on the belief that educational opportunity could be equalized only by eliminating single-race schools but also on the belief that something of value would occur if blacks and whites interacted with one another at an early age (Orfield 1993). The same dual rationale propelled the desegregation of other public facilities and of previously all-white residential areas. Harmful racial stereotypes would be reduced, it was assumed, and children who sat together in the classroom, played on the same team, and swam in the same public pool would be better equipped to maintain positive relations with one another as adults.

Here again, then, is the idea that propinquity breeds positivity, especially early in life. During the last quarter century, events have sometimes seemed to contradict this idea. However, because basic attitudes and behaviors tend to be acquired early in life and because children spend most of their time at school or at home, the character of the schools one attended and of the neighborhood in which one grew up can hardly fail to have shaped one's adult attitudes and behaviors. Thus, if there is a carryover effect from youth to adulthood, those who lived in a neighborhood or attended school with children of the other race should be more likely to seek out, or at least accept, interracial contact when they become adults.

The Influence of Personal Attributes

Regardless of where one grew up or currently spends one's time, one's personal attributes are likely to shape one's contact with members of the other race. Beyond the opportunities for greater contact that some social statuses confer (as we discuss below), socioeconomic attributes affect preferences for interracial contact. Some whites who live in all-white areas and some blacks who live in all-black areas are motivated, at least in part, by a desire to be surrounded by others of their own race; Farley et al. (1994) show that about 20% of blacks prefer living in an all-black neighborhood, and, in our survey, 30% of whites favored an all-white neighborhood. Of course, we could measure preference for interracial contact directly by looking at attitudes and opinions but that would beg the issue of whether preferences lead to contact or vice versa. Accordingly, we step back to look at the impact of [two] personal attributes that seem likely to underlie such preferences.

Age. Middle-aged people play more numerous and varied social roles than either the young or the elderly, for during middle age one is likely to function simultaneously as a spouse, parent, worker, and member of various informal groups and community, civic, and recreational organizations (Riley 1985). This surfeit of social roles provides extra op-

portunities for contact with others, including those of another race. People of different ages are also likely to have undergone different socialization experiences and to have learned different attitudes and values, including racial attitudes. Those who grew up during or after the mid-1960s are likely to have acquired more liberal racial and social attitudes than their parents (Hyman and Sheatsley 1956; Greeley and Sheatsley 1971; Schuman, Steeh, and Bobo 1985; Taylor, Sheatsley, and Greeley 1978).

The latter, attitude-based interpretation leads us to anticipate greater interracial contact among the young and middle-aged than among those who grew up prior to the mid-1960s. The opportunity-based interpretation, on the other hand, suggests greater interracial contact among middle-aged people than among their younger or older counterparts. If both interpretations are correct, as we expect, interracial contact should rise as a function of age until it peaks in middle age, after which it should decline at a steeper rate than it rose.

Socioeconomic Status. Because prejudice against blacks is more widespread among less educated, lower- and working-class whites and because estrangement from whites is more intense among less educated, lower- and working-class blacks (Sigelman and Welch 1991), interracial contact may vary according to gradations in socioeconomic status. Moreover, those higher on the status ladder are more likely to have opportunities for contact with members of the other race. The very poor may travel little outside their own neighborhood, but education and affluence lead to greater involvement in a range of social activities that bring blacks and whites into contact with one another. Because of the ghettoization of very poor blacks, we expect socioeconomic status to be an even more crucial determinant of interracial contact among blacks than it is among whites.

In one recent study, blacks with the most education and highest income were the most likely to prefer neighborhoods with significant numbers of whites, and whites with the most education were the least likely to hold negative stereotypes of blacks and to be uncomfortable living near blacks (Farley et al. 1994). However, income did not affect negative stereotyping among whites and had a curvilinear relationship with whites' discomfort about living in neighborhoods with blacks. Those in the $60,000–$80,000 income range expressed the greatest resistance to living in mixed neighborhoods; those with lower or higher incomes were less resistant (Farley et al. 1994). . . .

Summary and Discussion

. . . [The authors analyzed data on both casual and close contacts in the Detroit Area Study and found both propinquity and personal attributes to be important predictors of interracial relations. Over the past quarter century interracial contact has changed in Detroit.] On the one hand, whites in the 1990s are much more likely, and blacks are somewhat more likely, to interact with members of the other race than was the case a quarter century ago. It appears that since the late 1960s, Detroit has become more integrated in fact as well as in law. Indeed, very few residents of the Detroit area (only about 1% of the blacks and 6% of the whites in our 1992 survey) have no personal contact with members of the other race, and most have considerable casual contact. Moreover, in the hypersegregated Detroit area, where media reports of racial hostility appear almost every day, the fact that approximately one person in three has one or more close friends of the other race may be welcomed as unexpectedly good news. . . .

On the other hand, much contact between blacks and whites consists of brief, superficial encounters while shopping, attending sporting events, and the like. Nearly half of the city's black residents do not have a single white friend, and almost the same proportion of whites in the Detroit suburbs have neither a friend nor a social acquaintance who is black. These findings will undoubtedly strike some as bleak corroboration that black and white America are indeed separate. Moreover, some of the increased interracial contact might be of a negative character. Both the popular press and scholarly studies document instances of hostile treatment of blacks

who are simply trying to gain service in restaurants or stores or to walk in or even drive through predominantly white neighborhoods (Feagin 1991).

These findings provide fresh insights into the extent of interracial contact in a hypersegregated city. Indices of hypersegregation are based on aggregate racial housing patterns. Individual patterns of interracial contact are probably positively correlated with indices of housing segregation. Still, considerable interracial contact on the individual level can occur in the presence of hypersegregation, if, for example, white neighborhoods have at least some black residents even though most blacks live in segregated neighborhoods, or if such contact occurs in workplaces among fellow employees or between employees and customers. Thus, we found extensive and increasing interracial contact in Detroit, even in the context of a hypersegregated environment. The other side of the coin is that integrationist policies can promote interracial contact but can do relatively little to promote close interracial ties. Nor can increased interracial contact, or even close interracial ties, guarantee that blacks' and whites' attitudes toward one another will change. Still, the increased interracial contact we have observed in Detroit indicates a potential for improved race relations.

Our findings about the conditions under which interracial contact occurs are straightforward. For whites, propinquity—where one lives, works, and worships—is the key to the quantity and the quality of contact with blacks. However, for blacks, spatial considerations hardly matter. Blacks who work in the suburbs have more contact with whites than do blacks who do not work outside the home, but other spatial considerations are irrelevant. Living in the suburbs, living in a racially integrated neighborhood, and working outside the home but in the city do not bring blacks into more frequent contact with whites. Spatial factors are clearly secondary to early life experiences and personal attributes as influences on blacks' interracial contact. . . .

How might we account for this difference? Part of the answer is that, although within each race people have different preferences for interracial contact, blacks as a group have less of a free hand than do whites to live where they wish. Most blacks would prefer to live in a racially integrated neighborhood (Clark 1991; Farley et al. 1994). However, whereas most blacks want a more or less even mix of blacks and whites, most whites want just a few blacks: when asked in our 1992 survey whether they would rather live in a neighborhood that is all black, mostly black, half black and half white, mostly white, or all white, 44% of whites answered "mostly white" and 30%, "all white"; but 81% of blacks answered "half black and half white." Thus, blacks tend to see integration in terms of numerical equality, but whites are concerned about maintaining their majority status. Moreover, because blacks are often unable to put their residential preferences into practice, their friendship choices are less likely than those of whites to reflect the racial character of their neighborhood.

A different explanation is based on opportunity rather than preference. Other things being equal, members of a minority group should be expected to have more contact with the majority than members of the majority have with the minority. Thus, many whites who live in a predominantly white neighborhood have extremely limited opportunities for contact with blacks, but many blacks who live in a predominantly black neighborhood still have numerous opportunities for contact with whites. And most whites who attended an integrated school had very few black classmates, but many blacks attended predominantly white schools.

For both blacks and whites, interracial contact in general and interracial friendship in particular also reflect early life contact with members of the other race. To the extent that black-white contact and friendship have grown over the years, the greater frequency of early life contact with members of the other race is undoubtedly part of the reason why, and the consequences of such contact should continue well into the future. However, blacks are more likely than whites to be affected by these early life experiences, particularly by the racial composition of the neighborhood in which they grew up. This difference, we believe, is largely reflective of parental social class. For many blacks, having grown up in a racially mixed neighborhood reflects membership in a middle-class family, or at least an upwardly mobile one, but for many whites, having grown up in a racially mixed neighborhood may mean just the opposite.

Earlier we pointed out that increased interracial contact since the late 1960s has not been a purely spontaneous development. Rather, policies such as school integration, equal employment opportunity, and affirmative action have shaped patterns of behavior. Even fair housing laws, though largely ineffectual, may have had some effect, as suggested by the fact that approximately 60% of all whites in the Detroit area and more than 80% of all blacks live in neighborhoods that have at least some residents of the other race. Thus, civil rights policies seem not only to have reduced the sorts of outright discrimination that once kept blacks and whites physically apart; they have also enhanced many blacks' prospects for earning higher wages in better jobs and opened up a wider range of choices concerning the place where they live, the activities in which they are involved, and the people with whom they meet.

The continuing high levels of residential segregation pose a major impediment to further racial integration. We have seen that residential proximity is *the* major predictor of whites' contact with blacks. More intensive efforts to implement fair housing laws have the potential to increase interracial contact, especially among whites.

References

Alba, Richard, and John R. Logan, 1993. "Minority Proximity to Whites in Suburbs: An Individual Level Analysis of Segregation." *American Journal of Sociology* 98: 1388–1427.

Berscheid, Ellen, and Elaine Hatfield Walster. 1969. *Interpersonal Attraction.* Reading, MA: Addison-Wesley.

Blau, Peter. 1977. *Inequality and Heterogeneity.* New York: Free Press.

Clark, W. A. V. 1991. "Residential Preferences and Neighborhood Racial Segregation: A Test of the Schelling Segregation Model." *Demography* 28:1–19.

DuBois, David L., and Barton J. Hirsch. 1990. "School and Neighborhood Friendship Patterns of Blacks and Whites in Early Adolescence." *Child Development* 61: 524–36.

Farley, Reynolds, Charlotte Steeh, Maria Krysan, Tara Jackson, and Keith Reeves. 1994. "Stereotypes and Segregation: Neighborhoods in the Detroit Area." *American Journal of Sociology* 100:750–80.

Feagin, Joe R. 1991. "The Continuing Significance of Race: Antiblack Discrimination in Public Places." *American Sociological Review* 56:101–16.

Festinger, Leon, Stanley Schachter, and Kurt Back. 1950. *Social Pressures in Informal Groups: A Study of Human Factors in Housing.* New York: Harper.

Fischer, Claude S. 1982. *To Dwell Among Friends: Personal Networks in Town and City.* Chicago: University of Chicago Press.

Greeley, Andrew M., and Paul B. Sheatsley. 1971. "Attitudes Toward Racial Integration." *Scientific American* 225:13–19.

Hacker, Andrew. 1992. *Two Nations: Black and White, Separate, Hostile, Unequal.* New York: Scribner's.

Hallinan, Maureen T. 1982. "Classroom Racial Composition and Children's Friendships." *Social Forces* 61:56–72.

Hallinan, Maureen T., and Ruy A. Teixeira. 1987. "Opportunities and Constraints: Black-White Differences in the Formation of Interracial Friendships." *Child Development* 58:1358–71.

Hallinan, Maureen T., and Richard A. Williams. 1989. "Interracial Friendship Choices in Secondary Schools." *American Sociological Review* 54:67–78.

Hyman, Herbert H., and Paul B. Sheatsley. 1956. "Attitudes on Integration." *Scientific American* 195:35–39.

Jackman, Mary R., and Marie Crane. 1986. "'Some of My Best Friends Are Black': Interracial Friendship and Whites' Racial Attitudes." *Public Opinion Quarterly* 50:45 9–86.

Lee, Barrett A., Karen E. Campbell, and Oscar Miller. 1991. "Racial Differences in Urban Neighboring." *Sociological Forum* 6:525–50.

Massey, Douglas S., and Nancy A. Denton. 1993. *American Apartheid: Segregation and the Making of the Underclass.* Cambridge, MA: Harvard University Press.

Orfield, Gary. 1993. "School Desegregation after Two Generations: Race, Schools and Opportunity in Urban Society." Pp. 234–62 in *Race in America: The Struggle for Equality,* edited by Herbert Hill and James E. Jones. Madison: University of Wisconsin Press.

Riley, Matilda White. 1985. "Age Strata in Social Systems." Pp. 369–411 in *Aging and the Social Sciences,* edited by Robert Binstock and Ethel Shanas. New York: Van Nostrand Reinhold.

Rosenbaum, James E., Susan J. Popkin, Julie E. Kaufman, and Jennifer Rusin. 1991. "Social Integration of Low-Income Black Adults in Middle-Class White Suburbs." *Social Problems* 38:448–61.

Schuman, Howard, Charlotte Steeh, and Lawrence Bobo. 1985. *Racial Attitudes in America: Trends and Interpretations.* Cambridge, MA: Harvard University Press.

Sigelman, Lee, and Susan Welch. 1991. *Black Americans' Views of Racial Inequality: The Dream Deferred.* New York: Cambridge University Press.

Taylor, D. Garth, Paul Sheatsley, and Andrew M. Greeley. 1978. "Attitudes toward Racial Integration." *Scientific American* 238: 42–49.

Vander Zanden, James W. 1984. *Social Psychology.* New York: Random House.

Verbrugge, Lois M. 1983. "A Research Note on Adult Friendship Contact: A Dyadic Perspective." *Social Forces* 62: 78–83.

Affirmative Action

One of the most contentious issues on the current political scene is affirmative action. Some opinion polls indicate that support for affirmative action programs has eroded sharply, although the degree of support or opposition expressed by Americans depends heavily on the precise wording of poll questions (Bobo and Kluegel 1993; Steeh and Krysan 1996). For instance, according to a USA Today/CNN/Gallup poll of March 17–19, 1995, when asked "Do you favor or oppose affirmative action programs?" 53 percent of whites expressed support, as compared with only 35 percent who were opposed. As one might expect, African Americans indicated much greater approval of affirmative action (72 percent vs. 21 percent). However, only 30 percent of whites support racial and gender "quotas" for businesses, as compared with 66 percent of African Americans. Similar levels of white opposition surfaced in regard to quotas for school admissions, and requirements that business set up specific goals and timetables for hiring women and minorities (cited in Marable 1996). Further, Proposition 209, which prohibits the use of racial, ethnic, or gender preferences in all public sector programs and activities, was supported by approximately 55 percent of California voters in 1996. Also a series of court decisions have eliminated or scaled back the use of affirmative action in university admissions, government contracts, congressional redistricting, and other arenas.

With the future of affirmative action seemingly in doubt, it is not surprising that the issue has engaged politicians across the ideological spectrum (Skrentny 1996). In recent years, Republicans—even some long-time politicians who initially favored affirmative action— have increasingly come to oppose any use of racial, ethnic, or gender preferences. Thus, conservatives have attempted to use this as a "wedge issue," forcing their opponents to decide which constituencies to offend—suburban and working-class whites (especially men), or racial and ethnic minorities and women, who are increasingly central to the Democratic party coalition. Moderate and liberal leaders, who tend to endorse at least some use of affirmative action, have struggled to articulate a vision for "mending, but not ending" this practice as a tool in the struggle for racial and ethnic equality.

What is affirmative action? Today, this term generally refers to "any effort taken to expand opportunity for women or racial, ethnic, and national origin minorities by using membership in those groups that have been subject to discrimination as a consideration in decision-making or in the allocation of resources" (Edley 1996: 17). As Glasser (this volume) observes, this broad umbrella term is commonly used in discussing several classes of initiatives, including: (a) temporary efforts to provide various types of enhanced opportunities to racial and ethnic minorities (and other groups, such as women) as compensation for past (and perhaps contemporary) discrimination or exclusion; (b) legal remedies, often involving numerical targets or quotas, in response to documented practices or patterns of racial and ethnic (or gender) discrimination; and (c) attempts to ensure fair and visible representation of racial and ethnic minorities in positions when the public good is deemed to require it—e.g., to ensure African American or Latino/a police officers in heavily minority neighborhoods, to provide legitimate opportunities for the election of minority officials in heavily African American or Latino/a political districts, and so on. In practice, most discussions of affirmative action center on the first two types of initiatives.

Advocates of affirmative action argue passionately in favor of programs giving some preference to persons of color in hiring and promotions, college admissions, and other arenas, on grounds of morality and pragmatism (Bergmann 1996; Skrentny 1996; Glasser, this volume). They point out that various minority populations have suffered generations of despicable treatment in the United States. African Americans have experienced slavery, Jim Crow, and the far reaching, long-term legacy of these systemic abuses, while Native Americans have endured a succession of callous policies that border on social, economic, and cultural genocide. Despite the obvious differences in their experiences, these populations, and various other groups, have confronted persistent prejudice and discrimination, often enshrined in legal structures and state policies. Indeed, some observers wryly suggest that European Americans (whites) have benefited from a type of affirmative action for some 400 years. It has been widely argued that the impacts of slavery and colonization persist today, manifested in patterns of cumulative disadvantage that handicap many people of color in the struggle for education, employment, and other opportunities. Others hasten to add that discriminatory practices remain embedded in the everyday workings of corporations, universities, and other gateways to opportunity in American society. Seen from this perspective, because these institutions benefit whites disproportionately, laws that require merely "colorblind" practices and "equal" treatment are unlikely to reduce racial inequality. According to proponents, only affirmative policies that actively target opportunities to qualified people of color have any hope of altering the status quo and reversing these patterns. In turn, many supporters argue that these policies will help to ensure that diverse cultures and viewpoints—shaped by divergent racial/ethnic backgrounds—will have a voice in organizations and institutions which were previously dominated by European Americans (whites), and that peoples of color will have more successful role models to emulate (Carter 1991; Kennedy 1995). In this context, affirmative action is viewed as both morally appropriate and practically necessary (Bergmann 1996). Preference programs aim to compensate African Americans and other racial/ethnic minorities for this legacy of exclusion, and to open universities, corporations, and other institutions to people of color (Glasser, this volume).

Critics reject the moral arguments advanced by proponents of affirmative action (Skrentny 1996). They maintain that the use of racial/ethnic preferences in college admissions, hiring and promotions, government contracts, and other areas merely replaces one form of injustice with another. According to opponents of affirmative action, efforts to take race and ethnicity into account unfairly penalize some people of European American ancestry (and perhaps others, including Asian Americans), many of whom may have worked hard and deserve to reap rewards for their efforts and talents. From this perspective, instead of fulfilling a moral imperative to mitigate the effects of generations of racism and poverty that have been perpetrated against some groups in our society, affirmative action is seen as a form of reverse discrimination (Lynch 1992). Opponents argue that it violates a cardinal tenet of the civil rights movement, namely the belief that all people should be judged on the basis of universal criteria, such as standards of character and accomplishment, rather than on the basis of race, ethnicity, gender, or other ascribed characteristics. Thus, they insist that the allocation of resources and opportunities should be based on putatively race-neutral processes, such as aptitude and skills testing, which are thought to gauge individual merit without bias.

Supporters of affirmative action typically respond to this line of argument in two ways. First, they often point out that few systems actually operate entirely on "merit." Many individuals are hired for jobs through personal networks—they learn about job openings through social contacts, and they benefit via recommendations from insiders or influential members of the community. These advantages, however, are not equally accessible to everyone, and more importantly, they may have little bearing on one's ability to perform work-related tasks. Similarly, many colleges and universities reserve a certain number of admissions slots for "legacies," the progeny of their graduates. Interestingly, few have challenged the legitimacy of these and other deviations from "merit-based" processes.

Second, supporters of affirmative action challenge many conventional yardsticks used to gauge merit, on grounds that they are not race-neutral after all. For example, some scholars and activists allege that the SAT and other tests measure, in part, types of specialized cultural knowledge that is more accessible to middle-class European American students than, for example, to inner-city African American counterparts. If it is true that European Americans have a built-in advantage on these tests—not because of greater intelligence or effort, but because of these hidden biases in the construction of many such tests—then reliance on these "objective" standards of merit may only legitimize and deepen racial and ethnic inequalities.

Skeptics also raise a number of additional issues regarding the ethics of group preferences. For instance, how can we fairly judge the moral standing of the diverse racial and ethnic groups that might seek to benefit from some form of affirmative action? Certainly most observers would agree that, if affirmative action is to be enacted, African Americans and Native Americans should be included. But which segments of the very diverse Latino/a population should benefit from group preferences? And how should we evaluate the standing of groups that have suffered varying types and degrees of prejudice and discrimination but have attained significant aggregate socioeconomic success nevertheless? Examples would include Jewish Americans and some (but not all) segments of the Asian American and Pacific Islander populations. Critics raise these and numerous other examples to underscore the complexities of distributing group preferences based on differing collective histories and degrees of suffering and injustice (Sowell 1989).

Many opponents also believe that affirmative action—however well-intentioned at its inception—has a range of unintended consequences that actually render it counterproductive in the struggle for racial/ethnic equality. Certain of these arguments seem altruistic, expressing concern about the impact of affirmative action on the intended beneficiaries. For instance, some opponents allege that such programs institutionalize a sense of inferiority among African Americans and members of other racial and ethnic minority populations. Critics contend that people of color frequently are left to wonder whether their rewards result from their hard work and individual accomplishment, or from group preferences. Thus, affirmative action is seen as tainting the achievements of all members of racial and ethnic minority groups, sowing the seeds of self-doubt. Although some prominent African-American commentators have embraced this position (Steele 1990, and this volume), there is as yet little evidence that minority students or other people of color feel stigmatized by affirmative action. Some worry that affirmative action may also fuel resentment and backlash among European Americans and others, some of whom unfairly suspect that all people of certain racial and ethnic backgrounds have advanced through special and (in their view) illegitimate means (Lynch 1992). The spectre of affirmative action raises the salience of racial and ethnic categories, and highly successful people of color sometimes express frustration at being labeled as outstanding African-American scholars or top Latino/a engineers, rather than being recognized simply as leaders in their respective fields (Carter 1991).

There are also concerns about the broader social and economic impacts of affirmative action. Some observers maintain that the beneficiaries of these policies are disproportionately middle-class African Americans and Latinos/as, many of whom might well advance without group preferences. Why, the argument goes, should the son or daughter of an African American executive receive special consideration in college admissions, when the child of a European American (white) laborer would not? Despite the rhetorical claims of supporters, critics of affirmative action argue that the benefits rarely trickle down to those who desperately need them—e.g., the ghetto poor. These arguments have persuaded a number of commentators that class-based affirmative action should supplant prevailing systems of race and ethnic preference (Kahlenberg 1995). Indeed, this may be one way to salvage the principle of group preference in an increasingly inhospitable political environment. But others warn that a switch to class-based preferences would benefit mainly poor and working-class European Americans (whites) at the expense of African Americans and other people of color (Thernstrom 1995).

Other objections center on the allegedly destructive impact of the principle of affirmative action on U.S. society and its institutions. Some critics argue that the emergence of group preference programs has encouraged a bewildering array of mobilization campaigns (and even group redefinition), as new groups of aspiring beneficiaries scramble for a piece of the affirmative action pie. Indeed, it is clear that the list of "protected" groups has expanded over time in response to such mobilization, and some observers worry that the increased prominence of group preferences has exacerbated interethnic competition, promoted litigiousness, and eroded productivity (Sowell 1989).

Others express alarm that affirmative action can decrease incentives for skill acquisition and development (Loury 1992). After all, if members of a given group can receive jobs, promotions, and other social goods without obtaining certain skills, then they presumably will become less motivated to expend the extra energy and resources necessary to upgrade their skills. Moreover, the members of other groups will also decline to invest in skill enhancement if they perceive (correctly or incorrectly) that the members of favored groups will gain jobs and promotions denied to others who may be more qualified. Of course this argument is vigorously countered by supporters of affirmitive action who argue that the use of group preference can stimulate productivity by (a) bolstering hope and productivity among previously marginalized groups; and (b) mobilizing new sources of talent and initiative within these untapped populations.

How have affirmative action policies worked? Not surprisingly, opinions differ sharply on this point, and statistics can be marshalled on both sides of the debate. If raw numbers equal success, then there is some evidence that affirmative action has advanced the cause of racial equality. In the years since the advent of these policies, the numbers and proportions of African Americans (and other racial and ethnic minority populations) employed in white-collar (i.e., professional and managerial) occupations and admitted to leading colleges and universities have risen significantly (Hacker 1996). In addition, the numbers suggest that affirmative action has helped to increase minority representation in police and fire departments as well as in blue-collar jobs. Thus, several analyses have concluded that, on balance, the effects of affirmative action on opportunities for racial and ethnic minorities have been positive (Robinson and Spitz 1986–87; Jaynes and Williams 1989).

Predictably, however not everyone agrees; concerns about the implementation of affirmative action come from many different quarters. Some charge that the main beneficiaries of affirmative action have been European American (white) women, and that gains for racial and ethnic minorities, especially males of color, have been meager or nonexistent. While the evidence does suggest that women—especially minority women—enjoy enhanced educational and employment opportunities in the wake of preference programs, however, it does not appear that these gains have come at the expense of men of color (Badgett and Hartmann 1995; Hartmann 1996). Another common complaint from European American workers and managers around the country is that affirmative action has encouraged the hiring and promotion of underqualified employees of color, to the detriment of businesses (Gleckman et al. 1991), although large-scale, systematic evidence for this claim has been elusive (Robinson and Spitz 1986–87). Some sympathetic skeptics also point out that compliance efforts typically focus too narrowly on the *hiring* of minorities. Until recently, much less attention has been given to the retention and long-term development of employees of color or to addressing the resistance to diversity often found among European American managers and workers (Gleckman et al. 1991; Lynch 1997).

Other critics say that focusing solely on this type of result—i.e., the (apparently) improved prospects of people of color—misses the point. A sober evaluation of the performance of affirmative action requires attention to the various costs associated with these programs. To be sure, some supporters argue that most affirmative action is actually voluntary (Hartmann 1996). Government monitoring and enforcement has always been limited and may be declining further due to political opposition and shrinking budgets (Bergmann 1996). Still, opponents contend that the mere threat of a lawsuit by the Equal Employment Opportunity Commission (EEOC)—or, in the case of many firms, the threat of withdrawal of government contracts—has often driven corporations to adopt minority hiring goals and timetables, which are essentially quotas, even though quotas are officially banned by current civil rights laws (Brimelow and Spencer 1993).

Opponents argue that affirmative action entails three types of costs: (a) direct costs, or those incurred by government agencies that investigate and sanction non-compliance with current laws; (b) indirect costs, or the costs borne by the private sector in monitoring and complying with EEOC and other guidelines: filling out paperwork, recruiting workers from "protected" groups, and reorganizing the workplace to accomodate current laws; and (c) opportunity costs, or profits that businesses could have reaped had they been free to invest their resources as they saw fit, to hire the employees they really wanted, and so forth (Brimelow and Spencer 1993). Some estimates now place the total economic cost of affirmative action in the hundreds of billions of dollars annually. Taking this argument to its logical extreme, some conservatives even propose the complete elimination of anti-discrimination laws, claiming that competitive rigor and open bidding for labor in the free market would eventually eliminate most (though perhaps not all) racial and ethnic discrimination (Epstein 1992). They claim it would be cheaper and more efficient simply to pay members of "protected" groups directly, rather than to continue with the current regulatory regime.

Defenders argue that affirmative action has not yet had a fair chance to accomplish its objectives—after all, they point out, it may be unfair to expect a quarter century of preference programs to overcome the legacy of four centuries of slavery and discrimination against African Americans, or various acts and structures of oppression against other groups. Nevertheless, given the range and diversity of these attacks, the future of affirmative action as a tool in the struggle for racial equality is increasingly in doubt (Lipset, this volume). In addition to political reversals like California's Proposition 209, various court decisions have curtailed the circumstances under which affirmative action can be implemented. For instance, several decisions since the late 1980s have curtailed the use of minority contract set-aside programs by state and local governments, requiring specific evidence of discrimination and placing other limitations on these practices. A 1996 decision by the U.S. Fifth Circuit Appelate Court in *Hopwood v. University of Texas* has officiallly prohibited the consideration of race or ethnicity in university admissions in three states, and in Texas this logic has been extended to eliminate minority scholarships, fellowships, and other targeted programs. As this volume goes to press, some politicians have renewed their attempts to ban the use of racial, ethnic, or gender preferences in hiring and contracting by the federal government. A wide range of additional anti-preference initiatives are certain to follow, but they will be contested vigorously. As the scope of affirmative action narrows, the task of crafting new mechanisms for promoting equal opportunity for people of color (e.g., by criminalizing acts of discrimination) will present a formidable challenge for policymakers and citizens alike.

References

Badgett, M.V., and Heidi Hartmann. 1995. "The Effectiveness of Equal Opportunity Employment Policies." In *Economic Perspectives on Affirmative Action*, edited by M. Simms. Washington: Joint Center for Political and Economic Studies.

Bergmann, Barbara. 1996. *In Defense of Affirmative Action*. New York: Basic Books.

Bobo, Lawrence, and James Kluegel. 1993. "Opposition to Race-Targeting: Self-Interest, Stratification Ideology, or Racial Attitudes?" *American Sociological Review* 58: 443–464.

Brimelow, Peter, and Leslie Spencer. 1993. "When Quotas Replace Merit, Everybody Suffers."*Forbes*, February 15.

Carter, Stephen L. 1991. *Reflections of an Affirmative Action Baby*. New York: Basic Books.

Edley, Christopher. 1996. *Not All Black and White: Affirmative Action and American Values*. New York: Hill and Wang.

Epstein, Richard A. 1992. *Forbidden Grounds: The Case Against Employment Discrimination Laws*. Cambridge, MA: Harvard University Press.

Gleckman, Howard, Tim Smart, Paula Dwyer, Troy Segal, and Joseph Weber. 1991. "Race in the Workplace: Is Affirmative Action Working?" *Business Week*, July 8.

Hacker, Andrew. 1996. "Goodbye to Affirmative Action?" *New York Review of Books* (July 11): 21–29.

Hartmann, Heidi. 1996. "Who Has Benefited from Affirmative Action in Employment?" Pp. 77–98 in *The Affirmative Action Debate*, edited by George E. Curry. Reading, MA: Addison-Wesley.

Jaynes, Gerald, and Robin M. Williams, Jr. 1989. *A Common Destiny*. Washington: National Academy Press.

Kahlenberg, Richard. 1995. "Class, Not Race." *New Republic*, April 3. (Reprinted in *Affirm-*

ative Action, edited by A. Sadler. San Diego: Greenhaven Press, 1996.)

Kennedy, Duncan. 1995. "A Cultural Pluralist Case for Affirmative Action in Legal Academia." Pp. 159–176 in *Critical Race Theory*, edited by Kimberle Crenshaw, Neil Gotanda, Gary Peller, and Kendall Thomas. New York: New Press.

Loury, Glenn C. 1992. "Incentive Effects of Affirmative Action." *Annals of the American Academy of Political and Social Science* 523: 19–29.

Lynch, Frederick R. 1992. *Invisible Victims: White Males and the Crisis of Affirmative Action*. New York: Greenwood Press.

——. 1997. *The Diversity Machine: The Drive to Change the 'White Male Workplace.'* New York: Free Press.

Marable, Manning. 1996. "Staying on the Path to Racial Equality." Pp. 3–15 in *The Affirmative Action Debate*, edited by George E. Curry. Reading, MA: Addison-Wesley.

Robinson, William L., and Stephen L. Spitz. 1986–87. "Affirmative Action: Evolving Case Law and Shifting Philosophy." *Urban League Review* 10 (Winter): 84–100.

Skrentny, John D. 1996. *The Ironies of Affirmative Action: Politics, Culture, and Justice in America*. Chicago: University of Chicago Press.

Sowell, Thomas. 1989. "Affirmative Action: A Worldwide Disaster." *Commentary* (December), 21–41.

Steeh, Charlotte, and Maria Krysan. 1996. "Affirmative Action and the Public, 1970–1995." *Public Opinion Quarterly* 60: 128–158.

Steele, Shelby. 1990. *The Content of Our Character*. New York: St. Martins Press.

Thernstrom, Abigail. 1995. "A Class Backwards Idea." *Washington Post*, June 11.

28

Equal Chances Versus Equal Results

Seymour Martin Lipset

Affirmative action policies, perceived as special preferences or numerical goals for women, blacks, and other defined minorities, have become a major political issue, a subject for congressional debate and action in new civil rights legislation. These policies have introduced a new approach to the concern for equality in American life initially voiced in the Declaration of Independence. That early concern stressed equal opportunity for individuals. The new one focuses on equality of results for groups.

Two Peoples, Two Stratification Systems

From its beginning as a string of colonies, this country has been composed of two peoples in two different stratification systems. One system emphasized egalitarianism, respect across class lines, equal opportunity, meritocracy. For most of our history, the other has been a system of explicit hierarchy, caste, and hereditary inequality.

The treatment of blacks has been the foremost deviation from the American creed. Blacks have been here since the early 1600s. Until 1865, however, most were slaves; during the next 100 years, most worked as a lower caste under Jim Crow policies, with little chance to gain much education or money. The caste system of slavery and segregation was far more hierarchical and hereditary than European feudalism. Only since the 1950s and 1960s have blacks had a true claim to political equality and economic opportunity.

Thomas Jefferson and George Washington voiced their concern over how the treatment of blacks would affect the nation's future. Jefferson wrote, "I tremble for my country when I reflect that God is just."[1] Anticipating that the nation might break up because it could not resolve the problem, Washington told a friend that, if this happened, "he had made up his mind to move and be of the northern."[2]

Group Solutions

Growing attention to the caste situation of blacks from the 1950s on resulted in efforts to find a group solution. These have been called "affirmative action." The term has had two meanings. The first, emerging in the 1960s, involved attempts to incorporate blacks into the general race for success. Lyndon Johnson explained this policy at Howard University in 1965. He said that, as a society, we want all Americans to engage in the race, but some have shackles on their legs; hence programs are needed to remove the chains so that all can compete equally. These programs became the war on poverty, including Head Start, Aid to Families with Dependent Children, and other programs to help poor, predominantly black, families gain a better education and better skills.

These programs were backed by strong Fair Employment and Fair Housing acts designed to end discrimination against blacks in the workplace, education, housing, and clubs. The assumption was that, with equal education and the full political citizenship ensured by Voting Rights acts, blacks could win their legal rights as individuals in the courts and administrative tribunals.

Concern that these policies were not working as quickly as was hoped and that racial barriers still operated in various arenas led to the second type of affirmative action. It emphasizes group solutions: not equal opportunity for individuals but equal results for groups. It assumes that the best way to improve the situation of blacks is by numerical goals and preferences in education and jobs.

Such goals and preferences, advocated by the black leader Martin Delany as early as 1871,[3] were introduced in 1969 by the Nixon administration. George Shultz, Nixon's first

Secretary of Labor, concluded that antidiscrimination judgments by courts and administrative agencies would do little and take too long to open discriminatory parts of the labor market to blacks. He issued an order setting quotas for black apprentices in the Philadelphia construction trades, where both employers and unions excluded blacks. The policy was soon extended to other cities and industries. Similar programs for faculty and students in higher education were pressed by other officials with Nixon's approval.[4]

These policies were strongly opposed by a Johnson appointee, Comptroller General Elmer Staats, trade union leaders, and most congressional Democrats, who argued that the 1964 Civil Rights Act outlawed numerical hiring. Congress, however, rejected a rider to bar the so-called Philadelphia Plan. Republicans opposed the rider 124 to 41, while Democrats supported it 115 to 84.[5] George Bush, then a Texas congressman and planning a campaign against liberal Democratic Senator Ralph Yarborough, who opposed employment quotas, emphasized his vote for a fair-housing bill and racial job preferences. The leaders and the parties were soon to reverse their positions.

The government has applied the principle of group rights to other minorities and women, though opinion polls show that overwhelming majorities of white men and women and often a majority of blacks believe that only individuals, not groups, should be treated equally. Nonetheless, major segments of American elites believe in group remedies for blacks and other groups perceived to lack equal rights: Hispanics, Native Americans, Asians, women, and the handicapped.

The Case for Group Preference

Blacks are the quintessential distinctive American minority group, better able than any other ethnic or social group but Native Americans to justify a claim for preferential treatment. Some even argue for reparations as follows: whites profited greatly from the labor of slaves and the Jim Crow years when blacks, as outcasts under the law, did the hard, low-paid work of unskilled laborers, field hands, servants, and maids. Thereby whites acquired the leisure, education, and wealth of which they deprived blacks and for which blacks deserve compensation.

Parallel cases are the compensation of Indian tribes for removal from their lands; the acknowledgment by Congress of an obligation to recompense Japanese Americans for their detention during World War II; and the German government's reparations to Jews and Israel. Veterans receive preference for civil service jobs, special educational benefits, and cheap home mortgages.

Individualistic values handicap the socially depressed in all societies. People tend to hire and favor members of their own social and ethnic groups. Few institutions acknowledge such preferences. Many or most private universities, including Harvard, Chicago, and Stanford, have given preference to the children of alumni, faculty, and athletes, however. Many scholarships have been limited to persons from special regional, gender, ethnic, or religious groups; some but not all of these are now illegal.

In 1963, I noted, "Perhaps the most important fact to recognize about the current situation of the Negro is that *equality is not enough to assure his movement into the larger society.*[6] Other minorities and women have required only genuine equal opportunity, not special help. In any case, immigrants have no claim to preferential treatment, since any handicaps they may have are clearly not the fault of American society. Immigrants, including Hispanics and West Indians, generally do better economically the longer they are in this country.

Lawrence Fuchs has argued that preferential employment should be confined to jobs requiring adequacy or competence. Jobs requiring higher standards—for example, medicine, scholarship, sports, management, airline pilots—should not be subject to preferential policies. Thus affirmative programs for Navy pilots or ballet dancers should be "limited to special recruitment and training efforts," whereas numerical goals can serve to increase the number of minority "fire fighters, machinists, computer operators, and candidates for dental school."[7]

Whatever the merits of the distinction between mere competence and high ability, fire fighters, police officers, or assembly-line workers do not accept this disparaging assessment of their worth and skills. In many opinion polls, such workers favor meritocratic standards for their jobs. In fact, white elites, whose economic and social status is more secure, are more likely than workers to endorse preferences for minorities.

Public Opinion

Mass opinion remains opposed to preferential treatment. Thus the Gallup poll has repeated one question five times between 1977 and 1989: "Some people say that to make up for past discrimination, women and minorities should be given preferential treatment in getting jobs and places in college. Others say that ability, as determined by test scores, should be the main consideration. Which point of view comes close to how you feel on the subject?" In each survey, 81–84 percent replied "ability" and 10–11 percent, "preferential treatment." In 1989, 56 percent of blacks favored "ability, as determined in test scores"; only 14 percent, compared to 7 percent of whites, supported preferential treatment. Women and men responded alike: 85 percent favored ability and 10 percent, preferential treatment.[8]

Gallup presented the issue somewhat differently in 1987 and 1990: "We should make every effort to improve the position of blacks and other minorities even if it means giving them preferential treatment." In this formulation, with no mention of ability or test scores, 71–72 percent opposed and 24 percent supported preferential treatment in both years. Over two-thirds of blacks rejected preference, while 32 percent—and 18 percent of whites—favored it. Over four-fifths of Republicans and two-thirds of Democrats opposed preference.[9]

In 1991, when Gallup posed the issue in terms of equal qualifications, whites were still opposed, but blacks were more favorable. The question was this: "Do you believe that because of past discrimination against black people, qualified blacks should receive preference over equally qualified whites in such matters as getting into college or getting jobs?" Only 19 percent of whites but 48 percent of blacks said "yes," while 72 percent of whites and 42 percent of blacks opposed such preference.

Americans will, however, support affirmative action programs that do not involve quotas. In an ABC News-*Washington Post* poll in July 1990, 66 percent of whites and 84 percent of blacks responded favorably to the question, "All in all, do you favor or oppose affirmative action programs in business for blacks, provided there are no rigid quotas?" The Harris poll reported similar responses to comparable questions several times in the 1980s.

Many inconsistencies in racial attitudes point to a deep contradiction between two core values in the American creed—individualism and egalitarianism. Political debate often takes the form of one value opposing the other. Liberals and conservatives typically do not take opposing positions on issues of equality and freedom; instead, they appeal to one or the other value. Liberals stress egalitarianism and the social injustice that flows from unfettered individualism. Conservatives enshrine individual freedom and the social need for mobility and achievement as values endangered by the collectivism inherent in liberal nostrums. Both sides treat the entire American public as their natural constituency. In this sense, liberals and conservatives are less opponents than competitors, like two department stores on the same block trying to draw the same customers by offering different versions of what everyone wants.

The egalitarian element in the American creed created the consensus behind the civil rights revolution of the past thirty years. The more recent focus on group equality and preference, conflicting with the individualistic, achievement-oriented element, has broken the consensus.

Poll data reveal a pro-civil-rights consensus when only egalitarian questions are raised, but an anti-civil-rights consensus when an issue also challenges basic notions of individualism. Public opinion, even in the white South, is powerfully against racial discrimination. Many whites, however, deeply resent compulsory integration and quotas, believing that they violate their rights. Liberals note the inegalitarian consequences of de facto segregation, but most whites prefer individual freedom to compulsory social egalitarianism.

Most whites and many blacks feel it is better for disadvantaged groups to resolve their problems by individual effort and advancement than to demand benefits for all group members. Most oppose special treatment for blacks even when it does not involve preferences, because it violates the idea of racial equality. Thus, in a 1989 poll, 64 percent of whites and 44 percent of blacks disagreed with the statement "Because of past discrimination, blacks who need it should get some help from the federal government that white people in similar economic circumstances don't get."

The claims of women and of blacks and other minorities to full equality are now widely accepted. The General Social Survey, conducted by the National Opinion Research Center every two years, indicates steady improvement in attitudes toward racial equality in many spheres from 1972 through 1990. A large majority of white Americans believes that discrimination is wrong and that government should guarantee the application of competitive merit principles to all, blacks and whites. In a 1991 Gallup poll, 47 percent of whites and 63 percent of blacks said they "socialize regularly with members of another race." Only 6 percent of whites said they would be "uncomfortable working with members of another race" or "for a boss of another race."[10] But every national survey shows that a sizable majority of whites opposes giving special consideration in hiring or school admission to less formally qualified persons.

Americans distinguish compensatory action from preferential treatment. Few object to the former, which helps disadvantaged people improve their qualifications by special training and community development."[11] But most object to the latter, in which standards of admission or employment are lowered for disadvantaged people.

The major support for preferential policies seems to come from the liberal intelligentsia, the well-educated, and those who have studied liberal arts in college or have gone to graduate school. It is strong among the political elite, particularly Democrats but many Republicans as well. Congressional Democrats increasingly support such policies; the proportion of these Democrats with a liberal voting record has grown steadily since the 1960s. Universities, more liberal than other institutions, also support them. Their most extensive use of numerical goals occurs in the humanities and soft social sciences, whose faculty and students are more liberal than those in other academic fields.

Political Implications

The affirmative action debate shows no sign of moderating. Quotas were a major issue in several 1990 elections. HR 1, the first bill introduced by Democratic leaders of the House of Representatives in the 1991 session, was a civil rights measure called a quota bill by its opponents. A revised, but essentially similar bill was eventually passed and signed by George Bush.

The arguments over quotas or preferences appear increasingly to strengthen Republicans, who now vigorously emphasize meritocratic standards. Their earlier support for quotas has been forgotten. Most Democrats face a dilemma: how to respond to pressure from civil rights groups and the intelligentsia without alienating the party's traditional white working-class support. In 1965, in a private discussion of civil rights, Lyndon Johnson said, "We have to press for them as a matter of right, but . . . by doing so we will destroy the Democratic party." He anticipated that much of the white South and northern white workers would defect.[12] This has happened, particularly in presidential elections since 1968.

In 1990, North Carolina Senator Jesse Helms won reelection by exploiting the issue of affirmative hiring. Ex-Klansman David Duke did the same in Louisiana and received a majority of white votes in the senatorial primary. Democrat Dianne Feinstein's espousal of quotas in state government employment contributed to her losing the California gubernatorial race. Two studies commissioned by the Michigan Democratic Party in 1985 and 1987 showed that affirmative action played a major role in the party's loss of support. "Quotas and minority preferences were a primary source of anti-government, anti-Democrat anger among white blue-collar voters. Democratic campaign themes such as 'fairness,' 'equity,' and 'justice' had been perceived . . . as code words for quotas."[13]

National polls report similar findings. In 1986 and 1990, 70 percent or more of whites agreed that it was "very likely" or "somewhat likely" that "a white person won't get a job or promotion while an equally or less qualified black person gets one instead." A 1991 poll sponsored by the Leadership Conference on Civil Rights reported that "many white voters believe there is pervasive reverse discrimination in the work place and that civil rights leaders are more interested in special preference than in equal opportunity."[14] Commenting on this study, black columnist William Raspberry wrote, white Americans . . . do not see themselves as racists, or as opponents of equal opportunity . . . they oppose . . . preferential benefits for minorities."[15]

Black Progress—A Contentious Issue

Blacks remain considerably behind whites in income and employment levels but are much better off than they were before the civil rights movement and the adoption of various remedial programs. Awareness of such gains is not widespread, however, in part because black, Hispanic, and women's leaders do not admit to significant progress. In the mid-1980s, three-fifths of black leaders told pollsters the situation of blacks was "going backwards." Contrariwise, two-thirds of a national black sample said they were "making progress," though support for this view declined somewhat in the latter years of the Reagan era.[16] In July 1990, an NBC News-*Wall Street Journal* poll reported that 60 percent of blacks felt that blacks were "better off" than ten years before.

The refusal of black leaders to acknowledge improvement is understandable. The worse things seem, the more the leaders can demand. Yet their emphasis on how little progress has been made sustains the argument that programs to help blacks do not work, that some factors inherent in the black situation prevent progress. Most whites and many blacks have absorbed such negative images. In an ABC News-*Washington Post* survey in 1989, over half of whites and blacks agreed that "discrimination has unfairly held down blacks, but many of the problems blacks in this country have today are brought on by blacks themselves."

Black youths are often told that society is racist, that there is, therefore, no point in trying to work hard or study. Many develop the same invidious stereotypes about blacks as do whites. These images are sustained by the great social morbidity of poor blacks in the ghettos that is so very visible to the media and the public. Reports pour out about the high rate of black crime, homelessness, drug addiction, infant mortality, youth homicide and unemployment, and adult illness.

But the underclass, both black and white, is small. Paul Peterson reports that the metropolitan census tracts in which 40 percent or more of the people are poor—William J. Wilson's definition of the ghetto poor—contained "little more than one percent of the U.S. population in 1980."[17] An Urban Institute study estimates the size of the underclass, both white and black, as 2 or 3 million in 1980.[18]

The status of a major proportion of blacks has improved dramatically. From 1970 to 1988, the proportion comprising high school dropouts fell from 31 to 18 percent, compared to 14 percent of whites in both years.[19] The proportion of blacks living in poverty fell from 55 percent in 1959 to 31 percent in 1989.[20] The black middle class outnumbers the black poor.[21] The proportion of blacks living in urban ghettos has declined. Most blacks have steady jobs, are members of the middle or working class, and are married or in stable relationships. Middle-class black fertility is below that of middle-class whites.[22] The sharp rise in the proportion of black births in female-headed households—from 23 percent in 1960 to 62 percent in 1990—reflects not a big increase in the number of illegitimate births but a drastic fall in the birth rate of married black women.[23]

It is doubtful that racial preference has done or can do much for socially fatherless black ghetto youths who lack marketable skills. The federal contract compliance program has "raised demand for black males more in highly skilled white-collar and craft jobs than in the blue-collar operative, laborer, and service occupations." Antidiscrimination litigation has led to gains in white-collar, professional, and managerial positions.[24] Similar class differences have been reported in the effects of affirmative action on women's employment.[25]

As William J. Wilson observes, "affirmative action programs are not designed to deal with the unique problems of the black poor"[26] but with "minority individuals from the most advantaged families . . . [who are] most qualified for preferred positions—such as higher-paying jobs, college admissions, promotions and so forth."[27] One study showed that, from 1974 to 1981, young black college graduates "obtain[ed] more prestigious posts than their white counterparts," a result attributed to "employer sensitivity to affirmative action requirements" and the "concentration of educated blacks in the public sector."[28] This pattern declined with the early 1980s recession and the halt in the growth of government employment, however. By the late 1980s, the "earning gap between blacks and whites with college education [had] widened sharply."[29]

Conclusion

White opposition to various forms of special government assistance for blacks and other minorities is in part a function of a general antagonism to statism and a preference for personal freedom.

Although Americans are less willing than Europeans to use government as an instrument of income distribution, their egalitarianism leads them to approve certain programs to provide more opportunities for blacks—for example, expenditures on education, special schools, and Head Start. But Americans are much less prone to endorse general measures to help the underprivileged. Thus in 1987 only 21 percent agreed that "the government should provide everyone with a guaranteed basic income," compared to 50 percent or more of Germans, Austrians, Italians, Dutch, and Britons. Only 29

percent of Americans but 60 percent or more of Europeans agreed that "it is the responsibility of the government to reduce the differences in income between people with high incomes and those with low incomes."[30]

The greater American opposition to state intervention is not limited to such economic measures. For instance, only 49 percent of Americans but 80 percent or more of Europeans and Australians feel that "the wearing of seat belts should be required by law."[31]

The vast majority of Americans, including most blacks, believe this is still a land of opportunity where merit and ambition are rewarded. In 1988, 71 percent—compared to 23–43 percent of Dutch, Germans, Britons, and Italians—said they had a good chance to improve their standard of living. More Americans than Europeans believe "ambition is [essential or very important] for getting ahead in life."[32]

Most Americans still think their children will do well. Though still concerned about the economy in 1992, large majorities say their personal economic situation is good. The rates of social mobility into professional and other privileged positions, measured in elaborate detail by sociologists, remain high. Changes in the occupational structure accompanying the shift to a postindustrial economy have led to increased upward movement, as measured by comparing the occupations of respondents to those of their parents. Most Americans believe that ambition and hard work, not "lucky breaks," "help from other people," or "a wealthy family," is what enables people to move up.

Success in postindustrial society requires a good education. While the education of blacks has improved significantly, it is often well behind that of whites, in real knowledge, at the same grade level. The black underclass is proportionally much larger than the white. Preferences will not help poorly educated persons to secure good jobs. Extending and vastly improving education and training programs is the way to help poor people regardless of their race or ethnicity.

We can learn from the success of the integrated armed forces in offering stable employment, effective career training, and real economic opportunity to young black and white adults. If all youths were able to take part in a voluntary national service program for two or more years, those with inadequate education and skills could be trained for needed positions while helping to rebuild the national infrastructure.

Post-feudal European society was structured into a fixed hierarchy in which each lower class deferred to superior classes. Consequently, the emerging European working class responded to the political world in class terms marked by the development of socialist parties. Conversely, white America, the purest bourgeois and classically liberal society in the world, has treated class as an economic construct; its social class hierarchy was less visible and more open than the European.

Hence class-conscious politics and socialist demands for measures of economic equalization have been limited. As Walter Dean Burnham put it, "No feudalism, no socialism."[33]

The situation of American blacks is analytically comparable to that of European peasants and workers. Their post-caste situation has limited their economic and social prospects more than the post-feudal situation restricted those of their European counterparts. It is not surprising, therefore, if blacks are more group conscious than European workers or if many support a version of the old socialist emphasis on equality of results. Ninety percent vote Democratic, much more than any other ethnic group or union members. Blacks back Jesse Jackson's Rainbow Coalition, which supports stronger income redistribution policies and greater state involvement in the economy than socialists in other countries. At least three black congressmen are openly socialist. Poll data show blacks divided about how much to favor policies of group uplift or of individual opportunity. This debate goes back at least to the Reconstruction period, when Frederick Douglass ridiculed the idea of racial quotas as "absurd," as they implied, to him, that blacks "should constitute one-eighth of the poets, statesmen, scholars, authors and philosophers." Douglass opposed "special efforts" for the freedmen because "promoting an image of blacks as privileged wards of the state" might sustain prejudices that should

be banished.[34] Like Douglass, Shelby Steele, once a Rainbow Coalition activist, now argues that blacks "stand to lose more from . . . [affirmative action] than they gain." He rejects the idea of leaping "over the hard business of developing a formerly oppressed people to the point where they can achieve proportionate representation on their own" and suggests that preferences undermine morale, implying that successful blacks have not earned their positions but are inferior to whites.[35]

Civil rights leaders, liberals, and Democrats need to combat their identification with preferential policies and reverse discrimination. The American Left from Jefferson to Hubert Humphrey stood for equal opportunity. By a supreme irony, Richard Nixon, the man most hated by Democrats, initiated the policy that has placed them on the wrong side of this issue politically. The leaders of strong Democratic factions—of minorities, feminists, liberals, and the intelligentsia—strongly endorse numerical goals and preferential policies, but a substantial majority of Americans, including most Democrats, oppose them. Americans basically agree with an emphasis on equal rights for individuals and social programs that serve everyone or all those in a given condition such as poverty or illness, not people with fixed hereditary characteristics.

White Americans have emphasized individual rights more than any other people. Yet the situation of blacks has contradicted the principles on which the nation was established. The American dilemma persists. Until blacks are absorbed into our economy and society, we must, in Jefferson's words, be fearful of a just God.

Endnotes

1. Thomas Jefferson, *Notes on the State of Virginia* (New York: Harper & Row Torchbooks, 1964), p. 156.

2. James T. Flexner, *Washington: The Indispensable Man* (New York: New American Library, 1984), pp. 389–90.

3. Martin, Delany, *Homes for the Freedman* (Charleston, SC, 1871).

4. Hugh D. Graham, *The Civil Rights Era* (New York: Oxford University Press, 1990), pp. 326–31.

5. Ibid., pp. 339–40.

6. Seymour M. Lipset, *The First New Nation* (New York: Basic Books, 1963), p. 331; italics in original.

7. Lawrence H. Fuchs, *The American Kaleidoscope* (Middletown, CT: Wesleyan University Press, 1990), pp. 451–52.

8. *Gallup Poll Monthly*, p. 18 (Dec. 1989).

9. In the 1987 survey; the 1990 results were similar.

10. *Newsweek*, 6 May 1991, pp. 30–31.

11. S. M. Lipset and William Schneider, "The Bakke Case," *Public Opinion*, 1:38–44 (Mar.-Apr. 1978).

12. Nicholas Lemann, *The Promised Land* (New York: Knopf, 1991), p. 183.

13. Study report by Stanley Greenberg of the Analysis Group, cited in Frederick R. Lynch, *Invisible Victims* (Westport, CT: Greenwood Press, 1989), p. 3.

14. Thomas B. Edsall, "Rights Drive Said to Lose Underpinnings," *Washington Post*, 9 Mar. 1991.

15. William Raspberry, "Why Civil Rights Isn't Selling," *Washington Post*, 13 Mar. 1991.

16. Linda S. Lichter, "Who Speaks for Black America?" *Public Opinion*, 8:41–44, 59 (Aug.-Sept. 1985).

17. Paul E. Peterson, "The Urban Underclass and the Poverty Paradox," in *The Urban Underclass*, ed. Christopher Jencks and Paul Peterson (Washington, DC: Brookings Institution, 1991), p. 22.

18. Ronald B. Mincy et al., "The Underclass: Definition and Measurement," *Science*, 27 Apr. 1990, p. 451.

19. Ben J. Wattenberg, *The First Universal Nation* (New York: Free Press, 1991), p. 67.

20. U.S., Department of Commerce, Bureau of the Census, *Money Income and Poverty Status in the United States 1989*, Current Population Reports, Consumer Income, series P–60, 1990, no. 168, pp. 57–58.

21. James P. Smith and Finis R. Welch, *Closing the Gap* (Santa Monica, CA: RAND, 1986), p. ix.

22. Lemann, *Promised Land*, p. 283; Ben J. Wattenberg, *The Birth Dearth* (New York: Pharows Books, 1987), p. 7.

23. Christopher Jencks, "Is the American Underclass Growing?" in *Urban Underclass*, ed. Jencks and Peterson, pp. 86–89.

24. Jonathan S. Leonard, "The Impact of Affirmative Action Regulation and Equal Employment Law on Black Employment," *Journal of Economic Perspectives*, 4:53, 60 (Fall 1990).

25. James P. Smith and Michael Wood, "Women in the Labor Market and the Family," *Journal of Economic Perspectives*, 3:15 (Winter 1989).

26. William J. Wilson, "Race, Class, and Public Policy," *American Sociologist*, 16:126–27 (May 1981).

27. William J. Wilson, *The Truly Disadvantaged* (Chicago: University of Chicago Press, 1978), pp. 18–19.

28. In Soo Son et al., "Polarization and Progress in the Black Community," *Sociological Forum*, 4:323 (Sept. 1989).

29. Henry Aaron, "Symposium on the Economic Status of African Americans," *Journal of Economic Perspectives*, 4:5 (Fall 1990).

30. Tom Smith, "Social Inequality in Cross-National Perspective," in *Attitudes to Inequality and the Role of Government*, ed. J. E. Becker et al. (The Hague: CIP Gegevens Koninklije Bibliotheek, 1990), p. 24.

31. "America's Unique Outlook," *American Enterprise*, 1:116 (Mar.-Apr. 1990).

32. Tom Smith, "Social Inequality," p. 24; "America's Unique Outlook," p. 116.

33. Walter D. Burnham, "The United States: The Politics of Heterogeneity," in *Electoral Behavior*, ed. Richard Rose (New York: Free Press, 1974), p. 718.

34. Philip S. Foner, ed., *The Life and Writings of Frederick Douglass* (New York: International, 1955), 4:280–81, 67–68.

35. Shelby Steele, *The Content of Our Character* (New York: St. Martin's Press, 1990), p. 13.

Reprinted from: Seymour Martin Lipset, "Equal Chances Versus Equal Results." In *Annals of the American Academy of Political and Social Science* 523: 63–74. Copyright © 1992 by Sage Publications, Inc. Reprinted by permission.

29

Affirmative Action and the Legacy of Racial Injustice

Ira Glasser

Origins and Definitions

Because affirmative action has become something of an undifferentiated code word, for both its advocates and its opponents it is useful to define our terms. The concept of affirmative action, as distinct from the term, has two separate, though related, origins. Under one definition, affirmative action is a narrow, if drastic, *legal remedy*, temporarily imposed or approved by the courts in particular cases to redress the specific effects of past or current discrimination, where such discrimination has been proved. Under the second definition, affirmative action is a broad kind of moral reparation, a form of temporary *compensatory opportunity*, designed to make up generally for past injustices and to get things even again before allowing the race to continue on relatively equal terms. There is a third strain of thought as well, which defines affirmative action as an effort to achieve *fair and visible representation* for minorities for reasons of social or political effectiveness. Under this definition, for example, police forces in inner cities should reflect a fair proportion of blacks not only because that may be a remedy for specific discrimination or a compensation for prior exclusions, but also because we will have a better police force when blacks are included, especially if a large proportion of the community is black. This argument has also been applied to teachers

and other employment categories. The argument has been made most forcefully with respect to political representation on governing bodies such as local legislatures and school boards.

People who make such arguments claim that such representation in leadership roles is not only a legitimate extension of the right of suffrage itself, but also a manifestation of full citizenship and a crucial indicator that, at last, historic racial exclusions from the rights of citizenship have ended. Moreover, some political scientists, notably Philip Green (1981), have argued that only the creation of leadership classes that forcefully demonstrate the capabilities inherent in the communities excluded can begin to erode the internalized belief on the part of many in the excluded group that somehow the fault is theirs.

Although this line of argument provides a compelling justification for affirmative action, it is not itself affirmative action, as no one argues that such representation should be mandated in the absence of discriminatory exclusion or independently of whatever standards of merit otherwise apply. In fact, therefore, affirmative action is usually understood to mean either a specific legal remedy to specific discriminatory exclusion or a more general, if temporary, compensatory opportunity for the members of a group that has long been disadvantaged relative to the dominant social group. Both of these definitions will be examined below.

Affirmative Action as Legal Remedy

The problem that most easily illustrates this concept is jury discrimination. Imagine a southern town with 40% of its adult population black, not one of whom has ever served on a jury. A civil rights suit is brought, and after a trial, the judge finds that the town has discriminated on the basis of race and that this discrimination is illegal. An order is issued requiring the town to stop discriminating. A year later, the plaintiffs are back in court. Their complaint is that the town is still discriminating, despite the court order. The town defends itself by proving that 10 blacks have served or have been called to serve on juries during the past year. But the judge finds that 10 blacks amount to only one-tenth of 1% of the adult population. As all adults are qualified to serve and should be chosen at random, it is impossible to believe that so few blacks would be chosen unless racial discrimination was still being practiced. The town offers other explanations, but none is found to be persuasive. The judge rules that discrimination has continued and orders the town once again to stop, and to institute a new system for choosing jurors that will ensure nondiscrimination.

Six months later, everyone is back in court again. This time the plaintiffs seek an order requiring the town to meet a goal of 40% blacks in the jury pool within the next 3 months. The town again claims that it is no longer discriminating and says that it is trying as hard as it can to include blacks. But the facts show that only 10% of the jury pool is black—a vast improvement, but still far short of what one would expect if there were no discrimination. The judge closely examines the procedures used by the town as well as its explanations for why only 10% of the jury pool is black when 40% of the available qualified population is black and when the choice is supposed to be random. The judge also takes into consideration the history of entrenched racism in the town and the particular impact of that racism on jury selection. After the trial, the court finds that, despite significant improvement, the only explanation for the continued exclusion of blacks is discrimination. The town claims that it no longer intends to discriminate, but intent is hard to prove, and given the long history of purposeful discrimination, the court looks to the effect of the system for choosing jurors and finds that it continues to exclude disproportionate numbers of qualified blacks. As a result, the court now orders a more drastic remedy to rectify the continued exclusion: the town is ordered to adopt a system that results in approximately 40% blacks in the jury pool, plus or minus 3%, within 6 months. Moreover, an independent monitor is appointed by the court to review the town's progress and to report periodically to the court.

It is difficult to see why anyone would find this sort of specific remedy objectionable, under the circumstances described. Yet, all the elements of affirmative action to which people frequently object are present in this example. First of all, *the remedy is race-conscious, not color-blind.* It counts people based on race and measures the degree to which discrimination has stopped by comparing the percentage of blacks chosen to their percentage in the qualified pool. Second, *the remedy includes a numerical goal* (40%, plus or minus 3%) *and a timetable* (6 months, with periodic monitoring), or what would some would call a *quota.* The goal is established as a way of measuring whether discrimination has stopped; the timetable is set to put pressure on the town to stop dragging its heels.

Opponents of affirmative action regularly say that we should be color-blind, not race-conscious, and that goals and timetables are "reverse discrimination." They stigmatize such goals and timetables by calling them "quotas," in order to identify this sort of remedy with historical mechanisms that were used to place artificial ceilings on the inclusion of minorities. But in a case such as that described above, how can we fairly measure progress against the discriminatory exclusion of blacks except by counting blacks? And if 40% of the qualified population is black, why is it unreasonable to expect that something close to 40% would be included in the jury pool *if the choice were made fairly, and without discrimination?*

Jury discrimination is an easy case, of course. In cases of employment discrimination, the principles just established are much harder to apply. The reasons are fairly obvious. It is easy to tell who is qualified to be on a jury: anyone who has reached the age of majority. If 40% of the adult population is black, then 40% of the qualified population is black. The calculation is more complex and problematic in the area of employment. If 40% of the adult population is black, it does not necessarily follow that 40% of those qualified to teach high school, or to be firefighters, will be black. But it is possible to identify reasonable qualifications for these jobs and to assess the proportion of the qualified labor pool that is black. Suppose, for example, that careful studies showed that 20% of the population qualified to be firefighters was black, but no more than 3% were ever chosen. Wouldn't that present the same problem and justify the same remedy as the jury discrimination case?

Obviously, the determination of the proper percentage is much more difficult in the area of employment. Definitions of what constitute proper qualifications for given jobs differ. So do methods of measuring those qualifications. But so many "qualifications" in the past were not really bona fide qualifications related to job performance; rather, they were restrictions designed to exclude people for impermissible reasons. That's what literacy tests were in the area of voting, or college degree requirements for various manual labor jobs, or weight-lifting requirements that eliminated women even though such requirements were not related to the job.

The fact is that, traditionally, the definition of qualifications for particular jobs as well as the methods for evaluating the applicants have themselves often been reflections of discrimination rather than fair tests of job-related qualities. Affirmative action litigation has forced everyone to think more carefully and precisely about what qualifications are actually required for a given job, and to find better ways of measuring those qualifications. This process has undoubtedly reduced discrimination and made hiring fairer.

In any case, it is usually possible, for any job category, to determine, within a reasonable range, what percentage of the available qualified labor pool is black or female. Suppose, again taking our hypothetical town, that 20% of the population qualified to be firefighters was black, but no more than 3% blacks had ever been chosen. Assume that the figure of 20% is reasonably accurate, and that the town has a history of racial discrimination and persistently hires no more than 3% black firefighters. Why isn't that situation, in moral terms, exactly like the jury discrimination case?

Suppose, for example, that a number of blacks, who claim to be qualified for the job of firefighter but who were turned down, sue the town, claiming racial discrimination. Suppose further that, after trial, the court finds that the town has had a long history of racial discrimination in public employment and, in particular, in the hiring of firefighters.

Finally, suppose the court finds that the tests currently being used by the town to qualify firefighters disproportionately exclude blacks and are not validly predictive of job performance. The court then prohibits the use of that test and orders the town to develop a method of evaluating job applicants that is nondiscriminatory.

As in the jury case, a year passes and the proportion of blacks hired as firefighters hardly increases and does not come close to approaching the estimate of 20%, which is the proportion of available qualified blacks in the labor force. The town defends itself by showing that it now uses nondiscriminatory tests and has engaged in vigorous recruiting of minorities. It therefore claims that its failure to hire more blacks is not evidence of discrimination and that, in fact, it has acted in good faith to recruit and hire on a nondiscriminatory basis.

If, after hearing both sides and examining the evidence as well as the testimony of experts, the court accepts the town's arguments, then the lawsuit will be dismissed. Good-faith efforts to hire on a nondiscriminatory basis are enough. If, on the other hand, the court finds the town's arguments specious and a cover for continued, if more subtle, discriminatory acts, or if the court finds that the town's current methods are not sufficient to overcome the effects of past discrimination, then the court may order the town to reach a goal of, say, 15% blacks in its firefighter force within 2 years. As in the jury case, this goal would be established based on the court's finding that, in the absence of discrimination, approximately 15% of the firefighters would be black. Although the actual percentage used may well be open to dispute, the fact that more blacks would have been hired but for discrimination is difficult to dispute. In the face of persistent discriminatory exclusion, why is it unreasonable, much less immoral, for a court to order the offending employer to stop discriminating and then to measure compliance with that order by establishing a reasonable goal?

The examples I have used are relatively simple. Cases can and do arise that are much more complex and make the remedy of goals and timetables much more difficult to apply fairly. But the principle remains the same: If qualified blacks are available but are not being hired as the result of past or current discrimination, then they should be hired. And the only way to measure whether they are being hired on a nondiscriminatory basis is to count them and compare the percentage hired with the percentage of qualified people in the available population. To deny this sort of remedy in cases where discrimination has been proved, and where racial exclusion remains persistent, is to say that even though fundamental rights have been violated, we will not act to remedy such violations. That result seems profoundly immoral.

Affirmative Action as Compensatory Opportunity

Affirmative action as a specific remedy imposed in particular situations where discrimination has been proved is the easiest form of affirmative action to justify. More problematic is the broad provision of compensatory opportunities or entitlements, special advantages given on the basis of race in order to make up, in a general way, for disadvantages that were imposed on the basis of race. The earliest examples of such compensatory opportunities and entitlements occurred after the Civil War, when Congress established certain economic and educational programs to which only recently freed slaves and other blacks in the South were entitled. Whites were explicitly excluded (including poor whites), and some blacks were included who arguably had not personally been victims of discrimination. But the judgment was made that blacks as a group had suffered a special disadvantage—slavery—and therefore required certain special advantages to even things out. As it turned out, the special advantages weren't enough and hardly made up for the disadvantages, both past and continuing. But the principle seemed fair; indeed, it seemed the only moral stance.

In nonracial settings, the same principle has been applied without controversy. The GI bill and various other special benefits for war veterans following World War II did not require that each veteran prove personal disadvantage. Nor did these benefits allow nonveterans to apply on the basis of disadvantages

they might have suffered as a result of the war. Rather, the society made a judgment that, because all veterans, as a group, had been taken out of the race, as it were, by being conscripted to fight in a foreign land, all veterans, as a group, were entitled to various economic and educational benefits to get them even.

These programs were generally perceived to be morally justified. Why shouldn't similar programs be similarly justified in behalf of blacks, who as a group certainly have been more deeply and pervasively disadvantaged by government action than returning veterans? But from the beginning, unlike special programs for veterans, special programs for blacks were not seen as morally justified—indeed, were often seen as immoral, as being a form of "reverse racism." If the problem is seen in this way, it is compelling to believe that the sharp difference in perception between affirmative action programs for veterans and affirmative action programs for blacks is itself a reflection of race discrimination. . . .

In an influential book published in 1963, John F. Fischer, then the president of Teachers College, Columbia University, said explicitly that equal opportunity was not enough. He pointed out that the idea of treating black children in a special way was nothing new: "The American Negro youngster," he wrote, "happens to be a member of a large and distinctive group that for a very long time has been the object of special political, legal and social action." These special actions, Fischer said, were deeply destructive over a long period of time. To act now "as though any child is suddenly separable from his history is indefensible. In terms of educational planning, it is also irresponsible." And although he was very careful to recognize that every child, including every black child, is entitled to be treated as an individual, he also insisted that "every Negro child is the victim of the history of his race in this country. On the day he enters kindergarten, he carries a burden no white child can ever know." He ended his analysis by asking and answering the key question:

Is it not a reasonable contention—and a just one—that to compensate for past injustice, we should offer these children educational services beyond the level of what might be called standard equality? Could it be that to achieve total equality of opportunity in America we may have to modify currently accepted ideas about equality of opportunity? . . . We may need to substitute for our traditional concept of equal educational opportunity a new concept of *compensatory opportunity*. (p. 295)

These early thoughts, and others, began to suggest that there had to be a temporary imbalance in favor of blacks if we meant to achieve true equality of opportunity. It is important to emphasize that all these people were talking about *temporary* programs, and all resisted any notion of permanent, institutionalized preferential systems. Indeed, they were deeply opposed to permanent preferences based on race and were working hard, in some cases laying their lives on the line, for a color-blind society where individuals would be judged on the basis of merit, not skin color. But they were beginning to see that the disadvantages that had been imposed on blacks as a group could not be overcome by pretending that the race was even or that everyone had started together. They were beginning to understand that, in a country that had been so destructively race-conscious for so long, the road to a color-blind society required a transition period of constructive race consciousness. They knew it had to be temporary and they were not wholly comfortable with the idea. Nor did they know specifically how the idea should be implemented. But the principle had begun to take hold and it seemed both moral and necessary.

Even at this earliest of stages, however, fissures appeared on the horizon. . . . But the idea persisted—and grew. By 1965, it had reached the White House. In a now-famous speech at Howard University, President Lyndon Johnson observed:

Freedom is not enough. You do not wipe away the scars of centuries by saying: Now, you are free to go where you want, do as you desire, and choose the leaders you please. You do not take a man who for years has been hobbled by chains, liberate him, bring him to the starting line of a race, saying, "You are free to compete with all the others," and still justly believe you have been completely fair. Thus it is not enough to open the gates of opportunity.

But if it was not enough to open the gates of opportunity, no one knew exactly what was enough. . . . But the moral principle behind it was clear: Equal opportunity was not enough. In 1965, that seemed to be a moral principle that American society was ready to accept. Indeed, it seemed to be the next logical stage of the civil rights movement.

Today, that moral principle is under broad attack. . . . It behooves us to examine the basis of such moral criticisms.

Justifications and Criticisms

Merit

A major criticism of affirmative action is that it ignores merit in its relentless drive to achieve the desired proportion of blacks. According to this line of criticism, individual merit and only individual merit ought to be what determines whether a person gets a particular job or is admitted to a particular school. At first glance, this would appear to be an unobjectionable standard. Wasn't it the goal of the civil rights movement to achieve a society in which individuals would be judged, as Martin Luther King, Jr., said, by the content of their character and not by the color of their skin?

But "merit" is a tricky issue, hard to define and harder still to justify in terms of traditional practices. In fact, determinations of who gets a particular job and who gets admitted to a particular school have always been made, and continue to be made, on the basis of criteria other than individual merit.

As we've already pointed out, veterans receive preference when they apply for certain civil service jobs. This preference is bestowed on all veterans, whether they were drafted or not, whether they saw combat or not, whether they specifically can be shown to have been disadvantaged by their military service or not. Those who are not veterans are discriminated against even if, as individuals, they may be more disadvantaged in some way or arguably more qualified. This preferential system, which is not based strictly on individual merit, has not been seen by American society as unfair or immoral. The assumption was made that veterans were disadvantaged as a group and that fairness therefore required us to give them special, if temporary, advantages as a group.

Other preferential systems do not even attempt to justify compensatory advantages on the basis of fairness. Schools, for example, often prefer applicants who reside in the state where the school is located, even if these applicants show less merit than out-of-state applicants.

Schools also frequently prefer the children of alumni, even if other children show more merit as individuals. This sort of preference not only downgrades the importance of individual merit; it also perpetuates past discriminatory advantages. If prior patterns of admission to a particular school reflected discrimination, then a system that prefers the children of alumni perpetuates such discrimination. Yet, such preferential systems have not caused a storm of protest among those who champion the merit system, nor have such preferential systems been generally perceived by Americans as unfair or immoral.

Seniority rights in employment provide another example. The length of service in a particular job determines certain benefits relating to promotion, protection against layoff, training programs, and so on. These benefits accrue regardless of individual merit simply as the result of length of service. This system may well be justified on several grounds, but individual merit is not one of them. Moreover, in a system that has discriminatorily excluded people on the basis of race in the past, the seniority system perpetuates the disadvantages of this discrimination and continues its effects into the future.

Yet, often those—particularly labor union leaders—who talk most about merit when affirmative action programs are being discussed, manage to forget about merit when seniority systems are discussed.

Finally, those who oppose affirmative action on the ground that it is a diversion from the merit system must concede, if they have any respect for facts at all, that factors having nothing to do with merit have traditionally governed entry into many professions. Philip Green (1981) put it well:

> To make their case consistent, these opponents [of affirmative action] would also have to explain what "merit" has been possessed by those professionals who have enjoyed the rewards of restrictive rules of entry to their professions (e.g., lawyers and doctors); by businessmen, bankers and brokers who were privileged by virtue of coming from an acceptable social background; public employees who belonged to the right ethnic group in the right place at the right time; craftsmen whose acceptance by a trade union has been contingent on their recommendation by members of their own family; and academics who through most of their careers have engaged in neither productive scholarship nor innovative teaching but have rather been "good old boys," expertly mimicking the values of their superiors. (p. 79)

The fact is that, although everyone pays tribute to the idea of merit, factors extrinsic to merit often and routinely determine who gets particular jobs. "Only in the most technologically advanced and abstruse careers are factors extrinsic to any true ranking of skills totally discarded," Green concluded. "Most of the time, the question is not whether other facts . . . are going to be taken into account by us, but which ones" (p. 80).

People do discriminate. They take into account certain characteristics, which they believe are proxies for merit but which often are not. For many blacks, who have lived for generations knowing that, despite what individual merit they might possess, they would be passed over and others, less talented, would be chosen, the current concern by opponents of affirmative action about the idea of merit seems to be little more than an effort to change the rules in the middle of the game. . . .

No responsible advocate of affirmative action opposes merit or argues that employers should be required to hire unqualified applicants, or that standards should be reduced in order to meet affirmative action goals. What we do argue is that the rules should be the same for blacks as they have always been for whites. Standards should not be raised to higher levels when measuring black applicants. Merit should not be invoked in a new way to make it harder to end discrimination. Nondiscrimination means applying the same standards to everyone regardless of race. If those standards are high, they should remain high. But they should not be made higher as a response to affirmative action. . . .

Affirmative action is a method of ending such discrimination. It is not opposed to high standards, but it is opposed to double standards. And it does recognize that employers who have for years discriminated in their employment practices by using criteria extrinsic to merit cannot be expected suddenly to end such habits without a little push. Goals and timetables are such a push, and they are reasonable. They are also dangerous, because, although they are intended to be temporary remedies to end the habits of discrimination, they can be transformed into permanent quotas that institutionalize discrimination. Responsible advocates of affirmative action recognize that danger and are alert to it. But the existence of that danger does not justify abandoning the remedy.

Fairness

A major criticism of affirmative action—a criticism perceptually shared by many white workers—is that affirmative action requires employers to discriminate against better-qualified, or equally qualified, whites who themselves bear no responsibility for discrimination. This is what is sometimes called *reverse discrimination*. According to this criticism, if, in a given factory, there are 100 jobs, all held by whites, and the affirmative action goal requires 20% blacks, then ultimately 20 whites who would otherwise have been employed will not be employed, even though they, as individuals, were not responsible for the prior discrimination.

The issue of responsibility is an interesting one, but it does not come to grips with the fact that, even though such white workers were not themselves responsible for excluding blacks, they certainly benefited from that exclusion. Moreover, they benefited unjustly. Every discriminatory exclusion of a black worker unjustly benefited a white worker. The argument that such unjust benefits should be perpetuated is an argument for the continuation of discrimination against blacks, at least in a context where the number of jobs remains finite and smaller than the number of people seeking jobs. . . .

In baseball, although several teams did continue to resist hiring blacks for some time, the imposition of such a court-ordered remedy did not prove necessary. Discrimination was ended without it (at least with respect to players). But in many other employment contexts, discrimination was not ended. And that is why lawsuits were brought and, where discrimination was found, remedies were ordered.

To be sure, where the number of jobs is limited, fewer whites will be employed, just as fewer men will be employed if women are allowed to compete on a nondiscriminatory basis. But where there are too few jobs to go around, who gets those jobs cannot morally be determined on the basis of race or sex. The fact that the distribution of jobs was determined for so long on the basis of race and sex created an expectation among whites and males. The loss of that expectation may now seem unfair to them. But the expectation was not fair in the first instance. Fairness requires ending discrimination, not perpetuating it, and that includes ending the advantages that whites enjoyed as the result of discrimination against blacks.

But although individual whites were the beneficiaries of this discrimination, in many instances they did not, as individuals, cause it. The responsibility for employment discrimination lies with the employer, who may bear certain obligations, to both white workers and black, during the transition to a nondiscriminatory system.

For example, suppose a worker in a factory is unjustly fired. He contests the firing by grieving under his union contract. While the grievance proceeds, the employer hires a replacement. Six months pass. Finally, an impartial arbitrator hands down a decision in favor of the employee and orders him reinstated with back pay. The employer complies and lays off the replacement, who has now been working for 6 months. The employee who is now laid off was not responsible for the unjust firing of the original employee. But he was the beneficiary of it and now he has lost his job as a direct result of the remedy ordered by the arbitrator. Fairness triumphs, but the replacement employee is out of a job.

The first point to make is that no one would argue that the replacement employee was unjustly fired. He owed his job in the first instance to a vacancy created by illegally excluding the original employee. Now that the illegal exclusion has been rectified, he loses the benefit. Exactly the same moral analysis applies to racial discrimination lawsuits. Vacancies were created for white employees as the direct result of illegal exclusions of black workers. When those illegal exclusions are rectified, the benefits unjustly derived are ended.

Normally, the imposition of an affirmative action remedy does not result in white workers' getting fired. The remedy is prospective. Thus, white workers will now have to compete with black workers for the available jobs. Moreover, as whites have for so long enjoyed an unfair advantage, blacks have a lot of catching up to do. The terms of the competition, biased for so long in favor of whites, will now be temporarily reversed. The employer is required to hire a certain number of blacks within a certain period in order to end discrimination within a reasonable time. During this temporary period, the terms of competition may not be even. Blacks may be given the edge. That does not mean, or should not mean, that unqualified blacks will be hired. It does mean that, where qualifications are met, and are roughly equal, blacks will be given preference, not only because it is the only way to break the employer's habit of favoring whites but also because it is unfair to have maintained biased terms of competition for so long without reversing the bias for a period of time.

Reversing the bias, of course, is dangerous because it may institutionalize the legitimacy of bias and make it more difficult ultimately to achieve a color-blind, nondiscriminatory world. That is a danger that advocates of af-

firmative action must face up to and resolve to avoid. Affirmative action goals and timetables are a fair and moral remedy for institutionalized racism, but the remedy must be temporary and measured. Critics of affirmative action remedies perceive the danger but are insufficiently sensitive to the persistence of discrimination and its effects and to the need for drastic remedies. Chemotherapy is a drastic remedy for cancer. It has bad side effects. Used injudiciously, it can kill the patient. But used judiciously and with awareness of its side effects, it can stop cancer.

The cancer of racial discrimination is no less relentless. It has grown for a long time in the body politic. The danger of affirmative action remedies is real, but the argument that such remedies should be abandoned, and the cancer left alone before it is completely destroyed, is immoral.

Some critics of affirmative action remedies now argue that the time has come to abandon the temporary imposition of affirmative action goals and timetables because the procedures that require fairness have in large measure been institutionalized. In the view of these critics, not much would change if affirmative action remedies were ended now. As Robert J. Samuelson (1984) wrote:

[The aggressive uses of antidiscrimination laws, including affirmative action,] have changed the way labor markets work. Many firms have overhauled personnel policies. Recruitment has been broadened. Tests unrelated to qualifications have been abandoned. Promotions are less informal. When positions become open, they are posted publicly so anyone (not just the boss's favorite) can apply. Formal evaluations have been strengthened so that, when a manager selects one candidate over another (say, a white man over a woman), there are objective criteria. Equally important, women and blacks increasingly are plugged into the informal information and lobbying networks that remain critical in hiring and promotion decisions. (p. 8)

Although this description is undoubtedly accurate in some instances, it does not justify a general abandonment of affirmative action remedies for two reasons.

First, the situation Samuelson described is idealized and does not describe every employer. Affirmative action remedies are never imposed except when discrimination has been proved and a court, or the parties to a dispute, agrees that such a remedy is necessary to end discrimination. In some few cases where nondiscriminatory hiring has been firmly institutionalized, it may be possible to begin to discuss relaxing the temporary remedy of affirmative action procedures. But that should be very carefully done and should be monitored, on a case by case basis.

Second, much of the situation that Samuelson described is the direct result of pressures imposed by affirmative action goals and timetables. It is too soon to believe that the habits of discrimination and preferential systems for the hiring and promotion of whites, nurtured and institutionalized for generations, would not reemerge, at least in part, if affirmative action pressures were removed. The reification of a color-blind culture of nondiscrimination has not yet been accomplished. The truth is that the strongest advocates of ending affirmative action remedies now are those who never supported them in the first instance. It is, perhaps, time to begin discussing Samuelson's claims in specific instances. It is not yet time to begin a general relaxation of the pressures that have only begun to break the habits of racial discrimination.

The Internalization of Inferiority

The most ironic critics of affirmative action remedies argue that such remedies damage blacks themselves and retard their economic advancement. This line of argument takes several forms.

Charles Murray (1984), for example, argued that affirmative action remedies, or what he called "preferential treatment," perpetuate a feeling of inferiority among blacks. This feeling, he implied, derives from the suspicion by many blacks that they got their jobs not on their own merits but only because they were black, and also from the personal failures that resulted from being thrust into positions for which they were not qualified.

The latter argument is a straw man. Success surely breeds confidence, and failure, especially repeated failure, just as surely shatters confidence. But no one advocates placing people in positions for which they are not qualified. And no one wants to give people jobs they cannot do. If that is happening as a result of affirmative action, it should stop. But thrusting people into positions for which they are not qualified is not a necessary ingredient of affirmative action, nor is it a phenomenon limited to affirmative action.

Political patronage has forever been a mechanism for placing unqualified people in important jobs. So have family and business connections. When I was growing up, the phrase "It's not what you know, it's who you know" was an accepted cliche of life in the real world. This reality certainly troubled those who were thereby excluded from certain opportunities, but one never imagined that the beneficiaries of such connections spent many sleepless nights worrying about it.

It is true that, where affirmative action hiring goals are met in crude and mechanistic ways, the beneficiaries of those hiring goals may well wonder if they were hired on their own merits. Most often, however, minority applicants, like all of us, will assume that they are capable people who, if given a fair chance, will be able to perform satisfactorily. And they will perceive affirmative action goals as necessary to give them a fair chance, or, in Philip Green's phrase (1981), "to force their prospective employers to recognize and reward their abilities" (p. 80). After all, most blacks, like most whites, know full well that jobs often depend on who you know and on who you are rather than on innate abilities. In Green's telling words:

> Do all those corporate directors, bankers, etc., who got their jobs for extraneous reasons—first, because they were somebody's son, second, because they were male, third, because they were Protestant and fourth, because they were white—feel demeaned thereby? It would be interesting to ask them—or to ask the same question of those doctors who managed to get into good medical schools because there were quotas keeping out Jews, the skilled tradesmen who were admitted to the union because two members of their family recommended them and so on. Clearly implicit in this standard critique

of affirmative action, is a notion that whereas it's never painful to be rewarded because you are in the majority or the established elite, it's always painful to be rewarded because you're in the minority, or a marginal group. (p. 79)

A second line of argument suggests that black economic progress cannot be legislated and that the effort to do so through the imposition of affirmative action goals actually reinforces the idea among blacks that skills and hard work aren't important and that their lack of progress is society's fault.

Thomas Sowell (1984), an economist who is himself black, has been predominantly identified with this position:

Is it possible to din into the heads of a whole generation that their problems are all other people's fault; that the world owes them an enormous debt; that everything they have yet to achieve is an injustice; that violence is excusable when the world is flawed—and yet expect it all to have no effect on attitudes? Is the arduous process of acquiring skills and discipline supposed to be endured for years by people who are told, by word and deed, that skills are not the real issue? (sec. B, p. 4, col. 4)

Thomas Sowell is fond of chiding liberals for their failure to support their rhetorical claims with hard evidence, but he has cited no evidence to support his own rhetoric. No responsible advocates of affirmative action even suggest that skills and hard work are not important, nor is there any evidence of which I am aware that shows that blacks' willingness to devote themselves to "the arduous process of acquiring skills" has been eroded by affirmative action remedies. Indeed, I would argue that the opposite is true. By breaking down discriminatory barriers to employment, affirmative action remedies encourage the development of skills.

Sowell was right when he wrote that skills will not be developed by people who are told, by word and deed, that skills are not the real issue. That was what the reality of racial discrimination did. It told blacks, by word and deed, that no matter what skills they developed, no matter how hard they worked, opportunity would not be theirs and certain

jobs would simply not be available. It was discrimination, not the effort to end discrimination, that suffocated ambition and destroyed hope. It was the guarantee of exclusion from employment, not the expectation of inclusion, that made hard work futile.

Affirmative action remedies should certainly not be implemented in a way that diminishes standards or the importance of skills. To the extent that some affirmative action plans have diminished the importance of skills, they deserve criticism. But the idea of affirmative action itself cannot be diminished by reference to those instances where it has not worked well, or where it has abandoned some of the principles that justified it in the first instance.

Affirmative action remedies, properly conceived and implemented, ought only to open up opportunities for the development of skills, opportunities previously closed either by overt racial discrimination or by the habits that flourished in a discriminatory culture.

Sowell also made much of the inability of affirmative action remedies to solve all of the economic problems of blacks. He argued that affirmative action has a poor record in opening up opportunities for the poorest black Americans and implied that it should for that reason be abandoned. . . .

But if affirmative action remedies cannot reach the problems of poor education and institutionalized poverty, that does not mean they should be abandoned. Indeed, no advocate of affirmative action has claimed that it is a panacea, or a cure for all the racial and economic ills we face. Affirmative action is merely a means of breaking through a reified system of discrimination and of giving people who have long been handicapped by that system a temporary leg up.

Moreover, to the extent that black children growing up need to know that opportunities are available and that hard work matters, it is crucial to have visible examples. . . . Affirmative action will not today open up opportunities for the poor and the uneducated and the unskilled. But it will change how they look at the world, and it will say, by word and deed, that hard work pays off and that skills matter. Affirmative action remedies may not quickly solve every problem. But without such remedies, the suffocating impact of discrimination will continue.

Conclusion: Regaining a Moral Consensus

I have tried to demonstrate that there is a moral basis for the concept of affirmative action and that those who supported efforts to break down the legal barriers to racial justice a quarter century ago ought, for the same reasons, to support affirmative action remedies today. It is the same fight.

I have also conceded, and I think it is incumbent on advocates of affirmative action to concede, that such remedies must be temporary, must not result in diminishing the importance of skills, and must not be administered in a way that lowers standards or institutionalizes, however unintentionally, unfair practices. It is difficult for me to believe that a moral consensus behind these principles cannot be regained.

The residue of slavery and centuries of legal discrimination still stains our society and substantially limits the opportunities of many black children. Simple justice requires that those of us who do not suffer from the disadvantages caused by past and current racial discrimination—who, indeed, may have benefited from it—not abandon the fight to find reasonable remedies for those who do. Yet, white liberal support for such remedies, including affirmative action, has substantially dissolved since the height of the civil rights movement,

now nearly two decades ago. Blacks stand in danger of being isolated again, and this remains a major moral issue in American life.

Affirmative action is not the only element of this moral issue, but it has become a polarizing symbol for it. Somehow, the moral issue must regain its consensus and its place high on our social agenda, until the color of our skins no longer determines where we work, where we live, where we go to school, and whether we are treated fairly. We have made much progress, but there is still a long way to go.

References

Fischer, J. H. 1963. Educational problems of segregation and desegregation. In A. H. Passow (Ed.), *Education in depressed areas.* New York: Teachers College, Columbia University.

Green, P. 1981, March 30. The new individualism. *Christianity and Crisis,* 41, 79–80.

Johnson, L. B. 1965, June. Address, Howard University.

Murray, C. 1984, December 31. Affirmative racism. *The New Republic.*

Samuelson, R. J. 1984, July 11. Affirmative action's usefulness is passing. *Washington Post,* sec. D, p. 8, col. 1.

Sowell, T. 1984, August 12. Black progress can't be legislated. *Washington Post Outlook,* sec. B, p. 4, cols. 3, 4.

30

Affirmative Action:

The Price of Preference

Shelby Steele

In a few short years, when my two children will be applying to college, the affirmative action policies by which most universities offer black students some form of preferential treatment will present me with a dilemma. I am a middle-class black, a college professor, far from wealthy, but also well-removed from the kind of deprivation that would qualify my children for the label "disadvantaged." Both of them have endured racial insensitivity from whites. They have been called names, have suffered slights, and have experienced firsthand the peculiar malevolence that racism brings out in people. Yet, they have never experienced racial discrimination, have never been stopped by their race on any path they have chosen to follow. Still, their society now tells them that if they will only designate themselves as black on their college applications, they will likely do better in the college lottery than if they conceal this fact. I think there is something of a Faustian bargain in this.

Of course, many blacks and a considerable number of whites would say that I was sanctimoniously making affirmative action into a test of character. They would say that this small preference is the meagerest recompense for centuries of unrelieved oppression. And to these arguments other very obvious facts must be added. In America, many marginally competent or flatly incompetent whites are hired everyday—some because their white skin suits the conscious or unconscious racial preference of their employer. The white children of alumni are often grandfathered into elite universities in what can only be seen as a residual benefit of historic white privilege. Worse, white incompetence is always an individual matter, while for blacks it is often confirmation of ugly stereotypes. The Peter Principle was not conceived with only blacks in mind. Given that unfairness cuts both ways, doesn't it only balance the scales of history that my children now receive a slight preference over whites? Doesn't this repay, in a small way, the systematic denial under which their grandfather lived out his days?

So, in theory, affirmative action certainly has all the moral symmetry that fairness requires—the injustice of historical and even contemporary white advantage is offset with black advantage; preference replaces prejudice, inclusion answers exclusion. It is reformist and corrective, even repentant and redemptive. And I would never sneer at these good intentions. Born in the late forties in Chicago, I started my education (a charitable term in this case) in a segregated school and suffered all the indignities that come to blacks in a segregated society.

My father, born in the South, only made it to the third grade before the white man's fields took permanent priority over his formal education. And though he educated himself into an advanced reader with an almost professorial authority, he could only drive a truck for a living and never earned more than ninety dollars a week in his entire life. So yes, it is crucial to my sense of citizenship, to my ability to identify with the spirit and the interests of America, to know that this country, however imperfectly, recognizes its past sins and wishes to correct them.

Yet good intentions, because of the opportunity for innocence they offer us, are very seductive and can blind us to the effects they generate when implemented. In our society, affirmative action is, among other things, a testament to white goodwill and to black power, and in the midst of these heavy investments, its effects can be hard to see. But after twenty years of implementation, I think affirmative action has shown itself to be more bad than good and that blacks—whom I will focus on in this essay—now stand to lose more from it than they gain.

In talking with affirmative action administrators and with blacks and whites in general, it is clear that supporters of affirmative action focus on its good intentions while detractors emphasize its negative effects. Proponents talk about "diversity" and "pluralism"; opponents speak of "reverse discrimination," the unfairness of quotas and set-asides. It was virtually impossible to find people outside either camp. The closest I came was a white male manager at a large computer company who said, "I think it amounts to reverse discrimination, but I'll put up with a little of that for a little more diversity." I'll live with a little of the effect to gain a little of the intention, he seemed to be saying. But this only makes him a halfhearted supporter of affirmative action. I think many people who don't really like affirmative action support it to one degree or another anyway.

I believe they do this because of what happened to white and black Americans in the crucible of the sixties when whites were confronted with their racial guilt and blacks tasted their first real power.

In this stormy time white absolution and black power coalesced into virtual mandates for society. Affirmative action became a meeting ground for these mandates in the law, and in the late sixties and early seventies it underwent a remarkable escalation of its mission from simple anti-discrimination enforcement to social engineering by means of quotas, goals, timetables, set-asides and other forms of preferential treatment.

Legally, this was achieved through a series of executive orders and EEOC guidelines that allowed racial imbalances in the workplace to stand as proof of racial discrimination. Once it could be assumed that discrimination explained racial imbalances, it became easy to justify group remedies to presumed discrimination, rather than the normal case-by-case redress for proven discrimination. Preferential treatment through quotas, goals, and so on is designed to correct imbalances based on the assumption that they always indicate discrimination. This expansion of what constitutes discrimination allowed affirmative action to escalate into the business of social engineering in the name of anti-discrimination, to push society toward statistically proportionate racial representation, without any obligation of proving actual discrimination.

What accounted for this shift, I believe, was the white mandate to achieve a new racial innocence and the black mandate to gain power. Even though blacks had made great advances during the sixties without quotas, these mandates, which came to a head in the very late sixties, could no longer be satisfied by anything less than racial preferences. I don't think these mandates in themselves were wrong, since whites clearly needed to do better by blacks and blacks needed more real power in society. But, as they came together in affirmative action, their effect was to distort our understanding of racial discrimination in a way that allowed us to offer the remediation of preference on the basis of mere color rather than actual injury. By making black the color of preference, these mandates have reburdened society with the very marriage of color and preference (in reverse) that we set out to eradicate. The old sin is reaffirmed in a new guise.

But the essential problem with this form of affirmative action is the way it leaps over the hard business of developing a formerly oppressed people to the point where they can achieve proportionate representation on their own (given equal opportunity) and goes straight for the proportionate representation. This may satisfy some whites of their innocence and some blacks of their power, but it does very little to truly uplift blacks.

A white female affirmative action officer at an Ivy League university told me what many supporters of affirmative action now say: "We're after diversity. We ideally want a student body where racial and ethnic groups are represented according to their proportion in society." When affirmative action escalated into social engineering, diversity became a golden word. It grants whites an egalitarian fairness (innocence) and blacks an entitlement to proportionate representation (power). *Diversity* is a term that applies democratic principles to races and cultures rather than to citizens, despite the fact that there is nothing to indicate that real diversity is the same thing as proportionate representation. Too often the result of this on campuses (for example) has been a democracy of colors rather than of people, an artificial diversity that gives the appearance of an educational parity between black and white students that has not yet been achieved in reality. Here again, racial preferences allow society to leapfrog over the difficult problem of developing blacks to parity with whites and into a cosmetic diversity that covers the blemish of disparity—a full six years after admission, only about 26 percent of black students graduate from college.

Racial representation is not the same thing as racial development, yet affirmative action fosters a confusion of these very different needs. Representation can be manufactured; development is always hard-earned. However, it is the music of innocence and power that we hear in affirmative action that causes us to cling to it and to its distracting emphasis on representation. The fact is that after twenty years of racial preferences, the gap between white and black median income is greater than it was in the seventies. None of this is to say that blacks don't need policies that ensure our right to equal opportunity, but what we need more is the development that will let us take advantage of society's efforts to include us.

I think that one of the most troubling effects of racial preferences for blacks is a kind of demoralization, or put another way, an enlargement of self-doubt. Under affirmative action the quality that earns us preferential treatment is an implied inferiority. However this inferiority is explained—and it is easily enough explained by the myriad deprivations that grew out of our oppression—it is still inferiority. There are explanations, and then there is the fact. And the fact must be borne by the individual as a condition apart from the explanation, apart even from the fact that others like himself also bear this condition. In integrated situations where blacks must compete with whites who may be better prepared, these explanations may quickly wear thin and expose the individual to racial as well as personal self-doubt.

All of this is compounded by the cultural myth of black inferiority that blacks have always lived with. What this means in practical terms is that when blacks deliver themselves into integrated situations, they encounter a nasty little reflex in whites, a mindless, atavistic reflex that responds to the color black with alarm. Attributions may follow this alarm if the white cares to indulge them, and if they do, they will most likely be negative—one such attribution is intellectual ineptness. I think this reflex and the attributions that may follow it embarrass most whites today, therefore, it is usually quickly repressed. Nevertheless, on an equally atavistic level, the black will be aware of the reflex his color triggers and will feel a stab of horror at seeing himself reflected in this way. He, too, will do a quick repression, but a lifetime of such stabbings is what constitutes his inner realm of racial doubt.

The effects of this may be a subject for another essay. The point here is that the implication of inferiority that racial preferences engender in both the white and black mind expands rather than contracts this doubt. Even when the black sees no implication of inferiority in racial preferences, he knows that whites do, so that—consciously or unconsciously—the result is virtually the same. The effect of preferential treatment—the lowering of normal standards to increase black representation—puts blacks at war with an expanded realm of debilitating doubt, so that the doubt itself becomes an unrecognized preoccupation that undermines their ability to perform, especially in integrated situations. On largely white campuses, blacks are five times more likely to drop out than whites. Preferential treatment, no matter how it is justified in the light of day, subjects blacks to a midnight of self-doubt, and so often transforms their advantage into a revolving door.

Another liability of affirmative action comes from the fact that it indirectly encourages blacks to exploit their own past victimization as a source of power and privilege. Victimization, like implied inferiority, is what justifies preference, so that to receive the benefits of preferential treatment one must, to some extent, become invested in the view of one's self as a victim. In this way, affirmative action nurtures a victim-focused identity in blacks. The obvious irony here is that we become inadvertently invested in the very condition we are trying to overcome. Racial preferences send us the message that there is more power in our past suffering than our present achievements—none of which could bring us a *preference* over others.

When power itself grows out of suffering, then blacks are encouraged to expand the boundaries of what qualifies as racial oppression, a situation that can lead us to paint our victimization in vivid colors, even as we receive the benefits of preference. The same corporations and institutions that give us preference are also seen as our oppressors. At Stanford University minority students—some of whom enjoy as much as $15,000 a year in financial aid—recently took over the president's office demanding, among other things, more financial aid. The power to be found in victimization, like any power, is intoxicating and can lend itself to the creation of a new class of super-victims who can feel the pea of victimization under twenty mattresses. Preferential treatment rewards us for being underdogs rather than for moving beyond that status—a misplacement of incentives that, along with its deepening of our doubt, is more a yoke than a spur.

But, I think, one of the worst prices that blacks pay for preference has to do with an illusion. I saw this illusion at work recently in the mother of a middle-class black student who was going off to his first semester of college. "They owe us this, so don't think for a minute that you don't belong there." This is the logic by which many blacks, and some whites, justify affirmative action—it is something "owed," a form of reparation. But this logic overlooks a much harder and less digestible reality, that it is impossible to repay blacks living today for the historic suffering of the race.

If all blacks were given a million dollars tomorrow morning it would not amount to a dime on the dollar of three centuries of oppression, nor would it obviate the residues of that oppression that we still carry today. The concept of historic reparation grows out of man's need to impose a degree of justice on the world that simply does not exist. Suffering can be endured and overcome, it cannot be repaid. Blacks cannot be repaid for the injustice done to the race, but we can be corrupted by society's guilty gestures of repayment.

Affirmative action is such a gesture. It tells us that racial preferences can do for us what we cannot do for ourselves. The corruption here is in the hidden incentive *not* to do what we believe preferences will do. This is an incentive to be reliant on others just as we are struggling for self-reliance. And it keeps alive the illusion that we can find some deliverance in repayment. The hardest thing for any sufferer to accept is that his suffering excuses him from very little and never has enough currency to restore him. To think otherwise is to prolong the suffering.

Several blacks I spoke with said they were still in favor of affirmative action because of the "subtle" discrimination blacks were subject to once on the job. One photojournalist said, "They have ways of ignoring you." A black female television producer said, "You can't file a lawsuit when your boss doesn't invite you to the insider meetings without ruining your career. So we still need affirmative action." Others mentioned the infamous "glass ceiling" through which blacks can see the top positions of authority but never reach them. But I don't think racial preferences are a protection against this subtle discrimination; I think they contribute to it.

In any workplace, racial preferences will always create two-tiered populations composed of preferreds and unpreferreds. This division makes automatic a perception of enhanced competence for the unpreferreds and of questionable competence for the preferreds—the former earned his way, even though others were given preference, while the latter made it by color as much as by competence. Racial preferences implicitly mark whites with an exaggerated superiority just as they mark blacks with an exaggerated inferiority. They not only reinforce America's oldest racial myth but, for blacks, they have the effect of stigmatizing the already stigmatized.

I think that much of the "subtle" discrimination that blacks talk about is often (not always) discrimination against the stigma of questionable competence that affirmative action delivers to blacks. In this sense, preferences scapegoat the very people they seek to help. And it may be that at a certain level employers impose a glass ceiling, but this may not be against the race so much as against the race's reputation for having advanced by color as much as by competence. Affirmative action makes a glass ceiling virtually necessary as a protection against the corruptions of preferential treatment. This ceiling is the point at which corporations shift the emphasis from color to competency and stop playing the affirmative action game. Here preference backfires for blacks and becomes a taint that holds them back. Of course, one could argue that this taint, which is, after all, in the minds of whites, becomes nothing more than an excuse to discriminate against blacks. And certainly the result is the same in either case—blacks don't get past the glass ceiling. But this argument does not get around the fact that racial preferences now taint this color with a new theme of suspicion that makes it even more vulnerable to the impulse in others to discriminate. In this crucial yet gray area of perceived competence, preferences make whites look better than they are and blacks worse, while doing nothing whatever to stop the very real discrimination that blacks may encounter. I don't wish to justify the glass ceiling here, but only to suggest the very subtle ways that affirmative action revives rather than extinguishes the old rationalizations for racial discrimination.

In education, a revolving door; in employment, a glass ceiling.

I believe affirmative action is problematic in our society because it tries to function like a social program. Rather than ask it to ensure equal opportunity we have demanded that it create parity between the races. But preferential treatment does not teach skills, or educate, or instill motivation. It only passes out entitlement by color, a situation that in my profession has created an unrealistically high demand for black professors. The social engineer's assumption is that this high demand will inspire more blacks to earn Ph.D.'s and join the profession. In fact, the number of blacks earning Ph.D.'s has declined in recent years. A Ph.D. must be developed from preschool on. He requires family and community support. He must acquire an entire system of values that enables him to work hard while delaying gratification. There are social programs, I believe, that can (and should)

help blacks *develop* in all these areas, but entitlement by color is not a social program; it is a dubious reward for being black.

It now seems clear that the Supreme Court, in a series of recent decisions, is moving away from racial preferences. It has disallowed preferences except in instances of "identified discrimination," eroded the precedent that statistical racial imbalances are *prima facie* evidence of discrimination, and in effect granted white males the right to challenge consent degrees that use preference to achieve racial balances in the workplace. One civil rights leader said, "Night has fallen on civil rights." But I am not so sure. The effect of these decisions is to protect the constitutional rights of everyone rather than take rights away from blacks. What they do take away from blacks is the special entitlement to more rights than others that preferences always grant. Night has fallen on racial preferences, not on the fundamental rights of black Americans. The reason for this shift, I believe, is that the white mandate for absolution from past racial sins has weakened considerably during the eighties. Whites are now less willing to endure unfairness to themselves in order to grant special entitlements to blacks, even when these entitlements are justified in the name of past suffering. Yet the black mandate for more power in society has remained unchanged. And I think part of the anxiety that many blacks feel over these decisions has to do with the loss of black power they may signal. We had won a certain specialness and now we are losing it.

But the power we've lost by these decisions is really only the power that grows out of our victimization—the power to claim special entitlements under the law because of past oppression. This is not a very substantial or reliable power, and it is important that we know this so we can focus more exclusively on the kind of development that will bring enduring power. There is talk now that Congress will pass new legislation to compensate for these new limits on affirmative action. If this happens, I hope that their focus will be on development and anti-discrimination rather than entitlement, on achieving racial parity rather than jerry-building racial diversity.

I would also like to see affirmative action go back to its original purpose of enforcing equal opportunity—a purpose that in itself disallows racial preferences. We cannot be sure that the discriminatory impulse in America has yet been shamed into extinction, and I believe affirmative action can make its greatest contribution by providing a rigorous vigilance in this area. It can guard constitutional rather than racial rights, and help institutions evolve standards of merit and selection that are appropriate to the institution's needs yet as free of racial bias as possible (again, with the understanding that racial imbalances are not always an indication of racial bias). One of the most important things affirmative action can do is to define exactly what racial discrimination is and how it might manifest itself within a specific institution. The impulse to discriminate *is* subtle and cannot be ferreted out unless its many guises are made clear to people. Along with this there should be monitoring of institutions and heavy sanctions brought to bear when actual discrimination is found. This is the sort of affirmative action that America owes to blacks and to itself. It goes after the evil of discrimination itself, while preferences only sidestep the evil and grant entitlement to its *presumed* victims.

But if not preferences, then what? I think we need social policies that are committed to two goals: the educational and economic development of disadvantaged people, regardless of race, and the eradication from our society—through close monitoring and severe sanctions—of racial, ethnic, or gender discrimination. Preferences will not deliver us to either of these goals, since they tend to benefit those who are not disadvantaged—middle-class white women and middle-class blacks—and attack one form of discrimination with another. Preferences are inexpensive and carry the glamour of good intentions—change the numbers and the good deed is done. To be against them is to be unkind. But I think the unkindest cut is to bestow on children like my own an undeserved advantage while neglecting the development of those disadvantaged children on the East Side of my city who will likely never be in a position to benefit from a preference. Give my children fairness; give disadvantaged children a better shot at development—better elementary and secondary schools, job training, safer neighborhoods, better financial assistance for college, and so on. Fewer blacks go to college today than ten years ago; more black males of college age are in prison or under the control of the criminal justice system than in college. This despite racial preferences. The mandates of black power and white absolution out of which preferences emerged were not wrong in themselves. What was wrong was that both races focused more on the goals of these mandates than on the means to the goals. Blacks can have no real power without taking responsibility for their own educational and economic development. Whites can have no racial innocence without earning it by eradicating discrimination and helping the disadvantaged to develop. Because we ignored the means, the goals have not been reached, and the real work remains to be done.

Reprinted from: Shelby Steele, *The Content of Our Character*, pp. 111-125. Copyright © 1990 by Shelby Steele. Reprinted by permission of St. Martin's Press, Inc.

Diversity in Higher Education

As we stand on the threshold of the twenty-first century, one of the most compelling issues on the public agenda is how best to promote educational opportunity and equity for all Americans. Researchers and policymakers are concerned about the substantial racial and ethnic differences in rates of college enrollment, retention, and graduation. These variations have profound implications for the future of minority populations and intergroup relations in the U.S. By virtually any indicator, African Americans, Latino/a Americans, and other minority groups are disadvantaged in the arena of higher education. For example, the rate of college attendance was roughly 38 percent for European Americans (whites) in 1992, but it was substantially lower for African Americans (30.8 percent) and Latino/a Americans (28.7 percent) (Justiz 1994). On average, students from minority backgrounds are also less likely than European Americans (whites) to complete their bachelor's degrees within a five- or six-year period; they are also more likely to encounter academic probation or dismissal, and their average grades tend to be lower than those of whites. Further, although college attendance has been on the rise among African American and Hispanic females in recent years, observers note an alarming drop among minority males, especially African Americans (Wilson 1994). Overall, the number of bachelor's degrees awarded to Latino/a Americans rose more than 80 percent during the 1977–91 period, while the number of such degrees given to African Americans actually dropped (de los Santos and Rigual 1994).

The reasons for these racial/ethnic patterns are varied and complex. One critical piece of the puzzle is surely the unequal access to good primary and secondary education. In many areas, public schools have become resegregated, and the schools that are populated mainly by students of color tend to be underfunded when compared to white suburban schools, due to the overreliance on local taxation—typically property tax revenues, which tend to be smaller in poor districts despite relatively high tax rates. This situation can result in underqualified and underpaid teachers, dilapidated buildings, and a dearth of computers, up-to-date textbooks, and other key resources (Kozol 1991). Some critics note that these school districts often have very high per-pupil expenditures, for which high labor and administrative costs—and, in some cases, corruption—are blamed for undermining education. However, public school advocates counter that schools serving mostly poor and minority students are called upon to meet an exceptionally wide range of other social needs (such as health care and nutrition) in addition to severe educational needs.

Beyond this lack of key resources, some reports indicate that minority youths are ill-served by the educational system. For instance, they are more likely to repeat grades, more likely to be placed in remedial classes, and less likely to be placed in advanced placement or college preparatory courses. There is evidence that some teachers tend to hold low expectations of minority students, and research suggests that communicating these low expectations can have negative consequences for the self-confidence and achievement of these students. In a particularly disturbing pattern, researchers and activists argue that African American and Latino/a American youths are also more likely to be directed toward vocational tracks and are otherwise discouraged from pursuing higher education. Critics argue that wider use of culturally appropriate pedagogical strategies might well enhance achievement levels of many students of color. Among high school students, dropout (some prefer the term "pushout") rates are highest among Latino/a youths, especially those of Mexican American and Puerto Rican backgrounds, followed by African Americans.

Family and neighborhood factors may also help to explain the comparatively low levels of minority student preparation and success. One study reports that, even among students who perform adequately during the school year, African American children are more likely than whites to lose ground academically during the summer months; these differences are due mainly to the high levels of poverty among minority families (Entwisle and Alexander 1992). Parents of low socioeconomic status may be less able, on average, to participate in school activities, or to help with homework or to supplement school curricula with other outside learning opportunities. Due to poverty, discrimination, and other factors, many minority families may experience a broader array of stressful events and conditions (e.g., job loss and criminal victimization) that can disrupt children's academic success. Further, because of family and neighborhood environments, many poor minority youths may not identify with adult role models in which education is a stepping stone to career success (D'Augelli and Hershbetger 1993). According to some observers, the legacy of exclusion and discrimination against people of color has led to the emergence, in some areas, of an oppositional culture that distrusts white-dominated educational institutions and practices (Ogbu 1990).

One key dilemma in the area of higher education is the racial/ethnic disparities in average standardized test scores, including the Scholastic Aptitude Test (SAT). In 1990, for instance, 73 percent of African Americans who took the SAT scored below 400 on the verbal component; approximately 59 percent of Latinos and only 31 percent of European Americans (whites) received scores in this range. Significant racial/ethnic disparities also surface in math SAT scores (Justiz 1994). These gaps probably reflect the cumulative impact of unequal primary and secondary education, as well as the other influences mentioned above. Some critics also charge that the SAT is biased in favor of middle-class European American students, and that it does not adequately test the kinds of language skills and cultural capital at which many African American and Latino/a youths may excel. In any event, the pivotal role that is often assigned to SAT scores limits the numbers of minority students admitted to selective colleges and universities (Morganthau 1995). Many observers believe that admissions policies giving greater weight to factors besides SAT scores—particularly high school class rank—can increase campus diversity, especially where the use of affirmative action in admissions has been curtailed by ballot initiative or court decision. Some scholars advocate a broader philosophical shift, proposing that colleges should focus less on competing for status by landing "star" students, and more on developing the talents of students from diverse social backgrounds (Astin, this volume).

Compared with their European American (white) counterparts, students of color are disproportionately likely to enroll at community colleges and other two-year colleges. Due in part to worries about the social and academic climate at many predominantly white schools, a growing proportion of African American students are enrolling at historically black colleges and universities (Wilson 1994). While these schools may lack abundant material resources and academic prestige, some observers contend that the faculty and administrators at historically black institutions tend to devote more time and take greater personal interest in African American students than personnel at predominantly white schools. Graduation rates for African Americans are also generally higher at historically black colleges and universities than at mostly white institutions (Allen 1992).

Researchers and advocates report that students of color attending predominantly white institutions often face several types of obstacles. According to various indicators of academic achievement—such as grade point averages—African American, Latino/a, and Native American students tend to have, on average, somewhat lower grade point averages and higher attrition rates than European American (white) and Asian American students, for many of the complex reasons described in this section. Quite a few institutions have developed programs to address these disparities. In addition, funding constraints often cause problems for students of color from families of modest means. These young people are especially likely to rely on jobs and loans which diminish their study time and result in large financial debts. Changes in the college loan programs during the 1980s exacerbated many of these problems. Recent political attacks on scholarships and fellowships intended to aid minority students may also make matters more difficult in the future. Some studies indicate that African American and Latino/a college students are less likely than their Asian American counterparts to develop study groups within their social networks.

One of the critical problems in contemporary academia is the dearth of role models for minority students. Of particular concern is the fact that the percentage of African American faculty members at four-year institutions has increased only slightly over the past 15 years, despite strong efforts to recruit and tenure more minority faculty members during that period. Why have these efforts met with so little success? Although there are many factors that come into play here, part of the problem is clearly the shrinking number of newly minted African-American Ph.D.s—a pool that has never been especially large. Between 1977 and 1990, the number of African Americans (U.S. citizens) who were granted doctoral degrees each year declined by more than 25 percent, from 1,116 to 828. The low point during this period was 1987, when only 767 African Americans received Ph.D.s (Brown 1994). Note that for African Americans, the total number of doctorates is somewhat misleading, because for years more than half of all Af-

rican American doctorates have been granted in a single field: education. Meanwhile, the number of Ph.D.s given to Latino/a Americans improved by 65 percent during the 1977–90 period (from 423 to 698), and the number for Asian Americans rose by a striking 82 percent (from 339 to 617) (Brown 1994).

According to Blackwell (1990), the period from 1976-84 was important in reducing the size of the pool of eligible African American Ph.D.s. During that period, the number of African Americans enrolled in U.S. graduate schools dropped by approximately 22 percent. By comparison, the number of whites remained roughly constant, while the number of Latino/a Americans rose by around 14 percent. African American numbers have been slow to rebound from that steep decline. Graduate students competed for fewer loan dollars, which were available on less favorable terms, following a series of Reagan-era changes in education funding policies. For students of color, many of whom had just amassed large debts while financing their bachelor's degrees, jobs in the private sector may have seemed more attractive than graduate school. For those who did pursue advanced degrees, Blackwell (1990) has pointed out an intriguing disparity in funding: African American and Latino/a American graduate students tended to fund their graduate education through scholarships and fellowships. However, this may not have been as helpful as the research and teaching assistantships often received by white and Asian American (and international) students. Especially for aspiring academics, such assistantships may be more desirable in the long run because they help students build academic careers through applied experience and close contacts with faculty mentors.

In addition to the scarcity of coethnic academic role models, critics attribute low levels of minority achievement to an indifferent, even hostile, campus climate (Feagin, this volume; Vera and Imani 1996). As Feagin and other social scientists have documented, many minority students feel that they receive negative treatment from white students, faculty, and staff. They charge that campus police often treat African American and Latino/a Americans students (especially males) differently from whites, stopping and questioning them without cause, disrupting their parties, and sometimes using excessive force against them. Further, organizations that monitor race relations on campus confirm that intergroup tensions are on the rise—from casual expressions of aversion or indifference by whites, to hostile rhetoric and graffiti, racist fraternity parties, and even violence (Ehrlich 1994). Minority students also complain of mistreatment by European American (white) faculty. Such accounts make it clear that many students of color experience predominantly white colleges and universities as unwelcoming, and even hostile to their needs.

Skeptics discount these claims, noting that minority student complaints have skyrocketed in recent years, despite unprecedented educational opportunities for students of color. Further, they call attention to various administrative responses to the demands of minority students and community activists—the growth of ethnic theme dorms, minority student unions, and penalties against insensitivity and "hate speech," among others—as evidence of the schools' good faith. In fact, conservative author Dinesh D'Souza (1991) maintains that it is precisely such "special concessions" to minorities that have triggered an angry backlash among some white students. In his view, this helps to explain an intriguing paradox: several schools experiencing racial incidents are relatively progressive institutions such as Oberlin and Stanford. Some observers also criticize the apparent tendency for some minority students to avoid meaningful contact with whites and to focus on campus ethnic activism at the expense of their studies (Steele, this volume), although others dispute these charges (D'Augelli and Hershberger 1993).

In response to rising racial/ethnic tensions, some colleges and universities have instituted multicultural curriculum reforms. These changes typically require all students to pass certain courses with "multicultural" content—typically courses on the histories and cultures of groups that have traditionally been oppressed (e.g., African American literature, Latino/a sociology). Some schools define "multiculturalism" more expansively, to include exposure to Jewish, women's, gay/lesbian, and various area studies programs as well. Some observers remain skeptical of what they consider to be a "band-aid" approach to multiculturalism. They argue that instead of simply adding new courses—a move that can alienate students majoring in programs that already have rigid course requirements—schools should provide incentives for faculty members to incorporate coverage of diverse cultures and experiences into existing classes wherever feasible. Proponents of multiculturalism, whatever its precise form, hope that exposure to better information about racial/ethnic groups and cultures will foster a positive campus climate by instilling respect for others. They also suggest that the expansion of multiculturalism can send an important signal of validation to students of color, and may attract more minority faculty members, many of whom may specialize in these areas.

Not surprisingly, multiculturalism has drawn harsh criticism from some quarters. Some opponents voice fundamental objections to this entire approach. They tend to argue that institutions of higher learning should concentrate on teaching about our common (shared) history and values, rather than emphasizing racial/ethnic distinctiveness—or other sources of difference—that (they believe) tend to divide rather than unite us. Other critics worry that such courses can degenerate into political indoctrination, promoting a (generally liberal) "party line" on racial and ethnic issues. They also doubt the wisdom of requiring multicultural classes for all graduating seniors. Although such courses may foster positive attitudes among students who are already interested or open, critics worry that requiring these classes may be counterproductive, angering and alienating those less enthusiastic students. Further, some skeptics are concerned that the institutionalization of multiculturalism may enshrine ideologues and marginal scholars in positions of influence on campuses around the country (Schlesinger 1992).

While some of these objections may be viewed as expressions of cyncism or intolerance, others may be worth taking seriously as institutions move—however haltingly—in the direction of multicultural curriculum reform. To date, few if any studies have carefully examined the consequences of multicultural course requirements. Nevertheless, while multiculturalism may not offer a panacea for intergroup tensions on campus (or elsewhere), many observers believe that carefully designed multicultural coursework is vitally important in promoting greater understanding of the diverse experiences of various racial/ethnic populations, as well as an appreciation of their manifold contributions to our common past, present, and future as Americans.

As studies continue to demonstrate the importance of higher education for future earnings and career prospects, it is vitally important that we continue working to promote equity and inclusiveness in higher education. To be sure, this task has been complicated by recent court decisions (e.g., *Hopwood v. University of Texas* case) and political developments (e.g., Proposition 209 in California) that sharply limit or eliminate the consideration of race/ethnicity as a factor in college admissions decisions. Nevertheless, few issues are more urgent for an increasingly diverse society entering a new century.

References

Allen, Walter. 1992. "The Color of Success: African American College Student Outcomes at Predominantly White and Historically Black Public Colleges and Universities." *Harvard Educational Review* 62: 26-44.

Blackwell, James E. 1990. "Current Issues Affecting Blacks and Hispanics in the Educational Pipeline." Pp. 35-52 in *US Race Relations in the 1980s and 1990s: Challenges and Alternatives*, edited by Gail E. Thomas. New York: Hemisphere/Taylor and Francis.

Brown, Shirley Vining. 1994. "The Impasse on Faculty Diversity in Higher Education: A National Agenda." Pp. 314-333 in *Minorities in Higher Education*, edited by Manuel J. Justiz, Reginald Wilson, and Lars G. Bjork. Phoenix: Oryx Press/American Council on Education.

D'Augelli, Anthony R., and Scott L. Hershberger. 1993. "African American Undergraduates on a Predominantly White Campus: Academic Factors, Social Networks, and Campus Climate." *Journal of Negro Education* 62: 67-81.

D'Souza, Dinesh. 1991. Illiberal Education: The Politics of Race and Sex on Campus. New York: Free Press.

de los Santos, Alfredo, Jr., and Anthony Rigual. 1994. "Progress of Hispanics in American Higher Education." Pp. 173-194 in *Minorities in Higher Education*, edited by Manuel J. Justiz, Reginald Wilson, and Lars G. Bjork. Phoenix: Oryx Press/American Council on Education.

Ehrlich, Howard J. 1994. "Campus Ethnoviolence." Pp. 279-290 in *Race and Ethnic Conflict: Contending Views on Prejudice, Discrimination, and Ethnoviolence*, edited by Fred L. Pincus and Howard J. Ehrlich. Boulder, CO: Westview Press.

Entwisle, Doris R., and Karl L. Alexander. 1992. "Summer Setback: Race, Poverty, School Composition, and Mathematics Achievement in the First Two Years of School." *American Sociological Review* 57: 72-84.

Feagin, Joe R., Hernan Vera, and Nikitah Imani. 1996. *The Agony of Education: Black Students at White Colleges and Universities*. New York: Routledge.

Justiz, Manuel. 1994. "Demographic Trends and Challenges to American Higher Education." Pp. 1-21 in *Minorities in Higher Education*, edited by Manuel J. Justiz, Reginald Wilson, and Lars G. Bjork. Phoenix: Oryx Press/American Council on Education.

Kozol, Jonathan. 1991. *Savage Inequalities: Children in America's Schools*. New York: Crown.

Morganthau, Tom. 1995. "The University: Losing Ground in the Scramble for Qualified Black Applicants." *Newsweek* (April 3): 30-31.

Ogbu, John. 1990. "Racial Stratification and Education." Pp. 3-34 in *US Race Relations in the 1980s and 1990s: Challenges and Alternatives*, edited by Gail E. Thomas. New York: Hemisphere/Taylor and Francis.

Schlesinger, Arthur. 1992. *The Disuniting of America: Reflections on a Multicultural Society*. New York: W.W. Norton.

Wilson, Reginald. 1994. "The Participation of African Americans in American Higher Education." Pp. 195-209 in *Minorities in Higher Education*, edited by Manuel J. Justiz, Reginald Wilson, and Lars G. Bjork. Phoenix: Oryx Press/American Council on Education.

31

Educational Equity and the Problem of Assessment

Alexander Astin

Among proponents of "equal access" and "expanding opportunities" in higher education, there are few issues that generate as much heat as testing and assessment. The basis for much of the resistance to the use of assessment in higher education is easy to understand, given the following facts: 1) African Americans, Hispanics, and poor students are substantially underrepresented in American higher education, especially in the more select or elite institutions; 2) American higher education institutions rely heavily on two measures—the high school grade point average and scores on standardized college admission tests—to select their students; and 3) African Americans, Hispanics, and poor students tend to receive lower high school GPAs and lower test scores than other groups. Clearly, the continuing reliance on such measures by college and university admission offices will make it very difficult for any educationally disadvantaged or underrepresented group to attain equal or proportionate access to higher education opportunities.

The use of grades and test scores for admission to higher education has serious equity implications beyond the competitive disadvantage that it creates for certain groups in the college admissions process. Since the lower schools tend to imitate higher education in their choice and use of assessment technology, there is a heavy reliance on school grades and standardized tests all the way down to the primary schools. Given the normative nature of such measures—students are basically being compared with each other—students who perform below "the norm" are receiving powerful negative messages about their performance and capabilities. At best, they are being told that they are not working hard enough; at worst, they are being told that they lack the capacity to succeed in academic work. A young person who regularly receives such messages year after year is not likely to come to view academic work in a positive way and is not likely to aspire to higher education. Why continue the punishment? In other words, it seems reasonable to assume that the use of normative measures such as school grades and standardized test scores causes many students to opt out of education altogether, long before they reach an age where they might consider applying to college.

Even among students who will finish school and apply to college, the school's reliance on school grades and standardized test scores has a major impact on *where* any student chooses to send applications (Astin, Christian and Henson 1975). A great deal of college and university "selectivity" is, in fact, *self*-selection. Very few students with mediocre grades or test scores apply to highly selective institutions. While some high-scoring students do apply to nonselective institutions, most of them apply instead to the more selective institutions. As a matter of fact, the self-selection by student applicants is so extreme that most of the highly selective institutions could admit students at random from their applicant pools and end up with an entering class that differs only very slightly, in terms of high school grades and test scores, from those admitted through the usual applicant screening process (Astin 1971).

In short, colleges' and universities' continuing reliance on high school grades and test scores in the admissions process poses a serious obstacle to the attainment of greater educational equity for disadvantaged groups, not only because of the handicap that it poses in the admissions process, but also because of the profound effects that it has on students' decision making at the precollegiate level.

'Excellence' and Equity

In earlier writings (Astin 1982, 1985a and b), I have argued that the principal driving force behind the use of grades and test scores in the admissions process is adherence to the resources and reputational views of excellence. "Excellence" in American higher education has traditionally been equated either with an institution's academic reputation or with its resources as measured by money, faculty, research productivity, or highly able students. Students with high grades or high scores on standardized college admissions tests are seen as a valuable "resource" (and, by implication, lower-scoring students as a liability), and having a select (high-scoring) student body enhances an institution's reputation because it is regarded as a sign of "excellence." The educational folklore that has evolved out of this process consists primarily of a hierarchy or pecking order of institutions with the most selective ("highest quality") institutions at the top and the least selective ("lowest quality") ones at the bottom. That students, parents, teachers, and counselors are well aware of this folklore is reflected in the considerable amount of self-selection that takes place among high school students before they ever apply to college.

For several years now I have been arguing that the resources and reputational views should be replaced by a "talent development" conception, whereby an institution's excellence is judged in terms of how effectively it is able to educate the students who enroll. Under a talent development view, an "excellent" institution is one that is able to develop its students' talents to the fullest extent. . . .

Despite its hierarchical nature and its strong inclination to favor the best-prepared students, American higher education has made substantial efforts to mitigate the handicaps posed by selective admissions and reliance on norm-referenced tests and grades. First we have "special" admissions or "affirmative action" admissions, wherein an institution accepts African American or Hispanic applicants whose grades and test scores fall below the minimum levels required to admit other students. Practically all selective institutions practice some form of special admissions, and many invest substantial resources in actively recruiting minority students. Beyond this, most institutions have some form of remedial or "developmental" educational programs for specially admitted students, which provide special tutoring and counseling to help students raise their performance levels to those of regularly admitted students. Nevertheless, judging from the continuing underrepresentation of African Americans and Hispanics at both the admissions and graduation levels (Astin 1982), these special admissions and educational programs have not been able to achieve anything approaching proportional representation of Hispanics and African Americans among college students and college graduates.

Opportunity for What?

One of the problems that one frequently encounters in discussions of "equal access" and "equal opportunity" is a great deal of fuzziness about the meaning of the term "opportunity." Opportunity for what? Opportunity to do what?

Perhaps the best way to approach this issue is from the student's perspective. What sorts of benefits can a student derive by attending a postsecondary institution? I see three major types of benefits (Astin 1985a): *educational* benefits, *fringe* benefits, and *existential* benefits. Educational benefits have to do with the changes in the student—in intellectual capacity and skills, values, attitudes, interests, mental health, and so forth—that can be attributed to the college experience. Educational benefits, of course, relate directly to the talent development model: to what extent are students able to develop their talents as a result of being exposed to particular educational programs?

From the student's perspective, the "fringe benefits" of college include those postcollege outcomes that are related to the institutional credential that the student receives, rather than the student's personal attributes. This situation has been called the "sheepskin effect" by some educators. Having a degree from a particular institution can confer certain social and occupational advantages that have nothing necessarily to do with the graduate's personal characteristics or qualifications.

The last category of benefit, "existential benefits," refers to the quality of the undergraduate experience itself, independent of any talent development (educational benefits) or sheepskin effect (fringe benefits). Existential benefits have to do with the student's subjective satisfaction derived from the learning process, peer contacts, interactions with faculty, extracurricular and academic experiences, recreational activities, and so on. Such experiences may, of course, lead to educational benefits, but the existential aspects of attending college are important in and of themselves.

Defining 'Equity'

Some policy makers prefer to define educational equity in terms of the access concept. These observers would be content to believe that educational equity will be attained when *overall* enrollments in postsecondary education reach proportionate or near-proportionate representation for ethnic minorities, poor students, and other underrepresented groups. Indeed, measured by this standard, the United States, of all the countries in the world, has achieved the greatest degree of equity. If "opportunities" in American higher education were indeed equal, such a gross measure of equity might be acceptable. However, given the great disparities in educational resources and reputations that are associated with the institutional hierarchy, any definition of "equity" or "equality of access" must also take into consideration the quality of the opportunity offered. In other words, guaranteeing that opportunities are available for all does not ensure equity unless the opportunities themselves are comparable.

To provide some rough indication as to the great discrepancies among institutions in the United States, let us consider two extreme groups of institutions: the most selective (those whose entering freshmen average 1,300 or above on the SAT) and the least selective (those whose entering freshmen average below 775 on the SAT). Computed on a per student basis, for every dollar invested in

"educational and general" expenditures in the least selective institution, the most selective institutions invest three dollars. The most selective institutions pay their faculty 60 percent more than do the least selective institutions (Astin 1985b). And more than 90 percent of the freshmen entering the most selective institutions live in residential facilities, compared to fewer than half the students entering the least selective institutions. Furthermore, there is considerable evidence (e.g., Henson 1980) that graduates of selective institutions enjoy a great many fringe benefits not available to students at the least selective institutions. Among the several such benefits would be access to the best job opportunities and to the top graduate and professional schools, and increased lifetime earnings (Solomon 1975). Finally, there are certain educational benefits to consider: longitudinal research suggests that a student starting out at a selective institution has a much better chance of completing a degree program than a *comparable* student (in terms of academic preparation and family background) who starts at a nonselective institution (Dey and Astin 1989). . . .

[T]he issue of "equity versus excellence" is really more a matter of *how we define excellence*. If we accept the reputational or resource approach to excellence, there is clearly a conflict with the goal of equity: there are only so many resources to go around and there are only so many institutions with great reputations, so if we allocate more resources to the educationally unprepared or admit more of these students to the prestigious institutions, we end up spending less on the best-prepared students and admitting fewer of them to prestigious institutions. In other words, under the reputational and resource approaches, we are playing a zero-sum game when it comes to excellence: there is only so much of it to go around and if we want to distribute more of it in the direction of the underprepared students we must dilute the "excellence" of education provided to the best prepared students. In short, when it comes to affirmative action and the expansion of educational opportunities to disadvantaged students, it is the reputational and resource views, more than anything else, that pose the greatest obstacles.

The conflict has still other dimensions. From the perspective of an individual institution, admitting more underprepared students forces us to admit fewer of the best-prepared students, thereby diluting the "quality" of our institution ("quality" in this context being defined in terms of the level of preparation of the students who attend). Conversely, if we decide to become more "excellent" by raising our admission standards, we must necessarily deprive more of the less-prepared students of a place in our institution. Clearly, under this definition of excellence there is an inherent conflict between excellence and equity.

This zero-sum game also serves to foster a great deal of wasteful competition among institutions. If my institution succeeds in becoming more "excellent" by recruiting away some of your faculty stars or National Merit scholars, then your excellence is proportionally reduced. And the resources invested in this competition are lost from the system with no gain in overall "excellence."

A talent development approach to excellence creates a very different scenario. From this perspective, our excellence depends less on who we admit and more on what we *do* for the students once they are admitted. In other words, our excellence is measured in terms of how effectively we *develop* the educational talents of our students, rather than in terms of the mere level of developed talent they exhibit when they enter. . . . [T]here is nothing *inherently* competitive or normative about talent development. That is, if my institution manages to be highly successful in developing the talents of our students, this fact in no way constrains or limits what any other institution can do. As a matter of fact, under a talent development approach institutions can learn from each other's successes and failures in the talent development enterprise, thereby enhancing the talent development (human capital development) that occurs in the system as a whole. . . .

To me the most potent conceptual tool for expanding educational opportunities and achieving a greater degree of educational equity is the talent development approach. This is especially true in the case of our public institutions, since they are presumably committed to "serving the public." Clearly, the most appropriate public service that can be performed by such institutions is education. Since the explicit charter of the public institution is thus to serve society by educating its citizens, a public institution does not exist primarily to enhance its own resources and reputation or, to put it in the vernacular, merely to become as rich and as famous as it can. Indeed, public institutions exist primarily to confer educational (and possibly fringe and existential) benefits on large segments of the population.

What is particularly interesting about these issues is that many of the contemporary spokespersons for higher education have lately been arguing the "human capital" viewpoint as a basis for greater public support and funding. America's "competitiveness," they argue, depends upon educating all of our citizens to the greatest extent possible, not only to maximize the number of high-achieving scientists, inventors, and leaders, but also to minimize the number of lower-performing people who often represent a drain on the society's resources. The "human capital" argument, in other words, applies across the entire spectrum of ability and achievement. Such a view meshes very nicely, it seems to me, with the talent development approach. In both instances, we strive to maximize educational benefits.

Assessment and 'Academic Standards'

While I believe there is considerable evidence supporting the idea that the primary justification for the use of high school grades and standardized test scores in college admissions is to support the reputational and resource conceptions of excellence, many college faculty will argue that the fundamental reason for selective admissions is to establish and maintain "academic standards." But what, exactly, is meant by the term "academic standards?" I see at least two different meanings that can be extracted from this phrase. First, academic standards can be interpreted as referring to the level of performance the student must demonstrate in order to be awarded particular grades or to earn the bachelor's degree. When the term is used in this sense, the resistance to lowering admissions standards to accommodate more underprepared students is actually a concern that final (exit) performance standards will also be lowered. Those who make such an argument forget that changed admissions standards do not lead inevitably to changed performance standards, simply because performance standards can be maintained independently of admissions standards.

The lack of a necessary relationship between admissions standards and exit performance standards can perhaps best be understood with an analogy from the field of medicine. In much the same way that education seeks to develop the student's talent to a high level, the exit performance standard for all forms of medical treatment is a sound and healthy patient. . . .

[I]f a hospital admits a patient who is more seriously ill than the typical patient at the hospital, the hospital does not automatically set lower performance standards for that patient: It is hoped that all patients will eventually get over their illnesses and be healthy, productive citizens when they leave the hospital. It is true that the extremely ill patient may require a greater investment of resources to reach the hoped-for performance standards for discharge, and it is true that the probability of reaching those standards might be somewhat less than would be the case for an average patient, but the hospital does not automatically alter its performance standards simply because the patient has a poor prognosis at entry.

This medical analogy underscores one important reality about expanding educational opportunities. If an institution or a system of institutions wants to maintain exit performance standards *and* to enroll a greater proportion of underprepared students (students who, at college entry, have lower high school GPAs and lower standardized test scores than the average student), one or more of the following changes must occur: The underprepared students must be given more *time* to reach performance standards; a greater share of institutional resources must be deployed to deal effectively with the under-

prepared students; or the institution's dropout and failure rates must increase. In short, lowering admissions standards does not necessarily require any alteration in performance standards at the exit point.

In higher education our thinking about performance "standards" tends to be much more simplistic. Rather than attempting to achieve common performance standards by differential treatment, we try to "maintain standards" through selective admissions. This practice is basically no different in principle from trying to achieve performance standards in a medical setting by refusing to admit the sickest patients. Indeed, in American higher education we have developed a set of elite institutions that are so selective in their inputs that high performance standards are almost guaranteed, even if the institution contributes little to the students' educational development. Moreover, these same institutions have the best facilities and the most resources.

A second meaning of the "maintaining academic standards" argument expresses a concern for the talent development process itself. The argument goes as follows: If larger numbers of underprepared students are admitted to an institution, that institution's academic program will become less demanding and will therefore lose some of its potency in developing student talent. This argument implies that, in attempting to gear its program to greater numbers of underprepared students, the institution will slight its better-prepared students, giving them a watered-down education that will lead to less talent development among the better-prepared students. It should be emphasized that this argument revolves around a problem that all institutions face, regardless of their admissions policies: How to deal effectively with students who come to college differing significantly in their levels of academic preparation. . . . Good diagnostic assessment and appropriate guidance and course placement are among the techniques most commonly used to deal with differences in academic preparation. When such diagnostic assessment and differential placement is done thoroughly and thoughtfully, there is no reason why students at all levels of performance cannot be exposed to rigorous courses that challenge them to develop their talents.

The 'Prediction' Argument

When challenged about their reliance on high school grades and test scores in making admissions decisions, many faculty will respond that these assessment devices "predict grades in college." Many observers have argued, correctly I think, that grades leave much to be desired when it comes to their use as a college student performance measure. But even if we accept college grades as a valid performance measure, the prediction argument does not really hold up under scrutiny. Basically, the prediction argument asserts that students with high grades and high test scores should be favored in the admissions process because they are likely to "perform well" later on in college (i.e., get good grades). What this really means is that a high-scoring student is more likely than one with lower grades and test scores to do well on measures of academic performance (college grades, honors, retention, etc.). This argument is simply another way of saying that high school performance correlates with college performance. But does the argument really have anything to say about how much or how well the different students will actually *learn?* Does it say anything about how much talent development different students will eventually show? Unfortunately, it does not. . . . In other words, *traditional selective admissions does not necessarily further the talent development mission of a college or university.*

Supporters of selective admissions might respond that my argument is flawed because a student's college GPA is indeed a valid indicator of how much a student has learned in college. . . . [But] students who get mediocre grades in a course can be learning as much (as measured by score improvements in standardized tests given before and after the course) as students with the highest grades. . . . [T]he only requirement for high school performance to correlate with college performance is that the students' positions relative to each other show some consistency over time. Nothing in the correlation tells us how much learning has occurred or even whether there has been any learning at all. . . .

What Are the Social Responsibilities of Public Systems?

While the institutional hierarchy within the private sector of higher education developed more or less by historical accident, the hierarchies that exist within most of our state systems have been established as a matter of public policy. These systems, in turn, are sustained by a system of selective admissions that relies heavily on the students' high school grades and scores on standardized tests. In the typical state system, there are one or more "flagship" universities that occupy the top rungs in the hierarchy. The middle rungs of most public hierarchies are occupied by the state colleges and universities (many of them former teachers colleges), and the community colleges occupy the bottom rungs. . . . As with the private hierarchies, the resources and opportunities are unequally distributed within the public hierarchies, with the greatest resources and opportunities concentrated in the flagship universities and the fewest resources and opportunities at the community college level (Hayden 1986). While it is well known that poor students and members of educationally disadvantaged minority groups are severely underrepresented in higher education as a whole, it is often not recognized that poor and minority students are not equally distributed across different types of institutions *within* most public systems. To achieve proportional representation, large numbers of minority and poor students would have to be moved from the community colleges to the state colleges and flagship universities, and some would probably also have to be moved from the state colleges into the flagship universities. Thus, to achieve proportional representation in the flagship universities, the number of African Americans attending these institutions would have to be more than doubled, the number of Hispanics would have to be increased by more than 80 percent, and the number of Native Americans would have to be increased by more than 60 percent (Astin 1982). Note that "proportionate" in this context refers solely to the distribution of currently enrolled students *within* these public higher education systems. Given that all three of these groups are substantially underrepresented in higher education as a whole relative to their proportions in the population, the problem of equal access to higher education is far more serious than these substantial figures suggest.

A similar result occurs when we look at how low-income students are distributed among the public institutions (Astin 1985). If we define "low income" as including each student whose family's income falls in the lowest 20 percent for college students nationally, the number attending flagship universities would have to be more than doubled to achieve proportional representation in these institutions.

In an earlier study of the 65 flagship universities across the country (Astin 1982a), 56 had significant underenrollments of African Americans, 48 had significant Hispanic underenrollments, and 46 had significant underenrollments of Native Americans. Moreover, the degree of underenrollment was greatest in those states with the largest minority populations.

To attain proportionate representation of the underrepresented minorities in the flagship universities in New York, Texas, California, and most of the southern states, the numbers would have to be increased by between 200 and 600 percent!

The maldistribution of minorities and low-income students becomes even more pronounced if we look only at the 24 most selective flagship universities (that is, those whose entering freshmen score above 1,100 on the SAT composite test). While these institutions enroll 4.8 percent of all college students in the United States, they enroll only the following percentages of minorities: African Americans, 2.1; Hispanics, 2.5; and Native Americans, 2.3. It might be added that Asian Americans, who are slightly underrepresented in all public universities, are actually overrepresented by nearly 100 percent in the most selective public universities (these institutions enroll 9.3 percent of all Asian Americans compared to only 4.8 percent of all students).

The flagship universities and their supporters are willing to defend this state of affairs primarily because, in one way or another, they all support the resources and reputational views of excellence. But what of the public university's broader mandate? To what extent is the pursuit of institutional self-interest through resource acquisition and reputation enhancement compatible with the public university's mission of serving the public interest? Does not the "public interest" include the education of *all* the citizens and expansion of opportunities for minority and low-income students?

While it might be argued that the flagship universities are "not equipped" to educate underprepared students, most universities have explicitly acknowledged their responsibilities in this area by introducing special admissions programs, remedial and support services for underprepared students, and the like. Programs of this type are especially generous when it comes to academic assistance for specially admitted athletes. The real issue seems to be the numbers of such students that these universities are willing to take in. In this connection, it should be noted that several major research universities in the Midwest have a long-standing policy of open admissions. At the same time, virtually every state has acknowledged its commitment to expanding opportunities by providing all high school graduates with access to *some* type of public institution. This analysis indicates, however, that these "opportunities" tend to be confined to the community colleges and, to a lesser extent, the state colleges.

It seems clear that the flagship university's interest in expanding educational opportunities to disadvantaged groups directly conflicts with its quest for "excellence" in reputational and resource terms. Judging from the current distribution of low-income and minority students among our public institutions in most states, it appears that the quest for excellence has been given much higher priority than the issue of equal access. As a consequence, in most states low-income and minority students do not have equal access to the best educational opportunities. . . .

Let us return briefly to consider once more the role of assessment in promoting equal opportunity. Several years ago my colleagues and I obtained national college admissions test data from the College Entrance Examination Board and the American College Testing Program, which allowed us to determine just how the representation of minority and low-income students would be affected by changing the way in which high school grades, test scores, and other assessment information is used in the college admissions process. Following are some of the major findings of that simulation study:

- Both African Americans and Hispanics are put at a competitive disadvantage when high school grades and standardized admissions test scores are used in making admissions decisions. Test scores pose a greater handicap than high school grades do, especially for African Americans.

- The handicap resulting from the use of test scores and grades becomes greater as the selection ratio increases. A simple combination of test scores and grades produces an 80 percent underrepresentation of African Americans when the selection ratio is one and four, but only a 65 percent underrepresentation when the selection ratio is one in two.

- Much of the handicap posed by the use of test scores and grades can be mitigated by the use of a "disadvantagement index" based on the income and educational level of the student's parents. This index gives special credit for students whose parents are poor and/or relatively uneducated.

- Underrepresented minorities benefit differentially from the use of a disadvantagement index, but such an index must be given substantial weight to overcome the handicap imposed by test scores and grades.

- Given the considerable handicap posed by standardized test scores, the use of a disadvantagement index benefits minority students more if it is combined with grades alone rather than with grades and test scores.

This last finding is of particular relevance since a number of studies have shown that standardized test scores contribute little to the prediction of academic performance once the student's high school grades are taken into account.

Besides modifications in the use of different assessment devices for college admissions, there are other avenues available to public universities that may wish to enhance their enrollments of minority and low-income students. One such alternative relates to the structure of public higher education systems. The California model, with its three-tiered system, is not necessarily the only or even the best model. States such as Pennsylvania and Kentucky, for example, have developed public university systems that, in effect, combine the community college model with the research university model by means of two-year branch campuses that offer the first two undergraduate years. A student attending one of these branch campuses is admitted to the university for upper-division work without having to go through the usual application and transfer paperwork. Another version of this alternative would be for universities to "adopt" existing community colleges and to standardize the lower-division transfer curricula. Although these alternative structures may degenerate into an implicit hierarchy (through comparisons of the branch campus with the main campus, for example), they appear to represent some advance over more rigidly stratified systems.

Summary

The "conflict" between equity and excellence in American higher education is caused in part by our continuing reliance on the reputational and resource conceptions of excellence. Under these views, students with good grades and high test scores are highly sought after because they are seen as an important "resource" that enhances the institution's reputation; lower-scoring students, on the other hand, are shunned as a liability that detracts from institutional "excellence."

Under a talent development view, the performance level of *entering* students is of much less importance, since the institution's "excellence would depend primarily on how effectively the institution was able to *develop* its students' talents.

The traditional argument that lowered admissions standards necessarily erode "academic standards" is challenged, as is the argument that test scores and high school grades should be used in admissions because they "predict" college grades.

Considering that public systems of higher education, in particular, are responsible for extending equal educational opportunities to all citizens of a state, the existence of hierarchical public systems supported by selective admissions based on test scores and grades is questionable. There is reason to believe that the "flagship" universities in most states could substantially increase their enrollments of underrepresented minorities without seriously compromising "academic standards."

References

Astin, A. W. 1971. *Predicting Academic Performance in College.* New York: Free Press.

——. 1982. *Minorities in Higher Education: Recent Trends, Current Prospects, and Recommendations.* San Francisco: Jossey-Bass.

——. 1985a. *Achieving Educational Excellence: A Critical Assessment of Priorities and Practices in Higher Education.* San Francisco: Jossey-Bass.

——. 1985b. "Selectivity and Equity in the Public Research University." In *The Future of State Universities: Issues in Teaching, Research, and Service,* edited by L. W. Koepplin and D. Wilson. New Brunswick, NJ: Rutgers University Press.

Astin, A. W., C. E. Christian, and J. W. Henson. 1975. *The Impact of Students' Financial Aid Programs on Students' Choice.* Los Angeles: Higher Education Research Institute.

Dey, E., and A. W. Astin. 1989. *Predicting College Retention: Comparative National Data from the 1982 Freshman Class.* Los Angeles: Higher Education Research Institute.

Hayden, T. 1986. *Beyond the Master Plan.* Sacramento: Joint Publications Office.

Henson, J. W. 1980. "Institutional Excellence and Student Achievement: A Study of College Quality and its Impact on Education and Student Achievement." Ph.D. dissertation, University of California, Los Angeles.

Solomon, L. C. 1975. "The Definition of College Quality and its Impact on Earning." Explorations in Economic Research (Fall): 537–587.

32

The Recoloring of Campus Life:

Student Racism, Academic Pluralism, and the End of a Dream

Shelby Steele

In the past few years, we have witnessed what the National Institute Against Prejudice and Violence calls a "proliferation" of racial incidents on college campuses around the country. The nature of these incidents has ranged from open racial violence . . . to the harassment of minority students and acts of racial or ethnic insensitivity, with by far the greatest number of episodes falling in the last two categories. . . .

In response, black students around the country have rediscovered the militant protest strategies of the sixties. At the University of Massachusetts at Amherst, Williams College, Penn State University, University of California-Berkeley, UCLA, Stanford University, and countless other campuses, black students have sat in, marched, and rallied. But much of what they were marching and rallying about seemed less a response to specific racial incidents than a call for broader action on the part of the colleges and universities they were attending. Black students have demanded everything from more black faculty members and new courses on racism to the addition of "ethnic" foods in the cafeteria. There is the sense in these demands that racism runs deep. . . . I don't think so, not really. But if it is not a war, the problem of campus racism does represent a new and surprising hardening of racial lines within the most traditionally liberal and tolerant of America's institutions—its universities.

As a black who has spent his entire adult life on predominantly white campuses, I found it hard to believe that the problem of campus racism was as dramatic as some of the incidents seemed to make it. The incidents I read or heard about often seemed prankish and adolescent, though not necessarily harmless. There is a meanness in them but not much menace; no one is proposing to reinstitute Jim Crow on campus. On the California campus where I now teach, there have been few signs of racial tension.

And, of course, universities are not where racial problems tend to arise. . . . I wouldn't say that the phrase "campus racism" is a contradiction in terms, but until recently it certainly seemed an incongruence.

But a greater incongruence is the generational timing of this new problem on the campuses. Today's undergraduates were born after the passage of the 1964 Civil Rights Act. They grew up in an age when racial equality was for the first time enforceable by law. This too was a time when blacks suddenly appeared on television, as mayors of big cities, as icons of popular culture, as teachers, and in some cases even as neighbors. Today's black and white college students, veterans of "Sesame Street" and often of integrated grammar and high schools, have had more opportunities to know each other than any previous generation in American history. Not enough opportunities, perhaps, but enough to make the notion of racial tension on campus something of a mystery, at least to me.

To look at this mystery, I left my own campus with its burden of familiarity and talked with black and white students at California schools where racial incidents had occurred: Stanford, UCLA, and Berkeley. I spoke with black and white students—not with Asians and Hispanics—because, as always, blacks and whites represent the deepest lines of division, and because I hesitate to wander onto the complex territory of other minority groups. . . .

I have long believed that the trouble between the races is seldom what it appears to be. It was not hard to see after my first talks with students that racial tension on campus is a problem that misrepresents itself. It has the same look, the archetypal pattern, of

America's timeless racial conflict—white racism and black protest. And I think part of our concern over it comes from the fact that it has the feel of a relapse, illness gone and come again. But if we are seeing the same symptoms, I don't believe we are dealing with the same illness. For one thing, I think racial tension on campus is more the result of racial equality than inequality.

How to live with racial difference has been America's profound social problem. For the first hundred years or so following emancipation it was controlled by a legally sanctioned inequality that kept the races from each other. No longer is this the case. On campuses today, as throughout society, blacks enjoy equality under the law—a profound social advancement. No student may be kept out of a class or a dormitory or an extracurricular activity because of his or her race. But there is a paradox here: on a campus where members of all races are gathered, mixed together in the classroom as well as socially, differences are more exposed than ever. And this is where the trouble starts. For members of each race—young adults coming into their own, often away from home for the first time—bring to this site of freedom, exploration, and (now, today) equality, very deep fears, anxieties, inchoate feelings of racial shame, anger, and guilt. These feelings could lie dormant in the home, in familiar neighborhoods, in simpler days of childhood. But the college campus, with its structures of interaction and adult-level competition—the big exam, the dorm, the mixer—is another matter. I think campus racism is born of the rub between racial difference and a setting, the campus itself, devoted to interaction and equality. On our campuses, such concentrated micro-societies, all that remains unresolved between blacks and whites, all the old wounds and shames that have never been addressed, present themselves for attention—and present our youth with pressures they cannot always handle.

I have mentioned one paradox: racial fears and anxieties among blacks, and whites, bubbling up in an era of racial equality under the law, in settings that are among the freest and fairest in society. But there is another, related paradox, stemming from the notion of—and practice of—affirmative action. Under the provisions of the Equal Employment Opportunity Act of 1972, all state governments and institutions (including universities) were forced to initiate plans to increase the proportion of minority and women employees and, in the case of universities, of students too. Affirmative action plans that establish racial quotas were ruled unconstitutional more than ten years ago in *University of California v. Bakke*, but such plans are still thought by some to secretly exist, and lawsuits having to do with alleged quotas are still very much with us. But quotas are only the most controversial aspect of affirmative action; the principle of affirmative action is reflected in various university programs aimed at redressing and overcoming past patterns of discrimination. Of course, to be conscious of past patterns of discriminations—the fact, say, that public schools in the black inner cities are more crowded and employ fewer top-notch teachers than a white suburban public school, and that this is a factor in student performance—is only reasonable. But in doing this we also call attention quite obviously to difference in the case of blacks and whites, racial difference. What has emerged on campus in recent years—as a result of the new equality and of affirmative action and, in a sense, as a result of progress—is a *politics of difference*, a troubling, volatile politics in which each group justifies itself, its sense of worth and its pursuit of power, through difference alone.

In this context, racial, ethnic, and gender differences become forms of sovereignty, campuses become balkanized, and each group fights with whatever means are available. No doubt there are many factors that have contributed to the rise of racial tension on campus: What has been the role of fraternities, which have returned to campus with their inclusions and exclusions? What role has the heightened notion of college as some first step to personal, financial success played in increasing competition, and thus tension? But mostly, what I sense is that in interactive settings, fighting the fights of "difference," old ghosts are stirred and haunt again. Black and white Americans simply have the power to make each other feel shame and guilt. In most situations, we may be able to deny these feelings, keep them at bay. But these feelings are likely to surface on college campuses, where young people are groping for identity and power, and where difference is made to matter so greatly. In a way, racial tension on campus in the eighties might have been inevitable.

I would like, first, to discuss black students, their anxieties and vulnerabilities. The accusation black Americans have always lived with is that they are inferior—inferior simply because they are black. And this accusation has been too uniform, too ingrained in cultural imagery, too enforced by law, custom, and every form of power not to have left a mark. Black inferiority was a precept accepted by the founders of this nation; it was a principle of social organization that relegated blacks to the sidelines of American life. So when young black students find themselves on white campuses surrounded by those who have historically claimed superiority, they are also surrounded by the myth of their inferiority.

Of course, it is true that many young people come to college with some anxiety about not being good enough. But only blacks come wearing a color that is still, in the minds of some, a sign of inferiority. Poles, Jews, Hispanics, and other groups also endure degrading stereotypes. But two things make the myth of black inferiority a far heavier burden—the broadness of its scope and its incarnation in color. There are not only more stereotypes of blacks than of other groups, but these stereotypes are also more dehumanizing, more focused on the most despised human traits: stupidity, laziness, sexual immorality, dirtiness, and so on. In America's racial and ethnic hierarchy, blacks have clearly been relegated to the lowest level—have been burdened with an ambiguous, animalistic humanity. Moreover, this is made unavoidable for blacks by sheer visibility of black skin, a skin that evokes the myth of inferiority on sight. Today this myth is sadly reinforced for many black students by affirmative action programs, under which blacks may often enter college with lower test scores and high school grade point averages than whites. "They see me as an affirmative action

case," one black student told me at UCLA. This reinforces the myth of inferiority by implying that blacks are not good enough to make it into college on their own.

So when a black student enters college, the myth of inferiority compounds the normal anxiousness over whether he or she will be good enough. This anxiety is not only personal but also racial. The families of these students will have pounded into them the fact that blacks are not inferior. And probably more than anything it is this pounding that finally leaves the mark. If I am not inferior, why the need to say so?

This myth of inferiority constitutes a very sharp and ongoing anxiety for young blacks, the nature of which is very precise: it is the terror that somehow, through one's actions or by virtue of some "proof" (a poor grade, a flubbed response in class), one's fear of inferiority—inculcated in ways large and small by society—will be confirmed as real. On a university campus where intelligence itself is the ultimate measure, this anxiety is bound to be triggered.

A black student I met at UCLA was disturbed a little when I asked him if he ever felt vulnerable—anxious about "black inferiority"—as a black student. But after a long pause, he finally said, "I think I do." The example he gave was of a large lecture class he'd taken with over three hundred students. Fifty or so black students sat in the back of the lecture hall and "acted out every stereotype in the book." They were loud, ate food, came in late—and generally got lower grades than whites in the class. "I knew I would be seen like them, and I didn't like it. I never sat by them." Seen like what, I asked, though we both knew the answer. "As lazy, ignorant, and stupid," he said sadly.

Had the group at the back been white fraternity brothers, they would not have been seen as dumb whites, of course. And a frat brother who worried about his grades would not worry that he had been seen "like them." The terror in this situation for the black student I spoke with was that his own deeply buried anxiety would be given credence, that the myth would be verified, and that he would feel shame and humiliation not because of who he was but simply because he was black. In this lecture hall his race, quite apart from his performance, might subject him to four unendurable feelings—diminishment, accountability to the preconceptions of whites, a powerlessness to change those preconceptions, and finally, shame. These are the feelings that make up his racial anxiety, and that of all blacks on any campus. On a white campus a black is never far from these feelings, and even his unconscious knowledge that he is subject to them can undermine his self-esteem.

There are blacks on any campus who are not up to doing good college-level work. Certain black students may not be happy or motivated or in the appropriate field of study—*just like whites.* (Let us not forget that many white students get poor grades, fail, drop out.) Moreover, many more blacks than whites are not quite prepared for college, may have to catch up, owing to factors beyond their control: poor previous schooling, for example. But the white who has to catch up will not be anxious that his being behind is a matter of his whiteness, of his being racially inferior. The black student may well have such a fear.

This, I believe, is one reason why black colleges in America turn out 37 percent of all black college graduates though they enroll only 16 percent of black college students. Without whites around on campus, the myth of inferiority is in abeyance and, along with it, a great reservoir of culturally imposed self-doubt. On black campuses, feelings of inferiority are personal; on campuses with a white majority, a black's problems have a way of becoming a "black" problem.

But this feeling of vulnerability a black may feel, in itself, is not as serious a problem as what he or she does with it. To admit that one is made anxious in integrated situations about the myth of racial inferiority is difficult for young blacks. It seems like admitting that one is racially inferior. And so, most often, the student will deny harboring the feelings. This is where some of the pangs of racial tension begin, because denial always involves distortion.

In order to deny a problem we must tell ourselves that the problem is something different from what it really is. A black student

at Berkeley told me that he felt defensive every time he walked into a classroom of white faces. When I asked why, he said, "Because I know they're all racists. They think blacks are stupid." Of course it may be true that some whites feel this way, but the singular focus on white racism allows this student to obscure his own underlying racial anxiety. He can now say that his problem—facing a classroom of white faces, *fearing* that they think he is dumb—is entirely the result of certifiable white racism and has nothing to do with his own anxieties, or even that this particular academic subject may not be his best. Now all the terror of his anxiety, its powerful energy, is devoted to simply *seeing* racism. Whatever evidence of racism he finds—and looking this hard, he will no doubt find some—can be brought in to buttress his distorted view of the problem while his actual deep-seated anxiety goes unseen.

Denial, and the distortion that results, places the problem *outside* the self and in the world. It is not that I have any inferiority anxiety because of my race; it is that I am going to school with people who don't like blacks. This is the shift in thinking that allows black students to reenact the protest pattern of the sixties. *Denied racial anxiety–distortion–reenactment* is the process by which feelings of inferiority are transformed into an exaggerated white menace—which is then protested against with the techniques of the past. Under the sway of this process, black students believe that history is repeating itself, that it's just like the sixties, or fifties. In fact, it is not-yet-healed wounds from the past, rather than the inequality that created the wounds, that is the real problem.

This process generates an unconscious need to exaggerate the level of racism on campus—to make it a matter of the system, not just a handful of students. Racism is the avenue away from the true inner anxiety. How many students demonstrating for black theme dorms—demonstrating in the style of the sixties, when the battle was to win for blacks a place on campus—might be better off spending their time reading and studying? Black students have the highest dropout rate and the lowest grade point average of any group in American universities. This need not be so. And it is not the result of not having black theme dorms.

It was my very good fortune to go to college in 1964, when the question of black "inferiority" was openly talked about among blacks. The summer before I left for college, I heard Martin Luther King speak in Chicago, and he laid it on the line for black students everywhere: "When you are behind in a footrace, the only way to get ahead is to run faster than the man in front of you. So when your white roommate says he's tired and goes to sleep, you stay up and burn the midnight oil." His statement that we were "behind in a footrace" acknowledged that, because of history, of few opportunities, of racism, we were, in a sense, "inferior." But this had to do with what had been done to our parents and their parents, not with inherent inferiority. And because it was acknowledged, it was presented to us as a challenge rather than a mark of shame.

Of the 18 black students (in a student body of 1,000) who were on campus in my freshman year, all graduated, though a number of us were not from the middle class. At the university where I currently teach, the dropout rate for black students is 72 percent, despite the presence of several academic support programs, a counseling center with black counselors, an Afro-American studies department, black faculty, administrators, and staff, a general education curriculum that emphasizes "cultural pluralism," an Educational Opportunities Program, a mentor program, a black faculty and staff association, and an administration and faculty that often announce the need to do more for black students.

It may be unfair to compare my generation with the current one. Parents do this compulsively and to little end but self-congratulation. But I don't congratulate my generation. I think we were advantaged. We came along at a time when racial integration was held in high esteem. And integration was a very challenging social concept for both blacks and whites. We were remaking ourselves—that's what one did at college—and making history. We had something to prove. This was a profound advantage; it gave us clarity and a challenge. Achievement in the American mainstream was the goal of integration, and the best thing about this challenge was its secondary message—that we *could* achieve.

There is much irony in the fact that black power would come along in the late sixties and change all this. Black power was a movement of uplift and pride, and yet it also delivered the weight of pride—a weight that would burden black students from then on. Black power "nationalized" the black identity, made blackness itself an object of celebration, an allegiance. But if it transformed a mark of shame into a mark of pride, it also, in the name of pride, required the denial of racial anxiety. Without a frank account of one's anxieties, there is no clear direction, no concrete challenge. Black students today do not get as clear a message from their racial identity as my generation got. They are not filled with the same urgency to prove themselves because black pride has said, *You're already proven, already equal, as good as anybody.*

The "black identity" shaped by black power most forcefully contributes to racial tensions on campuses by basing entitlement more on race than on constitutional rights and standards of merit. With integration, black entitlement derived from constitutional principles of fairness. Black power changed this by skewing the formula from rights to color—if you were black, you were entitled. Thus the United Coalition Against Racism (UCAR) at the University of Michigan could "demand" two years ago that all black professors be given immediate tenure, that there is a special pay incentive for black professors, and that money be provided for an all-black student union. In this formula, black becomes the very color of entitlement, an extra right in itself, and a.very dangerous grandiosity is promoted in which blackness amounts to specialness.

Race is, by any standard, an unprincipled source of power. And on campuses the use of racial power by one group makes racial, ethnic, or gender difference a currency of power for all groups. When I make my *difference* into power, other groups must seize upon their difference to contain my power and maintain their position relative to me. Very quickly a kind of politics of difference emerges in which racial, ethnic, and gender groups are forced to assert their entitlement and vie for power based on the single quality that makes them different from one another.

On many campuses today academic departments and programs are established on the basis of difference—black studies, women's studies, Asian studies, and so on—despite the fact that there is nothing in these "difference" departments that cannot be studied within traditional academic disciplines. If their rationale is truly past exclusion from the mainstream curriculum, shouldn't the goal now be complete inclusion rather than separateness? I think this logic is overlooked because those groups are too interested in the power their difference can bring, and they insist on separate departments and programs as tribute to that power.

This politics of difference makes everyone on campus a member of a minority group. It also makes racial tension inevitable. To highlight one's difference as a source of advantage is also, indirectly, to inspire the enemies of that difference. When blackness (and femaleness) become power, then white maleness is also sanctioned as power. A white male student I spoke with at Stanford said, "One of my friends said the other day that we should get together and start up a white student union and come up with a list of demands."

It is certainly true that white maleness has long been an unfair source of power. But the sin of white male power is precisely its use of race and gender as a source of entitlement. When minorities and women use their race, ethnicity, and gender in the same way, they not only commit the same sin but also, indirectly, sanction the very form of power that oppressed them in the first place. The politics of difference is based on a tit-for-tat sort of logic in which every victory only calls one's enemies to arms.

This elevation of difference undermines the communal impulse by making each group foreign and inaccessible to others. When difference is celebrated rather than re-marked, people must think in terms of difference, they must find meaning in difference, and this meaning comes from an endless process of contrasting one's group with other groups. Blacks use whites to define themselves as different, women use men, Hispan-

ics use whites and blacks, and on it goes. And in the process each group mythologizes and mystifies its difference, puts it beyond the full comprehension of outsiders. Difference becomes inaccessible preciousness toward which outsiders are expected to be simply and uncomprehendingly reverential. But beware: in this world, even the insulated world of the college campus, preciousness is a balloon asking for a needle. At Smith College graffiti appears: "Niggers, spics, and chinks. Quit complaining or get out."

I think that those who run our colleges and universities are every bit as responsible for the politics of difference as are minority students. To correct the exclusions once caused by race and gender, universities—under the banner of affirmative action—have relied too heavily on race and gender as criteria. So rather than break the link between difference and power, they have reinforced it. On most campuses today, a well-to-do black student with two professional parents is qualified by his race for scholarship monies that are not available to a lower-middle-class white student. A white female with a private school education and every form of cultural advantage comes under the affirmative action umbrella. This kind of inequity is an invitation to backlash. . . .

The politics of difference sets up a struggle for innocence among all groups. When difference is the currency of power, each group must fight for the innocence that entitles it to power. To gain this innocence, blacks sting whites with guilt, remind them of their racial past, accuse them of new and more subtle forms of racism. One way whites retrieve their innocence is to discredit blacks and deny their difficulties, for in this denial is the denial of their own guilt. To blacks this denial looks like racism, a racism that feeds black innocence and encourages them to throw more guilt at whites. And so the cycle continues. The politics of difference leads each group to pick at the vulnerabilities of the other.

Men and women who run universities—whites, mostly—participate in the politics of difference because they handle their guilt differently than do many of their students. They don't deny it, but still they don't want to *feel* it. And to avoid this feeling of guilt they have tended to go along with whatever blacks put on the table rather than work with them to assess their real needs. University administrators have too often been afraid of guilt and have relied on negotiation and capitulation more to appease their own guilt than to help blacks and other minorities. Administrators would never give white students a racial theme dorm where they could be "more comfortable with people of their own kind," yet more and more universities are doing this for black students, thus fostering a kind of voluntary segregation. To avoid the anxieties of integrated situations blacks ask for theme dorms; to avoid guilt, white administrators give theme dorms.

When everyone is on the run from their anxieties about race, race relations on campus can be reduced to the negotiation of avoidances. A pattern of demand and concession develops in which both sides use the other to escape themselves. Black studies departments, black deans of student affairs, black counseling programs, Afro houses, black theme dorms, black homecoming dances and graduation ceremonies—black students and white administrators have slowly engineered a machinery of separatism that, in the name of sacred difference, redraws the ugly lines of segregation.

Black students have not sufficiently helped themselves, and universities, despite all their concessions, have not really done much for blacks. If both faced their anxieties, I think they would see the same thing: academic parity with all other groups should be the overriding mission of black students, and it should also be the first goal that universities have for their black students. Blacks can only *know* they are as good as others when they are, in fact, as good—when their grades are higher and their dropout rate lower. Nothing under the sun will substitute for this, and no amount of concessions will bring it about.

Universities can never be free of guilt until they truly help black students, which means leading and challenging them rather than negotiating and capitulating. It means inspiring them to achieve academic parity, nothing less, and helping them to see their own weaknesses as their greatest challenge. It also means dismantling the machinery of separatism, breaking the link between difference and power, and skewing the formula for entitlement away from race and gender and back to constitutional rights.

As for the young white students who have rediscovered swastikas and the word "nigger," I think that they suffer from an exaggerated sense of their own innocence, as if they were incapable of evil and beyond the reach of guilt. But it is also true that the politics of difference creates an environment that threatens their innocence and makes them defensive. White students are not invited to the negotiating table from which they see blacks and others walk away with concessions. The presumption is that they do not deserve to be there because they are white. So they can only be defensive, and the less mature among them will be aggressive. Guerrilla activity will ensue. Of course this is wrong, but it is also a reflection of an environment where difference carries power and where whites have the wrong "difference."

I think universities should emphasize commonality as a higher value than "diversity" and "pluralism"—buzzwords for the politics of difference. Difference that does not rest on a clearly delineated foundation of commonality is not only inaccessible to those who are not part of the ethnic or racial group, but also antagonistic to them. Difference can enrich only the common ground. Integration has become an abstract term today, having to do with little more than numbers and racial balances. But it once stood for a high and admirable set of values. It made difference second to commonality, and it asked members of all races to face whatever fears they inspired in each other. I doubt the word will have a new vogue, but the values, under whatever name, are worth working for.

Reprinted from: Shelby Steele, *Content of Our Character*, pp. 127–147. Copyright ©1990 by Shelby Steele. Reprinted by permission of St. Martin's Press, Inc.

33

The Continuing Significance of Racism:

Discrimination Against Black Students in White Colleges

Joe R. Feagin

In the last few years we have seen a growing concern among academic administrators and educational researchers about black student enrollment and attrition rates. A number of survey studies (Astin 1977, 1982) have found that college enrollment and graduation for black Americans have declined in many programs. . . .

Keller (1988–1989) notes traces of racism in the college subculture, but plays down the importance of this factor in explaining student attrition and the lack of black advancement in higher education. Like most of the authors he reviews, Keller emphasizes individual and family factors, including black attitudes toward education and the lack of black leadership. He concludes with the argument that no one knows with certainty what to do about attrition; he prefers the interpretive analysis of Glenn Loury, who argues that middle-class blacks bear the "responsibility for the behavior of black youngsters" and are failing to encourage young blacks to study hard (Loury and Anderson 1984, p. 5). . . . The burden is on black leaders and adults to encourage black youth to view education as the main way to overcome poverty and inferiority. Keller argues in effect that college subcultures no longer play a central role in the problems of black students.

An Alternative Perspective

Much of the recent educational literature has picked up on this old theme in the analy-

sis of black Americans: the emphasis on racial group deficits in personal, family, intellectual, and moral development as explanations for black problems, in this case college achievement and attrition problems. But there are important exceptions. Some researchers still place racial discrimination near the top of the list in explaining problems of minority student achievement and attrition. . . .

A Field Research Study

The purpose of this research project is (a) to provide a detailed description of the barriers faced by black college students in predominantly white colleges and universities, (b) to suggest a typology of kinds of discrimination, and (c) to offer a tentative theory of cumulative discrimination. The study draws on in-depth interviews with two dozen college students, administrators, and faculty members in a larger sample of 180 middle-class black Americans interviewed in 14 cities, from Boston and Baltimore to Houston, Dallas, and Los Angeles. The interviewers were black graduate students, undergraduate seniors, and professors. The first respondents were known to the black interviewers as members of white college communities, known to the author, or recommended by knowledgeable informants. Snowball sampling was then used. Those quoted here were interviewed, on average for one to one-and-a-half hours, between July 1988 and October 1989. . . .

A Preliminary Overview

Discrimination can be defined as the "differential practices carried out by members of dominant racial groups that have a negative impact on members of subordinate racial groups" (see Feagin and Eckberg 1980, p. 2). Beyond this general definition, one can distinguish an array of different types of discriminatory treatment. Although a detailed typology will be developed later, the following breakdown along the important dimension of potential discriminators will be used to organize the presentation: (a) white students, (b) white faculty members, (c) white administrators and staff members, (d) white alumni. Black students face numerous blatant and subtle discriminatory barriers from these four groups.

Specific Campus Barriers: White Students

Racist Comments and Racial Awareness

Several students discussed in interviews how they became fully conscious of being black only when they entered a white college. In talking about what made her conscious of being black, one student answered:

> I don't remember in high school being called a "nigger" before, and I can remember here being called a nigger.
> [When was this?]
> In my freshman year, at a university student parade. There was a group of us, standing there, not knowing that this was not an event that a lot of black people went to! [laughs] You know, our dorm was going, and this was something we were going to go to because we were students too! And we were standing out there and [there were] a group of white fraternity boys—I remember the Southern flag and a group of us, five or six of us, and they went by us, before the parade had actually gotten under way. And one of them pointed and said, "Look at that bunch of niggers!" I remember thinking, "Surely he's not talking to us!" We didn't even use the word *nigger* in my house. . . .
> [How did you feel?]
> I think I wanted to cry. And my friends—they were from a southwestern city—they were ready to curse them, and I was just standing there with my mouth open. I think I wanted to cry. I could not believe it, because you get here and you think you're in an educated environment and you're dealing with educated people. And all of this backward country stuff . . . you think that kind of stuff is not going on, but it is.

This black student's first memory of being called a "nigger" comes from her college years in the 1980s. In this case white fraternity members in a college parade pointed her and her friends out as "bunch of niggers." Note that she first could not believe what they were saying. She gave these white male students the benefit of the doubt. Her sense of

fairness is evident. Perhaps because she was inadequately prepared for her encounters with campus racism, she at first did not want to believe that she was being labeled in a derogatory way.

Racist Jokes

The student quoted above also commented on the racist jokes that are part of the white campus subculture:

> I hate to say that I've gotten bitter, but I've gotten bitter . . . last summer, I can remember people telling jokes, that's what I remember most, everyday there was a racial joke. And they found it necessary to tell me. It might be funny and then I'd laugh, and then I thought about it while reading that book [*Black Power*]. Even if they didn't mean any harm, how can they not mean any harm? How can they not, these people who are your classmates. And supposedly some of them are your friends. How can they not mean any harm? What do you mean they don't mean any harm? Why am I making excuses for their actions? I think that's what I was doing a lot of times was making excuses. . . .

Here we see another aspect of the college subculture: the racist jokes that white students like to tell. Some white students may not realize how offensive and troubling such jokes can be, while others may intentionally tell them because they know the jokes cause pain. For the latter, racial humor is probably an outlet for passive aggression. What makes the jokes even more painful is the experience of a regular diet of them. The student just quoted at first assumed that the joke tellers did not "mean any harm." But on reflection she changed her mind. And her recognition that the white students often do mean harm has made her both bitter and stronger. . . .

Student Opposition to Things Black

Another undergraduate student explains some one-way integration features of the campus subculture:

> It's a constant battle dealing with racism. It is so much a part of everything. To integrate means simply to be white. It doesn't mean fusing the two cultures; it simply means to be white, that's all. And we

spend so much effort in passing into the mainstream of American society. They have no reason to know our culture. But we must, in order to survive, know everything about their culture. . . .

When you look at something as simple as just a group of people talking, black people are given much more, a much higher, regard if they are seen in an all-white group than they would if they were to be seen in an all-black group. If you're seen in an all-white group laughing and talking, you're seen as respectable, and probably taking care of something important. You're not wasting time. You're all right. But if you're in an all-black group, regardless if they can even hear your conversation, white people think you're trying to, you're congregated, to take over the world. It's just that basic . . . you're just punished for expressing your black culture . . . you're just constantly forced to take on the culture of white America.

This student expresses a reflective concern with the Procrustean bed aspects of the white campus subculture. Integration has not meant the fusing of two subcultures. Blacks must learn the white subculture, but whites learn little or nothing about black American subculture.

So integration, in practice, means racial discrimination. Campus racism means preferring the straight (like-white) hairstyle to a natural Afro hair style. Campus racism means a preference for white English and slang over black slang. White preferences in these matters provide great pressure on black students to conform.

Particularly insightful is this student's discussion of the group behavior of university students. She suggests that to be respectable as a black student at this large white university involves mostly being seen with, and listening to, whites. One's presence in an all-black group may be taken by whites as a sign of aggressiveness. Whites may feel threatened. Black students quickly get the message that congregating in all-black groups is undesirable behavior. There is the constant reminder of one's racial group distinctiveness.

Seeing Blacks as 'All Alike.'

A student at another university suggested that many white students see black students as "all alike":

> That's the first question they'll ask you: "Are you an athlete?" Professors, students, everybody here will ask you, "Are you an athlete?" When you say, "No," they're like, "Oh!" And it's like you got here because you're black.

In many cases black students were assumed to be athletes. She commented further on her experiences in the dorm:

> Here in my dorm, there are four black girls. Me and my roommate look nothing alike. And the other two are short, and I'm tall. They [white students] called me by my roommate's name the whole semester, and I didn't understand that. [Maybe] I understood it, but I didn't want to have to deal with that whole thing. That's really upsetting. It's like they put their shutters on when they see a black person coming. And the few black people that do get along with the other students, they seem to sort of put on a facade. They pretend to be something they're not.

Noted here is the failure of white students to see very different black students as individuals. . . .

The Difficulty of Socializing on a White Campus

In part as a result of this stereotyping, making close friendships with white students is difficult for black students. Another student with whom we talked had this to say about a question asking, "Do you feel that you can trust white people?":

> I'm sure you could. But I just haven't been in a situation where I could find out because most of the white people that I've met here at college all seem to be reacting on a superficial basis. . . . People that I've met living in the dorm—you know most of the time there's a majority of people who are white in the dorm, and most of the people who really develop a close friendship are just white. People I start out knowing, though, I usually get phased out with toward the end of the year. I still don't know why. . . .

Now when I was in high school, it was different. We hung out with a lot of different people. We had a lot of Orientals, Mexicans—it was just a whole rainbow of friends I had in high school. I didn't think much of it, but when I came to this university, it seemed to change. I don't know if it was just me, or the environment, but somehow my view of intimacy with other people, especially white people, has soured since then.

This student had a rainbow of friends in his multiethnic high school, but at the white university he has found it difficult to make white friends. In his experience most white students react on a superficial friendship basis; most do not want to become long-term friends with black students.

The ostracism behavior of some whites is illustrated in this report by an attorney in her mid-20s on her predominantly white college:

I had an incident with discrimination, which really, basically took me by surprise. . . . I lived in the dorms for a couple of years. And you sit around in the dorms and eat food with the girls, eat popcorn and watch the soaps when you don't have classes. And I remember this particular incident, this girl, we had just socialized the night before, watching T.V., having popcorn, et cetera, and I saw her on campus the next day. And she turned her head to make sure she didn't have to speak to me. . . .

A suggested reason here for the socially isolating behavior of some white students is the unwillingness to let other whites see them befriending black students.

Professors

Seeing Blacks as Representatives of Their Race

Much analysis of the attrition rate of black students from white universities and colleges neglects the role of key college actors, especially faculty members and administrators, in that attrition rate. An important aspect of the white campus subculture is the chronic inability, not only of students but also of many white faculty members and administrators to see black students as individuals.

Like the students discussed above, many white faculty members view black students in stereotypical group terms. One graduate student described such an experience.

A black undergraduate in my department is doing some research on black and white achievement in college, and one of her advisers was once the head of a rather prestigious organization in my field, not to mention [being] chair of the department. Apparently she assumed that this one undergraduate somehow spoke for all black people. And this professor would ask her things like, "Well, I don't know what you people want. First you want to be called Negro, then you want to be called black. Now you want to be called African American. What do you people want anyway? And why don't black people show up in class more? Why is it that I can't get enough blacks to sit in on my classes?" So every now and then that sort of racist mentality comes out.

Attempting to do research on blacks and whites, this student went to one of her advisers, but she was treated by this white professor as a spokesperson for her racial group. In this case, the black student was not seen as an individual but rather as a source to explain what black people "want." A common complaint among black students at predominantly white colleges is that they are often not seen as individuals.

Another undergraduate at a major public university echoed this point and set it in a broader context in commenting on what angers her about whites:

Probably the thing that angers me the most about white people is their insensitivity and their total inability to see you as an individual. You're always seen as a black person. And as a black woman, you're seen as a black person before you're seen as a woman. It's just a constant struggle. You're always trying to assert your personality, or your style, your individuality. If you want recognition you practically have to go overboard to get people to see that you are unique with your own style and your own goals, and your own way of thinking about things. . . .

The White Model

One black college student described how a college English professor told her that she should not write essays about the black people she liked to write about because those experiences were not universal. She said that he told her:

If a white person, for example, picked up one of my stories he would not understand what the hell was going on. So therefore I shouldn't write about these things. But I should write about [other] things, and he quoted William Faulkner quite liberally. I should write about things that appeal to the human heart, that everybody can appeal to and can relate to. And, see me, in my nice trusting self, I said no, he's not saying that black people aren't people enough to be termed as universal. He's not saying that, he's meaning something else. He couldn't possibly be saying this to my face. I was very, very confused. I did not understand what the hell he meant by it, not just the racial implications, but the whole statement.

The professor regarded her stories about the distinctiveness of the black experience as somehow not as universalizable as classical stories about the white experience. Moreover, by citing Faulkner liberally he was clearly suggesting that the model for good writing is not only white but also male and Southern.

In an East Coast city a male banker reported on a recent experience in an English course:

The only thing that hurt me was certain white institutions. Instead of helping you and educating you, they will browbeat [you] and downplay the educational level that you have. I turned in a paper one time at a college, and I had an instructor tell me that I was speaking black English. I was the only black in the class, and it was a freshmen writing class. And she told me that I was speaking black English. And it kind of, in one sense, made me not want to be black, and, in another sense, wonder what was black English. Because, I had gone to white schools from the sixth grade on, and I had been speaking, not speaking but writing white English all my life. . . .

That really woke me up, because that really taught me to take a lot of English writing workshops. Where now, I guess you could say, my writing skills are above average. And that's great because by her hurting me, and telling me that I was speaking black English, now I'm able to speak black English in a white format, where I can get my point across and be understood.

This student describes the strong sense of inferiority that came from his teacher stereotyping his English writing patterns as black English without providing him the necessary framework for understanding the racism of making white English the standard. As a young student who had been to integrated schools, he thought he spoke English. Her white bias and insensitivity to the fact that there is not an independent scale for evaluating spoken language—all language is equally valid if it communicates—resulted in the teacher hurting this black student. Interestingly, his reaction was to become an expert in the standard English expected in the white-conformity perspective of such teachers.

A subtle example of the white model being applied to minority students can be seen in the common emphasis on conventional standards such as SAT test scores and on attendance at certain high schools. One student commented on her recent experiences:

When I got here it was an ignorance, a closed-minded ignorance that I didn't know how to handle. One of my professors—I went to him as a freshman asking for help, and he asked me my SAT scores. And I told him. And [he said], "I don't know why they let you in, you're not expected to do well. There are so many people like you here that aren't qualified, and I can try to help you and find a tutor." I [said], "Thanks!"

In this case her score on the SAT test, historically developed as a measure of white middle-class culture and education, was considered to be an excellent measure of a student's quality. The professor also asked her what high school she had gone to. When she told him that she had gone to an elite private white high school, "his face just went every which way, [his] eyes went big, and then he said, 'Well, I'll help you get a tutor, and we'll study, because I know you're prepared for this.' " . . . Apparently, the fact that she was tracked through an elite white school meant to these professors that they should take her more seriously. . . .

The Lack of Feedback and Reinforcement

A problem that many students, black and white, have with their college professors is a lack of appropriate feedback on course performance. But this lack of feedback and reinforcement is doubly difficult for a black student at sea in a white world. . . .

One graduate student described his undergraduate experiences this way:

And I can think of several courses where I honestly feel that I was very much discriminated against. One class was an honors course in social science. And it just so happened that the criteria for getting in the course was to have made a certain grade in a previous social science course, which I did. So I took the course, which I enjoyed very much.

But when it came time for grades, the grade that I got was not the grade I earned . . . and the professor actually never even respected me enough to sit down and talk to me about my grades. The only feedback I got from the guy was when I approached him after I got the grade. And he talked to me only the amount of time that it took him to walk out of his office and go to where he had to go, and I stood there as he walked through his door. And except for that he wouldn't even give me any feedback.

And essentially what he told me was that, first of all, my attendance was poor in class. And secondly he told me that some work which he gave as optional work—that I had done—was . . . poor work. So what I understood him to say was that he took off of my regular grade for extra credit work. And as far as attendance goes, he said that I never attended class. But in fact I only missed two classes the entire semester, and the only reason I missed those two classes was because I was required by the military to be out of town on those two days. And I think, it seemed like he had, he only had the practice of taking attendance on Fridays. And

those were two Fridays because those were the two scheduled times, and I guess he assumed that if you weren't there that Friday that you weren't there that week, But I personally always felt that for a college professor to take attendance was a little bit ludicrous anyway. But that was the explanation that he gave me, that my class attendance was poor, and that my extra credit work was poor. And I think that was no evidence to support the grade.

He gave yet another example:

Another case was in organic chemistry, which in fact I failed. Throughout the semester I would go to the professor, especially before the exams, to see if I could get some help and input for things I expected to encounter on the test. And the professor literally, literally, on several occasions kicked me out of his office, and said he didn't have time to talk to me, and for me to go study with some other students in the class. And so I really think that was racially motivated also. And actually there's probably a million other examples I could give you like that. . . .

In some cases a white professor's style may be brusque for all students, black and white, but this cold style brings an especially heavy burden to minority students in a setting that is already difficult for them. . . . Perhaps these professors would have done the same with white students; however, this insensitivity and lack of feedback can have a very negative impact, whether or not it was intentional. A persistent diet of this professorial behavior, as this student notes, is a factor in the dropout rate of black males from college.

Black students become especially sensitive to negative feedback from faculty members, as yet another graduate student reported:

After a while, I think that you become real sensitive to certain kinds of feedback, and I think that becomes self-defeating. Like, if the message that you receive from someone or some institution, from a school or a class, or a professor is that you're not quite as good, or you're not good enough, or your performance is not up to standard—whether or not that happens to be true—you tend to internalize that. And to the extent that you internalize that, I think that really affects your actual performance. You know, the self-fulfilling prophecy. If you really think that you're dumb, you'll act as a dumb person will.

And so I think that it's only in recent years that I've begun to realize that . . . I think things are starting to surface where I'm beginning to realize that when I got a bad grade and I didn't deserve it. . . . I'm making a special effort to distinguish between [when] my performance really is not up to par, and when somebody says it's not up to par, but it really is.

. . . Most of us have trouble assessing the feedback we get about our performance. Is the feedback fair or unfair? Is our performance really poor, as negative feedback suggests, or is the evaluator biased? And failure to read the feedback correctly can be a very serious liability in coping with college, and especially with graduate school. This general problem becomes very difficult for black students in a predominantly white college where there is a significant probability of racial bias. . . . Moreover, a lack of professorial feedback can be particularly devastating to minority students because they have often suffered denigration and discrimination in many other areas of college life. . . .

Lack of Receptiveness to Minority Research and Issues

Another student, a graduate student in the social sciences, commented on subtle discrimination he has faced from his professors:

If I go back to my first few days as a graduate student, I came in having done some work on stereotypes as an undergraduate. At my undergraduate school, my professor was really supportive and in fact the whole department was supportive of me doing that sort of work. When I got here, literally [on] the first day of class, the very professor who I had been referred to took a look at the work I'd done, and said, "Well, that was fine as an undergraduate, but you're in graduate school now."

And what I didn't realize was that that sort of work basically wasn't done in the department. . . . The example I just gave you where I would be hard-pressed to say well, that's dis-

crimination in itself. But what I found once I began graduate school four years ago was that it was quite difficult to match not only personal interests, but also personalities. . . . He added this in a similar vein:

I do remember my first year here being a bit disillusioned. A few faculty within my area were basically up-and-coming types who again gave lip service to notions of equality; [they] seemed not to really take my opinion as seriously as I thought they should have, just in terms of the research we were doing. And in fact, I received some rather negative feedback at the end of that year from those individuals. I thought, wait a minute, I haven't heard anything like this before, nobody confronted me with anything like this my whole first year. . . .

This graduate student came to the university with enthusiasm for social science research on racial and ethnic issues, for at his undergraduate college he had been encouraged to do research on stereotyping. But he quickly got the message in his graduate department that there was little support for such race-related research. He had gone into this social science field to be of help to black people, but now he has had to go outside the university classrooms to pursue that goal.

The same graduate student noted that his problem was not isolated. He commented on some of his classmates who did not feel welcome in the department:

I know of people who have been in my department who have left. I can think of a black woman, who I never actually met, who left the year before I got there, who felt that the department was so constricting in terms of not only the types of research that she could do, but in terms of attitudes. Apparently, she was told at one point [that] she wasn't thought of as a black person, largely because she was doing so well. She was outperforming the white students in a class. And apparently a faculty member told her something like, "Well, we don't think of you as one of them anymore." . . .

When white faculty members, in blatant or subtle ways, rule out research that minority students consider especially important, they are also likely to force some of those students out of their programs. Another graduate student also talked about the difficulties of doing research on black Americans:

> I guess the other thing that I would say is that obviously I have a vested interest in my heritage, so, although this is not my exclusive focus, there are times and places when I really would want to do some research specifically related to black issues. And my experience to this date is that in the larger educational community, there really is not that much of an interest in that kind of research. . . .
>
> So what I'll probably wind up doing is going to a predominantly black university. Or universities who have a tangential interest in black research to do any kind of work like that. And I think that's particularly a handicap because I really don't think the resources, research resources, at traditional black schools and smaller minority programs in major universities compare to what the resources are in other research deals.

This student reiterates the point that white professors are not sensitive to the need for research on issues of direct importance to black Americans. In fact, he has come to the conclusion that he will probably have to take a position at a predominantly black university in order to pursue his reasonable research goals. . . .

One signal that college and university subcultures are not integrated is the downplaying of research on black Americans. Such research is suspect and not considered to be truly scholarly—an attitude that signals institutionalized discrimination. . . .

Campus Police

Some of the most serious harassment faced by black students at predominantly white colleges and universities has come from the police. At one campus, a student reported that a number of black students had been harassed by white police officers. She has had spotlights put on her by the police; and some male friends, including her boyfriend, have had guns drawn on them. She commented:

> As far as my boyfriend. . . . This past year there have been some incidents, some attacks on campus. And he was at the gym playing basketball; and he was going to the gas station. He got out of the car at the gas station down the street. The [police] guy tells him to put his hands up, and he pulled a gun. It wasn't the campus police, but I feel they called him. Their reason was that they saw him leaving the gym, and they thought they heard a woman screaming at him. He said, there was no woman. . . .
>
> Do you want to see my ID? Give me a reason. You can't just ask me for my ID when I'm just walking down the sidewalk. There are 50 billion other white people walking on the same sidewalk and you didn't ask them for their ID. . . . You don't want to have your friends come here sometime because they'll be harassed. So, it's kind of bad. But I've heard a lot of campuses are like that, white campuses.

In addition to the problems created by white students and faculty members, black students—especially black male students on white campuses in cities with significant black populations—are sometimes treated differently by the campus and local city police. Police officers are trained, formally in classes or informally by older officers, to look for demographic cues or attributes that distinguish potential criminal offenders from other people. High on the list of these attributes are *black* and *male*. Black men often do make up a disproportionate percentage of urban criminals, but in most white areas they are not the majority of criminals. And recent research has demonstrated that in general whites tend to exaggerate greatly the role of blacks in crime (see Graber 1980). The consequence of this distorted white perspective is that many innocent blacks, such as black students on white campuses, will be stopped unnecessarily by the police. This differential treatment is clearly discriminatory on campuses, like the above, where there are only a few black students, whose faces could easily be memorized by the campus police. . . .

Conclusion: Toward a Theory of Cumulative Discrimination

In order to describe contemporary discrimination [within formally integrated settings such as white colleges and universities] more accurately, several salient dimensions should be considered. One dimension is the *location* of the discriminatory action. The experience of discrimination and hostility, and thus a black person's vulnerability, varies from the most private to the most public spaces: (a) home with family and friends, (b) work and school settings, (c) stores and public accommodations, (d) streets. If a student is in a protected site, such as with friends at home, the probability of hostile treatment is low. If that same person is in a moderately protected site, such as a black student in a setting within a predominantly white university, then the probability of experiencing racial hostility and discrimination increases. And as that student moves into the public places outside the university, such as stores and streets, the dangers increase.

A second dimension is the type of actor doing the discrimination. There are four classes that we have identified: students, faculty members, administrators and other staff members, and alumni. . . . A third dimension is the type of hostile or discriminatory action directed against blacks. We find the following continuum of practices: (a) aggression, verbal and physical; (b) exclusion, including social ostracism; (c) dismissal of subculture, including values, dress, and groups; (d) typecasting, including assuming blacks are all alike.

. . . Some campus obstacles are created mostly by white students. These include the range of possibilities: verbal aggression, exclusion and ostracism, dismissal of black subculture, and typecasting. Another line of barriers is provided by faculty members. Interviews for this project did not uncover the racist-epithets aggression, but there were examples of exclusion and ostracism, dismissal of black interests and models, and typecasting. Also documented are the common barriers—ranging from physical aggression and exclusion to typecasting and stereotyping—that administrators, staff, and alumni create.

Each barrier can take different forms. Sometimes the discrimination is blatant and overtly racist. At other times the discrimination is subtle or covert—that is, hidden behind the scenes. Each discriminatory obstacle can vary in its harmful impact, but even one instance can be quite harmful.

Cumulative Discrimination: A Broad Impact

Perhaps most importantly, black students experience the sustained obstacle of *cumulative discrimination*. Discrimination for most of these black students does not mean just the occasional or isolated discriminatory act in one of the enumerated categories, but rather a college career or lifetime series of blatant and subtle acts of differential treatment by whites which often cumulates to a severely oppressive impact. Some particular instances of discrimination may seem minor, or even misperceived, to outside (white) observers, especially if considered one at a time. But when blatant actions combine with subtle and covert slights, and these cumulate over weeks, months, years, and lifetimes, the impact is likely to be far more than the sum of the individual instances.

The cumulative impact of aggression, exclusion, dismissal, and typecasting can be seen in the more general comments of the students about the college environment. One black honors student at a predominantly white college was asked, "What is it like being a black person in white America today?" Situated in her white college environment, she replied:

Everything, everywhere I look, everywhere I turn, right, left, is white. It's lily white, it's painted with white. And it's funny, because I was reading this article about how America is synonymous with white people. I mean, I'm sure when Europeans—or Asians or Africans for that matter—think of America they think of white people, because white people are mainstream. White people are general. "White is right" as my daddy tells me. White is right, at least they think it is. So, if you're a black person trying to assert yourself, and express your culture, there's something wrong with you, because to do that is to be diametrically opposed to everything this country stands for. And everything this country stands for is what is white. I'm sorry. I mean, I hate to be that simplistic about it . . . you're a fool if you don't realize that to a certain degree. I'm not saying that white people are all out to get us, because I don't think they think about us that much, where they sit down and actually plot, in some dark smoke-filled room, how they're going [to] stomp on black people. They don't have to because it's ingrained in the system. . . .

Ensconced in a large public college with a student body 97% white, she feels hemmed in by the omnipresent white student body and white subculture. . . . When she says *white* is an omnipresent problem, she is not just talking about a color or racial identification. When she and other students talk about everything around them being "lily white," they are reporting being at sea in a strange and hostile environment of white ways of being and of thinking.

When asked to comment on the black student's general situation, one black professor responded as follows:

When a black student walks into a predominantly white environment that student gets the same feeling that I get when I walk into a predominantly white situation. I immediately become fearful and defensive: fearful that someone will openly show hostility, that someone will openly show that I'm not wanted there; defensive, trying to set myself up so that if I face that, I can deal with it. . . .

That's what happens to so many of these youngsters on these campuses, they're dealing with kids who are sons and daughters of bigots. And as soon as they find a friend who accepts them, and they feel real good and start to relax, they run into this young bigot who brings back all the pain. . . .

So, they're constantly in a state of stress. There's not a time when they feel that they can afford to let down. And when they let down, they're hurt. They

are constantly in a situation where people don't understand, don't know. They don't know black people, they don't know black kids, so you're constantly answering questions. . . .

From this perspective the college subculture is white-normed; discrimination is reinforced by the everyday, unstated assumptions about the priority of whiteness. As a result, blacks must be on guard; they regularly find themselves, even subconsciously, on the defensive. This array of barriers, ranging from aggression and social exclusion to dismissal of subculture and typecasting, combines to create the white campus subculture and subsociety that daily confront those black students courageous enough to enter the predominantly white colleges.

References

Astin, A. W. 1977. *Preventing Students From Dropping Out.* San Francisco: Jossey-Bass.

——. 1982. *Minorities in Higher Education.* San Francisco: Jossey-Bass.

Feagin, J. R., and D. Eckberg. 1980. "Discrimination: Motivation, action, effects, and context." *Annual Review of Sociology, 6,* 1–23.

Keller, G. 1988–1989. "Black students in higher education: Why so few?" *Planning for Higher Education, 17,* 50–56.

Loury, G., and B. Anderson. 1984. *Black Leadership: Two Lectures.* Princeton, NJ: Urban and Regional Research Center.

Reprinted from: Joe R. Feagin, "The Continuing Significance of Racism" In *Journal of Black Studies* 22(4): 546–578. Copyright © 1992 by Sage Publications, Inc. Reprinted by permission.

Crime and Criminal Justice

Among the biggest news items in the United States in the 1990s were the well-known incidents involving Rodney King and O.J. Simpson. Readers may recall that King was the victim of a savage beating at the hands of several Los Angeles police officers, who were initially acquitted of criminal charges, but were later found guilty of civil rights violations. Simpson, a former pro football star, was acquitted on charges of murdering his estranged wife and her male companion, but subsequently lost a civil suit for wrongful death in the case. As these events unfolded, public opinion polls and in-depth interviews conducted around the country showed that African Americans and whites tended to view the facts, issues, and meanings associated with these incidents in very different ways. These events generated extensive popular debate about the links between race and crime: interracial differences in patterns of criminal behavior and victimization; the role of race in shaping public perceptions of, and responses to, crime; and racial/ethnic variations in the adjudication of cases and in the administration of justice. In this section introduction, we briefly outline several (though certainly not all) of the key issues within this broad domain.

We begin this discussion with a cursory examination of racial and ethnic differences in rates of criminal perpetration and victimization. Most previous studies compare rates of perpetration and victimization for whites (European Americans) and African Americans; systematic data on Latino Americans, Asian Americans, and Native Americans remain sketchy. Available data indicate that crime rates are much higher among African Americans than among whites, and are probably not due to black/white differences in socioeconomic status (LaFree, this volume). Analyzing data on arrests from the Uniform Crime Reports (UCR), Harris and Meidlinger (1995) report that "the ratio of blacks to whites arrested for homicide is 8.3; [comparable figures are] 5.2 for homicide, 10.8 for armed robbery, and 4.3 for aggravated assault (p. 116). Racial disparities in arrest rates are somewhat lower for property offenses—such as burglary, larceny-theft, motor vehicle theft, and arson—than for crimes against people. Further, it seems unlikely that these racial disparities in arrest rates are due entirely to biases in police practices. Evidence of racial differences in rates of criminal activity also surfaces in victim reports (e.g., the National Crime Victimization Survey), in studies of inmates (e.g., the Rand Inmate Survey), and in the Justice Department's felony conviction data. In all, African American arrests account for a disproportionate share of arrests for virtually every category of crime for which the Federal Bureau of Investigation compiles statistics, save for driving while intoxicated (Hacker 1992: 181).

The types of data cited above suggest that African Americans commit a disproportionate number of crimes against people and property offenses. While these disparities seem clear with regard to crime "in the streets," the evidence concerning white collar offenses is somewhat more mixed. On the one hand, African Americans, who constitute 12–13 percent of the US population, account for more than 30 percent of arrests for embezzlement, forgery, and fraud, according to UCR data (Harris and Meidlinger 1995: 140). However, these may not be "white collar" crimes in the usual sense of that term—i.e., the offenses usually are not occupationally related. Further, the limited available information on white-collar criminals suggests that, while African Americans may be overrepresented among lower-level offenders, whites are overrepresented among higher-level offenders—i.e., middle- and upper-level managers and executives. Their crimes can legitimately be labelled "silk collar" offenses, or crimes "in the suites." For instance, partly because of the limited access of racial and ethnic minorities to leadership roles in business and finance, whites are more likely to be implicated in most illegal stock manipulations, monopolistic trade practices, tax evasion, and other illicit business practices (Harris and Meidlinger 1995).

But if African Americans are more likely to commit most types of crimes than whites, then who are the most common victims? According to Harris and Meidlinger (1995), "Even when additional factors such as income are taken into account, the statistically overrepresented victim of street crime clearly resembles the statistically overrepresented offender: male, young, poor, and black" (p. 122). They summarize data from the National Crime Victimization Surveys (NCVS) of the early 1990s, which indicate that for the most serious of violent offenses (i.e., rape, aggravated assault, armed robbery), African American victimization rates were at least 50 percent higher than white rates. Such disparities in victimization also hold for property crimes, such as burglary, motor vehicle theft, and others (Harris and Meidlinger 1995). For robbery, the African American victimization rate exceeds the white rate by more than 200 percent! A disproportionate amount of violent crime in the US involves African Americans assaulting other African Americans; contrary to some popular myths, fewer than 10 percent of murders or rapes are interracial—i.e., involving African Americans assaulting whites or whites victimizing African Americans (Hacker 1992).

How might we explain the higher rates of most types of street crime (i.e., violent and property offenses) among African Americans? Sociologists have tended to focus on the role of social factors in shaping patterns of criminal behavior and victimization. Per-haps the most popular explanations for racial differences in crime rates have centered on the higher rates of unemployment and deprivation, and the dearth of opportunities for economic mobility, among African Americans. But while these hypotheses strike many researchers as reasonable, empirical support for them has been mixed; at the very least, the relationships are more complex than previously assumed (LaFree, this volume).

One interesting line of investigation has examined changes in white and African American crime rates since the late 1950s, via annual time-series analyses. Although the results of these studies are complicated, several conclusions seem clear: Income levels and unemployment rates are related to changes in arrest rates for violent and property crimes during this period only among whites, and not among African Americans (LaFree et al. 1992). However, inequality—especially *intra*racial inequality—is a consistent predictor of changes in arrest rates for both African Americans and whites over the same period of time (LaFree and Drass 1996). Further, during those years when the income gap within the African American population widened most dramatically, black educational gains were actually associated with increases in African American arrest rates. These findings suggest that a growing sense of relative deprivation—the frustration of feeling "left behind"—among the least-advantaged segments of the African American population—the urban "underclass" (Wacquant and Wilson, this volume)—may account for the high African American crime rates discussed above.

Another approach to this issue uses cross-sectional data (i.e., data collected at one point in time) and examines the association between various characteristics of metropolitan areas or census tracts (which are similar to, but not exactly the same as, neighborhoods) within metropolitan areas, and crime rates, especially among African Americans. One recent study conducted in Columbus, Ohio showed that "extremely disadvantaged" census tracts—defined as those with high levels of poverty, female-headed households, and male joblessness—have qualitatively higher levels of violent crime than other tracts (Krivo and Peterson 1996). However, the effects of neighborhood context on property crime rates are less striking. The findings of this study suggest that high rates of violent crime among urban African Americans may be due to their disproportionate location in such "underclass" census tracts.

Why do these areas tend to have high crime rates? Although research to pin down these casual mechanisms will continue for some time, sociologists have suggested several possible reasons (Sampson and Wilson 1995; Krivo and Peterson 1996). First, these communities have fewer employed residents to provide role models and guidance for young people, and the "old heads" that remain tend to lack credibility and moral authority. With fewer working- and middle-class families in the area, there may also be fewer community organizations (e.g., clubs, churches, etc.) that can cushion the effects of unemployment and poverty. The dissolution of social networks in these communities is also thought to erode informal mechanisms of social control— i.e., the everyday processes of monitoring and influence that promote conformity with laws and norms (Sampson and Wilson 1995). And high levels of poverty, unemployment, and inequality can also result in family disruption— i.e., higher percentages of single-parent, female-headed households in blighted neighborhoods—which, in turn, can lead to higher crime rates (Sampson 1987; Shihadeh and Steffensmeier 1994).

While these neighborhoods typically lack the structures that would ordinarily buffer individuals and communities from crime, aggravating factors may be present in abundance. For one thing, individuals may be exposed to criminal role models, gangs, and others who encourage or legitimize illegal behavior. With increasing regularity, residents may witness crimes and become victims of crime. And crime begets more crime, as some of these residents respond to neighborhood changes by projecting toughness, carrying weapons, and so on. Moreover, given the dearth of social and economic opportunities, idle residents (especially young people) may spend a significant portion of their time in public spaces—on street corners, in pool halls, and in other such settings—where they are vulnerable to social and community influences. The congregation of groups of residents in these contexts tends to increase the likelihood of criminal activity and victimization (Krivo and Peterson 1996).

Still another (complementary) perspective identifies the residential patterning, and particularly the (hyper-)segregation, of many U.S. cities as a key correlate of African American crime (Massey 1995). Studies in this tradition have analyzed cross-sectional comparative data on major U.S. metropolitan areas. To date, researchers have shown that rates of serious crime (i.e., homicide, robbery, rape, assault, burglary, larceny/theft, and auto theft) among African Americans in large cities increase with the degree of suburbanization in the metropolitan areas (Shihadeh and Ousey 1996). On closer inspection, the apparent effects of suburbanization on crime may result from its association with the deterioration and isolation of central-city African American communities. Other studies report that urban violence by African Americans is positively related to the degree of residential segregation in the metropolitan area (Peterson and Krivo 1993) and to the degree of African American social isolation from whites (Shihadeh and Flynn 1996). For the most part, these residential dynamics seem to have little bearing on white crime rates.

Despite their differences, the approaches outlined above share the view that racial disparities in crime rates result primarily from social causes, particularly differences in the social and geographical positioning of African Americans and whites. But not everyone accepts this assumption. Indeed, some analysts and opinionmakers argue that crime—like unemployment, family disruption, and other problems—results primarily from deviant or flawed values (Wilson 1975). They are particularly concerned about the possible emergence of a self-sustaining, oppositional subculture within inner-city African American neighborhoods which can include, among other things, normative support for violence. According to some observers, partly in response to the dearth of opportunities for upward mobility through legitimate channels, significant numbers of young African

American males have embraced a "code of the streets" in which traits like strength, aggressiveness, and fearlessness are especially valued, and gaining and maintaining the respect of others is seen as the paramount achievement (Anderson 1994). Aware that they could die at any time, these young males may feel that they have little to lose, and thus react to real or perceived slights ("dissing," even if unintended) with violence.

Of course such arguments about the emergence of a culture of violence among some urban African Americans—like claims about a culture of poverty—are not necessarily at odds with structural perspectives. Nevertheless, if such a subculture within these communities now plays a causal role in producing criminal behavior, then policies to mend the social fabric of neighborhoods, reduce residential segregation, or lower income inequality may have little impact on crime rates. For proponents of "culture of violence" perspectives, stronger deterrent efforts and tougher punishment often seem like more attractive solutions to the vexing problem of urban crime.

There are important and ominous connections between the disproportionately high rates of African American crime (especially violent crime), whites' fears of crime, and contemporary racial/ethnic prejudice. As we noted earlier (introduction to Section 6, this volume; Sniderman and Piazza, this volume), public opinion polls show that a significant percentage of whites tend to stereotype African Americans (as well as Latino Americans) as aggressive and violence-prone, and to associate people of color with drug use and other types of criminal activity. Moreover, one recent study found a substantial positive association between the *perceived* number of African Americans residing nearby and whites' fears of crime; interestingly, the *actual* neighborhood racial composition was virtually unrelated to white fearfulness (Chiricos et al. 1997). These negative images have implications for the ways in which African Americans, Latino/a Americans, and other peoples of color are treated, by law enforcement officers and fellow citizens (Mann and Zatz 1998). For instance, many African Americans, especially black males, report being stopped and questioned by police while driving through predominantly white neighborhoods, often for what seems to be flimsy justification. Anecdotal accounts and unobtrusive studies show that racial/ethnic minorities are often treated with suspicion and hostility by shopkeepers and security personnel in malls, stores, and numerous other public settings. And the list goes on. Some commentators blame media for promoting stereotypes of African Americans, Latinos, and other persons of color as criminals. They object to movies that depict violent crime by racial/ethnic minorities, as well as sensationalized new accounts that have fueled a "moral panic" concerning urban African American and Latino/a youth gangs (Rome 1998; Portillos 1998). Critics also call attention to the advent of the "reality-based" police television genre (i.e., "cop doc" shows like COPS, America's Most Wanted, and others), noting that these shows often represent persons of color as perpetrators of crime (Oliver 1994).

Some suggest that there are racial undertones to white punitiveness as well. For instance, in one recent experimental study, researchers showed simulated "news" broadcasts to several (randomly-assigned) groups of white subjects (Gilliam and Iyengar 1998). In the broadcasts shown to some of these groups, a brief news item reporting a robbery-murder at an automated teller machine was embedded. A subset of these broadcasts included a picture of the suspect in this violent crime; half of these dummy broadcasts depicted an African American suspect, while the remainder showed a white suspect. Following their viewing of the broadcast, study subjects were asked a series of questions about their recall of the crime report, and about their attitudes toward crime, punishment, and racial/ethnic issues. Those who saw the crime story that lacked information about a specific suspect were likely to say the suspect was non-white. Further, those subjects who had just viewed the broadcast depicting an African American suspect consistently expressed harsher, more punitive orientations toward criminals than did the other study participants.

Is there evidence of racial discrimination in the criminal justice system? While this issue remains the focus of heated debate, many criminologists answer this question in the affirmative. Clearly African American males are incarcerated at a rate that is approximately seven times higher than the rate for the U.S. population as a whole. Of course, such a racial disparity in incarceration could be due simply to the fact that African American men are more likely to commit the types of crimes that result in imprisonment. But a recent review of 38 previous studies concludes that, on average, African Americans are more likely than whites to be imprisoned, even when the offenses are comparable in key features and seriousness and the background characteristics, including prior criminal records of the offenders, are similar (Chiricos and Crawford 1995). Strong evidence of racial disparity exists only for in/out decisions; among those who are imprisoned, most research shows few (if any) racial differences in sentence length. Further, the evidence of discriminatory incarceration practices is strongest in certain contexts: in the South, in areas with large percentages of African American residents, and in areas characterized by high unemployment (Chiricos and Crawford 1995).

Critics cite other evidence of discrimination as well. For instance, Joseph (1995) finds disparities in the treatment of African American and white youths at every phase of the juvenile justice system, from arrest and processing to sentencing. Some criminologists charge that the "war on drugs" has taken a disproportionately heavy toll on African American and Latino communities since its inception in the 1980s (Tonry 1994, and this volume). They contend that law enforcement officials tend to target minority neighborhoods, where drug trafficking and consumption tends to take place outdoors, in public space, and under conditions that are more easily observed and documented by police. But critics also point to apparent sentencing disparities: According to Tonry and others, penalties prescribed for the types of drug possession that are more common among African Americans and other minorities (e.g., crack cocaine) are much more severe than penalties for possessing the types of drugs (e.g., powder cocaine) that are more popular among whites. Growing sensitivity to the negative impact of drug-related convictions on African American individuals, families, and communities has led some critical legal scholars to advocate "jury nullification"—a controversial suggestion that African American jurors consider summarily acquitting African American defendants who are accused of non-violent offenses (Lewis 1997).

Some criminologists, jurists, and activists believe that capital punishment is applied in a racially discriminatory manner—i.e., that African Americans convicted of premeditated murder are more likely to be sentenced to die than whites. This hotly-debated issue is more complex than it might appear, because the likelihood of receiving a death sentence depends heavily on the race of the victim (i.e., those who kill white victims are much more likely to receive capital sentences than persons who kill African Americans or Latinos), as well as on the circumstances under which homicides are committed, and a range of additional factors (White 1991). Throughout most of the twentieth century, African American males convicted of raping white women were more likely to receive death sentences than other convicted rapists, especially in the South. By removing rape charges from the reach of capital punishment, legal reforms eliminated one source of discrimination against African Americans. But some studies have also suggested that capital punishment is still applied in racially uneven manner in murder cases in some areas of the U.S. (Chiricos and Crawford 1995). To be sure, various legal changes have been introduced with the aim of eliminating racially discriminatory sentencing practices. These reforms have included new laws designed to increase the likelihood that minority jurors will be impaneled, and more specific guidelines that require juries to balance aggravating and mitigating circumstances when sentencing capital defendants. Nevertheless, many observers remain skeptical that these loose reforms have significantly reduced sentencing discrimination (White 1991). Given the extraordinarily high stakes in this debate, one hopes that this controversy will continue to receive widespread attention in the future.

In light of the issues discussed above, it is not surprising that African Americans, Latinos, and whites view crime and criminal justice issues very differently. Public response to the events surrounding the Rodney King beating, and to the trial and verdict in the O.J. Simpson case, demonstrated clearly that African Americans harbor a profound mistrust of the justice system and of law enforcement officers in particular; whites tend to support and trust police, prosecutors, and other representatives of this system. Studies show that disadvantaged minority youths are especially likely to grow up in environments characterized by animosity toward law enforcement and other criminal justice personnel (Hagan and Peterson 1995), often coming to view police as "bullies," while white and Asian American youths tend to see them as "guardians" (Waddington and Braddock 1991). Much of this attitudinal chasm is probably due to the high rates of arrest within many minority communities and to the history of police brutality and other forms of maltreatment (real and perceived) within this system (Mann 1993). Indeed, according to data reported by Hacker (1992: 189), African Americans were roughly three times more likely than whites to be killed by law enforcement officers during the 1970s and 1980s. However, part of the problem may also be the underrepresentation of African Americans, Latinos, and other minorities in virtually every aspect of the criminal justice system (Joseph 1995; Nalla and Corley 1996). This, in turn, is probably exacerbated by the widespread mistrust of police in some communities, which may discourage African Americans, Latinos, and other minorities from seeking careers in law enforcement and other areas of the criminal justice system.

With a few exceptions, such as the long tradition of research on racial and ethnic disparities in sentencing, many of the issues discussed above have been understudied until recently. As we noted at the beginning of this section, events such as the high-profile trials of Rodney King and O.J. Simpson have enhanced public awareness of the dramatic racial and ethnic chasm in the experience and perception of crime and criminal justice in the United States. If the promise of "liberty and justice for all" is to be more than empty rhetoric, a better understanding of these complex phenomena must be an important priority for scholars, policymakers, and informed citizens alike in the twenty-first century.

References

Anderson, Elijah. 1994. "The Code of the Streets." *Atlantic Monthly* (May): 81– 94.

Chiricos, Ted G., and Charles Crawford. 1995. "Race and Imprisonment: A Contextual Assessment of the Evidence." Pp. 281–309 in *Ethnicity, Race, and Crime*, edited by D.F. Hawkins. Albany: SUNY Press.

Chiricos, Ted G., Michael Hogan, and Marc Gertz. 1997. "Racial Composition of Neighborhoods and Fear of Crime." *Criminology* 35: 107–129.

Gilliam, Franklin D., Jr., and Shanto Iyengar. 1998. "Prime Suspects: Effects of Local News on the Viewing Public." Unpublished manuscript, Department of Political Science, UCLA.

Hacker, Andrew. 1992. *Two Nations: Black and White, Separate, Hostile, Unequal.* New York: Scribners.

Hagan, John, and Ruth D. Peterson. 1995. "Criminal Inequality in America." Pp. 14–36 in *Crime and Inequality*, edited by J. Hagan and R.D. Peterson. Stanford, CA: Stanford University Press.

Harris, Anthony R., and Lisa R. Meidlinger. 1995. "Criminal Behavior: Race and Class." Pp. 115–143 in *Criminology: A Contemporary Handbook*, 2nd edition, edited by J.F. Sheley. Belmont, CA: Wadsworth.

Joseph, Janice. 1995. *Black Youths, Delinquency, and Juvenile Justice.* Newport, CT: Praeger.

Krivo, Lauren J., and Ruth D. Peterson. 1996. "Extremely Disadvantaged Neighborhoods and Urban Crime." *Social Forces* 75: 619–648.

LaFree, Gary, and Kriss A. Drass. 1996. "The Effect of Changes in Intraracial Income Inequality and Educational Attainment on Changes in Arrest Rates for African Americans and Whites, 1957 to 1990." *American Sociological Review* 62: 614–634.

LaFree, Gary, Kriss A. Drass, and Patrick O'Day. 1992. "Race and Crime in Postwar America: Determinants of African American and White Arrest Rates, 1957–1988." *Criminology* 30: 157–188.

Lewis, Neil A. 1997. "Race Theory Challenges Goal of a Colorblind Society." *Austin American-Statesman*, June 8, J1, J6.

Mann, Coramae Richey. 1993. *Unequal Justice: A Question of Color*. Bloomington, IN: Indiana University Press.

Massey, Douglas S. 1995. "Getting Away With Murder: Segregation and Violent Crime in Urban America." *University of Pennsylvania Law Review* 143: 1203–1232.

Mauer, Marc. 1990. *Young Black Men and the Criminal Justice System: A Growing National Problem*. Washington: The Sentencing Project.

Nalla, Mahesh K., and Charles Corley. 1996. "Race and Criminal Justice: Employment of Minorities in the Criminal Justice System." Pp. 139–155 in *Justice with Prejudice: Race and Criminal Justice in America*, edited by M.J. Lynch and E.B. Patterson. Guilderland, NY: Harrow and Heston.

Oliver, Marybeth. 1994. "Portrayals of Crime, Race, and Aggression in 'Reality-Based' Police Shows: A Content Analysis." *Journal of Broadcasting and Electronic Media* 5: 179–191.

Peterson, Ruth D., and Lauren J. Krivo. 1993. "Racial Segregation and Black Urban Homicide." *Social Forces* 71: 1001–1026.

Portillos, Edwardo L. 1998. "Images of Crime and Punishment: Latinos, Gangs, and Drugs." Pp. 156–165 in *Images of Color, Images of Crime*, edited by Marjorie S. Zatz and Coramae Richey Mann. Los Angeles: Roxbury.

Rome, Dennis M. 1998. "Stereotyping by the Media: Murderers, Rapists, and Drug Addicts." Pp. 85–96 in *Images of Color, Images of Crime*, edited by Marjorie S. Zatz and Coramae Richey Mann. Los Angeles: Roxbury.

Sampson, Robert J. 1987. "Urban Black Violence: The Effect of Male Joblessness and Family Disruption." *American Journal of Sociology* 93: 348–382.

Sampson, Robert J., and William Julius Wilson. 1995. "Toward a Theory of Race, Crime, and Urban Inequality." Pp. 37–54 in *Crime and Inequality*, edited by J. Hagan and R.D. Peterson. Stanford, CA: Stanford University Press.

Shihadeh, Edward S., and Nicole Flynn. 1996. "Segregation and Crime: The Effect of Black Social Isolation on the Rates of Black Urban Violence." *Social Forces* 74: 1325–1352.

Shihadeh, Edward S., and Graham Ousey. 1996. "Metropolitan Expansion and Black Social Dislocation: The Link Between Suburbanization and Center-City Crime." *Social Forces* 75: 649–666.

Shihadeh, Edward S., and Darrell J. Steffensmeier. 1994. "Economic Inequality, Family Disruption, and Urban Black Violence: Cities as Units of Stratification and Social Control." *Social Forces* 73: 729–751.

Tonry, Michael. 1994. *Malign Neglect: Race, Crime, and Punishment in America*. New York: Oxford University Press.

Waddington, P.A., and Q. Braddock. 1991. "Guardians or Bullies? Perceptions of the Police Amongst Adolescent Black, White, and Asian Boys." *Police and Society* 2: 31–45.

White, Welsh S. 1991. *The Death Penalty in the Nineties: An Examination of the Modern System of Capital Punishment*, revised edition. Ann Arbor: University of Michigan Press.

Wilson, James Q. 1975. *Thinking About Crime*. New York: Basic Books.

Zatz, Marjorie S., and Coramae Richey Mann (eds.). 1998. *Images of Color, Images of Crime*. Los Angeles: Roxbury.

34

Race and Crime Trends in the United States, 1946–1990

Gary LaFree

... [T]here are ... compelling reasons to carefully examine crime differences by race. First and most obviously, the criminal justice system, especially for African-Americans, has entered a period of unprecedented crisis. Although blacks represent only 12 percent of the U.S. population, they now account for 64 percent of robbery arrests, 55 percent of homicide arrests, and 32 percent of burglary arrests (Federal Bureau of Investigation 1989). Similarly, black incarceration rates have reached alarming proportions. Black males born in the U.S.A. today now face a one-in-five lifetime chance of serving a sentence in an adult state prison (U.S. Bureau of Justice Statistics 1985, p. 5). For the age range 20–29, the U.S.A. now has substantially more black men in prison or on probation or parole (609,690) than in colleges and universities (436,000; Mauer 1990; Langan 1991). Clearly, our failure to study the connection between race and crime has not made race-related crime problems and stereotypes go away.

Second, given that most crime is intraracial, blacks are disproportionately affected by high crime rates. African-American men now face a one-in-21 lifetime chance of being murdered (U.S. Bureau of Justice Statistics 1985, p. 8)....

Finally, the fact that most researchers have ignored race does not mean that it has become less important in everyday thinking about crime. On the contrary, the Willie Horton story illustrates how the basest kind of prejudice is free to flourish in the absence of more objective analysis. Wilson (1984, p. 90) notes that because there has been so little recent systematic research on blacks, racial stereotypes have not been sufficiently rebutted.

In this paper I consider some of the practical difficulties of examining the relationship between race and crime in the United States. I begin with cross-sectional data on arrest rates for African-Americans, American Indians, Asian-Americans, and whites, and consider some of the issues raised by these data. For blacks and whites only, I next present arrest trend data from 1946 to 1990 and then consider the differing implications of several common social-structural theories for black and white crime trends.

Measuring Crime Trends by Race

In terms of crime trends by race, data options in the United States are limited. Neither self-report nor victimization surveys have been collected systematically for a long enough period to permit annual time-series analysis. Moreover, neither of these data sources include yearly estimates for the 1960s—a period when the largest crime increases in the postwar period began. This means that the only annual time-series data available for the United States in the postwar period are from the Federal Bureau of Investigation's Uniform Crime Report (UCR) system....

Arrest Rates

... The most unique aspect of the UCR is its reliance on the voluntary cooperation of thousands of individual police departments across the country to provide crime information. In general, UCR coverage has been most complete for major metropolitan areas in which about 98 percent of the population is represented and least complete for rural areas in which about 90 percent of the population is represented (U.S. Federal Bureau of Investigation, 1985).

The UCR has consistently collected two main types of crime information: total crimes *known to police* and total arrests. ...

However, the UCR measure of crimes known to police does not report the suspect's race. Thus, the only U.S. crime measure that includes race and has been collected for the entire postwar period is the UCR measure of arrests.

The most common criticisms of UCR data point to its scope and validity. Many critics (Geis 1972; Chambliss 1988; Harris 1991) have argued that the UCR emphasis on street crime focuses attention on crimes that are more common among minorities and the poor, and less common among nonminorities and the wealthy. However, the incompleteness of the UCR should not be seen as a fatal deficiency. While it is true that the seven index crimes for which the UCR includes the most complete data are only a subset of all crimes, it is also true that they are of substantial policy interest. Few would argue that we should reject data on murder, for example, just because we do not have equally valid data on embezzlement.

The validity of UCR statistics, especially arrest statistics, has been hotly debated for more than half a century (Warner 1931; President's Commission 1967; Gove, Hughes, and Geerken 1985; Blumstein, Cohen, and Rosenfeld 1991). Apart from the many technical issues, most of the criticisms reflect a concern with either citizen or police reporting. Both of these concerns have important implications for conclusions about crime trends by race. For example, if nonminorities are more likely than minorities to report crimes to police, then conclusions about crime rates by race will be erroneous. Similarly, if police arrest decisions are influenced by race, then conclusions about crime from different race groups will also be biased.

Fortunately, the National Crime Survey (NCS) victim surveys now provide a comparative data source independent of the criminal justice system that allows us to partially assess these concerns. In general, analysis of the NCS and other victim survey data shows little variation in reporting by race (Block, 1974; Hindelang, 1978). . . .

The possibility that UCR arrest statistics by race are determined more by police decision-making than actual behavior has also been frequently examined (Hindelang, 1978;

O'Brien, 1985). To the extent that racial correlates of arrest rates are the same as offending rates measured by the NCS, researchers can have greater confidence in the validity of UCR data. Indeed, systematic comparisons of UCR index arrest rates with offending rates for robbery and burglary estimated from the NCS show remarkable similarity. . . .

More generally, a large and reliable body of evidence shows that crime seriousness is consistently the strongest predictor of arrest (Black and Reiss 1970; Gottfredson and Gottfredson 1980). Thus, in their exhaustive analysis of the validity of UCR reports, Gove et al. (1985) conclude that "the perceived seriousness of the crime . . . accounts for most of the variance in whether a crime is reported and officially recorded; personal characteristics of the offender and victim have only minor effects" (p. 451). Hence, after providing the appropriate words of caution, the available evidence suggests that UCR arrest data, especially for serious crimes, provides information that is at least highly correlated with actual crime trends by race.

However, the measurement of race and ethnicity in UCR arrest statistics raises further limitations and difficulties. First, the UCR does not allow an analysis of Hispanic arrest rates over time. . . . Second, because the UCR system is based on the voluntary compliance of police agencies, and because American Indians fall under the jurisdiction of a complex combination of native and nonnative legal entities, UCR trend data for American Indians are also problematic (Peak and Spencer, 1987; Zatz, et al., 1991). Third. . .there is no obvious way of constructing trend data for Asian-Americans in the postwar period based on UCR arrest statistics. . . .

To summarize, the UCR is currently the only U.S. data source that includes longitudinal crime data by race for the postwar period. However, the difficulties of using the UCR for this purpose are such that we should think of analysis as more similar to archeology than econometrics. However, I would argue that just as a serious archeologist would not throw out relevant information—no matter how imperfect—so too a responsible criminologist cannot afford to ignore the major source of longitudinal data on race and crime in North America. Even so, because of changes in the way the UCR collected arrest data over time, trend analysis for groups other than blacks and whites is probably not defensible. And even with the analysis of blacks and whites, we should proceed with the utmost caution. . .

Having offered these warnings, can we nonetheless draw any useful interpretations from these data? First, note that crime rates for these racial and ethnic groups follow the same sequence for all seven UCR crimes [ie., murder, rape, robbery, aggravated assault, burglary, theft, and motor vehicle theft]. For each, black rates are highest, followed by American Indians, whites, and Asians. These are not trivial differences. Black robbery rates are more than eleven times higher than white rates. They are more than twenty-one times higher than Asian-American rates.

Second, differences by race vary by crime type. The largest discrepancy by race is for robbery, where blacks account for 62 percent of all arrests, followed by murder (55 percent), rape (44 percent), aggravated assault and motor vehicle theft (33 percent), and burglary and theft (31 percent). In general, the greatest discrepancies for blacks are for violent street crime (robbery, murder, rape) and the least, are for property crimes involving no direct contact between victim and offender (burglary, theft).

Even allowing for the fact that UCR crime data are imperfect, these data raise some serious issues for criminology. Given our worst fears about police racism, can we reasonably conclude that police discrimination accounts for a difference of the magnitude shown in [these figures]. . . .

Both critics (O'Brien 1985) and supporters (Gove et al. 1985; Devine, Sheley, and Smith 1988; Harer and Steffensmeier 1992) of UCR data agree that its quality is generally highest for more serious crimes, in which citizens are more likely to report crimes to police and police arrest is more likely. Following this reasoning, discriminatory behavior on the part of police might be expected to be most pronounced for those less serious crimes for which police have the greatest discretion.

However . . . the greatest differences by race are precisely for the most serious and presumably most reliably measured crimes (robbery, murder) and lowest for the least serious and, presumably, least reliably measured crimes (burglary, theft). In short, even accepting the limitations of UCR arrest data, the differences. . . are so large and exhibit patterns that are so distinctive that the hypothesis of no difference by race seems unlikely. . . .

Trends in African-American and White Crime Rates, 1946–1990

. . . [I]n addition to the arguments already presented in a longitudinal analysis of murder, robbery, and burglary rates, 1957–1988, my colleagues and I (LaFree and Drass 1992; LaFree, Drass, and O'Day 1992) tested the association by combining UCR arrest rates disaggregated by race and then comparing them to the more widely used UCR measure of crimes known to police. This analysis showed a strong correspondence between the disaggregated arrest rates and the measures of crimes known to police for the crimes we analyzed: robbery, $r = .98$; murder, $r = .97$; burglary, $r = .95$.

Figure 34.1
Murder Arrests per 100,000, United States, 1946-1990.

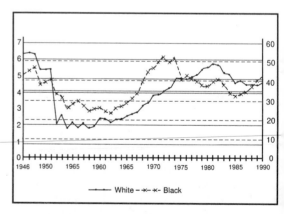

. . . [Comparing] black and white arrest trends for murder, robbery and burglary . . . permit[s], at least two related conclusions. First, while the size of differences [in Figure 34.1 to 34.3] varies greatly by specific crime type and period, black arrest rates are substantially higher than white rates for all three crimes and from 1946 to 1990. Second, despite the fact that black arrest rates are generally much higher than white rates, both black and white trends show important similarities. Correlations between black and white rates for all three crimes are highly significant: burglary ($r = .95$), robbery ($r = .81$), and murder ($r = .70$).

Figure 34.2
Robbery Arrests/100,000 United States, 1946-1990.

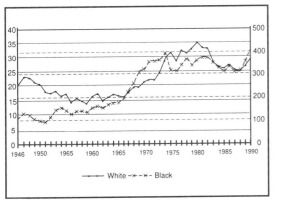

Figure 34.3
Burglary Arrests/100,000 United States, 1946-1990.

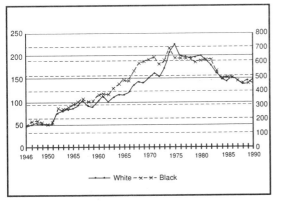

These patterns suggest that some part of the postwar variation in crime rates for blacks and whites may have similar causes, other sources of variation may be distinct, and that the balance may depend on crime

type. Thus, the correlation between black and white burglary rates is so high that we might suspect largely similar underlying dynamics. By contrast, correlations for murder and robbery allow the possibility of substantially different dynamics by race. It could be that a close examination of different crime trends might help us sort out some of the differences and similarities between black and white crime in the postwar period. For example, compared to other crimes, why are burglary trends similar for blacks and whites? By contrast, why are murder trends so different?

If we examine these three figures for general patterns, the most consistent similarity is a rapid increase in the 1960s and early 1970s for both blacks and whites. Similarly, arrest rates for all three crimes have leveled off or even declined since the 1970s. Detailed analysis of changes such as these could be important in advancing our understanding of crime in the United States.

. . . [I]n 1990 blacks were arrested 8.53 times more often than whites for murder. . . . Compared to white rates, black rates are generally highest for violent crimes (murder, robbery, assault, rape) and lowest for property crimes (burglary, theft, motor vehicle theft). If we limit comparisons to the period 1960–1990, the period for which UCR data are most valid, black to white arrest ratios are consistently highest for robbery and murder, and consistently lowest for burglary, theft, and motor vehicle theft.

These data raise important research issues. First, what explains variation in the rates? For example, why did the ratio of black to white murder arrests decline by more than 50 percent from 1971 to 1984? Second, what explains the long-term differences between black and white arrest rates? For example, although there is substantial variation over the postwar period, compared to whites, black arrest rates for robbery range from a low of 4.83 times greater (1950) to a high of 16.35 times greater (1971). That is, regardless of other considerations, black robbery arrest rates have been consistently much higher than white robbery arrest rates. . . .

To summarize, when we compare black and white arrest rates in the postwar years, we find intriguing similarities and differences. Both blacks and whites generally experienced rapid arrest increases in the 1960s and early 1970s. Black and white trends are most similar for theft and burglary. Regardless of crime type or year, black arrest rates are substantially higher than white rates. The differences are greatest for the violent crimes of robbery, murder, and rape.

Explanations for Crime Differences by Race

Deterrence Perspectives

For both laypersons and legal agents, the single most popular explanation for crime in the postwar period has probably been some form of the deterrence argument. Elaborated in the eighteenth century by social reformers like Bentham and Beccaria, and jurists like Blackstone, Romilly, and Feuerbach, deterrence theorists argue that crime can be reduced by increasing the costs of criminal behavior or increasing the awards of noncriminal behavior.

Deterrence perspectives among social researchers were not common in the early part of the postwar period, but gained momentum beginning in the 1970s (Wilson 1975; Tittle 1980; Murray 1984). The implications of the theory are straightforward: criminal behavior will be deterred to the extent that punishment for it is more severe, certain, and swift.

Deterrence perspectives have generally assumed similar dynamics across race and ethnic groups (Tittle 1980; Ross and LaFree 1986). However, given the extraordinarily high rates of legal punishment African-Americans have experienced in recent years, they are an interesting test case of deterrence models. In fact, the limitations of deterrence perspectives are especially clear in the case of blacks. While aggregate incarceration rates for the United States are now among the highest in the world, rates become truly staggering when estimated separately for African-Americans (Langan 1991). A study by Mauer (1990) shows that 23 percent of all black men, ages 20 to 29, are currently in prison or on probation or parole in the United States on any given day. Despite these unprecedented punishment levels, black crime

rates remain at historically high levels. Even as a purely practical matter, it seems obvious to question the logic of a social policy that applies serious sanctions to nearly one-quarter of a major segment of the population.

Social Disorganization Perspectives

Social disorganization theory first gained popularity in the U.S.A. in the early part of the twentieth century (Shaw et al. 1929; Shaw and McKay 1942) and can be traced in part to Durkheim's ([1893] 1947) assessment of the transition from traditional to modern industrial society. According to Shaw and McKay (1942), social disorganization increases in communities characterized by high rates of population turnover and heterogeneity. The disruption of established systems of role allocation and the emergence of new roles not yet fully institutionalized and integrated into society make normative guidelines ambiguous and may disrupt traditional support mechanisms. Bursik (1988, p. 521) argues that the strongest argument can be made by conceptualizing social disorganization as "a group-level analog of control theory." This approach emphasizes the negative impact social disorganization has on informal sources of social control, especially the ability of family and neighborhoods, to effectively socialize and integrate their members.

The idea that crime rates, especially black crime rates, are directly linked to increasing family disorganization has been popular throughout the postwar period (Frazier 1950; Moynihan 1965; Rainwater 1970; Sampson 1987; Jencks 1992). Indeed, by the early 1980s, 48 percent of black families with children under 18 were headed by women (compared to 14 percent for white; Bureau of the Census 1984), 68 percent of births to black women aged 15 to 24 were outside marriage (U.S. Bureau of the Census 1983), and 69 percent of all black women had never been married (Bureau of the Census 1981). Black women are more likely to head their own families, have more children outside marriage, and are less likely to marry and remarry; black children are less likely to live with both biological parents.

However, despite the popularity of the argument, empirical support from the extensive cross-sectional literature has been limited (Robins and Hill 1966; Chilton and Markle 1972; Ross and Sawhill 1975; Rosen and Nielson 1978; Montare and Boone 1980; Harris 1991). In our recent time-series analyses of black robbery, burglary, and homicide arrest rates in the postwar period (LaFree et al. 1992; LaFree and Drass 1992), we found that increasing rates of female-headed households were generally associated with decreases rather than increases in black crime arrests. In fact, several considerations lead us to question the widely assumed link between female-headed households and crime—especially for blacks.

First, comparative and historical research do not consistently support the view. For example, many countries of western Europe have relatively high rates of divorce and female-headed households (Rogers and Norman 1985; Popenoe 1988) and yet, compared to the U.S.A., very low crime rates. Similarly, some of the largest increases in female-headed households in the U.S.A. came not in the 1960s when crime was dramatically increasing, but rather in the mid-1970s and 1980s, when crime rates had already stabilized.

Second, although the linkage between female-headed households and declining income is well documented for both blacks and whites (Farley 1984), the longitudinal connections between crime and poverty are inconsistent. Moreover, the assumption that women are always *pushed* into heading families by economic necessity is questionable. In fact, there is growing evidence that when given the economic opportunity, a large proportion of women—especially black women—choose something other than husband-wife families. Hill (1981, p. v) reports that between 1970 and 1979, female-headed families increased ten times faster among college educated (and presumably, more economically marketable; 308 percent) than grade-school educated (32 percent) black women. Similarly, using quasi-experimental data from New Jersey, Bishop (1980) found that marital dissolution rates were 66 percent *higher* for black families receiving guaranteed incomes compared with a control group that did not receive such economic guarantees. In contrast, Bishop found no difference

between the experimental and control groups for white families.

Third, the economic stress produced by heading a household for women is also dependent on the income of the spouse. Throughout the postwar period, this fact has had different implications for black and white women. Given that median income for African-American and white women is now identical, but that median income for black men continues to lag far behind that of white men (Farley 1984 p. 79), the relative economic impact of female-headed households for black women may be less than it is for white women.

Finally, social disorganization theories link female-headed households to crime by emphasizing the role of the family in controlling the delinquent and criminal behavior of children. But this reasoning does not take into account a situation in which frequent contacts with the legal system have become nearly normative. For example, as we have seen, on any given day in the U.S.A., nearly a quarter of all black men, ages 20 to 29, are either in prison or on probation or parole (Mauer 1990). Clearly, this calls into question assumptions about the role of husband-wife families in controlling the delinquency of children.

Economic Stress Perspectives

The idea that African-American and white crime rates in the postwar period are related to deteriorating economic conditions has probably produced the largest body of research to date (Long and Witte 1981; Cantor and Land 1985; Chiricos 1987). Merton's (1938) well-known anomie theory applied economic stress arguments directly to the United States by linking crime to a social structure that bombards Americans with the goal of monetary success, but does not equally distribute legitimate economic opportunities for attaining this goal. This imbalance creates isolated, anomic individuals with new, unpredictable, and potentially unfillable desires. Building on Merton's work, Cloward and Ohlin (1960, p. 86) constructed an influential *opportunity and crime* theory that attributes high crime rates in the U.S.A. to "limitations on legitimate avenues of access to conventional goals." Economic stress arguments have led researchers to study either the absolute effect of economic well-being (especially unemployment and poverty, Cantor and Land 1985; Sampson 1987), or the relative effect of economic inequality (Blau and Blau 1982; Stack 1984) on crime.

Given that economic conditions for blacks have been (and remain) far worse than they are for whites, economic stress arguments would appear to be especially relevant for blacks. However, when we (LaFree, et al. 1992; LaFree and Drass 1992) examined the effect of unemployment and income measures on black and white rates of robbery, burglary and homicide, 1957–1988, we found that none of these measures had expected effects for blacks, although many did for whites. Similarly, when we included relative deprivation measures in our longitudinal analyses (based on comparing black to white economic stress measures), we found no significant effect for black crime rates.

While researchers have most often measured black relative deprivation by comparing blacks to whites (but see Harer and Steffensmeier 1992, p. 1036), relative deprivation theorists (Runciman 1966; Merton 1968; Clark 1972) have long argued that comparisons that result in relative deprivation are most likely made to groups sharing important status attributes. Research showing that blacks generally do not use whites as referents for feelings about themselves (McCarthy and Yancey 1971; Heiss and Owens 1972) and research on the past (Molotch 1972; Pearce 1979) and continuing (Massey and Fong 1990) racial segregation of the U.S.A., lends support to the hypothesis that lower-class blacks might more readily compare themselves to middle-class and upper-class blacks than to whites. Conceptualized in this way, relative deprivation is related to the concept of "polarization."

Farley (1984, p. 9) defines polarization as intraracial inequality. The concept can be traced back to the mid-1960s research of Moynihan (1965, pp. 5-6), who claimed that African-Americans were increasingly dividing into a relatively stable and steadily growing middle class and an increasingly disorganized and disadvantaged lower class. Simi-

larly, Clarke (1965, p. 28) argued that "the masses of Negroes are now starkly aware of the fact that recent civil rights victories benefitted a very small percentage of middle-class Negroes while their predicament remained the same or worsened." More recently, Wilson (1987) has claimed that many seemingly anomalous findings for African-Americans may be explained by the widening gap between successful middle-class blacks and a growing black *underclass*. If lower-class blacks have experienced an increasing sense of injustice and frustration as they have witnessed the gains made by middle-class blacks, increasing intraracial inequality may be associated with higher black crime rates.

In our analyses of black and white robbery, murder, and burglary rates for the United States, 1957–1988 (LaFree and Drass 1992), we found evidence for a polarization argument. Our measures of income polarization had significant effects on street crime rates for both blacks and whites. Our results strongly suggest that both black and white crime rates increased in the postwar period along with increases in intraracial inequality.

Conclusions

Based on our review, it seems fair to conclude that thus far efforts to explain black crime rates in the postwar years using deterrence, social disorganization, and economic stress perspectives have been only partially successful. The most promising of these to date looks at the impact of growing intraracial inequality on crime for the black lower class. However, much work remains to be done. The best evidence suggests that black crime rates—especially for violent street crimes—are much higher than white rates or rates for other minorities, and that while black crime rates have fluctuated a good deal during the postwar years, they have nonetheless been considerably higher than comparable rates for whites throughout the period.

My major assumption in preparing this paper is that it is time for social researchers in the United States to face issues of race squarely and forthrightly. While criminologists have largely ignored connections between race and crime during the past three decades, the involvement of African Americans in the legal system has reached crisis proportions. The story of Willie Horton clearly illustrates how racial stereotypes operate in the absence of more objective analysis. I am arguing that paradoxically, it is only by bringing race issues to the fore that we may be able, at long last, to develop an uneasy truce among ourselves and ultimately, lay race issues to rest.

References

Bishop, John. 1980. "Jobs, Cash Transfers and Marital Instability: A Review and Synthesis of the Evidence." *Journal of Human Resources* 15:301–34.

Black, Donald, and Albert J. Reiss, Jr. 1970. "Police Control of Juveniles." *American Sociological Review* 35:63–77.

Blau, Judith R., and Peter M. Blau. 1982. "The Cost of Inequality: Metropolitan Structure and Violent Crime." *American Sociological Review* 47:114–29.

Block, Richard. 1974. "Why Notify the Police: The Victim's Decision to Notify the Police of an Assault." *Criminology* 11:555–69.

Blumstein, Alfred, Jacqueline Cohen, and Richard Rosenfeld. 1991. "Trend and Deviation in Crime Rates: A Comparison of UCR and NCS Data for Burglary and Robbery." *Criminology* 29:237–63.

Bursik, Roben J., Jr. 1988. "Social Disorganization and Theories of Crime and Delinquency: Problems and Prospects." *Criminology* 26:519–52.

Cantor, David I., and Kenneth C. Land. 1985. "Unemployment and Crime Rates in the Post-World War II United States: A Theoretical and Empirical Analysis." *American Sociological Review* 50:317–32.

Chambliss, William J. 1988. *Exploring Criminology.* New York: MacMillan.

Chilton, Roland J., and G. E. Markle. 1972. "Family Disruption, Delinquent Conduct, and the Effect of Subclassification." *American Sociological Review* 37:93–99.

Chiricos, Theodore. 1987. "Rates of Crime and Unemployment: An Analysis of Aggregate Research Evidence." *Social Problems* 34:187–212.

Clark, Robert E. 1972. *Reference Group Theory and Delinquency.* New York: Human Sciences.

Clarke, Kenneth B. 1965. *Dark Ghetto: Dilemmas of Social Power.* New York: Harper & Row.

Cloward, Richard A., and Lloyd E. Ohlin. 1960. *Delinquency and Opportunity: A Theory of Delinquent Gangs.* New York: Free Press.

Devine, Joel A., Joseph F. Sheley, and M. Dwayne Smith. 1988. "Macroeconomic and Social-Control Policy Influences in Crime Rates, 1948–1985." *American Sociological Review* 53:407–21.

Durkheim, Emile. [1893] 1947. *The Division of Labor in Society.* Tr. by George Simpson. Glencoe, IL: Free Press.

Farley, Reynolds. 1984. *Blacks and Whites: Narrowing the G.P.* Cambridge, MA: Harvard University Press.

Federal Bureau of Investigation, 1946–1991. "Crime in the United States." *Uniform Crime Reports.* Washington, DC: Government Printing Office.

Frazier, E. Franklin. 1950. "Problems and Needs of Negro Children and Youth Resulting from Family Disorganization." *Journal of Negro Education,* summer: 269–77.

Geis, Gilbert. 1972. "Statistics Concerning Race and Crime." Pp. 61–69 in *Race, Crime and Justice,* edited by C. E. Reasons and J. C. Kuykendall. Pacific Palisades, CA: Goodyear.

Gottfredson, Michael R., and Don Gottfredson. 1980. *Decision Making in Criminal Justice.* Cambridge, MA: Ballinger.

Gove, Walter R., Michael Hughes, and Michael Geerken. 1985. "Are Uniform Crime Reports a Valid Indicator of the Index Crimes? An Affirmative Answer with Minor Qualifications." *Criminology* 23:451–501.

Harer, Miles, D., and Darrell Steffensmeier. 1992. "The Differing Effects of Economic Inequality on Black and White Rates of Violence." *Social Forces* 70:1035–54.

Harris, Anthony R. 1991. "Race, Class and Crime." Pp. 95–120 in *Criminology,* edited by Joseph R Sheley. Belmont, CA: Wadsworth.

Heiss, Jerald, and Susan Owens. 1972. "Self-Evaluation of Blacks and Whites." *American Journal of Sociology* 78:360–70.

Hill, Robert. 1981. *Economic Policies and Black Progress: Myths and Realities.* Washington, DC: National Urban League.

Hindelang, Michael J. 1978. "Race and Involvement in Crime." *American Sociological Review* 43:93–109.

Jencks, Christopher. 1992. *Rethinking Social Policy.* Cambridge: Harvard University Press.

LaFree, Gary, and Kriss A. Drass. 1992. "Race, Crime and Polarization in Postwar America, 1957–1987." Paper presented at the annual meetings of the American Society of Criminology, New Orleans.

LaFree, Gary, Kriss A. Drass, and Patrick O'Day. 1992. "Race and Crime in Postwar America: Determinants of African-American and White Rates, 1957–1988." *Criminology* 30:157–88.

Langan, Patrick A. 1991. *Race of Prisoners Admitted to State and Federal Institutions, 1926–1986.* U.S. Department of Justice. Washington, DC: Government Printing Office.

Long, Sharon K., and Anne D. Witte. 1981. "Current Economic Trends: Implications for Crime and Criminal Justice." Pp. 69–143 in *Crime and Criminal Justice in a Declining Economy,* edited by Kevin Wright. Cambridge, MA: Oelgeschiager, Gunn, and Hain.

Massey, Douglas S., and Eric Fong. 1990. "Neighborhood Quality: Blacks, Hispanics and Asians in the San Francisco Metropolitan Area." *Social Forces* 69:15–32.

Mauer, Marc. 1990. *Young Black Men and the Criminal Justice System.* Washington, DC: The Sentencing Project.

McCarthy, John, and William L. Yancey. 1971. "Uncle Tom and Mr. Charlie: Metaphysical Pathos in the Study of Racism and Personal Disorganization." *American Journal of Sociology* 76:648–72.

Merton, Robert K. 1938. "Social Structure and Anomie." *American Sociological Review* 3:672–82.

——. 1968. *Social Theory and Social Structure.* Glencoe, IL: Free Press.

Molotch, Harvey. 1972. *Managed Integration: The Dilemmas of Doing Good in the City.* Berkeley: University of California Press.

Montare, A., and S. L. Boone. 1980. "Aggression and Paternal Absence: Racial-Ethnic Differences Among Inner-City Boys." *Journal of Genetic Psychology* 137:223–32.

Moynihan, Daniel P. 1965. *The Negro Family: The Case for National Action.* Office of Policy Planning and Research, Department of Labor, Washington, DC: Government Printing Office.

Murray, Charles. 1984. *Losing Ground: American Social Policy, 1950–1980.* New York: Basic Books.

O'Brien, Robert. 1985. *Crime and Victimization.* Beverly Hills, CA: Sage. Another 'Trail of Tears.'" *Journal of Criminal Justice* 15:485–94.

Peak, K., and J. Spencer. 1987. "Crime in Indian Country: Another 'Trail of Tears'" *Journal of Criminal Justice* 15:485–494 @RT = Pearce, Diana M. 1979. "Gatekeepers and Homekeepers: Institutional Factors in Racial Steering." *Social Problems* 26:325–42.

Popenoe, David. 1988. *Disturbing the Nest: Family Change and Decline in Modern Societies.* New York: Aldine DeGruyter.

President's Commission on Law Enforcement and Administration of Justice. 1967. *Task Force Report: Crime and Its Impact—An Assessment.* Washington, DC: U.S. Government Printing Office.

Rainwater, Lee. 1970. *Behind Ghetto Walls: Black Families in a Federal Slum.* Chicago: Aldine.

Robins, Lee N., and Shirley Y. Hill. 1966. "Assessing the Contribution of Family Structure. Class and Peer Groups to Juvenile Delinquency." *Journal of Criminal Law, Criminology, and Police Science* 57:325–34.

Rogers, John, and Hans Norman, eds. 1985. *The Nordic Family: Perspectives on Family Research.* Uppsala University.

Rosen, Lawrence, and Kathleen Nielson. 1978. "The Broken Home and Delinquency." Pp. 406–15 in *Crime in Society,* edited by Leonard D. Savitz and Norman Johnston. New York: Wiley.

Ross, H. Laurence, and Gary LaFree. 1986. "Deterrence in Criminology and Social Policy." Pp. 129–52 in *Behavioral and Social Science Knowledge: Discovery, Diffusion and Social Impact.* Washington, DC: National Research Council.

Ross, Heather, and Isabel Sawhill. 1975. *Time of Transition: The Growth of Families Headed by Women.* Washington, DC: Urban Institute.

Runciman, Walter G. 1966. *Relative Deprivation and Social Justice.* Berkeley: University of California Press.

Sampson, Robert J. 1987. "Urban Black Violence: The Effect of Male Joblessness and Family Disruption." *American Journal of Sociology* 93:348–82.

Shaw, Clifford R., and Henry McKay. 1942. *Juvenile Delinquency and Urban Areas.* Chicago: University of Chicago Press.

Shaw, Clifford R., Henry D. McKay, Frederick M. Zorbaugh, and Leonard S. Cottrell, Jr. 1929. *Delinquency Areas.* Chicago: University of Chicago Press.

Stack, Steven. 1984. "Income Inequality and Property Crime: A Cross-National Analysis of Relative Deprivation Theory." *Criminology* 22:229–57.

Tittle, Charles. 1980. *Sanctions and Social Deviance.* New York: Praeger.

U.S. Bureau of the Census. 1981. "Marital Status and Living Arrangements, March 1980." *Current Population Reports.* Washington, DC: Government Printing Office.

——. 1983. "Fertility of American Women, June 1981." *Current Population Reports,* Series P–20. Washington, DC: Government Printing Office.

——. 1984. "Household and Family Characteristics, March 1983." *Current Population Reports.* Series P–20. no. 388. Washington, DC: Government Printing Office.

U.S. Bureau of Justice Statistics. 1985. *The Risk of Violent Crime: Department of Justice Special Report.* Washington, DC: Government Printing Office.

Warner, S. B. 1931. "Crimes Known to the Police— An Index of Crime." *Harvard Law Review* 45:307–34.

Wilson, James Q. 1975. *Thinking About Crime.* New York: Basic.

Wilson, William Julius. 1984. "The Urban Underclass." In *Minority Report,* edited by Leslie W. Dunbar. New York: Pantheon.

——. 1987. *The Truly Disadvantaged: The Inner City, the Underclass and Public Policy.* Chicago: University of Chicago Press.

Zatz, Marjorie S., Carol Chiago Lujan, and Zoann K. Snyder-Joy. 1991. "American Indians and Criminal Justice: Some Conceptual and Methodological Considerations." Pp. 100–112 in *Race and Criminal Justice,* edited by M.J. Lynch and E. B. Patterson. New York: Harrow and Heston.

35

Racial Politics, Racial Disparities, and the War on Crime

Michael Tonry

Racial disparities in arrests, jailings and imprisonment steadily worsened after 1980 for reasons that have little to do with changes in crime patterns and almost everything to do with two political developments. First, conservative Republicans in national elections "played the race card" by using anticrime slogans (remember Willie Horton?) as a way to appeal to anti-black sentiments of black voters. Second, conservative politicians of both parties promoted and voted for harsh crime control and drug policies that exacerbated existing racial disparities.

The worsened disparities might have been ethically defensible if they had been based on good faith beliefs that some greater policy good would thereby have been achieved. Sometimes unwanted side effects of social policy are inevitable. Traffic accidents and fatalities are a price we pay for the convenience of automobiles. Occupational injuries are a price we pay for engaging in the industries in which they occur.

The principal causes of worse racial disparities have been the War on Drugs launched by the Bush and Reagan administrations, characterized by vast increases in arrests and imprisonment of street-level drug dealers, and the continuing movement toward harsher penalties. . . .

Crime Reduction Effects of Crime Control Policy

There is no basis for a claim that recent harsh crime control policies or the enforcement strategies of the War on Drugs were based on good faith beliefs that they would achieve their ostensible purposes. In this and other countries, practitioners and scholars have long known that manipulation of penalties has few, if any, effects on crime rates.

Commissions and expert advisory bodies have been commissioned by the federal government repeatedly over the last 30 years to survey knowledge of the effects of crime control policies, and consistently they have concluded that there is little reason to believe that harsher penalties significantly enhance public safety. In 1967, the President's Commission on Law Enforcement and Administration of Justice observed that crime control efforts can have little effect on crime rates without much larger efforts being directed at crime's underlying social and economic causes. . . .

In 1978, the National Academy of Sciences Panel on Research on Deterrent and Incapacitative Effects, funded by President Ford's department of justice and asked to examine the available evidence on the crime-reductive effects of sanctions, concluded: "In summary, we cannot assert that the evidence warrants an affirmative conclusion regarding deterrence" (Blumstein, Cohen, and Nagin 1978). Fifteen years later, the National Academy of Sciences Panel on the Understanding and Control of Violent Behavior, created and paid for with funds from the Reagan and Bush administrations departments of justice, surveyed knowledge of the effects of harsher penalties on violent crime (Reiss and Roth 1993). A rhetorical question and answer in the panel's final report says it all: "What effect has increasing the prison population had on violent crime? Apparently very little. . . .

I mention that the two National Academy of Sciences panels were created and supported by national Republican administrations to demonstrate that skepticism about the crime-preventive effects of harsher punishments is not a fantasy of liberal Democrats. Anyone who has spent much time talking with judges or corrections officials knows that most, whatever their political affiliations, do not believe that harsher penalties significantly enhance public safety. . . .

There is no better evidentiary base to justify recent drug control policies. Because no other western country has adopted drug policies as harsh as those of the United States, a bit of background may be useful before I show why there was no reasonable basis for believing recent policies would achieve their ostensible goals. In drug policy jargon, the United States has adopted a prohibitionistic rather than a harm-reduction strategy and has emphasized supply-side over demand-side tactics (Wilson 1990). This strategic choice implies a preference for legal threats and moral denunciation of drug use and users instead of a preference for minimizing net costs and social harms to the general public, the law enforcement system, and drug users. The tactical choice is between a law enforcement emphasis on arrest and punishment of dealers, distributors, and importers, interdiction, and source-country programs or a prevention emphasis on drug treatment, drug-abuse education in schools, and mass media programs aimed at public education. The supply-side bias in recent American policies was exemplified throughout the Bush administration by its insistence that 70% of federal antidrug funds be devoted to law enforcement and only 30% to treatment and education (Office of National Drug Control Policy 1990).

It has been a long time since most researchers and practitioners believed that current knowledge justifies recent American drug control policies. Because the potential income from drug dealing means that willing aspirants are nearly always available to replace arrested street-level dealers, large-scale arrests have repeatedly been shown to have little or no effect on the volume of drug trafficking or on the retail prices of drugs (e.g., Chaiken 1988; Sciridoff, Sadd, Curtis, and Grinc 1992). Because the United States has long and porous borders, and because an achievably large proportion of attempted smuggling would have to be stopped to affect drug prices significantly, interdiction has repeatedly been shown to have little or no effect

on volume or prices (Reuter 1988). Because cocaine, heroin, and marijuana can be grown in many parts of the world in which government controls are weak and peasant farmers' incentives are strong, source-country programs have seldom been shown to have significant influence on drug availability or price in the United States (Moore 1990).

The evidence in support of the demand-side strategies is far stronger. In December 1993, the President's Commission on Model State Drug Laws, appointed by President Bush, categorically concluded, "Treatment works." That conclusion is echoed by more authoritative surveys of drug treatment evaluations by the U.S. General Accounting Office (1990), the National Institute of Medicine (Gerstein and Jarwood 1990), and in *Crime and Justice* by Anglin and Hser (1990). Because drug use and offending tend to coincide in the lives of drug-using offenders, the most effective and cost-effective way to deal with such offenders is to get and keep them in well-run treatment programs.

A sizable literature now also documents the effectiveness of school-based drug education in reducing drug experimentation and use among young people. (e.g., Botvin 1990; Ellickson and Bell 1990). Although there is no credible literature that documents the effects of mass media campaigns on drug use, a judge could take judicial notice of their ubiquity. It is not unreasonable to believe that such campaigns have influenced across-the-board declines in drug use in the United States since 1980 (a date, incidently, that precedes the launch of the War on Drugs by nearly 8 years). . . .

Racial Disparities in Arrests, Jail, and Prison

Racial disparities, especially affecting blacks, have long bedeviled the criminal justice system. Many hundreds of studies of disparities have been conducted and there is now widespread agreement among researchers about causes. Racial bias and stereotyping no doubt play some role, but they are not the major cause. In the longer term, disparities in jail and prison are mainly the result of racial differences in offending patterns. In the shorter term, the worsening disparities since 1980 are not primarily the result of racial differences in offending but were foreseeable effects of the War on Drugs and the movement toward increased use of incarceration. These patterns can best be seen by approaching the recent increases in racial disparities in imprisonment as a mystery to be solved. (Because of space limitations, jail data are not discussed here at length, but the trends parallel those for prisons. Between 1980 and 1991, e.g., the percentage of jail inmates who were black increased from 40% to 48%.)

. . . [T]he percentages of prison inmates who were black or white from 1960 to 1991 reveal two trends. First, for as long as prison population data have been compiled, the percentage of inmates who are black has by several times exceeded the percentage of Americans who are black (10% to 13% during the relevant period). Second, since 1980 the black percentage among prisoners has increased sharply.

Racial disproportions among prison inmates are inherently undesirable, and considerable energy has been expended on efforts to understand them. In 1982, Blumstein showed that around 80% of the disproportion could be explained on the basis of racial differences in arrest patterns. Of the unexplained 20%, Blumstein argued, some might represent bias and some might reflect racial differences in criminal history or arguably valid case-processing differences. Some years later, Langan (1985) skipped over the arrest stage altogether and showed that racial patterns in victims' identifications of their assailants explained about 80% of disparities in prison admissions. In 1990, Klein, Petersilia, and Turner showed that, after criminal history and other legitimate differences between cases were taken into account, the offender's race had no independent predictive effect in California on whether he was sent to prison or for how long. There the matter rests. Blumstein (1993a) updated his analysis and reached similar conclusions (with one important exception that is discussed below).

Although racial crime patterns explain a large part of racial imprisonment patterns, they do not explain why the black percentage rose so rapidly after 1980. . . . Within narrow bands of fluctuation, racial arrest percentages have been stable since 1976. Comparing 1976 with 1992, for example, black percentages, among people arrested for murder, robbery, and burglary were slightly up and black percentages among those arrested for rape, aggravated assault, and theft were slightly down. Overall, the percentage among those arrested for violent crimes who were black fell from 47.5% to 44.8%. Because prison sentences have traditionally been imposed on people convicted of violent crimes, Blumstein's and the other analyses suggest that the black percentage among inmates should be flat or declining. That, however, is not [the case]. Why not?

. . .Arrests of blacks for violent crimes may not have increased since 1980, but the percentage of blacks among those sent to prison has increased starkly, reaching 54% in 1991 and 1992. Why? The main explanation concerns the War on Drugs.

. . . Blacks today make up about 13% of the U.S. population and, according to National Institute on Drug Abuse (1991) surveys of Americans' drug use, are no more likely than whites ever to have used most drugs of abuse. Nonetheless, the percentages of blacks among drug arrestees were in the low 20% range in the late 1970s, climbing to around 30% in the early 1980s and peaking at 42% in 1989. The number of drug arrests of blacks more than doubled between 1985 and 1989, whereas black drug arrests increased only by 27%. Figure 35.1 shows the stark differences in drug arrest trends by race from 1976 to 1991.

Drug control policies are a major cause of worsening racial disparities in prison. In the federal prisons, for example, 22% of new admissions and 25% of the resident population were drug offenders in 1980. By 1990, 42% of new admissions were drug offenders and in 1992 were 58% of the resident population. In state prisons, 5.7% of inmates in 1979 were drug offenders, a figure that by 1991 had climbed to 21.3% to become the single largest category of prisoners (robbers, burglars, and murderers were next at 14.8%, 12.4%, and 10.6%, respectively) (Beck et al. 1993).

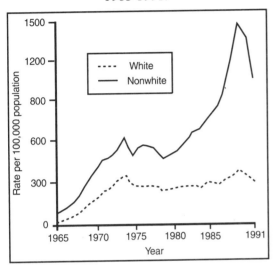

Figure 35.1
Arrest Rates for Drug Offenses by Race, 1965-1991.

Source: Blumstein 1993b.

The effect of drug policies can be seen in prison data from a number of states. [For instance] Figure 35.2 shows prison admissions for drug crimes in Virginia from 1983 to 1989; the racial balance flipped from two-thirds White, one-third non-White in 1983 to the reverse in 1989.

Why, if blacks in their lives are no more likely than whites to use illicit drugs, are blacks so much more likely to be arrested and imprisoned? One possible answer, which is almost certainly wrong, is that blacks are proportionately more likely to sell drugs. We have no representative surveys of drug dealers and so cannot with confidence paint demographic pictures. However, there is little reason to suspect that drug crimes are more interracial than are most other crimes. In addition, the considerations that make arrests of black dealers relatively easy make arrests of black dealers relatively hard.

Drug arrests are easier to make in socially disorganized inner-city minority areas than in working- or middle-class urban or suburban areas for a number of reasons. First, al-though drug sales in working- or middle-class areas are likely to take place indoors and in private spaces where they are difficult to observe, drug sales in poor minority areas are likely to take place outdoors in streets, alleys, or abandoned buildings, or indoors in public places like bars. Second, although working- or middle-class drug dealers in stable areas are unlikely to sell drugs to under-cover strangers, dealers in disorganized areas have little choice but to sell to strangers and new acquaintances. These differences mean that it is easier for police to make arrests and undercover purchases in urban minority areas than elsewhere. Because arrests are fungible for purposes of both the individual officer's personnel file and the department's year-to-year statistical comparisons, more easy arrests look better than fewer hard ones. And because, as ethnographic studies of drug trafficking make clear (Fagan 1993; Padilla 1992), arrested drug dealers in disadvantaged urban minority communities are generally replaced within days, there is a nearly inexhaustible potential supply of young minority Americans to be arrested.

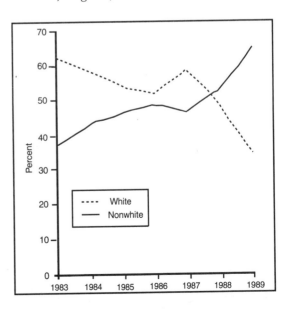

Figure 35.2
Percentage of New Drug Commitments by Race, Virginia, Fiscal Years 1983-1989.

Source: Austin and McVey 1989.

There is another reason why the War on Drugs worsened racial disparities in the justice system. Penalties for drug crimes were steadily made harsher since the mid-1980s. In particular, purveyors of crack cocaine, a drug used primarily by poor urban blacks and Hispanics, are punished far more severely than are purveyors of powder cocaine, a pharmacologically indistinguishable drug used primarily by middle-class whites. The most notorious disparity occurs under federal law which equates 1 gram of crack with 100 grams of powder. As a result, the average prison sentence served by black federal prisoners is 40% longer than the average sentence for whites (McDonald and Carlson 1993). Although the Minnesota Supreme Court and two federal district courts have struck down the 100-to-1 rule as a denial of constitutional equal protection to blacks, at the time of writing, every federal court of appeals that had considered the question had upheld the provision.

The people who launched the drug wars knew all these things—that the enemy troops would mostly be young minority males, that an emphasis on supply-side antidrug strategies, particularly use of mass arrests, would disproportionately ensnare young minority males, that the 100-to-1 rule would disproportionately affect blacks, and that there was no valid basis for believing that any of these things would reduce drug availability or prices.

Likewise, as the first section showed, there was no basis for a good faith belief that the harsher crime control policies of recent years—more and longer mandatory minimum sentences, tougher and more rigid sentencing guidelines, and three-strikes-and-you're-out laws—would reduce crime rates, and there was a good basis for predicting that they would disproportionately damage blacks. If blacks are more likely than whites to be arrested, especially for drug crimes, the greater harshness of toughened penalties will disproportionately be borne by blacks. Because much crime is intraracial, concern for black victims might justify harsher treatment of black offenders if there were any reason to believe that harsher penalties would reduce crime rates. Unfortunately, as the reports of

National Academy of Sciences Panels funded by the administrations of Republican Presidents Ford, Reagan, and Bush all agree, there is no reason to believe that harsher penalties significantly reduce crime rates.

Justifying the Unjustifiable

There is no valid policy justification for the harsh drug and crime control. . . . The justification, such as it is, is entirely political. Crime is an emotional subject and visceral appeals by politicians to people's fears and resentments are difficult to counter.

It is easy to seize the low ground in political debates about crime policy. When one candidate campaigns with pictures of clanging prison gates and grief-stricken relatives of a rape or murder victim, and with disingenuous promises that newer, tougher policies will work, it is difficult for an opponent to explain that crime is a complicated problem, that real solutions must be long term, and that simplistic toughness does not reduce crime rates. This is why, as a result, candidates often compete to establish which is tougher in his views about crime. It is also why less conservative candidates often try to preempt their more conservative opponents by adopting a tough stance early in the campaign. Finally, it is why political pundits congratulate President Clinton on his acumen in proposing federal crime legislation as or more harsh than his opponents. He has, it is commonly said, "taken the crime issue away from the Republicans." . . .

The story of Willie Horton is [well-known]. . . . Horton, who in 1975 had been convicted of the murder of a 17-year-old boy, failed to return from a June 12, 1986, furlough. The following April, he broke into a home in Oxon Hill, Maryland, where he raped a woman and stabbed her companion.

Lee Atwater, Bush's campaign strategist, after testing the visceral effects of Willie Horton's picture and story on participants in focus groups, decided a year later to make Horton a wedge issue for Republicans. . . .

The sad reality is that tragedies like the crimes of Willie Horton are inevitable. So are airplane crashes, 40,000 to 50,000 traffic fatalities per year, and defense department cost overruns. Every person convicted of a violent crime cannot be held forever. Furloughs are used in most corrections systems as a way to ease offenders back into the community and to test their suitability for eventual release on parole or commutation. Horton had successfully completed nine previous furloughs, from each of which he had returned without incident, under a program established in 1972 not by Michael Dukakis but by Governor Francis Sargent, a Republican.

Public discourse about criminal justice issues has been debased by the cynicism that made Willie Horton a major participant in the 1988 presidential election. That cynicism has made it difficult to discuss or develop sensible public policies, and that cynicism explains why conservative politicians have been able year after year successfully to propose ever harsher penalties and crime control and drug policies that no informed person believes can achieve their ostensible goals.

Three final points, arguments that apologists for current policies sometimes make, warrant mention. First, it is sometimes said to be unfair to blame national Republican administrations for the failures and disparate impacts of recent crime control policies. This ignores the efforts of the Reagan and Bush administrations to encourage and, through federal mandates and funding restrictions, to coerce states to follow the federal lead. Attorney General William Barr (e.g., 1992) made the most aggressive efforts to compel state adoption of tougher criminal justice policies, and the Bush administration's final proposed crime bills restricted eligibility for federal funds to states that, like the federal government, abolished parole release and adopted sentencing standards no less severe than those in the federal sentencing guidelines. In any case . . . the use of crime control issues (among others including welfare reform and affirmative action) to elicit anti-black sentiments from white voters has long been a stratagem of both state and federal Republican politicians.

Second, sometimes it is argued that political leaders have merely followed the public will; voters are outraged by crime and want tougher policies (DiIulio 1991). This is a half-truth that gets the causal order backwards.

Various measures of public sentiment, including both representative surveys like Gallup and Harris polls and work with focus groups, have for many years consistently shown that the public is of two minds about crime (Roberts 1992). First, people are frustrated and want offenders to be punished. Second, people believe that social adversity, poverty, and a troubled home life are the principal causes of crime, and they believe government should work to rehabilitate offenders. A number of surveys have found that respondents who would oppose a tax increase to pay for more prisons would support a tax increase to pay for rehabilitative programs. These findings of voter ambivalence about crime should not be surprising. Most people have complicated views about complicated problems. For example, most judges and corrections officials have the same ambivalent feelings about offenders that the general public has. Conservative politicians have seized upon public support of punishment and ignored public support of rehabilitation and public recognition that crime presents complex, not easy, challenges. By presenting crime control issues only in emotional, stereotyped ways, conservative politicians have raised its salience as a political issue but made it impossible for their opponents to respond other than in the same stereotyped ways.

Third, sometimes it is argued that disparate impacts on black offenders are no problem and that, because much crime is intraracial, failure to adopt tough policies would disserve the interests of black victims. As former Attorney General Barr (1992) put it, perhaps in ill-chosen words, "the benefits of increased incarceration would be enjoyed disproportionately by black Americans" (p. 17). This argument also is based on a half-truth. No one wants to live in unsafe neighborhoods or to be victimized by crime, and in a crisis, people who need help will seek it from the police, the public agency of last resort. Requesting help in a crisis and supporting harsh policies with racially disparate effects are not the same thing. The relevant distinction is between acute and chronic problems. A substantial body of public opinion research (e.g., National Opinion Research Center surveys conducted throughout the 1980s summarized in Wood 1990) shows that blacks far more than whites support establishment of more generous social welfare policies, full employment programs, and increased social spending. The congressional black and Hispanic caucuses have consistently opposed bills calling for tougher sanctions and supported bills calling for increased spending on social programs aimed at improving conditions that cause crime.

Thus, in claiming to be concerned about black victims, conservative politicians are responding to natural human calls for help in a crisis while ignoring evidence that black citizens would rather have government support efforts to ameliorate the chronic social conditions that cause crime and thereby make calls for help in a crisis less necessary.

The evidence on the effectiveness of recent crime control and drug abuse policies, as the first section demonstrated, cannot justify their racially disparate effects on blacks, nor, as this section demonstrates, can the claims that such policies merely manifest the peoples' will or respect the interests of black victims. All that is left is politics of the ugliest kind. The War on Drugs and the set of harsh crime control policies in which it was enmeshed were adopted to achieve political, not policy, objectives, and it is the adoption for political purposes of policies with foreseeable disparate impacts, the use of disadvantaged black Americans as means to the achievement of black politicians' electoral ends, that must in the end be justified. It cannot.

References

Anglin, M. Douglas, and Yih-Ing Hser. 1990. "Treatment of Drug Abuse." In *Drugs and Crime*, edited by M. Tonry and J. Q. Wilson. Chicago: University of Chicago Press.

Austin, James, and Aaron David McVey. 1989. *The Impact of the War on Drugs.* San Francisco: National Council on Crime and Delinquency.

Barr, William P. 1992. "Case for More Incarceration." Washington, DC: U.S. Department of Justice, Office of Policy Development.

Beck, Allen et al. 1993. *Survey of State Prison Inmates, 1991.* Washington, DC: Bureau of Justice Statistics.

Blumstein, Alfred. 1982. "On the Racial Disproportionality of United States' Prison Populations." *Journal of Criminal Law and Criminology* 73:1259–81.

———. 1993a. "Racial Disproportionality of U.S. Prison Populations Revisited." *University of Colorado Law Review* 64:743–60.

———. 1993b. "Making Rationality Relevant—The American Society of Criminology 1992 Presidential Address." *Criminology* 31:1–16.

Blumstein, Alfred, Jacqueline Cohen, and Daniel Nagin. 1978. *Deterrence and Incapacitation.* Report of the National Academy of Sciences Panel on Research on Deterrent and Incapacitative Effects. Washington, DC: National Academy Press.

Botvin, Gilbert J. 1990. "Substance Abuse Prevention: Theory, Practice, and Effectiveness." In *Drugs and Crime*, edited by M. Tonry and J. Q. Wilson. Chicago: University of Chicago Press.

Chaiken, Marcia. ed. 1988. *Street Level Enforcement: Examining the Issues.* Washington, DC: U.S. Government Printing Office.

Clark, Stover. 1992. "Pennsylvania Corrections in Context." *Overcrowded Times* 3:4–5.

Clarke, Stevens H. 1992. "North Carolina Prisons Growing." *Overcrowded Times* 3:1, 11–13.

DiIulio, John J. 1991. *No Escape: The Future of American Corrections.* New York: Basic Books.

Edsall, Thomas, and Mary Edsall. 1991. *Chain Reaction: The Impact of Race, Rights, and Taxes on American Politics.* New York: Norton.

Ellickson, Phyllis L., and Robert M. Bell. 1990. *Prospects for Preventing Drug Use Among Young Adolescents.* Santa Monica, CA: RAND.

Fagan, Jeffrey. 1993. "Political Economy of Drug Dealing Among Urban Gangs." In *Drugs and the Community*, edited by R. C. Davis, A. J. Lurigio, and D. P. Rosenbaum. Springfield, IL: Charles C. Thomas.

Gerstein, Dean R., and Henrik J. Jarwood, eds. 1990. *Treating Drug Problems.* Report of Committee for Substance Abuse Coverage Study, Division of Health Care Services, National Institute of Medicine. Washington, DC: National Academy Press.

Klein, Stephen, Joan Petersilia, and Susan Turner. 1990. "Race and Imprisonment Decisions in California." *Science* 247:812–16.

Langan, Patrick A. 1985. "Racism on Trial: New Evidence to Explain the Racial Composition of Prisons in the United States." *Journal of Criminal Law and Criminology* 76:666–83.

McDonald, Douglas, and Ken Carlson. 1993. *Sentencing in the Federal Courts: Does Race Mat-*

ter? Washington, DC: U.S. Department of Justice, Bureau of Justice Statistics.

Moore, Mark H. 1990. "Supply Reduction and Drug Law Enforcement." In *Drugs and Crime,* edited by M. Tonry and J. Q. Wilson. Chicago: University of Chicago Press.

Moynihan, Daniel Patrick. 1993. "Iatrogenic Government—Social Policy and Drug Research." *American Scholar* 62:351–62.

National Institute on Drug Abuse. 1991. *National Household Survey on Drug Abuse: Population Estimates 1990.* Washington, DC: U.S. Government Printing Office.

Office of National Drug Control Policy. 1990. *National Drug Control Strategy—January 1990.* Washington, DC: Author.

Padilla, Felix. 1992. *The Gang as an American Enterprise.* New Brunswick, NJ: Rutgers University Press.

Reiss, Albert J., Jr., and Jeffrey Roth. 1993. *Understanding and Controlling Violence. Report of the National Academy of Sciences Panel on the Understanding and Control of Violence.* Washington, DC: National Academy Press.

Roberts, Julian V. 1992. "Public Opinion, Crime, and Criminal Justice." In *Crime and Justice: A Review of Research,* vol. 16, edited by M. Tonry. Chicago: University of Chicago Press.

Sviridoff, Michele, Susan Sadd, Richard Curtis, and Randolph Grinc. 1992. *The Neighborhood Effects of Street-Level Drug Enforcement.* New York: Vern Institute of Justice.

Tonry, Michael. 1994. *Malign Neglect: Race, Crime, and Punishment in America.* New York: Oxford University Press.

U.S. General Accounting Office. 1990. *Drug Abuse: Research on Treatment May Not Address Current Needs.* Washington, DC: U.S. General Accounting Office.

Wilson, James Q. 1990. "Drugs and Crime." In *Drugs and Crime,* edited by M. Tonry and J. Q. Wilson. Chicago: University of Chicago Press.

Wood, Floris W. 1990. *An American Profile: Opinions and Behavior, 1972–1989.* New York: Gale Research.

36

Persistent Poverty, Crime, and Drugs:

The U.S.-Mexican Border Region

Avelardo Valdez

The highest indicators of poverty in the United States are along the Rio Grande Valley in Texas. The scarcity of institutional resources and economic development, relative to other areas of the state, is attributed to the fact that this area is identified as a Mexican American region. Social mobility is, nonetheless, possible for a small proportion of Mexican Americans whose class interests often conflict with the majority of this population. The interests of these Mexican Americans usually coincide with those of the dominant Anglos. As a result, most Mexican Americans occupy a subordinate status based on ethnicity and class. Recent economic changes have exacerbated social differences among Mexican Americans, solidifying the dominant position of the middle class and the subordinate position of the working-poor.

This study focuses on the impact of this economic transformation on Mexican Americans in Laredo, Texas, who comprise 90 percent of the population. The research explores how sectors of Laredo's poor have adapted alternative social strategies to survive economically. It also examines how the presence of the international border, combined with high poverty rates, generates disproportionate levels of illicit behavior, particularly related to drugs.

Wilson and others argue that during the last two decades an underclass has formed among urban blacks as a result of national economic restructuring (Wilson 1987; Harrington 1984). The underclass is associated with chronic poverty, joblessness, residential segregation, and the breakdown of community institutions. Among the most significant impacts of these economic changes was the disappearance of a stable wage-based economy in urban areas. As a result, many economic activities in black ghettos were now generated outside the formal wage market (Wilson 1985). This included increased governmental dependency and criminal activities centered on the ghetto's illegal economy. Although the discourse on the underclass often alludes to this underground economy, few studies have focused on it, particularly as it concerns the Mexican American community (Moore 1989). . . .

Laredo: Portrait of a U.S.–Mexico Border City

Laredo is a major commercial and retail link between the Mexican state of Tamaulipas and Texas. The city's primary economic activities are international transportation, manufacturing, and retail trade. Laredo's major transportation artery is Interstate 35, which leads 150 miles north to San Antonio and the rest of the United States. Laredo's shopping mall and upscale restaurants and popular night spots are also located along or adjacent to this highway. The interstate is flanked by fast-food restaurants, motels, international auto insurance companies, money exchange houses, gas stations, tire stores, and other businesses catering to U.S. and Mexican tourists.

The interstate leads directly to the new international bridge crossing into Nuevo Laredo, Tamaulipas. The older bridge is several blocks to the west. Most of the businesses catering to Mexican shoppers, American and Mexican tourists, and travelers are near the older bridge. There is a constant flow of pedestrians, automobiles, trucks, and commercial busses here, for just across this bridge is the heart of downtown Nuevo Laredo.

Laredo's downtown is north of the old bridge, centered around a plaza bustling with shoppers, schoolchildren, office workers, peddlers, undocumented Mexicans, Nuevo Laredo shoppers, elderly pensioners, and other residents from both cities. Laredo's city busses reach all parts of the city from this plaza. The city's new municipal building, county courthouse, county jail, financial institutions, hotels, and other services and businesses are located

Northwest of the central city lies a huge railyard where the National Railyard of Mexico and the Missouri Pacific lines meet. Much of U.S.—Mexico trade is shipped through here. The tracks lead south to a railroad bridge that crosses into Mexico. Surrounding the railyard are acres of parked semitrailers used to transport goods. Semitrailers are also seen on the interstate access roads entering Laredo from the north, where a concentration of import/export brokers and warehouses cater to the maquiladora industry.

East of downtown Laredo is a warehouse and manufacturing district served by rail lines and trucking firms. Highway 83 runs southeast through this area to Zapata, Texas. This highway, as it runs from downtown through south Laredo, is an important retail corridor for local residents, lined with auto-parts stores, grocery stores, restaurants, nightclubs, and other businesses. The homes in this part of the city are predominantly single-family houses on large lots in older subdivisions off the main highway. Neighborhood roads and streets are mostly unpaved and without sidewalks. Many residents are migrant farm workers who travel to the Midwest during the summer and reside here in the water.

The disproportionate percentage of families in poverty is reflected in the dispersion of the poor through all areas of Laredo. The poorest neighborhoods are adjacent to the central business district, transportation and shipping facilities, and the Rio Grande River. In these neighborhoods small clapboard houses sit on single lots. Many of the streets are unpaved, and are hot and dusty during the summer. Inadequate drainage causes flooding in many of these neighborhoods during the rains. Barrios such as El Azteca, El Cuarto, Canta Ranas, and Los Colonias, are highly enclosed neighborhoods, with long-term multigenerational residents, that have developed distinctive identities. There are other still poorer neighborhoods on the outskirts of the city called *colonias*, newer areas best described as poor subdivisions lacking many essential services.

There are sections of Laredo that are associated with the wealthy. The city's traditional upper class tends to reside in the near northwest side of the city. This area, south of Martin High School, is filled with large homes on perfectly manicured lawns with thick foliage. The streets are all paved and have sidewalks. Many of these houses are built in a Spanish-stucco style and surrounded by large walls. Newer middle-class subdivisions lie on the far north side and in an area surrounding the city's airport. These subdivisions are home to many middle-level managers recently moved to Laredo as well as lower-middle-class residents native to this region.

Mexican Americans are found throughout the class structure. As in other south Texas border cities there is a small Mexican American upper class of bankers, ranchers, and professionals. A larger middle class has also developed. It consists of small businessmen, teachers, lawyers, health workers, semiprofessionals, public employees, and politicians. Additionally there is a working class that is employed in civil service, blue-collar jobs, and retail and clerical work. The majority of Laredo residents, nonetheless, are poor and only marginally integrated into the local economy, primarily as unskilled workers.

Nuevo Laredo residents, as is true of other Mexicans living along the border, have a special legal status that allows them limited access to U.S. border areas. This allows Mexican residents to shop, visit, and conduct business in U.S. border regions. The free flow of Mexican residents into Laredo is typical of other U.S. border cities. Many Mexicans along the border, however, abuse this privilege by working, which is prohibited by U.S. immigration laws. Some estimates conclude that 20 percent of Laredo's work force is comprised of Mexicans who commute daily or weekly into the city. These workers often are employed at salaries and under conditions unacceptable to Mexican Americans. The presence of Mexican workers in Laredo and other border cities contributes to the low salary structures, high unemployment levels, and poverty of these regions.

The predominance of persons of Mexican origin throughout the class structure and Laredo's proximity to Mexico create a homogeneous cultural milieu. Although English is the official language, Spanish is the dominant language of the city. Mexican Americans are found in all levels of business, government, education, mass media, and religion.

Many Mexican Americans from throughout the class structure, who are natives of Laredo, claim never to have experienced ethnic prejudice and/or discrimination in this community. Poverty and inequality for most Mexican Americans in Laredo appears to be more the result of class differences than ethnic or racial prejudice. . . .

Economic Reconstruction along the U.S.-Mexico Border: The Case of Laredo, Texas

The border separates Laredo from Nuevo Laredo, Tamaulipas, in Northern Mexico. These two cities have populations of 113,000 and 500,000, respectively. Together the cities have played a traditionally dominant role in the region's economy (south Texas and northern Mexico), particularly in the retail and service trade and as an export/import center. The economic interdependence of these two cities has resulted in a series of regional booms and busts over the past fifty years (Martinez 1983). Prior to the 1970s Laredo's economy was based on ranching, tourism, retail trade, and international trade. A large portion of its Mexican American population migrated to work as temporary agricultural workers in other areas of the United States. More recently, Laredo's economy has benefitted from the maquiladora industry, with non-Mexican-owned companies assembling and producing products in Mexico yet maintaining administrative control in the United States and other countries.

The Economic Boom: 1970 and 1982

During the 1970s and early 1980s Laredo experienced an economic boom. The economy was based primarily on ranching, oil and gas, retail trade, and international trade. Laredo served as a major point of U.S.-Mexico commercial trade because it was located on one of the most direct routes between these two regions. A daily average of 151 railroad freight cars entered Laredo in 1978 (Hanson 1981). The city during this period had one of the highest retail sales per resident in the nation (Harrell and Fischer 1985), based primarily on purchases made by Mexican residents. Furthermore the Mexican middle class invested their inflationary pesos in businesses and real estate on the U.S. border. Between 1970 and 1980 Laredo's population grew from about 70,000 to 90,000 as its labor force swelled by 75 percent. Poverty declined from 45 to 35 percent (Miller 1983). This growth offset the loss in 1972 of a military base that was Laredo's single largest employer.

As Laredo retailers expanded their businesses by two- and threefold, the city became northern Mexico's primary shopping center. Prices for housing, land, and other property rose. Economic prosperity, however, was unequally distributed within the population. . . . As a result Laredo's economic prosperity during this period did little to change the status of the poor in this community.

The Post-1982 Period

In 1982, the Mexican Government lowered the value of the peso by 80 percent and Laredo's economic boom was shaken. . . .

Unemployment and underemployment along the international border increased throughout the eighties. In the early 1980s Laredo's unemployment rate stood at 10 percent, and in 1983 the unemployment rate increased to 25 percent, which represented 11,000 workers. From 1984 to 1988 unemployment levels fluctuated between 16 and 13 percent, about double the overall rate in Texas. Not until 1989 and 1990 did unemployment level off, at approximately 10 percent.

The leveling-off of the unemployment rate was a result of the overall increase in Laredo's labor force in 1989–1990. The number of nonagricultural wage and salaried employees rose from 40,800 to 42,700 between 1988 and 1989. Employment also climbed 8 percent in wholesale and retail trade, and 5 percent in total manufacturing. Finance, insurance, real estate, and government employment, however, saw a decrease in jobs (Texas Employment Commission 1990).

Official unemployment rates in Laredo, however, are understated because they do not include persons who have ceased to look for work and other legal residents who are not considered. These official statistics also do not include unemployed Mexicans from Nuevo Laredo. Thousands of these jobless Mexicans, who face high unemployment and extreme inflation in their country, commute to Laredo in search of work. This unemployed sector, estimated as high as 40 percent of Nuevo Laredo's population, exacerbates the social and economic problems experienced by Laredo residents.

The Maquiladora Industry: Laredo's Contemporary Economy

Laredo's contemporary economy continues to serve a Mexican market, but has moved to one based primarily on international manufacturing, export, and trade. This economy is largely dependent on maquiladoras, which are non-Mexican owned factories and assembly plants along the border. The Mexican government provides the maquiladora industry with substantial duty and tariff advantages. Most U.S. companies involved in maquiladoras have established labor-intensive twin plants along the U.S.-Mexico border. These firms are involved in cloth and fabric production, leather production, clay products, electronic and electrical equipment, and transportation equipment. Rising labor costs in the United States make the relatively cheap labor in Mexican border communities attractive to U.S. manufacturers. These companies have the best of both worlds with low-cost, quality production in Mexico and well-developed markets in the United States. . . .

[T]he growth of the maquiladora industry has not had a significant impact on the economic status of this population, particularly that of Mexican Americans in Laredo. This industry has done little, overall, to develop Laredo and other Texas border communities economically. Most maquiladora factories adjacent to Laredo, for instance, purchase their primary raw materials from non-Texas suppliers, and industrial supplies and services from non-border cities.

Laredo has benefited from the maquiladora industry mainly through income spent by maquiladora workers in the service trade sector and increased business to transportation and warehousing firms. In service trades Mexican Americans often find themselves competing with Mexican nationals, particularly at the entry-level positions. Mexican Americans were hired to some extent at blue-collar positions in the transportation and warehouse industry. However, many of the managerial positions generated by this industry went to persons from outside south Texas. Native Mexican-origin persons in Laredo were in the main not hired for these jobs, owing to their lack of education and/or job experience and in some cases discrimination.

Persistent Poverty

Although poverty levels fluctuated during the 1980s, by 1989 they had reached levels consistent with those of the previous decades. Laredo's economic transformation favored upper-class and middle-class Mexican Americans and skilled managers and professionals from outside south Texas. These were the persons who had the skills and capital to take advantage of the opportunities offered by these economic changes. The majority of Laredo's Mexican Americans, however, continued to survive at economically low-subsistence levels.

In 1990, 37 percent (52,635) of the total population of Laredo (Webb County) lived below the official poverty line as compared to 34.5 percent (31,291) in 1980. The poverty rate in Laredo runs more than double that of Texas and triple that of the United States. In 1980, 30 percent of families were impoverished compared to 39 percent in 1970. Despite the decrease of families living in poverty from 1970 to 1980, the rate was still 100 to 200 percent higher than the state or the nation. Laredo also has a disproportionate share of female-headed households . . .

During the 1980s . . . the instances of teen pregnancies steadily increased (from 23 percent of all births in 1983 to 28 percent in

1986). The demand on public and private assistance programs rose after the devaluation crisis of 1982. In 1990, 2300 families were on federal Aid to Families with Dependent Children (AFDC) for a total of 5172 children. . . .

Poverty levels are reinforced by low levels of human capital skills. [(i.e., low median years of schooling completed, low high school graduation rates)]. . . Laredo also has a disproportionate percentage of foreign-born. . . The majority of these were Mexican nationals, but these figures do not include the undocumented Mexicans living in this city. This large immigrant population influences language and other ethnic variables. In Laredo, for instance, 94 percent of all persons age 5 years or older speak a language other than English.

Table 36.1
Number of New Applications for Food Stamps and Total Caseload, 1983–1988

Year	New Applications	Total Case Load
1983	5676	36,306
1984	3996	37,363
1985	3652	35,955
1986	4068	36,084
1987	3816	36,879
1988	4212	37,494

Source: Texas Department of Human Resources, 1989.

Poverty has had a devastating effect on the psychic well-being of residents as well. According to Laredo social service workers, caseloads have continued to increase over the last few years. Many clients exhibited anxiety and stress disorders. Children's referrals have doubled, with slight increases in the number of people applying for mental disability under the federal Supplemental Security Income (SSI) program.

Crime Indicators, Drug Violations, and Drug-Related Murders

Persistent poverty among large segments of Laredo's population generates various adaptation patterns as the poor find innovative means to subsist economically. This may include government assistance programs, self-employment with undeclared income, and/or

illicit behavior, particularly related to drugs in the 1980s.

Borders politically divide economic markets by restricting the exchange of goods, services, and people between two nations. This situation structurally creates conditions conducive to illicit commerce and contraband. The large discrepancy in economic status between the United States and Mexico reinforces the opportunity structures for these types of illegal activities.

In Laredo, as in many other U.S.-Mexico border communities, contraband retail trade is a major economic activity, often involving legitimate business and commercial sectors. Stock in trade includes stolen vehicles, guns, and the traffic of undocumented immigrants. Laredo is a city with extensive trafficking in drugs, primarily marijuana, heroin, and cocaine. The exact proportion of the population involved in some illicit activity in Laredo is difficult to determine, but compared to non-border communities the proportion is certainly high. The extensiveness of these illicit activities, moreover, creates a climate and culture of permissiveness toward this type of behavior.

The official crime rate in Laredo in 1984 was 68 (crimes per 10,000 inhabitants) and had increased to 89 by 1988. . . . According to the Laredo Police Department, increases in crime were largely related to drug activity. For instance, 85 percent of burglaries are estimated to be drug-related. The most significant increase was in the category of theft under $50, which consist mostly of shoplifting cases that are associated with drug addicts.

The Uniform Crime Report data on Webb County show that overall drug violations increased 46 percent from 1987 to 1988. . . . These data indicate that violations related to possession of illegal substances increased overall by 60 percent and marijuana possession by 79 percent.

Use and marketing of drugs and contrabanding of illegal aliens across the U.S./Mexican border are linked in the Laredo area. In 1988 there was a slight decrease, compared to 1987, in alien apprehension. As alien smuggling decreased, however, narcotics smuggling increased. The Border Patrol reports the total value of drugs confiscated increased 60 percent (U.S. Border Patrol 1989). Marijuana was the primary drug seized, followed by cocaine and heroin. . . .

Law enforcement officials claim that Texas, along with New Mexico, Arizona, and California, is becoming the preferred route for smuggling drugs into the United States. Some estimate that about 40 percent of all drugs smuggled into the United States pass through south Texas (U.S. Border Patrol 1989). . . .

Drug-trafficking activities were a causal factor in the majority of murders from 1985 to 1989. Although most murders in the Laredo area are not officially designated as drug-related, most persons familiar with the circumstances involved disagree. Based on discussions with different sources [between] 1985 to 1989 . . . 68 persons were murdered in Laredo; 61 percent (42 persons) of these murders were drug-related.

Increased levels of crime in Laredo are also related to the population's disproportionate substance-abuse problems, particularly related to its intravenous drug (IVD) users. Estimates of the number of intravenous drug users in Laredo vary. Use of the National Institute of Drug Abuse's (NIDA) method of estimating drug prevalence during a six-month period results in an estimate of 4530 persons in Webb county who use intravenous drugs (Balli 1989). Others have estimated that the population involved in IVD use is as high as 12,000. A reasonable estimate, based on the cumulative data in this analysis, would be approximately 5000 to 6000 IVD users in the Laredo area out of a total population of 113,000.

The social pathology generated by these IVD addicts and users reverberates throughout the community, particularly affecting the users' immediate families, friends, and neighborhoods. For instance, many arrests for shoplifting, burglary, and auto theft are in neighborhoods with a high proportion of addicts. As previously mentioned, these offenses are closely associated with intravenous drug users.

The Impact of Poverty and Crime: Three Distinct Neighborhoods

By focusing on three specific low-income neighborhoods, this section analyzes how social, economic, and ecological factors facilitate the development and continuation of illicit activities. Most of these data were gathered from field observation and interviews.

The pervasive poverty of Laredo means that low-income residential areas are found throughout the city. In this type of environment, impoverished families experience various forms of disorganization. As a result, the poor often engage in innovative behavior as a means to adapt to the social and economic conditions they confront. Many Laredo residents turn to drugs and alcohol as an escape from reality. Others take advantage of the opportunity presented by the international border to engage in various types of illicit activities.

La Azteca

La Azteca, located on the Rio Grande River east of the new international bridge and west of the power plant, is one of the oldest barrios in Laredo. Most of its residents are elderly first-generation Mexican Americans, recent Mexican immigrants, and young Mexican American families. Many who live here are Mexican nationals with relatives in the residential area located immediately on the opposite bank of the river in Nuevo Laredo. The barrio covers about ten square blocks, consisting of densely built single-family clapboard homes and a labyrinth of narrow unpaved streets that often end in cul-de-sacs. Many of these structures are weather-beaten wooden shacks that seem ready to fall over from age and neglect. The majority of the homes are owner-occupied, but the residents are too poor to invest in repairs. Other properties in the area are owned by speculators who patiently await development of this area.

The major characteristic of the Azteca is its accessibility to Nuevo Laredo, particularly its sister community, La Victoria, across the river, The shallowness of the Rio Grande, and Azteca's proximity to downtown Laredo, provides an ideal environment for contrabanding. Once across the border, individuals can hide in the dense foliage on the islands that separate the two banks of the Rio Grande, then find cover in the Azteca neighborhood, and finally slip unnoticed into the streets of downtown Laredo. The location is so convenient that many Mexicans living in Nuevo

Laredo with day jobs in Laredo use this crossing daily.

Many residents of Azteca are involved in smuggling undocumented immigrants into the United States. . . . Other forms of illicit activities in the Azteca area include smuggling goods such as guns, electrical appliances, and other retail merchandise.

Much of the illicit drug activity in La Azteca centers around a group of young men between the ages of 17 and 25, most of whom are intravenous drug users addicted to heroin. These individuals are in the early stages of the drug-use life cycle typical of Laredo's male IVD population. Many of these young men begin drinking beer, smoking marijuana, sniffing glue, and taking pills in their early teens. They often come from broken families, where there is little parental supervision. They have been raised in poor neighborhoods, socially and geographically isolated in some of the worst barrios in Laredo. Schools and other public institutions are not perceived as challenging viable alternatives. Most of them are unemployed high school dropouts, their identity centered around cliques of family and neighborhood peers.

In the Azteca many of the addicts support their addiction by illicit activities facilitated by the neighborhood's strategic geographic location. As in other communities along the Rio Grande, many of Azteca's young IVD users secure resources by transporting Mexicans and Central Americans. One 19-year-old IVD user is living with his parents:

> He shoots up once or twice a week. He makes his money for drugs by stealing and transporting aliens from this side of the river to the downtown area. He gets paid $30 for each person.

This activity has a fast yield and does not take a lot of organization. Young IVD users in La Azteca are familiar with the patterns of the Border Patrol and have developed a system to minimize risks.

Dealing in drugs is another source of income for many young users. Throughout these low-income neighborhoods dealers bring in small quantities of heroin and marijuana to distribute within Laredo. Larger quantities of drugs destined for outside markets (Houston, San Antonio, and other major cities) are smuggled through isolated crossings. The Azteca area is used by those with more limited resources, especially small-time drug pushers and users. These persons do not have the connections or experience to deal drugs at a higher level. Usually, if trust has been established with neighborhood pushers, established dealers may front them small amounts of heroin to distribute. The more extensive dealing is conducted by older IVD users.

La Ladrillera

Ladrillera is located across a series of railroad tracks by the river adjacent to the U.S.-Mexico border. This is one of the poorest communities in Laredo. The area is flat and dusty from the heavy truck and rail traffic. Many streets are unpaved with no sidewalks. Housing is predominately single-family clapboard homes on large lots set back some twenty yards from the street. Many streets dead-end on the banks of the Rio Grande or in the railyards.

To enter Ladrillera, you cross the tracks joining the National Railroad of Mexico and the Missouri Pacific, then pass acres of parked semitrailers to reach the community. Much of the legitimate U.S.-Mexico export and import trade ships through this area. Furthermore, much illegitimate trade in marijuana, cocaine, and heroin goes through Ladrillera. Authorities continually intercept semitrailers leaving this area with large loads of marijuana. The trains are also used by undocumented Mexicans and other immigrants to leave the border region.

Ladrillera is characterized by long-term residents with multigenerational family ties. Although a majority of these families are Mexican American, there is a minority of Mexican immigrant families in this community. Residents comprise close-knit exclusive networks where loyalty to extended family and neighborhood takes precedence over everything else. These characteristics, as well as the opportunities offered by the accessibility of the river, ecological isolation, and access to transportation, make it an ideal location for large-scale contrabanding.

As in communities all along the U.S.-Mexico border, several groups here are involved in high-volume alien and drug smuggling. Some of these networks are more elaborate than others, but the basic unit of organization is the family and/or neighborhood-based friendship cliques. These types of groups control a vast amount of marijuana, heroin, and cocaine, smuggled across the border. There is no large organized syndicate of drug dealers that dominates the drug trade in this region. The permeable border and the easy availability of these drugs preclude such dominance.

People involved in illicit activities are often supported by family and community networks. For those who leave their family of orientation and form their own nuclear families, marriage shifts the support system from parents to wives and the new relationships that accompany this change in status. Wives and children now must endure the many social and personal crises that are part of this subculture. For the wife, this often means being married to a person who holds no steady job, leads a life centered around illicit activities, and is incarcerated for long periods of time.

Ladrillera has a disproportionate number of IVD users. This means that their life is often centered on illicit activities essential to support their addiction. Throughout the different stages of the life cycle, these individuals find a social sanctuary within the family. Informants repeatedly referred to heroin users who return to live with their parents after long prison terms, during which time they had been divorced by their wives. Others live with brothers, uncles, or other close relatives. These families continue to support the intravenous drug user despite all the problems of living with them.

Santo Niño

Located on the southern fringes of the city along the Zapata Highway, Santo Niño is characterized as a highly exclusive and closely knit community of working-poor Mexican American families. Neighborhoods in this area have high levels of crime and drug abuse. The highway that runs through this area is lined with auto parts stores, tire shops, junkyards, automobile repair shops, and auto body shops. Several of these businesses

are known as "chopshops," where stolen cars are stripped and the parts resold on the black market. Other businesses, particularly restaurants and nightclubs, are legitimate fronts for known drug dealers and other participants in the border's underground economy. Many of the tire-repair shops are known as "copping places" and "shooting galleries" for drugs. That is, heroin addicts may buy drugs and intravenously use them at these locations.

Santo Niño is dominated by owner-occupied homes. Neighborhood roads and streets are mostly unpaved and without sidewalks. Because many families are migrant farm workers who travel throughout the Midwest during the summer and only reside here during the winter, many of these homes are often boarded up. Children of the migrants often do not attend school for the full nine months and have disproportionately high drop-out rates. These children frequently become involved in illegal drugs and other unlawful activities.

Santo Niño residents are involved in a wide array of crimes, which include smuggling guns and undocumented aliens, stolen-car rings, and the distribution of marijuana, cocaine, and heroin, both locally and to areas throughout the United States. These neighborhoods have a high proportion of heroin addicts, many of them young men 17–25 years old. Being on heroin at this stage in life makes it difficult to hold steady employment, particularly since most young users have little education or marketable job skills. Most of their energy is spent getting cash to buy drugs for the day. This type of user cannot usually deal drugs successfully, and will not be able to use this means to supply his own habit. Their only access to cash is through shoplifting, breaking and entering into homes and businesses, and hustling and conning parents, family, and anyone else gullible enough to fall for their tactics.

Another type of intravenous drug user in these communities is a more mature and stable male. He usually starts shooting heroin as a young man and continues to do so throughout his life. He might have ceased using heroin intermittently, for instance, during periods of incarceration or detoxication attempts. This user might support his habit by dealing heroin himself. Maturity and extensive contacts cultivated over years of involvement in this life-style provide the discipline and knowledge to deal successfully. Others in this category might support their habit by shoplifting, often with a female partner who is a junkie herself. Shoplifting among these *veteranos*, compared to the younger *tecatos*, is more sophisticated, elaborate, and lucrative. Others within this group are involved in more organized crime activities, usually working with or for others. This includes well-organized stolen-car rings, Mexican-immigrant-smuggling operations, large-scale drug dealing, and other high-level criminal activity.

Pecos Street, typical of the many neighborhoods in Santo Niño, is located off the Zapata Highway in the southern part of this area. Pecos Street intersects with the major highway leading south from Laredo to Zapata, Texas. This neighborhood consists of single-family clapboard homes and unpaved, pot-holed streets that turn into mud during the rainy season. Fifteen years ago the Pecos Street neighborhood began to change substantially. One resident recalls:

> When we moved here about 18 years ago, we were one of the few houses in this area. The area was all monte [brush country]. You could see all the way down to the creek beds from our back yards.

Today the neighborhood has been absorbed in Laredo's metropolitan expansion and is densely populated.

For years the Pecos Street area was a small barrio where neighbors were close acquaintances and could rely on each other for favors. Families were poor, but they grew up in a community that offered sanctuary from the outside world. Residents left their homes unlocked without worrying about burglaries or vandalism. That has all drastically changed.

One resident has lived on Pecos Street for twenty years, not far from his mother, who is 70 years old and who has lived alone ever since her husband died. This person returned from military service about twelve years ago, bought a house trailer, and moved it onto his parent's lot after marrying a woman from Nuevo Laredo. The neighborhood has drastically changed during the last five years. This person has put up a six-foot-high chain link fence around his property, and he keeps two large Dobermans that viciously bark at everything that gets within thirty feet of the lot. The fence and dogs are a result of the burglaries that now characterize Pecos Street. . . .

The burglaries coincided with the appearance of heroin in the Pecos Street area. Conditions have deteriorated since two heroin dealers set up business within a block of each other. He said, "I got one heroin dealer on that side [pointing east] and another [pointing west]." The availability of heroin in the neighborhood now means that more young men are hooked.

> We never had so much crime in the area. And, you can't talk to these kids. The other day I woke up and my trailer was getting bombarded by bricks thrown by some neighborhood kids. The next day, I went to their father. He said that I shouldn't approach the kids. He would handle it. They are too dangerous.

The problems faced by families such as these are typical in these communities. They are the victims of the changing economic structure of the border economy.

Conclusion

Mexican Americans in this region traditionally have had exceedingly high levels of poverty. Laredo's recent economic prosperity did little to change the social composition of the Mexican American population in this border community . . .

A major difference between Laredo's poor communities and those associated with the [mostly African-American urban] underclass (Wilson 1987), however, is that these communities are more institutionally complete. Strong extended families are the major sustaining social structure in Laredo barrios. Mexican American neighborhoods are more residentially stable, and have a high proportion of home ownership. There are also greater interclass relations found in Mexican American neighborhoods. These social factors, along with a dominant ethnic culture, create a strong sense of community structure and identification missing in the black underclass.

One of the major differences between to-day and previous periods is that Laredo's poor are being increasingly affected by criminal activities. This study has indicated that a wide segment of the Laredo community is taking advantage of the illicit opportunities offered by the U.S.-Mexican border for their economic survival. Among the poor, crime centers around smuggling undocumented immigrants, guns, and stolen automobiles, and in particular drugs. Drug activities are carried out by exclusive networks of family and friends usually based in multigenerational neighborhoods. These networks may be small, and their operations limited to Laredo, whereas others are larger, organized drug networks with connections in Mexico and other cities throughout the United States.

These activities and conditions make drugs widely accessible in this community. The availability of heroin in particular means that many young men and women become addicts and are forced to support their habits from their local neighborhoods—by breaking and entering, shoplifting, conning relatives and friends, and other predatory behavior. Addicts in a community are socially and economically disruptive, and linked to increased crime rates in Laredo over the last ten years, primarily thefts and burglaries. This aspect of Laredo's poor closely resembles under-class conditions and may indicate a trend toward the formulation of an underclass in this community and others along the U.S.-Mexico border. The recent economic transformations and related social characteristics, however, have not at this period created an underclass in this region as it may have among groups elsewhere in the United States.

References

Balli, Jakim. 1989. "The Development of a Drug Abuse Prevalence Estimate in Webb County, Texas." Unpublished paper, Our Lady of the Lake University. School of Social Work, San Antonio, Texas.

Hanson, N. 1981. *The Border Economy*. Austin: University of Texas Press.

Harrell, L., and D. Fischer. 1985. "The 1982 Mexico Peso Devaluation and Border Area Employment." *Monthly Labor Review* 108: 25–32.

Harrington, M. 1984. *The New American Poverty*. New York: Penguin Books.

Martinez, O. 1983. "The Foreign Orientation of the Mexican Border Economy." *Border Perspectives*, no. 2. El Paso, TX: Center for Interamerican and Border Studies, University of Texas, El Paso.

Miller, M.J. 1983. "Recent Growth in Texas Border Metropolitan Areas: Progress or Illusions for the Mexican-American Community." Unpublished paper.

Moore, J. 1989. "Is There a Hispanic Underclass?" *Social Science Quarterly* 70: 265–283.

Texas Employment Commission. 1990. "South Texas Source Delivery Area." *Planning Information PY 1991*. Austin: ERA Department.

U.S. Border Patrol, Laredo Sector 1989. "End of the Month News Releases." Laredo, TX, June.

Wilson, W.J. 1985. "Cycles of Deprivation and the Underclass Debate." *Social Service Review* 59: 541–591.

———. 1987. *The Truly Disadvantaged: The Inner City, the Underclass, and Public Policy*. Chicago: University of Chicago Press.

Interracial and Interethnic Conflict*

During the 1980s and 1990s, major cities around the U.S. have witnessed a surge in interracial and interethnic tensions, which have sometimes erupted in violence. A few prominent examples illustrate this disturbing trend.

- Perhaps the best-known such conflict emerged following the original verdict in the trial of Los Angeles police officers accused of beating an African American man, Rodney King, in 1992. In the rioting (some prefer the term "rebellion") that followed, numerous businesses in South-Central Los Angeles were destroyed and there was widespread looting and violence. While angry African American residents were involved in many of these incidents, much of their animosity was directed not at European Americans, but instead at Asian Americans who owned stores in the area. Adding to the complexity of this incident, approximately half of those arrested in the aftermath were Latinos, including many recent immigrants from Mexico and Central America (Miles 1992).

- In Los Angeles (Ong et al., this volume) and several other cities (e.g., New York, Chicago), there have been recurrent conflicts between inner-city African American residents and Asian American (especially Korean American) merchants (Min 1996; Yoon 1997). On several occasions, local black leaders and activists have organized protests and boycotts against these shopkeepers because of various practices and slights (real and alleged), which are discussed further below.

- In Miami, longstanding tensions between inner-city African Americans and Cuban Americans have boiled over into violence on several occasions in the past two decades (Portes and Stepick 1993). On one occasion, rioting was sparked by the acquittal of a Latino police officer who killed an African American man. Another violent dispute centered on the poor treatment of Nelson Mandela—at that time, leader of the anti-apartheid movement in South Africa—by Cuban-American city officials and conservative radio talk show hosts during his visit to that city.

- In May of 1991, several Washington, D.C. neighborhoods erupted in two days of rioting. Commercial businesses were looted, small fires were set, and numerous acts of vandalism and attacks on police were also reported. These "civil disturbances" followed an incident in which an African American policewoman shot a Salvadoran immigrant while attempting to arrest him for public intoxication. Latinos (mainly Salvadorans) engaged in various acts of violent protest against what was perceived to be a longstanding pattern of police abuse of racial and ethnic minorities in the District. African Americans, and

---

* This Introduction was written by Velma McBride Murry of the University of Georgia and the editors.

even some European Americans from adjacent neighborhoods, subsequently joined the unrest (Manning 1996).

- In Compton, California, a predominantly African American suburb of Los Angeles, the rapidly growing Latino/a minority has clashed with city officials in their quest for a larger share of police, fire, and other civil service jobs. Latino/a residents have also accused the primarily African American police of using excessive force against Latino/a suspects.

- In a widely publicized incident, tensions between African Americans and members of a Hasidic Jewish community in the Crown Heights area of Brooklyn (NY) boiled over into violence. Although the underlying dynamics of the long-running conflict are complex, the violence was sparked by an auto accident in which a chauffeur driving the spiritual leader of the Hasidic community ran over and killed a seven-year-old African-American boy.

In some respects, these confrontations seem to mark a return to the levels of urban violence that were evident during the 1960s and early 1970s. However, there is at least one critical difference: Whereas the intergroup tensions of that period almost always involved African Americans and whites, prominent conflicts now routinely pit African Americans against Latino/a Americans, Asian Americans, and other persons and groups of color. The black-white paradigm which traditionally guided our view of intergroup relations in America has clearly become obsolete.

These clashes over residential space, economic mobility, social status, and political power are best understood within a larger historical and structural context. The dynamics of contemporary urban conflicts may have parallels in earlier historical eras. Successive waves of immigration from southern, central, and eastern Europe in the late 1800s and early 1900s were accompanied by significant interethnic and interreligious antagonisms. Then large numbers of African Americans migrated from the South to the urban North in the early decades of the twentieth century, often taking jobs in manufacturing

and service occupations, including domestic work (Lemann 1991). These African American migrants provided cheap labor for Northern enterprises, and were sometimes recruited to serve as strikebreakers and to fill domestic industrial labor shortages during World War I. As African Americans competed for working-class jobs and residential space with ethnic whites, those whites employed a range of strategies, including violence, to preserve their social distance and relative advantage vis-à-vis blacks (Wilson 1978; Lieberson 1980). During the 1880–1914 period, anti-black and other forms of ethnic violence were especially likely in those cities that faced economic stagnation, rising unemployment rates, and high levels of immigration (Olzak 1992).

Broadly similar structural dynamics may underlie more recent episodes of interracial and interethnic conflict in our cities (Olzak and Shanahan 1996). Since the 1960s there has been a dramatic increase in the numbers and proportions of immigrants of color—particularly those from Mexico (and from violence-torn regions of Central America) and from various Asian countries. These new immigrants have clustered overwhelmingly in urban areas. While New York, Chicago, and other East Coast or Midwestern cities received the lion's share of immigrants prior to 1960, Los Angeles has become the single most popular destination for new arrivals; in recent years, approximately one in every five immigrants to the U.S. has chosen to live in the Los Angeles metro area (Bozorgmehr et al. 1996).

Industrial restructuring has taken a heavy toll on African Americans, Puerto Ricans, and other immigrant groups in Northern and Eastern cities like New York (Waldinger 1996). Cities in the Northeastern and Midwestern United States have lost large numbers of relatively high-paying blue-collar jobs, as plants and firms have closed down or relocated to more profitable areas. Remaining businesses have implemented labor-saving technologies that have reduced demand for workers, especially those with modest skill levels. These changes have been accompanied by some growth in the numbers of service sector jobs, but many of those openings require education or special skills that are beyond the immediate reach of most minority inner-city residents or new immigrants. Although not all observers agree on this point, many have concluded that the realistic available employment options for unskilled or low-skill workers in these cities have declined since 1970, or at best, have failed to keep up with rising demand. The transformation of New York, Washington (DC), and other Snowbelt cities into "postindustrial" economies has also caused fiscal shortfalls, creating severe problems for local governments seeking to fund infrastructure, education, and various social services (Waldinger 1996; Manning 1998).

Until recently, Sunbelt cities like Los Angeles have fared better than their cities in other regions of the country. In the late 1980s and early 1990s, however, Southern California experienced an economic downturn, due to military base closures and declines in military procurement (e.g., new weapons systems) at the end of the Cold War, along with stagnation in some high-tech industries (e.g., semiconductor manufacturing). Overall manufacturing employment in Los Angeles rose from 881,000 in 1969 to 925,000 in 1987, but then dropped to 895,000 in 1991 (Bozorgmehr et al. 1996). During roughly the same period, the Los Angeles area underwent a substantial transformation in the composition of its manufacturing employment. The proportion of manufacturing employment in low-tech, labor-intensive industries (e.g., textiles, clothing, furniture) jumped from 16 percent in 1970 to 26 percent in 1990, with many of these jobs going to Latino/a and Asian immigrants. This shift was accompanied by gradual declines in the shares of manufacturing jobs in high-tech fields (e.g., electronics, aerospace) and metallurgical and mechanical industries (Scott 1996). Some analysts suggest that the changes have hurt African Americans especially, and that frustration over layoffs and other symptoms of this transformation may have played a role in the urban unrest that rocked Los Angeles in the early 1990s (Johnson et al. 1992).

These structural dilemmas are exacerbated by the dearth of affordable housing in major cities, and by the disturbing pattern of large-scale "white flight." Middle-class European Americans (and many upwardly mobile African Americans, Latino/a Americans, and Asian Americans as well) have been moving to the suburbs that ring central cities since the 1960s, leaving behind those who lack the resources or ability to follow. Moreover, recent evidence indicates that significant numbers of whites are now migrating well beyond the suburban rim. Whereas California was once the premier destination for white migrants from the Eastern and Midwestern U.S., many whites are now leaving California (and other racially and ethnically diverse states) for regions of the country with very small numbers of African Americans and other persons of color (e.g., the Mountain states and the Pacific Northwest). Although these relocation patterns are occurring ostensibly because of public concerns about crime, declining schools, and other problems in urban settings, some observers suspect that racial and ethnic biases are at work, and they warn about the consequences of continued balkanization (Frey 1996).

These migratory flows, together with large-scale immigration and the other processes mentioned above, are leaving large and growing populations of color in major cities, where they are often competing for a stagnant or decreasing pool of resources. Not surprisingly, the shifts in population composition have been especially stark in Los Angeles (Sabagh and Bozorgmehr 1996). In 1960, non-Hispanic whites made up approximately 80.5 percent of that city's population; 30 years later, that figure had dropped to only 40.8 percent. By contrast, the Latino/a share exploded during the same period, from under 10 percent to 36.4 percent. While African Americans outnumbered Asian Americans (including Pacific Islanders) by more than 3-to-1 in 1960 (7.6 percent vs. 2.2 percent), their respective shares of the Los Angeles population were virtually even by 1990 (11.2 percent vs. 11.0 percent), with the Asian American component growing more rapidly due to high levels of immigration (Bozorgmehr et al. 1996).

Miami has also undergone a dramatic transformation. The Greater Miami population is now more than half Latino; clearly the majority of this Latino segment is of Cuban birth or descent. Nearly 25 percent of the areas' residents are black—native-born African Americans or immigrants from the Caribbean (primarily, though not exclusively, Haitians). In the meantime, the numbers of non-Hispanic white residents declined by 24 percent during the 1980s, due largely to high mortality rates among the elderly and the diversion of new retirees to other parts of Florida (Grenier and Perez 1996). Other cities have experienced substantial, albeit less dramatic, changes in population composition in recent decades.

In light of these variegated social processes, what are the specific mechanisms that foster diverse expressions of interracial and interethnic animosity, within our major cities and beyond? As we suggested earlier, some areas may be characterized by what ecologists call "niche overlap," in particular, competition between African Americans and other persons of color for similar types of employment opportunities. While many of the jobs in question (e.g., service, light manufacturing) are neither lucrative nor prestigious, access to such positions remains important for both African Americans and immigrant populations. To date, the evidence regarding job competition remains mixed. In general, reviews of econometric studies have revealed few, if any, effects of immigration on the wages of African Americans (e.g., Heer 1996; Waldinger 1996). Nevertheless, some recent studies provide evidence of displacement and exclusion in specific occupations (Scott 1996; Waldinger 1997). It appears that certain niches that were traditionally "held" by African Americans are increasingly occupied by Latino/a Americans, including recent immigrants from Central America. One example of this trend involves domestic servants (i.e., housekeepers, gardeners), especially in the Southwestern United States (Miles 1992, Hondagneu-Sotelo 1994; Baker 1997; Hagan 1998). However, the precise degree of direct labor market competition and displacement of African Americans by immigrants remains the focus of ongoing research and debate (see Hamermesh and Bean 1997).

In addition to competing for employment opportunities, African Americans and various immigrant populations also engage in other forms of competition that generate tension and conflict. African Americans constitute the majority of residents in many urban neighborhoods, and may perceive the incursions of other groups (e.g. Latino and Asian immigrant populations) into these traditionally black areas as threatening. These processes of residential succession may even predate the onset of other forms of interracial and interethnic competition (e.g. in labor markets). In an intriguing analysis supporting this view, Bergesen and Herman (1998) show that fatalities during the 1992 riot in Los Angeles were highest in those Census tracts in which African American hegemony was being threatened. Indeed, measures of ethnic residential succession were stronger predictors of riot fatalities than standard measures of economic deprivation or decline, such as changes in unemployment rates or earnings.

Besides the threat of (real or perceived) competition for jobs and other resources, there have been perennial disputes between the residents of inner-city neighborhoods—mostly African Americans—and members of other racial and ethnic groups serving as economic "middlemen." These middlemen are merchants who sell products in predominantly black neighborhoods while usually residing elsewhere (Ong et al., this volume). In the 1960s, this description fit significant numbers of Jewish shopkeepers in inner-city areas (Aldrich 1973); in many cities today, these merchants are Asian American, particularly Korean American. In Los Angeles, Brooklyn (NY), Chicago, and other cities, African American groups have initiated boycotts and other actions aimed at undermining Korean-owned businesses in black neighborhoods, and/or forcing changes in the practices and customer relations of these establishments (Yoon 1997).

Relations between African Americans and Korean American shopkeepers have been strained by a number of factors. Some of the problems are traceable to the "middleman minority" role of these Korean businesses (Min 1996). African American activists in various cities have charged that Korean merchants gouge their customers by charging high prices for low-quality merchandise. This may occur in some cases. However, because the businesses are usually small, and because inner-city markets can be limited, these merchants are frequently unable to benefit from economies of scale, and they also confront high costs of doing business in these areas (e.g., crime, high insurance rates). Korean entrepreneurs also tend to rely heavily on family and coethnic labor, frustrating many African Americans who prefer that these businesses help the community by hiring more neighbohood residents, especially black youths. Critics also point out that some "middleman minority" enterprises are unwholesome (e.g., pawnshops, liquor stores); such businesses profit from poverty and despair, but generate few benefits for the surrounding communities (Ong et al., this volume).

Further, African Americans in several cities have mobilized against particular Korean American shopkeepers who seem to stereotype and discriminate against neighborhood residents, particularly young black males. Critics charge that Korean merchants routinely treat African American customers discourteously, and that they view young blacks as potential criminals, and monitor their actions closely. Indeed, there have been several well-publicized incidents in Los Angeles and elsewhere in which Korean American shopkeepers have used violence against young African American customers, allegedly to thwart robbery attempts. On several of these occasions, community residents have been outraged when the merchants were treated with leniency by the courts (Yoon 1997).

Cultural differences have also heightened the suspicion and mistrust between communities. For instance, many Korean immigrants were not accustomed to policies that provide for refunds or exchanges in case of defective products. Their initial reluctance to allow such policies fueled resentment among many African Americans (Yoon 1997). In addition, the limited English language facility of some Korean shopkeepers has occasionally resulted in miscommunication with African American customers (Min 1996).

More broadly, many African Americans in inner-city neighborhoods tend to resent the rapid social and economic mobility of some recent immigrant groups—particularly Asian Americans on the West Coast and Cuban Americans in the Miami area (Miles 1992; Grenier and Perez 1996). Some community activists believe—often incorrectly—that immigrant entrepreneurs have received favorable treatment from banks and other institutions that is unavailable to native-born African Americans. The feelings of exploitation and dependency that sometimes result from dealings with "middleman minority" groups are particulary frustrating to individuals and organizations advocating greater economic autonomy for urban African American communities.

Despite these problems, observers caution against exaggerating the tensions between African Americans and Korean immigrants. Many of the disputes between Korean merchants and black customers have resulted from simple business matters (e.g., haggling over prices, return policies), and have been resolved without major incident. Boycotts of Korean-owned businesses in cities around the country have drawn only minimal African American support, and most campaigns have been organized by activists and black nationalist groups outside the neighborhoods (Min 1996). Some observers also blame slanted and sensationalistic media coverage for fueling black-Korean tensions (Abelmann and Lie 1995). In the wake of these conflicts, some Korean American merchants and business groups in Los Angeles and other cities have undertaken various efforts to improve relations with their African American neighbors and customers (Light and Bonacich 1988: 320-24; Min 1996: 126-45).

At a broader level, some interracial and interethnic tensions have also been exacerbated by policy disputes. This has been particularly important in the conflict between African Americans and Jews (Ginsberg 1993; Morris and Rubin, this volume), although it also bears upon the rift between African Americans and other groups, notably Cuban Americans in the Miami area (Portes and Stepick 1993, and this volume). In brief, some African American elected officials and others (especially those connected with the Nation of Islam, such as Louis Farrakhan) have expressed support for the Palestinian Liberation Organization (PLO), and for the leaders of various Muslim nations that remain hostile to the state of Israel. This has angered and alienated many Jewish Americans, who have traditionally supported African Americans and other minority groups in civil rights struggles (Ginsberg 1993). Several African-American academics and other public figures have made unfortunate and inflammatory public statements that seemed anti-Semitic in spirit—for example, charging (apparently inaccurately [Friedman 1997]) that Jews spearheaded the slave trade in the antebellum period. Some African-American commentators have also advocated reconsideration of Black-Jewish harmony in light of (a) the longstanding opposition of many otherwise liberal Jews to affirmative action and other racial/ethnic preference programs, and (b) the growth of neoconservatism among some relatively affluent Jewish business leaders and intellectuals. Nevertheless, while Black-Jewish tensions have received extensive media coverage, it is important not to exaggerate these rifts; some observers find reasons for optimism concerning the long-term relations between African Americans and Jews in the U.S. (Morris and Rubin, this volume).

Finally, no discussion of recent racial and ethnic tensions would be complete without some mention of emerging *intra*-ethnic divisions. A partial listing of these would include the generational, nationality, and class cleavages now observed among Latino/a and Asian Americans in areas of California, Texas and elsewhere, as well as the sometimes-competitive relations between native-born African Americans and recent Haitian immigrants in the Greater Miami area (Grenier and Perez 1996). According to some accounts, divisions within the Latino/a community were underscored during and after the Los Angeles rioting (or rebellion), in which new Mexican and Central American immigrants participated extensively, to the chagrin of many second- and third-generation Latinos (Miles 1992). In California nearly one-third (31 percent) of Latino/a voters and a clear majority (57 percent) of Asian American voters backed Proposition 187 (Martin 1997).

The complex structural dynamics and shifting urban environments described above defy easy summary. However, one lesson seems clear: Given the competitive dynamics among persons and groups of color, outlined above, creative leadership will be essential to minimize inter- and intragroup conflict, and to build a sense of community and shared destiny in the cities of the twenty-first century.

References

Abelmann, Nancy, and John Lie. 1995. *Blue Dreams: Korean Americans and the Los Angeles Riots.* Cambridge, MA: Harvard University Press.

Aldrich, Howard. 1973. "White-Owned Businesses in Black Ghettos." *American Journal of Sociology* 78: 1403–1426.

Baker, Susan Gonzalez. 1997. "A Window on Economic Restructuring: Domestic Service Workers in the Urban Economy." Paper presented at the annual meeting of the Population Association of America, Washington, D.C.

Bergesen, Albert, and Max Herman. 1998. " Immigration, Race, and Riot: The 1992 Los Angeles Uprising." *American Sociological Review* 63: 39-54.

Bobo, Lawrence, and Vincent L. Hutchings. 1996. "Perceptions of Racial Group Competition: Extending Blumer's Theory of Group Position to a Multiracial Social Context." *American Sociological Review* 61: 951–972.

Bozorgmehr, Mehdi, Georges Sabagh, and Ivan Light. 1996. "Los Angeles: Explosive Diversity." Pp. 346–359 in *Origins and Destinies: Immigration, Race, and Ethnicity in America,* edited by S. Pedraza and R. Rumbaut. Belmont, CA: Wadsworth.

Cummings, Scott, and Thomas Lambert. 1997. "Anti-Hispanic and Anti-Asian Sentiments Among African Americans." *Social Science Quarterly* 78: 338–353.

Frey, William. 1996. "Immigration, Domestic Migration, and Balkanization: New Evidence for the 1990s." *Population and Development Review* 22: 741–763.

Friedman, Saul S. 1997. *Jews and the American Slave Trade.* New Brunswick, NJ: Transaction.

Ginsberg, Benjamin. 1993. *The Fatal Embrace: Jews and the State.* Chicago: University of Chicago Press.

Grenier, Guillermo J., and Lisandro Perez. 1996. "Miami Spice: The Ethnic Cauldron Simmers." Pp. 360–372 in *Origins and Destinies: Immigration, Race, and Ethnicity in America,* edited by S.

Pedraza and R. Rumbaut. Belmont, CA: Wadsworth.

Hagan, Jacqueline Maria. 1998. "Social Networks, Gender, and Immigrant Incorporation: Resources and Constraints." *American Sociological Review* 63: 55-67.

Hamermesh, Daniel, and Frank D. Bean (eds.). 1997. *Help or Hindrance? The Economic Implications of Immigration for African Americans*. New York: Russell Sage Foundation.

Heer, David. 1996. *Immigration in America's Future*. Boulder, CO: Westview Press.

Hondagneu-Sotelo, Pierette. 1994. *Gendered Transitions: Mexican Experiences of Immigration*. Berkeley: University of California Press.

Johnson, James, Colyzelle Jones, Walter Farrell, and Melvin Oliver. 1992. "The Los Angeles Rebellion: A Retrospective." *Economic Development Quarterly* 6: 356–372.

Lemann, Nicholas. 1991. *The Promised Land: The Great Black Migration and How it Changed America*. New York: Alfred Knopf.

Lieberson, Stanley. 1980. *A Piece of the Pie: Blacks and White Immigrants Since 1880*. Berkeley: University of California Press.

Light, Ivan, and Edna Bonacich. 1988. *Immigrant Entrepreneurs: Koreans in Los Angeles, 1965–1982*. Berkeley: University of California Press.

Manning, Robert D. 1996. " Washington, D.C.: The Changing Social Landscape of the International Capital City." Pp. 373-389 in *Origins and Destinies: Immigration, Race, and Ethnicity in America*, edited by S. Pedraza and R. Rumbaut. Belmont, CA: Wadsworth.

——. 1998. "Multicultural Washington, D.C.: The Changing Social and Economic Landscape of a Post-Industrial Metropolis." *Ethnic and Racial Studies*.

Martin, Philip. 1997. "Proposition 1987 in California." Pp. 325–332 in *New American Destinies,* edited by Darrell Y. Hamamoto and Rodolfo D. Torres. New York: Routledge.

Miles, Jack. 1992. "Blacks vs. Browns (African Americans and Latinos)." *Atlantic Monthly* (October): 41–61.

Min, Pyong Gap. 1996. *Caught in the Middle: Korean Merchants in America's Multiethnic Cities*. Berkeley: University of California Press.

Olzak, Susan. 1992. *The Dynamics of Ethnic Competition and Conflict*. Stanford, CA: Stanford University Press.

Olzak, Susan, and Suzanne Shanahan. 1996. "Deprivation and Race Riots: An Extension of Spilerman's Analysis." *Social Forces* 74: 931–961.

Portes, Alejandro, and Alex Stepick. 1993. *City on the Edge: The Transformation of Miami*. Berkeley: University of California Press.

Sabagh, Georges, and Mehdi Bozorgmehr. 1996. "Population Change: Immigration and Ethnic Transformation." Pp. 79–107 in *Ethnic Los Angeles*, edited by Mehdi Boborgmehr and Roger Waldinger. New York: Russell Sage Foundation.

Scott, Allen J. 1996. "The Manufacturing Economy: Ethnic and Gender Divisions of Labor." Pp. 215–244 in *Ethnic Los Angeles*, edited by Mehdi Bozorgmehr and Roger Waldinger. New York: Russell Sage Foundation.

Waldinger, Roger. 1996. *Still the Promised City? African Americans and the New Immigrants in Post-Industrial New York*. Cambridge, MA: Harvard University Press.

Waldinger, Roger. 1997. "Black/Immigrant Competition Re-assessed: New Evidence from Los Angeles." *Sociological Perspectives* 40: 365–386.

Wilson, William Julius. 1978. *The Declining Significance of Race: Blacks and Changing Social Institutions*. Chicago: University of Chicago Press. 5/20/98

Yoon, In-Jin. 1997. *On My Own: Korean Businesses and Race Relations in America*. Chicago: University of Chicago Press.

37

The Turbulent Friendship:

Black-Jewish Relations in the 1990s

Milton D. Morris
Gary E. Rubin

For almost three decades now, the Black and Jewish communities have been debating the state of their relationship. On both sides the prevailing consensus is that a productive, long-standing relationship has been deteriorating, even though a wide variety of effective interactions continue. There is no agreement, however, about the extent of the deterioration or the forces contributing to it.

Analysts have given considerable attention to specific incidents or disagreements involving Blacks and Jews as indicators of the state of their relationship. . . . Invariably, commentators have viewed such incidents against a heavily retouched historical backdrop of a warm and trouble-free relationship. The result has been widespread failure to recognize and appreciate the broad currents and little complexities that have shaped Black-Jewish relations historically and continue to do so now.

This article suggests that claims of serious deterioration in Black-Jewish relations are exaggerated and often oversimplify a complex reality. Such claims reflect serious misperceptions of the history of Black-Jewish relations; inadequate knowledge and understanding of each community by the other; and failure to view the relationship in the context of profound changes in the circumstances of the two groups, in the bases for their interaction, and in the larger society. The study argues, further, that Blacks and Jews continue to share a relatively strong and mutually beneficial relationship and that this relationship needs to continue. But continuing it to maximum effectiveness will not be easy. . . .

Our Faulty Recollection of the Past

A common yet appropriate observation of Black-Jewish relations is that the good old days were never as good as we remember them. Claims of a rapidly deteriorating Black-Jewish relationship rest in part on the false assumption that there was once warm, conflict-free relationship. . . . The result is that most discussions aimed at improving Black-Jewish relations are steeped in nostalgic recollections of these presumably good old days, and implicit advocacy of recapturing that relationship.

Reality differed substantially from these recollections, however. Black-Jewish relations throughout more than 100 years of interaction were always substantially limited in scope and depth. Both groups found common cause as their needs and circumstances permitted. Jews became very early supporters of Black efforts to cope with the harsh legacy of slavery. They assisted Black migrants to the northern cities from the rural south after World War I, and they became strong, resourceful allies in the long, costly struggle for civil rights in the courts and in the streets. Throughout, the Jewish community consistently stood out to Blacks as the most supportive white population group by far. Through these activities, Black and Jewish leaders gradually forged strong, close ties that probably reached their peak in the major legislative triumphs of the mid-1960s.

The epic joint struggle for Black civil rights had implications for the Jewish community as well. During the years of struggle, Jews had themselves been victims of discrimination throughout the United States, not to speak of the hate and discrimination to which they had been subject elsewhere in the world for centuries. They therefore felt rightfully threatened by any form of hate and intolerance, and, in fighting with Blacks, they were actually fighting for their own interests. Historian Hasia Diner points out in this regard that:

many of the issues raised by Black civil rights groups spoke directly to the problems faced by American Jews. Job discrimination, restrictive housing markets, exclusion from universities and professional schools were concerns of Jews also. . . . Through race issues, Jews could show America how useful they had become. . . . In doing this, they not only drew links between themselves and the rhetoric of American democracy, but they illustrated the compatibility of their own heritage and culture with that of America.[1]

This sense of common interest undoubtedly constituted a special basis for the close Black-Jewish relationship that emerged around civil rights. Yet, even during those years of a close, cooperative relationship between leaders of the two communities, there were significant tensions, especially below the leadership level. . . . Even at the height of the civil rights struggle, some Black analysts were pointing to numerous irritants, from the daily encounters of the two groups in the urban ghetto to the chafings of Black leaders at what they perceived as overly patronizing attitudes by Jews. Thus the highly successful Black-Jewish collaboration on civil rights occurred alongside significant conflicts and tensions and undoubtedly some anti-Semitism.

By the late 1960s, the bases and nature of Black-Jewish conflict had begun to change significantly. The change, reflected most sharply in the emergence of a young cadre of Black leaders advocating Black Power, in battles for control of local schools in New York and Chicago, and in vigorous disagreements with those Jews opposed to strong forms of affirmative action, signified a major shift in direction by relative newcomers to the leadership struggle. Moving beyond the broad principles of equal rights and racial tolerance that were bases for Black-Jewish cooperation, new voices sought to direct their own search for increased political influence and economic opportunity. The conflict at this juncture became more pronounced and more substantive than at any time in the past. But it hardly signified a breaking point in the relationship.

Clearly, the history of Black-Jewish relations is one of both close and constructive relations as well as conflicts and tensions. Major civil rights victories were won, even as tensions were clearly evident. That this pattern continues today should not be surprising or alarming and need not indicate significant, overall deterioration in the relationship. On the contrary, amid the expressions of conflict, there are widespread indications of strong, effective relations between the two groups. . . .

Our Poor Understanding of Each Other

. . . Black leaders from Martin Delany to Alexander Crummell, Frederick Douglass, and Marcus Garvey all invoked the Jewish experience over the centuries for insight and inspiration as they pondered the prospects of Black people in America for dignified survival as a small and despised minority. In this century, most of the civil rights leadership encountered the Jews as generous and stalwart partners in the fight for civil rights and, in the post-civil rights era, as sometime political allies. But, in the gritty, harsh struggle to survive and make progress in the teeming urban ghettos, with their formidable barriers of racial discrimination and segregation, other Blacks at times vented their frustrations on the Jews they came in contact with or even the Jews they only heard of. In their view, the Jews had functioned profitably as intermediaries between them and a hostile white establishment, and their extraordinarily rapid progress, socially and economically, merely intensified the frustrations these Blacks felt. As the years of close collaboration on civil rights recede into the past, and the Black civil rights leaders of that era leave the active scene, these angry urban voices seem to gain greater prominence.

A few aspirants to power in the largely Black inner cities continue to find the increasingly distant image of Jews a useful target for expressing the rage of the young and poor and for gaining attention. The anti-Semitic utterances of these personalities are too often viewed benignly by much of the Black public, partly because of their limited understanding of the experiences and fears of the seemingly secure and successful Jewish community and partly because of their perception that angry rhetoric has limited significance. There are notable exceptions to this reaction. . . . Nonetheless, benign attitudes to anti-Semitic remarks constitute one of the prime indicators of growing Black anti-Semitism for many Jews.

The Jewish community has expressed anger and anxiety with each anti-Semitic or otherwise unfriendly utterance and has demanded that more responsible Black leaders denounce the statement at issue and the individuals associated with it. They worry that unrepudiated anti-Semitic utterances could help make hatred of Jews widely acceptable. However, neither Black nor Jewish leaders and analysts have done enough to increase understanding of this disturbing behavior as a basis for responding to it appropriately and effectively. In the absence of such understanding, the Jewish community might well misperceive the scale of the problem in the Black community and seek responses that exacerbate rather than solve it.

One of the most controversial and damaging issues in the debate about Black-Jewish relations is the now routine claim by Jews that, in contrast to the rest of the population, there is a high and growing level of anti-Semitism among Blacks and that this level rises as education increases. These perceptions are now a prominent part of folk wisdom in the Jewish community. These claims of a disturbing and distinctive anti-Semitic trend among Blacks rest in large part on a number of survey-based studies conducted between 1967 and 1992.[2] . . .

One of the most recent studies is by Tom Smith of the National Opinion Research Center, who reviewed data from the General Social Survey for 1990. Smith underscored the specter of rising Black anti-Semitism. . . . Smith concludes his review of attitudes toward Jews by observing, "While Black anti-Semitism is not a major force at present, it is the only potential source of an invigorated anti-Semitism that is being pushed by leaders with non-trivial followings."[3]

This view of Blacks as the only likely source of anti-Semitism is reinforced by even more recent surveys sponsored by the Anti-Defamation League (ADL) and the American Jewish Committee. . . . The [American Jewish Committee] survey showed evidence of extensive anti-Semitism among Black New Yorkers. Illustrative of this is the study's finding that 47 percent of all respondents felt that Jews had too much influence, while 63 percent of Blacks thought so.[4] Since Jewish analysts of anti-Semitism consider this perception of too much influence the single strongest indicator of anti-Semitism, the results would seem to confirm the Smith portrayal of Blacks as the source of an invigorated anti-Semitism.

The claim that anti-Semitism is most prevalent among African Americans, presumably confirmed by these surveys, raises some troubling questions for Black-Jewish relations. . . .

Most of the anti-Semitism surveys employ a battery of 9–11 questions that tap a variety of attitudes toward Jews. The mix of questions has varied slightly from one study to the next, but they constitute a fairly consistent anti-Semitism index. While they provide extremely valuable attitudinal information, it is not clear that they are a consistently reliable measure of anti-Semitism. For example, the survey item traditionally considered by Jewish analysts to be the strongest indicator of anti-Jewish sentiment, whether the respondent thought that Jews had too much influence, has been questioned by African American analysts as to how accurately it denotes anti-Semitic attitudes. Their assessment is that, especially among African Americans, who frequently compare influence across groups and assess their position in relation to others, the fact that Jews hold a proportion of prominent public offices much higher than their proportion of the population while the reverse is true for African Americans might make the affirmative response of the latter informed rather than hateful. In fact, in one opinion survey, 35.8 percent of Jewish respondents felt that African Americans had too little political influence.[5] A test using such measures to confirm alleged Black anti-Semitism might well be unhelpful, though a response that Jews have too much power cannot be dismissed out of hand. . . .

Virtually all the surveys done by Jewish and other sponsors examining attitudes toward various ethnic groups yield two compelling findings concerning Jews. First, they are the most admired population group in the United States, and this admiration holds across every other group, including African Americans. Second, even those respondents classified as anti-Semitic because of the number of questions to which they give a qualifying answer exhibit a number of highly positive assessments of or attitudes toward Jews. . . . The most reliable conclusion one can draw from these findings is that the potential for both warm and tense relations coexist in attitudes toward Jews. Which will emerge as dominant will depend on how circumstances in one's experience bring out one or the other.[6]

Paralleling the concern of Jews about anti-Semitism among African Americans are growing claims of Jewish racism. Several factors seem to contribute to this perception among African Americans. One is that the strong image of Black-Jewish cooperation in pursuit of civil rights that was very pronounced up to the mid-1960s has all but disappeared even though a substantial level of such cooperation continues. A contributing factor in the declining image of cooperation in this area is the declining number of prominent civil rights issues in contention. . . .

A second factor is the evidence from opinion surveys that the attitudes of Jews toward African Americans is mixed, providing some evidence of racism along with friendly and supportive attitudes. Virtually all recent surveys of racial attitudes show that Jews hold consistently more favorable attitudes toward Blacks than do other whites and generally favor school and housing integration. A substantial segment of the Jewish population, however, does not share these views. In his study of Jewish attitudes toward Blacks, Tom Smith used data from the National Opinion Research Center to analyze Jewish feelings toward Blacks.

He found that Jews had moderately favorable feelings toward Blacks, but only 15.2 percent identified closely with Blacks. At the same time, Jews are very cool to those Blacks they identify as "militants."[7] This barely "warm" attitude combined with a handful of openly racist or socially conservative Jews contributes to the growing complaints of Jewish racism.

Third, and perhaps most important, although Blacks and Jews agree on a number of important issues, there are fundamental differences between them that contribute to the perception of Jewish racism. Smith sums up these differences with the observation that among Jews, "while the principle of equal treatment and non-discrimination on the basis of race is widely endorsed, the idea of special efforts to help Blacks is less popular, especially if couched in the language of preferential treatment."[8] Specifically, Smith reports, "a majority of Jews do not favor government measures to help Blacks, more government spending for Blacks, and the use of busing to achieve school integration, though . . . Jewish support for these positions is far from negligible."[9]

These attitudes are in sharp conflict with the expectation of most Blacks that Jews would be supportive of what had become most important to Blacks—civil rights. Such supportive images have not been readily evident in the post-civil rights era, however. Instead, Jews are now seen by many African Americans as vigorous opponents of what now matters most to them—increased economic opportunities through strategies like numerically based affirmative action programs. Another factor is that for younger African Americans who have little knowledge or recollection of Black-Jewish collaboration on civil rights or of Jews as strong proponents of open housing, Jews are an increasingly distant part of white America, distinguished only by their extraordinary success. This whitening of the Jews, while itself an indication of the triumph of the struggle for pluralist values, almost forces many Blacks to view them as attitudinally just like the other whites. . . .

Survey data indicate that, as with Black attitudes toward Jews, the attitudes of Jews toward Blacks are mixed. Virtually all the recent polls show that compared to other whites, Jews consistently hold more favorable attitudes toward Blacks. On measures of social distance, Jews rate themselves as having moderately warm feelings toward Blacks, feeling neither particularly distant nor intimate. While most Jewish respondents favor school integration and would have little hesitancy sending their children to racially integrated schools, most would not send their children to schools with a Black-majority enrollment.

While most Jews had a favorable opinion of "Black civil rights leaders," they were decidedly less favorable toward those they characterized as "Black militants."[10] Furthermore, virtually all the opinion surveys indicate that in sharp contrast to Jews, African Americans consistently fall at or very near the bottom of every ranking of distinct racial or ethnic groups. Along with Hispanics, they consistently are given the highest negatives and lowest positives by others, including Jews.[11] When these findings are linked to the whitening phenomenon, they lead to perceptions of Jewish racism, especially in the absence of significant offsetting experiences. Still, higher than average positive attitudes of Jews toward Blacks consistently emerge from the surveys. . . .

Changing Times and Priorities

Relationships like those involving Blacks and Jews are subject to changing times and circumstances. Unfortunately, discussions about the relationship by both communities occur with little attention to how profound changes in the circumstances of both communities and in the rest of society affect the relationship. At a minimum, efforts to understand and improve Black-Jewish relations require that we take into account the changing context of the relationship. At least four broad, interrelated areas of change seem especially noteworthy: the socioeconomic circumstances of the two groups, the level and character of their political participation, their issue orientations, and the treatment of ethnicity and diversity in the society. Together, these will determine both the form and the substantive bases of future relations.

Different Socioeconomic Experiences

. . . [A]lthough the Black population had been experiencing substantial gains in education and income since the end of World War II, and the pace of those gains was picking up

in the 1960s, Blacks still lagged very far behind the rest of the population. The urban disorders of the mid-1960s dramatically underscored the demand for economic opportunity, spawned a cadre of angry and impatient urban leaders, and prompted a combination of urban development initiatives and race-specific policies to expand opportunities. Although analysts and politicians disagree about the effectiveness of these policies, they clearly provided important new economic opportunities. By the late-1970s, however, Black economic progress had stalled and a painful stagnation had begun to set in. Black families, already handicapped by the strains of rapid urbanization, began to disintegrate under the strain of economic stagnation and the social dislocations resulting from increased migration from the central cities by those Blacks able to benefit from open housing opportunities. By the early 1980s, analysts were describing what they characterized as a "new urban underclass," consisting mostly of Black urban residents hopelessly mired in poverty, lacking many of the social structures essential to effective community life, and enmeshed in crime and other dysfunctional life-styles.

Even though many Blacks continue to experience significant progress, overall, their economic gains have all but stalled, and about a third of the population remains in poverty. . . . Moreover, the large poverty population hangs like a dark cloud over the Black community, defining the status of the group and its policy priorities. The crises of long-term poverty and social disintegration, coupled with the twin scourges of illegal drugs and violent crime, have contributed to a profound sense of disillusionment and hopelessness, even among those Blacks not directly affected. This grim economic outlook continues to define the world of Black America.

On the other hand, by virtually any measure, the Jewish population has experienced dramatic social and economic gains in the postwar years and especially in the past three decades. These gains were not primarily the result of the civil rights movement, but the movement undoubtedly helped to remove some remaining barriers to opportunity for

Jews. Rapid socioeconomic advancement enabled most of those Jews who were inner-city residents to move to the suburbs or to wealthier urban neighborhoods. Success also enabled them to give up the roles of inner-city merchants, landlords, and other service providers of the Black inner-city poor. Thus the sharply contrasting experiences of the two communities have helped increase the physical distance and, to an extent, decrease their common concerns.

The Changed Political Relationship

Easily the most dramatic change in the experience of African Americans is their greatly increased political participation as voters and office-holders. . . . That change, combined with major expansion of the concept of equal representation by the courts and the gradually increasing willingness of whites to vote for Black candidates, has resulted in dramatic increases in the number and types of elective offices they hold. . . . These accomplishments constitute considerable potential political influence. . . .

What has not changed significantly over the past three decades is the similarity in Black-Jewish voting patterns, a fact that continues to contribute to the image of a Black-Jewish political alliance. . . . [B]lacks and Jews have consistently backed the Democratic Party and Democratic presidential candidates. . . . Similarities in partisan voting show up in the partisanship of Blacks and Jews in Congress. The Congress, beginning in 1993, has 39 Black representatives—38 Democrats and 1 Republican. It also has 33 Jewish representatives—27 Democrats and 6 Republicans. In the Senate, there is 1 Black Democrat, along with 9 Jewish Democrats and 1 Jewish Republican.

The perception of Black-Jewish political collaboration has been particularly strong at the municipal level. In a number of highly visible mayoral races involving Black candidates, Jewish voters provided the critical margin of victory, emerging, as a result, as a critical ally. This was true starting with the first of the major mayoral races of the 1960s. . . .

In spite of their similar voting patterns, strong identification with the Democratic Party, and support for Black candidates in key mayoral races, the Black-Jewish political relationship has never been as deliberate or deep as the term "alliance" might suggest. Although Jewish votes did provide the margin of victory in key mayoral races when the electorate was otherwise divided along racial lines, the level of Jewish support never reached a majority of their votes. What was distinctive was that a much higher proportion of Jews supported these candidates than was the case for other whites. . . .

But even the modest level of Jewish electoral support for Black candidates may be shrinking as relations between the two groups become increasingly complex. Some of this shrinkage may well be coincidental as prominent Black mayoral figures were followed by less prominent ones or as the political climate changed in some cities. . . . Heightened ethnic and racial tensions in major cities, the growing preoccupation by the Jewish community with anti-Semitic expressions by some Blacks, and the declining novelty of Black electoral success are likely to weaken Black-Jewish electoral alliances at the municipal level. Simultaneously, growing differences in overall policy agendas as well as on specific issues may be diminishing prospects for meaningful alliances at this level in the future.

Black-Jewish political collaboration may be declining for major substantive reasons as well. Their collaboration has been most effective on basic civil rights issues, but the number of such issues has been declining. Although Blacks and Jews both support liberal policies and activist government, the two communities seem to mean very different things by "liberal policies." On racial matters, most Jews see the goal of activist government as that of achieving equal opportunity; however, they oppose policies they view as favoring one group over another. Thus, while they support programs in job training, education, and health care, most Jews oppose racially targeted programs, as well as school busing. For Blacks, on the other hand, the goal of equal opportunity requires some race-specific policies to help achieve a level playing field. The sharp disagreements between the two groups over numerically based affirmative action programs illustrate the deep substantive division between the two communities. Most Jews view strong forms of affirmative action programs as a form of racial quotas that threaten their continued access to opportunities and violate their strong commitment to performance or merit-based achievement.

Of course, many Jews do support some affirmative action programs, but they distinguish between those programs that rely on general equal opportunity goals and timetables from those that appear to impose firm numerical quotas. For example, the American Jewish Committee has been on record in support of several affirmative action programs while opposing others.

Although Black-Jewish political collaboration at the municipal level appears to be eroding, recent broad gains by Blacks in state legislatures, in Congress, and in the federal executive branch are likely to provide important new bases for cooperation. The more than 500 Black state legislators are close to composing an average of 10 percent of the approximately 40 state legislatures in which they serve. Because most are Democrats in Democratic Party-controlled legislatures, they have been moving rapidly into key leadership positions. As state governments have gained prominence in policymaking over the past decade, this Black presence has become an increasingly important source of influence.

The growing Black presence in Congress is an even more promising basis for a future political relationship between Blacks and Jews. . . . Although the two communities disagree on some domestic policy issues, they also share a broad range of domestic policy concerns. . . .

The interests of the Jewish community have come to focus increasingly on defense and foreign policy issues relevant to Israel's well-being. African Americans, too, after having been only occasionally involved with foreign affairs, are becoming more interested in U.S. foreign policy, especially in relation to Africa and other developing areas. It is likely that future Black-Jewish collaboration might focus more on common interests in Congress and particularly in international affairs. The prospects here are for important new successes for their joint efforts on such issues as humanitarian and development aid to developing countries. On the other hand, there may be new conflicts over policies in the Middle East on what constitutes fair treatment of Palestinians or security for Israel and over allocations of foreign assistance dollars. . . .

Changing Attitudes Toward Diversity and Identity

Black-Jewish relations have been complicated by powerful new currents in group attitudes toward race and ethnicity and in the way these attitudes are expressed. Historically, the great divide in American society has been racial. The civil rights struggle was fundamentally about whether Blacks would be fully incorporated into society with the same rights and opportunities as whites. . . . Gradually, this simple Black-white dichotomy has been changing to a more complex multiethnic picture, aided in large part by the heavy immigration of the past two decades. Along with this change has come a broader range of group conflicts, new concerns and insecurities by African Americans about their position and opportunities, and greater emphasis on group identity than at any time in the recent past.

In this changing environment, African Americans have been seeking to affirm their identity and assert their cultural autonomy with renewed vigor and controversy. They are demanding greater attention to their African heritage and their distinctive contributions to a common American culture. . . . Use of the term "African American," demands for an Afrocentric curriculum in the public schools, increased conflicts with some newly arrived groups like Koreans, and increasingly angry expressions in speech, music, and literature are all reflections of this development.

In this environment, the Black community has tended to accommodate or tolerate a very wide range of expression, some of it angry, distinctly antiwhite, and anti-Semitic. . . . This tradition of accommodating diverse viewpoints has made many Blacks less perturbed about, and less condemnatory of, extremist rhetoric and hateful expressions than might be expected or desirable.

Of course, such acceptance of within-group diversity is not peculiar to Blacks. The Jewish community, too, has long been characterized by a very wide array of beliefs and attitudes about most major issues, including race relations. Indeed, the conflict that plagued the Crown Heights neighborhood is a clear example of the diversity within each of the two communities, involving as it did a small sect of Jews and a mostly Caribbean-born Black population. So is the current, highly charged debate about race and ethnicity in the two communities. There are visible, vocal Jewish proponents of racist views, opponents of relationship building, and opportunistic proponents of the view that Blacks are enemies of the Jews. More broadly, a concern with Jewish continuity and fears of population erosion through intermarriage have caused many in the Jewish community to turn inward and place less emphasis on building relations with others. In many respects, these trends parallel similar attitudes and expressions in the Black community. What is noteworthy and encouraging is the fact that the hostile fringes in both communities have been and remain small. . . .

One factor that now magnifies Black anti-Semitic expression and tends to exacerbate Black-Jewish tensions is the communications revolution, which allows easy access to mass media, and the greater availability of major public forums for nontraditional, angry, even hateful expression. Thus the Nation of Islam preached its antiwhite and anti-Semitic views in the 1950s much as it does now, but today those views are expressed via talk radio and from the podium of major universities. We live in an age when outrageous expression has market appeal and when little is taboo. Yet, public and widely broadcast expressions of hatred have unprecedented potential to affect public attitudes. . . .

Revitalizing the Relationship

. . . While claims of serious deterioration seem exaggerated, there clearly has been change, and it is important that both communities use those changes as starting points in revitalizing the relationship. . . . The challenge . . . is to determine how they can most effectively proceed to forge a relationship that appears likely to meet their respective interests. Three steps seem essential in that effort: to accept the principle of limited partnership, one that acknowledges the inevitability of disagreements and builds on areas of agreement; to choose issue areas of importance to both sides for long-term collaborations—a social policy agenda for expanding opportunities is one such area; and to resolve to serve as special guardians of the society's pluralist values.

Limited Partnerships

Black-Jewish relations have been set back by a tendency on both sides to stress the issues on which there is disagreement and to overlook the broad areas of agreement and common interests. . . . [I]t is unrealistic to expect full, across-the-board agreement on issues or approaches to problems from two large, diverse communities. The success of Black-Jewish relations depends in large part on the willingness of both sides to accept the inevitability of differences, to respect reasoned disagreements, and to keep litmus-test issues to a minimum.

The Jewish and African American communities already share a commitment to the core issues for each group. Both sides, for practical reasons as well as on principle, share an especially strong opposition to hate and bigotry whether expressed as anti-Semitism or racism. Both sides, too, share a strong commitment to basic civil and human rights and equal opportunity. In addition, the Black community has a long unassailable commitment to the security of Israel, a fundamental concern of the Jewish community, and Jews have been prominent in the struggles against apartheid in South Africa and oppression in Haiti. . . . Fundamental to this view of relationship is mutual respect as equals in society. . . .

Focused Collaboration

Relationships invariably are forged through cooperative action rather than through debates. It is not surprising that the two groups seemed closer and may have felt closer as they worked toward a clear set of shared goals. Currently, those goals—the civil rights agenda—have been partly replaced by a quality-of-life or economic opportunity agenda for African Americans. The relationship might be considerably enhanced by a joint effort on this front. . . .

The data show clearly that while education helps, it does not do nearly enough to narrow the Black-white opportunity gap. Some form of affirmative action that pushes both public and private sectors to expand opportunities is critical. Yet indications are that the strategies that evolved out of the 1960s and 1970s affirmative action efforts might need rethinking, not only because of Jewish opposition but because the expanding categories of beneficiaries are rapidly undermining their effectiveness. Those sectors of the Jewish community like the American Jewish Committee that already provide qualified support for affirmative action by distinguishing between those that have the effects of firm quotas and those that do not might be in a good position to help fashion more effective and widely supportive measures. Such an effort would respond to the concern among many Blacks that, while Jews support the broad principle of equal opportunity, they oppose any practical means of getting there.

Guardians of Pluralism

Finally, this collaboration would not only serve to advance the interests of both communities and improve economic fairness in society broadly; it would also demonstrate that two communities can overcome differences to work toward common goals. In the current fractured atmosphere of American life, this demonstration of working pluralism would reaffirm the value of diversity and the potential for cooperation to overcome ethnic and racial division. The future of relations between the Jewish and African American communities will tell much about the potential of U.S. society to live fruitfully within its pluralistic structure, repudiate hatred, and secure a better future for all.

Endnotes

1. Haisa Diner, *In the Almost Promised Land* (Westport, CT: Greenwood Press, 1977), pp. xv–xvi.

2. These are reviewed and analyzed in Jennifer Golub, *What Do We Know about Black Anti-Semitism?* (New York: American Jewish Committee, 1990).

3. Tom W. Smith, *What Do Americans Think about Jews?* (New York: American Jewish Committee, 1991), p. 27.

4. *1992 New York City Intergroup Relations Survey* (New York: American Jewish Committee, 1992), p. 27.

5. Tom W. Smith, *Jewish Attitudes toward Blacks and Race Relations* (New York: American Jewish Committee, 1990), p. 22.

6. Gary E. Rubin, "A No-Nonsense Look at Anti-Semitism," *Tikkun*, 8(3):46–48, 79–81 (May-June 1993).

7. Smith, *Jewish Attitudes toward Blacks and Race Relations*, p. 6.

8. Ibid.

9. Ibid., p. 5.

10. Ibid., passim.

11. Smith, *What Do Americans Think about Jews?* pp. 5–12; *1992 New York City Intergroup Relations Survey.*

Reprinted from: Milton D. Morris and Gary E. Rubin, "The Turbulent Friendship: Black-Jewish Relations in the 1990s." In *Annals of the American Association for Political and Social Science*, 530 (Nov., 1993), pp. 42–60. Copyright ©1993 by Sage Publications, Inc. Reprinted by permission.

38

The Korean-Black Conflict and the State

Paul Ong
Kye Young Park
Yasmin Tong

. . . Beginning in the 1970s, Korean merchants, many operating "mom-and-pop" stores, have emerged as visible economic actors in South Central, the geographic home for low-income Blacks in Los Angeles. The conflict between the two groups is partially embedded in the prejudices held by members of each population, which magnify economic-derived tensions by reinterpreting disagreements and points of friction into ethnic-racial terms. The resulting conflicts include over-the-counter hostilities and group protest. Violence directed at Korean merchants reached a peak during the 1992 Los Angeles riot/rebellion, in which Korean merchants suffered a disproportionately large share of the economic losses. Government-sponsored efforts to address the conflicts have evolved over time, with the 1992 riot/rebellion being a watershed. The strategy to manage race relations was replaced by limited economic initiatives that, unfortunately, balanced the grievances of Black residents against the financial interests of Korean merchants. . . .

Structural Foundation of Intergroup Tensions

The Koreans reached their extraordinary level of entrepreneurship by mobilizing class, ethnic, and familial resources (Light and Bonacich 1988; Min 1984). The high rate of self-employment was also the product of limited employment opportunities in the larger labor market caused by language problems, the lack of transferability of education and training received in Korea, and discriminatory practices. Self-employment promised substantial financial rewards, and success was not an impossible dream, as the income data from the 1990 census indicate. Those who "made it" served as powerful and seductive role models, instilling and reinforcing the American dream of economic success based on entrepreneurial spirit. . . .

The abandonment of South Central by mainstream capital and corporations and by the public in the 1970s and 1980s, along with the aging of a previous generation of non-Black merchants, created an opening for aspiring Korean entrepreneurs. South Central, home to about a million people, contained some of the poorest neighborhoods in Los Angeles. Although the population changed during the 1970s and 1980s from predominantly Black to nearly equally Latino and Black (Ong and Lawrence 1992), South Central continued to be the home of inner-city Blacks. Racial recomposition was not the only notable change. South Central is like many other inner-city ghettos in terms of recent economic developments. These communities had been marginalized for most of this century, and structural changes in the urban economy over the last quarter century made conditions worse, creating, in some situations, an urban underclass (Wilson 1987). South Central suffered the brunt of deindustrialization of heavy manufacturing in Los Angeles. Between 1978 and 1982, South Central lost seventy thousand high-wage, stable, blue-collar jobs (Soja 1989). Major companies such as General Motors, Goodyear, Firestone, and Bethlehem Steel closed plants in or around the area (Johnson et al. 1992). According to a study by the United Way, a total of 321 plants or industries left South Central over a 15-year period (Hamilton 1988–1989).

. . . [M]any Blacks became trapped in poverty-stricken, deteriorating neighborhoods with little hope of moving up or out (Norman 1992, 8). The 1990 census showed that approximately one in three residents lived in households with incomes below the official poverty line, a rate more than twice that for the county. More than a quarter of all households survived on public assistance. Poverty in South Central, however, was not primarily a problem of welfare dependency. The community had a large and growing number of working poor, whose earnings often left a family near the poverty level. The average hourly wage in the South Central area was $9.12 in 1989, 58 percent of the average for Los Angeles County (Ong et al., 1992). Poverty was also tied to joblessness. In 1990, only 59 percent of adults aged 20 to 64 in South Central worked, a rate 16 percentage points lower than the county rate.

These broad economic trends set the stage for the appearance of high numbers of Korean merchants in South Central. The absence of large chain retailers meant that smaller operations would not be squeezed out by bigger and more efficient ones. At the same time, increasing poverty, along with a growing crime rate, made old-time merchants want to leave the community. Some were forced to, abandon their businesses with no compensation, particularly after the 1965 Watts riot/rebellion, but others found buyers among the Korean immigrants. Once the original cohort of Korean merchants became established in South Central, others followed in increasing numbers.

Although opening a South Central business was cheaper than purchasing a business in other areas of Los Angeles, the costs were nonetheless high. Given the sizable demand for self-employment business by Korean immigrants, buyers competed against one another, and with a fixed supply of businesses, prices rose to the point where the potential for high profits was dissipated. The total cost of starting up a business, which included the purchase price and investments in inventory, could run into the hundreds of thousands of dollars (Duignan-Cabrera 1992, B8). To raise the funds, some Koreans took great personal risks by mortgaging their homes; thus failure would mean losing not only their business but also their home. The costly investments forced Koreans to operate at the margins, cutting costs by relying on unpaid family workers and cheap co-ethnic labor and by forgoing adequate insurance coverage.

The relative importance of Korean Americans in the South Central subeconomy depends on the frame of reference. In the context of overall Korean entrepreneurship, Korean businesses in this area accounted for a small fraction of all Korean-owned businesses. According to Eui-Young Yu, a sociologist who had closely followed the development of the Korean community, the customer base of Korean-owned businesses in Los Angeles County by the early 1990s was only 10 percent African American and another 17 percent Latino (*LA Weekly*, 3-9 January 1992). Since many of the businesses serving minorities operated outside South Central, it is likely that only about a fifth of the customer base was in South Central.

On the other hand, Koreans operated a visible proportion of the stores in this community. According to some estimates for the mid-1980s, Koreans owned more than two-thirds of the gas stations and about one-third of the small markets and liquor stores in South Central (*Los Angeles Times*, 15 April 1985). Given the continued growth in the number of Korean merchants, the proportions were probably considerably higher by the end of the decade. The economic importance of Korean-owned stores in South Central, then, centered on their prominence in this low-income community, which persisted until 1992. The events of that year, which are discussed in detail later, made the presence of Korean merchants in South Central problematic.

In one sense, the emergence of a Korean merchant class in South Central can be conceptualized as ethnic succession of outside merchants in a low-income, minority community. Koreans were not the first nonBlack ethnic group to operate extensively in poor African American neighborhoods. They had been preceded by Jewish merchants, many of whom sold their shops to Koreans (Pleasant 1992). The succession, however, was not just, from Jews to Koreans. There were also smaller numbers of Japanese and Chinese owners, along with some Black owners, who also sold their businesses (Takahashi and Hee 1992). In some cases, these original owners retained control over the property while selling the business operation (Ong and Hee

1993), thus profiting through both the sales and continuing rents. Many of the absentee landlords were not residents of South Central, so the income generated by these transactions leaked out of the community.

The ethnically based practices of Korean merchants perpetuated the economic leakage and isolated them from the rest of the community. The isolation was reinforced by the fact that most Koreans resided outside South Central and were thus removed from the daily life of the community. The interactions between Blacks and Koreans were effectively limited to those between outside merchants and local customers. This restrictive relationship had broader economic consequences. Like the previous generation of merchants, Koreans took their profits and income out of South Central. . . .

In their drive to adapt to the U.S. economy, the Korean merchants also played a minor role in urban restructuring as it affects South Central. Korean Americans were not party to the disinvestment and abandonment of South Central, but they helped reshape the local economy. The emergence of the Korean merchant class was more than simply a process of a one-to-one replacement. At the very time the community was losing its manufacturing jobs, large retailers, and banking services, other economic activities were selectively maintained or expanded through Korean American investments.

This selectivity can be seen in the abundance of liquor stores and grocery stores with liquor licenses. According to one estimate, there was one store with a liquor license for every 700 residents by the early 1990s, a proportion three to four times higher than the ratio for the rest of Los Angeles (Lacy 1992). Koreans played a significant role in this trend through their purchases and investments in liquor licenses, which made them the intermediary in the sales (Light and Bonacich 1988, 232–233). The purveying of this self-destructive commodity to an oppressed population was motivated by a search for profits that precluded any social commitment to the overall well-being of the community. The aggregate sum of rational individual actions by Koreans in combination with the exodus of mainstream capital and corporations contrib-

uted to the unbalanced economic development of South Central.

Koreans also contributed to restructuring by being active agents of innovation rather than simple passive buyers of existing businesses. The creation of new forms is most apparent in the development of indoor swap meets, the vast majority of which were operated by Koreans (Chang 1990). These malls operated in large buildings where space was leased to numerous small vendors who sold low-cost clothing, shoes, electronic goods, and other retail merchandise. By the late 1980s, there were more than a thousand Korean-operated booths in indoor swap meets in South Central (Chang 1990, 98). Similar operations could be found in other parts of Los Angeles, but those in South Central were dearly a product of the absence of large chain retailers.

Interracial Conflicts

The discrete class positions occupied by Koreans and Blacks in South Central created a set of interactions potentially filled with conflicts. Many points of confrontation were rooted in economics—the disparate interests of sellers and buyers. In the U.S. economy, the potential explosiveness of market transactions is minimized when fairness is imposed by competitive forces or governmental regulations that prevent monopolistic or oligopolistic behavior. As we argue below, however, South Central residents did not perceive such fairness, but rather shared a sense of being victims of inherent economic injustice. While economics was at the base of potential conflict, the problems between Korean sellers and Black buyers were also social because the roles were strongly defined along racial-ethnic lines. The overlapping categorization by class and race-ethnicity was not perceived as coincidental or tangential in importance. Race and ethnicity became a basis for individual and collective action. This tendency was further strengthened by racially based and racially distinct perceptions and misperceptions (Stewart 1989) and by sharp cultural and linguistic differences that produced a gulf of misunderstanding. Like most Korean merchants, many of those operating retailing stores had a poor command of English.

Regardless of whether Korean merchants provided much-needed services, many South Central Black residents saw them as another link in a long historical chain of exploitative outsiders. A 33-year-old cosmetologist who is representative of this view stated, "Blacks see the Koreans as taking their money and making money off them in their neighborhood." In numerous interviews, residents repeated the litany of common complaints: the lack of employment for Blacks, exorbitant prices for inferior goods, and poor service.

For some residents, the exploitative relation involved a broader conspiracy by whites and the government. In reviewing the history of outside merchants, one 29-year-old male cosmetologist stated: "Now that Jews have left and the Asians come in—which the whites have consciously allowed . . . the whites, or the system, won't allow Blacks to get into these business positions." According to another informant, the government was an active agent that allocated Koreans "money to get another family member over as long as they open businesses or something similar." While these arguments are specious, they played a role in casting Korean Americans on the side of whites and the "system."

The judicial system's lenient treatment of Koreans added to the perception of their relative privilege. That was particularly true after the 1991 killing of Latasha Harlins by Korean-born grocer Soon Ja Du and the subsequent trial. What had started as a dispute over a bottle of orange juice in Du's Empire Liquor Market Deli on South Figueroa Street in South Central ended in the shooting death of the 15-year-old Harlins. The ruling by Judge Joyce Karlin, a white female, which gave Du probation, became a heated point of controversy. In the eyes of many Blacks, the trial was another blatant case of antiBlack racism within the justice system.

The potentially conflict-filled relationship was intensified by Black perceptions of Korean Americans as racially prejudiced. A 28-year-old vital statistics clerk stated, "Korean merchants have bought into the attitude that Blacks are below human. . . . They look at Black people as if they were animals." For

one resident, this perceived prejudice explains the actions of Korean merchants: "Korean Americans always watch you. They are very suspicious. They think Blacks are thieves." Some residents however, believed that these prejudices were the product of the larger society, which, according to a 40-year-old manager at a law firm, portrays Blacks "as belonging in gangs, uneducated, and as people who steal." Korean Americans, according to a 45-year-old hair stylist, "have a negative attitude towards African Americans because of the way television portrays them."

It is difficult to judge how pervasive these anti-Korean sentiments were among South Central Blacks. Clearly, the views were not monolithic, for the interviews with residents also uncovered more sympathetic and understanding attitudes toward Korean merchants. Nonetheless, the anti-Korean view was given currency by the opinions expressed and disseminated by the local Black newspapers, especially the *Los Angeles Sentinel*. For example, the newspaper published a series of articles in 1986 that accused Asian and Korean merchants of greed, poor services, and high prices and of failing to contribute to the community's social and economic well-being. . . .

Regardless of the validity of [Blacks'] anti-Korean perceptions, these views, in combination with the history of economic exploitation and racial injustice, played a powerful role in interpreting and magnifying confrontations. A perceived absence of a proper check on the economic power of merchants made every transaction suspect of being an unfair one. Although the Koreans were only actors in a play scripted by larger forces, they were nonetheless the immediate agents conducting business. High prices, poor-quality merchandise, no-return policies, and the like were seen as small but persistent incidents of exploitation. Many of these practices are understandable, given the marginal existence of many Korean stores, which force owners to cut cost and service; nonetheless, those at the receiving end as customers would find it difficult rationally to disregard these practices when confronted with them repeatedly.

Korean Americans also held stereotyped, race-based perceptions, as evident in the statement by a Korean woman shopkeeper:

> We are enlightened not to steal, unlike African Americans in this neighborhood. Their parents do not pay attention to their children's education. Especially, since doing businesses in this South Central, I found that they do not have work. Lack of work—they usually do not work. They do not study and therefore they remain children.

The choice of the term "enlightened" is indicative of the way Korean Americans differentiated themselves from Blacks. Although racial stereotypes existed, it would be unfair to say that all Korean Americans were prejudiced. Just as the interviews revealed that anti-Korean perceptions were not universal among Blacks, it was clear that prejudices against Blacks were not shared by all Koreans. Nonetheless, there was a broadly accepted view that the two groups were divided by tremendous cultural differences, which often contributed to intergroup misunderstanding and tension.

The perceptions held by Korean merchants were also shaped by daily exposure to potential crime. Operating in low-income areas obviously carried with it high risks. Shoplifting was regarded not simply as a petty crime but also as a sign of disrespect toward Koreans and a drain on meager profits. Robberies, some of which were violent, were far more serious. At times, the number of incidents was extremely high, and during one tragic month, four Korean merchants were killed. One would be hard pressed to argue that these murders were racially motivated, but some Koreans could not help associating criminal action and race. One Korean male stated, "As Blacks have been oppressed for a long time, they have accumulated their hostility toward others, including us." The racial interpretation was reinforced by continuing coverage in the Korean newspapers, which often played up the role of race (Chang 1990, 199–200). The race-based perceptions, along with the anxiety over the lack of personal safety, made some Korean merchants react defensively to their Black customers, thus adding to tensions over daily transactions.

Although over-the-counter conflicts were an important element of Korean-Black interaction, racial hostility was not limited to the interpersonal level. Black boycotts of Korean-owned stores were a form of collective action against what the protesters saw as unacceptable business practices. . . .

Boycotts were frequently tied to specific incidents, but they had deeper roots in the resentment over racism in general and outside merchants in particular. This sentiment endowed boycotts with a greater political meaning than a simple grievance against any one store or owner. The boycotts took on a symbolic aspect that sometimes became entangled with race. This symbolic importance was not lost on some Black activists, who used boycotts to promote their own political agenda, which often included Black nationalism.

Korean businesses were also caught in a growing movement to limit the sale of liquor. Many inner-city residents saw liquor outlets as undesirable because they contributed to alcoholism and served as meeting places for individuals with antisocial behavior (Lacy 1992, A14). What further inflamed residents was that larger outside economic interests profited by actively promoting sales. The manufacturing industry developed cheap but potent products targeted at inner-city residents (White and Lacy 1992). The issue of liquor sales, then, involved not merely personal freedom to consume a beverage but also corporate exploitation.

What started as individual concerns developed into a political campaign both in Los Angeles and in urban areas throughout the nation. (Sims 1992). In South Central, the Community Coalition for Substance Abuse Prevention and Treatment emerged as a driving force behind this movement. It actively lobbied governmental agencies and elected officials to reduce the number of liquor outlets, and it organized residents to fight the sale of liquor. Not surprisingly, the movement became enmeshed with broader issues of racism and exploitation. Consequently, the anti-liquor movement, like the store boycotts, assumed political importance beyond the immediate issue.

The controversy over liquor sales need not have been racial. The Community Coalition attempted to prevent the racialization of the issue, and its executive director, Karen Bass, worked extensively with Asian Americans to find mutually acceptable options. Nonetheless, keeping events nonracial proved to be difficult because of the way that opposing sides were mobilized. More often than not, protesters were Black (and Latino) residents, some of whom interjected the recurring complaint of outside exploitation.

At the same time, Korean merchants banded together in reactive solidarity to counter the boycotts and the anti-liquor movement. Some sought to demonstrate that Koreans were willing to be responsive to community needs by hiring local residents, contributing to neighborhood scholarship, and adopting a better code of business conduct. Unfortunately, there were structural limitations to this response. The larger economic dynamics of South Central and the ethnic foundation of the Koreans' entrepreneurship precluded radical changes in their practices and choice of business activities.

The Riot/Rebellion of 1992

The nature of Korean-Black conflict changed dramatically during the riot/rebellion of 29 April to 1 May 1992 in Los Angeles. This event was spontaneous, albeit highly predictable in retrospect. Civil unrest exploded in Los Angeles after a jury in Simi Valley, a white suburb, found four Los Angeles Police Department officers not guilty of beating Black motorist Rodney King. For residents of South Central, as well as millions of citizens throughout the nation, the verdict was incomprehensible, given the visual evidence captured on a videotape and broadcast innumerable times by local and national television. The reaction in Los Angeles was a riot/rebellion of unprecedented proportions, leaving in its wake 43 deaths, 2,383 injured persons, more than 16,000 arrests, and $1 billion in damages and losses (Bobo et al. 1992). Although the riot/rebellion was concentrated in the inner-city neighborhoods of Los Angeles, looting and violence occurred over a large territory ranging from the San Fernando Valley in the north to Long Beach in the south. This civil unrest shared some of the features of the riot/rebellions of the 1960s but differed in its multiracial complexity (Tierney 1993). The participants in the violence and their victims included whites, Blacks, Latinos, and Asians.

Apart from injuries and deaths, some consequences are proving to be long-term, The potential direct and indirect employment losses from the destruction to businesses are enormous: 11,500 jobs with an annual payroll of $240 million (California Employment Development Department 1993, 67). Many of these jobs are not easily replaceable. The rebuilding has been slow in South Central, where less than a third of all damaged buildings were repaired one year later (Reinhold 1993). Despite the grand aspirations of Rebuild L.A. (RLA), a nonprofit organization created by Mayor Tom Bradley to coordinate and stimulate the rebuilding of Los Angeles, many of the announced commitments by large corporations for new investments in this community have no substance or will not materialize in the near future (Brooks and Weinstein 1992). Some areas in South Central will remain devastated into the next century.

Asian Americans, especially Korean Americans, bore a disproportionate share—perhaps more than a third—of the losses during the three days of civil disorder (Ong and Hee 1993; Tierney 1993). Koreans far outnumbered all other Asian victims. . . . Korean stores in South Central accounted for more than a third of the total losses to all Korean establishments, with Koreatown being the second hardest hit area. According to one analysis, 761 Korean stores in South Central were looted, damaged, or both, creating a loss of $158 million (Ong and Hee 1993). Disentangling the reasons why Korean stores were heavily hit is difficult. There is no question that they were easy targets of opportunity with lootable merchandise in large part because of the refusal or inability of the police department to provide timely protection to South Central merchants. Korean owners had neither the political nor the economic clout to prompt the city into action. Moreover, most of these stores were left unprotected, because their owners feared entering South Central during the civil unrest, given the antiwhite and anti-Asian nature of the attacks on persons.

Race also played a direct role: "preexisting racial conflicts provided both the motivation and rationale for such action" (Ong and Hee 1993, 10). Not only did Blacks attack Korean-owned stores in South Central, but Latinos attacked Korean-owned stores in other parts of town. In many respects, Korean victims were no different than business victims of earlier race riot/rebellions who were singled out because they were unwelcome outsiders (Dynes and Quarantelli 1968).

Even if race did not play a central role in the motivations and actions of the rioters, the devastating outcomes added to the racial tension and mistrust between Koreans and Blacks. The events of April-May 1992 are part of a broader escalation of racial conflicts from interpersonal, over-the-counter hostilities to interest-group political clashes and finally to collective violence. This transformation moved the Korean-Black conflict closer to the center stage of the discourse on race relations, as can be seen in the coverage by the media. By mid-1992, the Korean-Black conflict had pushed its way onto the front pages and the evening news. Although reporters still had a strong tendency to see the riot/rebellion in terms of Blacks and whites, there was a growing acknowledgment that contemporary urban racial conflict is "multicolor." In other words, the redefinition of race is unfolding.

State Response

. . . The pre-riot/rebellion policy of managing racial conflicts included efforts to incorporate and mobilize the elites in each community, to ameliorate symptoms, and to focus on interpersonal conflicts. Even before Korean merchants moved into South Central, this orientation was well established, as illustrated by the history of the Los Angeles County Commission on Human Relations, one of the primary local agencies handling race-related issues. The commission was founded in 1944 in response to the zoot-suit riots, "to seek out the causes of racial tension

and devise all means possible to eliminate them" (Los Angeles County Commission on Human Relations, 1969, 5). This goal, however, quickly proved to be unrealistic, because the commission did not have the power to tackle the profound underlying causes of racial tension. The mission was scaled back a few years later: "To engage in research and education of the public for the purpose of lessening racial, religious and sexual prejudice, and to develop and administer programs and plans designed to promote full acceptance of all citizens" (Los Angeles County Commission on Human Relations, 1969, 8). The commission essentially defined minority-majority conflict in terms of interpersonal relations and, in doing so, defined the problem, away from systemic structural racism.

Even with its more modest mission, the Human Relations Commission was ill-equipped to address the Korean-Black conflict. Beginning in the mid-1970s, declining local revenues and greater conservative power on the County Board of Supervisors combined to gut the commission's budget, forcing it to reduce its staff of one hundred in the 1970s to only 15 professionals by the early 1990s (Feldman 1990; Wong 1992). These cutbacks occurred at the very time that the demand for services increased: the minority population was growing, along with greater cultural heterogeneity (Ong and Lawrence 1992; Pearlstone 1990, 33) and an escalating number of hate crimes (Chavez 1992). Even when the commission gained public visibility, its recommendations carried little political weight. The commission organized high-profile hearings addressing hate crimes against Asians, the quality of life in South Central, and changing demographics in Los Angeles (Los Angeles County Commission on Human Relations 1984, 1985, 1991). But the supervisors rarely implemented or acted on the recommendations emanating from these hearings (Wong 1992).

Given the commission's limitations, other institutional forms emerged to address interracial conflicts. The Black-Korean Alliance (BKA) was established in 1986 with the assistance of Los Angeles County's Human Relations Commission after four Korean merchants were killed in four weeks in April

1986. BKA operated outside the administrative and procedural confines of the county bureaucracy to improve relations between Korean merchants and Black residents in South Central. The alliance included representatives from the mayor's office and local small business associations, academics, and workers from the human relations profession, in addition to business, church, and other leaders from the Korean and Black communities (George 1992). The BKA'S objective was to establish an interethnic dialogue enabling people to air their differences as well as become more informed about one another. . . .

Despite [some notable] achievements, the efforts could not eliminate intergroup tension or substantially reduce the level of hostilities. The limitations of the approach of managing racial conflict with the most meager of resources became very apparent during the 1992 riot/rebellion. In the case of the BKA, its ineffectiveness ultimately led to its demise in December 1992, because, to paraphrase the sentiments of some members, "talking was not enough" (Doherty 1992). Even before the riot, there was considerable tension among its participants, and the fallout from the 1992 riot/rebellion proved fatal. Although the dispute resolution centers continued to operate after April-May 1992 and received funding to form the joint Asian-Black mediation team, their resources continued to be grossly inadequate to address the complex economic and social problems that fostered the Korean-Black conflict. Of course, it would be unfair to blame any limited set of institutions for society's failure. Both the BKA and the dispute resolution centers had noble intentions and some highly dedicated people, but they had only marginal support at best from the state. The failure was not so much of individual organizations but of the underlying approach to managing racial conflict. . . .

The policies that emerged were not race neutral, and in relation to the Korean-Black conflict they placed Korean merchants at a disadvantage with only limited compensation. This approach can be seen in the mechanisms that the city of Los Angeles adopted to guide reconstruction. Along with incentives to attract new investments, new barriers were enacted to discourage the reestablishment of "undesirable" businesses. Which businesses fell into each category was based as much on politics as on objective criteria.

As stated earlier, liquor outlets were among the most controversial businesses. Even before the outbreak of mass violence the city had moved cautiously to address the issue. Responding to growing political pressure from South Central residents and organizations, Los Angeles mayor Bradley established the South Central Liquor Task Force in April 1992, ironically only a few weeks before the riot/rebellion. Koreans and Blacks were among its members, which included community residents, representatives of elected officials, and community activists. Its objective was to limit the number of liquor outlets through enforcing land-use restrictions and using a revocation process to eliminate problem stores. Events quickly overtook the task force.

The riot/rebellion accomplished what the antiliquor movement had been unable to do—the removal of large numbers of liquor outlets. During the unrest, more than half the South Central stores with a liquor license (an estimated 400 of 728) were damaged or destroyed (McMillan, 1992). An analysis of one list (South Central Community/Merchant Liquor Task Force, 1992. 23–26) indicates that an overwhelming majority were owned by Koreans. The widespread destruction enabled the movement to shift from demanding removal of existing outlets to preventing the reopening of the closed operations. In the few months following the riot, the movement was able to gather 34,000 signatures on a petition demanding a reduction in the number of liquor stores in South Central (APPCON, 1992).

Korean merchants resisted this demand, not surprisingly, since the owners stood to lose a substantial part of their investments. The average financial value of a license was about $12,000, with some as high as $25,000 to $30,000 (McMillan, 1992). Although the liquor manufacturers and wholesale distributors also played a role in protecting the "right to sell liquor," they operated in the background through their influence on elected officials (White and Lacy, 1992). Koreans, on the other hand, were on the front line, and their visibility gave a distinctly ethnic appearance to those protecting the interest of liquor sales.

In the battle over the liquor stores, the antiliquor movement made greater gains than their Korean adversaries. Working through the task force and city council representatives from South Central, the antiliquor movement partially achieved its new objective through a special provision achieved its new objective through a special provision in local law (Ordinance no. 167, 909). To facilitate reconstruction, the city waived certain fees eliminated some red tape, and allowed firms to rebuild according to older and less stringent codes. Not all businesses could benefit from these provisions, however, "Establishments dispensing alcoholic beverages for consideration," that is, liquor outlets, along with "swap meets, gun shops, pawnshops, and automobile repair establishments," were excluded. The outcome, then, was a victory for the residents and organizations fighting the presence of liquor outlets.

Although the exclusions did not explicitly target any ethnic group, the de facto effect was to disadvantage a disproportionately large number of Korean merchants. Although corporate-backed operations, such as 7–Eleven stores, had the resources to undergo rigorous hearing process and to meet newer building code requirements, few Koreans were able to overcome the barriers (Duignan-Cabrera, 1992; Rainey, 1992).

Korean merchants received only minor compensation in the form of financial incentives and programs to help them convert their establishments to other lines of business. The initiative to assist displaced Korean liquor store owners came from the Asian Pacific Planning Council (APPCON), an umbrella organization of social service providers. APPCON accepted the need to reduce the number of liquor outlets in South Central but added that the city must provide "compensation for liquor licensees and assistance for store owners to relocate or convert . . . to another business" (APPCON 1992).

. . . Clearly, the interjection of [Koreans] into what had been seen as largely a Black-white situation precipitated new economic and social conflicts. From the start, the state used approaches that defined the problems away from a majority-minority framework and avoided fundamental structural issues.

The 1992 riot/rebellion brought about some new initiatives. The restrictions on the rebuilding of liquor stores and the incentives for conversion can be seen as efforts to bring about economic change. But they also represented a reactive adaptation of the state's use of regulatory powers and financial incentives to direct economic development, which had been applied on a much larger scale to benefit corporate America through programs such as urban renewal. The reforms that were adopted for South Central suffered serious constraints. The most obvious limitation is that at best the efforts can only chip away at the underlying social and economic structure of racial inequality, which would be acceptable if the efforts were complemented by more comprehensive changes, but this does not appear to be the case. . . .

References

APPCON (Asian Pacific Planning Council). 1992. "Proposal for Liquor Store Business Conversion Program." Mimeographed.

Bobo, Lawrence D., James H. Johnson, Melvin L. Oliver, James Sidanius, and Camile Zubrinsky. 1992. "Public Opinion before and after a Spring of Discontent: A Preliminary Report on the 1992 Los Angeles County Social Survey." Occasional Working Paper Series, vol. 3, no. 1. Los Angeles: Center for the Study of Urban Poverty, University of California.

Brooks, Nancy Rivera, and Henry Weinstein. 1992. "19 of 68 Firms Question Listing by Rebuild L.A." *Los Angeles Times*, 18 November, pp. A1, A18–19.

California Employment Development Department. 1993. *Analysis of the 1992 Los Angeles Civil Unrest*. Los Angeles.

Chang, Edward. 1990. "New Urban Crisis: Korean-Black Conflicts in Los Angeles." Ph.D. dissertation, University of California, Berkeley.

Chavez, Stephanie. 1992. "Mediators Work to Defuse Racial Tensions." *Los Angeles Times*, 19 April, p. Al.

Duignan-Cabrera, Anthony. 1992. "As Some Reopen, Other Stores Caught in Red Tape." *Los Angeles Times*, 25 June, pp. B1,B8.

Dynes, R. R., and E. L. Quarantelli. 1968. "What Looting in Civil Disturbances Really Means." *Trans-Action* (May): 9–14.

Feldman, Paul. 1990. "L.A. County Agency Tries a Mail Appeal for Money," *Los Angeles Times*, 10 February, p. A1.

George, Lynell. 1992. "Going Between: Mediators Bridge the Culture Gap." *LA Weekly*, 3 January, pp. 14–17.

Hamilton, Cynthia. 1988–1989. "Apartheid in American City: The Case of Blacks in Los Angeles." *LA Weekly*, 30 December–5 January.

Johnson, James, Cloyzelle Jones, Walter Farrell, and Melvin Oliver. 1992. "The Los Angeles Rebellion, 1992: A Preliminary Assessment from Ground Zero." Los Angeles: Center for the Study of Urban Poverty, University of California.

Lacy, Marc. 1992. "Last Call for Liquor Outlets." *Los Angeles Times*, 14 December, pp. A1, A14–A15.

Light, Ivan, and Edna Bonacich. 1988. *Immigrant Entrepreneurs: Koreans in Los Angeles, 1965–1982*. Berkeley: University of California Press.

Los Angeles County Commission on Human Relations. 1969. *A Twenty-five-Year History, 1944–1969*. Los Angeles.

——. 1984. *The New Asian Peril: Report of a Hearing on Rising Anti-Asian Bigotry*. Los Angeles.

——. 1985. *McCone Revisited: Focus on Solution to Continuing Problems in South Central Los Angeles*. Los Angeles.

——. 1991. *Hate Crime in Los Angeles County, 1990: A Report to the Los Angeles County Board of Supervisors*.

Los Angeles Times Poll. 1993. "Asians in Southern California." *Los Angeles Times*, 20 August, p. A1.

McMillan, Penelope. 1992. "Task Force on Liquor Stores Is Unveiled." *Los Angeles Times*, 30 June, pp. B1, B8.

Min, Pyong Gap. 1984. "From White Collar Occupations to Small Business: Korean Immigrants' Occupational Adjustments." *Sociological Quarterly* 25:333–352.

Norman, Alex. 1992. "Black-Korean Relations: From Desperation to Dialogue; Or, From Shouting and Shooting to Sitting and Talking." Paper presented at the Conference on Black-Korean Encounters, California State University, Los Angeles, 22–23 May.

Ong, Paul, and Suzanne Hee. 1993. "Korean Merchants and the L.A. Riot/Rebellion." In *Losses in the Los Angeles Civil Unrest*, pp. 7–14.

Los Angeles: Center for Pacific Rim Studies, University of California.

Ong, Paul, and Janette Lawrence. 1992. *Pluralism and Residential Patterns in Los Angeles*. Discussion Papers, D9202. Los Angeles: Graduate School of Architecture and Urban Planning, University of California.

Pearlstone, Zena. 1990. *Ethnic L.A.* Los Angeles: Hillcrest Press.

Pleasant, Betty. 1992. "A Tale of Two Riots." *Los Angeles Sentinel*, 7–13 May, pp. A1, A16.

Rainey, James. 1992. "Four Liquor Stores Destroyed in Riots Get OK to Rebuild." *Los Angeles Times*, 20 November, p. B4.

Reinhold, Robert. 1993. "Rebuilding Lags in Los Angeles a Year after Riots." *New York Times*, 10 May.

Sims, Calvin. 1992. "Under Siege: Liquor's Inner-City Pipeline." *New York Times*, 29 November, sec. 3, pp. 1, 6.

Soja, Edward. 1989. *Postmodern Geographies: The Reassertion of Space in Critical Social Theory*. London and New York: Verso.

Stewart, Ella. 1989. "Ethnic Cultural Diversity: An Ethnographic Study of Cultural Differences and Communication Style between Korean Merchants and Employees and Black Patrons in South Los Angeles." Master's thesis, California State University, Los Angeles.

Takahashi, Jane, and Suzanne Hee. 1992. "The 1965 Watts Riots and Asian Americans." Mimeographed. Asian American Studies Center, University of California, Los Angeles.

Tierney, Kathleen J. 1993. "Los Angeles, 1992: First Urban Unrest of the Twenty-First Century." Paper presented at the Annual Meeting of the Southern Sociological Society, Chattanooga, Tenn., 1–4 April.

White, George, and Marc Lacy. 1992. "Liquor Industry Takes on Activists in Political Arena." *Los Angeles Times*, 15 December, pp. A1, A32–33.

Wilson, William J. 1987. *The Truly Disadvantaged: The Inner City, the Underclass, and Public Policy*. Chicago: University of Chicago Press.

Wong, Jai Lee. 1992. Interview of Jai Lee Wong, of the Los Angeles County Human Relations Commission, by Yasmin Tong, 1 April.

39

A Year to Remember:

The Riot and the Haitians

Alejandro Portes
Alex Stepick

Blacks and Refugees

... The anti-Mariel campaign. . . [caused] an increase in the mood of tension in the city. Not only Mariel Cubans but also Haitians were coming (sometimes washing) ashore, and the sense of being under invasion by the Third World fused with the unresolved racial tensions of this southern city. Even as the local establishment battled the Cubans in its effort to fend off new waves of immigrants, it persisted in its old ways with regard to the native ethnic proletariat—the Blacks. These ways involved relegating Blacks to a permanently subservient status and then, when civil rights legislation made this impossible, simply ignoring them. . . .

Although middle-class Cubans in the 1960s took whatever jobs were available and in this sense "displaced Blacks," their stay in those jobs was relatively brief. Subjectively, the exiles did not see themselves competing with the native minority; they were simply making do until they could return to Cuba. As those prospects became progressively dimmer, many moved rapidly into self-employment in such areas as garment subcontracting, landscaping, and residential construction. This evolution did not so much displace Blacks as transform the local economy. Indeed, figures on ethnic employment by industry indicate that the rising representation of Latins (overwhelmingly Cuban) was primarily at the expense of native whites rather than Blacks. . . .

There was no one-to-one substitution of Blacks by Cubans in the labor market, nor was there direct exploitation of one minority by the other. There was, however, a new urban economy in which the immigrants raced past other groups, leaving the native minority behind. Hence, after decades of striving for a measure of equality with whites, Miami Blacks found that the game had drastically changed. Anglos were leaving, and other whites who spoke a foreign language were occupying their positions. As a result, most Blacks were in a similar position as before. . . .

It was . . . in the development of small enterprises that the differences became most visible. Perhaps most devastating to the Black community was the apparent ease with which the Cubans ensconced themselves in the local economy, all the while claiming that their stay was temporary for they would soon return to their island. In 1977, only eighteen years after the Cuban Revolution, Cuban-owned firms in Dade County exceeded eight thousand in number, or four times as many as were owned by Blacks; average gross receipts of Cuban firms amounted to almost $84,000, or twice as much as the typical Black enterprise.[1] By 1980, approximately half of the largest banks and enterprises owned by Spanish-origin groups in the United States were in Miami, even though the area claimed a mere 5 percent of the country's Spanish-origin population. By contrast, only one Miami Black business made the list of the three hundred top Black enterprises in the nation.[2] . . .

During the 1970s, the two minorities never clashed directly; each remained absorbed in its own situation and problems. Yet the immigrants' presence increasingly altered the character of the city, adding a new twist to the perennial subordination of Blacks and to their rising discontent.

The Riot

. . . By 1980, this situation of double marginalization had not yet been articulated into a coherent Black discourse, although the reality of powerlessness was there for all to see. At the street level, powerlessness was reflected in the traditional police practice of treating Blacks with relative impunity. Seen by respectable white citizens as the vice-ridden "bad" parts of town, Liberty City and other Black ghetto areas were places where the police were given a freer hand. People living in these areas had to fear not only violence from crime, but also violence from their would-be protectors. This adversarial culture between the Black citizenry and the local police departments then became exacerbated in the wake of the civil rights movement, just as an increasing number of officers came to bear Spanish names.

"McDuffie," as the case was known locally, represented the culmination of this hostile trend. In March 1980, a thirty-three-year-old Black insurance agent named Arthur McDuffie died in Miami's Jackson Memorial Hospital from injuries sustained after being chased by city and county police units. The cause of the chase was a rolling stop at a red light plus an obscene gesture toward a nearby officer. Police claimed that McDuffie had died as the result of accidental injuries during the chase. Black Miami knew better. On March 31, four white Dade County Public Safety Department officers were charged with playing some role in the beating of McDuffie and subsequent attempts to cover up the cause of his death. Sensing the mood of tension in the city, a local judge granted a change of venue to Tampa. As he put it, the case was "a time bomb."[3]

Mariel had not yet started at the time of the March indictment, but by mid-May, when the jury's verdict came in, some fifty thousand new refugees were camped in the Orange Bowl and in public land under I-95, the city's main north-south thoroughfare. Their visibility was compounded by dire forebodings in the press about their presence. Just a week before, the *Miami Herald* had published its survey of significant negative reactions to the new refugees and the "potentially dangerous disagreements" among native whites, Blacks, and Latins.[4] The anti-Mariel campaign only added to the rising tension in the city. Hence, as Cuban exiles and native whites focused their attention on the comings and goings in the Straits of Florida, Black Miami remained fixed on that Tampa courtroom.

For Miami native whites, the city was under siege from the outside; as Blacks saw things, *their* city had long been under siege by the forces of the local establishment.

The verdict, reached in less than three hours of deliberation by an all-white jury, was broadcast by the Miami media on a clear Saturday afternoon. All four white officers were acquitted of all charges.

It took the Black community about as much time to react to this verdict as it had taken the white jury to arrive at it. The news was known in Miami at 2:42 p.m.; less than three hours later the first rocks and bottles were flying in Liberty City.

The 1980 Miami riot was different from similar urban uprisings in three ways: first, it was isolated rather than part of a national trend; second, it was unusually violent; third, it took place with at least the tacit approval of many Black leaders, who under other circumstances could have been trusted to oppose it.

It had been twelve years since the other great Black Miami uprising. But unlike the 1968 riot, which was timed to coincide with the National Democratic Convention in Miami Beach, the 1980 civil disorders were not matched by similar events in other cities. Black Miami rose alone. Its action stood as yet another manifestation of the singularity of the city, and as a reflection of the uncommonly harsh conditions endured by its nonwhite citizenry.

The riot was also different in its viciousness. Porter and Dunn estimate that total property loss reached about $80 million. All kinds of businesses were hit, including manufacturing plants where no consumer goods were to be found. White-, Cuban-, and Black-owned businesses were torched indiscriminately. By the end of the disorders, commercial life in many parts of Liberty City had virtually ceased to exist.[5] Nevertheless, the pent-up anger reflected in the rioters' drive not just to steal but to destroy was nothing in comparison with the way they went after random whites, Anglo and Latin alike. There was an eye-for-an-eye mood which led hitherto powerless Blacks to attack any unfortunate representatives of their perceived oppressors who happened by. Driving down the wrong street during those days could lead to a nightmarish experience, if not death. Whites were doused with gasoline and set afire in their cars; others were dragged out and beaten repeatedly with chunks of concrete and bricks, run over by cars, stabbed with screwdrivers, and shot. One was left dying in the street, a red rose in his mouth. Eight whites died in such terrible ways, most on the first day of the riot.[6]

Similar uprisings in other cities have brought Black leaders into the streets to calm down the masses, and older Black citizens have generally tried to rein in ghetto youth. There were such attempts in Liberty City and other Black areas of Miami, but they were countermanded by the opposite trend. A peaceful rally called by the local branch of the NAACP the day the verdict was announced turned into a full-scale riot involving both ghetto teenagers and Black professionals. During the incident, the seat of Dade County's justice system, the courthouse itself, was broken into and torched. Adults on ghetto street corners were observed egging on youths as they stopped and attacked cars driven by whites.[7] "During the riot, we hit everybody, Anglo, Cuban, it didn't matter," a Black community leader told us in 1985—the pronoun "we" speaking volumes; "it was the only way left for this community to show its ire."[8] The local head of the Urban League refused to go into the streets and calm the crowds, noting that "anyone who had any understandings of the ramifications of dehumanization and social isolation could understand the riots. . . . Whites thought it was irresponsible . . . because they assumed that Black leaders were there to protect them and not to lead Black folks."[9]

The 1980 riot expressed in actions what words had not been able to. American Blacks have always defined their reality in reaction to the subordination and discrimination laid on them by whites; indeed, this is the core of a nationwide Black discourse. In their study of American race riots, for example, Stanley Lieberson and Arnold Silverman noted that cities where riots occurred as a rule had: (1) too few Black police officers relative to the Black population; (2) too few Black entrepreneurs and store owners; and (3) an electoral system that led to too few Black representatives in local government.[10] Miami fulfilled all three conditions amply, but in addition the native minority confronted the reality of a changed city, where a new immigrant group was elbowing them aside. "McDuffie" was, without doubt, the trigger for the riots, but the resentment of being always left out, of remaining invisible and forgotten as other groups marched forward, was the background against which the extremely violent actions of May took place.

Mariel and the Black riot had this in common: they galvanized the two ethnic communities and provided the basis for a vigorous effort at reinterpretion. The stigma of Mariel compelled the Cubans to invent a "new Miami" in which their own role was both central and positive. Similarly, the deaths and deliberate destruction during the May uprising forced Black leaders to rethink the city in terms not bounded by the standard urban-minority frame. The militant double-subordination perspective that took shape during the next decade was born out of these events.[11]

The Boat People

My name is Jean and I came to the United States in 1978. Well, what happened to me was that a Macoute[12] came to rent a bicycle from me for a dollar. When I asked for it back, he told me, "Don't you know that I bought this bicycle from you for a dollar?" I held the bicycle and took it away from him. Right away he hit me with a club. As I was trying to get away, four more came and started beating on me. I ran and hid in the woods.

A cousin came to tell me that they had taken one of my brothers. When he couldn't tell them where I was they took him to a park in front of everybody and killed him. I spent two or three months hiding, and then I went to the Northwest to find a boat. That wasn't hard, but I had to get the $1,500 for the passage. I sold one of my small plots. Anyway, I thought that, once in Miami, I could earn enough to buy it back and probably more. Other families in the town received as much as $200 a month from relatives in Miami. . . . That's more than most could earn in three years.[13]

Between Port-de-Paix and Cap-Haitien on the north coast of the Republic of Haiti, there were at the start of the 1980s some sixty boats capable of carrying people on a long sea voyage. Charging two or three times the commercial air fare and packing dozens of people in every trip, the captains of those boats created one of the most lucrative businesses in the country. The destination was Miami.

People sold everything they had, including land that had been in their family since the Haitian Revolution in 1804, to buy passage aboard those boats. Their desperation was understandable. In May 1980, the military commander of Haiti's Northwest Province called together all the area's pastors to inform them that the government wanted to stop the exodus. He asked the religious community for its assistance. In fact, the flow did stop for about a week. But after the brief embargo, the first boat to leave departed from directly below the military commander's headquarters. All along, his intent had been not to control outmigration but to obtain a monopoly on kickbacks.[14]

To try to leave the poorest country with one of the most corrupt regimes in the hemisphere is a rational course of action. Indeed, for several decades Haitians of all classes had been streaming out. During the 1960s and 1970s their main destination was New York City. As with other immigrants, New York simply absorbed the newcomers. Middle-class professionals escaping the Duvaliers' oppression were followed by artisans and workers, who simply overstayed their temporary visas. No matter: New York took them in, adding them to its global mix.

Miami, however, was different. Between 1977 and 1981, approximately sixty thousand Haitians arrived by boat in South Florida. The number was only about one-fifth the size of New York's Haitian population, but the impact that these "boat people" had in the receiving city was immeasurably greater.[15]

More than numbers, it was the manner of their arrival that garnered attention, both locally and nationwide. Photographs of shirtless Black refugees huddled aboard barely seaworthy craft evoked images buried deep in the American collective mind. Like the slave ships of yore, these boats also brought a cargo of Black laborers, except that this time they came on their own initiative, and this time nobody wanted them. Still more pathetic were those Black bodies washing ashore Florida's pristine beaches when their craft did not make it. For native whites, this new immigrant wave reinforced the state-of-siege mentality created by Mariel.

In 1980, the Third World laid claim to Miami. The Haitian boat flow peaked right at the time of the Cuban flotilla, the two becoming one in the public mind. Yet despite this conflation, the two refugee streams were very different.[16] Mariel had been, after all, sponsored from Miami, the creation of nostalgic Cuban-Americans. The majority of Mariel entrants had relatives awaiting them and a strong community that understood their language and culture. Cubans, moreover, had been a familiar presence in South Florida for two decades.

Haitians were not sponsored by Miami, nor did they have any solid ethnic networks on which to rely. Few people in South Florida understood either Haitian Creole or the abysmal conditions that the would-be refugees were leaving behind. Not surprisingly, the reaction of native whites was to reject the new arrivals and to try to stop their entry. Unlike Mariel, this effort met with greater success.

In response to representations made by Miami leaders and local staff of the INS, federal officials in Washington initiated a "Haitian Program" in 1979. The core of the program involved accelerating deportation proceedings and making a concerted effort to discourage Haitian boat people from applying for political asylum. Those who did apply did not have much luck: "Five minute answers to such questions as 'What do you think would happen to you if you return to Haiti?' were reduced to a single sentence in translation. 'Why did you come to the United States?' was virtually always answered on the official form as 'I came here to find work,' as if each of the Haitians had used precisely the same words."[17] The INS would either fail to advise Haitians of their right to a lawyer or else tell them that a lawyer would only get them into trouble. A favorite tactic was to schedule multiple hearings simultaneously. Attorneys for the would-be refugees were expected to argue fifteen different cases in five different locations at the same time.

The culmination of this campaign came not in government offices, but on the high seas. Soon after the installation of the Reagan administration, Coast Guard cutters were ordered to patrol Haitian waters around the clock so that Miami-bound boats could be intercepted at sea before reaching U.S. jurisdiction.[18] Faced with such determined efforts to prevent their arrival, it is remarkable that so many Haitians managed to slip through and remain in South Florida.

Ironically, the reason the "Haitian Program" did not thoroughly succeed was its victims' own defenselessness. Their plight elicited public compassion and the concern of churches and philanthropic organizations. The National Council of Churches sponsored the Haitian Refugee Center (HRC), led by an activist Haitian priest named, most appropriately, Gerard Jean-Juste. The three or four young attorneys who worked pro bono at the center, with support from national law firms, probably did as much to sustain the fledgling Haitian community as the refugees themselves. These lawyers in effect interposed the American legal system between the powerless newcomers and the government's efforts to be rid of them. Their efforts culminated in a class action suit heard in Miami's Federal District Court the same week that the first boats from Mariel came streaming in.[19]

Cuban-Americans also provided unwitting support for the Haitian refugees through their efforts to bring their own kin from Mariel. The coincidence of the two flows only underscored the glaring disparities in the receptions accorded to each group. No government official ever attempted to summarily deport a Mariel refugee; U.S. Coast Guard cutters towed and escorted boats carrying Cubans to Key West, not back to Cuba. No matter how disparaged Mariel entrants were by the media, they were still Cuban and thus effectively insulated from the fate awaiting the boats from Cap-Haitien and Port-de-Paix.

The U.S. government's justification for the differential treatment hinged on the distinction between "political" refugees and "economic" migrants. The argument did not wash. Clearly many Mariel refugees had left in search of better opportunities, while many Haitians had experienced genuine persecution. . . .

In fact, the difference between the Cubans and Haitians streaming into Miami had less to do with individual motivations than with the country they left behind, the community that received them, and their color. This last realization mobilized the Black political establishment in defense of the Haitians. . . .

Faced with this combined offensive, the government relented. Processing of the two flows was assigned to a new administrative entity—the Cuban-Haitian Task Force, housed in the State Department. The creation of this task force and the appointment of a new "Cuban-Haitian refugee coordinator" by the Carter administration further stigmatized the Mariel arrivals, but proved invaluable to Haitians seeking stays from deportation. From then on, any government action toward the "entrants" (as both Mariel Cubans and Haitians were now officially labeled) would have to be on an equal basis.[20] . . .

[However,] the Black community had reason to look upon the Haitians with ambivalence. True, prominent Black figures had defended the newcomers against government deportation, but they had done so in the interest of racial equality—because they were Black, not because they were immigrants. Once settled, however, the newcomers proceeded to compete directly with Black Americans for manual labor jobs, accepting almost any wages and work conditions. For Liberty City, Overtown, and other Black ghetto areas reeling under the impact of double marginalization, the appearance on the labor scene of yet another competitor was not welcome. Black leaders never publicly attacked the Haitians, but confrontation between the two groups mounted nevertheless. The Creole-speaking newcomers were too docile, too subservient to white employers, and, above all, too foreign to the realities of Black America.

Discrimination on the part of native Blacks did not go unreciprocated; Haitians did not see the common circumstance of race as sufficient reason to join a subjugated minority. Instead they set their sights higher, seeking to become an entrepreneurial group. The self-conscious attempt to pattern Little Haiti after the business community of Little Havana was part of this effort. The Haitian quarter abuts Liberty City on the east, but contacts between the fledgling immigrant neighborhood and the Black ghetto were scarce and uneasy. A Haitian-American community leader described the situation in the early eighties thus: "Haitians rarely cross 7th Avenue or I-95 (the locally agreed-upon limits of Liberty City). They call the area 'Black Power' and do not want to live close to it. Haitians will not melt into the larger Black community. There is just too much animosity between both groups both in school and at work. The competition for jobs is tremendous."[21]

The difficult circumstances of arrival and the indifference, if not hostility, of the local population combined to make the initial years in the United States a trying experience for the boat people.". . .

Although Haitian entrants were somewhat better educated, more highly skilled, and more urban than their compatriots still in Haiti, they nevertheless compared poorly with American Blacks or Mariel Cubans. On average, none had advanced beyond the fifth or sixth grade, and about four-fifths spoke little or no English. In Haiti, about a third had been jobless (unemployed or not looking for work) before they decided to leave.

By 1983, the Haitians' tribulations had not yet begun to pay off. True, over half were enrolled in English and other courses in order to improve their labor market chances, but fully two-thirds (and 80 percent of the women) were jobless. By way of comparison, that figure is about twice the jobless rate among Mariel refugees and, for males, three times the jobless rate reported by the Census for all pre-1980 Haitian residents nationwide.[22] As a result, the average household income for Haitian entrants was less than half that reported for the pre-1980 U.S. Haitian population; indeed, close to 60 percent of the new households were below the poverty line. Despite their dire situation, only 29 percent of the immigrants received any form of public or private assistance during their initial years in the United States—a clear indicator of the social environment they confronted here. Of those lucky enough to have found jobs, the overwhelming majority had done so with the aid of kin and friends or by themselves; fewer than 4 percent had been helped by any public or private agency.

The pariah status of Haitian boat people was a consequence of both their race and the highly visible manner of their arrival, which contrasted with the low profile that their conationals had been keeping in New York for years. The two factors combined to insure a negative reception by both the federal government and the local population. For the latter, the pathetic image of the arriving Haitian boats suggested that not only Cuba, but the entire Caribbean, was about to empty itself in Miami. The association in the public mind of incoming Cubans and Haitians became one of the few lucky things going for the latter. Yet despite this coincidence and the help of churches and private charities, the situation three years after arrival was anything but enviable.

Haitians were not so much at the bottom of the labor market as outside it; they were neglected by public welfare agencies and looked down on by all other segments of the local community, including native Blacks. Reflecting this situation, 53 percent of our 1983 Haitian entrant respondents [part of our broader study of immigrants in South Florida] reported that they were discriminated against by Black Americans; 65 percent indicated that Anglo-Americans considered them inferior; and 86 percent had few or no contacts with a single native white.

The City at Mid-Year

Now picture the situation by the late summer of 1980: Mariel had added some ninety thousand to Dade County's Cuban population. The exile community had gotten away with the boatlift, but Fidel Castro had succeeded in stigmatizing the rescue effort. Although most Mariel refugees had integrated themselves quietly into the community, a visible minority was causing enough trouble to garner national attention. Seriously disturbed mental patients roamed the streets of Little Havana, overwhelming the local mental health system[23]; former convicts survived by preying on Jewish retirees in South Miami Beach; Mariel drug gangs peppered each other with gunfire in any neighborhood shopping center.

Meanwhile, much of the Black northwest section of Miami lay in shambles following the latest assault by its own citizens, a rebellion against the city that immigrant newcomers were overcoming all obstacles to reach. The May riot had made abundantly clear just how tall the barriers were separating native whites, Latins, and Blacks. Next to the wasted Black ghetto, immigrants of the same color but a different mind-set had started building a community of their own. For old-time Miamians, this activity was a harbinger of things to come. French Creole was now added to Spanish in what was quickly becoming a polyglot boardinghouse.

Monolingual Anglos, meanwhile, responded by voting solidly for the primacy of English. Cubans paid no attention. Haitians enrolled in English classes, but they learned Spanish on the job too. By now, *Miami Herald* columnists had run out of expressions to describe the new events, each one a blow to the city as they had known it. Their cries of anguish also went unheeded. Miami was a very different place eight months into the year because the remarkable happenings beforehand had fundamentally altered its ethnic makeup and, in the process, subverted an entire social order. . . .

Endnotes

1. Bruce Porter and Marion Dunn, *Miami Riot of 1980: Crossing the Bounds*, Lexington, MA: DC Heath, 1984, 195-96. Alejandro Portes, "The Social Origins of the Cuban Enclave Economy of Miami," *Sociological Perspectives* 30 (October 1987): 340-72.

2. Portes, "Social Origins of the Cuban Enclave Economy"; Marvin Dunn and Alex Stepick, "Blacks in Miami," in *Miami Now! Immigration, Ethnicity, and Social Change*, ed. G.J. Grenier and A. Stepick (Gainesville: University Press of Florida, 1992), 41-56.

3. Joan Didion, *Miami*,41. New York: Simon and Schuster, 1987.

4. "Dade Fears Refugee Wave," *Miami Herald*, May 11, 1980.

5. Ibid., 129-30.

6. Ibid., 47-60; Didion, *Miami*, 45.

7. Porter and Dunn, *Miami Riot of 1980*, 60-68.

8. Field interview with head of a major social services agency in Liberty City, 1985.

9. Porter and Dunn, *Miami Riot of 1980*, 68.

10. Stanley Lieberson and Arnold R. Silverman, "The Precipitants and Underlying Conditions of Race Riots," *American Sociological Review* 30 (December 1965): 887-98.

11. By the time of the Overtown uprising of January 1989, the distinct positions of the Miami Black community had become well articulated. See, for example, Dorothy Gaiter, "Lozano Verdict Brought Relief and Long-delayed Justice," *Miami Herald*, December 8, 1989, 31A.

12. Tonton Macoutes is the name given by Haitians to the bands of thugs hired by the successive Duvalier regimes to intimidate the population.

13. This story is an amalgamation of affidavits of Haitian refugees who testified in *Haitian Refugee Center v. Civiletti*, 503 F. Supp. 442 (S.D. Fla 1980), modified *Sub nom. Haitian Refugee Center v. Smith*, 676 F. 2d 1023 (5th Cir. 1982), including especially the case of Odilius Jean. Parts were also derived from Stevan Petrow, "What Did the Haitians Do?" *St. Petersburg Times*, November 11, 1979, 8ff.; and Bruce Keldan, "Tales of the Tonton Macoutes from Haitians Who Fled," *Philadelphia Inquirer*, October 8, 1979, A1, 10A.

14. Alex Stepick, *Haitian Refugees in the U.S.*, Minority Rights Group (MRG) no. 52 (London: MRG, 1986), 11.

15. Alex Stepick and Alejandro Portes, "Flight into Despair: A Profile of Recent Haitian Refugees in South Florida," *International Migration Review* 20 (Summer 1986): 329-50.

16. The combination was sanctioned officially by the creation of the federal Cuban-Haitian Interagency Task Force in mid-1980. This agency is described below.

17. Stepick, *Haitian Refugees*, 14.

18. Task Force on Immigration and Refugee Policy, "Issue Paper—Subject: What Policy Should the United States Adopt with Regard to Foreign Persons Who Enter South Florida Without Visas?" (June 26, 1981), Memorandum to President Reagan from task force established by him March 6, 1981. Subsequently, the policy became formal and legal via U.S. Department of State, "Migrants—Interdiction," Agreement Between the United States of America and Haiti, Effected by Exchange of Notes, Signed at Port-au-Prince, September 23, 1981, Treaties and Other International Act Series,

10241, pursuant to PL 89-497, approved July 8, 1966 (80 Sta. 271; 1 U.S.C. 113).

19. Stepick, *Haitian Refugees*, 14-15.

20. In December 1980, the task force was moved to the Department of Health and Human Services. Its first coordinator was Ambassador Victor Palmieri. See White House, "New Cuban-Haitian Plan," *Fact Sheet #114* (Washington, D.C., July 1980).

21. Field interview conducted as part of the Cuban/Haitian immigration project, August 1983.

22. Stepick and Portes, "Flight into Despair"; Portes and Stepick, "Unwelcome Immigrants."

23. Camayd-Freixas, *Crisis in Miami*, chaps. 5 and 6.

The Conflict Over Immigration

Immigration, legal and illegal, has become the focus of intense public debate. Since the mid-1980s, this concern has yielded a series of legislative attempts to reform U.S. immigration and naturalization policies (Baker 1997; Bean and Fix 1992). In more recent years, there have been other efforts to diminish benefits for legal immigrants, such as the restrictions included in the welfare reform legislation passed by Congress in 1996. The Immigration and Naturalization Service (INS), the Border Patrol, and other agencies have stepped up efforts to reduce unlawful entry, especially from Mexico, and to apprehend and return undocumented immigrants in various areas of the U.S. (Dunn 1996). Public concern about high levels of legal and undocumented immigration can be seen in various opinion polls, and opposition to current trends has fueled the growth of public interest groups devoted to the issue, such as the Federation of Americans for Immigration Reform (FAIR). States that are popular destinations for undocumented entrants have formulated their own responses to the perceived crisis, most notably California's Proposition 187, the ballot initiative aimed at slashing benefits for undocumented immigrants (e.g., education, public health), which passed by a sizeable majority vote in 1994. California and Florida have sued the federal government to recover some costs associated with providing various benefits for undocumented immigrants, charging that federal agencies failed to carry out their responsibilities to control the nation's borders. Other states are contemplating similar lawsuits in the future.

At first glance, the current brouhaha over the costs, benefits, and ethics of immigration may seem strangely out of place. After all, it is often said that the U.S. is "a nation of immigrants." Indeed, virtually everyone reading this anthology is descended from immigrants. However, it is important to remember that immigration has been the focus of recurrent and heated debate, and various immigrant groups have been subject to oppression at the hands of native-born elements. Not surprisingly, many of the themes raised by both sides in today's immigration debate have surfaced repeatedly throughout U.S. history (Rumbaut 1997).

After the initial entry of European Americans (chiefly from England, Scotland, and Wales) prior to the American Revolution, assimilation occurred with decades of migration, contact, and adjustment. However the Revolution, severe economic depressions, and the War of 1812 caused immigration to the new United States to slow dramatically. As the numbers of new entrants swelled again by the mid-19th century, the initial European Americans became concerned about the impact of large-scale immigration from Ireland, Germany, and other European countries. This concern was exacerbated by the numbers of entrants, which grew from approximately 300,000 during the 1830s to 980,000 in the 1840s, peaking in the early 1850s (Bogue 1969). As they sought jobs, housing, and other resources in the U.S., these new Americans (especially the Irish immigrants) were often met with suspicion and unflattering stereotypes, and sometimes with violence.

By the 1880s, many in the native-born U.S. population were becoming worried about a new stream of immigrants. This influx peaked during the first decade of the 20th century, when nearly 9 million immigrants entered the U.S.; almost 70 percent of these newcomers were from southern and eastern Europe. Though fewer in numbers, Asian immigrants—mainly Chinese and Japanese—increased sharply during the 1880–1920 period as well. There were various efforts aimed at impeding immigration flows, and especially at reducing the influx of laborers who were seen as driving down wages and diminishing the quality of life enjoyed by native-born European Americans. Examples of this trend included the anti-contract labor provisions of the 1880s, as well as subsequent efforts to limit immigration from Mexico. (Interestingly, the first efforts to restrict cross-border traffic were not aimed primarily at reducing the influx of Mexicans, who were desired as workers in certain economic sectors, but rather at keeping out Chinese laborers who entered the U.S. from Mexico.) In California, a series of draconian steps were taken in the early 20th century to curb the dramatic gains of Japanese Americans in agriculture. Throughout the late 19th and early 20th century, Asian immigrants were subjected to noxious treatment throughout much of the western U.S.

The anti-immigration climate of this era resulted in legislation aimed specifically at stopping most Asian immigration—especially entry by working-class Chinese and Japanese—and culminated in far-reaching restrictions, such as the National Origins Quota Acts of 1921 and 1924. The 1921 law restricted immigration in any year from any given country to no more than 3 percent of the foreign-born stock from that country in the 1910 Census. The 1924 law modified this provision, lowering the percentage from 3 percent to 2 percent, and basing this calculation on the 1890 Census, rather than the 1910 Census. Because of the 1924 law, immigration into the U.S. dropped dramatically, and most observers mark this as the end of the second major migratory stream in American

history. Figures remained low until after World War II, but have been rising dramatically since the mid-1960s, when U.S. immigration laws underwent another fundamental overhaul.

Today's debate over immigration revolves around several important issues. First, there is disagreement over the magnitude of current immigration trends. How dramatic are the contemporary immigration trends? What do they mean for the future of U.S. society? The answers to these questions depend partly on which statistics we choose to emphasize. In the 1990 Census year, foreign-born persons made up 7.9 percent of the total U.S. population. Pro-immigration groups often point out that this is a lower percentage than in many other countries, and well below the peak of 14.7 percent reported in the 1910 Census (U.S. Bureau of the Census 1992). Further, in absolute numbers, the 7.34 million legal immigrants recorded during the 1980s was smaller than the total during the 1900–10 period (Immigration and Naturalization Service 1990–92). Why the current uproar over immigration?

Critics of current immigration practices argue that these figures largely miss the point. They note that the 7.9 percent figure is the highest recorded in any Census year since 1940 (when the figure was 8.8 percent), and it has been increasing steadily since the mid-1960s, when massive changes in immigration laws were first instituted. And such numbers typically count legal immigrants; it is estimated that the population of undocumented immigrants is increasing at some 300,000 per year (Rumbaut 1997). Some demographers also emphasize the importance of calculating net immigration—i.e., adjusting the official INS figures to undocumented entrants, refugees, and other special categories of immigrants, as well as the departures of legal immigrants from U.S. shores. (The proportion of immigrants choosing to remain in the U.S. is significantly higher today than in previous decades.) According to one estimate, net immigration during the 1980s was 8.2 million, as compared with only 4.9 million from 1900–10 (Passel and Edmonston 1992).

Further, given low and declining fertility among much of the native-born U.S. population, net immigration accounted for nearly 40 percent of U.S. population growth during the 1980s, a figure which represents a dramatic increase over previous decades, and equals or surpasses the 20th century peak mark of the 1900–10 decade (U.S. Bureau of the Census 1992; Passel and Edmonston 1992). And if current immigration patterns continue unabated, this figure is likely to increase sharply in future decades; according to one estimate, by the year 2050, more than one-third (36 percent) of the U.S. population will be post-1970 immigrants and their descendants (Bouvier and Grant 1994). What are we to make of such numbers? One of the most outspoken critics of current trends, Peter Brimelow (himself an immigrant from Britain), uses such figures to argue that "Immigration policy is quite literally driving a wedge between the American nation, as it had evolved by 1965, and its future" (1995: 46). Brimelow and others reject the implication that current trends represent continuity with the past, or fidelity to America's self-understanding as a "nation of immigrants." To the contrary, they insist that unless something is done to limit absolute numbers of immigrants, or to change the composition of the immigrant pool, or both, American society will undergo fundamental, destablizing changes in its structure and character.

Supporters of immigration reform blame certain provisions of the 1965 immigration law for many of the current problems they perceive. In particular, this overhaul of U.S. immigration policy emphasized family reunification, permitting immigrants from various parts of the world to bring significant numbers of both immediate and extended kin to the U.S. According to critics of the policy, the effects of this provision of U.S. immigration law have been exacerbated by the well-documented tendency of immigrants to settle in communities which already have large coethnic populations and established ethnic institutions. This tendency is understandable, and partly reflects the preference of many new entrants for cultural and linguistic familiarity; moreover, coethnic networks are important in facilitating the social and economic incorporation of immigrants—helping them to locate formal or in-

formal employment opportunities, providing information about unfamiliar laws and customs, and so forth. One consequence of such settlement patterns has been the heavy concentration of immigrants from various sources in a small number of states (e.g., California, Texas) and metropolitan areas (e.g., Honolulu, Los Angeles, New York). Proponents of immigration reform assert that this can alter the cultures, institutions, and politics of those areas in ways that are incompatible with the preferences of long-time residents.

Economic issues figure prominently in the current immigration debate. According to supporters of immigration reform, by privileging family reunification over scarce skills, the 1965 immigration law has contributed to declines in the average skill levels of recent and current immigrants (Brimelow 1995, and this volume), creating the potential for several undesirable socioeconomic consequences. While recognizing that many recent entrants are highly educated (e.g., engineers, computer and high-tech workers), some proponents of reform worry that large numbers of unskilled immigrants will undermine overall economic productivity, and over the long term will reduce the base of taxpayers needed to sustain entitlements and other state programs. Moreover, there are concerns that large numbers of unskilled entrants will have difficulty finding jobs in our evolving economy, because the need for unskilled labor in the U.S. has been declining over the past two decades (Borjas 1990).

According to critics of current immigration policies, unskilled and low-skilled entrants are thrust into direct competition for employment, housing, and other resources with some of the least advantaged Americans—for example, in the search for low-level service positions, domestic work, and other jobs. The main losers, in this view, may be African Americans, as well as other historically impoverished groups. To date, the evidence on this point has been mixed (for a review, see Hamermesh and Bean 1997). Many empirical analyses over the past decade have turned up little connection between numbers of immigrants and unemployment or wage rates in the native population as a whole. And after recently reviewing a series of studies investigating niche overlap between African Americans and Latino immigrants in California, one prominent observer concluded: "[N]one of the studies reviewed so far provide evidence of harm to blacks . . . due to high levels of immigration from Mexico" (Heer 1996: 187). However, other research suggests a somewhat different conclusion. For instance, some studies indicate that high levels of immigration may contribute to the widening gap between the annual earnings of white and African American males. According to data from the 1991 Current Population Survey, individual earnings are lower in low-skilled occupations that have higher proportions of immigrants; this apparent negative effect of immigration is not present within higher-skilled occupations (Camarota 1997).

Based on in-depth interviews with managers and employers in several types of firms (e.g., restaurants, hotels, printers) in the Los Angeles area, Waldinger (1997) found that a number of factors incline employers to hire Latino/a immigrants over African Americans for low-level positions. Many employers harbor anti-black bias, due in some cases to previous negative experiences with African American employees. Latino immigrants, on the other hand, are widely viewed as more productive and tractable workers. Moreover, Waldinger found that many Latino immigrants were hired through their personal networks (e.g., connections with friends or relatives already working at the firm). These network ties in the workplace may increase the pressure on immigrant workers to perform well, because new employees are "on the spot" not to embarrass their references. In turn, these hiring practices are thought to enhance the cohesion of work groups, and to make on-the-job training by coworkers much easier. Further, many employers in Waldinger's study believe that inserting an African American worker into a predominantly Latino crew erodes productivity, due to friction between African Americans and Latinos (Waldinger 1997). While considerably more research is needed to see whether these findings are generalizable to other contexts, this study offers valuable hints about the possible employment competition and displacement in some sectors that may be due to immigration.

Defenders of current immigration policies include an intriguing mix of Latino and other immigrant groups (e.g., the National Council of La Raza), which tend to embrace left-of-center positions on human rights matters and a range of policy issues, and libertarian conservatives, who endorse free-market economic policies and relatively open national borders to permit the free flow of labor. These groups maintain that throughout much of U.S. history, immigration has resulted in a net increase in jobs for our economy (Simon 1989; Borjas 1990). They argue that an influx of new entrants actually creates new employment niches (e.g., jobs to satisfy the additional demand from a new pool of consumers) and that immigrants often take jobs that native-born workers cannot or will not fill (e.g., as agricultural workers, or as employees in ethnic restaurants), rather than competing with native-born residents. Pro-immigration forces also correctly point out that rates of entrepreneurship are exceptionally high among immigrant groups (e.g., Light and Rosenstein 1995; Waldinger, Aldrich, and Ward 1990). Many new entrants into the U.S. start their own small businesses, which may offer goods and services primarily to coethnics and may employ mainly coethnics. To many observers, this makes immigrants seem like an economic asset rather than a liability, although some worry that the high rate of immigrant business startups in minority neighborhoods may stifle entrepreneurial activity among native-born residents. Given that calls for immigration reform have gained the greatest political ground in California, during a period of economic stagnation due partly to cutbacks in U.S. military procurement and related spending, pro-immigration forces tend to view the current anti-immigration climate as a product of scapegoating and political opportunism by some elected officials.

One persistent concern of anti-immigration groups has been the burden of high immigration levels on taxpayers, at the state and federal levels. Especially in light of the low skill levels of some current immigrants, it has become popular to argue that many immigrants require extensive social services, including welfare, health care, and education

Miles 1992). Critics of current policy often argue that large numbers of immigrants come in order to give birth to their children on U.S. soil, so that their offspring will automatically be U.S. citizens, entitled to all of the rights and benefits that citizenship confers. Critics also warn that immigrants may be crowding out native-born racial and ethnic minorities and poor whites, who also draw upon many of these services and benefits. As a matter of principle, they assert that—especially in an era of government fiscal crisis—scarce resources should be devoted to the needs of native-born U.S. residents first, rather than new entrants, including some who are not yet citizens. Similar arguments were advanced to defend provisions in the 1996–97 federal welfare reform legislation, which curtailed access to many services even for legal immigrants. California's Proposition 187 was also based on this premise, and required that teachers, health care workers, and other public sector employees deny services to undocumented immigrants.

What is the evidence that immigration burdens taxpayers? Although a host of studies have addressed aspects of this question, scholars and policymakers remain far from a consensus on the matter. Researchers have identified a significant distributional problem with regard to taxpayer burden: While the social services utilized by immigrants tend to be funded by states and localities, a disproportionate share of the taxes paid by immigrants goes to the federal government (Rothman and Espenshade 1992). This suggests that federal assistance to states and communities with large numbers of immigrants may be appropriate. More recently, several studies have attempted to calculate the overall costs of immigration to U.S. taxpayers, and to the taxpayers of various high-immigration states (e.g., California, Texas) and localities. However, estimates vary wildly, with some high-profile studies reporting that immigration imposes huge burdens (e.g., Huddle 1993) and others disputing such alarmist estimates (e.g., Passel 1994). One reason for these discrepancies is that studies differ widely in methodology (e.g., in which types of revenues and outlays they consider, and in whether to calculate costs and benefits at one point in time only, or over the lifetime of immigrants). According to one careful review of existing studies, the lack of agreement on a uniform accounting framework, and the absence of high-quality data on many of the most important issues, make it impossible to draw firm conclusions at this time about the overall costs and benefits of immigration to U.S. taxpayers (Vernez and McCarthy 1996).

While some celebrate the growth of Latino and Asian American populations in the U.S., and argue that Americans should embrace the multicultural diversity that will result, proponents of restrictionist immigration reforms sometimes paint a picture of cultural and institutional anarchy. Many conservatives maintain that key features of the U.S. experience—democratic political structure, capitalism, human rights (including property rights), work ethic, and more—have been based on a so-called "Anglo-Saxon cultural core," to which successive streams of immigrants have (more or less) assimilated throughout U.S. history (Brimelow 1995). They worry that given the rapid growth of immigrant populations from Latin America and Asia—and their sheer size and spatial concentration—new entrants may successfully resist pressures for assimilation, although contemporary trends in intermarriage suggest that such concerns may be overblown. Assuming that shared language (i.e., English) and shared values are key ingredients in social stability, conservative critics fear that over the long term, these dynamics could lead to unprecedented and irreversible ethnic balkanization and social upheaval.

Such arguments outrage pro-immigrant groups, who see anti-Latino and anti-Asian sentiment behind the strident rhetoric and gloomy predictions. They are concerned that supporters of immigration reform seem to marginalize non-European cultures and groups, discounting or ignoring their past, present, and future contributions to U.S. society. Moreover, is it appropriate to presume that the U.S. should remain dominated by European American values? Are those customs and values superior? Or do some anti-immigration arguments really imply beliefs about racial superiority? This is explosive symbolic and emotional terrain. Taken to their logical extreme, some anti-immigration arguments raise fundamental questions about identity, about who should be considered a "real American." Even some cultural conservatives decry anti-immigrant scapegoating, noting that many immigrants seem to embody so-called "middle-American values" (e.g., commitment to family, work ethic, thrift and enterprise) more fervently than members of the native-born population (Fukuyama 1993).

The debates surrounding immigration policy raise wrenching and complicated human rights issues. For example, advocates for immigrants argue that the provisions of California's Proposition 187 direct state employees to act as agents of the Immigration and Naturalization Service (INS), and that in some instances individuals may be required to violate their professional ethics or standards. Pro-immigrant groups also worry that passage of Proposition 187 may discourage immigrants—perhaps legal entrants, as well as undocumented—from seeking medical care, immunizations for children, or public education, either (a) because they will assume they are ineligible or (b) because they will fear negative treatment (or, if undocumented, they will fear detection and deportation). In addition to adversely affecting immigrant families themselves, such reluctance to use public agencies could also lead to a rise in public health problems (e.g., untreated epidemics) and other social problems (e.g., poorly-educated youth) in California and other states which may pass restrictive immigration legislation.

Opinion polls suggest a hardening of popular attitudes toward immigrants, especially in states with large immigrant populations. Immediately following the passage of Proposition 187 in California, pro-immigrant groups publicized accounts of negative treatment toward Latino/a Americans, including some who were naturalized citizens. For instance, the Coalition for Humane Immigration Rights of Los Angeles (CHIRLA) released a report in late 1995, reviewing 229 cases of discrimination, denial of services, civil rights violations, hate speech, and hate crimes that CHIRLA was able to verify in follow-up interviews after initial screening by attorneys (CHIRLA 1995). The time period covered by the report is from the summer of

1994, when anti-immigrant and pro-187 sentiment were building, through the fall of 1995; most of the incidents were reported after CHIRLA set up a hot line in late 1994, immediately following the passage of Proposition 187. More than 60 percent of these cases of abuse were committed against U.S. citizens and legal permanent residents, all Latino. The CHIRLA report focuses on 157 (of the 229 total) incidents that occurred in settings not targeted by Proposition 187—i.e. not in schools or clinics, but in banks, restaurants, grocery stores, traffic stops, and so on. Most acts of discrimination and abuse were perpetrated by European Americans who (a) incorrectly assumed that most Latinos are undocumented immigrants and (b) mistakenly cited Proposition 187 as justification for their actions. (It bears mentioning that while most discussions of undocumented immigration focus exclusively on Latinos and Asians, large numbers of illegal entrants from various European countries are present in New York and other East Coast cities.) Advocates worry that abuses will become more widespread as anti-immigrant scapegoating continues.

The recent militarization of U.S. border enforcement, involving several federal agencies, has apparently led to an increase in maltreatment and brutality against Latinos in border communities throughout the Southwest (Dunn 1996, and this volume). Again, such abuses have been experienced by numerous Latinos, including native-born and naturalized citizens, as well as undocumented immigrants. For the undocumented, this compounds the risks already associated with immigration, which include: accidents; dehydration and starvation; robbery and violence at the hands of bandits and drug merchants in border areas; as well as exploitation by unscrupulous guides (who obtain money and other favors in exchange for arranging passage to the U.S.), and by employers in search of cheap and pliant labor in garment industries and other sweatshops. While the data available from county medical examiners and other official sources are sometimes limited, researchers at the University of Houston estimate that nearly 1,200 persons died, mostly in various types of accidents, while attempting to cross the U.S.-Mexican border between 1993–96 (Bailey et al. 1997). The dangers to these immigrants may be exacerbated by recent changes in border enforcement strategy, which has pushed border crossing attempts into increasingly isolated and rugged terrain (Dunn, this volume). As U.S. policymakers and citizens sort out the difficult issues that lie at the center of the immigration wrangle, it is crucial that we push for humane policies that respect the rights, dignity, and due process of all parties.

References

Bailey, Stan, Karl Eschbach, Jacqueline Hagan, and Nestor Rodriguez. 1997. *Migrant Death at the Texas-Mexico Border.* Houston: Center for Migration Studies, University of Houston.

Baker, Susan Gonzalez. 1997. "The 'Amnesty' Aftermath: Current Policy Issues Stemming From the Legalization Programs of the 1986 Immigration Reform and Control Act." *International Migration Review.* 31:5–27.

Bean, Frank D., and Michael Fix. 1992. "The Significance of Recent Immigration Policy Reforms in the United States." Pp. 41–55 in *Nations of Immigrants: Australia, the United States, and International Migration,* edited by Gary P. Freeman and James Jopp. Melbourne: Oxford University Press.

Bogue, Donald J. 1969. *Principles of Demography.* New York: Wiley and Sons.

Borjas, George. 1990. *Friends or Strangers: The Impact of Immigrants on the U.S. Economy.* New York: Basic Books.

Bouvier, Leon, and Lindsey Grant. 1994. *How Many Americans? Population, Immigration, and the Environment.* New York: Sierra Club.

Brimelow, Peter. 1995. *Alien Nation: Common Sense About America's Immigration Disaster.* New York: HarperCollins.

Camarota, Steven A. 1997. "The Effect of Immigrants on the Earnings of Low-Skilled Native Workers: Evidence from the June 1991 Current Population Survey." *Social Science Quarterly* 78: 417–431.

CHIRLA [Coalition for Humane Immigrant Rights of Los Angeles]. 1995. *Hate Unleashed: Los Angeles in the Aftermath of 187.* Los Angeles: CHIRLA (November).

Dunn, Timothy J. 1996. *The Militarization of the U.S.-Mexico Border, 1978–1992: Low-Intensity Conflict Doctrine Comes Home.* Austin: Center for Mexican American Studies, University of Texas.

Fukuyama, Francis. 1993. "Immigrants and Family Values." *Commentary* (May): 26–32.

Hamermesh, Daniel S., and Frank D. Bean (eds.). 1997. *Help or Hindrance? The Economic Implications of Immigration for African Americans.* New York: Russell Sage Foundation.

Heer, David. 1996. *Immigration in America's Future.* Boulder, CO: Westview Press.

Huddle, Donald. 1993. *The Net National Costs of Immigration.* Washington, DC: Carrying Capacity Network.

Light, Ivan, and Carolyn Rosenstein. 1995. *Race, Ethnicity, and Entrepreneurship in Urban America.* New York: Aldine de Gruyter.

Miles, Jack. 1992. "Blacks vs. Browns (African Americans vs. Latinos)." *Atlantic Monthly* (October): 41–64.

Passel, Jeffrey. 1994. *Immigrants and Taxes: A Reappraisal of Huddle's The Cost of Immigrants.* Washington: Urban Institute, PRIP-UI-29, January.

Passel, Jeffrey, and Barry Edmonston. 1992. *Immigration and Race: Recent Trends in Immigration the U.S.* Washington: Urban Institute.

Rothman, Eric, and Thomas Espenshade. 1992. "Fiscal Impacts of Immigration to the United States." *Population Index* 58: 381–415.

Rumbaut, Ruben G. 1997. "Origins and Destinies: Immigration to the United States Since World War II." Pp. 15–46 in *New American Destinies: A Reader in Contemporary Asian and Latino Immigration,* edited by Darrell Y. Hamamoto and Rodolfo D. Torres. New York: Routledge.

Simon, Julian L. 1989. *The Economic Consequences of Immigration.* Cambridge, MA: Basil Blackwell.

U.S. Bureau of the Census. 1992. *Statistical Abstracts of the United States, 112th ed.* Washington: U.S. Government Printing Office.

U.S. Immigration and Naturalization Service. 1990–1992. *Statistical Yearbook.* Washington: U.S. Government Printing Office.

Vernez, Georges, and Kevin F. McCarthy. 1996. *The Costs of Immigration to Taxpayers: Analytical and Policy Issues.* Santa Monica, CA: RAND.

Waldinger, Roger. 1997. "Black/Immigrant Competition Re-assessed: New Evidence from Los Angeles." *Sociological Perspectives* 40: 365-386.

Waldinger, Roger, Howard Aldrich, Robin Ward, and associates. 1990. *Ethnic Entrepreneurs: Immigrant Business in Industrial Societies.* Beverly Hills: Sage.

40

Immigration and the Social Contract

Frank D. Bean
Robert G. Cushing
Charles W. Haynes
Jennifer V. W. Van Hook

Immigration issues once again occupy a prominent place on the public policy agenda of the United States (Fix and Passel 1994; Teitelbaum and Weiner 1995; U.S. Commission on Immigration Reform 1994). Concomitantly, public opinion polls show increasing numbers of persons who think current U.S. immigration levels are "too high" (Bean et al. 1997; Espenshade and Calhoun 1993). To understand why policymakers and the public have grown increasingly concerned about immigration, it is helpful to examine recent trends in the magnitude of flows of persons coming into the country compared with those at earlier time periods. In addition, it is also useful to inquire into the texture of these flows. Increasing anxiety about immigration may reflect worries about the size of flows less than concerns about their national origin and racial/ethnic composition (Massey 1995). Finally, the relatively diminished economic prospects facing American workers in recent years may also contribute to growing doubts about immigration. Thus, the specific purposes of this paper are (1) to develop a portrait of the recent major migration flows to the United States, (2) to assess their implications for the racial/ethnic composition of the U.S. population, and (3) to examine the economic context in which they have occurred. Our general goal is to try to explain not only why recent

migration flows have come to be negatively perceived, but also why they appear increasingly to be seen as violating the prevailing sense of social contract in the United States.

Major Flows into the United States

The major features of post-World War II migration flows to the United States include (1) rising numbers of legal immigrants; (2) increasing numbers of refugees and asylees; (3) increasing numbers of undocumented migrants; and (4) enormously increasing numbers of persons admitted for short periods of time on so-called nonimmigrant visas. Although these flows are not always mutually exclusive (e.g., many refugees eventually become immigrants), the share of persons from Hispanic and Asian countries has been increasing and now constitutes a majority of each flow, whereas the share from European countries has been decreasing. This pattern has occurred at the same time that economic growth has slowed and wages have stagnated.

In part, recent concerns about levels of immigration in the United States may stem from anxieties about changes in the size and composition of racial/ethnic groups or from worries about economic competition and job opportunities. In order to assess which of these contributes the most to rising opposition to immigration, we analyze recent changes in each of these migration flows to the United States and assess changes in the social, demographic, and economic contexts in which they have occurred. We seek to discern the most important sets of forces driving current reactions to U.S. immigration trends and policies.

Legal Immigrants

After a lull from 1925 through 1945, legal immigration to the United States has risen steadily, reaching by the early 1990s levels approaching the all-time highs set in the early part of the twentieth century (Bean, Vernez, and Keely 1989). If the legalizations resulting from the Immigration Reform and Control Act (IRCA) are included in the totals, the levels in 1990 and 1991 exceed all previous annual highs (U.S. Immigration and Naturalization Service 1995).

The national origins of U.S. immigrants have also been changing. Prior to 1960, the vast majority came from Europe or Canada (often over 90 percent when examined on a per decade basis). Even as late as the 1950s, 67.7 percent of all arrivals were from these areas. Things changed rapidly during the 1960s, when family reunification criteria rather than national-origin quotas became the basis for granting entry visas (Reimers 1983; Bean, Vernez, and Keely 1989). By the 1980s, only 12.5 percent of legal immigrants came from Europe or Canada, whereas 84.4 percent were from Asian or Latin American countries (U.S. Immigration and Naturalization Service 1995).

These relatively recent changes in the national-origin composition of immigrants have begun to convert the United States from a largely biracial society consisting of a sizable white majority, a small black minority, and a very small American Indian minority of less than 1 percent into a multiracial, multiethnic society consisting of several racial/ethnic groups (Passel and Edmonston 1994). This trend became discernible in the 1950s, but began to accelerate in the 1960s. By 1990, nearly a quarter of the U.S. population designated itself as black, Hispanic, Asian, or American Indian. The growth of other groups has meant that the proportion of blacks in the minority population has been declining. In fact, by 1990, blacks no longer constituted a majority of the minority population (Passel and Edmonston 1994).

Refugees and Asylees

The United States, like most other Western democracies, did not begin to focus explicitly on refugees in immigration policy until after World War II. At that time, it recognized the victims of political persecution as "a distinct category of international migrants to whom [it] owed special obligations" (Zohlberg 1992: 55). Essentially crafted and implemented on an *ad hoc* basis, U.S. postwar refugee policy introduced another source of new U.S. entrants. Since the end of World War II, nearly three million refugees and asylees have been granted lawful permanent resident

status by the United States (U.S. Immigration and Naturalization Service 1995).

During the 1940s and the 1950s, the number of refugees and asylees averaged about fifty thousand per year, a figure that declined to about twenty thousand per year during the 1960s, before rising again to over fifty thousand per year during the 1970s and to well over one hundred thousand per year in the 1990s. As with legal immigrants, the vast majority come from Asia, Latin America, and the Caribbean (49.2 percent overall since 1945, and 82.2 percent during the 1980s), although both the relative and the absolute numbers coming from the former Soviet Union have increased substantially since 1990. In short, the category of refugee and asylee admissions has constituted an increasing flow of persons, predominantly Asian and Latino, into the country since 1945.

Illegal Migrants

Persons who enter the United States illegally and persons who enter legally and then stay illegally constitute another major flow into the country. The former are called "EWI's" by the U.S. Immigration and Naturalization Service (or simply undocumented migrants by other observers) because they "enter without inspection"; the latter are called "visa-overstayers," because they stay beyond the expiration date of their visas. Almost all of the undocumented migrants enter at the U.S.-Mexico border, and the vast majority originate in Mexico, although in recent years substantial members have also come from Central American countries (Bean, Passel, and Edmonston 1990). The visa-overstayers do not come predominantly from any one country, but as a group, they appear to represent almost half of the illegal population resident in the country in recent years (Warren 1990, 1992; New York Times 1995).

The stock of undocumented migrants, together with the stock of visa-overstayers, started to grow in the 1960s and to increase rapidly in the 1970s. That this number has become substantial is indicated by the fact that the U.S. Bureau of the Census includes an annual net gain of two hundred thousand illegal immigrants in its annual population estimates and projections (Campbell 1994).

Other sources estimate the current size of this net component in the range of two hundred thousand to three hundred thousand persons (Warren 1992).

Obviously, the racial/ethnic composition of illegal immigrants is not known with the same degree of certainty as that of legal immigrants, but the available evidence suggests that the group, like contemporary legal immigrants in general, is mainly Asian and Latin American in origin (Warren and Passel 1987; Warren 1990, 1992). This would suggest that the effect on racial/ethnic composition is not greatly different from that of legal immigration. This conclusion is corroborated by the national-origin composition of the persons who became legal immigrants under the provisions of the 1986 Immigration Reform and Control Act, nearly 69.9 percent of whom were of Mexican origin and 92.4 percent of whom were either of Latin American or Asian origin (U.S. Department of Justice 1992).

Nonimmigrant Entrants

Nonimmigrant admissions are an important source of flows into the country and have implications for immigration issues that go beyond sheer magnitude. During fiscal year 1993, 21.4 million nonimmigrant admissions to the United States were recorded, an increase of 650,000 (3.1 percent) over fiscal year 1992 (U.S. Immigration and Naturalization Service, 1995). The dramatic increases in nonimmigrant admissions in recent years reflect the mounting demand both for tourism and for business- and employment-related entry resulting from the increased globalization of the economy. Nonimmigrant flows constitute the source from which visa-overstayers develop and have been estimated to make up about half of all illegal residents currently in the United States (Warren 1992). The picture that emerges from numerous ethnographic studies of migration implies that many visa-overstayers eventually become legal immigrants. Hence, as the volume of nonimmigrant admissions continues to climb steeply, pressures on the legal immigration system are likely to increase, even if the rate of visa-overstaying remains constant.

While the number of nonimmigrant entrants has steadily increased over the past decade, the national origins of people in this flow have been somewhat more diverse than is the case for other kinds of flows. The percentage of nonimmigrant entrants from Asia, Latin America, and the Caribbean was about 54 percent in 1993, up from about 41 percent in 1965. In addition to the fact that nonimmigrant entrants compose the pool from which visa-overstayers emerge, the number and racial/ethnic composition of persons in the United States on nonimmigrant visas are also likely to affect public perceptions about immigration to the country. The average citizen seems rarely to distinguish among different kinds of immigrants, let alone among different kinds of immigrants, let alone among different kinds of nonimmigrants or between nonimmigrants and immigrants (Bean, Telles, and Lowell 1987). Thus, the rapidly rising number of nonimmigrants, over half of whom are from Hispanic and Asian countries, undoubtedly contributes to the impression that Latino and Asian immigration to the United States is higher than is actually the case.

Immigration and Trends in U.S. Racial/Ethnic Composition

Because recent concerns about immigration often appear to be rooted in fears about the country's changing racial/ethnic composition and the role that immigration plays in contributing to that process, it is important to examine more precisely the contribution of immigration per se to population growth and changing population composition. . . . [Consider] immigration's contribution since 1900 to population growth (as opposed to growth resulting from an excess of births over deaths among pre-1900 natives) for the major racial/ethnic groups in 1990. Almost all of the growth in the Hispanic and Asian populations is attributable to twentieth-century immigration (85.7 percent and 97.3 percent, respectively). Although post-1990 immigration has accounted for about 30 percent of the growth of the total U.S. population since 1900, its contribution to the growth of the various major racial/ethnic subgroups varies enormously and accounts for nearly all of the growth among Asians and Hispanics and virtually none of the growth among blacks.

Given that immigration has recently affected U.S. racial/ethnic composition, what will the racial/ethnic composition of the U.S. population look like in the future if current immigration and other demographic trends continue? One answer is provided by population projections undertaken by the U.S. Bureau of the Census (Campbell 1994). These are based on what the Bureau thinks are the most reasonable assumptions about extrapolations of current demographic trends. Although the Bureau projects the Hispanic and non-Hispanic white populations separately (because Hispanics may be of any race, although almost all are white), we subtracted the Hispanic numbers from the numbers for non-Hispanic whites so that the totals for these two groups would be mutually exclusive. Expressed as a percentage of the total population, the four largest racial/ethnic minority groups combined are projected to increase from 24.8 percent of the total population in 1990 to 37.5 percent in 2020. Thus, given current trends (including immigration), the size of the U.S. minority population will grow considerably in just thirty years. . . .

Apart from assumptions about demographic processes, projections about the future racial/ethnic composition of the U.S. population depend on two other critical assumptions: first, that racial/ethnic categories are immutable; second, that interracial and interethnic marriage patterns have little effect on racial/ethnic identification or on projections of their future composition. Neither of these assumptions seems totally warranted.

Exogamy affects estimates of the future racial/ethnic composition of the United States directly by affecting fertility, mortality, migration, and other factors that shape racial/ethnic composition; indirectly, it affects racial/ethnic composition; indirectly, it affects racial/ethnic composition by means of racial/ethnic identification. Measuring racial/ethnic identification is always complex, and special problems may arise in the case of mixed-ancestry individuals whenever patterns of endogamy/exogamy vary substantially among racial/ethnic groups and by age and sex cohorts. In 1970, the U.S. Census changed data collection procedures, replacing face-to-face interviews with self-enumeration schedules. This resulted in the use of self-identification questions as the basis for measuring racial/ethnic status, a practice that has been followed ever since. Because the factors that influence self-identification of racial/ethnic status are not yet well understood, particularly for people with multiple ancestries (Waters 1990), self-identification of ancestral roots presents a problem for any attempt to project racial/ethnic populations (Edmonston, Lee, and Passel 1994: 9).

. . . Data from the Public Use Micro Samples (PUMS) from the 1990 U.S. Census . . . [i]llustrate that exogamy varies among different racial/ethnic categories has been increasing over time. . . . A comparison of the odds ratios for 1980 and 1990 shows that the likelihood of in-group marriage declined appreciably over time; conversely, intermarriage increased substantially.

The percentage of endogamous marriages by age cohort gives another indication of trends over time for each racial/ethnic group. . . . In general, there is a lower in-group marriage rate among the younger age cohorts for most groups, also suggesting that exogamy is increasing over time among racial/ethnic groups.

This conclusion is buttressed by National Center for Health Statistics intermarriage data on blacks and whites in the United States, reported by Kalmijn (1993) and Berg (1995). Both of these authors report that the incidence of black-white marriages among couples increased more than five times within twenty years, from 1.6 percent of all marriages involving African Americans in 1968 to 8.9 percent in 1988. Intermarriage rates between blacks and other groups and between whites and other groups have also been increasing (Berg 1995; Hacker 1995).

While increasing rates of intermarriage among racial/ethnic groups in the United States provide evidence of a more favorable climate of opinion toward intergroup relations, it must also be kept in mind that statistics like those just cited may mostly reflect the changing behavior of persons of higher socioeconomic status. Persons of lower socioeconomic status from all races and ethnicities in the United States have been less inclined to intermarry in recent years (McLanahan and Casper 1995). Thus, any greater tolerance of intermarriage may primarily indicate greater tolerance of higher-socioeconomic-status intermarriage. Even if this were the case, the near-universality of the increasing exogamy patterns across all racial/ethnic groups is impressive and undoubtedly indicates a rise in the tendency toward out-group marriage, thus blurring further the sharpness of boundaries among groups. . . .

The Economic Context

As these trends make clear, the substantial rise in immigration occurring since World War II has consisted of several kinds of flows and is beginning to change the country's racial/ethnic composition. The increases in each of the flows may be seen as rooted to some extent in conditions that emerged out of the postwar economic expansion. From the end of World War II to the early 1970s, the United States experienced rising economic prosperity and increasing affluence. Levels of productivity were high and wages and personal incomes rose (Levy 1987; Landau 1988). Not by coincidence, in 1965 the country eliminated the restrictive and discriminatory national-origins criteria for the admission of immigrants that were embodied in the 1924 National Origins Quota Act and ratified in the 1952 McCarran-Walter Act. Adopted in their place were more inclusionary family-reunification criteria reflecting the era's domestic policy emphasis on improving civil rights and the foreign policy emphasis on establishing better relations with newly independent Third World countries (Cafferty et al. 1983). As a result of such policies in general and the family reunification provisions in particular, legal immigration began to rise substantially (Reimers 1983, 1985). At about the same time, because of the termination of the Bracero program in 1964 and because of growing demand for inexpensive labor, undocumented (mostly Mexican)

immigration began to increase (Massey 1981). Unlike the so-called old immigrants, who were mostly European in origin, the so-called new immigrants (both legal and undocumented) came mostly from Third World Hispanic and Asian countries (Bean and Tienda 1987).

In the mid-1970s, growth in real wages began to level off, unemployment rose as the country experienced a recession, and calls for immigration reform began to emerge (Bean, Telles, and Lowell 1987). Frequently, these consisted of restrictionist outcries against the new immigration, often stated in the form of unsubstantiated claims about the pernicious nature of immigration and its harmful effects on the country. During the 1980s, a substantial body of social science research emerged that found little basis for the claims that immigration was generating strongly negative demographic, economic, or social effects. In fact, the research tended to show that immigrants were assimilating socioeconomically within a reasonable period of time, were not exerting very large labor market effects on the wages and unemployment of natives, and were not consuming more in the way of public benefits than they were paying in taxes (Borjas and Tienda 1987; Simon 1989, Butcher and Card 1991; Clark et al. 1994).

In part because the national-origin composition of immigration has been changing, questions have been raised about whether the skill levels of immigrants have been declining, both within and across countries of origin (Borjas 1990; Lalonde and Topel 1991). The general conclusion is that immigration does not appear to be generating much in the way of either large positive or large negative effects.

The coincidence of trends in economic growth and immigration growth, though *not* indicative of a causal relationship between the variables, can nonetheless be informative concerning the emergence of conditions likely to influence the reaction of natives to immigration. . . . During the first ten years of this century, when immigration reached the highest levels of any decade in the nation's history (and with respect to a population base less than half the current base), the economy grew faster than either population or inflation. For example, from 1900 to 1910, the average inflation- and population-adjusted growth rate was 2.8 percent. In other words, the economy expanded 2.8 percent faster than did population after adjusting for inflation. In the 1950s, this differential was 1.6 percent; in the 1960s, 2.5 percent; in the 1970s, 1.8 percent; and in the 1980s, 1.6 percent. From 1991 through 1995, it was 1.1 percent. When U.S. economic growth began to increase again in 1992, wage stagnation and decline continued, at least at the middle and bottom of income distribution. It is impossible to say whether the recent relatively low rates of economic growth will continue. Because of IRCA's legalization programs and because the Immigration Act of 1990 boosts legal immigration by as much as 40 percent (Bean and Fix 1992), however, it is a certainty that high levels of immigration to the United States will persist unless Congress changes U.S. immigration policy.

In thinking about the implications of these trends, it is useful to remember that the last decade with both high levels of immigration *and* low levels of real per capita economic growth was 1911-1920. This, of course, was the decade that preceded the outburst of nativism, which led to the passage of the National Origins Quota Act in 1924 (Higham 1963).

U.S. Immigration Patterns and the Social Contract

Three overarching conclusions emerge from the analyses presented to this point: (1) migration flows have been increasing significantly and are beginning to diversify the racial/ethnic composition of the U.S. population; (2) wage stagnation and uncertainty about employment security continue as features of the economic context within which immigrants arrive; and (3) recent substantial increases in interracial and interethnic marriage indicate not only the current and future blurring of boundaries between U.S. racial and ethnic groups (Alba 1990), but also the resilience and growth of levels of racial and ethnic tolerance. What are the implications of these major trends regarding the kinds of factors most responsible for the emergence of recent concerns in the United States about immigration?

In our view, these trends suggest that economic anxiety, more than concern over the possibility of increased racial/ethnic competition and tensions stemming from racially and ethnically diverse immigration flows, is at the root of current perceptions that immigration levels are too high. Otherwise, the dramatic trends toward increased racial and ethnic intermarriage documented earlier are difficult to reconcile with the results of public opinion polls showing increased opposition to rising immigration.

Even if economic anxiety more than growing ethnic prejudice is responsible for rising concerns about immigration, the public's concern about immigration is still significant, because the combination of the withering of the American Dream and rising immigration levels hold implications for the nature of the social contract in the United States. This contract implies that citizens (and, in certain instances, other residents) who work hard and obey the law are eligible for government assistance in the form of health and education benefits and other social services at certain points in their lives, including those times when they are especially economically vulnerable. It is important to emphasize that immigrants do not threaten the social contract per se; that is, they do not jeopardize the social contract just because they are not yet citizens. If they succeed economically, do not exert harmful effects on others, and do not receive a disproportionate share of benefits, their entry and the policies regulating (or failing to regulate) their entry are comparatively nonproblematic (Borjas and Tienda 1987). But to the extent that they are less successful in becoming incorporated into the socioeconomic mainstream, create economic problems for others, or disproportionately consume social services and benefits, then immigrants and the policies governing their entry may be seen as potentially threatening the implicit social contract that undergirds the legitimacy of the welfare state.

Even if immigrants are not the direct or indirect *cause* of negative effects, aggregate economic opportunities may change in ways that may lead to the perception that immigrants are detrimental to the national interest. The slowdown in the growth rate of the civilian labor force, the stagnation of wages over the past twenty years, the changing spatial and sectoral distribution of jobs by race and ethnicity, and the continuing increase in the growth rate of immigration thus pose challenges for both analysts and policymakers. Between 1989 and 1992, very little growth occurred in the number of employed persons in the United States (as evidenced by a growth rate of less than 0.1 percent). Beginning in early 1993, job growth moved strongly upward until mid-1995, when it again slowed, only to rise once again. The growth in the number of new jobs, however, was accompanied by continued economic restructuring (layoffs) and wage stagnation.

Over roughly the same period, total legal immigration continued to increase, boosted early in the period by IRCA-related immigration in particular. And starting in 1994, those immigrants who legalized under IRCA (including over two million Mexicans) became eligible for citizenship. Thus, after they naturalize they can then petition on an unrestricted basis for the additional entry of immediate family members, a phenomenon experts predict will soon raise immigration levels even further. . . .

Many observers have argued that an integral part of the country's social contract with immigrants has consisted of a tacit agreement that good-faith efforts to control undocumented immigration are the price paid for the continuation and growth of a moderately expansionist legal immigration policy (Fuchs 1990; Schuck 1990, 1992; Bean and Fix 1992). This contract may have been rendered somewhat more fragile by the apparent failure of IRCA to curb, or to slow more than briefly, the flow of undocumented migration to the United States (Bean, Passel, and Edmonston 1990; Donato, Durand, and Massey 1992). And the current squeeze on state and local governmental budgets deriving from federal mandates makes it more and more difficult for governments to pay for generous spending policies vis-à-vis immigrants (Fix and Passel 1994).

The challenge to policymakers, then, and one often obscured by the strident and denunciatory claims made by both anti-immigration and pro-immigration advocacy groups alike, remains to devise policies that foster, rather than undermine, the sense of distributive justice on which the viability of the social contract depends. . . .

References

Alba, Richard D. 1990. *Ethnic Identity: The Transformation of White America*. New Haven, CT: University of Connecticut Press.

Bean, Frank D., Rodolfo O. de la Garza, Bryan R. Roberts, and Sidney Weintraub, eds. 1997. *At the Crossroads: Mexico and U.S. Immigration Policy*. Lanham, MD: Rowman & Littlefield.

Bean, Frank D., and Michael Fix. 1992. "The Significance of Recent Immigration Policy Reforms in the United States." Pp. 41-55 in Gary P. Freeman and James Jupp, eds., *Nations of Immigrants: Australia and the United States in a Changing World*. New York: Oxford University Press.

Bean, Frank D., Jeffrey S. Passel, and Barry Edmonston. 1990. *Undocumented Migration to the United States: IRCA and the Experience of the 1980s*. Washington, D.C.: Urban Institute Press.

Bean, Frank D., Eduardo Telles, and Lindsay Lowell. 1987. "Undocumented Migration to the United States: Perceptions and Evidence." *Population and Development Review* 13: 671-690.

Bean, Frank D., and Marta Tienda. 1987. *The Hispanic Population of the United States*. New York: Russell Sage Foundation.

Bean, Frank D., George Vernez, and Charles B. Keely. 1989. *Opening and Closing the Doors: Evaluating Immigration Reform and Control*. Washington, D.C.: Urban Institute Press.

Berg, Ruth. 1995. "Low Fertility among Intermarried Mexican-Americans: An Assessment of Three Hypotheses." Ph.D. dissertation, University of Texas at Austin.

Borjas, George. 1990. *Friends and Strangers: The Impact of Immigrants on the U.S. Economy*. New York: Basic Books.

Borjas, George, and Marta Tienda. 1987. "The Economic Consequences of Immigration." *Science* 235: 645-651.

Butcher, Kristin F., and David Card. 1991. "Immigration and Wages: Evidence from the 1980s." *Economic Impact of Immigration* 81: 292-296.

Cafferty, Phyllis, Barry R. Chiswick, Andrew Greeley, and Teresa A. Sullivan. 1983. *The Dilemma of American Immigration*. New Brunswick, NJ: Transaction.

Campbell, Paul R. 1994. *Population Projections for States, by Age, Sex, Race, and Hispanic Origin: 1993-2020*. Washington, D.C.: U.S. Bureau of the Census, P25-1111.

Clark, Rebecca L., Jeffrey S. Passel, Wendy N. Zimmermann, Michael E. Fix, with Taynia L. Mann and Rosalind E. Berkowitz. 1994. *Fiscal Impacts of Undocumented Aliens: Selected Estimates for Seven States*. Washington, D.C.: The Urban Institute.

Donato, Katharine M., Jorge Durand, and Douglas Massey. 1992. "Changing Conditions in the U.S. Labor Market: Effects of the Immigration Reform and Control Act of 1986." *Population Research and Policy Review*.

Edmonston, Barry, Sharon M. Lee, and Jeffrey S. Passel. 1994. "Ethnicity, Ancestry, and Exogamy in U.S. Population Projections." Paper presented at the Population Association America meetings, Miami.

Espensade, Thomas J., and Charles A. Calhoun. 1993. "An Analysis of Public Opinion Toward Undocumented Migration." *Population Research and Policy Review* 12: 189-224.

Fix, Michael, and Jeffrey S. Passel. 1994. *Immigration and Immigrants: Setting the Record Straight*. Washington, D.C.: Urban Institute Press.

Fuchs, Lawrence H. 1990. *The American Kaleidoscope: Race, Ethnicity, and the Civic Culture*. Boston, MA: University Press of New England and Wesleyan University Press.

Hacker, Andrew. 1995. *Two Nations: Black and White, Separate, Hostile, and Unequal*. New York: Ballantine Books.

Higham, John. 1963. *Strangers in the Land*. New Brunswick, NJ: Rutgers University Press.

Kalmijn, Matthijs. 1993. "Trends in Black/White Intermarriage." *Social Forces* 72: 119-146.

Lalonde, R.J., and R.H. Topel. 1991. "Immigrants in the American Labor Market: Quality, Assimilation, and Distributional Effects." *American Economic Review Papers and Proceedings* 91: 297-302.

Landau, Ralph. 1988. "U.S. Economic Growth." *Scientific American* 258: 44-52.

Levy, Frank. 1987. *Dollars and Dreams: The Changing American Income Distribution*. New York: Russell Sage.

Massey, Douglas S. 1981. "Dimensions of the New Immigration to the United States and the Prospects for Assimilation." *Annual Review of Sociology* 7: 57-85.

———. 1995. "The New Immigration and Ethnicity in the United States." *Population and Development Review* 21: 631-652.

McLanahan, Sara, and Lynne Casper. 1995. "Growing Diversity and Inequality in the American Family." Pp. 1-46 in Reynolds Farley, ed., *State of the Union: America in the 1990s*, Vol. 2, *Social Trends*. New York: Russell Sage Foundation.

Passel, Jeffrey S., and Barry Edmonston. 1994. "Immigration and Race: Recent Trends in Immigration to the United States." Pp. 31-72 in Edmonston and Passel, eds., *Immigration and Ethnicity: The Integration of America's Newest Arrivals*. Washington, D.C.: Urban Institute Press.

Reimers, David M. 1983. "An Unintended Reform: The 1965 Immigration Act and Third World Migration to the United States." *Journal of American Ethnic History*: 9-28.

Schuck, Peter. 1990. "The Great Immigration Debate." *The American Prospect*: 100-118.

———. 1992. "The Politics of Rapid Political Changes: Immigration Policy in the 1980s." *Studies in American Political Development* 6: 37-82.

Simon, Julian L. 1989. *The Economic Consequences of Immigration*. Cambridge, England: Basil Blackwell.

Teitelbaum, Michael S., and Myron Weiner, eds. 1995. *World Migration and U.S. Policy*. New York: Norton.

U.S. Commission on Immigration Reform. 1994. *U.S. Immigration Policy: Restoring Credibility*. Washington, D.C.: U.S. Government Printing Office.

U.S. Department of Justice. 1992. *Immigration Reform and Control Act: Report on the Legalized Alien Population*. Washington, D.C.: U.S. Government Printing Office.

U.S. Immigration and Naturalization Service. 1995. *Statistical Yearbook of the U.S. Immigration and Naturalization Service, 1994*. Washington, D.C.: U.S. Government Printing Office.

Warren, Robert. 1990. "Annual Estimates of Nonimmigrant Overstays in the United States: 1985-1988." Pp. 77-101 in Bean, Edmonston, and Passel, eds., *Undocumented Migration to the United States: IRCA and the Experience of the 1980s*. Washington, D.C.: Urban Institute Press.

———. 1992. "Estimates of the Unauthorized Immigrant Population Residing in the United States, by Country of Origin and State of Residence: October 1992." Washington, D.C.: Immigration and Naturalization Service Statistics Division.

Warren, Robert, and Jeffrey S. Passel. 1987. "A Count of the Uncountable: Estimates of Undocumented Aliens Counted in the 1980 United States Census." *Demography* 24: 375-394.

Waters, Mary C. 1990. *Ethnic Options: Choosing Identities in America*. Berkeley & Los Angeles: University of California Press.

Zohlberg, Aristide R. 1992. "Response to Crisis: Refugee Policy in the United States and Canada." Pp. 55-109 in Barry R. Chiswick, ed., *Immigration, Language, and Ethnicity: Canada and the United States*. Washington, D.C.: AEI Press.

41

Border Enforcement and Human Rights Violations in the Southwest

Timothy J. Dunn

Immigration enforcement along the U.S.-Mexico border has steadily increased since the late 1970s in response to periodic waves of political anxiety over undocumented immigration—the current wave was recently demonstrated by the overwhelming passage of Proposition 187 in California. The politically popular "war on drugs" has brought additional enforcement resources to the southwest border—including the U.S. military—some of which have also been directed toward immigration enforcement. Broadly speaking, this expanded southwest border enforcement has overwhelmingly focused on people of Mexican origin (i.e., Mexican immigrants and Mexican Americans). Yet U.S. immigration authorities estimate that half of all undocumented immigrants do not illegally cross the southwest border but rather enter the country legally and then overstay their visas (U.S. General Accounting Office 1995: 8). Moreover, the undocumented immigrant population is diverse and not solely Mexican. For example, the three largest groups of undocumented immigrants in New York (home of the nation's second largest such population) are from Italy, Ecuador, and Poland (A. Dunn 1995). Nonetheless, the southwest border and Mexican immigrants are still the focal points of contemporary enforcement efforts.

Border Enforcement Trends

The expansion in southwest border enforcement resources is most apparent in the growth of the budget of the Border Patrol unit of the U.S. Immigration and Naturalization Service (INS), the nation's principle immigration enforcement body, which has positioned 88 percent of all its agents in the southwest border region (GAO 1995: 2). The Border Patrol's 1996 budget stands at $582.6 million (Public Law 104–134), an increase of 79 percent since only 1992. The authorized staffing level for the Border Patrol in 1996 is an estimated 6,263 agents, a jump of 27 percent above the 1992 level (U.S. Congress, House Committee on Appropriations 1993: 13; 1995: 1086). In addition, the Immigration Bill of 1996 calls for this unit to be expanded by 5,000 agents over the next five years. The Border Patrol has also been increasingly staffed by Latino American agents, who by 1993 made up 41 percent of the unit's personnel.

Along with additional funds and staff, the formal legal authority of the Border Patrol has also been expanded well beyond its traditional immigration focus. In 1986, Border Patrol agents were deputized to enforce federal drug and contraband laws; in 1991, the unit was designated as the primary force responsible for drug enforcement between official border crossings. In addition, agents were granted the authority to enforce *any* federal law by the 1990 Immigration Act; by 1991, they had received similar authority under state law in New Mexico and Arizona (Dunn 1996: 53, 80–81). Although immigration law enforcement has remained the Border Patrol's principal responsibility, its agents now wield the legal authority of a national (and in some cases, state) police force, which affords agents much broader discretionary power. The politically popular objective of drug enforcement has been enthusiastically adopted by the Border Patrol, although by 1993, many agents apparently were still not trained for it (McDonnell and Rotella 1993). Drug enforcement is a far more dangerous task than the relatively low-key apprehension of undocumented immigrants, who are typically nonthreatening and cooperative. The Border Patrol has increasingly combined these two very different law enforcement activities, however, particularly as drug trafficking and undocumented immigration often occur in adjacent or sometimes overlapping border corridors.

Along with its expanded role and authority, the Border Patrol has also been outfitted with increasingly sophisticated equipment and technology, much of it military in origin. This includes electronic ground sensors, assorted infrared and night vision surveillance equipment, some 53 helicopters by 1992 (up from just two in 1980), and even M-16 rifles, which are available for use in some circumstances. Perhaps the most notable new equipment afforded the Border Patrol during the 1990s has been the U. S. military's construction of border walls constructed of military surplus landing mat (thin corrugated steel), 10-12 feet high (Dunn 1996: 38, 53, 66–69). Thus far, walls have been built in seven high-traffic illegal border crossing zones in California and Arizona, ranging from two to 14 miles in length, the longest running between San Diego and Tijuana. In addition, the Immigration Act of 1996 calls for the construction of two additional layers of wall and fencing just behind the San Diego-Tijuana wall.

Through the drug issue, the Border Patrol has engaged in an ongoing and multifaceted collaboration with the U.S. military. This budding relationship was facilitated by a series of legal changes begun in 1981 that, under the justification of aiding drug enforcement, gradually weakened century-old restraints that had strictly limited U.S. military involvement in domestic law enforcement activities. Although troops are still forbidden from directly participating in arrests, searches, or seizures, the military can nonetheless provide a wide range of support (Dunn 1996: 106–145). In practice, this has included staffing observation and listening posts, ground patrol, aerial reconnaissance, construction and engineering, intelligence analysis, equipment loans, transportation and maintenance support, intelligence analysis, and training in assorted military tactics (U.S. Army Corp of Engineers 1994: 4–2; Palafox 1996).

In recent years, INS-military collaboration has begun to focus more directly on immigra-

tion enforcement. During the autumn of 1994, the INS drew upon the military to help design expanded immigration enforcement efforts along the border (Ostrow 1994). Also in 1994, the California National Guard began to deploy its 120 counterdrug troops whenever possible in a manner that would benefit both the immigration and drug enforcement efforts of the Border Patrol (U.S. Congress, House Committee on the Judiciary 1995: 114, 121). In January 1996, the Clinton Administration announced that some 350 military troops would provide support explicitly for the Border Patrol's accelerated immigration enforcement efforts along the southwest border in California and Arizona (McDonnell and Rotella 1996).

Recent Border Patrol Immigration Enforcement Operations

As immigration enforcement has once again occupied a central role in the nation's political debates, a series of new, escalated immigration enforcement efforts have been implemented by the Border Patrol at various points along the southwest border. The first and most successful of these was the El Paso Border Patrol's "Operation Blockade" (later renamed "Operation Hold the Line"), which began on September 19, 1993, and continues to the present, though on a smaller scale. Initially, some 400 agents were deployed on a round-the-clock basis in vehicles directly adjacent to the Rio Grande in a stationary, highly visible fashion at short-distance intervals along a 20 mile stretch between El Paso and Ciudad Juarez. This massive show of force was intended to deter potential undocumented border crossers (most of whom were local commuters) in advance rather than apprehending them at crossing points. Arrests fell 72 percent the first year of the operation, though apprehension levels have since rebounded. There was also a noticeable decrease of the disorder that had prevailed in border towns frequented by undocumented border crossers (U.S. Congress, House Committee on the Judiciary 1995: 33–34, 39). Meanwhile, the bulk of the remaining undocumented crossings were forced toward the edges of these towns during night hours, thereby greatly reducing public visibility. In addition, certain categories of crime (notably auto theft) decreased, though the overall crime rate was already falling before the operation began (Bean et al. 1994: 95).

The operation proved enormously popular with El Paso residents (registering over 80 percent support in opinion polls during 1994), including Mexican Americans who make up some three-quarters of the local population and who were no longer subjected to routine surveillance and questioning about their citizenship by Border Patrol agents. This positive reaction was perhaps also partly fueled by the tendency among local Anglos to look disfavorably on people of Mexican origin and among local Mexican Americans to differentiate themselves from Mexicans and vice versa (Vila 1994). The operation created much expanded opportunities for this sort of differentiation, as nationalist tensions were heightened markedly during the early weeks of the operation (Fried 1994). Also, the new Border Patrol chief who initiated the blockade was himself Mexican American.

Hoping to replicate the successes of the El Paso operation, the INS implemented new border enforcement operations in California and Arizona during late 1994. "Operation Gatekeeper" was implemented in September, 1994, on the border between San Diego and Tijuana, the site of an estimated one half of all undocumented crossings, most of which largely take place at night (U.S. Congress, House Committee on the Judiciary 1995: 44–46). It also involved a mass deployment of agents near the border and was initiated with great fanfare less than two months before the 1994 elections (at a cost of $46 million), amid the rising tide of anti-immigrant sentiment in California. The objective of Operation Gatekeeper was to effectively close off the most frequently used illegal border crossings in the western portion of the San Diego sector, rendering such activities so difficult that many would-be immigrants would give up or at least be forced to try more remote and forbidding areas further east. Border Patrol apprehensions were down significantly (40 percent) on the western side during the first year, while increasing greatly on the east side. (However, the veracity of these data is pres-

ently in doubt and under investigation [Graham 1996]). Unlike the El Paso operation, overall apprehensions in the sector did not decrease, nor have they yet.

In response to an expected increase in undocumented immigration across the Arizona side of the border following these escalated enforcement efforts in the El Paso and San Diego areas, the INS announced "Operation Safeguard" for the Arizona border in October 1994. This area, where drug trafficking had been a stronger enforcement focus, had not traditionally been a high-volume crossing point for undocumented immigrants until recently. The new operation's objective was again to force potential undocumented border crossers away from urban border areas into more remote, difficult, and dangerous desert terrain. Nevertheless, Border Patrol apprehensions have remained high. On the whole, the thrust of recent U.S. border enforcement efforts is consistent with the growing tendency to view undocumented immigrants as a security threat—despite the fact that they do not physically threaten the United States (Andreas 1995).

Human Rights Consequences of Increased Border Enforcement

While most observers are preoccupied with the effectiveness of border enforcement measures in reducing the flow of undocumented immigrants and illegal drugs, it is also important to consider how these efforts affect the status of human rights in the border region. However, the nature of the issue and the limits of the available data make it difficult to obtain more than a glimpse of the dimensions of the problem today, as there is no comprehensive borderwide effort to record and document human and civil rights abuses. Nonetheless, there are some systematic though incomplete data gathered by human rights groups, which have documented repeated offenses committed by U.S. authorities along the southwest border. These include beatings and physical abuse, shootings and inappropriate use of firearms, sexual assault, inhumane detention conditions, denial of due process, false deportation, illegal and inappropriate searches and seizures, destruction of property, verbal and psychological abuse, and reckless high-speed pursuits (Immigration Law Enforcement Monitoring Project 1990, 1992; Americas Watch 1992, 1993; Human Rights Watch/Americas 1995). Despite this record, the 1996 Immigration Act greatly limits judicial review over immigration enforcement practices.

Some of the more exceptional recent cases of abuse by Border Patrol agents have included the fatal shooting of an unarmed man, the beating of and deadly threats against a drug suspect, the rape of a young woman, the skull fracture of a handcuffed man, and the denial of medical treatment to people injured during arrest (HRW/A 1995: 6–18). In addition, the San Diego federal public defender's office has documented some 400 incidents of serious beatings by Border Patrol agents during a five-year period ending in April 1993 (McDonnell and Rotella 1993). The same source has also reported that some Border Patrol agents complained about supervisors who tolerated and even encouraged abusive practices, concluding that "[physical] abuse is deep-rooted in the Border Patrol culture, according to some veteran agents." Recurring evidence of similar types of physical abuse over sustained periods of time suggests the existence of an institutionalized pattern. Yet, the level of abuse seems to be less than that typically found among police agencies in Mexico and many other developing countries. Nonetheless, the rights abuses committed by U.S. border enforcement agents are extremely problematic and totally unacceptable.

Drug enforcement, in particular, is more likely to lead to excessive use of force, which in turn often spills into immigration enforcement. Former National Chief Border Patrol Agent Mike Williams noted that a "war-zone or drug-zone mentality" existed among agents in Arizona (McDonnell and Rotella 1993). The dangers of this mentality were most clearly exemplified by Tucson Agent Michael Elmer who in 1992 killed an unarmed, undocumented Mexican border crosser during a drug stakeout, shooting him in the back as he was trying to run back to Mexico. Earlier, this same agent had opened fire on a group of undocumented immigrants on foot

in the desert carrying their belongings in bags, which he allegedly mistook for drugs. This was in direct contradiction to the official agency policy that Border Patrol agents must fire warning shots over the heads of suspected drug couriers (Dunn 1996: 87–89).

Improper gunplay was nothing new for the Border Patrol. In a 1991 study, the Department of Justice reported that firearms regulations were violated by agents in one-third of 66 reported Border Patrol shootings (McDonnell and Rotella 1993). Agents were also involved in a number of questionable shootings during the late 1980s (U.S. Congress, House Committee on Foreign Relations 1990: 50–60) and 1990, though such episodes subsequently declined in frequency. Granted, undocumented border-crossing areas are often dangerous at night, rife with assailants committing violent crimes mainly against undocumented immigrants, particularly in the heavily trafficked San Diego-Tijuana area. However, a special Mexican immigration police unit called Grupo Beta, operating in this same area since 1990, has been extremely effective at reducing crime without using deadly force.

In examining reports of official rights abuse data for the INS (1,322 official complaints registered against all INS agents, including Border Patrol, from 1989 through 1994; see HRW/A 1995: 32), the ratio of abuse complaints to arrests seems to range from 1/10,000 to 1/6,666. This ratio is undoubtedly low, because the official abuse complaint process records only a portion of all abuses for various, often bureaucratic reasons. The procedures for filing a complaint against Border Patrol and other INS agents are largely inaccessible to the public, no information is provided that such a complaint procedure exists, nor is there even a standardized complaint form (HRW/A 1995:26; Salopek 1993). Such basic flaws in the INS complaint process have been noted by civil rights authorities since 1980 (U.S. Commission on Civil Rights 1980) but have yet to be addressed adequately. Moreover, the complaint process is so complex that even some officials from the agencies involved seem to be unclear about it (HRW/A 1995: 27). It is common for Border Patrol and INS agents to discourage the filing of complaints by, for example, stonewalling would-be complainants, losing their statements (Salopek 1993), or even using threats, such as retaliatory countercharges (e.g., assaulting an officer or resisting arrest [HRW/A 1995: 25]). Further, abuse reports are discouraged internally by a strict code of silence among Border Patrol agents, preventing agents themselves from reporting misconduct among their colleagues (McDonnell and Rotella 1993).

One concludes that the official data on such rights abuse complaints drastically understates the problem, particularly in light of a mounting body of quantitative data from other sources. For example, a leading nongovernmental human rights organization in the border region documented 1,326 abuses (52.6 percent due process violations, 22.2 percent verbal/psychological, 21.3 percent physical, and 4.5 percent other) against 772 persons from May 1988 through May 1991 (ILEMP 1990, 1992). Border Patrol staff accounted for 50.1 percent of the abuses, other INS personnel 27.7 percent (for a cumulative INS share of 77.8 percent), while Customs Service and local police agents accounted for the remainder. Official complaints were filed with the government in only 24 percent of the cases. Of half the victims for whom such data was recorded, the majority had some form of legal immigration status (including 17.7 percent who were U.S. citizens), and 90 percent of the victims were Latino. Likewise, survey research in two small, overwhelmingly Latino border-region communities in Arizona and Texas found 18.1 percent and 10.2 percent of the residents questioned in the respective communities had experienced mistreatment by U.S. border enforcement authorities (Koulish et al. 1994).

During four months in 1991, data on undocumented immigrants returned to Mexico by the Border Patrol at the Tijuana ports of entry indicated a significant frequency of abuse by these agents (Santibanez, Valenzuela, and Velasco 1993). A survey of some 5,400 returned undocumented immigrants there found that some 5.9 percent had experienced "injuries or abuses of authority by the Border Patrol." (Unfortunately, the study does not indicate how this term was defined by researchers or interpreted by respondents.) The authors estimate that some 8,769 of the undocumented immigrants returned by the Border Patrol at the Tijuana ports of entry experienced injuries or abuses of authority by the Border Patrol. In addition, a nonabusive human rights problem exists in the fact that many accidental deaths are suffered by undocumented immigrants trying to enter the country. Researchers estimate that during the 1985–1994 period, there were from 1,900 to 3,300 accidental deaths (mostly by drowning) of undocumented immigrants along the Texas-Mexico border alone (Bailey et al. 1996: 27–29).

Of course, Border Patrol agents also face certain dangers. For example, in 1992, they were victims of 167 assaults (most of them from rock throwing) which resulted in 49 injured agents, four of them seriously. From 1980 through 1992, eleven agents were killed in the line of duty, ten in vehicle accidents and one shot by a suspected smuggler (McDonnell and Rotella 1993). In 1995, a Border Patrol agent died after falling off a cliff while chasing undocumented border crossers through night brush. During January and February of 1996, three agents were shot in three separate incidents in Texas and Arizona, apparently by corrupt Mexican police and drug smugglers. Border Patrol agents (and the public) also face safety problems stemming from a highly flawed agent screening process, combined with political pressure to rapidly increase the size of the unit during the late 1980s. This has led to the hiring and placement in the field of a number of agents with histories of serious misconduct, including criminal behavior (McDonnell and Rotella 1993). Finally, agents also face enormous frustrations arising from difficult working conditions (e.g., operating at night, often alone), the highest arrest rates of any U.S. police force, inexperience due to high agent turnover rates, and the seeming futility and thanklessness of their job. According to veteran agents, these frustrations can often lead to abuse. A leading border-region human rights activist came to a similar conclusion, proposing that agents have been assigned a "mission impossible," which "is a recipe for disaster and grossly unfair" (U.S. Congress,

House Committee on Foreign Relations 1990: 29–30).

Human Rights and Special Border Enforcement Operations

Operation Blockade (or 'Hold the Line')

Operation Blockade (later renamed "Hold the Line") was implemented in El Paso in September 1993 and involved a massive high-visibility deployment of Border Patrol agents directly next to the river boundary in stationary vehicles within sight of each other. This operation was explicitly designed to deter the entry of undocumented crossers, especially in long-established, highly visible areas near downtown El Paso. It originated as the result of a federal injunction to force the Border Patrol to cease the practice of detaining people solely on the basis of ethnic (i.e., Latino) appearance (Dubose 1992), and partly as a response to the rising tide of abuse complaints. Operation Blockade removed most agents from established Mexican American and Mexican immigrant neighborhoods near the river boundary, thus greatly reducing confrontations and abusive encounters with residents.

Immediately after Operation Blockade went into effect, rights abuse claims against Border Patrol agents declined dramatically, a trend which continued for over a year through the end of 1994. The decrease can largely be attributed to the fact that Border Patrol agents were no longer in frequent contact with the public. Apprehensions dropped 72 percent during the first year of the operation, and the river-boundary deployment strategy halted most neighborhood patrolling by agents. However, reports of human rights abuse began to climb again in 1995, although illegal or inappropriate seizures of persons constituted a much lower share of complaints (El Paso Border Rights Coalition 1996).

Another significant change was the location in which Border Patrol abuses were occurring. Most pre-blockade abuses were concentrated in long-established Mexican American and Mexican immigrant neighborhoods in the central and south side areas of the city.

In contrast, abuses reported in 1995 were concentrated in the peripheral areas of El Paso. One cluster of abuse complaints centered on a small New Mexico community, where much of the undocumented border crossing had shifted and where the Border Patrol had increased its roving patrols. Such complaints involved illegal and inappropriate searches and seizures of persons, such as Border Patrol agents routinely entering the grounds of a Catholic church to apprehend suspected undocumented immigrants (interview with anonymous resident, September 1995). Another cluster of reported abuses was based in a poor, rural subdivision (*colonia*) east of El Paso. These included psychological and verbal abuse as well as inappropriate seizure and destruction of immigration documents. Border Patrol agents targeted a *colonia* for escalated enforcement efforts shortly after the residents filed a legal challenge to get the subdivision developer to provide water service. Agents also staked out a local school, which led to great anxiety among some students who feared apprehension and separation from their parents (interview with anonymous resident, October 1995). Both of these new sites of abuse are very low-income areas and made up largely of recent Mexican immigrants. Thus, reported abuses were not nearly as visible nor as detectable as in other settings. In a more severe and publicized case in 1992, two undocumented Guatemalan women reported that they were sexually assaulted in a Border Patrol station just east of the city. Meanwhile, however, the previously affected areas in central and south El Paso have remained much more tranquil than they were before the operation.

In the broader meaning of human rights, Operation Blockade had been designed to increase hardships for would-be border crossers. During the early weeks of the operation, the Border Patrol discouraged undocumented crossing by shipping those whom they had apprehended to a return border crossing 60 miles away, where they were left to walk back to Juarez. In addition, Border Patrol officials hope that their new 1.3-mile-long, ten-foot-high chain-link fence along the border will push undocumented border crossers even further west out into more remote and dangerous desert areas. This outcome may likely lead to an increase in accidental injuries or deaths due to exposure.

Beyond the Border Patrol itself, there seem to have been substantial abuses of authority by INS and Customs officials who staff the official ports of entry, where bridge crossers have been more aggressively scrutinized. In 1996, an informal newspaper survey of 1,050 respondents in El Paso (three quarters of whom were Mexican citizens) found that almost one third (31.4 percent) reported that they had suffered an abusive incident by U.S. officials at the local international bridges—the most frequent being "arbitrary detention" (34 percent) and "insults or threats" (24 percent) (Giovine 1996).

Operation Gatekeeper

Operation Gatekeeper was implemented in September 1994, after a year of increasing clamor from the San Diego-Tijuana area for something that would replicate the success of El Paso's Operation Blockade. This area had long accounted for the most Border Patrol apprehensions, as well as complaints of abuse committed by these agents. Although complete information is still lacking, it seems that under Operation Gatekeeper, rights abuses have continued to a greater extent than under Operation Blockade; but they too have changed in character and geographic location. During the first six months of the operation, rights abuse claims increased, especially regarding inhumane detention conditions, during the marked rise in apprehensions (Alvarez 1995).

However, as time wore on and much of the undocumented immigration flow and Border Patrol apprehension activity shifted to more isolated border areas, it has become increasingly difficult to monitor human and civil rights conditions for immigrants and the nature of the border enforcement activity there.

Despite the lack of information on what is happening in these remote areas, several human rights consequences are becoming apparent. Perhaps the most obvious problem is the increased occurrence of risky high-speed flights by smugglers in vehicles loaded with undocumented immigrants to evade apprehension by Border Patrol and other law enforcement authorities. Such activity led, for example, to the infamous beatings of immigrants by Riverside County Sheriff's Deputies, which was caught on film in April 1996. In the same month, similar high-speed vehicle flights in the Southern California area led to four fatal accidents, which left 10 people dead and at least 34 people injured, all of whom were occupants of the immigrant-smuggler vehicles (Smith 1996). Although Border Patrol policy strictly limits their involvement in high-speed pursuits, these vehicles fled after being initially followed by Border Patrol vehicles. Though such tragic episodes are not new, it does seem that as undocumented immigrants find it more difficult to cross the border, they are willing to confront greater risks to avoid apprehension.

There are other apparent dangers for undocumented immigrants. First, there is an increased potential for more injuries and deaths from exposure to harsh conditions, especially in the desert; at least 14 such deaths were reported in the first half of 1996 (Nathan 1996). There is also the possibility that they may stumble into a large-scale anti-drug operation in the Imperial Valley area, where the military and over a dozen law enforcement agencies are deployed and of which only the INS and Border Patrol have any expertise in immigration enforcement. Meanwhile, the increased flow of undocumented crossers through the eastern San Diego County area has led to more frequent, and sometimes violent, confrontations with local residents.

Operation Safeguard

Operation Safeguard is the latest major border enforcement program to be implemented, and relatively little is known about its impact on human and civil rights. Designed to address the increased flow of undocumented immigrants through southern Arizona, it has generally relied on additional deployments of Border Patrol agents near the border in urban areas and, like Operation Gatekeeper, on the erection of border walls. Even before the operation was implemented, it was clear that the newly expanded border wall in Nogales was having adverse human rights consequences for undocumented border crossers. First, the wall diverted undocumented crossers underground to a cross-border sewer system, where they were more frequently assaulted and robbed by assailants. Subsequently, numerous injuries were reported among persons who attempted to scale and jump over the high metal walls (12 feet high in some places), resulting in an average of three emergency room calls per week in 1994 at the local hospital (Sahagun 1994).

Once again, a deadly consequence of the increased border enforcement effort is that immigrants are increasingly trying to cross in more remote and dangerous desert areas. In June 1996, six out of a group of seven undocumented border crossers died from dehydration and exposure attempting to cross a desert area 40 miles west of Tucson. Although this is a problem every year, according to a local human rights activist, it appears to be worsening due to increased border enforcement efforts. As of September, ten immigrants had died in the Arizona desert in 1996 (Nathan 1996). Such tragic consequences stemming from the operation seem to directly contradict its "Safeguard" moniker.

Conclusion

Recent escalations in immigration enforcement operations along the southwest border are analogous to squeezing a balloon: Applying pressure (i.e., increasing enforcement) in one area causes bulges (i.e., increased undocumented immigration) elsewhere. Likewise, overall Border Patrol apprehensions have continued to rise in recent years. This approach has also caused numerous, though largely unacknowledged, human rights problems. Moreover, it seems that U.S. policymakers have not considered what might happen if the balloon is squeezed so hard in so many places simultaneously that it bursts. A more constructive strategy would be to let some of the air out of the balloon by addressing the key underlying conditions that fuel undocumented immigration from Mexico. Specifically, policymakers would do well to promote economic development in Mexico that more broadly benefits the urban working class, peasants, the middle class,

and small businesses—unlike current policies (e.g., the 1995 peso bailout loan package) that are structured to benefit only finance markets, big investors, large corporations and banks, while forcing austere measures on the bulk of the population.

References

Alvarez, Fred. 1995 (April 7). "Border Woes." *Los Angeles Times.*

Americas Watch. 1992. *Brutality Unchecked: Human Rights Along the U.S. Border With Mexico.* New York: Americas Watch, Human Rights Watch.

Americas Watch. 1993. "United States Frontier Injustice: Human Rights Violations Along the U.S. Border With Mexico Persist amid Climate of Impunity." *News from Americas Watch,* vol. 5, no. 4, pp. 1–46.

Andreas, Peter. 1995 (Sept.). "The Retreat and Resurgence of the State: Liberalizing and Criminalizing Flows Across the U.S.-Mexico Border." Paper delivered at Latin American Studies Association Meetings, Washington, DC.

Bailey, Stanley R., Karl Eschbach, Jaqueline Maria Hagan, Nestor Rodriguez. 1996 (Jan.). "Migrant Deaths at the Texas-Mexico Border, 1985–1994." Center for Immigration Research, University of Houston.

Bean, Frank D., Roland Chanove, Robert G. Cushing, Rodolfo de la Garza, Gary Freeman, Charles W. Haynes, and David Spener. 1994. "Illegal Mexican Migration and the United States/Mexico Border: The Effects of Operation Hold the Line on El Paso/Juarez." Prepared for the U.S. Commission on Immigration Reform. Population Research Center, University of Texas at Austin.

Dubose, Louis. 1992 (Dec. 11). "Suing the Border Patrol: The Battle at Bowie High." *Texas Observer.*

Dunn, Ashley. 1995 (Jan. 3). "Greeted at Nation's Front Door, Many Visitors Stay on Illegally." *New York Times.*

Dunn, Timothy J. 1996. *The Militarization of the U.S.-Mexico Border, 1978–1992: Low Intensity Conflict Doctrine Comes Home.* Austin, Texas: Center for Mexican American Studies, University of Texas at Austin.

El Paso Border Rights Coalition. 1996. "Statistical Report of Abuse Complaints Made to the BRC from El Paso Sector: Border Patrol Complaints, 1993–1995."

Fried, Jonathan. 1994. *Operation Blockade: A City Divided.* Report from the American

Friends Service Committee's Immigration Law Enforcement Monitoring Project. Philadelphia: American Friends Service Committee.

Giovine, Patricia. 1996 (May 11). "Vicitimas de abusos, 1 de 3 usarios." *Diario de Juarez.*

Graham, Wade. 1996 (July). "Masters of the Game." *Harpers Magazine*, pp. 35–50.

Human Rights Watch/Americas. 1995 (April). *United States Crossing the Line: Human Rights Violations Along the U.S. Border With Mexico Persist Amid Climate of Impunity.* New York: Human Rights Watch/Americas.

Immigration Law Enforcement Monitoring Project. American Friends Service Committee. 1990. *Human Rights at the U.S.-Mexico Border.* Second annual report. Houston: ILEMP.

Immigration Law Enforcement Monitoring Project. American Friends Service Committee. 1992. *Sealing Our Borders: The Human Toll.* Third annual report. Philadelphia: American Friends Service Committee.

Koulish, Robert E., Manuel Escobedo, Raquel Rubio-Goldsmith, and John Robert Warren. 1994. *U.S. Immigration Authorities and Victims of Human Civil Rights Abuses: The Border Interaction Project Study of South Tucson, Arizona, and South Texas.* Working Paper Series, no. 20. Tucson: Mexican American Studies and Research Center, University of Arizona.

McDonnell, Patrick, and Sebastian Rotella. 1993 (April 22–24). "Crossing the Line: Turmoil in the U.S. Border Patrol." Special series. *Los Angeles Times.*

McDonnell, Patrick, and Sebastian Rotella. 1996 (Jan. 12). "Military, Police to Aid in New Push by Border Patrol." *Los Angeles Times.*

Nathan, Debbie. 1996 (Sept. 16–29). "Dangerous Crossings." *In These Times*, v. 20, no. 22, pp. 12–14).

Ostrow, Ronald. 1994 (Oct. 14). "Border has Tightened, Official Says." *Los Angeles Times.*

Palafox, Jose. 1996 (Spring). "Militarizing the Border." *Covert Action Quarterly*, no. 56, pp. 14–19.

Public Law 104–134 ("Omnibus Consolidated Recessions and Appropriations Act of 1996"). 1996. *United State Code Congressional and Administrative News*, 104th Cong., 2nd Sess. St. Paul, MN: West Publishing.

Sahagun, Louis. 1994 (Sept. 8). "Nogales Wall Takes Toll in Injuries—and Costs." *Los Angeles Times.*

Salopek, Paul. 1993 (March 12). "La Migra: The Border Patrol's Wall of Silence." *Texas Observer.*

Santibanez, Jorge, Javier Valenzula, and Laura Velasco. 1993 (May). "Migrantes devueltos por la Patrulla Fronteriza." Paper presented at conference on The Facets of Border Violence, University of Texas at El Paso.

Smith, Claudia E. 1996 (April 29). "Weigh the Risk of Chasing Border Crossers." *Los Angeles Times.*

U.S. Army Corps of Engineers. Fort Worth District. 1994 (April). *Programmatic Environmental Impact Statement: JTF-6 Activities Along the U.S.-Mexico Border.*

U.S. Commission on Civil Rights. 1980. *The Tarnished Door: Civil Rights Issues in Immigration Enforcement.* Washington, DC. U.S. Commission on Civil Rights.

U.S. Congress, House Committee on Appropriations. 1993. *Departments of Commerce, Justice, and State, and the Judiciary, and Related Agencies. Appropriations for 1994.* Part 2B. 103rd Cong., 1st sess. Washington, DC: Government Printing Office.

U.S. Congress, House Committee on Appropriations. 1995. *Departments of Commerce, Justice, and State, and the Judiciary, and Related Agencies. Appropriations for 1994.* Part 2. 104th Cong., 1st sess. Washington, DC: Government Printing Office.

U.S. Congress, House Committee on Foreign Relations. *1990 Allegations of Abuse Along the United States-Mexico Border.* 101st Cong., 2nd sess. Washington, DC: Government Printing Office.

U.S. Congress, House Committee on the Judiciary. 1995. *Border Security.* 104th Cong., 1st sess. Washington, DC: Government Printing Office.

U.S. General Accounting Office. 1995. *Border Control: Revised Strategy is Showing Some Positive Results.* Washington, DC: GAO.

Vila, Pablo. 1994. "Everyday Life, Culture, and Identity on the Mexican-American Border: The Ciudad Juarez-El Paso Case." Ph.D. diss., University of Texas at Austin.

42

Immigration Has Consequences:

Economics

Peter J. Brimelow

Immigration, The 1965 Immigration Act (Not the Same Thing), and Economics

. . . [T]he] discussion of immigration in principle has little to do with immigration in practice, as governed by the 1965 Immigration Act. Today, immigration to the United States is not determined by economics: it is determined—at least profoundly distorted—by public policy. *Current U.S. immigration is not an economic phenomenon; it is a political phenomenon.*

. . . [T]he effect of the 1965 reform has been *to uncouple legal immigration from the needs of the U.S. economy*. A low point was reached in 1986, when less than 8 percent of over 600,000 legal immigrants were admitted on the basis of skills—of whom about half were accompanying family members.

The 1990 Immigration Act was allegedly designed in part to rectify this situation. But in 1992, only 13 percent of the 914,000 non-IRCA legal admissions were employment-based—of whom half were accompanying family. Most legal immigrants, 55 percent, entered under the law's various "family reunification" provisions. And this proportion does not include the accompanying family members of humanitarian or "diversity" immigrants. Of course, some of the family-reunification immigrants will have skills. But it is purely an accident whether their skills are wanted in the U.S. economy.

The family-reunification policy inevitably contributes to two striking characteristics of the post-1965 flow:

- Firstly: the post-1965 immigrants are, on average, less skilled than earlier immigrants. And getting even less so. As George Borjas put it in his *Friends or Strangers:* "The skill level of successive immigrant waves admitted to the U.S. has declined *precipitously* in the past two or three decades."[1] (My italics—but you see the point.)

- Secondly: the post-1965 immigrants unmistakably display more mismatching between what they can do and what America needs. They seem not to be fitting as well into the economy as did earlier immigrants. Instead, they are showing a greater tendency to become what used to be called a "public charge."

Post-1965 Immigration: Skill Levels Down[2]

Put another way, in 1970 the *average* recent immigrant had 0.35 less years schooling than native-born Americans. By 1990, the average recent immigrant had 1.32 years less schooling. (And note that "native" here includes American blacks and Puerto Ricans. Both these groups systematically lag behind American whites in educational achievement. If we were to look only at native-born, non-Hispanic American whites, average educational attainment might increase by as much as a year. Which makes the immigrant performance appear really grim. . . .

"But everyone knows American education is going down the tube—a high school diploma just doesn't mean what it used to," immigration enthusiasts extemporize desperately.

Maybe. But economists, in their unromantic way, view earnings as a proxy for skills. And the relative decline in immigrant education seems to be confirmed by the relative decline in their earnings that has occurred over the same period.

In 1970, immigrants on average actually earned some 3 percent more than native-born Americans. (That slight inferiority in average education was apparently counterbalanced, perhaps by higher average age.) But in 1990, this immigrant achievement had disappeared: immigrants on average earned 16.2 percent less than native-born Americans.

Examined more closely, the trend is even more alarming. In 1970, immigrants who had just arrived—within the previous five years—earned some 16.6 percent less than the native-born population. But by 1990, the gap had nearly doubled: immigrants who had arrived within the previous five years earned some 31.7 percent less than natives.

In other words, the decline in *average* immigrant earnings masked an even sharper deterioration in the earnings of the *most recent* immigrants.

The evidence, George Borjas has concluded, no longer supports another of the immigration enthusiasts' favorite claims: *"Immigrants soon catch up with and outstrip native-born Americans in earnings"*—thus proving what desirable citizens they are (at least economically). He says:

> My research indicates that if a particular immigrant cohort is tracked across Censuses, there is relatively little wage convergence between the immigrants and natives. Because more recent immigrant waves start off poorly, *it is unlikely that the earnings of the "new immigrants" will ever catch up with those of natives.* In fact, the wage differential between immigrants and natives may exceed 20 percent even after two or three decades after immigration. [My emphasis again.]

Borjas, incidentally, thinks that the skill decline would have occurred even apart from the 1965 Immigration Act's preference for family reunification above skills. This is because of a paradox in the way the 1965 reform works:

> Besides favoring "family reunification," the 1965 Act also allowed immigration from the Third World. And Third World countries typically have comparatively unequal income distributions. By contrast, First World countries, such as the welfare states of Western Europe, have relatively equal income distributions, reinforced by government policies that tax the rich and spend on the poor.
>
> So a skilled worker in the Third World has less incentive to emigrate, relative to his unskilled countrymen—who have enormous incentives. Whereas in egalitarian Western Europe, skilled workers have relatively more to gain by emigrating to the United States . . . if they could get in.

Borjas's theory seems to work: First World immigrants are indeed disproportionately skilled and successful. As he puts it, Third World immigrants tend to be *"negatively selected."* Thus current immigration is tending to

1. lower the average quality of the U.S. workforce; and

2. stratify it, with the post-1970 immigrants tending to the bottom.

This is why immigration enthusiasts have been able to get away with arguing that immigrants are more highly skilled than native-born Americans. It's true. They are. But they are also, simultaneously, lower-skilled.

You hear a lot about Ph.D. immigrants working in California's Silicon Valley computer complex. Just under 3 percent of recent immigrants had Ph.D.s, as opposed to just over 1 percent of native-born Americans. But that's only, say, 30,000 immigrant Ph.D.s a year. And have you heard that surveys show some 10 percent of Mexican illegal immigrants (suggesting, say, 30,000 to 50,000 of the net illegal influx each year) were *totally illiterate in any language?*[3] . . .

Note also this: *by 1990, the immigrant advantage in college graduates had disappeared.* This reflects the sharp relative deterioration in immigrant skills in the most recent years. It happened at the other, unskilled pole too: at various times in the 1980s the proportion of newcomers who had not graduated from high school was running in excess of 40 percent.

"Immigrants have never been more educated," immigration enthusiasts sometimes argue. Maybe not. But in a rapidly developing and increasingly competitive world, *relative skill levels are what count.* . . .

Most people realize that the U.S. economy at the beginning of the twentieth century was much less skill-based. It could use laborers and sweatshop workers. But few people realize, in addition, that native-born Americans were, on average, much less skilled.

For example, only 13.5 percent of the over-twenty-five adult population had four or more years of high school in 1910.[4] The ideal that everyone should go through high school came surprisingly late in American history—really after World War II. So the contrast with unskilled immigrants was not as sharp as it is today.

Post-1965 Immigration: Welfare Up

The second striking characteristic of the post-1965 immigrant flow: *increased mismatching with the U.S. labor market*. This shows up in immigrants' increasing tendency to go n welfare.

In the early 1980s, immigration researchers were generally pretty complacent about immigration's impact on the United States. It became an article of faith, still echoed by some of the less alert immigration enthusiasts, that immigrants earned more, and went on welfare less, than native-born Americans.

The reason for this complacency, of course: the researchers were looking at old data. It still substantially reflected the pre-1965 immigrants.

By the early 1990s, the scene had changed completely. It was becoming clear that, among the post-1965 immigrants, welfare participation rates were sharply higher. *Immigrant welfare participation was, on average, higher than native-born Americans (9.1 percent vs. 7.4 percent)*. And what's more, *immigrant households on welfare tended to consume more, and increasingly more, than native-born households on welfare.* (In 1970, 6.7 percent of all welfare cash benefits went to immigrants; in 1990, 13.1 percent.) Some immigrant groups, such as Dominicans (27.9 percent on welfare), were far above the welfare participation even of American-born blacks (13.5 percent). (And note that "welfare" means just cash programs like Aid to Families with Dependent Children, Supplementary Security Income, and other general assistance—not non-cash programs like Food Stamps and Medicaid, for which there are no good numbers.)

Even pro-immigration researchers like the Urban Institute, while downplaying immigrant welfare participation, have reported that the immigrant proportion of those people living in areas of concentrated poverty

had nearly tripled in twenty years, to over 10 percent in 1990. . . .

Both American blacks and Puerto Ricans are disproportionately heavy users of welfare. One estimate suggests that looking only at native-born, non-Hispanic American whites, might drop the welfare-participation rate by more than two percentage points, to somewhere above 5 percent.[5] Which makes the immigrant performance appear, once again, really grim. . . .

And, as with immigrant skill levels, examining the welfare participation of just the most recent immigrants makes the trend more alarming. The 1990 Census reported that those arriving in the previous five years were significantly more likely to be on welfare (8.3 percent) than were their counterparts in 1970 (5.5 percent).

Which is particularly interesting news. Because according to the law, legal permanent residents are liable to be deported as a "public charge" *if they use public benefits during their first five years in the United States*. But as a practical matter (look at the numbers!), the whole concept of a "public charge" has collapsed. Only some forty-one people were deported on these grounds from 1961 to 1982. At that point, the INS just stopped bothering to report the category separately.[6]

Similarly, U.S. authorities now make no real effort to enforce the guarantees given by the sponsors of any immigrants—not just refugees—who then become public charges.

This passivity is unprecedented in American history. When immigration was handled by the states, prior to the 1875 Supreme Court ruling establishing federal jurisdiction, they legislated repeatedly and frantically to block European countries from dumping their "paupers"—potential welfare cases—in America. . . .

But even if the American authorities were enforcing the law, they would have to deal with rampant fraud. One indicator: an INS study found that *83 percent* of illegal immigrants amnestied under IRCA had false Social Security numbers.[7] But local agencies are now essentially forbidden by confidentiality laws from reporting fraud to the INS.[8]

Similarly, the Internal Revenue Service makes no effort to prevent illegal aliens from receiving Earned Income Tax Credit refunds, which are sometimes payable even if no income tax is due and can exceed two thousand dollars. Of course, the IRS computers often choke on those false Social Security numbers. If necessary the IRS *will then assign a temporary number.* . . .

Unquestionably, the largest loophole in welfare-eligibility provisions, however, is the birthright-citizenship provision of the Fourteenth Amendment. Whole nations are coming through it.

It works like this: the minor "citizen children" of illegal immigrants have the full entitlements of American citizens—for example, to cash payments under the federal Aid for Families with Dependent Children (AFDC) program. Naturally, their illegal parents collect it for them. And, equally naturally, no U.S. government is going to deport the parents of an American citizen. So having a child in the United States gives the illegal immigrant a secure, taxpayer-funded foothold here. And when the child turns eighteen, it can sponsor the legal immigration of its relatives.

Examining the group of immigrants arriving in the five years before 1970 reveals even more depressing news: welfare participation actually *increased* the longer they were in the United States. Originally, their rate was 5.5 percent; the 1990 Census reported it at 9.8 percent. All waves of immigrants show a similar drift. The conclusion is unavoidable: *immigrants are assimilating into the welfare system.*

Immigrants from different countries differ enormously in how likely they are to go on welfare. Cambodians and Laotians show astonishing welfare-participation rates—close to half (48.8 percent and 46.3 percent, respectively). Vietnamese are above a quarter (25.8 percent).

The apparent reason for these extreme welfare-participation rates: many members of these groups are refugees. And refugees are immediately entitled to welfare. And it's addictive.

Even after twenty years, refugees are still more likely to be on welfare than either native-born Americans or other immigrants. Even refugee groups that Americans think of as successful, such as the pre-1980 non-*Marielito* Cubans or refuseniks from the former

Soviet Union, in fact participate heavily in welfare (15.3 percent and 16.3 percent, respectively). . . .

Unavoidable conclusion, looking at these numbers:

> The post-1980 approach to refugees has created a catastrophe—even by the generally disastrous standards of immigration policy.

Still, Borjas says, the refugee presence is not enough to account for the immigrant slide into welfare. That trend remains even after refugee households are factored out. (Non-refugee immigrants are 7.8 percent into welfare, as opposed to native-born American participation of 7.4 percent.)

And immigrants from different countries still differ sharply in their likelihood to go on welfare even when none are refugees. The basic pattern: immigrants from developed countries are significantly less likely to go on welfare (the United Kingdom, 3.7 percent; Germany, 4.1 percent) than immigrants from the Third World (Haiti, 9.1 percent; Mexico, 11.3 percent).

Borjas's conclusion echoes that of the Urban Institute: a significant number of recent low-skilled immigrants now go to swell the ranks of the underclass. . . .

Post-1965 Immigration: 'An Excellent Investment?'

So the post-1965 immigrants are less successful economically and more inclined to use welfare. Does that mean they are now taking more from the various levels of American government than they pay in taxes—that immigration is a net cost to the public purse?

Immigration enthusiasts deny it vehemently. They are fighting a desperate battle to defend the proposition that, as Julian Simon put it in *The Economic Consequences of Immigration,* "an immigrant family is an excellent investment."[9] But they are clearly losing.

In part, the immigration enthusiasts are being driven back by the sheer volume of horror stories slowly emerging from the local level. For example, in California, *fully a third of all public assistance* goes to immigrant-headed households. And Californians are reacting. . . .

George Borjas suggests that a back-of-the-envelope cost-to-government calculation should look like this:

> . . . Assume immigrants are charged a proportionate "fair share" of all government expenditures. Assume also that they take the same proportion of non-cash benefits as cash benefits (13.1 percent). Thus in 1990, about 8.9 percent of government revenues are used to fund cash and non-cash programs. And in 1990, immigrants earned about $285 billion (net of welfare payments) and, combining federal, state and local taxes, probably face an estimated 30 percent tax rate. That adds up to some $85 billion in immigrant tax payments. So 8.9 percent of immigrants' $85 billion taxes ($7.6 billion) can be set against their use of cash and other benefits (about $23.8 billion). *Net cost to native-born American taxpayers: over $16 billion*.

Three Big Questions: Education, Social Security, and Unequal Impact

Note that Borjas's calculation doesn't include the immense costs of educating immigrant children. A year for one student in the New York City public school system, for example, involves an average annual expenditure of nearly $7,400.[10] By comparison, the annual per capita national income of Mexico is about $4,000. In Haiti, it's just $320 per capita.[11]

Arguably, some of that cost will be paid back, as the immigrant children's skill levels are improved and they eventually earn more than they would otherwise have done. And, on the other side of the ledger, some immigrants arrive already educated and presumably benefit native-born Americans with their skills—although capturing much of the surplus in their own earnings. So the net impact of education costs is hard to figure out.

But meanwhile, *education costs money now.* Note also that Borjas is not taking into account immigrants' payments into the Social Security system. Which may seem surprising, because for many workers these payments now exceed income taxes. But (as with education) there's another side to the question: *immigrants*

paying into the system also represent a future claim upon it.

Amazingly, there have been no full-blown academic studies of the net impact of immigration on the Social Security system. But, since the median age of immigration is thirty, many immigrants will pay into the system for a much shorter period than will the native-born. Yet the benefits they receive will be substantially the same. If you work fifteen years, you receive only slightly less than for working thirty years. So it looks ominous.

"But immigrants are going to bail out the Social Security system!" This is a favorite claim of immigration enthusiasts. It works like this. Social Security is not really an insurance system: it's actually a direct hand-over, via the government, from working Americans to retired Americans. The benefits that retired Americans receive far surpass the value of their earlier payments. While working Americans far outnumber retired Americans, as they do while the Baby Boom generation is in the labor force, the system teeters in balance. But what happens when the Baby Boomers retire—and the succeeding Baby Bust generation is all that's available to support them?

"IMMIGRANTS!" say the immigration enthusiasts. . . . But . . . the immigration enthusiasts' numbers don't add up. The Dallas-based National Center for Policy Analysis has calculated that to keep payments constant and the Social Security payroll tax at current levels, the U.S. workforce would have to be doubled by immigration in less than three decades. Since parents will bring children, this could involve the departure of *about half the nonelderly population of Latin America*.[12]

There is, however, a third point in the cost-to-government debate on which everyone agrees:

> Whatever the overall balance between immigrant taxes and costs, the impact on specific states and cities is severe.

This is because many of the taxes that immigrants pay go to Washington—for example, their Social Security deductions—whereas the services they receive are paid for by the local community.

It's easy enough to argue that Washington must step in with money to repair the damage. But this almost certainly means further loss of control by the state governments, further erosion of the founding American principle of federalism in favor of centralization in Washington.

. . . As the [Wall Street] investment firm Sanford C. Bernstein commented tersely in downgrading the state of California's bond rating in 1991:

The primary reasons for the state's credit decline are above-average population growth and shifting demographics. . . . The degree of public assistance required by two of the fastest growing groups, Latinos and political/ethnic refugees (most of whom are Southeast Asians), is substantially higher than that of the general population[13] . . .

George Borjas has drawn the inevitable moral as well as it can be done:

A welfare state cannot afford the large-scale immigration of less skilled persons.[14]

Endnotes

1. George J. Borjas, *Friends or Strangers? The Impact of Immigration on the U.S Economy*. New York: Basic Books, 1990), 219.

2. Unless otherwise indicated, data are drawn from the work of George J. Borjas (Professor of Economics, University of California, San Diego, Research Associate, National Bureau of Economic Research). Principal sources are "The Economics of Immigration," *Journal of Economic Literature*, December 1994; "Immigration Research in the 1980s: A Turbulent Decade," in *Research Frontiers in Industrial Relations and Human Resources*, ed. D. Lewin, O. Mitchell, P. Sherer (Industrial Relations and Research Association, 1992); "Immigration and Ethnicity," *NBER Reporter*, National Bureau of Economic Research, Fall 1993; "The Economic Benefits from Immigration," forthcoming; "Assimilation and Changes in Cohort Quality Revisited: What Happened to Immigrant Skills in the 1980s," *Journal of Labor Economics*, forthcoming; "Ethnic Capital and Intergenerational Mobility," *Quarterly Journal of Economics*, February 1992.

   See also George Borjas, Richard B. Freeman, eds., *Immigration and the Work Force: Economic Consequences for the United States and Source Areas* (Chicago: University of Chicago Press, 1992); George Borjas, *Friends or Strang-*

ers: The Impact of Immigration on the U.S. Economy (New York: Basic Books, 1990).

   Borjas's conclusions are widely echoed in the literature on the recent migration: for example, Michael Baker and Dwayne Benjamin, "The Performance of Immigrants in the Canadian Labor Marker," *Journal of Labor Economics*, forthcoming; Deborah A. Cobb-Clark, "Immigrant Selectivity and Wages: The Evidence for Women," *American Economic Review*, September 1983; Rachel M. Friedberg, "The Labor Market Assimilation of Immigrants in the United States: The Role of Age at Arrival," Brown University, 1992; Robert J. LaLonde and Robert H. Topel, "The Assimilation of Immigrants in the U.S. Labor Market," in *Immigration and the Work Force*, ed. G. Borjas and R. Freeman, above.

3. Stephen Moore, *Insight*, November 22, 1993.

4. Spokesman, Office of Educational Research and Improvement, Education Information Branch, Department of Education, interview.

5. House Committee on Ways and Means, Subcommittee on Human Resources, *Patterns of Public Assistance Receipt Among Immigrants: Results from the 1990 and 1980 Censuses*, report prepared by Frank D. Bean et al. Population Research Center, University of Texas at Austin, presented November 15, 1993.

6. 1992 Statistical Yearbook of the INS (Washington, D.C.: U.S. Government Printing Office), table 66, 162.

7. "The Immigration and control Act: A Report on the Legalized Alien Population"; John Bjerke, Project Director (INS: U.S. Government Printing Office, 1992).

8. House Committee on Ways and Means, Subcommittee on Human Resources, testimony by Mark J. Lefcowitz, Department of Human Development, Fairfax County, Va., November 15, 1993.

9. Julian L. Simon, *The Economic Consequences of Immigration* (Cambridge, Ma.: Basil Blackwell, 1989), 128.

10. Interview with New York City Board of Education spokesman.

11. Department of State office, interview by author.

12. John C. Goodman and Aldona Robbins, *The Immigration Solution* (Dallas, Tex.: National Center for Policy Analysis, 1992).

13. Sanford C. Bernstein and Company, Municipal Research, *The State of California* (New York: Sanford C. Bernstein and Company, 1991) 4, 7.

14. George J. Borjas, *National Review*, December 13, 1993, 42–43.

Renegotiating Identities, Rethinking Categories[*]

"An ethnic/group identity is a complex interaction between personal and social definitions" (Thornton 1996, p. 115). Racial and ethnic identity is therefore both a psychological and social phenomenon. Each of these aspects of identity encompasses a distinct but interrelated aspect of our understanding of the issue. Within both a psychological and a social approach, the concept of identity can be broken down even further to focus on whether the point of reference is individuals or groups of individuals.

Psychological Approach to Racial/Ethnic Identity

The formation of an individual identity is viewed by many child development theorists as crucial to maturity. Erikson focuses on identity development as an important stage of adolescence that is necessary in order for individuals to function effectively in the next stage of development, which focuses on the maintenance of relationships. Thus, one must define one's own identity before one can enter successfully into relationships with others. The psychological approach toward racial and ethnic identity can also focus on a group's perceptions of its own characteristics, values, or orientations, and the resulting collective identity that emerges from this common conceptualization. For example, the collective group identity of African Americans highlights such values as cooperation and sharing, and places emphasis on the extended family and the importance of religion, music, and education (McAdoo 1996 and Billingsly 1992). Collective identity provides the impetus for group cohesion, as it delineates the source of group pride. Collective identity also provides criteria from within that determine who is and is not a group member.

Social Approach to Racial/Ethnic Identity

A social approach to identity focuses on characterizations of an individual or group from the outside. Around the world, individuals are forced to identify themselves as part of a particular racial or ethnic group; the forced categorization of individuals into racial and ethnic groups on census and other governmental forms in the United States is a good example. The number and nature of racial and ethnic categories from which people have been able to choose has changed many times since the end of the nineteenth century, sometimes making distinctions among people of color (i.e., Colored [blacks], Colored [mulattoes], Chinese, and Indian in the 1870 census; white, black and other in the 1950 census; and white, black, Asian, Hispanic, and Indian on federal forms in the 1990s) (Spickard 1992; Cornell and Hartmann 1998).

[*] This introduction was written by Melissa Landers–Potts and Trellis Smith with the assistance of Velma McBride Murry, all of the University of Georgia.

Societies identify individuals as belonging to racial and ethnic groups without regard to their psychological orientations or self-characterizations. All societies impose these identifications differently. In Brazil, for example, there are many categories for people of color that distinguish between various skin shades. Categorization of different racial and ethnic groups is significant in that privileges and resources (such as economic opportunities, civil rights, social interaction with the majority group, etc.) are often granted on the basis of membership in these groups. Societies create strict guidelines by which they view individuals as identifying with or belonging to a particular group, and often place sanctions on individuals who challenge these guidelines (e.g., biracial or multiracial individuals), or who dare to challenge the social norms established to maintain the power structure. In addition, society imposes identities on racial and ethnic groups, which may be very much at odds with the collective, insider identity of the group. The negative stereotypes historically and presently generated by the majority society regarding the African American racial/ethnic group have served the purpose of justifying slavery, injustice, and prejudice for the benefit of the majority group for centuries. The complexity of the various aspects of identity and the importance of racial and ethnic identity in so many areas of peoples' lives create constant dilemmas for individuals whose psychological identities do not mesh with those of the society in which they live. Dissonance between these aspects of identity may affect bi- or multiracial individuals whose individual psychological identities do not coincide with the way in which society views them, or for a racial or ethnic group member whose positive characterization of his or her group's collective identity is not embraced by the society.

In order to completely understand the nuances of these discussions, it is important to understand the differences and similarities between racial and ethnic identity. Race, in reference books and social science literature, is aligned with biological or physical characteristics: skin color, blood type, nose or eye shape, hair texture, and body shape, among others. Racial identity refers to the percep-

tions of individuals, groups, and societies of group membership based on these biological and/or physical characteristics. Ethnic groups and ethnic identity, in contrast, are based on culturally derived characteristics that presume no genetic component. Ethnic identity, instead, focuses on social characteristics, historical circumstances, ideas, values, or orientations that individuals or groups of individuals have in common, as perceived by individuals, group members, and/or societies. All of the articles in this section touch on the intersection between racial and ethnic identity, although most of the articles emphasize one or the other. Neither race nor ethnicity is a concrete, scientifically substantiated category, which makes them social constructs or creations which have meaning only in the particular society or context in which they were created. We will discuss racial identity and ethnic identity in separate sections, as each form of identity contains its own set of issues and implications. Finally, we will discuss common themes and suggest future directions for research.

Racial and Ethnic Identity
[Racial] Identity

Jim and I decided that as grandparents, we were going to take the baby. We knew that that baby was a part of our daughter, Alison, and we loved her so much. When Alison told me that three couples have been to look at Lauren and they don't want her, I was, I was just, I can't tell you. I was so devastated. I didn't know how to react. I said to Jim, 'I'm going to get this baby and bring it home.' So we went to Houston to visit the hospital and later I told my mom, 'Lauren is Black.' My mom said, 'Oh no, no she isn't.' I said, 'Oh yes, mother, she is. I can see. I know she is. I know she is.'

Once in a store, Skip heard a black cashier spar with Alison. "Yes, it is my baby," Alison said. "No, it's not!" the cashier insisted. Finally Alison walked away. . . . The real pain for Skip came when the outside world begin to get inside Lauren's head and she asked, "Daddy, why is my skin brown and yours is white?"

Above is an account of a true story that happened to a white American family. The grandmother of the newly born baby is expressing to her own mother how she felt when she found out that her daughter, Alison, had a baby, Lauren, by a black man. The grandmother did not know that the baby was biracial until after she was born. Before the birth of the baby, Alison married an old boyfriend, who was white. Thus, the biracial child began life in an environment where she is apparently "different." After spending time with the baby outside of their home, Alison and Skip realized the potent issue of race and/or racial identity that Lauren will face for the rest of her life. She is a minority in a majority-dominated society, a member of the "out-group" that sticks out as such because of the color of her skin.

According to Goodstein and Ponterotto (1997), a tendency exists among all humans to delineate boundaries between those who are and are not a part of their cultural group. The most salient aspect of the social self that lends itself to such delineation is race. The construction of race has affected relationships between different cultures of people in the American society, and has had both positive and negative impacts. Throughout history, race has emerged from sociohistorical processes of dominance and subjugation. Populations termed "white" and "black" and the idea of two distinct races emerged as a product of the European colonization of the New World through the extensive slave trade, and the historical events that followed slavery. As people from various ethnic groups in Africa were separated from families and friends and forced to leave their homeland, they began to forge new bonds. They began to take the first steps toward the formation of an Afro-American culture, under conditions of great duress. Many of the slaves on a given boat did not speak a common language but they quickly formed the beginnings of a community. The community that they formed provided emotional and instrumental support to help them cope with stressful life events. As the diverse Africans who made up the slave population increasingly created their own unique culture, their actions evoked responses from their supposed owners. In all areas of the New World, slave owners and merchants paid careful attention to the cultural innovations and developments of the slaves, often responding with harsh measures to try and stamp out activities that they, the masters, deemed dangerous or insubordinate. Perhaps the most conspicuous of these measures in North America, was the widespread ban on teaching slaves to read (Reed and Gaines 1997).

After the Civil War, African Americans struggled for political and social equality, but failed to achieve it. The demands of freed slaves for access to the basic means of life, economic and civic, were met with a massive attack from other parts of the American society. This attack included a significant ideological component in which the concept of a supposedly degraded Negro race played a dominant role. In order to justify slavery and increasingly harsh treatment of ex-slaves, white Americans invented the myth of a primitive African or black culture. And, as most mythological systems require a polar structure, they located white or European culture at the opposite pole from the allegedly degraded African culture. All white Americans stood to gain psychologically and financially from a social structure that consigned persons of African descent to the lowest rung on the socioeconomic ladder. Every nonwhite group encountered by the Anglos in the United States was exploited economically and psychologically. Native Americans faced genocide, blacks were subjected to racial slavery, Mexicans were invaded and colonized, and Asians faced exclusion. In general, white European Americans placed themselves at the center of the sociopolitical and socioeconomic universe and consistently behaved in bad faith toward people of color (Reed and Gaines 1997).

Literature on racial identity suggests that in American society, children of all races are socialized by various institutions to believe that goodness is manifested solely in biological and cultural whiteness, and that badness is manifested in anything other than whiteness. Therefore, white children begin with the assumption that their race is superior to all others, and children of color begin with the assumption that their race is inferior to the white race. Institutions throughout American society are controlled by European Americans and perhaps reinforce images of the goodness of biological and cultural whiteness along with corresponding images of the badness of nonwhiteness. Radio, newspaper, television, the internet, and all other mass media outlets are dominated by European Americans.

In a study conducted by Ruth Horowitz in 1939, line drawings were used to study racial awareness among white and black nursery school children who were asked to indicate which drawings looked most like themselves. The findings of the study were that black children more often identified with white rather than black figures, and perceived them as having more favorable attributes. This led to the inference that blacks had negative connotations of their race, and actually wanted to be white. This research also indicated that children are aware of racial differences at young ages. In a similar study conducted by Clarke and Clarke (1947), children were offered choices between two colors of dolls, white and dark brown. The researchers noted that 23 percent of medium- and dark-skinned black children and 80 percent of light-skinned black children identified with the white doll. A study conducted by Hraba and Grant (1970), in an era when the idea that "black is beautiful" was prevalent, showed that black children turned to the black doll in making preferential choices. The results of this research illustrate that the formation of racial identity is closely linked to the ideas of dominant members in society. Other literature on racial identity indicates that experiences of racism provide a unique set of societal restrictions that create dilemmas for developing racial identity and self-esteem.

Racial identity is the degree to which a person believes he or she shares a common racial heritage with a particular group. Feelings about the self are often developed by separating one's personal sense of self from the negative perceptions attached to one's racial group. Mixed feelings toward the group exist among minorities who must contend with the negative images of their group that permeate society. Research has shown that positive racial identification is stronger for black

elders than for their younger counterparts (Smith and Thornton 1993). This, perhaps, is due to a stronger sense of community that evolved through shared experiences throughout history. The well-educated are alienated from the core of black society but remain ambiguous toward those who are outside and work against the white-dominated system. Persons attempting to move in to a new setting with a group reluctant to accept them may become strangers to both the old and new settings. Caught between two conflicting social groups, these people are prone to social ambiguity, divided loyalties, and psychological distress. Feelings of isolation and divided loyalties are documented among middle-class blacks living in predominantly white neighborhoods (Tatum 1987).

Ethnic Identity

Ethnicity is a broader and more inclusive concept than race, as ethnic groups can be based not only on physical traits, but also on other factors such as religious beliefs, language, or common history. This section will focus primarily on issues of ethnic identity; however, it is impossible to discuss ethnicity without discussing race, as racial identities comprise some of the most salient ethnic identities in our society. Ethnicity is one of an individual's most socially significant attributes, particularly because societies commonly assign social status on the basis of ethnic identity. Evidence for this can be found through examination of world events over the last 50 years. Extermination of Jews on the basis of their religious ethnicity occured during World World II, terrorism between Isrealis and Palistinians as a result of religous and historical ethnicity continues, and discrimination against individuals on the basis of their skin color in Western society persists.

Social perceptions of some ethnic groups change over time. During the first half of this century in the United States, for example, Italian and Irish ethnic identity was assigned a negative status, causing many of those whose parents immigrated from Italy or Ireland to deny their ethnicity and work hard to assimilate into mainstream American culture. These white European immigrant groups, over time, have been 'accepted' into mainstream America and their heritage no longer elicits negative connotations. The following is a discussion of a third-generation Italian immigrant (one of the authors of this paper) who is describing (to the other author) her mother's feelings about her Italian identity:

> My mom's parents were Italian immigrants who came to the U.S. in the 1930s. When my parents were dating, because of the fact that being Italian was really looked down on, my dad's parents visibly expressed their dislike for my mom and their dissatisfaction that my dad intended to marry her. So I think my mom tried not to associate herself with being Italian. When I was little, she would get embarrassed if I told my friends that my grandparents came over from Italy. Today, though, my mom is really proud of her heritage. She has traveled to Italy three times, twice in the past two years, and after her last trip, she said to me, "I was just so proud to be Italian!"

The second-generation woman described above attempted to conceal her Italian identity throughout her childhood and early adulthood, but reclaimed her ethnic identity in middle age with pride, as have many other individuals with similar European immigrant histories. The ability of white European immigrants such as Italians and Irish to become successful in America through traditional means (i.e., the labor market and social organizations) and to consequently shed the negativity associated with their ethnic identity is not an experience common to all immigrant groups. In particular, dark-skinned immigrant ethnic groups (e.g., Latinos/as, West Indians, and Haitians), who now comprise the majority of immigrants to this country (Spickard, this volume), do not have the same access to traditional avenues of success in America. Neither do they have the opportunity to assimilate into the majority culture, if that is what is desired. These growing ethnic groups, whose members look different than those of the majority group, are identified in society as members of a different "race." Physical appearance, and skin color in particular, is extremely relevant in determining social status in the United States and in many countries around the world. Ethnic identification therefore takes on a different meaning for the dark-skinned ethnic immigrant groups that are now most prevalent in this country than for those immigrant ethnic groups that arrived during the first half of the century. Members of dark-skinned ethnic groups therefore have a different set of identities from which to choose.

Mary Waters (this volume) found that second-generation Caribbean immigrant children identified with three different ethnic groups: black American nonimmigrants (American-identified), their ethnic immigrant community in America (ethnic-identified), and their homeland (immigrant-identified). It is significant that Caribbean-American children did not identify with white Americans. The specific nature of ethnic identity is therefore determined in part by the meanings assigned to skin and other physical attributes associated with 'race.' Waters found that specific behaviors, opinions, and values were associated with each type of identity, many of which had implications for adolescents' success in school.

Recently, and partly as a result of the increasing number of interracial/interethnic marriages and the subsequent increase in bi- and multiethnic children born of these unions (Fundenburg 1994; Daniel 1996), multiracial children have founded advocacy groups such as I-Pride, and have begun to lobby against the way in which they are categorized in this society. Self-categorization of race/ethnicity is basic and frequent in our daily lives, as it is required on birth certificates, school records, and employment applications. Yet, the categories available on such forms are inadequate. Consider the following excerpt of a woman's diary entry in Pat Bell Scott's book, *Life Notes* (1994, pp. 69–70):

> My mother ended up having an affair with a Japanese man. . . . I was born barely seven months later, on October 21, 1947, in my great-grandmother's house in Albany, Texas . . . My great grandmother Maggie was Irish and African-American. My great-grandfather was Dutch and Choctaw Indian. My mother's father was African-American. My great-grandfather's mother, who was Choctaw, and his father

who was Dutch, had moved to Texas from Oklahoma, where many Choctaws had been relocated by Andrew Jackson . . . All I know is my great-grandfather's family name was Waggoner, but when he was born, the birth certificate was changed and his last name became Smith, because they said Waggoner was a white man's name. My own birth certificate lists me as the child of my mother's husband, with a "C," I assume for "Colored," under race.

The writing of this multiethnic, multiracial woman clearly illustrates the complexity of the issue of race and ethnicity in America. The fact that a single letter in a box on her birth certificate served as a substitute for the complexity of her racial/ethnic background exemplifies the inadequacy of our social frameworks for conceptualizing race and ethnicity. Her ethnic identity could be one of many, and the negotiation of her own identity could potentially take a variety of routes. These routes have the potential to be influenced by a variety of personal factors, including her experiences, relationships that she develops, attitudes of significant others in her life (primary caregivers, in particular), and contact with specific family members, as well as an array of societal factors which include the political climate, employment and residential opportunities, the nature of social institutions such as schools and banks, and the culture of the society in which she lives (Cornell and Hartmann 1998).

Finally, some members of the majority deny the importance of race and ethnicity in modern American society, which has the consequence of also denying that power and status differences exist as a function of race and/or ethnicity (Frankenburg, this volume). Additionally, some parents of multiracial children teach their children that they are members of a world culture, and that all people share a common ancestry (Root 1996). The connotation of such a perspective is that ethnic and/or racial identities are irrelevant or erroneous. These parents are technically correct in that we are all of one species, and there are no biological characteristics which successfully place us into groups (i.e., races), yet it is no more possible to deny the existence of the intangible, unmeasurable ethnic differences that distinguish us from, and that bind us to one another than it is to deny the existence of culture. Our individual perceptions of our culture and our place within it allow us to define our own identities, which are the means by which we organize our actions and behaviors.

Conclusion

Controversy concerning issues of racial and ethnic identity may or may not be apparent after the introduction of this topic. However, explicitly stated, controversy and conflict exist due to the subjectivity of the constructs and fluidity of their boundaries. Race does not have a scientific justification in human biology, and there is as much genetic variability between two different people from the same 'racial' group as there are between two people from any two different 'racial' groups. In addition to the variability of genetic material that is characteristic of people within and outside of racial groups, the distribution of human physical characteristics is persistently irregular. Blood types, hair textures, skin colors, and body forms all vary, sometimes dramatically, both between and within populations. Categories of race and ethnicity vary across time, with social criteria for membership in particular racial and ethnic groups constantly changing throughout history and varying according to the social or geographical context in which people live. For example, during the early part of this century, Jewish and Irish people were considered to comprise their own racial groups. Today, however, neither is viewed as its own racial group, or as having a unique racial identity.

Another aspect of race and ethnicity that is often overlooked is the variation of ethnicity within racial groups. For example, Caribbeans, Jamaicans, Trinidadians, and Haitians may be assigned by members of society to the black American racial group, but have separate ethnic identities from African Americans. Factors that may contribute to differences in ethnic identities within racial groups are socioeconomic status, stage of individual identification, contact with outside group members, and impacts of historical events.

According to Smith (1989), individuals can occupy different stages of racial and ethnic identities. The first stage might be conceptualized as movement *toward* the aggressor, or the desire for acculturation and assimilation to mainstream society. The second stage might be viewed as movement *against* the aggressor, in which people of a different race/ethnicity are seen as "the enemy." The third stage might be conceptualized as movement *away* from the aggressor, and the fourth stage seems to be the stage of incorporation. An alternative perspective to Smith's stage theory is to view each stage as a typology so that some individuals may experience the stages in a different order and/or may arrive at any of the six stages as their "final destination." However, the underlying tenet of both approaches is that racial/ethnic identity is fluid and dynamic throughout the life course. Some people may feel that they have gone beyond the issue of race, even though they recognize racial/ethnic differences and the impact of lingering racism. Racial categories change as people struggle to establish, overcome, assign other people to, escape, and/or interpret them.

A closer look at race and ethnicity should reveal a greater need to understand how the two constructs are related to the overall development of personality, when people evaluate others primarily in terms of "different-from-me," and under what conditions other modes of evaluation will emerge to replace those that already exist. A closer look at race and ethnicity should also reveal the extent to which degrading messages are internalized, and how they are buffered by members of different groups. As we are challenged to rethink race and ethnicity in this section, issues of justification for inequalities, and long- and short-term effects of racial/ethnic categorization should ignite further development of curiosity and reasoning that will result in the dissolution of artificial separateness.

References

Ai. 1994. Arrival. In P.B. Scott (Ed.), *Life Notes* (pp.69–70). New York: W.W. Norton and Company.

Bell-Scott, P. 1994. *Life Notes*. New York: W.W. Norton & Company.

Billingsly, A. 1992. *Climbing Jacob's Ladder: The Enduring Legacy of African-American Families*. New York: Simon & Schuster.

Clarke, K.B. & M.P. Clarke. 1947. "Racial Identification and Preference in Negro Children." In T. M. Newcomb and E.L. Hartley, eds., *Readings in Social Psychology*, Pp. 169-178. New York: Holt.

Cornell, S. and D. Hartmann. 1998. *Ethnicity and Race: Making Identities in a Changing World*. Thousand Oaks: Pine Forge Press.

Daniel, G.R. 1996. "Black and white identity in the new millenium: Unsevering the ties that bind." In M. Root (Ed.), *The Multiracial Experience: Racial Borders as the New Frontier* (pp.101–120). Thousand Oaks, CA: Sage.

Fundenburg, L. 1994. *Black, White, Other: Biracial Americans Talk About Race and Identity*. New York: William Morrow.

Goodstein, R., & J. G. Ponterotto. 1997. "Racial and ethnic identity: Their relationship and their contribution to self-esteem." *Journal of Black Psychology*, 23(3), 275–292.

Hraba, J., & Grant, P. 1970. "Black is Beautiful: A Reexamination of Racial Preference and Identification." *Journal of Personality and Social Psychology* 16, 398–402.

McAdoo, H.P. (Ed.) 1996. *Black Families*, Third Edition. Thousand Oaks, CA: Sage Publications, Inc.

Pomerantz, G. M. 1997. (October 21). "The father whom Lauren has known from birth." *The Atlanta Journal/The Atlanta Constitution*, pp. B6.

Reed, E. S., & S. O. Gaines, Jr. 1997. "Not everybody is 'different-from-me': Toward a historico-cultural account of prejudice." *Journal of Black Psychology*, 23(3), 245–274.

Root, M.P. (Ed.). 1996. *The Multiracial Experience: Racial Borders as the New Frontier*. Thousand Oaks, CA: Sage.

Smith, E. 1989. "Black racial identity and development: Issues and concerns." *The Counseling Psychologist*, 17(2), 277–288.

Smith, R., and M. Thornton. 1993. "Identity and consciousness: Group solidarity among older Black Americans." In J. Jackson, L. Chatters, and R. Taylor (Eds.), *Aging in Black America* (pp.203–216). Newbury Park, CA: Sage.

Spickard, P.R. 1992. "The illogic of American racial categories." In M. Root (Ed.), *Racially Mixed People in America* (pp.12–23). Thousand Oaks, CA: Sage.

Tatum, B. 1987. *Assimilation Blues*. New York: Greenwood.

Thornton, M.C. 1996. "Hidden agendas, identity theories, and multiracial people." In M. Root (Ed.), *The Multiracial Experience: Racial Borders as the New Frontier* (pp.101–120). Thousand Oaks, CA: Sage.

Thornton, M. C., Tran, T. V., and Taylor, R. J. 1997. "Multiple dimensions of racial group identification among adult Black Americans." *Journal of Black Psychology,* 23(3), 293–309.

Vaugh, G. M. 1986. "Social change and racial identity: Issues in the use of picture and doll measures." *Australian Journal of Psychology* 38(3), 359-370.

43

Thinking Through Race

Ruth Frankenberg

... In the present chapter I will explore how white women think through race and pursue in ... detail questions about white women's inscription into discourses on race difference.

The very use of the term "race" raises the idea of difference, for race is above all a marker of difference, an axis of differentiation. What kind of difference race is and what difference race makes in real terms are the questions that are contested in competing modes of thinking through race. Thus, for example, some women said that race makes, or should make, no difference between people. Others discussed the significance of race in terms of cultural differences or economic and sociopolitical differences. The women also placed different kinds of value on "seeing difference": for some, seeing race differences at all made one a "racist," while for others, not seeing the differences race makes was a "racist" oversight.

The discourse that views race as a marker of ontological, essential, or biological differences—a discourse that dominated white thinking on race for much of U.S. history and that I refer to here as essentialist racism ... is in many ways the absent presence in these women's discussions of race and difference. None of the women I interviewed described herself as consciously or explicitly espousing the idea of race as an axis of ontological or biological difference and inequality. However, I suggest that much of what the women said about the kind of difference race makes refers back to that mode of thinking through race.

Essentialist racism has left a legacy that continues to mark discourses on race difference in a range of ways. First, precisely be-cause it proposed race as a significant axis of difference, essentialist racism remains the benchmark against which other discourses on race are articulated. In other words, the articulation and deployment of essentialist racism approximately five hundred years ago marks the moment when, so to speak, *race was made into a difference* and simultaneously into a rationale for racial inequality. It is an ongoing response to that moment that movements and individuals—for or against the empowerment of people of color—continue to articulate analyses of difference and sameness with respect to race. Thus, for example, when the women I interviewed insisted that "we are all the same under the skin," within what I have described as a color-evasive and power-evasive discursive repertoire, they did so partly in response to essentialist racism. Second, in significant ways the notion of ontological racial difference underlies other, ostensibly cultural, conceptualizations of race difference. ... Third, essentialist racism—particularly intentional, explicit racial discrimination—remains, for most white people, including many of the women I interviewed, paradigmatic of racism. This, as I have argued, renders structural and institutional dimensions of racism less easily conceptualized and apparently less noteworthy. ... Finally, although essentialist racism is not the dominant discursive repertoire on race difference in the United States, its corollary, racially structured political and economic inequity, continues to shape material reality. Given this, all of the women I interviewed were forced to grapple in one way or another with the material reality of racial inequality.

By pointing to an early and significant moment of essentialist racism in the United States, I do not intend to reduce all subsequent thinking to that moment. For while referring back implicitly to essentialist racism, these women also drew, for the most part much more consciously and explicitly, on later moments in the history of ideas about race and ethnicity in the United States. Centrally, I will argue that the majority of the women were in fact thinking through race within or against a second moment of race discourse. This moment, whose elements, I would argue, remain dominant in the United States today, is characterized by variations on color-evasive and power-evasive themes, which themselves built directly on the assimilationist theories that challenged essentialist racism in the first decades of the twentieth century. Some of the women also drew on elements of a third, race-cognizant, moment in U.S. race discourse that opposes both the first and second moments. For it articulates the new characterizations of race difference (including awareness of structural and institutional inequity and valorization of subordinated cultures) that emerged out of civil rights and later movements for the cultural and economic empowerment of people of color from the late 1950s to the present day.

These three moments—essentialist racism, color-and power-evasiveness, and race-cognizant reassertions and reorientations of race difference—can . . . be considered as the first, second, and third phases in U.S. race discourse in the sense that they originated in that order; however, past the point of their emergence they can no longer be conceptualized as unfolding chronologically in any simple sense. Rather, each, in different contexts, takes center stage as the organizing paradigm or retreats to the status of a repertoire that provides discursive elements but does not dictate overarching form or structure. From the point of view of white women thinking through race, these three moments together constituted the universe of discourse within which race was made meaningful, with elements combined and recombined, used in articulation with or against one another, and deployed with varying degrees of intentionality. . . .

The women frequently referred to the universe of discourse on race that framed the interview and their lives. At times they described the United States in terms of a changing scenario of race relations; some, for example, noted with approval the end of the Jim Crow era, and others expressed disappointment over what they perceived to be the separatism or "extremism" of autonomous movements of people of color. At other times they described *themselves* as changing, moving out of one mode of thinking through race and into another (for example, several southern-raised women described themselves as having moved from unquestioning acceptance of racial segregation to contact and friendship with people of color after moving to California).

They also commented on their own shifting attitudes and worldviews: many white feminists described themselves as "waking up" from past unconsciousness of racism. Others very consciously set limits on their willingness to accept or participate in critique of racism.

The women's language and thought about race was idiosyncratic and individual. But again, idiosyncratic strategies were linked to the larger picture, whether consciously or not. Some of the women described (or enacted in our conversations) conscious decisions about how to talk about race in the context of their estimation of the "racist status quo" in American society. For example, choices of how to name African American men and women indicated cognizance of how *girl* and *boy* have been used as racist appellations for Black people. Thus, when Pat Bowen described her twelve-year-old African American schoolfriends as "women," she was, I believe, overcompensating for the possibly derogatory implications of calling them "girls." Sandy Alvarez, speaking of a Black "boy" who asked her out on a date in junior high school, was at pains to add that "of course he really was a boy then." In a similar vein, women named and renamed particular groups in the course of speaking about them, vacillating, for example, among "Spanish," "Mexican," "Mexican American," and "Chicano." Each of these names evokes a particular moment in racial and colonial history, recalling the presence of the colonizer or the agency of the colonized in diverse ways.

Beyond the details of language, the struggle to deal personally with a particular dimension of the racial order seemed to run through some of the women's entire life stories. For example, as Debby Rothman spoke to me about racial tensions in her workplace, she repeatedly expressed her concern that, were I to write about her experience, I might discourage my white readers from participating in multiracial activity. This kind of concern over "damage control" given a racist society was a repeated theme in my interviews with Debby. She had hesitated to tell anyone about the physical violence in her eleven-year relationship with an African American man for fear of feeding whites' racist hostility, toward either Black men or interracial relationships. . . . She also described having once been mugged in Queens, New York: repeatedly questioned by white friends and relatives about the race of her assailant, she was relieved to have been able to report that although he was Black, so were the police officers who chased him down and the passersby who stopped to help her. . . .

Color Evasion: Dodging 'Difference'

Among the reasons to begin this exploration of discursive repertoires by examining color- and power-evasiveness is that it remains dominant in U.S. "public" race discourse. For many white people in the United States, including a good number of the women I interviewed, "color-blindness"—a mode of thinking about race organized around an effort to not "see," or at any rate not to acknowledge, race differences—continues to be the "polite" language of race. Second, I want to suggest that color evasion actually involves a selective engagement with difference, rather than no engagement at all. Third, it is crucial to examine this discursive repertoire because of its contradictions: it has in its various guises been taken to be antiracist, but color evasion, with its corollary of power evasion, ultimately has had reactionary results through most of the twentieth century. It is useful, then, to follow the logic and pathways of color evasiveness through the women's narratives and to examine both the ways in which it has been deployed against essentialist racism and the ways it leads white women back into complicity with structural and institutional dimensions of inequality. In this regard, it seems to me that there are some salutary lessons to be learned about the new kinds of selectivity currently emerging in U.S. society—selectivities that apparently embrace cultural and other parameters of diversity, but do so in ways that leave hierarchies intact and, in this sense, remain as power evasive as their "color-blind" antecedents. . .

> To me, they are like me or anyone else— they're human—it's like I told my kids, they work for a living like we do. Just because they are Black is no saying their food is give to them [sic]. If you cut them, they bleed red blood, same as we do.

. . . [T]he women's strategies for talking about race difference often implicitly responded to *other* strategies. In her insistence here that African Americans are "human," Ginny Rodd referred to a recent past (both nationally and in her own life) in which people of African descent were, precisely, *not* viewed as human. But at the same time as it sought to undo essentialist racism, there was something chilling and distancing about the way Ginny voiced her opinion.

Ginny grew up and spent her early married life in rural Alabama, in the 1930s, 1940s, and 1950s. . . . In this context, Ginny's insistence on the common humanity of African American and white people was an explicit rejection of the essentialist racism with which she was raised. The blood metaphor Ginny used is crucial, for it located sameness in the body—precisely the location of *difference* in genetic or biological theories of white superiority. Further, of course, blood is under the skin, and skin has been and remains the foremost signifier of racial difference.

Ginny's statement that African Americans "work for a living, just like we do" was particularly significant, for throughout our discussions Ginny's articulation of her own identity focused on work and on her ability to work long hours and survive on poor wages. Thus, when I asked her to describe herself at the start of the interview, she began, "I've worked hard all of my life." Ginny several times critically measured others' prejudices against both African Americans and Latinos against her respect for them as workers who did jobs that white workers rejected. In this way, her description moved beyond cliche to an assertion of sameness based on what she held most dear about herself.

Ginny was not alone in emphasizing sameness as a way of rejecting the idea of white racial superiority. Irene Esterley, a native of

Detroit ten or fifteen years Ginny's senior, told me that she wanted her grandchildren to meet people with a range of racial and cultural origins because "the more you do so, the more you realize there *is* no difference." A third example is seventy-three-year-old Joan Bracknell, raised in the Bay Area—as she put it, "an Okie from Oakland":

> RF: So you think that's the best way to be—color-blind?
>
> OAN: Yes. Don't just look at them and immediately say,"Oh, I shouldn't like them."

. . . It became clear through the interview that Joan did *not* claim not to see race differences so much as to take the position that either one should find something nice to say about every ethnic group or one should say nothing at all. She emphasized the importance in her adult life of "meeting people halfway" and described her reaction to the increasing presence of people of "other" ethnic groups in San Francisco with the words "So what?" She remembered being friends with a Black child at school who shared her first name:

> It was funny. There was the Black Joan and the White Joan.

Joan described her childhood sense of racial and cultural difference using an image drawn from the world of her favorite creatures— cats:

> I really don't think I even thought I was different from them. I just took it in stride—like a bunch of kittens—all of them are different colors.

There is, perhaps, a mixed message here: to "not notice" is different from "taking it in stride," which implies noting a potential obstacle but managing not to trip over it. The metaphor, on the one hand, clarifies the desire underlying Joan's position: an acknowledgment of differentiation that is innocent of hostility. But, on the other hand, the idea that noticing a person's "color" is not a good thing to do, even an offensive thing to do, suggests that "color," which here means nonwhiteness, is bad in and of itself.

White women who grew up before the 1960s came to adulthood well before the emergence and public visibility of the movements that emphasized cultural pride and renewal among people of color. During their formative years, there were only two ways of looking at race difference: either it connoted hierarchy or it did not (or should not) mean anything at all. Theirs was, then, a historically situated rejection of the salience of race difference. To expect women of Ginny's, Irene's, and Joan's ages to talk, particularly about their childhood years, in terms other than these is to risk the error of ahistoricity— to ask them to "preinvent" discourses on racial and cultural identity that did not emerge until much later.

However, it was striking that not only these older women continued to think about their lives in the 1980s in "color-blind" terms: much *younger* women did so also, underscoring the continued significance of color evasiveness as the dominant language of race in the United States. For many of the women, to be caught in the act of seeing race was to be caught being "prejudiced" "racism" was not for the most part a term that this group of women used). This automatic link came through in the words of Marty Douglass, who was under thirty at the time of the interview:

> RF: Do you remember the first time you noticed that somebody else was a different color from you?
>
> MARTY: I never paid that much attention. . . . I guess [my father] was prejudiced, in a sense, but we [kids] never became prejudiced. I'm still not prejudiced.

Given that within this discourse it was "bad" to see difference and "good" not to, it is perhaps not surprising that more generalized images of innocence and guilt, purity and impurity also came into play with respect to racism or "prejudice." Joan's image of the youthful innocence of kittens was paralleled in this regard by other women's linkage of innocence and guilt to youth and age. Both Marty Douglass and Evelyn Steinman told anecdotes that emphasized that their children were too young to be tainted by racial prejudice. Evelyn described an encounter between her son (then six) and an aunt that clearly captured this mental map:

One day I came home [and] Aunty Jean had been taking care of him. And he, very, very serious, took me into the study, and he said, "Mother, Aunty Jean said something very bad today." And I said, "She did? Because she's such a sweet little person. What did she say?" He said, "She said 'nigger.'" . . . And he was so upset about this. And I said, "Well, honey, we have to forgive Aunty Jean, she doesn't really mean it the way it sounds," and I said, "We just must try to forgive her that. Because she's a very kind person, and she's very kind, to you and to me." All right, he would accept that. But that was very distressing to him.

The terms of Evelyn's analysis are as interesting as her conclusions. There are, in effect, two "Innocents" involved. The "most innocent" party is Evelyn's son, whose youthful virtue is established on two counts: first by his horror at Aunty Jean's language and second by his willingness to forgive her transgression. The second is Aunty Jean (not coincidentally also described as "a little person"). Her use of racist language is "forgiven" or overridden by her essential goodness in other spheres of life. A number of possibilities are thus generated within the terms of the story, all of which have both Christian and legalistic overtones. Children are conceived as too young to be corrupt. Adults may be found "not guilty" by reason of lack of intent, by recourse to a balance sheet of good and bad acts, and by their honorary "littleness" (essential innocence). Finally, those who are "real racists" or, in the language of this discourse, "really prejudiced," who would by implication have to be adult and fully cognizant of their racism prejudice (essentially bad), are an absent presence in Evelyn's story.

Whereas earlier, seeing race meant being racist and being racist meant being "bad," causation here is reversed: a person who is good cannot by definition be racist, hence "little" Aunty Jean cannot really emerge as complicit with racism within the logic of Evelyn's analysis. This is an important moment in the color- and power-evasive repertoire, for this is the logic that undergirds legislative and judicial approaches to both workplace race discrimination and hate crime, placing the burden of proof on the intent of the perpetrator rather than on the effects of an event or situation on its victim(s). The issues of sin, guilt, and innocence resurfaced in some of the other women's attempts to think through the question of their own complicity with white power structures. . . .

This discursive repertoire intersects in several ways with liberal humanism as a philosophical discourse. First, it proposes an essential human sameness to which "race" is added as a secondary characteristic. This assertion of a distinction between selfhood and racialness makes it possible for white women to claim that they do not see the color, or race, of those with whom they interact, but rather see "under the skin" to the "real" person beneath. . . .

One concomitant of viewing people in terms of universal sameness overlaid with individual difference is the disinclination to think in terms of social or political aggregates. In these narratives, emphasis on the individual over the group either as cause or as target of racism had a leveling effect that made room for charges of discrimination against white people in institutional settings.

Thus, Irene . . . described her frustration at looking for a teaching job in a school district that was at that time primarily recruiting teachers of color:

> I resent it particularly because I feel that people should be considered for who they are as a human being and not as this, that, or the other—who you are, regardless of outside trappings—[there's an] inner person, shouting to get out. . . .

Irene's commitment to respecting the individual in this context is more likely to work against greater racial equality than for it, leading her to overlook the *social* context for affirmative action programs that seek to remedy years of structured inequality and thereby promote expression of the talents and merit of individuals of color. Here we hit the limits of philosophical humanism, for it does not enable Irene to think in social or collective terms about the life chances of individuals.

Now You See It, Now You Don't: Difference and Power Evasion

These women's efforts to "not see" race difference despite its continued salience in society and in their own lives generated a fault line or contradiction in their consciousness. In this context, a number of strategies for talking about race and culture emerged, effectively dividing the discursive terrain into areas of "safe" and "dangerous" differences, "pleasant" and "nasty" differences, and generating modes of talking about difference that evaded questions of power. In this way, the women I interviewed grappled with and tried to pacify the contradiction between a society structured in dominance and the desire to see society only in terms of universal sameness and individual difference. The peace was an uneasy one, however, always on the brink of being disturbed.

A number of euphemisms used by these women appeared to serve the function of avoiding naming power. Evelyn . . . for example, consistently described Black people as "colorful," simultaneously acknowledging and dodging their Blackness. Some women used the familiar cliche "I don't care if he's Black, brown, yellow, or green," a phrase that camouflages socially significant differences of color in a welter of meaningless ones.

There were also at times hints at the possibility that, for some women, descriptions of people of color that evaded naming race (and therefore power) differences formed what one might describe as a "polite" or "public" language of race that contrasted with other, private languages. For instance, in talking to me, Ginny . . . most often referred to her son-in-law, whose heritage was Mexican Filipino, as "Spanish," choosing an appellation that avoided drawing attention to his color and to the inequality between colonizer and colonized. At one point, however, she cheerfully described playful interactions between her "Spanish" son-in-law and his small son (Ginny's grandson) in which, as Ginny described it, they referred to one another affectionately as "Mexican."

. . . Irene was probably in her early sixties. . . . Her earliest memories were of the Depression years, when her family was poor.

But by the time of World War II, her father had made enough money for the family to move to a wealthier neighborhood, and for Irene to attend an exclusive girls' school. Her statement ran as follows:

> IRENE: I was born and raised in the Detroit area, so there are very few cultures or races that I haven't been exposed to in my lifetime. During the years that I was growing up, the melting pot theory was . . . being used, so there was a lot of mixing up, and people didn't feel separate as much as they do today, with the different cultures and races feeling that they need to be completely separate to preserve their heritage.
>
> I went to the University of Michigan, which had the very first exchange program, so I also was exposed to people, maybe not personally, but of a foreign element. So I didn't think much about it. Then, since I've been in California I've done a lot of teaching . . . so I was exposed to different races and cultures there also. So that just gives you a little smattering of why I feel I have been exposed to other races and cultures. And sometimes the two overlap.
>
> RF: Yeah. Well good. That gives me an idea—
>
> IRENE: —of what to ask me—
>
> RF: —of things to come back to.
>
> IRENE: I have other notes and things. I did go through the Detroit race riot as well as the Watts race riot.
>
> RF: Oh. OK, I'd definitely like to ask you about that.
>
> IRENE: And I have had, you know, help, live-in, you know, had some Black ladies living in my home when I was a girl, so I—and other friends of mine—had Black servants. I went to the University of Mexico [on a student exchange program] where I lived with a Protestant minister who had Mexican maids in his home, so I've been exposed to that. But I don't consider that a different race, it's a different culture. . . .

On the surface, the burden of Irene's message is proliferation and inclusiveness: much contact with many people, almost to the point of being blase—"I didn't think too much about it." However, there is actually a highly variegated set of differentiations here.

The melting pot, race riots, and separatism are historical markers and also indicators of degrees of rapprochement and opposition between "different" people. Irene preferred the melting pot, with its connotations of intercultural communication, to the later moments. But later discussion clarified that she did not apply the melting pot and separatist images to the same groups. The melting pot involved her (German) family's connections with Scottish, Welsh, Jewish, and Anglo (in short, white) Americans, while separatism was a choice she associated with people of color.

There is a range of class and power relationships in the contacts she described: while the "melting pot," exchange programs, and friendships suggested peer status, the presence of live-in domestic workers and teacher-student relationships did not. The most obviously power-imbalanced relationship—that with domestic workers—was the cause, perhaps coincidentally, of the most hesitation and rephrasing. The choice of "ladies" is also a rephrasing of history, since white people probably referred to Black women as "girls" in the period of which Irene is speaking. . . .

It was striking that while Irene cheerfully discussed with me her interactions with "foreigners" and cultural Others, as well as her feelings about them, she approached talk about her relationships with African Americans much more cautiously. What becomes clearer about color evasiveness, then, is that more than evading questions of difference wholesale, this discursive repertoire selectively engages difference, evading questions of power. While certain kinds of difference or differentiation can be seen and discussed with abandon, others are evaded if at all possible. A comparison of the ways Irene constructs difference, beginning with her connection to Jewish culture, clarifies all of these points and makes them concrete.

Before high school, in the Depression years, Irene grew up in her grandmother's house, a member of the only non-Jewish family in a Jewish neighborhood. Irene spoke with pleasure of her childhood involvement with Jewish culture:

> The Jewish holiday [Hanukkah], they give you a present every day, and because my friends were getting a present every day, my mother and grandmother thought that they didn't want me to feel left out. So they followed the Jewish tradition, and I got a different present every day. And that was the best year I ever had!

Irene was familiar with Jewish food partly thanks to Miriam, a Jewish woman who was a boarder in the house. And Irene's grandmother, like their Jewish neighbors, bought bagels and matzos and made noodles:

> RF: So there were some similarities—
>
> IRENE: Well, it's European. But as far as that goes it could be that some of our family was Jewish before they became gentile. . . . After all, it's a religion, it's really not a race. . . . However, I feel very comfortable with the Jewish culture because of being exposed, I suppose.

What comes across first here is Irene's pleasurable connection with Jewish culture and her family's active role in enabling it. Similarities between Irene's own family and European (or Ashkenazi) Jews was perceived as possibly extending to kinship. Jewishness, for Irene, was thus a mutable category of belonging: Irene could travel into that culture and Jewish people could travel out. "Not a race" in this context seemed, then, to indicate impermanence and the absence of a biological basis. But Irene maintained a sense of difference from Jewish people, as her return to the "exposure" metaphor clarified. Further, Irene added, her parents definitely expected her to marry within her own religious and ethnic group. . . .

Irene's descriptions of Black people were very different, as were her relationships with them. . . . In addition to a sense of social distance, Irene described her interaction with African Americans in more explicitly oppositional terms. She drew on the white "popular memory" of Detroit to tell an apocryphal story:

> When I was in high school we'd go downtown shopping. And I remember one day

specifically I was going into the big department store, and they had the revolving door. And as I got in, this great big fat Black lady got in with me and I could hardly breathe, and I got through, and I thought, "Wow, that was crowded," and I found out afterwards that they had something called "push day," where, that day of the week, anybody who was white who was downtown, they would do something to harass them. And until then, that had never been a problem. And it wasn't too long after that that the Belle Isle race riot occurred.

Irene's story seemed somehow to naturalize the Detroit race riot, to explain it in terms of Black "unruliness" rather than Black grievances. Irene spoke of inequality in a contradictory manner. She noted, for example, that in Detroit during her childhood years, African Americans did not have access to middle-class and upper-middle-class levels of income. Here, she was apparently recognizing injustice. But immediately afterward, she added that Black people "deservedly" had a reputation for destroying property, so that realtors were correct in keeping Blacks out of white neighborhoods.

It is perhaps not surprising in this context that Irene's description of the Detroit race riots of 1944 posed but immediately rejected the possibility that Black people had legitimate grievances. This ambivalence produced a description that was thoroughly self-contradictory:

I really don't know what precipitated it. Because, as far as I know, I think that Black people had jobs, or work. I don't remember many Black people having the skilled labor jobs, however. They did mostly things like the gardening, domestic help, doormen, a lot of Black people working in the hotels downtown, and [as] doormen for the department stores. As far as in factory work, or skilled labor, I don't think there were many Black people involved in that, but then there were no Jewish people involved in it either. Jewish people would not do manual labor. Mostly the Jewish people were the doctors and the lawyers and the businesspeople.

Something other than a simple denial, a straightforward failure to take note of race

and cultural difference, is clearly going on here. For in fact Irene was quite willing and able—albeit apparently inaccurately, since she had grown up in a poor, Jewish neighborhood whose residents were presumably neither doctors nor lawyers, nor even business owners—to associate different sectors of the job market with different groups of people. Contradictions and nonsensical statements proliferated at the point of examining the variance in power and resources that those differences might have implied. . . .

Because Irene could name differences only when they did not entail acknowledging differences of power, power evasion frequently led to a kind of flight from feelings. Irene's description of a Black neighborhood (in response to my question) was interesting in the way it seemed to repress potentially "bad" feelings about race difference:

IRENE: There was one other Black area of Detroit . . . you had to drive through it to get to downtown, but nobody felt any fear.

RF: Do you remember what you did feel?

IRENE: Nothing! That was just the Black area.

Irene repeated this pattern at one point in talking about her relationship to the Jewish boarder in her grandmother's house:

We knew she was Jewish and she knew we were Protestant, and that was as far as it went. There was no feeling of "I'm Jewish; you're gentile."

As we have seen, Irene's feelings went much further and deeper than a mere "knowing." Given what we already know about Irene's warm relationship with Miriam and others in the Jewish community, it is clearer in this instance that flight from feeling accompanies a desire to "not see" difference at moments when the act of noticing difference might involve noticing potential for mutual hostility or opposition. . . .

If the sharp edge of color evasion resides in its repression or denial of the differences that race makes in people's lives, power evasion is a permutation of that repression: rather than complete nonacknowledgment of any kind of difference, power evasion involves a selective attention to difference, allowing into conscious scrutiny—even conscious embrace—those differences that make the speaker feel good but continuing to evade by means of partial description, euphemism, and self-contradiction those that make the speaker feel bad. The latter, as I have shown, involved the naming of inequality, power imbalance, hatred, or fear. As with color evasion, one senses in some of these narratives a desire to overcome interracial hostility behind the impulse toward power-blindness. The outcome of this attempt, however, was frequently a lack of attention to the areas of power imbalance that in fact generate hostility, social distance, and "bad feelings" in general. . . .

Race Cognizance: Rethinking Race, Rethinking Power

While the discursive repertoire of color evasion was organized around the desire to assert essential *sameness*, the discursive repertoire that I will here describe as race cognizant insisted on the importance of recognizing *difference*—but with difference understood in historical, political, social, or cultural terms rather than essentialist ones. As I will show, the race-cognizant women differed from one another in important ways. However, they shared two linked convictions: first, that race makes a difference in people's lives and second, that racism is a significant factor in shaping contemporary U.S. society.

While opposite in principle the color-power-evasive and race-cognizant repertoires were by no means separable in practice. For one thing, these two repertoires in fact responded to one another's terms, so that, as we will see, some women described in explicit terms their own passage out of color-"blindness" and into race cognizance. Secondly, race-cognizant women, some more than others, continued to articulate their analyses of racism in dualistic and moralistic terms that deployed the structure of liberal humanism and elements of power evasiveness.

44

Ethnic and Racial Identities of Second-Generation Black Immigrants in New York City

Mary C. Waters

The growth of nonwhite voluntary immigrants to the United States since 1965 challenges the dichotomy which once explained different patterns of American inclusion and assimilation—the ethnic pattern of assimilation of immigrants from Europe and their children and the racial pattern of exclusion of America's nonwhite peoples. The new wave of immigrants includes people who are still defined "racially" in the United States, but who migrate to the United States voluntarily.

. . . The children of black immigrants in the United States face a choice about whether they will identify as black Americans or whether they will maintain an ethnic identity reflecting their parents' national origins. First-generation black immigrants to the United States have tended to distance themselves from American blacks, stressing their national origins and ethnic identities as Jamaican or Haitian or Trinidadian, but they also face overwhelming pressures in the United States to identify only as "blacks" (Strafford 1987; Foner 1987; Sutton and Makiesky 1975; Woldemikael 1989; Kasinitz 1992). . . . The children of black immigrants, because they lack their parents' distinctive accents, can choose to be even more invisible as ethnics than their parents. Second-generation West Indians in the United States will

most often be seen by others as merely "American"—and must actively work to assert their ethnic identities.

The types of racial and ethnic identities adopted by a sample of second-generation West Indians and Haitian Americans in New York City are explored here, along with subjective understandings these youngsters have of being American, of being black American, and of their ethnic identities. . . .

Longstanding tensions between newly arrived West Indians and American blacks have left a legacy of mutual stereotyping (see Kasinitz, 1992). The immigrants see themselves as hard-working, ambitious, militant about their racial identities but not oversensitive or obsessed with race, and committed to education and family. They see black Americans as lazy, disorganized, obsessed with racial slights and barriers, with a disorganized and *laissez faire* attitude toward family life and child raising. American blacks describe the immigrants as arrogant, selfish, exploited in the workplace, oblivious to racial tensions and politics in the United States, and unfriendly and unwilling to have relations with black Americans. The first generation believes that their status as foreign-born blacks is higher than American blacks, and they tend to accentuate their identities as immigrants. Their accent is usually a clear and unambiguous signal to other Americans that they are foreign born.

The dilemma facing the second generation is that they grow up exposed to the negative opinions voiced by their parents about American blacks and exposed to the belief that whites respond more favorably to foreign-born blacks. But they also realize that because they lack their parents' accents and other identifying characteristics, other people, including their peers, are likely to identify them as American blacks. . . .

The young people we talked to . . . include teens who are facing very limited socioeconomic mobility or downward social mobility (the inner city public school students and the street group), students in the church sample who are on an upward social trajectory and have a high chance of going to college, and teens whose families are doing well and who themselves would seem to have bright futures. Overall, 16 percent of the 83 teens were from very poor families on public assistance, 49 percent were from families with at least one parent working at a low wage job, and 35 percent were from middle-class families with at least one parent in a job requiring a college degree. The age of respondents ranged from 14–21. The average age was 17. The vast majority were aged 16–18. We included teenagers who had spent at least three years in the United States and who had immigrated before age 16. They included 34 (41%) who comprise the classic second generation—born in the United States of immigrant parents. Another 14 (17%) immigrated to the United States before age 7. The rest of the sample included 35 young people who had immigrated after age 7 and had spent at least three years in the United States. The actual age at immigration for these more recent immigrants varied from 7 [to] 15. . . .

[T]he youth described here, who seem to be on different socioeconomic trajectories, understand their racial and ethnic identities differently. Some of the adolescents we interviewed agree with their parents that the United States holds many opportunities for them. Others disagree with their parents because they believe that racial discrimination and hostility from whites will limit their abilities to meet their goals. By contrasting the ideas these youngsters have about their own identities and the role of race in American society, I suggest that social capital among the first generation and the type of segmented assimilation among the second generation varies within ethnic groups as well as between them. Some Jamaican Americans, for example, are experiencing downward social mobility while others are maintaining strong ethnic ties and achieving socioeconomic success.

The key factor for the youth I studied is race. The daily discrimination that the youngsters experience, the type of racial socialization they receive in the home, the understandings of race they develop in their peer groups and at school affect strongly how they react to American society. The ways in which these youngsters experience and react to racial discrimination influences the type of racial/ethnic identity they develop.

Patterns in the Second Generation

The interviews suggest that while there is a great deal of individual variation in the identities, perceptions and opinions of these teens, their racial and ethnic identities can be classified into three general types: identifying as Americans, identifying as ethnic Americans with some distancing from black Americans, or maintaining an immigrant identity that does not reckon with American racial and ethnic categories.

A black American-identified identity characterized the responses of approximately 42 percent of the 83 second-generation respondents interviewed. These youngsters identified with other black Americans. They did not see their "ethnic" identities as important to their self-image. When their parents or friends criticized American blacks or described what they perceived as fundamental differences between Caribbean-origin people and American blacks, these youngsters disagreed. They tended to downplay an identity as Jamaican or Trinidadian and described themselves as American.

Another 30 percent of the respondents adopted a very strong ethnic identity which involved a considerable amount of distancing from American blacks. It was important for these respondents to stress their ethnic identities and for other people to recognize that they were not American blacks. These respondents tended to agree with parental judgments that there were strong differences between Americans and West Indians. This often involved a stance that West Indians were superior to American blacks in their behaviors and attitudes.

A final 28 percent of respondents had more of an immigrant attitude toward their identities than either the American-identified youth or the ethnic-identified youth. Most, but not all, of these respondents were more recent immigrants themselves. A crucial factor for these youngsters is that their accents and styles of clothing and behavior clearly signaled to others that they were foreign born. In a sense, their identity as an immigrant people precluded having to make a "choice" about what kind of American they were. These respondents had a strong identity as Jamaican or Trinidadian, but did not evidence much distancing from American blacks. Rather their identities were strongly linked to their experiences on the islands, and they did not worry much about how they were seen by other Americans, white or black.

A number of factors influence the type of identity the youngsters develop. These include the social class background of the parents, the social networks the parents were involved in, the type of school the child attended, and the family structure. All of these factors affect the ability of parents and other family members to shield children from neighborhood peer groups that espouse antischool values.

There tended to be a strong relationship between the type of identity and outlook on American race and ethnic relations that the youngsters developed and their social class background and/or their social class trajectory. The ethnic-identified youngsters were most likely to come from a middle-class background. Of the total of 83 second-generation teens and young adults interviewed, 57 percent of the middle-class teens identified ethnically, whereas only 17 percent of the working class and poor teens identified ethnically. The poorest students were most likely to be immigrant or American-identified. Only one out of the twelve teens whose parents were on public assistance identified ethnically. The American-identified, perhaps not surprisingly, were also more likely to be born in the United States—67 percent of the American-identified were born in the United States, as opposed to only 13 percent of the immigrant-identified or 42 percent of the ethnically identified. . . .

Each of the different identity types adopted by these teens [is] described below.

The Ethnic Response

All of the teenage respondents reported comments by their parents about American blacks which were very similar to those recorded in our interviews with the first generation. The differences were in how the teens interpreted what their parents were saying. In general, the ethnic-identified teens agreed with their parents and reported seeing a strong difference between themselves and black Americans, stressing that being black is not synonymous with being black American. They accept their parents' and the wider society's negative portrayals of poor blacks and wanted to avoid any chance that they will be identified with them. They described the culture and values of lower-class black Americans as including a lack of discipline, lack of a work ethic, laziness, bad child-rearing practices and lack of respect for education. They contrast these with their parents' ethnic groups' values which include valuing education, strict discipline for children, a strong work ethic and social mobility. They try to impress to others that they are Jamaican or Haitian and most definitely not American black. This allows them less dissonance with their parents' negative views of American blacks. They do not reject their parents' culture and identities, but rather reject the American social system that would identify them as American black and reject strongly the African-American peer group culture to which they would be assigned by whites and others if they did not consciously transmit their ethnic identities.

. . . [T]he second-generation ethnic teens believed that being black American involves more than merely having black skin. One young woman criticized American blacks in this way:

> Some of them [black Americans] think that their heritage includes not being able to speak correctly or walk correctly, or act loud and obnoxious to make a point. I don't think they have to do that. Just when I see black Americans, it depends on how I see you on the street. Walking down the street with that walk that moves a little bit too much. I would say, I'd think you dropped out of high school.

These teens also differentiated themselves from black Americans in terms of their sensitivity to racism, real or imagined. Some of the ethnic-identified second generation echo the feelings we heard from the first generation that American blacks are too quick to use race as an explanation or excuse for not doing well. . . .

The second-generation teens who are doing well try to understand how it is that they are so successful when black Americans are not—and often they chalk it up to family values. They say that their immigrant families have close-knit family values that stress education. Aware of, and sometimes sharing, the negative images of black Americans that the whites they encounter believe, the second generation also perceives that whites treat them better when they realize they are not "just" black Americans. When asked if they benefitted ever from their ethnicity, they responded "yes": "It seems white Americans don't tend to put you in the same category as black Americans." . . .

The dilemma for the second generation is that while they have a strong sense of their own identities as very different from black Americans, this was not clear to other people. Often both whites and blacks saw them as just black Americans and did not notice that they were ethnically different. When people did comment on their ethnic difference it was often because of the way they talked and the way they walked. . . . Whites tend to let those of the second generation know that they think of them as exceptions to the rule, with the rule being that most blacks are not good people. However, these young people also know that unless they tell people of their ethnicity, most whites have no idea they are not black Americans.

Many of these teens coped with this dilemma by devising ways to telegraph their identities as second-generation West Indians or Haitians. One girl carried a Guyanese map as part of her key chain so that when people looked at her keys they would ask her about it and she could tell them that her parents were from Guyana. One young woman described having her mother teach her an accent so that she could use it when she applied for a job or a place to live. Others just try to work it into the conversation when they meet someone. . . .

The teens who were around many black Americans felt pressure from their peers to be part of the group and to identify as black American. These teens would consciously talk about passing for American at some points and passing for Haitian or Jamaican at others by changing the way they talked or acted:

> When I'm at school and I sit with my black friends and, sometimes I'm ashamed to say this, but my accent changes. I learn all the words. I switch. Well, when I'm with my friends, my black friends, I say I'm black, black American. When I'm with my Haitian-American friends, I say I'm Haitian. Well, my being black, I guess that puts me when I'm with black Americans, it makes people think that I'm lower class. . . . Then, if I'm talking like this [regular voice] with my friends at school, they call me white.

The American-Identified Second Generation

The American-identified second-generation teenagers differ . . . in how little they stressed their immigrant or ethnic identities to the interviewers. They follow a path which is more similar to the model posed in the straight line theory. They stress that they are American because they were born here, and they are disdainful of their parents' lack of understanding of the American social system. Instead of rejecting the black American culture, it becomes their peer culture and they embrace many aspects of it. This brings them in conflict with their parents' generation, most especially with their parents' understandings of American blacks. The assimilation to America that they undergo is most definitely to black America; they speak black English with their peers, they listen to rap music, and they accept the peer culture of their black American friends. They are aware of the fact that they are considered black American by others and that they can be accused of "acting white" if they don't speak black English and behave in particular ways. Most included their ethnic identities as background, but none of them adopted the stance that they were not, in a major sense, black American. . . .

Some of the young people told us that they saw little if any differences between the ethnic blacks and the American blacks. Many stressed the Caribbeanization of black New

York and described how all the Americans were interested in being Caribbean now:

> It use to be Jamaicans and American blacks did not get along because everyone was afraid of Jamaicans. But now I guess we are closer now. You tell an American that you are Jamaican and it is no big deal. Americans are acting more like Jamaicans. Jamaicans are acting like Americans.
>
> Q. What do you mean by acting like each other?
>
> A. Sure there are a lot of Americans out there speaking Patois. And then all the Jamaicans are coming over here and they are like "Yo, what's up" and they are like that. Pretty soon you can't really tell who is Jamaican and who is American.

However, the parents of the American-identified teens have expressed to their children the same negative impressions of American blacks that the ethnic-identified teens reported. These teenagers report many negative appraisals of American blacks by their parents:

> They always say Haiti is better in this way or in that way. They say the kids here have no respect. The kids here are brought up without any supervision. My father is always talking about they [American blacks] be hanging out on the corner. And he says you won't find Haitians doing that. My mom always says you will marry a Haitian. Why are you talking to those American boys?. . . .

In marked contrast to the ethnic-identified teens, though, the American-identified teens either disagreed with their parents' statements about American blacks, reluctantly agreed with some of it but provided qualifications, or perhaps most disturbingly accepted the appraisals as true of American blacks in general and themselves as American blacks. . . .

The fact that the teens are identifying as American and that their parents have such negative opinions of Americans causes some conflict. The teens either adopt a negative opinion of themselves or disagree with their parents' assessments of American blacks. But it is not just their parents who criticize black

Americans. These youngsters are very aware of the generalized negative view of blacks in the wider culture. In answer to the question "do whites have an image of blacks," all of them responded that whites had a negative view of blacks seeing them as criminal, lazy, violent and uncaring about family. . . . This knowledge that the society in which they live devalues them because of their skin color and their identity affected these teens deeply.

The Immigrant-Identified Teens

The more recently arrived young people who are still immigrant-identified differed from both the ethnic and the American-identified youth. They did not feel as much pressure to "choose" between identifying with or distancing from black Americans as did either the American or the ethnic teens. Strong in their identities with their own or their parents' national origins, they were neutral toward American distinctions between ethnics and black Americans. They tended to stress their nationality or their birthplace as defining their identity. . . .

While an ethnic-identified Jamaican American is aware that she might be seen by others as American and thus actively chooses to present herself as Jamaican, an immigrant-identified Jamaican could not conceive of herself as having a choice, nor could she conceive of being perceived by others as American. While an ethnic-identified teen might describe herself as Jamaican American, for the immigrant teen Jamaican would be all the label needed. Most teens in this category were recent immigrants themselves. The few U.S.-born teens classified as immigrant-identified had strong family roots on the islands, were frequent visitors to the islands, and had plans to return to live there as adults. A crucial factor that allows these youngsters to maintain this identity is that their accents and styles of clothing and behavior clearly signaled to others that they were foreign born.

> Q. How important is it to you that your friends think of you in terms of your ethnicity?
>
> A. Oh, very important. You know, I try hard not to lose my roots, you know, when I come to the United States. A lot of

people who come here try to lose their accent, you know. Even in the workplace, you know, because they fear what other people might think of them. Even in the workplace. Me, I never try to change, you know, the way I am. I always try to, you know, stay with them, the way of my culture.

Q. So it's something you want people to recognize?

A. Yeah, definitely, definitely, absolutely.

Q. Why?

A. Why? I'm proud of who I am, you know. I'm proud of where I'm from and I'm not going to change because somebody might not like the way I walk, talk or dress, you know. . . .

Some who adopt this strong identity with the immigrant country were born in the United States, but the combination of strong family roots on the island, frequent visits, and plans to go live there when they are older allows them to think of themselves as not really American at all. . . .

While the ethnics tended to describe people treating them better when they described their ethnic origins, and the Americans tended to stress the antiblack experiences they have had and the lack of difference between the foreign born and the American, the immigrant teens spoke about anti-immigrant feelings and discrimination and responded with pride in their national origins.

Contrasting Identities

In some sense one can see each of these identities as being an embrace of a particular identity, as well as an opposition to another identity. The American-identified youth are in fact assimilating to the American black subculture in the neighborhood. It is the American black cultural forms they are adapting to, and they do so in distinction to their parents' ethnic identities and the wider mainstream white identities. These students adopt some of the "oppositional" poses that American black teenagers have been observed to show toward academic achievement: the idea of America, the idea of oppor-

tunity, and the wider society (Ogbu, 1990; Fordham, 1988; Portes and Zhou, 1993).

They are also opposed to their parents' outlooks and ideas, stressing that what worked as an outlook and a life strategy and a child-raising technique in the islands does not work in the United States. These teens tend to adopt a peer culture of racial solidarity and opposition to school authorities. What is clear from the interviews is that this stance of opposition is in part a socialized response to a peer culture, but the vast majority of it comes about as a reaction to their life experiences. Most specifically, the teens respond to their experiences with racial discrimination and their perceptions of blocked social mobility. The lives of these youngsters basically lead them to reject the immigrant dream of their parents toward individual social mobility and to accept their peers' analysis of the United States as a place with blocked social mobility where they will not be able to move very far.

The American-identified teens do not seem to be aware of . . . perceptions . . . that the foreign born are higher social status than the American born. In the peer culture of the neighborhood and the school, these teenagers describe a situation in which being American is higher social status than being ethnic. For instance, several girls described "passing" as black American in order not to be ridiculed or picked on in school. . . .

When asked about the images others held of being from the islands, most of the teens described neutral attributes, like styles of dress. However, many who identified as Americans also described negative associations with the immigrants' identities. The Jamaicans said most people thought of drug dealers when they thought about Jamaicans. A few of the teens also intimated that the people from the islands were backwards in not knowing how to live in a big city. . . .

Not one of the American-identified teens voiced the opinion of the overwhelming majority of the ethnic teens that whites were more likely to like the foreign born. In part, this reflected the differences the groups had in their contact with whites. Most of the inner city ethnic-identified teens had almost no contact with whites, except for teachers.

They also are in schools where the vast majority of the students are foreign born or second generation. The larger number of middle-class teens who were ethnic-identified were more likely to have white classmates in citywide magnet high schools, in parochial schools or in suburban schools or workplaces.

The inner city American-identified teens also voiced more positive appraisals of black Americans than did the immigrant or the ethnic-identified teens. Their descriptions also reflect the reality of living in neighborhoods where there is crime and violence. A majority of the American-identified teens said that a good trait of black Americans is that they work hard and they struggle. These are the very same children whose parents describe black Americans primarily as lazy and unwilling to take advantage of the opportunities available to them. The children seem to be perceiving a reality that the parents cannot or will not.

Many of these teens live in neighborhoods that are all black and attend schools that are all black, too. So, aside from teachers, these young people have almost no contact with white Americans. This does not stop them from absorbing the fact that whites have negative stereotypic views of blacks. But unlike the middle-class blacks who come in contact with whites who tell them that they are "good blacks," these youths live in the urban areas that are associated with crime, they dress like the typical black urban youth, and they talk with Brooklyn accents and black American slang. When they do encounter whites in public places, the whites do not ask about their parents' backgrounds:

Q. Have you ever experienced any discrimination or hostility in New York?

A. From being Trinidadian, no. But because of being black, you know, everybody stereotypes. And they say "blacks, they tend to steal, and stuff like that." So, like, if I am walking down the street and a white lady go by and they smile and I smile. They put their bag on the other side.

The parents of these teens grew up in situations where blacks were the majority. The parents do not want their children to be "racial" in the United States. They define "being racial" as being overly concerned with race and with using race as an excuse or explanation for lack of success at school or on the job. The first generation tends to believe that, while racism exists in the United States, it can be overcome or circumvented through hard work, perseverance and the right values and attitudes. The second generation experiences racism and discrimination constantly and develops perceptions of the overwhelming influence of race on their lives and life chances that differs from their parents' views. These teens experience being hassled by police and store owners, not being given jobs, even being attacked on the streets if they venture into white neighborhoods. The boys adopt black American culture in their schools, wearing flattops, baggy pants, and certain types of jewelry. This contributes to the image that they project of the "cool pose" which in turn causes whites to be afraid of them. This makes them angry and resentful. The media also tells these youngsters that blacks are disvalued by American society. While parents tell their children to strive for upward mobility and to work harder in the face of discrimination, the American-identified teens think their chances of success by doing that are very slim.

This causes a wide gulf between the parents and their children. These parents are absolutely terrified of their children becoming Americans. For the children to be American is to have freedom from the strict parental controls of the immigrant parents. This is an old story in the immigrant saga that one can see in novels and movies about conflicts between Jewish and Italian immigrants and their children. But the added dimension in this situation is that these parents are afraid of the downward social mobility that becoming an American black represents to them. And these parents have that idea reinforced constantly by whites who tell them that they are better than American blacks.

. . . The result of these different world views is that the parents' view of an opportunity structure that is open to hard work is systematically undermined by their children's peer culture and more importantly, by the actual experiences of these teens.

On the other hand, the ethnic-identified teens, whose parents are more likely to be middle class and doing well or who attend parochial or magnet schools and not the substandard neighborhood high schools, see clearer opportunities and rewards ahead, despite the existence of racism and discrimination. Their parents' message that hard work and perseverance can circumvent racial barriers does not fall on unreceptive ears. The ethnic-identified youngsters embrace an ethnic identity in direct line from their parents' immigrants identity. Such an identity is basically in part in opposition to their peers' identities and in solidarity with their parents' identities. These youngsters stress that they are Jamaican Americans and that, while they may be proud of their racial identity as black, they see strong differences between themselves and black Americans. They specifically see their ethnic identities as keys to upward social mobility, stressing, for instance, that their parents' immigrant values of hard work and strict discipline help them to succeed in the United States when black-Americans fail. This ethnic identity is very much an American-based identity—it is in the context of American social life that these youngsters base their assumptions of what it means to be Jamaican or Trinidadian.

In fact, often the pan-ethnic identity as Caribbean or West Indian is the most salient label for these youngsters, as they see little differences among the groups and it is more important to differentiate themselves as second-generation nonblack Americans. The distancing that these teens show from black Americans often leads them to accept many negative stereotypes of black Americans. These youngsters tend to have ethnic friends from a West Indian background, white American friends, and very few, if any, black American friends.

The immigrant-identified teens are different from either of the other two, in part because of how they think about who they are not, as well as how they think about who they are. These teens have a strong identity as Jamaican or Trinidadian, but this identity tends to be related to their interactions with other Jamaicans or Trinidadians rather than their interactions with black or white Americans. These youngsters identify with their homelands or their parents' homelands, but not in opposition to black Americans or in opposition to white Americans. . . .

These identities are fluid and change over time and in different social contexts. There are cases we found of people who describe being very black American-identified when they were younger and who became more immigrant-identified when they came to high school and found a large immigrant community. Most new arrivals to the United States start out as immigrant-identified, and the longer they are in the United States the more they begin to think of themselves in terms of American categories. The kind of social milieu the child faces, especially the school environment, has a strong influence on the outcome. A school with many black Americans leads to pressure to identity racially; likewise a neighborhood and school with many immigrants makes it possible to avoid thinking much about American categories. In the face of much pressure in the neighborhood school environment not to follow the rules and not to succeed academically, youngsters who are doing well in school and do value education increasingly come to stress their ethnic backgrounds as an explanation for their ambition and success.

The American racial classification system which tends to push toward an either/or designation of people as black or white tends to make the immigrant option harder to hold onto. When others constantly identify the individual as a black and refuse to make distinctions based on black ethnicity, there tends to be pressure for the individual to adapt their identity to that outside identification—either to say "Yes, I am black," and to accept categorization with black Americans or to resent the characterization and strongly make an ethnic identification as Trinidadian American. The American myopia about ethnic differences within the black community makes the middle ground immigrant identity unstable. Because every young person is aware of the negative images held by whites and the wider society of black Americans, the acceptance of an American black identity also means the acceptance of the oppositional character of that identity. Oppositional identities, as Ogbu (1990) clearly argues, are self- and group-affirming identities for stigmatized groups—defining as good and worthy, traits and characteristics which are the opposite of those valued by the majority group. This tends to operate to downwardly level the aspirations of the teens.

Implications of the Patterns

Some of the distancing shown by the ethnic-identified teens in the sample vis-a-vis underclass black identity and behaviors is the same for middle-class black Americans. . . . Being an ethnic black in interactions with whites seems to be a shorthand way of conveying distance from the ghetto blacks. Thus, the second generation reserves their ethnic status for use as an identity device to stress their distance from poor blacks and to stress their cultural values which are consistent with American middle-class values. This same use of an ethnic identity is present among first-generation immigrants of all social classes, even those in racially segregated poor neighborhoods in New York.

The second generation in the segregated neighborhoods, with little chance for social mobility, seems to be unaware that status as a black ethnic conveys higher social status among whites, in part because as of yet they have not had much contact with whites. The mass media conveys to them the negative image of American blacks held by whites, but does not convey to them the image among intellectuals, middle-class whites and conservative scholars, such as Thomas Sowell, that they have cultural capital by virtue of their immigrant status. They do get the message that blacks are stereotyped by whites in negative ways, that the all black neighborhoods they live in are violent and dangerous, and that the neighborhoods of whites are relatively safe. They also encounter a peer culture which values black American cultural forms. The immigrant culture of struggle, hard work and educational success that their parents try to enforce is experienced in negative ways by these youngsters. They see their parents denying them privileges that their American

peers enjoy and, unlike the middle-class youth, they do not automatically associate hard work, lack of dating and partying, and stress on scholastic achievement with social mobility. In the peer culture of the school, immigrant and ethnic-identified teens tend to be the best students. In the neighborhood inner city schools, newly arrived immigrants who have attended better schools in the islands tend to out-perform the students who have spent their lives in the substandard New York City public schools. This tends to reinforce the association between ethnicity and school success—and the more American identified adopt an adversarial stance toward school. . . .

Middle-class blacks realize this and try to convey their class status to others in subtle and not so subtle ways (Feagin 1991). . . . The white New Yorkers we interviewed do notice differences among blacks, and they use ethnic differences as clues for class differences. If the association found here between social class and ethnic identity is widespread, this perception could become a self-fulfilling prophesy. It could be that the children of poor parents will not keep an ethnic identity and the children whose parents achieve social mobility will keep the ethnic identity. This will reinforce the image in the minds of whites that the "island people" are "good blacks," thus giving the edge in employment decisions and the like to ethnic blacks over American blacks.

[I]t remains to be seen how long the ethnic-identified second-generation teens will continue to identify with their ethnic backgrounds. This is also related to the fact that whites tend to make racial judgements about identity when it comes to blacks. The second generation does not have an accent or other clues which immediately telegraph their ethnic status to others. They are aware that, unless they are active in conveying their identities, they are seen as black Americans and that often in encounters with whites the status of their black race is all that matters. It could be that by the time they have their children they will have decided that the quest not to be seen as a black American will be a futile one.

References

Feagin, J. R. 1991. "The Continuing Significance of Race—Antiblack Discrimination in Public Places," *American Sociological Review*, 56(1):101–116.

Foner, N. 1987. "The Jamaicans: Race and Ethnicity among Migrants in New York City." In *New Immigrants in New York*. Ed. N. Foner. New York: Columbia University Press. Pp. 131–158.

Fordham, S. 1988. "Racelessness as a Factor in Black Students' School Success: Pragmatic Strategy or Pyrrhic Victory," *Harvard Education Review*, 58(1). February.

Kasinitz, P. 1992. *Caribbean New York: Black Immigrants and the Politics of Race*. Ithaca, NY: Cornell University Press.

Ogbu, J. 1990. "Minority Status and Literacy in Comparative Perspective," *Daedalus*, 119(2):141–168. Spring.

Portes, A., and M. Zhou. 1993. "The New Second Generation: Segmented Assimilation and Its Variants," *The Annals of the American Academy of Political and Social Science*, 530:74–97. November.

Stafford, S. B. 1987. "Language and Identity: Haitians in New York City." In *Caribbean Life in New York City: Sociocultural Dimensions*. Ed. C. R. Sutton and E. M. Chaney. New York: Center for Migration Studies.

Sutton, C. R., and S. P Makiesky. 1975. "Migration and West Indian Racial and Ethnic Consciousness." In *Migration and Development: Implications for Ethnic Identity and Political Conflict*. Ed. H. I. Safa and B. M. Du Toit. Paris: Mouton and Co.

Woldemikael, T.M. 1989. *Becoming Black American: Haitians and American Institutions in Evanston, Illinois*. New York: Ams Press.

Reprinted from: Mary C. Waters, "Ethnic and Racial Identities of Second-Generation Black Immigrants in New York City," *International Migration Review* 28 (4): 795–820. ©1994 by Center for Migration Studies. Reprinted by permission.

45

Pacific Islander Americans and Multiethnicity:

A Vision of America's Future?

Paul R. Spickard
Rowena Fong

At a recent basketball game in a schoolyard in Kaneohe, Hawai'i, two players began to argue. As basketball players will, they started talking about each other's families. One, who prided himself on his pure Samoan ancestry, said, "You got a Hawaiian grandmother, a Pake [Chinese] grandfather. Your other grandfather's Portegee [Portuguese], and you mom's Filipino. You got Haole [White] brother-in-law and Korean cousins. Who da heck are you?" The person with the bouquet of ethnic possibilities smiled (his team was winning) and said, simply, "I all da kine [I'm all of those things]. Le's play." This article attempts to explain that interaction. Specifically, it seeks to understand how ethnicity works for Pacific Islander Americans and what that might mean for other kinds of people.

Multiethnicity

. . . [Scholars] recognize that most people in fact are descended from multiple, not single, ethnic sources. They know that most African Americans are in fact part European American and Native American, that most Jews have some Gentile ancestry, and that most Scandinavian Americans have some German relatives. But the dominant and subdominant paradigms treat ethnicity as if each person had only one ethnic identity. They say, along with census takers and school forms, "choose one box." Thus, persons of mixed African, Native American, and European ances-

try have long been regarded—and have regarded themselves—as African American. Even as they may have acknowledged privately that they were descended from multiple roots, nonetheless they identified with only one. Reginald Daniel (1992) refers to this as the "rule of hypodescent"—the one-drop rule, whereby whites and blacks agree that one drop of black blood makes one black. The system was not so clear-cut for other groups, some measure of mixture was acknowledged in the cases of people whose ancestry came from several European sources, for instance. But even then, people tended to see themselves as predominantly one sort of person, ethnically speaking (Spickard 1989; Waters 1990).

In recent years, two things have happened that have caused this to begin to change. In the first place, for about two decades intermarriage across racial as well as religious and national lines has increased enormously. Almost no White American extended family exists today without at least one member who has married across what two generations ago would have been thought an unbridgeable gap. . . . Because of the increase in intermarriage, there has appeared a larger number of mixed people than ever before. In the 1980 census and again in 1990, the fastest growing ethnic category was "other," and most of these people were probably mixed (U.S. Bureau of the Census 1983:22, 1992:3). The cover of a recent *Time* magazine proclaimed mixed people to be "The New Face of America" (*Time* 1993).

The second thing that has happened to change the discourse of American ethnicity is that, in just the last few years, people of mixed ancestry have begun to claim both or all parts of their ancestry. They claim multiethnicity; they refuse to choose one box (Daniel 1992; Funderburg 1994; Hall 1992). This has gone so far as to result in the formation of organizations of multiethnic persons. Some of those organizations engage in serious lobbying for changes in the census (hence, school forms, etc.) to allow people to check more than one box (AMEA 1993; Multiracial Americans of Southern California 1993). The situation of Pacific Islander Americans can provide some clues to what may lie in store for other American ethnic groups in an age of ever-more mixed ethnicities.

Pacific Islander American Multiethnicity

The term *Pacific Islander Americans* is a bit problematic, for, like Asian Americans and Hispanic Americans, Pacific Islander Americans are not an ethnic group, but rather an artificial collection of groups. They appear as a subcategory of the human species in the U.S. census, on affirmative action forms, and the like, often mixed with Asian Americans, and paralleled by Native, African, Hispanic, and White Americans. Yet almost no person arises in the morning thinking of herself or himself as a Pacific Island American. Most think of themselves as Tongans (or Tongan Americans), Samoans, Fijians, and so on. A few would recognize the terms *Polynesian, Melanesian,* and *Micronesian* as somewhat larger categories that they have been told apply to them. But those are not indigenous categories, either. They are constructs of northwestern European imaginations (Scarr 1994). . . .

Pacific Islanders historically have constructed their ethnic identities rather more complexly than many other peoples. Pacific Islanders have long had a greater consciousness than other American groups of being mixed peoples, of having multiple ethnic identities—Samoan and Tongan, Marquesan and Tahitian, Maori and European, and so forth. They seem more comfortable than other Americans with holding in tension two or more ethnic identities, with being deeply involved in more than one at the same time.

Consider William Kauaiwiulaokalani Wallace, a Hawaiian rights activist and lawyer. When he speaks in public he begins by chanting his genealogy for five minutes and playing his nose flute and drum. His parents were Hawaiian, and he grew up on the island of Moloka'i where his first language was Hawaiian. He dug taro and talked story and knew himself to be completely Hawaiian.

Then at the age of ten or eleven Bill went to live with his grandmother in La'ie on the island of O'ahu. There he discovered—much to his dismay, at first—that he was Samoan. He spent time with his Samoan cousins and their friends. He learned some Samoan words, ate Samoan food, and began to feel *fa'a samoa*—the Samoan way. So he was half Hawaiian and half Samoan. But then, on questioning his elders, he found that his Samoan side had relatives in Tonga. And he found that his Hawaiian family went back to Tahiti. So he was Hawaiian and Samoan and Tongan and Tahitian.

Then, as he emerged into adulthood, Bill married a Maori woman from New Zealand. In time, he visited her family and was accorded a position of honor. And he began to discover other pieces of himself. He worked for a couple of years in Samoa, and discovered that his Samoan side included a fair amount of British and some German ancestry, that some of his relatives were members of what some call the *afakasi* class, part-Samoan and part-European. Back in Hawai'i Bill learned that the name Wallace stemmed from a Scottish ancestor. And he found that among his plantation ancestors on Moloka'i was a Chinese woman, back some three or four generations. Bill has a pretty clear hierarchy of these identities. The Hawaiian side has organized his life's activities, shaped his values, and determined his identity more than the others. Next comes the Samoan, although the Maori connection is not far behind. The other ethnic connections are quite dim. He confesses to feeling an occasional twinge of fellow-feeling for each of the peoples that contributed smaller portions to his genealogy, but only the three—Hawaiian, Samoan, and Maori—organize much of his life.

Bill Wallace is not at all unusual. The Pacific Islander American Research Project surveyed people in three rural villages on the windward coast of the island of O'ahu, Hawai'i, in 1992 (Nautu and Spickard 1994). Eight Pacific Islander American interviewers went house to house with a questionnaire aimed at gathering data on people's images of various Pacific Islander American groups and on the social distance perceived by various groups toward one another. The questionnaire was written in English, but the interviewers spoke a variety of Pacific Islander languages and used them when necessary to conduct the interviews. The survey included 406 people, of whom 289 said they had at least some Pacific Islander ancestry. Of those, 91 said they were purely one or another sort of Pacific Islander, and 198—more than two thirds—said they were biologically mixed. . . .

Many mixed people interviewed chose to identify with all parts of their ancestry: 42 out of 115 people who had part-Hawaiian ancestry; 32 out of 86 part-Samoans; 13 out of 38 part-Tongans. . . . One suspects that even some people who said they were unmixed actually possessed some mixed ancestry. . . .

Features of Pacific Islander American Multiethnicity

Pacific Islander ethnicity is perhaps not unique in the way it is constructed and operates, but it has several features that mark it as unusual. In the first place, Pacific Islander American ethnicity seems to be *situational* (Nagata 1974; Patterson 1975). Dorri Nautu has Hawaiian, Filipino, Portuguese, and several other ancestries. She lives in a mixed community of part-Hawaiians, Hawaiians, and several other ethnic groups, and she is qualified to attend university on an ethnic Hawaiian scholarship. She identifies herself more than anything else as Hawaiian. But, she says, "If I'm with my grandmother I'm Portuguese. If I'm with some of my aunts on my dad's side I'm Filipino. If I'm hanging around I'm just local. If I'm on the mainland I'm Hawaiian."

Dorri reports that her Filipino relatives accept her as a Filipina. But they see her (and she sees herself) as a little less completely Filipina than other family members. This is primarily, she says, because she has less cultural knowledge (about food, language, and so forth) than do other family members. Secondarily, it is because she has a smaller historic quantum of Filipino ancestry. Dorri says that her relatives excuse her lack of cultural knowledge because she is not purely Filipina in ancestry or upbringing, whereas they would be critical if a pure Filipina exhibited a similar cultural deficiency. Her Hawaiian relatives, on the other hand, do not seem to make any distinction regarding purity of ancestry. So how Dorri identifies herself de-

pends on which of her groups she is with—she feels significantly connected with each of her major ethnic derivations, and she is accepted in each of the groups as an insider.

Dorri seems to associate with the ethnicity of whichever set of relatives or friends she happens to be with. Lori Atoa reports the opposite situation—being treated as a Samoan by her mother's Idaho Haole fancily and as *palagi* by her relatives and schoolmates at home in Samoa. Alexis Siteine reports a more complex dynamic:

> My high school friend asked me, "What do you tell people that you are?" My answer was, "It depends on who's doing the asking." I do not choose to sometimes be one thing and at other times another, but I have learned to identify what I think people are really asking. Sometimes they are actually asking, "What makes you the same as me?" Yet, more often it is, "What makes you different?" If asked this question in New Zealand by a non-Samoan, I identify myself as Samoan. If the asker is Samoan, I acknowledge my heritage: "My mother is palagi and my father is Samoan." When I am out of New Zealand and am asked by a non-Samoan, I identify myself as a New Zealander; if a Samoan asks, my answer is the same, but I qualify it with "but my father is Samoan." These replies are generally satisfactory.

These various testimonies also point to some geographical differences. How one thinks about one's ethnicity seems to vary depending on where one is. Dorri Nautu feels "local"—mixed, polyglot, native to Hawai'i but not specifically ethnically Hawaiian—most of the time when she is in Hawai'i. On the mainland she feels Hawaiian, not just placed in that box by others but actively, primarily, ethnically Hawaiian in her own imagination. Some of that may be due to the difference between active and latent ethnicity. When one is with one's ethnic fellows, one seldom thinks about one's ethnicity except on ritual occasions. One just *is* ethnic—behaves in ways that embody the ethnic culture and associates with other ethnic people. The time when one feels one's ethnicity more vividly is when one is confronted by a large group of outsiders. . . .

The greater recognition of one's Pacific Islander identity when in a contrast situation also may be related to a phenomenon one may observe among Tongans and Samoans in California, Washington, or Utah. Pacific Islanders are more willing to express their multiplicity in an overtly multiple place like Hawai'i than they are on the U.S. mainland. The same person who, in Hau'ula or on the multicultural campus of BYU-Hawai'i, is primarily a Samoan but also recognizes some *palagi* and Asian Indian ancestors, in Los Angeles sees himself or herself and is treated only as a Samoan without the multiethnic consciousness (Misa 1992).

Even farther afield from centers of Pacific Islander American population, one's Pacific Islander identity may become fuzzier, not necessarily in one's own mind but in the minds of the people around. In several western metropolitan areas, most non-Pacific people know that there are Samoans and Hawaiians, and they may know that there are Tongans, although other groups such as Fijians, Marshall Islanders, and I-Kiribati are beyond their ken. But elsewhere in the U.S., Pacific Islanders are frequently mistaken for someone else. . . .

Another feature of Pacific Islander American multiethnicity is the common practice of *choosing one* from among the available identities for emphasis, at the same time holding onto other identities. Thus, Bill Wallace and Dorri Nautu have many ethnicities, but they choose to be mainly Hawaiian most of the time. Debbie Hippolite Wright is English and French in part, but chooses to be Maori in her primary identity. Jon Jonassen is Rarotongan and Norwegian and several other things, but is vociferously a Cook Islander. Lori Atoa is Samoan and *palagi*, but chooses Samoan because she grew up in Western Samoa and because she feels she looks more Samoan. Tupou Hopoate Pau'u has ancestors from Germany, Portugal, England, Fiji, and Samoa, but she is militantly Tongan even as she acknowledges the others.

The survey showed people choosing to simplify their ancestry. . . . There were discernible patterns in these simplifyings. Since the survey was taken in Hawai'i, and since in recent decades there has been a resurgence of the prestige of Hawaiian identity, it should surprise no one that many people who knew of mixed ancestry chose to identify with the Hawaiian branch of their family tree more than with any other. In general, the ancestry most likely to be left out in the simplifications was European. The second ancestry most likely to be left out was Asian. Only very seldom did any of the people interviewed choose to ignore a Pacific Islander ancestry; in most cases where they did that, it was when a person chose to embrace a single Hawaiian identity.

The choice of which identity to emphasize can shift in the course of one's life. Kookie Soliai says she feels more strongly Maori than anything else in her heart. But when she lived on the mainland she identified herself as Hawaiian because that was easier for most people to discern, and because it gave her a bond of sisterhood with other islanders far from home. Back in Hawai'i, she identifies publicly as part-Hawaiian despite her greater psychic affiliation with her Maori heritage, for reasons both political and financial. (There are tangible benefits to being Hawaiian.)

The pattern of simplifying one's ethnicity, and of choosing one heritage to emphasize while still acknowledging some others, is a bit like the pattern among White Catholics that Mary Waters found in *Ethnic Options* (1990). In both situations, the people in question acknowledge more than one possible identity; many simplify their ethnicity in practice; and many emphasize just one ethnic identity. The difference between Waters's White Catholics and the Pacific Islander Americans interviewed for this study has to do with the *importance* of ethnicity. . . . For Pacific Islander Americans . . . ethnicity is much more important. As for White Catholics, ethnicity for Pacific Islander Americans is multiple, but theirs is no mere symbolic ethnicity. It is not something to be put on and taken off, not something to be trotted out only for ceremonial occasions. In the case of all the Pacific Islander Americans interviewed, the ethnicity is powerful, it is deeply felt, and it organizes much of the person's life. The fact of multiplicity and the act of choosing do not imply lack of content to ethnicity, and they in no way diminish ethnicity's importance.

A final feature of Pacific Islander American multiethnicity is that the group tends to admit individuals who have mixed ancestry on more or less the same basis as people who have pure ancestry. That is not always the case in the Pacific, as indicated by the ridicule heaped on *afakasis* in Samoa (Shankman 1989). But it seems to be true of Pacific Islanders in America. There is little residue of the Samoan pure-blood/half-blood split in the U.S., either in Hawai'i or on the mainland. The same is true for other Pacific Islander groups in the U.S. Dorri Nautu is accepted by both Filipinos and Hawaiians, although she is treated a bit more specially by the Filipinos on account of her mixture than by the Hawaiians. The difference in her reception is probably partly because Hawaiians and other Pacific peoples see themselves as fundamentally mixed peoples, whereas Filipinos and other Asians see themselves each as more purely one thing. It may also be because Pacific Islander American ethnicity focuses not on the boundaries between groups but on the centers of group ethnicity and the glue that holds the group together—not on who is out but on who is in, and on what they do together. . . .

Bases of Pacific Islander American Multiethnicity

The identity choices of Pacific Islanders who possess multiple inheritances are based on several factors. A person's ethnicity may proceed from any of several bases, and the group seems willing to admit people to membership on the basis of any of several items. One such basis is consciousness of *ancestry*—bloodline, as many would call it. Samoans, especially, talk a lot about the importance of "blood," but all the Pacific Islanders interviewed stressed ancestry as an essential basis of ethnic identity.

In order to identify yourself as a Hawaiian, you must possess at least one Hawaiian ancestor. Being able to trace that ancestor gives you location. . . . Most Hawaiians do not begin their conversations in Pizza Hut by reciting their entire genealogies. But if one is meeting someone in an only slightly more formal way—if one, say, is being introduced to the aunt of one's friend—then the conversation is likely to begin with each person telling the other about who their relatives are and where they are from, until the two people arrive at a point of recognition, where each can place where the other is located among the Hawaiian people. And reciting the genealogy is something that the *Ali'i*, the Hawaiian nobility, are said to have done of old; the memory of that act anciently performed resonates for many modern Hawaiians. Like Hawaiians, Maori in New Zealand are likely to introduce themselves on formal occasions by means of a genealogical chant.

It is probably true that the idea of blood as the carrier of identity is not native to the Pacific; in fact, it seems to have come quite late—as late as the 1870s in Hawai'i (Jonassen 1993; Kame'eleihiwa 1992; Wallace 1993). And the idea of blood quantum, of calculating percentages, is found only in Hawai'i, and can be traced to American government impositions from the 1920s onward. But genealogy is nonetheless a very old Pacific imperative. *The Kumulipo* and other ancient chants recite long genealogies that give location and substance to the Hawaiian people (Beckwith [1951] 1972). . . . This celebration of the mystic chords of memory is perhaps as important as the actual content of the genealogical account in gluing together Hawaiians as a people.

There is something incantatory about certain ethnic political speech. It is as invigorating to ethnicity when a Pacific Islander American politician recites the history of abuse that her people have suffered, as when an island spiritual leader chants a genealogy. The ground of ethnicity in this case is almost rhetorical. It is publicly remembering. Like Thomas Jefferson's recitation in the *U.S. Declaration of Independence* of the dastardly deeds done by King George, such a catalogue of wrongs galvanizes the slumbering feeling of a people. Thus, for example, it is essential to the reawakening of Hawaiian political identity that Haunani-Kay Trask (1993) begin her book on Hawaiian nationalism by recounting the wrongs done to Hawaiians by Americans and others. It is true history, but it is more than that: it is the act of rhetorically, publicly remembering and thus it serves to strengthen the ethnic bond.

On a more prosaic level, who one's relatives are constitutes an essential ingredient in one's identifying with a Pacific Islander American group and being accepted by one. If you have relatives in a particular Pacific Islander American people, then you are a legitimate member of that group. As a mixed New Zealander, Alexis Siteine, puts it: "Maoris seem to have adopted the 'one drop' rule about themselves: If you can claim any Maori ancestor, then you are part of the *tangata whenua* (people of the land). The members of the Maori club [in school] then, ranged in appearance from the blonde, blue-eyed, freckled variety to dark-haired, dark-eyed brownness."

Much of what happens that is ethnic happens within the extended family. Almost all community ceremonies and obligations are organized on a family basis. The place, above all others, where Tongan or Fijian or, Samoan culture is passed on is in the *family*. As Lori Atoa says: "In the Samoan way of life, the extended family is first priority. Anytime there is a crisis in the family, we are always ready to give whatever is needed. . . . the aunts and cousins on the Samoan side were always around to follow through on straightening us out. There again, we were totally exposed to the Samoan way of doing things." Among Maori, both in New Zealand and in the U.S., it is not just ancestry or phenotype, but ties to the *marae* that give one ethnic location. . . .

The family tie does not necessarily have to be genetic in order to be powerful. Ricky Soliai (Kookie's husband) is biologically Hawaiian-Tongan-Irish, but his father was adopted and raised by a Samoan family. Ricky regards himself as full Samoan, his family and other people—Samoans and non-Samoans—treat him as a Samoan without qualification, and he insists on raising the couple's children as Samoans only, despite their strongly Maori-Hawaiian-Japanese mother. Contrast that to the situation of many other interethnic adoptees—we call some of them African Americans raised by White families, and others we call Korean babies in Swedish American families (Ladner 1977). Growing up, everyone thinks of them

as interracial adoptees, not as natural members of the group of their adopted parents. On reaching their teen years, many such people go searching for their ancestral roots (there is in fact a thriving industry that puts Korean youths from the American Midwest in touch with the land and culture of their biological ancestors). There seems to be less of this in the Pacific Islander case. One's adoption into a particular Pacific Islander ethnic group seems to entitle one to a more complete membership in that group than is the case with other American groups.

Bill Wallace's experience suggests that you may be able to marry into another ethnic group, although Dorri Nautu's and Kookie Soliai's experiences suggest that identity acquired through marriage may not be as strong as identity that comes from one's childhood home. There is also a possibility that Hawaiians may be more accepting of outside infusions than other peoples for identifiable historical reasons. Bill Wallace points out that, in the middle of the nineteenth century, "with the Hawaiian people dying out, the kings brought in people from the Pacific Rim—Chinese, Japanese, Koreans—to try to restock the Hawaiian blood." Whatever the case in specific historical situations, and whether or not people may marry into or be adopted into specific ethnic groups, it remains clear that the family is one of the primary bases of Pacific Islander American ethnicity.

Equally important with bloodlines and family connections in determining Pacific Islander American ethnicity is *cultural practice* (Bentley 1987). One is Tongan because one behaves like a Tongan, speaks the Tongan language, has a Tongan heart. Inoke Funaki (1993), in a moving personal exploration of "Culture and Identity in the Pacific," finds Tongan identity in *fe'ofo'ofani* (brotherly love), in family spirit, in the willingness to help each other, in kindness and neighborly generosity, and in the art of living together in harmony and peace. One is Samoan because one speaks Samoan and one understands and lives *fa'a samoa*. Many Pacific Islander Americans would argue, indeed, that language is the sine qua non of ethnicity, the essential variety of cultural practice, because so much that is powerful is shared through language. . . .

Another basis of Pacific Islander American ethnic connectedness is one's relationship to *place*. In Hawaiian, it is the *aina*, the land, and one must *malama aina*—care for the land. The caring is reciprocal, for the land also cares for the people, and the relationship is a deep, family bond (Kame'eleihiwa 1992). Leaders of the Hawaiian cultural and political renaissance of the past two decades have stressed the importance of reclaiming the *aina* above almost everything else (Trask 1993). But it is not only ethnic nationalist politicians who revere the land. Elderly Hawaiians of no particular political convictions speak of feeling roots reaching down through their feet, deep into the earth of their islands. . . .

Pacific Islanders of other derivations also celebrate their ethnicity by reference to place. Tupou Hopoate Pau'u, a Tongan raised in Australia who now lives in California, fled her Tongan ethnicity until her mother forced her to return to Tonga. She now speaks in hushed tones of her first encounter with the village and the hut where she was born, and the intense love for her people and her culture that grew from that encounter to become one of the central forces of her life (Pau'u 1994). . . . Pau'u's subsequent life choices—to work as a missionary in Tonga, to attend a university made up mainly of Pacific Islander students, to marry a Tongan American, to live in a Tongan community in southern California, to become a lawyer so she can serve her people—have all stemmed from her experience of that intensely Tongan place.

Not all Pacific Islander Americans have had personal contact with places that symbolize their ethnicity. But nearly all have heard about such places from their relatives, and the collective memory of those ethnic places is a powerful reinforcer of their ethnic identity. . . .

Conclusion: Multiple Ethnic Centers

. . . Pacific Islander Americans are in some ways a model of what is happening to America at large. The American people are becoming a people of multiple identities. We are, at last, biologically . . . a mixed America, but we are not melting. Instead, we are becoming vividly multiethnic within each person (Root

1992). Some other American ethnic groups are beginning to face up to this multiethnic reality. It used to be (and still is for the Orthodox) that to be a Jew one had to be either a convert or the child of a Jewish mother. Now, mindful of dwindling numbers in an era of 40% out-marriage or more, not a small number of Reform Jewish synagogues are holding "Get to Know Your Jewish Roots" classes and encouraging anyone who can identify a Jewish ancestor to consider joining the faith. In similar fashion, where a generation ago the small number of mixed offspring of Japanese American intermarriages were shunned by Japanese American community institutions, now one sees their pictures in Japanese community newspapers quite regularly, and their numbers are quite large (Spickard 1989). In an age of emerging multiplicity, Pacific Islander American formulations of multiethnicity are especially fruitful for understanding ethnicity as it is coming to be in the U.S. . . .

Now, for Pacific Islander Americans at least, it seems possible to reconcile two or more ethnic identities in one person without torment, and without one being subordinated to the other. Perhaps what is needed in our era is an understanding of ethnicity that does not presume that a person must check just one box. Perhaps, by focusing as Pacific Islander Americans do on the centers of ethnicity, and not on boundaries between groups, we can better prepare ourselves for an age when most if not all of us will be biologically and functionally multiethnic.

References

AMEA. 1993. "AMEA Testifies before Congressional Subcommittee." *AMEA Networking News* 4(5):1.

Beckwith, Martha Warren. [1951] 1972. *The Kumulipo*. University of Hawai'i Press.

Bentley, G. Carter. 1987. "Ethnicity and Practice." *Comparative Studies in Society and History* 29:24–55.

Daniel, G. Reginald. 1992. "Passers and Pluralists: Subverting the Racial Divide." Pp. 91–107 in *Racially Mixed People in America*, edited by Maria P.P. Root. Sage.

Funaki, Inoke. 1993. "Culture and Identity in the Pacific: A Personal Expression." Convocation address, BYU-Hawai'i.

Funderburg, Lise. 1994. *Black, White, Other: Biracial Americans Talk about Race and Identity.* Morrow.

Hall, Christine C.I. 1992. "Please Choose One: Ethnic Identity Choices of Biracial Individuals." Pp. 250–64 in *Racially Mixed People in America*, edited by Maria P.P. Root. Sage.

Jonassen, Jon. 1993. Former Executive Secretary, South Pacific Commission. Interview by author. La'ie, Hawai'i.

Kame'eleihiwa, Lilikala. 1992. *Native Land and Foreign Desires.* Honolulu: Bishop Museum.

Ladner, Joyce A. 1977. *Mixed Families: Adopting across Racial Boundaries.* Doubleday.

Misa, Pona. 1992. Interviewed by the author. La'ie, Hawai'i.

Multiracial Americans of Southern California. 1993. *Spectrum* 7(4).

Nagata, Judith. 1974. "What Is a Malay? Situational Selection of Ethnic Identity in a Plural Society." *American Ethnologist* 1331–50.

Nautu, Dorri, and Paul Spickard. 1994. "Ethnic Images and Social Distance among Pacific Islander Americans." *Social Process in Hawai'i* 36:69–85.

Patterson, Orlando. 1975. "Context and Choice in Ethnic Allegiance: A Theoretical Framework and Caribbean Case Study." Pp. 305–49 in *Ethnicity: Theory and Experience*, edited by Nathan Glazer and Daniel P. Moynihan. Harvard University Press.

Pau'u, Tupou Hopoate. 1994. "My Life in Four Cultures." *Social Process in Hawai'i* 36:1–15.

Root, Maria P.P. (ed.). 1992, *Racially Mixed People in America.* Sage.

Scarr, Deryck 1994. "Deconstructing the Island Group in Pacific History." *Pacific History Association Newsletter* 31:7.

Shankman, Paul. 1989. "Race, Class, and Ethnicity in Western Samoa." Pp. 218–43 in *Ethnicity and Nation-Building in the Pacific*, edited by Michael C. Howard. United Nations University.

Spickard, Paul R. 1989. *Mixed Blood: Intermarriage and Ethnic Identity in Twentieth-Century America.* University of Wisconsin Press.

Time. 1993. "Special Issue: The New Face of America."

Trask, Haunani-Kay. 1993. *From a Native Daughter.* Common Courage Press.

U.S. Bureau of the Census. 1983. *1980 Census of Population. 1B. General Population Characteristics. United States Summary* (PC80–1–B1). Government Printing Office.

——. 1992. *1990 Census of Population. General Population Characteristics. United States* (CP–1–1). Government Printing Office.

Wallace, William Kauaiwiulaokalani M. 1993. Director of Pacific Islands Studies, BYU-Hawai'i. Interviewed by the author. La'ie, Hawai'i.

Waters, Mary C. 1990. *Ethnic Options: Choosing Identities in America.* University of California Press.

46

The New Second Generation:

Segmented Assimilation and Its Variants

Alejandro Portes
Min Zhou

. . . Growing up in an immigrant family has always been difficult, as individuals are torn by conflicting social and cultural demands while they face the challenge of entry into an unfamiliar and frequently hostile world. And yet the difficulties are not always the same. The process of growing up American oscillates between smooth acceptance and traumatic confrontation depending on the characteristics that immigrants and their children bring along and the social context that receives them. In this article, we explore some of these factors and their bearing on the process of social adaptation of the immigrant second generation. We propose a conceptual framework for understanding this process and illustrate it with selected ethnographic material. . .

Research on the new immigration—that which arose after the passage of the 1965 Immigration Act—has been focused almost exclusively on the first generation, that is, on adult men and women coming to the United States in search of work or to escape political persecution. Little noticed until recently is the fact that the foreign-born inflow has been rapidly evolving from single adult individuals to entire family groups, including infant children and those born to immigrants to the United States. By 1980, 10 percent of dependent children in households counted by the census were second-generation immigrants.[1] . . .

The great deal of research and theorizing on post-1965 immigration offers only tentative guidance on the prospects and paths of adaptation of the second generation because the outlook of this group can be very different from that of their immigrant parents. For example, it is generally accepted among immigration theorists that entry-level menial jobs are performed without hesitation by newly arrived immigrants but are commonly shunned by their U.S.-reared offspring. . . .

Nor does the existing literature on second-generation adaptation, based as it is on the experience of descendants of pre-World War I immigrants, offer much guidance for the understanding of contemporary events. . . . Two such differences deserve special mention.

First, descendants of European immigrants who confronted the dilemmas of conflicting cultures were uniformly white. Even if of a somewhat darker hue than the natives, their skin color reduced a major barrier to entry into the American mainstream. For this reason, the process of assimilation depended largely on individual decisions to leave the immigrant culture behind and embrace American ways. Such an advantage obviously does not exist for the black, Asian, and mestizo children of today's immigrants.

Second, the structure of economic opportunities has also changed. Fifty years ago, the United States was the premier industrial power in the world, and its diversified industrial labor requirements offered to the second generation the opportunity to move up gradually through better-paid occupations while remaining part of the working class. Such opportunities have increasingly disappeared in recent years following a rapid process of national deindustrialization and global industrial restructuring. This process has left entrants to the American labor force confronting a widening gap between the minimally paid menial jobs that immigrants commonly accept and the high-tech and professional occupations requiring college degrees that native elites occupy.[2] The gradual disappearance of intermediate opportunities also bears directly on the race between first-generation economic progress and second-generation expectations, noted previously.

The New Americans at a Glance

Before examining this process in detail, it is important to learn a little more about today's second generation. In 1990, the foreign-born population of the United States reached an estimated 21.2 million. In absolute terms, this is the highest number in the history of the nation, although relative to the native-born population, the figure is lower than that at the turn of the century. A century ago, in 1890, immigrants represented 14.8 percent of the total population, almost double today's figure of 8.6 percent. The foreign-stock population, composed of immigrants and their descendants, is, however, much higher. In 1990, roughly 46 million, or 18.5 percent of the total U.S. population, were estimated to be of foreign stock. This yields a net second-generation total of 24.8 million, or 10.9 percent of the American population.[3]

As an estimate of the new second generation, this figure is inflated by the presence of offspring of older immigrants. A team of demographers at the Urban Institute have estimated the contribution of post-1960 immigration, including immigrants and their children, to the total 1990 U.S. population. . . . [T]he new second generation, formed by children of post-1960 immigrants represents 7.7 million, or 3.4 percent of the native-born population. . . .

More important, however, is the prospect for growth in future years. Given the record increase of immigration since 1960, the second generation as a whole is expected to grow rapidly, surpassing its former peak of roughly 28 million in 1940 sometime during the decade [of the 1990s]. . . . [T]he racial and ethnic composition of the component of the second generation attributable to post-1960 immigration is quite different from that which peaked just before World War II. Over 85 percent of children of immigrants in 1940 were born to Europeans, or, in current terminology, non-Hispanic whites. By contrast, approximately 77 percent of post-1960 immigrants are non-Europeans. Of the post-1960 immigrants, 22.4 percent are classified as Asians, 7.6 as blacks, and 47 percent as Hispanics. The latter group, which originates in Mexico and other Latin American countries, poses a problem in terms of phenotypical classification since Hispanics can be of any race.[4]

According to the 1990 census, 51.7 percent of the 22.3 million Hispanics counted were white, 3.4 percent black, and 42.7 percent of another race. The latter figure, possibly corresponding to the category of mixed race, or mestizos, was slightly larger among Mexicans, who constitute 60.4 percent of the total Hispanic population. Applying these figures with some adjustments to the post-1960 immigrant flow, it is reasonable to assume that approximately half of Hispanic immigrants would be classified as nonwhite. This phenotypical category would hence comprise a majority, roughly 54 percent, of the total inflow.[5] . . .

Assimilation as a Problem

The Haitian immigrant community of Miami is composed of some 75,000 legal and clandestine immigrants, many of whom sold everything they owned in order to buy passage to America. First-generation Haitians are strongly oriented toward preserving a strong national identity, which they associate both with community solidarity and with social networks promoting individual success.[6] In trying to instill national pride and an achievement orientation in their children, they clash, however, with the youngsters' everyday experiences in school. Little Haiti is adjacent to Liberty City, the main black inner-city area of Miami, and Haitian adolescents attend predominantly inner-city schools. Native-born youths stereotype Haitians as too docile and too subservient to whites and they make fun of French and Creole and of the Haitians' accent. As a result, second-generation Haitian children find themselves torn between conflicting ideas and values: to remain Haitian they would have to face social ostracism and continuing attacks in school; to become American—black American in this case—they would have to forgo their parents' dreams of making it in America on the basis of ethnic solidarity and preservation of traditional values.[7]

An adversarial stance toward the white mainstream is common among inner-city minority youths who, while attacking the newcomers' ways, instill in them a consciousness of American-style discrimination. A common message is the devaluation of education as a vehicle for advancement of all black youths, a message that directly contradicts the immigrant parents' expectations. Academically outstanding Haitian American students . . . have consciously attempted to retain their ethnic identity by cloaking it in black American cultural forms, such as rap music. Many others, however, have followed the path of least effort and become thoroughly assimilated. Assimilation in this instance is not into mainstream culture but into the values and norms of the inner city. In the process, the resources of solidarity and mutual support within the immigrant community are dissipated.

An emerging paradox in the study of today's second generation is the peculiar forms that assimilation has adopted for its members. As the Haitian example illustrates, adopting the outlooks and cultural ways of the native-born does not represent, as in the past, the first step toward social and economic mobility but may lead to the exact opposite. At the other end, immigrant youths who remain firmly ensconced in their respective ethnic communities may, by virtue of this fact, have a better chance for educational and economic mobility through use of the material and social capital that their communities make available.[8]

This situation stands the cultural blueprint for advancement of immigrant groups in American Society on its head. . . [T]he expectation is that the foreign-born and their offspring will first acculturate and then seek entry and acceptance among the native-born as a prerequisite for their social and economic advancement. . . .

[T]he expected consequences of assimilation have not entirely reversed signs, but the process has become segmented. In other words, the question is into what sector of American society a particular immigrant group assimilates. Instead of a relatively uniform mainstream whose mores and prejudices dictate a common path of integration, we observe today several distinct forms of adaptation. One of them replicates the time-honored portrayal of growing acculturation and parallel integration into the white middle-class; a second leads straight in the opposite direction to permanent poverty and assimilation into the underclass; still a third associates rapid economic advancement with deliberate preservation of the immigrant community's values and tight solidarity. This pattern of segmented assimilation immediately raises the question of what makes some immigrant groups become susceptible to the downward route and what resources allow others to avoid this course.

Vulnerability and Resources

Along with individual and family variables, the context that immigrants find upon arrival in their new country plays a decisive role in the course that their offspring's lives will follow. This context includes such broad variables as political relations between sending and receiving countries and the state of the economy in the latter and such specific ones as the size and structure of preexisting coethnic communities. The concept of modes of incorporation provides a useful theoretical tool to understand this diversity. As developed in prior publications, modes of incorporation consist of the complex formed by the policies of the host government; the values and prejudices of the receiving society; and the characteristics of the coethnic community. . . .

To explain second-generation outcomes and their segmented character, however, we need to go into greater detail into the meaning of these various modes of incorporation from the standpoint of immigrant youths. There are three features of the social contexts encountered by today's newcomers that create vulnerability to downward assimilation. The first is color, the second is location, and the third is the absence of mobility ladders. As noted previously, the majority of contemporary immigrants are nonwhite. Although this feature may appear at first glance as an individual characteristic, in reality it is a trait belonging to the host society. Prejudice is not intrinsic to a particular skin color or racial type, and, indeed, many immigrants never experienced it in their native lands. It is by virtue of moving into a new social environment, marked by different values and prejudices, that physical features become redefined as a handicap.

The concentration of immigrant households in cities and particularly in central cities, as documented previously, gives rise to a second source of vulnerability because it puts new arrivals in close contact with concentrations of native-born minorities. This leads to the identification of the condition of both groups—immigrants and the native poor as the same in the eyes of the majority. More important, it exposes second-generation children to the adversarial subculture developed by marginalized native youths to cope with their own difficult situation.[9] This process of socialization may take place even when first-generation parents are moving ahead economically and, hence, their children have no objective reasons for embracing a counter-cultural message. If successful, the process can effectively block parental plans for intergenerational mobility.

The third contextual source of vulnerability has to do with changes in the host economy that have led to the evaporation of occupational ladders for intergenerational mobility. As noted previously, new immigrants may form the backbone of what remains of labor-intensive manufacturing in the cities as well as in their growing personal services sector, but these are niches that seldom offer channels for upward mobility. The new hourglass economy, created by economic restructuring, means that children of immigrants must cross a narrow bottleneck to occupations requiring advanced training if their careers are to keep pace with their U.S.-acquired aspirations. This race against a narrowing middle demands that immigrant parents accumulate sufficient resources to allow their children to effect the passage and to simultaneously prove to them the viability of aspirations for upward mobility. Otherwise, assimilation may not be into mainstream values and expectations but into the adversarial stance of impoverished groups confined to the bottom of the new economic hourglass.

The picture is painted in such stark terms here for the sake of clarity, although in reality things have not yet become so polarized. Middle-level occupations requiring relatively modest educational achievements have not completely vanished. By 1980, skilled blue-collar jobs—classified by the U.S. census as "precision production, craft, and repair occupations"—had declined by 1.1 percent relative to a decade earlier but still represented 13 percent of the experienced civilian labor force, or 13.6 million workers. Mostly clerical administrative support occupations added another 16.9 percent, or 17.5 million jobs. In 1980, occupations requiring a college degree had increased by 6 percent in comparison with 1970, but they still employed less than a fifth—18.2 percent—of the American labor force.[10]

Even in the largest cities, occupations requiring only a high school diploma were common by the late 1980s. In New York City, for example, persons with 12 years or less of schooling held just over one half of the jobs in 1987. Clerical, service, and skilled blue-collar jobs not requiring a college degree represented 46 percent.[11] Despite these figures, there is little doubt that the trend toward occupational segmentation has increasingly reduced opportunities for incremental upward mobility through well-paid blue-collar positions. The trend forces immigrants today to bridge in only one generation the gap between entry-level jobs and professional positions that earlier groups took two or three generations to travel.

Different modes of incorporation also make available, however, three types of resources to confront the challenges of contemporary assimilation. First, certain groups, notably political refugees, are eligible for a variety of government programs including educational loans for their children. The Cuban Loan Program, implemented by the Kennedy administration in connection with its plan to resettle Cuban refugees away from South Florida, gave many impoverished first and second-generation Cuban youths a chance to attend college. The high proportion of professionals and executives among Cuban American workers today, a figure on a par with that for native white workers, can be traced, at least in part, to the success of that program.[12] Passage of the 1980 Refugee Act gave to subsequent groups of refugees, in particular Southeast Asians and Eastern Europeans, access to a similarly generous benefits package.[13]

Second, certain foreign groups have been exempted from the traditional prejudice endured by most immigrants, thereby facilitating a smoother process of adaptation. Some political refugees, such as the early waves of exiles from Castro's Cuba, Hungarians and Czechs escaping the invasions of their respective countries, and Soviet Jews escaping religious persecution, provide examples. In other cases, it is the cultural and phenotypical affinity of newcomers to ample segments of the host population that ensures a welcome reception. The Irish coming to Boston during the 1980s are a case in point. Although many were illegal aliens, they came into an environment where generations of Irish Americans had established a secure foothold. Public sympathy effectively neutralized governmental hostility in this case, culminating in a change of the immigration law directly benefiting the newcomers.[14]

Third, and most important, are the resources made available through networks in the coethnic community. Immigrants who join well-established and diversified ethnic groups have access from the start to a range of moral and material resources well beyond those available through official assistance programs. Educational help for second-generation youths may include not only access to college grants and loans but also the existence of a private school system geared to the immigrant community's values. Attendance at these private ethnic schools insulates children from contact with native minority youths, while reinforcing the authority of parental views and plans.

In addition, the economic diversification of several immigrant communities creates niches of opportunity that members of the second generation can occupy, often without a need for an advanced education. Small-business apprenticeships, access to skilled building trades, and well-paid jobs in local government bureaucracies are some of the ethnic niches documented in the recent literature.[15] In 1987, average sales per firm of the smaller Chinese, East Indian, Korean, and Cuban enterprises exceeded $100,000 per year and they jointly employed over 200,000 workers. These figures omit medium-sized and large ethnic firms, whose sales and work forces are much larger.[16] Fieldwork in these communities indicates that up to half of recently arrived immigrants are employed by coethnic firms and that self-employment offers a prime avenue for mobility to second-generation youths.[17] Such community-mediated opportunities provide a solution to the race between material resources and second-generation aspirations not available through competition in the open labor market. Through creation of a capitalism of their own, some immigrant groups have thus been able to circumvent outside discrimination and the threat of vanishing mobility ladders.

In contrast to these favorable conditions are those foreign minorities who either lack a community already in place or whose coethnics are too poor to render assistance. The condition of Haitians in South Florida, cited earlier, provides an illustration of one of the most handicapped modes of incorporation encountered by contemporary immigrants, combining official hostility and widespread social prejudice with the absence of a strong receiving community.[18] From the standpoint of second-generation outcomes, the existence of a large but downtrodden coethnic community may be even less desirable than no community at all. This is because newly arrived youths enter into ready contact with the reactive subculture developed by earlier generations. Its influence is all the more powerful because it comes from individuals of the same national origin, "people like us" who can more effectively define the proper stance and attitudes of the newcomers. To the extent that they do so, the first-generation model of upward mobility through school achievement and attainment of professional occupations will be blocked.

Three Examples

Mexicans and Mexican Americans

Field High School (the name is fictitious) is located in a small coastal community of central California whose economy has long been tied to agricultural production and immigrant farm labor. About 57 percent of the student population is of Mexican descent. An intensive ethnographic study of the class of

1985 at Field High began with school records that showed that the majority of U.S.-born Spanish-surname students who had entered the school in 1981 had dropped out by their senior year. However, only 35 percent of the Spanish-surname students who had been originally classified by the school as limited English proficient (LEP) had dropped out. The figure was even lower than the corresponding one for native white students, 40 percent. LEP status is commonly assigned to recently arrived Mexican immigrants.[19]

Intensive ethnographic fieldwork at the school identified several distinct categories in which the Mexican-origin population could be classified. Recent Mexican immigrants were at one extreme. They dressed differently and unstylishly. They claimed an identity as Mexican and considered Mexico their permanent home. The most academically successful of this group were those most proficient in Spanish, reflecting their prior levels of education in Mexico. Almost all were described by teachers and staff as courteous, serious about their schoolwork, respectful, and eager to please as well as naive and unsophisticated. They were commonly classified as LEP.

The next category comprised Mexican-oriented students. They spoke Spanish at home and were generally classified as fluent English proficient (FEP). They had strong bicultural ties with both Mexico and the United States, reflecting the fact that most were born in Mexico but had lived in the United States for more than five years. They were proud of their Mexican heritage but saw themselves as different from the first group, the *recien llegados* (recently arrived), as well as from the native-born Chicanos and Cholos, who were derided as people who had lost their Mexican roots. Students from this group were active in soccer and the Sociedad Bilingue and in celebrations of May 5th, the anniversary of the Mexican defeat of French occupying forces. Virtually all of the Mexican-descent students who graduated in the top 10 percent of their class in 1981 were identified as members of this group.

Chicanos were by far the largest Mexican-descent group at Field High. They were mostly U.S.-born second- and third-genera-tion students whose primary loyalty was to their in-group, seen as locked in conflict with white society. Chicanos referred derisively to successful Mexican students as "schoolboys" and "schoolgirls" or as "wannabes." According to M. G. Matute-Bianchi,

> To be a Chicano meant in practice to hang out by the science wing . . . *not* eating lunch in the quad where all the "gringos" and "schoolboys" hang out . . . cutting classes by faking a call slip so you can be with friends at the 7-11 . . . sitting in the back of classes and not participating . . . *not* carrying your books to class . . . *not* taking the difficult classes . . . doing the minimum to get by.[20]

Chicanos merge imperceptibly into the last category, the Cholos, who commonly seen as "low riders" gang members. They were also native-born Mexican Americans, easily identifiable by their deliberate manner of dress, walk, speech, and cultural symbols. Chicanos and Cholos were generally regarded by teachers as "irresponsible," "disrespectful," "mistrusting," "sullen," "apathetic," and "less motivated," and their poor school performance attributed to these traits.[21] According to Matute-Bianchi, Chicanos and Cholos were faced with what they saw as a forced-choice dilemma between doing well in school or being a Chicano. To act white was regarded as disloyalty to one's group.

The situation of these last two groups exemplifies losing the race between first-generation achievements and later generations' expectations. Seeing their parents and grandparents confined to humble menial jobs and increasingly aware of discrimination against them by the white mainstream, U.S.-born children of Mexican immigrants readily join a reactive subculture as a means of protecting their sense of self-worth. Participation in this subculture then leads to serious barriers to their chances of upward mobility because school achievement is defined as antithetical to ethnic solidarity. Newly arrived Mexican students are at risk of being socialized into the same reactive stance, with the aggravating factor that it is other Mexicans, not native-born strangers, who convey the message. The principal protection of *mexicanos* against this type of assimilation lies in their strong identification with home-country language and values, which brings them closer to their parents' cultural stance.

Punjabi Sikhs in California

Valleyside (a fictitious name) is a northern California community where the primary economic activity is orchard farming. Farm laborers in this area come often from India; they are mainly rural Sikhs from the Punjab. By the early 1980s, second-generation Punjabi students already accounted for 11 percent of the student body at Valleyside High. Their parents were no longer only farm laborers, since about a third had become orchard owners themselves and another third worked in factories in the nearby San Francisco area. An ethnographic study of Valleyside High School in 1980–82 revealed a very difficult process of assimilation for Punjabi Sikh students. According to its author, M. A. Gibson, Valleyside is "redneck country," and white residents are extremely hostile to immigrants who look different and speak a different language: "Punjabi teenagers are told they stink . . . told to go back to India . . . physically abused by majority students who spit at them, refuse to sit by them in class or in buses, throw food at them or worse."[22]

Despite these attacks and some evidence of discrimination by school staff, Punjabi students performed better academically than majority Anglo students. About 90 percent of the immigrant youths completed high school, compared to 70–75 percent of native whites. Punjabi boys surpassed the average grade point average, were more likely to take advanced science and math classes, and expressed aspirations for careers in science and engineering. Girls, on the other hand, tended to enroll in business classes, but they paid less attention to immediate career plans, reflecting parental wishes that they should marry first.

This gender difference is indicative of the continuing strong influence exercised by the immigrant community over its second generation. According to Gibson, Punjabi parents pressured their children against too much contact with white peers who may "dishonor" the immigrants' families, and defined "becoming Americanized" as forgetting one's roots and adopting the most disparaged traits of the majority, such as leaving home at age 18, making decisions without parental consent, dating, and dancing. At the same time, parents urged children to abide by school rules, ignore racist remarks and avoid fights, and learn useful skills, including full proficiency in English.[23]

The overall success of this strategy of selective assimilation to American society is remarkable because Punjabi immigrants were generally poor on their arrival in the United States and confronted widespread discrimination from whites without the benefit of either governmental assistance or a well-established coethnic community. In terms of our typology of vulnerability and resources, the Punjabi Sikh second generation was very much at risk except for two crucial factors. First, immigrant parents did not settle in the inner city or in close proximity to any native-born minority whose offspring could provide an alternative model of adaptation to white-majority discrimination. In particular, the absence of a downtrodden Indian American community composed of children of previous immigrants allowed first-generation parents to influence decisively the outlook of their offspring, including their ways of fighting white prejudice. There was no equivalent of a Cholo-like reactive subculture to offer an alternative blueprint of the stance that "people like us" should take.

Second, Punjabi immigrants managed to make considerable economic progress, as attested by the number who had become farm owners, while maintaining a tightly knit ethnic community. The material and social capital created by this first-generation community compensated for the absence of an older coethnic group and had decisive effects on second-generation outlooks. Punjabi teenagers were shown that their parents' ways paid off economically, and this fact, plus their community's cohesiveness, endowed them with a source of pride to counteract outside discrimination. Through this strategy of selective assimilation, Punjabi Sikhs appeared to be winning the race against the inevitable acculturation of their children to American-style aspirations.

Caribbean Youths in South Florida

Miami is arguably the American city that has been most thoroughly transformed by post-1960 immigration. The Cuban Revolution had much to do with this transformation, as it sent the entire Cuban upper class out of the country, followed by thousands of refugees of more modest backgrounds. Over time, Cubans created a highly diversified and prosperous ethnic community that provided resources for the adaptation process of its second generation. Reflecting this situation are average Cuban family incomes that, by 1989, approximated those of the native-born population; the existence in 1987 of more than 30,000 Cuban-owned small businesses that formed the core of the Miami ethnic enclave; and the parallel rise of a private school system oriented toward the values and political outlook of this community.[24] In terms of the typology of vulnerability and resources, well-sheltered Cuban American teenagers lack any extensive exposure to outside discrimination, they have little contact with youths from disadvantaged minorities, and the development of an enclave creates economic opportunities beyond the narrowing industrial and tourist sectors on which most other immigrant groups in the area depend. Across town, Haitian American teenagers face exactly the opposite set of conditions, as has been shown.

Among the other immigrant groups that form Miami's ethnic mosaic, two deserve mention because they represent intermediate situations between those of the Cubans and Haitians. One comprises Nicaraguans escaping the Sandinista regime during the 1980s. They were not as welcomed in the United States as were the Cuban exiles, nor were they able to develop a large and diversified community. Yet they shared with Cubans their language and culture, as well as a militant anti-Communist discourse. This common political outlook led the Cuban American community to extend its resources in support of their Nicaraguan brethren, smoothing their process of adaptation.[25] For second-generation Nicaraguans, this means that the preexisting ethnic community that provides a model for their own assimilation is not a downtrodden group but rather one that has managed to establish a firm and positive presence in the city's economy and politics.

The second group comprises West Indians coming from Jamaica, Trinidad, and other English-speaking Caribbean republics. They generally arrive in Miami as legal immigrants, and many bring along professional and business credentials as well as the advantage of fluency in English. These individual advantages are discounted, however, by a context of reception in which these mostly black immigrants are put in the same category as native-born blacks and discriminated against accordingly. The recency of West Indian migration and its small size have prevented the development of a diversified ethnic community in South Florida. Hence new arrivals experience the full force of white discrimination without the protection of a large coethnic group and with constant exposure to the situation and attitudes of the inner-city population. Despite considerable individual resources, these disadvantages put the West Indian second generation at risk of bypassing white or even native black middle-class models to assimilate into the culture of the underclass. . . .

Conclusion

. . . Fifty years ago, the dilemma of Italian American youngsters studied by Irvin Child consisted of assimilating into the American mainstream, sacrificing in the process their parents' cultural heritage in contrast to taking refuge in the ethnic community from the challenges of the outside world.[26] In the contemporary context of segmented assimilation, the options have become less clear. Children of nonwhite immigrants may not even have the opportunity of gaining access to middle-class white society, no matter how acculturated they become. Joining those native circles to which they do have access may prove a ticket to permanent subordination and disadvantage. Remaining securely ensconced in their coethnic community, under these circumstances, may be not a symptom of escapism but the best strategy for capitalizing on otherwise unavailable material and moral resources. As the experiences of Punjabi Sikh and Cuban American students suggest, a strategy of paced, selective assimilation may prove the best course for immigrant minorities. But the extent to which this strategy is possible also depends on the history of each group and its specific profile of vulnerabilities and resources. . . .

Endnotes

1. Defined as native-born children with at least one foreign- born parent or children born abroad who came to the United States before 12. See Leif Jensen, *Children of the New Immigration: A Comparative Analysis of Today's Second Generation*, paper commissioned by the Children of Immigrants Research Project, Department of Sociology, Johns Hopkins University, reprinted as Institute for Policy Research and Evaluation Working Paper no. 1990–32 (University Park: Pennsylvania State University, Aug. 1990).

2. See, for example, Saskia Sassen, "Changing Composition and Labor Markey Location of Hispanic Immigrants in New York City, 1960–1980," in *Hispanics in the U.S. Economy*, ed. George J. Borjas and Marta Tienda (New York: Academic Press, 1985), pp. 299–322.

3. Jeffrey S. Passel and Barry Edmonston, "Immigration and Race: Recent Trends in Immigration to the United States" (Paper no. PRIP–UI–22, Urban Institute, May 1992), tab. 2.

4. Ibid. , tab. 9.

5. U.S., Department of Commerce, Bureau of the Census, *Race by Hispanic Origin, 1990 Census of Population and Housing*, special tabulation prepared by the Ethnic and Hispanic Branch (Washington, DC: U.S. Department of Commerce, 1992).

6. See Alex Stepick, "Haitian Refugees in the U.S." (Report no. 52, Minority Rights Group, London, 1982); Alex Stepick and Alejandro Portes, "Flight into Despair: A Profile of Recent Haitian Refugees in South Florida," *International Migration Review*, 20:329–50 (Summer 1986).

7. This account is based on fieldwork in Miami conducted in preparation for a survey of immigrant youths in public schools.

8. On the issue of social capital, see James S. Coleman, "Social Capital in the Creation of Human Capital," *American Journal of Sociology*, supplement, 94:S95–121 (1988); Alejandro Portes and Min Zhou, "Gaining the Upper Hand: Economic Mobility among Immigrant and Domestic Minorities," *Ethnic and Racial Studies*, 15:491–522 (Oct. 1992). On ethnic entrepreneurship, see Ivan H. Light, *Ethnic Enterprise in America: Business and Welfare among Chinese, Japanese, and Blacks* (Berkeley: University of California Press, 1972); Kenneth Wilson and W. Allen Martin, "Ethnic Enclaves: A Comparison of the Cuban and Black Economies in Miami," *American Journal of Sociology*, 88:136–60 (1982).

9. See Mercer L. Sullivan, *"Getting Paid": Youth, Crime, and Work in the Inner City* (Ithaca, NY: Cornell University Press, 1989), chaps. 1, 5.

10. U.S., Department of Commerce, Bureau of the Census, *Census of Population and Housing, 1980: Public Use of Microdata Samples A (MRDF)* (Washington, DC: Department of Commerce, 1983).

11. Thomas Bailey and Roger Waldinger, "Primary, Secondary, and Enclave Labor Markets: A Training System Approach," *American Sociological Review*, 56:432–45 (1991).

12. Professionals and executives represented 25.9 percent of Cuban-origin males aged 16 years and over in 1989; the figure for the total adult male population was 26 percent. See Jesus M. Garcia and Patricia A. Montgomery, *The Hispanic Population of the United States: March 1990*, Current Population Reports, ser. P–20, no. 449 (Washington, DC: Department of Commerce, 1991).

13. Portes and Rumbaut, *Immigrant America*, pp. 23–25; Robert L. Bach et al., "The Economic Adjustment of Southeast Asian Refugees in the United States," in *World Refugee Survey, 1983*, (Geneva: United Nations High Commission for Refugees, 1984), pp. 51–55.

14. The 1990 Immigration Act contains tailor-made provisions to facilitate the legalization of Irish immigrants. Those taking advantage of the provisions are popularly dubbed "Kennedy Irish" in honor of the Massachusetts Senator who coauthored the act. On the 1990 act, see Michael Fix and Jeffrey S. Passel, "The Door Remains Open: Recent Immigration to the United States and a Preliminary Analysis of the Immigration Act of 1990" (Working paper, Urban Institute and RAND Corporation, 1991). On the Irish in Boston, see Karen Tumulty, "When Irish Eyes Are Hiding . . ." *Los Angeles Times*, 29 Jan. 1989.

15. Bailey and Waldinger, "Primary, Secondary, and Enclave Labor Markets"; Min Zhou, *New York's Chinatown: The Socioeconomic Potential of an Urban Enclave* (Philadelphia: Tem-

ple University Press, 1992); Wilson and Martin, "Ethnic Enclaves"; Suzanne Model, "The Ethnic Economy: Cubans and Chinese Reconsidered" (Manuscript, University of Massachusetts at Amherst, 1990).

16. U.S., Department of Commerce, Bureau of the Census, *Survey of Minority-Owned Business Enterprises, 1987*, MB–2 and MB–3 (Washington, DC: Department of Commerce, 1991).

17. Alejandro Portes and Alex Stepick, "Unwelcome Immigrants: The Labor Market Experiences of 1980 (Mariel) Cuban and Haitian Refugees in South Florida," *American Sociological Review*, 50:493–514 (Aug. 1985); Zhou, *New York's Chinatown*; Luis E. Guarnizo, "One Country in Two: Dominican-Owned Firms in New York and the Dominican Republic" (Ph.D. diss. Johns Hopkins University, 1992); Bailey and Waldinger, "Primary, Secondary, and Enclave Labor Markets."

18. Stepick, "Haitian Refugees in the U.S."; Jake C. Miller, *the Plight of Haitian Refugees* (New York: Praeger, 1984).

19. M. G. Matute-Bianchi, "Ethnic Identities and Patterns of School Success and Failure among Mexican-Descent and Japanese- American Students in a California High School," *American Journal of Education*, 95:233–55 (Nov. 1986). this study is summarized in Rubén G. Rumbaut, "Immigrant Students in California Public Schools: A Summary of Current Knowledge" (Report no. 11, Center for Research on Effective Schooling for Disadvantaged Children, John Hopkins University, Aug. 1990).

20. Matute-Bianchi, "Ethnic Identities and Patterns," p. 253.

21. Rumbaut, "Immigrant Students," p. 25.

22. M. A. Gibson, *Accommodation without Assimilation: Sikh Immigrants in an American High School* (Ithaca, NY: Cornell University Press, 1989), p. 268.

23. Gibson, *Accommodation without Assimilation*. The study is summarized in Rumbaut, "Immigrant Students," pp. 22–23.

24. Garcia and Montgomery, *Hispanic Population*; U.S., Department of Commerce, Bureau of the Census, *Survey of Minority-Owned Business Enterprises*, MB–2.

25. Portes and Stepick, *City on the Edge: The Transformation of Miami*, chap. 7.(Berkely: University of California Press, 1993).

26. Child, Irvin L. *Italian or American? The Second Generation in Conflict*. New Haven: Yale University Press, 1943.

Reprinted from: Alejandro Portes and Min Zhou, "The New Second Generation: Segmented Assimilation and Its Variants." In *Annals of the American Academy of Political and Social Sciences*, 530, November 1993. Pp. 74–96. Copyright © 1993 by Sage Publications, Inc. Reprinted by permission.